Community Policing

PARTNERSHIPS FOR PROBLEM SOLVING

Seventh Edition

Community Policing

PARTNERSHIPS FOR PROBLEM SOLVING

Seventh Edition

Linda S. Miller

Former Executive Director of the Upper Midwest Community Policing Institute
Sergeant (Retired), Bloomington, Minnesota, Police Department

Kären Matison Hess, Ph.D.

Normandale Community College, Bloomington, Minnesota

Christine Hess Orthmann, M.S.

Orthmann Writing & Research, Inc.

DELMAR
CENGAGE Learning®

Australia • Brazil • Japan • Korea • Mexico • Singapore • Spain • United Kingdom • United States

DELMAR
CENGAGE Learning·

Community Policing: Partnerships for Problem Solving, Seventh Edition
Linda S. Miller, Kären Matison Hess, Christine Hess Orthmann

Vice President, Careers & Computing:
Dave Garza

Director of Learning Solutions:
Sandy Clark

Senior Acquisitions Editor:
Shelley Esposito

Director, Development-Career and
Computing: Marah Bellegarde

Senior Product Development Manager:
Larry Main

Senior Product Manager: Anne Orgren

Editorial Assistant: Diane Chrysler

Brand Manager: Kristin McNary

Market Development Manager:
Michelle Williams

Senior Production Director:
Wendy Troeger

Production Manager: Mark Bernard

Senior Content Project Manager:
Jennifer Hanley

Cover image(s):
Main image: ©Lawrence Migdale/
Photo Researchers, Inc.

Inset images, left to right: ©Larry
Mulvehill/Corbis; ©Michael Rolands/
shutterstock; ©SVLuma/shutterstock;
©Thinkstock Images/Comstock
Images/Getty Images

For product information and technology assistance, contact us at
Cengage Learning Customer & Sales Support, 1-800-354-9706

For permission to use material from this text or product,
submit all requests online at **www.cengage.com/permissions**.
Further permissions questions can be e-mailed to
permissionrequest@cengage.com

Library of Congress Control Number: 2012948099

ISBN: 978-1-285-09667-4

Delmar
5 Maxwell Drive
Clifton Park, NY 12065-2919
USA

Cengage Learning is a leading provider of customized learning solutions with
office locations around the globe, including Singapore, the United Kingdom,
Australia, Mexico, Brazil, and Japan. Locate your local office at:
international.cengage.com/region

Cengage Learning products are represented in Canada by
Nelson Education, Ltd.

To learn more about Delmar, visit **www.cengage.com/delmar**
Purchase any of our products at your local college store or at
our preferred online store **www.cengagebrain.com**

Printed in the United States of America
1 2 3 4 5 6 7 17 16 15 14 13

BRIEF CONTENTS

CONTENTS

3   Understanding and Involving the Community   59

Section II: Building Relationships and Trust   147

6   Communicating with a Diverse Population   148

Section III: Community Policing in the Field: Collaborative Efforts   235

9 Early Experiments in Crime Prevention and the Evolution of Community Policing Strategies 237

10 Safe Neighborhoods and Communities: From Traffic Problems to Crime   271

11 Community Policing and Drugs   307

13 The Challenge of Gangs: Controlling Their Destructive Force   383

14 Understanding and Preventing Violence 414

15 Understanding and Preventing Terrorism 451

16 What Research Tells Us and a Look to the Future   483

FOREWORD

A democratic society has to be the most difficult environment within which to police. Police in many countries operate for the benefit of the government. The police of America operate for the benefit of the people policed. Because of that environment, we are compelled to pursue ways to advance our policing approach, involve people who are part of our environment, and enhance our effectiveness. Our policing methodology is changed or molded by trial and error, the daring of some policing leaders, the research and writing of academics, and the response of our communities to the way we do business.

For more than 40 years, we have tried a variety of approaches to doing our job better. Some have remained. Many have been abandoned, thought to be failures. They may, however, have been building blocks for our current policing practices and for what is yet to come. For instance, the community relations and crime prevention programs of the 1960s and the experiments with team policing in the 1970s are quite visible in the business of community policing. So should be the knowledge gained from research such as that conducted in the 1970s and 1980s associated with random patrol, directed patrol, foot patrol, one-officer/two-officer cars, and the effectiveness (or lack thereof) of rapid response to all calls for service. If we look at our past, we should not be surprised at the development of and support for community policing as the desired policing philosophy in our country today. It merely responds to the customers' needs and their demand for our policing agencies to be more effective. And therein lies the most important outcome of community policing—effectiveness. Yes, we have responded to millions of calls for service, made millions of arrests, and added thousands to our policing ranks. If we're honest about it, however, we may be hard-pressed to see the imprint of our efforts in our communities. Community policing, involving problem solving, community engagement, and organizational transformation, can contribute significantly to the satisfaction of the community policed and to those policing.

This text provides insight into the meaning of community policing and presents many dimensions necessary to consider when developing a community policing strategy. Its content should help readers to understand the practical side of community policing, recognize the necessary community considerations, and develop methods applicable to their unique environments.

Donald J. Burnett
General Partner
Law Enforcement Assistance Network

PREFACE

Welcome to *Community Policing: Partnerships for Problem Solving,* Seventh Edition. The complex responsibilities of departments embracing the community policing philosophy are challenging. Changes in technology and society continually present new challenges to police officers, requiring them to be knowledgeable in a wide variety of areas.

Community policing offers one avenue for making neighborhoods safer. Community policing is not a program or a series of programs. It is a philosophy, a belief that by working together the police and the community can accomplish what neither can accomplish alone. The synergy that results from community policing can be powerful. It is like the power of a finely tuned athletic team, with each member contributing to the total effort. Occasionally heroes may emerge, but victory depends on a team effort.

Community policing differs from earlier efforts such as team policing, community relations, crime prevention programs, or neighborhood watch programs. Community policing involves a rethinking of the role of the police and a restructuring of the police organization. Its two core concepts are community–police collaboration and partnerships and a problem-solving approach to policing. These dual themes are present throughout the text.

ORGANIZATION OF THE TEXT

Section I of this text discusses the evolution of community policing and the changes in our communities and our law enforcement agencies that have occurred over time. The section then examines the problem-solving approach to policing and how community policing might be implemented.

Section II emphasizes the development of the interpersonal skills needed to build good relationships with all those the police have sworn "to serve and protect." This includes those who are culturally, racially, or socioeconomically different from the mainstream; those who are physically or mentally disabled; and those who are elderly. It also includes youths (both as victims and as offenders), gangs and gang members, and victims of crime. In addition, building partnerships and interacting effectively with members of the media are vital to the success of community policing.

Section III describes community policing in the field. It begins with a look at early experiments in crime prevention and the evolution of community policing strategies. The remainder of the section is entirely new material dealing with community problems ranging from traffic to crime to the fear of crime. It then takes a close look at the drug problem, bringing youths into community policing, addressing the gang problem, and understanding and preventing violence, including domestic violence, workplace violence, and terrorism. The final chapter explains what researchers have found and explores what the future might hold for community policing.

NEW TO THIS EDITION

The Seventh Edition has been thoroughly revised with hundreds of new citations and a plentiful amount of new terms, figures, tables, and photographs. Chapter-specific additions made to the Seventh Edition include:

» Chapter 1: The Evolution of Community Policing
- New "Ideas in Practice" box: El Protector Program (Metropolitan Nashville Police Department)
- New data on COPS Office funding for FY 2012

» Chapter 2: Inside Police Agencies: Understanding Mission and Culture
- Updated data on the number of local police departments with community policing mission statement
- Updated statistics on the numbers of minority and women police officers
- Updated data on the number of U.S. citizens reporting contact with police, including data on perceived use of excessive force
- Revised definition and discussion of *discretion*
- New content on ethics and corruption

» Chapter 3: Understanding and Involving the Community
- Updated population data (2010 census) and new content on the increasing ethnic diversity of communities
- New content on the diversity of officers
- New content on public–private police partnerships
- New data on false burglar alarms
- New material on citizen oversight of police
- New table for a sample Citizen Police Academy Agenda

» Chapter 4: Problem Solving: Proactive Policing
- New terms: *geographic information system (GIS)*, *routine activity theory*
- New content on CompStat, hot spots policing
- Expanded discussions on crime mapping and geographic profiling
- New content on geospacial statistical analysis and routine activity theory
- New "Ideas in Practice" box: Halloween on State Street

» Chapter 5: Implementing Community Policing
- New content regarding change management
- New content about decentralization and an improved citation

» Chapter 6: Communicating with a Diverse Population
- New census data on immigrants, foreign-born residents, limited-English proficient (LEP) residents in the United States, the homeless, persons with disabilities, the elderly
- New coverage of federal legislation (Title VI of the Civil Rights Act of 1964 and Executive Order 13166)
- New content on cultural differences as a barrier to communication

- New material on tackling trust and communication issues in Arab American communities
- New content on racial profiling
- New material on religious diversity and Arab Americans
- New material about homelessness, constructive alternatives to criminalization, and violence against the homeless
- New research on suicide by cop (SBC) and new case: *Adams v. Fremont* (1998)
- New content on Alzheimer's disease (AD)
- Modified discussion on learning disabilities in youth to reflect updates in terminology and classification by NIH and ACLD

» Chapter 7: Building Partnerships: A Cornerstone of Community Policing
- Streamlined discussion on 311 systems
- New updated content on community prosecution, community courts
- New content on consolidation of services
- Additional material on partnerships with volunteers in law enforcement
- New content on older volunteers

» Chapter 8: Forming Partnerships with the Media
- New graphic of media advisory card for crime victims and witnesses
- New "Technology in Community Policing" box: PIOs and Digital Media

» Chapter 9: Early Experiments in Crime Prevention and the Evolution of Community Policing Strategies
- New "Technology in Community Policing" box: Neighborhood Watch Goes High Tech
- Added discussion of findings from the Philadelphia Foot Patrol Experiment

» Chapter 10: Safe Neighborhoods and Communities: From Traffic Problems to Crime
- Updated traffic data: speeding fatality statistics, red-light running, seat belt use (or nonuse)
- New "Technology in Community Policing" boxes: Red-Light Cameras; Mobile Multimodal Biometrics
- New content on identifying hot spots
- New examples of technology being used by police agencies
- New data about identity theft
- Updated content on human trafficking

» Chapter 11: Community Policing and Drugs
- Updated statistics on drug use, offender data
- Additional content on synthetic marijuana (spice)
- Inclusion of the FY 2012 national drug control budget
- Expanded material on drug courts
- New case: *United States v. Jones* (2012), GPS tracking of a suspect's vehicle is a search under the Fourth Amendment
- New "Technology in Community Policing" box: Identifying Pharmacy Robbers
- New Problem-Solving Partnership in Action example

» Chapter 12: Bringing Youths into Community Policing

- Additional terms: *protective factor, risk factor*
- Discussion of several new programs aimed at youth violence prevention, building partnerships between youth and the community
- Expanded content on protective factors to modify focus to what kids should be exposed to (from a proactive, programming perspective), not what they shouldn't be
- Updated content regarding SORNA compliance, America's Promise Alliance, Project Safe Childhood
- Deletion of Building Blocks for Youth—program discontinued in 2005
- Updated data on school crime and violence, bullying, shootings
- New "Technology in Community Policing" box: Preventing Loitering and Vandalism with the Mosquito
- New "Ideas in Practice" box: Urban High School Disorder Reduction Project

» Chapter 13: The Challenge of Gangs: Controlling Their Destructive Force

- Updated data/statistics on gang membership, gang growth
- New "Ideas in Practice" box: examples of antigang efforts being implemented around the country

» Chapter 14: Understanding and Preventing Violence

- New term: *intimate partner violence (IPV)*
- Updated crime and violence data and statistics throughout (hate crimes, gun violence, sexual assault, IPV, child abuse, workplace violence)
- New brief mention of Minneapolis Domestic Violence Experiment because it is a well-known study within the field—despite later criticism of methodology, it got researchers to examine effects of arrest on IPV
- Additional content about specialized domestic violence units

» Chapter 15: Understanding and Preventing Terrorism

- Adjusted list of designated state sponsors of terrorism
- Updated statistics on methods used by terrorists, number of attacks and fatalities, etc.
- New content on how the community policing philosophy fits with homeland security
- New material on law enforcement–private security partnerships to prevent terrorism
- New "Technology in Community Policing" box: NYPD and Microsoft Partner to Create Real-Time Crime Prevention and Counterterrorism Technology Solution

» Chapter 16: What Research Tells Us and a Look to the Future

- New content on the impact of the economic downtown on American policing
- New material on a rethinking of the "get tough" approach to crime control
- Expanded coverage of new and emerging technologies in policing

HOW TO USE THIS TEXT

This text is a carefully structured learning experience. The more actively you participate in it, the greater your learning will be. You will learn and remember more if you first familiarize yourself with the total scope of the subject. Read and think about the Contents, which provides an outline of the many facets of community policing. Then follow these steps for *triple-strength learning* as you study each chapter.

1. Read the objectives at the beginning of the chapter. These are stated as "Do You Know …" questions. Assess your current knowledge of the subject of each question. Examine any preconceptions you may hold. Look at the key terms and watch for them when they are used.

2. Read the chapter, underlining, highlighting, or taking notes—whatever is your preferred study method.

   a. Pay special attention to all highlighted information.

    Two themes apparent in the various definitions of community policing are problem solving and partnerships.

   The key concepts of the text are highlighted in this way and answer the "Do You Know …" questions.

   b. Pay special attention to the terms in bold print. The key terms of the chapter appear this way the first time they are defined.

3. When you have finished reading the chapter, read the summary—your third exposure to the chapter's key information. Then return to the beginning of the chapter and quiz yourself. Can you answer the "Do You Know …" questions? Can you define the key terms?

4. Read the Discussion Questions and be prepared to contribute to a class discussion of the ideas presented in the chapter.

By following these steps, you will learn more information, understand it more fully, and remember it longer.

A Note: The material selected to highlight using the triple-strength learning instructional design includes only the chapter's key concepts. Although this information is certainly important in that it provides a structural foundation for understanding the topics discussed, do not simply glance over the "Do You Know …" highlighted boxes and summaries and expect to master the chapter. You are also responsible for reading and understanding the material that surrounds these basics—the "meat" around the bones, so to speak.

EXPLORING FURTHER

The text also provides an opportunity for you to apply what you have learned or to go into specific areas in greater depth through discussions and through the Gale Emergency Services Database Assignments. Complete the assignments as directed by the text or by your instructor. Be prepared to share your findings with the class. Good learning!

ANCILLARIES
Book-Specific Supplement for Students

CourseMate Criminal Justice CourseMate is available for *Community Policing: Partnerships in Problem Solving,* 7th edition. This CourseMate includes:

» An interactive eBook, with highlighting, note taking, and search capabilities.
» Interactive learning tools including:
  - Quizzes
  - Flashcards
  - Videos
  - Crossword puzzles
  - And more!

To learn more about this resource and access free demo CourseMate resources, go to www.cengagebrain.com, and search by this book's ISBN (9781285096674). To access CourseMate materials that you have purchased, go to login.cengagebrain.com, enter your access code, and create an account or log into your existing account.

Book-Specific Supplements for Instructors

Instructor's Resource Manual with Test Bank This manual offers you learning objectives, key terms, chapter outlines, and chapter summaries. Also included is a test bank of hundreds of questions in multiple-choice, true/false, short answer, and essay formats, along with a full answer key. ISBN: 9781285096681

PowerLecture This one-stop lecture and class preparation tool makes it easy for you to assemble, edit, and present custom lectures for your course using Microsoft® PowerPoint®. PowerLecture™ includes lesson plans, real-world resources, text-specific lecture outlines, art from the text, and more. The DVD-ROM also contains ExamView® computerized testing, which allows you to create tests in minutes using items from the test bank in electronic format. ISBN: 9781285096742

CourseMate with Engagement Tracker Criminal Justice CourseMate is available for *Community Policing: Partnerships in Problem Solving,* 7th edition. The instructor version of CourseMate includes Engagement Tracker, a first-of-its-kind tool that monitors student engagement in the course. Instructors also have full access to the interactive eBook and other student CourseMate resources.

To access this CourseMate with Engagement Tracker, go to login.cengage .com, sign in with your SSO (single sign-on) login, and add this title to your bookshelf. (Note: Engagement Tracker monitors students who have purchased access to CourseMate.)

Companion Web Site The Instructor Companion Web site to accompany *Community Policing: Partnerships in Problem Solving,* 7th edition, features PowerPoint® lecture slides, lesson plans, real-world resources, the instructor's resource manual, and test banks in ExamView®, Blackboard, and rich text format. ISBN: 9781285096803

WebTUTOR™ Advantage Plus on Blackboard® with eBook Jumpstart your online course with customizable, rich, text-specific content—all easily and immediately accessible within your existing learning management system. Simply load a WebTutor™ cartridge into your course management system and add, edit, reorganize, or delete content—quizzes, learning objectives, flashcards, games, and more—as you see fit. Plus, use your book's test bank and your own grade book to make assessment easier than ever. Whether you want to Web-enable your class or put an entire course online, WebTutor delivers. Visit www.cengage.com/webtutor to learn more. ISBN: 9781285096766 (Instant Access Code) or 9781285096759 (Printed Access Code)

Discipline-Wide Supplement Related to This Text

The following supplement, referenced in this text but not produced specifically for this text, is available to qualified adopters. Instructors, please consult your Cengage Learning sales representative for details.

Gale's Custom Journals Database for Emergency Services and Criminal Justice *Community Policing: Partnerships for Problem Solving*, 7th edition, contains exercises referencing Gale's Custom Journals Database for Emergency Services and Criminal Justice, available for bundling with criminal justice titles. Containing customized portions of the Gale journal database (which is known for its accurate and authoritative reference content), this Custom Journals Database provides a 24/7 library reference of the latest information and research in this topic area. Learners who desire additional resources and research beyond the scope of their textbook will find this to be a useful tool.

Instructors, talk to your Cengage Learning sales representative to find out about adding the database to your adoption of this textbook. Students, talk to your instructors to find out whether you have access to this database.

Features include:

» Material drawn from magazines, academic journals, books, news, and multimedia resources
» Digital access allowing easy-to-use, powerful search capabilities, creating a great reference tool
» Current articles to help students prepare for their careers by way of industry journal information
» Additional tools such as citation tools, downloads, and even translation features

ISBN: 9781435482326

Additional Discipline-Wide Supplements

The following supplements can also help supplement your course. Instructors, please consult your Cengage Learning sales representative for details.

Careers in Criminal Justice Web Site The Careers in Criminal Justice Web site offers extensive career profiling information and self-assessment testing designed to help students investigate and focus on the criminal justice career choices that are right for them. This resource-rich Web site includes over 70 Career Profiles and more than 25 video interviews with links and tools to assist students in finding a professional position. It also features a career Rolodex, interest assessments, and a career planner with sample résumés, letters, interview questions, and more. View a demo at academic.cengage .com/criminaljustice/careers. ISBN: 9780495595236 (Instant Access Code) or 9780495595229 (Printed Access Card)

Careers in Criminal Justice and Related Fields: From Internship to Promotion, 6th edition (J. Scott Harr and Kären M. Hess) This supplemental book helps students develop a job-search strategy through résumés, cover letters, and interview techniques. It also provides students with extensive information on various criminal justice professions, including job descriptions, job salary suggestions, and contact information. ISBN: 9780495600329

Wadsworth's Guide to Careers in Criminal Justice, 3rd edition (Caridad Sanchez-Leguelinel, John Jay College of Criminal Justice) This handy, concise booklet provides a brief introduction to the exciting and diverse career choices in the criminal justice field. Students learn about opportunities in law enforcement, courts, and corrections—and how to get those jobs. ISBN: 9780495130383

ACKNOWLEDGMENTS

A number of professionals from academia and the field have reviewed the previous editions of *Community Policing: Partnerships for Problem Solving* and provided valuable suggestions. We thank them all: James S. Albritton, Marquette University; Vince Benincasa, Hesser College; Michael B. Blankenship, Memphis State University; W. D. Braddock, Boise State University; William Castleberry, The University of Tennessee at Martin; Bobbie Cox, Gardner-Webb University; Vincent Del Castillo, John Jay College of Criminal Justice; Burt C. Hagerman, Oakland Community College; Robert Ives, Rock Valley College; Deborah Jones, California State University–San Bernardino; William King, Bowling Green State University; Alan Kraft, Seminole Community College; James J. Lauria, Pittsburgh Technical Institute; Richard H. Martin, Auburn University at Montgomery; Deborah Wilkins Newman, Middle Tennessee State University; James E. Newman, Rio Hondo Community College; Willard M. Oliver, Glenville State College; Greg Osowski, Henry Ford Community College; Bernadette Jones Palomobo, Louisiana State University–Shreveport; Carroll S. Price, Penn Valley Community College; Charles L. Quarles, University of Mississippi; Mittie D. Southerland, Murray State University; Jeanne Stinchcomb, Florida Atlantic University; B. Grant Stitt, University of Nevada–Reno; Christine L. Stymus, Bryant and Stratton College, Rochester, New York; Gregory B. Talley, Broome Community College; Gary T. Tucker, Sinclair Community College; and Jay Zumbrun, Community College of Baltimore County.

The following reviewers contributed numerous suggestions to the Seventh Edition: Steven Ellwanger, East Tennessee State University; Clayton Steenberg, Copper Mountain (Arizona) Community College; and Steven Ellwanger, Central Lakes College (Minnesota). We greatly appreciate the input of these reviewers. The sole responsibility for all content, however, is our own.

We are especially grateful to Officer Kim Czapar for her perspectives contained in the feature "On the Beat." We extend a special thank you to Terri Wright, our photo researcher; Shelley Esposito and Anne Orgren, our editors at Cengage Learning; Jennifer Hanley, our project manager at Cengage Learning; Isabel Saraiva, our permissions editor; Michele Bassett, our copyeditor; and Sara Dovre Wudali, our production editor at Buuji, Inc. Finally, we thank our families and colleagues for their continuing support and encouragement throughout the development of *Community Policing: Partnerships for Problem Solving.*

Linda S. Miller
Kären M. Hess
Christine H. Orthmann

ABOUT THE AUTHORS

This text is based on the practical experience of Linda S. Miller, who has spent 26 years in law enforcement; the expertise of Kären Matison Hess, who developed instructional programs for 30 years; and Christine Hess Orthmann, who has been deeply involved with this text since its inception. The text has been reviewed by numerous experts in the various areas of community policing as well.

Linda S. Miller is the former executive director of the Upper Midwest Community Policing Institute (UMCPI) as well as a former sergeant with the Bloomington (Minnesota) Police Department. She was with the department for 22 years, serving as a patrol supervisor, a crime prevention officer, a patrol officer, and a police dispatcher. She also worked as the training coordinator for the Minnesota Coalition against Sexual Assault.

Ms. Miller is a member of the International Police Association, the International Association of Women Police, and the Public Safety Writers Association. In 1990 she was a member of the People-to-People's Women in Law Enforcement delegation to the Soviet Union.

Kären Matison Hess, Ph.D. (1939–2010) was the author who first developed this text with Miller and carried it through five very successful revisions. Dr. Hess held a Ph.D. in English and in instructional design from the University of Minnesota, was an instructor at Normandale Community College (Bloomington, Minnesota), and crafted a line of enduring, practical textbooks in the fields of law enforcement and criminal justice. Other Cengage texts Dr. Hess coauthored include *Criminal Investigation* (10th edition), *Introduction to Law Enforcement and Criminal Justice* (9th edition), *Introduction to Private Security* (5th edition), *Juvenile Justice* (5th edition), *Management and Supervision in Law Enforcement* (4th edition), *Police Operations* (5th edition), and *Careers in Criminal Justice: From Internship to Promotion* (6th edition).

Dr. Hess was a member of the Academy of Criminal Justice Sciences (ACJS), the American Association of University Women (AAUW), the American Society for Industrial Security (ASIS), the International Association of Chiefs of Police (IACP), the International Law Enforcement Educators and Trainers Association (ILEETA), the Justice Research and Statistics Association (JRSA), the Police Executive Research Forum (PERF), and the Textbook and Academic Author's Association (TAA). In 2006 Dr. Hess was honored by the University of Minnesota College of Education and Human Development at the school's 100-year anniversary as one of 100 alumni who have made a significant contribution to education and human development. Her tireless dedication to authorship and the education of criminal justice students will forever be an inspiration to us.

Christine Hess Orthmann, M.S. has been writing and researching in various aspects of criminal justice for more than 25 years. She is a coauthor of numerous Cengage books, including *Constitutional Law and the Criminal Justice System* (5th edition), *Criminal Investigation* (10th edition), *Introduction to Law Enforcement and Criminal Justice* (10th edition), *Juvenile Justice* (6th edition), *Management and Supervision in Law Enforcement* (6th edition), and *Police Operations: Theory and Practice* (6th edition), as well as a major contributor to *Introduction to Private Security* (5th edition), and *Careers in Criminal Justice and Related Fields: From Internship to Promotion* (6th edition).

Ms. Orthmann is a member of the Academy of Criminal Justice Sciences (ACJS), the American Society of Criminology (ASC), the Text and Academic Authors Association (TAA), and the National Criminal Justice Honor Society (Alpha Phi Sigma), and is a reserve officer with the Rosemount (Minnesota) Police Department. Orthmann has a Master of Science Degree in criminal justice from the University of Cincinnati.

About the Contributor

Officer Kim Czapar, a police officer since 2004 with the St. Louis Park Police Department in the Twin Cities metro area, has held a variety of job responsibilities, including patrol duty, community outreach, crime prevention programming, overseeing the Neighborhood Watch program, and facilitating the Crime Free Multi-Housing program. Officer Czapar is a certified trainer for the Crime Free Multi-Housing program and has trained hundreds of landlords and property managers in maintaining safe and desirable housing options for residents.

Certified as a crime prevention specialist, Officer Czapar has extensive training in crime prevention and community policing, active shooter response, surviving violent encounters, survival pistol courses, and advanced Crime Prevention Through Environmental Design. Officer Czapar is a board member of the Minnesota Crime Prevention Association and board president of the Hennepin County Chiefs of Police Crime Prevention Committee. Officer Czapar has a B.A. degree in criminal justice from St. Cloud State University and an M.A. degree in police leadership from the University of St. Thomas.

An Overview

The community and the police depend on each other. The common police motto—"To serve and protect"—suggests a target population of individuals who require service and protection. Most police departments stress the importance of community relations, and many have taken community relations beyond image enhancement and crime prevention programs and have started involving the community itself in policing.

This section begins with a discussion of the evolution of police-community relations. Since people first came together in groups, they have had some responsibility for ensuring that those within the group did as was expected. The U.S. method of "preserving the peace," modeled after that used in England, has evolved through several stages. The relationship between the community and its police has been severely strained at times, and attempts

© AP Photo/Jeff Roberson

to improve it have taken several forms. Recently, emphasis on improved public relations and crime prevention has expanded to a more encompassing philosophy of community policing, including problem-solving policing in many jurisdictions (Chapter 1).

Next, an in-depth look at the police is presented (Chapter 2). Who are the people behind the badges? How have they changed over the years? How might they change in the future? How does the public generally view the police? What aspects of the police role contribute to this view?

© AP Photo/Dan Loh

The focus in Chapter 3 is on the people and agencies involved in community-police relations. Who are the members of a community? How do communities differ? How have they changed over the years? What future changes might be anticipated? What aspects of a community must be understood by those working within it? What is expected of community members? What do community members expect?

This is followed by an examination of problem-solving policing, a key component of the community policing philosophy (Chapter 4). The section concludes with a discussion on implementing community policing guidelines and cautions (Chapter 5).

CHAPTER 1

The Evolution of Community Policing

> The police are the public and the public are the police.
>
> —*Sir Robert Peel*

DO YOU KNOW ...

» What community policing is?

» What two themes are apparent in the various definitions of community policing?

» When "modern" policing began?

» What Sir Robert Peel's principles emphasize?

» What the three eras of policing are?

» What the police relationship with the community was in each era?

» What the professional model of policing emphasizes?

» What some common types of crime prevention programs are?

» What four essential dimensions of community policing are?

CAN YOU DEFINE ...

community policing
community relations
frankpledge system
hue and cry
human relations
paradigm
paradigm shift
patronage system
political era
proactive
professional model
progressive era
public relations
reactive
reform era
spoils system
thin blue line
tithing
tithing system

INTRODUCTION

Community policing is often regarded as one of the most significant trends in the history of American policing (Rosenthal et al., 2000). However, community policing did not just magically appear as a panacea for society's ills. Its roots can be traced back several centuries to policing in another country, and its evolution in the United States has spanned many decades. Some scholars and practitioners suggest that community policing continues to evolve, now serving as a stepping stone to new innovations and further emerging trends in American law enforcement. Indeed, as society's needs change, so do the methods it uses to "keep the peace."

Community policing is not an isolated phenomenon. Efforts to involve the community are occurring throughout the entire criminal justice system as many criminal justice professionals explore and research the concept of community justice and the contention that all citizens have the right and the responsibility to participate in the justice system. Community justice is both a strategy and a philosophy.

This chapter begins with some definitions of *community,* followed by a brief history of policing and its evolution in the United States. Then the three strategic eras of policing and the paradigm shifts that occurred are described. Next, the influence of public relations, community relations, and crime prevention programs is explored. The chapter concludes with an in-depth look at community policing, including major features, potential problems, and the incorporation of a problem-solving approach.

WHAT IS COMMUNITY POLICING?

Community policing is a challenging concept to define, and no single definition can satisfy all those who study it or practice it. The following definitions illustrate the various ways community policing has been described:

» "Community policing is a philosophy that promotes organization strategies; it supports the systematic use of partnerships and problem-solving techniques to proactively address the immediate conditions that give rise to public safety issues, such as crime, social disorder, and fear of crime" (*Community Policing Defined*, 2009, 3).

» "It is a philosophy and not a specific tactic; a proactive, decentralized approach, designed to reduce crime, disorder, and fear of crime, by involving the same officer in the same community for a long-term basis" (Trojanowicz and Bucqueroux, 1990, 154).

» "Four general principles define community policing: community engagement, problem solving, organizational transformation, and crime prevention by citizens and police working together" (Skogan, 2004, 160).

» "In its simplest form, community policing is about building relationships and solving problems" (Melekian, 2001, 14).

community policing
A philosophy or orientation that emphasizes working proactively with citizens to reduce fear, solve crime-related problems, and prevent crime.

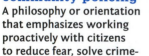

Community policing is an organization-wide philosophy and management approach that promotes (1) community, government, and police partnerships; (2) proactive problem solving to prevent crime; and (3) community engagement to address the causes of crime, fear of crime, and other community issues (Upper Midwest Community Policing Institute, n.d.).

Ford (2007, 321) presents another way to view community policing: "Community policing is an organizational strategy that emerged in the 1980s and '90s for dramatically improving the delivery of police services. ... The strategy requires greater emphasis on knowledge management, teamwork, and partnerships with the community in order for the police agency to become more proactive and adaptable in dealing with crime as well as becoming more focused on enhancing the quality of life for the community." As Kelling (1994) points out: "Whether one calls community policing a philosophy, a strategy, a model, or a paradigm, it is a complex set of ideas that simply cannot be put into a simple one-sentence definition."

Although no one has been able to define community policing in a way that satisfies everyone, most will agree that it includes two vital components: a problem-solving approach to crime and disorder and partnerships involving both the police and the community in solving the problems.

 Running through definitions of community policing are two basic themes: police–community partnerships and a proactive, problem-solving approach to the police function.

These are also the two core components identified by the Community Policing Consortium, comprised of the International Association of Chiefs of Police (IACP), the National Organization of Black Law Enforcement Executives (NOBLE), the Police Executive Research Forum (PERF), the National Sheriffs' Association (NSA), and the Police Foundation. Without solving the problems they encounter, the police are doomed to handle the same problems and suspects again and again. Without community partnerships, the chances that the police can successfully solve problems also are slim. A community without input and ownership in the solutions will unintentionally or even intentionally undermine police efforts.

A look at the history of policing helps in understanding how community policing has evolved.

A BRIEF HISTORY OF POLICING

Throughout history societies have established rules to govern the conduct of individuals and have devised punishments for those who break the rules. The earliest record of an ancient society's rules for controlling human behavior dates back to approximately 2300 BCE, when Sumerian rulers codified their concept of offenses against society. Since then such rules have been modified and adapted: "The beginnings of just laws and social control were destroyed during the Dark Ages as the Roman Empire disintegrated. Germanic invaders swept into the old Roman territory of Britain, bringing their own laws and customs. These invaders intermarried with those they conquered, the result being the hardy Anglo-Saxons" (Hess and Orthmann, 2012, 7).

The Anglo-Saxons grouped their farms around small, self-governing villages that policed themselves. This informal arrangement became more structured under King Alfred the Great (849–899 CE), who required every male to enroll for police purposes in a group of 10 families, known as a **tithing**. The **tithing system** established the principle of collective responsibility for maintaining local law and order.

The tithing system worked well until 1066, when William the Conqueror, a Norman, invaded and conquered England. William, concerned about national

tithing
A group of 10 families.

tithing system
The Anglo-Saxon principle establishing the principle of collective responsibility for maintaining local law and order.

security, replaced the tithing system of "home rule" with 55 military districts called shires,[1] each headed by a Norman officer called a reeve, hence the title shire-reeve (the origin of the word *sheriff*). William also established the **frankpledge system** which required all free men to swear loyalty to the king's law and to take responsibility for maintaining the local peace.

frankpledge system
The Norman system requiring all free men to swear loyalty to the king's law and to take responsibility for maintaining the local peace.

By the 17th century, law enforcement duties were divided into two separate units, a day watch and a night watch. The day watch consisted of constables who served as jailers and fulfilled other government duties. Citizens worked on the night watch. Each citizen was expected to take a turn watching for fires, bad weather, and disorderly individuals. Some towns also expected the night watchman to call out the time.

If a watchman or any other citizen saw a crime in progress, he was expected to give the **hue and cry** summoning all citizens within earshot to join in pursuing and capturing the wrongdoer. Preserving the peace was the duty of all citizens.

hue and cry
The summoning of all citizens within earshot to join in pursuing and capturing a wrongdoer.

By the end of the 18th century, most people with sufficient means paid others to stand their assigned watch for them, marking the beginning of a paid police force and, in effect, the original neighborhood watch.

The system of day and night watchmen was very ineffective. Because wealthy citizens could avoid the watch duty by hiring someone to take their place, those they hired were hesitant to invoke their authority against the well-to-do. According to Richardson (1970, 10), by the mid-1700s New York City's night watch was "a parcel of idle, drinking, vigilant snorers, who never quelled any nocturnal tumult in their lives … but would, perhaps, be as ready to join in a burglary as any thief in Christendom."

London, suffering from the impact of the Industrial Revolution, was experiencing massive unemployment and poverty. It had become a disorderly city with enormous, crime-ridden slums and a significant juvenile delinquency problem. Some citizens had even begun to carry weapons for self-protection. In an attempt to address the problems, Parliament convened five parliamentary commissions of inquiry between 1780 and 1820. When Sir Robert Peel was appointed home secretary, he proposed that London appoint civilians, paid by the community, to serve as police officers. The Metropolitan Police Act was passed in 1829 and modern policing began.

THE BEGINNINGS OF "MODERN" POLICE FORCES

 "Modern" policing began with the formation of the London Metropolitan Police, founded by Sir Robert Peel in 1829.

Peel set forth the following principles on which the police force was to be based:

» The duty of the police is to prevent crime and disorder.
» The power of the police to fulfill their duties is dependent on public approval and on their ability to secure and maintain public respect.

[1] A shire is equivalent to a U.S. county.

» Public respect and approval also mean the willing cooperation of the public in the task of securing observance of the law.

» The police must seek and preserve public favor not by pandering to public opinion but by constantly demonstrating absolutely impartial service to law.

» The police should strive to maintain a relationship with the public that gives reality to the tradition that the police are the public and the public are the police.

» The test of police efficiency is the absence of crime and disorder, not the visible evidence of police action in dealing with these problems.

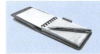 Peel's principles emphasized the interdependency of the police and the public as well as the prevention of crime and disorder.

Peel envisioned a close police–citizen relationship that helped the police maintain order in London. As originally envisioned by the architects of London's Metropolitan Police, a police officer's job was primarily crime prevention and social maintenance, not crime detection. Police were to serve as local marshals who actively maintained order by interacting with the neighborhoods they served.

Policing in the United States

Those who came to America in 1620 and their descendants, through the American Revolution, rejected the British Crown's rule that permitted British soldiers to take over homes and to have complete authority over the colonists. Our founders wanted to ensure that no such power would exist in the newly created nation. As former Chief Justice of the U.S. Supreme Court Warren E. Burger (1991, 26) stated: "The Founders, conscious of the risks of abuse of power, created a system of liberty with order and placed the Bill of Rights as a harness on government to protect people from misuse of the powers." Nonetheless, the system of policing and maintaining order in the northern part of the United States was modeled on the police system developed in England.

At the time the Metropolitan Police Force was established in London, the United States was still operating under a day-and-night watch system similar to the one that had been used in England. In the 1830s several large cities established separate paid day watches. In 1833 Philadelphia became the first city to pay both the day and night watches. Boston followed in 1838 with a six-officer police force. In 1844 New York City took the first step toward organizing a big-city police department similar to those that exist today across the country when it consolidated its day and night watches under the control of a police chief. The police department was modeled on the London Metropolitan Police and Peel's principles. Other cities followed the example set by New York. By 1857 Boston, Chicago, New Orleans, Newark, Cincinnati, Philadelphia, and Baltimore had consolidated police departments modeled on London's Metropolitan Police. The new police chiefs of these departments faced the beginning of tremendous personnel problems and disarray among their officers:

> What those first chiefs of police found in their newly consolidated forces was a motley, undisciplined crew composed, as one commentator on the era described it, principally of "the shiftless, the incompetent, and the ignorant." Tales abounded of police officers in the 1850s who assaulted their superior officers, who released prisoners from the custody of other officers, who were found sleeping or drunk on duty, or who could be bribed for almost anything. (Garmire, 1989, 17)

Despite these problems, and because there were also many honest, dedicated police officers, the citizens considered the police a source of assistance. Early police officers' duties included more community assistance and service than often imagined. Even at the beginning of the 20th century, law enforcement was one of the only government-sanctioned services to help citizens around the clock. Welfare, parole, probation, and unemployment offices did not exist. Police in New York, for example, distributed coal to the poor, monitored the well-being of vulnerable citizens, served as probation and parole officers, and helped establish playgrounds.

It was more than a decade after the formation of the first police forces in the United States that attempts were made to require police officers to wear uniforms. Police officers' well-known resistance to change was apparent even then. The rank-and-file reaction against uniforms was immediate. Police officers claimed that uniforms were "un-American" and "a badge of degradation and servitude." In Philadelphia, police officers even objected to wearing badges on their coats. It was a bitter 4-year struggle before they were finally persuaded to wear a complete uniform.

In 1856 New York City required its officers to be uniformed, but each local ward[2] could determine the style of dress. As a result, in some sections of the city, police officers wore straw hats, whereas in others they wore felt hats. In some wards summer uniforms were white "duck" suits; in other wards they were multicolored outfits.

Policing in the Southern States Policing in the South had different origins—the slave patrols found in the Southern colonies and states. By 1700 most Southern colonies, concerned about the dangers the oppressed slaves could create, had established a code of laws to regulate slaves. These codes prohibited slaves from having weapons, gathering in groups, leaving the plantation without a pass, or resisting punishment.

Predictably, many slaves resisted their bondage. According to Foner (1975) the resistance usually consisted of running away, criminal acts, and conspiracies or revolts. Compounding the problem, in some Southern states slaves outnumbered the colonists. For example, in 1720 South Carolina's population was 30 percent White and 70 percent Black (Simmons, 1976). As Reichel (1999) notes, the White colonists' fear of the slaves as a dangerous threat led to the development of special officers with general enforcement powers as a transition

---

[2] A ward is an administrative division of a city or town.

to modern police. Thus, a strong argument exists that these slave patrols were the first truly American police system (Williams and Murphy, 1990; Dulaney, 1996). In fact, by 1750 every Southern colony had a slave patrol that formally required all White men to serve as patrollers (Dulaney, 1996). In actuality, however, the patrollers were generally poor White men.

In most colonies and states, patrols could enter any plantation and break into slaves' dwellings; punish slaves found outside their plantation; and search, beat, and even kill any slaves found to be violating the slave code: "Twentieth-century Southern law enforcement was essentially a direct outgrowth of the nineteenth-century slave patrols employed to enforce curfews, catch runaways, and suppress rebellions. Even later on, in Northern and Southern cities alike, 'free men of color' were hired as cops only in order to keep other African Americans in line [enforcing Jim Crow laws supporting segregation]. Until the 1960s Black cops, by law or by custom, weren't given powers of arrest over White citizens, no matter how criminal" (Asirvatham, 2000, 2).

The evolution of law enforcement in both the North and South is often divided into three distinct eras.

THE THREE ERAS OF POLICING

Three major paradigm shifts have occurred in the evolution of policing in the United States. A **paradigm** is a model or a way of viewing a specific aspect of life such as politics, medicine, education, and even the criminal justice system. A **paradigm shift** is simply a new way of thinking about a specific subject. Kelling and Moore (1991) describe these paradigm shifts as specific "eras" of policing in the United States.

paradigm
A model or a way of viewing a specific aspect of life such as politics, medicine, education, and the criminal justice system.

paradigm shift
A new way of thinking about a specific subject.

 The three eras of policing are political, reform, and community.

The Political Era (1840 to 1930)

The **political era** extended into the first quarter of the 20th century and witnessed the formation of police departments. During this era police were closely tied to politics. This was dissimilar to the situation in England, where the police were centralized under the king and the police chief had the authority to fire officers. In the United States the police were decentralized under the authority of the municipality in which they worked. The chief had no authority to fire officers; therefore, the police were often undisciplined. "The image of 'Keystone Cops'—police as clumsy bunglers—was widespread and often descriptive of realities in U.S. policing" (Kelling and Moore, 1991, 9).

political era
Extended into the first quarter of the 20th century and witnessed the formation of police departments.

Police officers usually lived in their community and were members of the majority group. Because foot patrol was the most common policing strategy used, officers became close to the public.

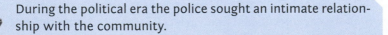 During the political era the police sought an intimate relationship with the community.

During this era chiefs of police were politically appointed and had a vested interest in keeping those who appointed them in power. Politicians rewarded those who voted for them with jobs or special privileges. This was referred to as the **patronage system**, or the **spoils system** from the adage "To the victor go the spoils."

In 1929 President Herbert Hoover appointed the National Commission on Law Observance and Enforcement to study the criminal justice system. Hoover named George W. Wickersham, former U.S. attorney general, as its chairman. When the report was published in 1931, it became one of the "most important events in the history of American Policing" (Walker, 1997, 154). The Wickersham Commission focused two reports on the police. Report 11, Lawlessness in Law Enforcement, described the problem of police brutality, concluding that "the third degree—the inflicting of pain, physical or mental, to extract confessions or statements—is extensively practiced." Specific tactics included protracted questioning, threats and intimidation, physical brutality, illegal detention, and refusal to allow access of counsel to suspects (National Commission on Law Observance and Enforcement, 1931, 4). Report 14, The Police, examined police administration and called for expert leadership, centralized administrative control, and higher standards for personnel—in effect, for police professionalism. The inefficiency and corruption of the police led to the second era of policing, the reform era.

The Reform Era (1930 to 1980)

The **reform era** is often referred to as the **progressive era**. August Vollmer and O.W. Wilson are usually attributed with spearheading the reform movement that called for a drastic change in the organization and function of police departments.

August Vollmer is often credited as the father of American policing. He was elected to be the Berkeley city marshal in 1904, a position changed to chief of police in 1909. Vollmer was chief until 1932. During his tenure at Berkeley, Vollmer created a police force that became a model for the country. His innovations included radios in patrol cars, a fingerprint and handwriting classification system, a workable system for filing and using modus operandi (MO) files, motorcycles and bicycles on patrol, and a police school at his department. Vollmer believed police should be trained professionals who were also social workers with a deeper responsibility to the community than simply fighting crime. Vollmer's book, *The Police and Modern Society* (1936), is still a classic in law enforcement. Vollmer also helped create the first college police program at the University of California at Berkeley.

O.W. Wilson, a protégé of Vollmer, continued the move toward professionalizing the police. One of Wilson's greatest strengths was his firm belief in honest law enforcement. Although very aware that the police had little control over the root causes of crime, Wilson advocated the concept of preventive patrol. Wilson's most noted works are *Police Administration* (1950) and *Police Planning* (1952).

One basic change during this era was to disassociate policing from politics, which was accomplished in a variety of ways. In Los Angeles, for example, the chief of police position became a civil-service job that required applicants to

---

patronage system
Politicians rewarded those who voted for them with jobs or special privileges; prevalent during the political era. Also called the *spoils system.*

spoils system
Politicians rewarded those who voted for them with jobs or special privileges; prevalent during the political era. Also called the *patronage system.*

reform era
Emphasized preventive automobile patrol and rapid response to calls for service. Also called the *progressive era.*

progressive era
Emphasized preventive automobile patrol and rapid response to calls for service. Also called the *reform era.*

pass a civil-service test. In Milwaukee the chief of police was appointed for life by a citizen commission.

With the disassociation of policing from politics came a change in emphasis in the police role as citizens began to equate policing with fighting crime. The police considered social-service-type functions less desirable and avoided them when possible.

The relationship between the police and the public also changed during the reform era: "Police leaders in the reform era redefined the nature of a proper relationship between police officers and both politicians and citizens. Police would be impartial law enforcers who related to citizens in professionally neutral and distant terms" (Kelling and Moore, 1991, 12). The public viewed the police as professionals who remained detached from the citizens they served.

 During the reform era the police relationship with the community they served was professionally remote.

During this era the concept of the **thin blue line** developed, a phrase referring to the line that separates law-abiding, peaceful citizens from the murderous, plundering villains who prey upon them. The phrase also suggests a distance between the police and the public they serve. The thin blue line describes the dangerous threats to communities, with police standing between that danger and law-abiding citizens. It suggests both police heroism and isolation.

thin blue line
The distancing of the police from the public they serve.

Adding to the distancing of police from the public during the reform era was the replacement of foot patrols with motorized patrols. O.W. Wilson's preventive patrol by squad car, coupled with an emphasis on rapid response to calls for service, became the dual focus of policing during this era. The police image became one of professional crime fighters roaring through city streets in high-powered squad cars, lights flashing and sirens wailing. Consequently, policing during the reform era is often referred to as the professional model.

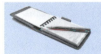 The **professional model** emphasized crime control by preventive automobile patrol coupled with rapid response to calls.

professional model
Emphasized crime control by preventive automobile patrol coupled with rapid response to calls. The predominant policing model used during the reform era (1970s and 1980s).

The problems the first police administrators faced did not change much, but under the professional model their answers did. Many police methods were challenged during the 1960s, when social change exploded in the United States as the result of several significant events occurring almost simultaneously.

The Civil Rights Movement began in the late 1950s as a grassroots effort to change the blatantly unequal social, political, and economic systems in the United States. Confrontations between African Americans and the police, who were almost completely male and White, increased during this time. Representing the status quo and defending it, the manner in which the police handled protest marches and civil disobedience often aggravated these situations.

Punctuated by the assassinations of President Kennedy, Malcolm X, Martin Luther King, Jr., Medgar Evers, and Robert Kennedy, the events of the decade were, for the first time in history, documented in detail and viewed by millions of Americans on television. The antiwar movement, based on college campuses, was also televised. When demonstrators at the 1968 Democratic convention in Chicago were beaten by the Chicago police, the demonstrators chanted: "The whole world is watching." Watching what was later termed a police riot, Americans were shocked.

Plagued by lack of training and confronted by a confusing array of social movements and an emerging drug culture, the police became the "enemy." Officers heard themselves referred to as "pigs" by everyone from students to well-known entertainers. They represented the status quo, the establishment, and everything that stood in the way of peace, equality, and justice. Police in the 1960s were at war with the society they served. Never had the relationship between the law enforcement community and the people it served been so strained.

The 1960s changed the face of the United States, and law enforcement was no exception. In addition to the questionable way police handled race riots and antiwar demonstrations during this decade, several big-city police departments were facing corruption charges. Studies in the 1970s on corruption and criminal behavior among police agencies brought great pressure to bear on the entire criminal justice system. Media coverage of law enforcement practices educated the public, who ultimately demanded change in police methods, attitudes, and image. *Understanding Community Policing* (1994, 6–7) describes the social and professional "awakening" that occurred during the 1960s and 1970s:

> Antiwar protesters, civil rights activists, and other groups began to demonstrate in order to be heard. Overburdened and poorly prepared police came to symbolize what these groups sought to change in their government and society. Focusing attention on police policies and practices became an effective way to draw attention to the need for wider change. Police became the targets of hostility, which ultimately led police leaders to concerned reflection and analysis. . . .
>
> A number of organizations within the policing field also became committed to improving policing methods in the 1970s. Among those on the forefront of this movement for constructive change were the Police Foundation, the Police Executive Research Forum, the National Organization of Black Law Enforcement Executives, the Urban Sheriffs' Group of the National Sheriffs' Association, and the International Association of Chiefs of Police. These organizations conducted much of the basic research that led police to reevaluate traditional policing methods.

Commissions Established to Examine Police Services   During the 1960s and early 1970s, considerable turmoil existed throughout the country related to issues of police and race relations, corruption, and use of force. During that period, five national Blue Ribbon Commissions, or ad hoc, short-term investigations of law enforcement, were initiated to examine various aspects of police services and the criminal justice process (Walker and Macdonald, 2009), and resulted in written reports with recommendation for reform:

» The President's Commission on Law Enforcement and Administration of Justice was influenced by urban racial turmoil. An outgrowth of its report published in 1967 and 1968 was the Safe Streets Act of 1968 and the Law Enforcement Assistance Administration, which provided significant funding for police-related programs.

» The National Advisory Commission on Civil Disorders (popularly known as the Kerner Commission) was also inspired by the riots and other disorders in many U.S. cities in the summer of 1967. Its report examined patterns of disorder and prescribed responses by the federal government, the criminal justice system, and local government.

» The National Commission on the Causes and Prevention of Violence was established after the assassinations of Martin Luther King, Jr., and Robert Kennedy in 1968. Its report, "To Establish Justice, To Insure Domestic Tranquility," was published in 1969.

» The President's Commission on Campus Unrest was established following student deaths related to protests at Kent State and Jackson State universities in 1970.

» The National Advisory Commission on Criminal Justice Standards and Goals issued six reports in 1973 in an attempt to develop standards and recommendations for police crime control efforts.

In response to the negative police image that emerged during the 1960s, several departments across the country established programs to enhance their relationships with the communities they served. These programs included public-relations programs, community-relations programs, and crime prevention programs.

Efforts to Enhance Relations between the Police and the Community

To avoid confusion, it is helpful to distinguish among public relations, community relations, and human relations because these terms are used frequently throughout this text and in other literature on policing.

» **Public relations**: Efforts to enhance the police image—"We'll tell you what we're doing, but leave us alone to fight crime"

» **Community relations**: Efforts to interact and communicate with the community—team policing, community resource officers, and school resource officers

» **Human relations**: Efforts to relate to and understand other people or groups of people—the focus of Section II

Public-relations efforts are usually one-way efforts to raise the image of the police. These efforts by police departments include hosting departmental open houses and providing speakers for school and community events. Many police departments have established a public-relations office or division and have assigned specific officers to the public-relations effort. Such efforts reflect the growing recognition by police administrators that they need public support.

In the past several decades, especially in the late 1970s and also as a result of the widening gap between the police and the public, many police departments began community-relations programs. Unlike public-relations efforts, which were primarily one-to-one communications and often media generated, community-relations programs sought to bring the police and the community closer through isolated police tactics such as team policing and community resource officers. Efforts to enhance community relations also frequently involved citizens through crime prevention programs.

public relations
Efforts to enhance the police image. See also *community relations*.

community relations
Efforts to interact and communicate with the community—team policing, community resource officers, and school liaison officers. See also *public relations*.

human relations
Efforts to relate to and understand other individuals or groups.

Crime Prevention Programs Such programs, which continue to be strategies used in many community policing efforts, are discussed in detail in Section III.

 Crime prevention programs that enlist citizens' aid include Operation Identification programs, neighborhood- or block-watch programs, and home and automobile security programs.

The Law Enforcement Assistance Administration Another response to the negative image of the police was the establishment of the Law Enforcement Assistance Administration (LEAA) in 1968. Over the next several years LEAA provided billions of dollars to the "war on crime," funding studies and programs for law enforcement. LEAA awarded more than $9 billion to state and local governments to improve police, courts, and correctional systems; to combat juvenile delinquency; and to finance innovative crime-fighting projects. Tens of thousands of programs and projects were supported with LEAA funds, and millions of hours were applied to identify effective, efficient, economical ways to reduce crime and improve criminal justice.

Although the consensus among law enforcement officials today is that LEAA was mostly mismanaged, there was also a very positive aspect of LEAA. This was the Law Enforcement Education Program (LEEP), which provided thousands of officers with funding for higher education.

The Courts The courts also had a major impact on criminal justice during the 1960s. Several legal decisions limited police powers and clarified the rights of the accused. The exclusionary rule, established in *Weeks v. United States* (1914), mandated that federal courts must refuse to consider evidence obtained by unreasonable, and therefore unconstitutional, search and seizure, no matter how relevant the evidence was to the case. In 1961 *Mapp v. Ohio* extended the exclusionary rule to every court and law enforcement officer in the country.

In 1963 in *Gideon v. Wainwright* the Supreme Court ruled 9 to 0 that the due process clause of the Fourteenth Amendment requires states to provide free counsel to indigent (impoverished) defendants in all felony cases. Another landmark case came the following year in *Escobedo v. Illinois* (1964), when the Court ruled that if individuals confess without being told of their right to have a lawyer present, the confessions are not legal.

In 1966 this right to have a lawyer present, and at public expense if necessary, and other rights were reaffirmed in what is probably the best-known Supreme Court case to date—*Miranda v. Arizona*. The Court held that evidence obtained by police during custodial interrogation of a suspect cannot be used in court unless the suspect is informed of the following four basic rights *before* questioning:

» The suspect's right to remain silent
» The right of the police to use in a court of law any statement made by the suspect
» The suspect's right to have an attorney present during questioning

» The suspect's right to have a court-appointed attorney before questioning if he or she cannot afford one

Another landmark decision was handed down in 1968 in *Terry v. Ohio*. This case established police officers' right to stop and question a person to investigate suspicious behavior and to frisk that person if the officer has reason to believe the person is armed:

> The police have the authority to detain a person for questioning even without probable cause to believe that the person has committed a crime. Such an investigatory stop does not constitute an arrest and is permissible when prompted by both the observation of unusual conduct leading to a reasonable suspicion that criminal activity may be afoot and the ability to point to specific and articulable facts to justify the suspicion. Subsequently, an officer may frisk a person if the officer reasonably suspects that he or she is in danger. (del Carmen and Walker, 2012, 28)

Other Problems and Challenges during the Progressive Era

Despite this decision, reported crime increased and the public's fear of crime intensified. An influx of immigrants added to the problems of major cities. The deinstitution-alizing of mental patients in the 1970s brought thousands of individuals who were mentally disabled into the mainstream of the United States, often without means to support themselves. This, coupled with the return of many Vietnam veterans who found it difficult to reenter society, resulted in a large homeless population.

Another challenge to the effectiveness of the professional model was the Kansas City Preventive Patrol Study. This classic study found that increasing or decreasing preventive patrol efforts had no significant effect on crime, citizen fear of crime, community attitudes toward the police, police response time, or traffic accidents. As Klockars (1983, 130) notes: "It makes about as much sense to have police patrol routinely in cars to fight crime as it does to have firemen patrol routinely in fire trucks to fight fire."

Many law enforcement officials view the Kansas City Preventive Patrol Study as the beginning of a new era in policing. It was considered by police to be the first experimental design used in policing and, as such, was a landmark. It set the stage for further research in policing and is viewed as the first true movement in the professionalization of policing. Its findings are also controversial. There were problems with the research design and implementation of this study; however, it called into question many assumptions about policing. It concluded what many police officials already knew but did not want publicized for fear of the impact on police budgets. Other research conducted in the 1970s also questioned police effectiveness:

> Research about preventive patrol, rapid response to calls for service, and investigative work—the three mainstays of police tactics—was uniformly discouraging.

> Research demonstrated that preventive patrol in automobiles had little effect on crime, citizen levels of fear, or citizen satisfaction with police. Rapid response to calls for service likewise had little impact on arrests, citizen satisfaction with police, or levels of citizen fear. Also, research into criminal investigation effectiveness suggested that detective units were so poorly administered that they had little chance of being effective. (Kelling, 1988, 4)

By the mid-1970s the general period of reform in policing in the United States slowed. Many promising reforms, such as team policing, had not caused any major changes. (Chapter 5 discusses team policing and its demise.) The reform movement was called into question by two articles: Herman Goldstein's "Problem-Oriented Policing" in 1979 and James Q. Wilson and George L. Kelling's "Broken Windows" in 1982.

Other reasons for reevaluating police methods were the changing nature of the people who became police and their frustration with the traditional role of the patrol officer. Although patrol was given lip service as the backbone of policing, it was seen as the least desirable assignment. A change was needed at the patrol level to attract more highly educated and less militaristic recruits. The patrol officer had to become more important to the department in accomplishing its mission.

Finally, many businesses and individuals began to hire private security officers to ensure their safety. The public assumed that the police alone were unable to "preserve the peace." Whereas some called for greater cooperation between public and private policing, others argued that the public should collaborate with all policing efforts.

A combination of the dissatisfaction with criminal justice and the role of patrol officers, research results, the trend toward private policing, and the writings of Goldstein and Wilson and Kelling led to the third era of policing—the community era.

The Community Era (1980 to Present)

In the 1980s many police departments began experimenting with more community involvement in the "war on crime." Also during this decade several cities tested Goldstein's problem-oriented approach to policing. The emphasis in many departments began to shift from crime fighting to crime prevention.

According to some historians, the community era had its roots in the Kerner Commission Report, released in February 1968 by the President's National Advisory Committee on Civil Disorder. The report condemned racism in the United States and called for aid to African American communities to avert further racial polarization and violence.

Mentel (2008) suggests: "Because it fosters mutual trust and respect between police and the public, community policing should be the operational force guiding agencies in a democratic society." Mentel outlines several core principles that guide fair and democratic policing:

» Engaging the community to create and maintain trust relationships
» Maintaining rights to privacy while protecting national security
» Taking diversity into account when devising policing strategies; diversity includes not only racial and ethnic considerations but also concerns the homeless, released offenders, youths, and immigrant populations.
» Making a commitment to police integrity and combating racially biased policing
» Building successful working relationships between law enforcement and the media
» Encouraging openness and policing innovations through technological and other strategic advances

Gradually law enforcement has become more responsive to the public's desire for a different kind of policing. Today there is considerable citizen–police interaction and problem solving. Although still resistant to change, police agencies are now more likely to respond to the needs and wishes of the communities they serve. The significant changes in the way police address sexual assault, domestic violence, sexual abuse of children, drunk driving, and missing children attest to this new responsiveness. The public wants the police to be proactive; citizens want police to try to prevent crime in addition to apprehending criminals after they have committed a crime.

 During the community era the police sought to reestablish a close relationship with the community.

Highlights of the three eras of policing are summarized in Table 1.1.

The community era goes by many names: community policing, community-oriented policing (COP), neighborhood policing, and the like. Currently the term *community policing* is most commonly used. At the heart of most "new" approaches to policing is a return to the ancient idea of community responsibility for the welfare of society—police officers become a part of the community, not apart from it. A comparison of traditional policing and community policing is made in Table 1.2.

Whereas traditionally policing has been **reactive**, responding to calls for service, community policing is **proactive**, anticipating problems and seeking solutions to them. The term *proactive* is beginning to take on an expanded definition. Not only is it taking on the meaning of anticipating problems, but it is also taking on the Stephen Covey slant, that of accountability and choosing a response rather than reacting the same way each time a similar situation occurs. Police are learning that they do not obtain different results by applying the same methods. In other words, to get different results, different tactics are needed. This is the focus of Chapter 4.

reactive
Responding after the fact; responding to calls for service. The opposite of *proactive*.

proactive
Anticipating problems and seeking solutions to those problems, as in community policing. The opposite of *reactive*.

Table 1.1	The Three Eras of Policing		
	Political Era (1840s to 1930s)	**Reform Era (1930s to 1980s)**	**Community Era (1980s to Present)**
Authorization	Politics and law	Law and professionalism	Community support (political), law, and professionalism
Function	Broad social services	Crime control	Broad provision of services
Organizational design	Decentralized	Centralized, classical	Decentralized, task forces, matrices
Relationship to community	Intimate	Professional, remote	Intimate
Tactics and technology	Foot patrol	Preventive patrol and rapid response to calls	Foot patrol, problem solving, public relations
Outcome	Citizen, political satisfaction	Crime control	Quality of life and citizen satisfaction

Source: Based on George L. Kelling and Mark H. Moore. "From Political to Reform to Community: The Evolving Strategy of Police." In *Community Policing: Rhetoric or Reality*, edited by Jack R. Greene and Stephen D. Mastrofski. New York: Praeger Publishers, 1991, pp. 6, 14–15, 22–23.

Table 1.2 Comparison of Traditional Policing and Community Policing

Question	Traditional Policing	Community Policing
Who are the police?	A government agency principally responsible for law enforcement.	Police are the public and the public are the police: The police officers are those who are paid to give full-time attention to the duties of every citizen.
What is the relationship of the police force to other public service departments?	Priorities often conflict.	The police are one department among many responsible for improving the quality of life.
What is the role of the police?	Focusing on solving crimes.	A broader problem-solving approach.
How is police efficiency measured?	By detection and arrest rates.	By the absence of crime and disorder.
What are the highest priorities?	Crimes that are high value (e.g., bank robberies) and those involving violence.	Whatever problems disturb the community most.
What, specifically, do police deal with?	Incidents.	Citizens' problems and concerns.
What determines the effectiveness of police?	Response times.	Public cooperation.
What view do police take of service calls?	Deal with them only if there is no real police work to do.	Vital function and great opportunity.
What is police professionalism?	Swift, effective response to serious crime.	Keeping close to the community.
What kind of intelligence is most important?	Crime intelligence (study of particular crimes or series of crimes).	Criminal intelligence (information about the activities of individuals or groups).
What is the essential nature of police accountability?	Highly centralized; governed by rules, regulations, and policy directives; accountable to the law.	Emphasis on local accountability to community needs.
What is the role of headquarters?	To provide the necessary rules and policy directives.	To preach organizational values.
What is the role of the press liaison department?	To keep the "heat" off operational officers so they can get on with job.	To coordinate an essential channel of communication with the community.
How do the police regard prosecutions?	As an important goal.	As one tool among many.

Source: Malcolm K. Sparrow. *Implementing Community Policing*, U.S. Department of Justice, National Institute of Justice, November 1988, pp. 8–9.

Although community policing is considered innovative, one of its central tenets of involvement with and responsiveness to the community is similar to the principles set forth by Sir Robert Peel in 1829 when he established the London Metropolitan Police. He stated: "The police are the public and the public are the police." Policing has strayed so far from these principles in the past century that the concepts central to community policing seem fresh and sensible today. These central concepts include the goals of community policing, its major features, and its essential elements.

Consider next some major features of community policing.

FEATURES OF COMMUNITY POLICING

Several major features associated with community policing are regular contact between officers and citizens; a department-wide philosophy and department-wide acceptance; internal and external influence and respect for officers; a well-defined role including both proactive and reactive policing—a full-service officer; direct service—the same officer takes complaints and gives crime prevention tips; citizens identify problems and cooperate in setting up the police agenda; police accountability is ensured by the citizens receiving

Police attempt to guide angry protesters onto the sidewalk during the march to Union Square from Bryant Park during Occupy Wall Street "May Day" protests on May 1, 2012, in New York, NY. Often, mere police presence is enough to keep protest groups from crossing the line to civil disobedience.

© Glynnis Jones/Shutterstock.com

the service in addition to administrative mechanisms; and the officer is the leader and catalyst for change in the neighborhood to reduce fear, disorder, decay, and crime:

> Community policing goes beyond simply putting officers on foot or bicycle patrols, or in neighborhood stations. It redefines the role of the officer on the street, from crime fighter to problem solver and neighborhood ombudsman. It forces a cultural transformation of the entire department including a decentralized organizational structure and changes in recruiting, training, awards systems, evaluation, promotions, and so forth. Furthermore, this philosophy asks officers to break away from the binds of incident-driven policing and to seek proactive and creative resolution to crime and disorder. (Peak and Barthe, 2009)

The chief of police is an advocate and sets the tone for the delivery of both law enforcement and social services in the jurisdictions. Officers educate the public about issues (such as response time or preventive patrol) and the need to prioritize services. Increased trust between the police officer and citizens because of long-term, regular contact results in an enhanced flow of information to the police. The officer is continually accessible in person, by telephone, or in a decentralized office with regular visibility in the neighborhood.

Officers are viewed as having a stake in the community. They are role models, especially for youth, because of regular contact with citizens. Influence is from the bottom up—citizens receiving service help set priorities and influence police policy, meaningful organizational change, and departmental restructuring—ranging from officer selection to training, evaluation, and promotion. When intervention is necessary, informal social control is the first choice. Officers encourage citizens to solve many of their own problems and volunteer to assist neighbors. Officers encourage other service providers such as animal control workers, firefighters, and mail carriers to become involved in community problem solving. Officers mobilize all community resources, including citizens, private and public agencies, and private businesses. Success is determined by a reduction in citizen fear, neighborhood disorder, and crime.

Identification and awareness of these features have allowed law enforcement departments nationwide to implement the principles and philosophy of community policing. Also important to understanding community policing is knowledge of the essential elements identified by researchers and practitioners.

ESSENTIAL ELEMENTS OF COMMUNITY POLICING

Three essential elements of community policing are partnerships, problem solving, and organizational change (Morabito, 2010). Partnerships describe the indispensable relationship between the community and law enforcement. Partnerships are central to modern-day policing because they recognize a basic truth—law enforcement cannot do it alone (Peed, 2008). Although partnerships are critical to policing, they must be purposeful, directed toward improving the quality of life through the second essential element of community policing—problem solving—which seeks to reduce problems by addressing their immediate underlying causes (Peed, 2008). However: "Partnerships and problem-solving will not occur spontaneously within our agencies. These two vital aspects of modern-day policing will only come about if we nurture them in our departments and officer" (Peed, 2008, 23). In other words, without organizational change, problem solving and partnerships will not happen.

In a study of how the actual implementation of community policing affects individual officers' feelings about community policing, a pre- and post-implementation survey found that implementation officers felt they had less communication with other officers, less independence and discretion, less participation in decision making and more meetings with agencies and businesses but less contact with citizens (Lord and Friday, 2008). The officers also indicated that the problem-oriented policing projects were too formal and time-consuming. The study concluded: "Community policing is a philosophy that can be translated into practice in as many ways as there are communities. … The *context of policing* is an important element in the success of COP implementation. Traditional policing has some important police–police interactions that add personal value to the job. There needs to be congruity between the philosophy of COP and its local implementation" (Lord and Friday, 2008, 236).

Rosenberg and colleagues (2008) examined, over a 19-month period, police officer attitudes toward community policing in Racine, Wisconsin, and found that patrol officers' and investigators' attitudes were less favorable toward community policing concepts, programming, decentralization of substations, and the community policing unit than those of senior command officers and, in some cases, sergeants. Both patrol officers and investigators indicated strained relationships with supervisors and were more supportive of a decentralized organizational structure than were sergeants and senior command officers. Research by the Rand Center on Quality Policing, presented in *Community Policing: What Makes It Work?* (2008), suggests that little is really known about what makes implementation of community policing work: "The extent to which the implementation of community policing varies across time and place is

EL PROTECTOR PROGRAM

Metropolitan Nashville Police Department

Together We Make a Difference, Juntos Hacemos La Diferencia.

This motto of the Metropolitan Nashville Police Department's El Protector initiative captures the essence of a programmatic approach aimed at utilizing community participation to solve and prevent crime. El Protector has worked to build trust between the Metropolitan Nashville Police Department (MNPD) and the Hispanic/Latino community in the Nashville metropolitan area, which is 7.2 percent of the city total, to reduce DUIs, traffic fatalities, and domestic violence, as well as promote crime prevention among people with limited English-speaking skills. This bilingual/bicultural program achieves these goals by providing public education and facilitating a dialogue between the police and the Hispanic community, instead of focusing specifically on law enforcement. The key to El Protector's success has been the involvement of officers of Hispanic ancestry or other officers who are bilingual and bicultural. MNPD has dedicated two such full-time sworn officers to be stationed in the two most heavily populated Spanish-speaking communities in Nashville in order to build relationships with those residents and communicate that it is safe to come to the police.

Research has shown that the Spanish-speaking population—mainly Cuban, Dominican, Guatemalan, Honduran, Mexican, Nicaraguan, and Puerto Rican immigrants and first-generation citizens—is often reluctant to seek help from the police when they are victimized or to come forward when they have witnessed a crime because of the corruption of law enforcement in their native countries and their perception that police in this country are equally corrupt. Fear of immigration enforcement is another concern. As one of the El Protector officers explains: "We need to let them know that we're here to protect and serve this community, and you're a part of this community." Not only is it important that residents know that they are entitled to services from the police, but that they are needed to assist the police in solving crimes. The message that the officers most urgently want to bring to Hispanic residents is that, "If you do not cooperate, we cannot help solve these crimes and recurring problems in your communities."

In order to further break down barriers between law enforcement officials and the Hispanic community, MNPD holds several annual events that include a Hispanic community festival, Hispanic Teen Academy, and a soccer tournament where they interact with community members outside of their regular police duties. Program events are held all over the city on residential streets, in apartment complexes, at churches, and in mall parking lots, allowing residents to have better access and opportunities to connect on their own turf: "Residents are more likely to participate when an event is at their local church, favorite restaurant, or even on their block. We try to be innovative about that so events take place where people will feel comfortable," says one police administrator.

El Protector officers also mobilize volunteers to organize and run many of the programs and events. One notable program—the Cricket Volunteer Interpreter Program—organizes Spanish-speaking dispatchers to translate for officers and residents during traffic stops, domestic violence calls, and other events involving Spanish-speaking witnesses to crimes. Engaging residents in this capacity—making them a part of programs that support their neighborhoods, friends, and families—is a hallmark of El Protector.

The benefits of establishing an open line of trust and communication with Hispanic residents have become apparent. Initially, the program saw a spike in the number of calls for service in the two precincts where the two El Protector Hispanic officers were stationed, which MNPD attributed to new resident confidence to access police support: "What appears as a spike in calls is actually a spike in the trust the community has in its police department, and specifically, the trust that has improved among the Hispanic population of Nashville." Since inception of the program the number of Hispanic victims of violent crimes has gone down and the program has effectively engaged area business owners and residents in crime prevention efforts through community engagement rather than enforcement measures.

El Protector was recognized by the Vera Institute of Justice, which chose MNPD out of 200 departments nationally to win one of the six best practices awards for its work in bridging the language divide in Nashville. In the future, El Protector is looking toward expanding their services to reach out to other ethnic groups, such as the growing Somali and Kurdish populations.

Source: Retzlaff, Christine. *Proactive Outreach to Hispanic Community Encourages Trust and Participation: Metropolitan Nashville Police Department's El Protector Program*. Local Initiatives Support Corporation's Community Safety Initiative, MetLife Foundation Community-Police Partnership Awards program, February 22, 2012. Retrieved May 7, 2012 from http://www.lisc.org/content/publication/detail/20015

ON THE BEAT

I was first introduced to the concept of community policing back in college. In fact, one of my first classes was "Police and Community." I recall the first day of the class when the instructor asked how many people in the room wanted to be police officers. Most everyone in the class raised their hands, except me. When the instructor asked me what I wanted to be, I stated, "I want to be a *peace officer*!" You can imagine the looks I got from my classmates.

The terms "police officer" and "peace officer" are interchangeable, as they should be. The further I go in my career, the more I see the importance of being a "peace officer." When you decide to go into police work, you will find yourself wearing hats you never thought you would wear. I am not talking about a physical hat you place on your head. You find yourself becoming an educator in many situations, a counselor, a mediator, someone who consoles,

a mentor, and the list goes on. That is what it means to police a community. It is also about partnering with community members and nonprofit organizations for the betterment of the whole. It is about getting to the root of neighborhood concerns and looking for some long-term resolutions.

If you find yourself going to the same address time after time, maybe it's time to look at all the issues involved and consider the entire situation. Often it may be easier to respond on a case-by-case basis, but this approach may not necessarily solve a problem. It is important to look at the causes of a problem and attempt to resolve some of those issues. Again, this calls for other agency involvement and this is where partnerships play in. I have found this to be the best way to serve a community.

—*Kim Czapar*

uncertain. The factors that influence its implementation are unclear, and statistically sensitive measures of implementation are lacking." Implementing community policing is the focus of Chapter 5.

Cordner (1999, 137) suggests: "It [community policing] started out as a fuzzy notion about increasing police–citizen contact and reducing fear of crime, then settled into a period during which it was seen as having two primary components—problem solving and community engagement." He provides a framework consisting of four dimensions for viewing community policing and determining whether the essential elements are in place.

 Cordner's four dimensions of community policing are the philosophical, strategic, tactical, and organizational dimensions.

The Philosophical Dimension

Many advocates of community policing stress that it is a philosophy rather than a program, and it does have that important dimension. The three important elements within this dimension are citizen input, a broadened function, and personalized service. Cordner (1999, 138) contends that citizen input meshes well with an agency that "is part of a government 'of the people, for the people, and by the people.'" A broadened police function means expanding responsibility into areas such as order maintenance and social services and protecting and enhancing the lives of our most vulnerable citizens: juveniles, the elderly, minorities, the disabled, the poor, and the homeless. The personal service element supports tailored policing based on local norms and values and on individual needs.

The Strategic Dimension

A philosophy without means of putting it into practice is an empty shell. This is where the strategic dimension comes in. This dimension "includes the key operational concepts that translate philosophy into action" (Cordner, 1999, 139). The three strategic elements of community policing are reoriented operations, a geographic focus, and a prevention emphasis.

The reorientation in operations shifts reliance on the squad car to emphasis on face-to-face interactions. It may also include differential calls for service. The geographic focus changes patrol officers' basic unit of accountability from time of day to location. Officers are given permanent assignments so they can get to know the citizens within their area. Finally, the prevention emphasis is proactive, seeking to raise the status of prevention/patrol officers to the level traditionally enjoyed by detectives.

The Tactical Dimension

The tactical dimension translates the philosophical and strategic dimensions into concrete programs and practices. The most important tactical elements, according to Cordner, are positive interactions, partnerships, and problem solving. Officers are encouraged to get out of their vehicles and initiate positive interactions with the citizens within their beat. They are also encouraged to seek out opportunities to partner with organizations and agencies and to mediate between those with conflicting interests, for example, landlords and tenants, adults and juveniles. The third essential element, problem solving rather than responding to isolated incidents, is the focus of Chapter 4.

The Organizational Dimension

Cordner's fourth dimension, the organizational dimension, is discussed in Chapter 5.

Other Views of the Elements of Community Policing

Maguire and Mastrofski (2000) examined the dimensionality of the community policing movement and found that the number of dimensions underlying the community policing movement varied significantly according to the source of the data:

» Skolnick and Bayley (1988) described four recurring elements of community policing found internationally: community-based crime prevention, reorientation of patrol activities, increased police accountability, and decentralization of command.

» Bayley (1994) defined community policing using four dimensions: consultation, adaptation, mobilization, and problem solving.

PARTNERSHIPS

Graffiti Hurts®

Graffiti Hurts®—Care for Your Community is a grass-roots community education program developed in 1996 by Keep America Beautiful. The Graffiti Hurts® Program is dedicated to raising awareness about the harmful effects of graffiti vandalism on communities. While graffiti vandals believe their actions harm no one, the reality is that graffiti hurts everyone: homeowners, communities, businesses, and schools. And those who practice it risk personal injury, violence, and arrest.

Graffiti on public transit property contributes to lost revenue associated with reduced ridership, reduced retail sales, and declines in property value. In addition, graffiti heightens fear of gang activity and is often perceived by residents and passers-by as a sign that a downward spiral has begun, even though this may not be true. Patrons of buildings, parks, or public facilities where graffiti vandalism has occurred may feel that if graffiti is tolerated, then other more serious crimes, such as theft and assault, may also go unchallenged. Approximately half of all schools across the country report incidents of vandalism, with about one-third of students reporting they saw hate-related graffiti at school. Although the cost of graffiti vandalism in the United States has yet to be definitively documented, for many communities, private property owners, and public agencies the cost is rising each year.

At the heart of the Graffiti Hurts program are four goals:

1. Educate citizens about the importance of graffiti prevention and abatement

2. Provide communities with tools and resources to respond to graffiti vandalism

3. Help foster partnerships that will encourage involvement from all members of the community in addressing graffiti vandalism

4. Help communities establish antigraffiti programs that get results, creating healthier, safer, and more livable communities

Communities are tackling graffiti vandalism with a variety of tools. While each of these best practices can be effective, the most successful programs use a comprehensive, systematic approach that includes changing the environment to prevent graffiti vandalism, ongoing education and community involvement, improved technologies for removal, updated ordinances, and consistent enforcement and prosecution.

Effective community graffiti prevention programs coordinate closely with local law enforcement. Police are critical to enforcing antigraffiti laws: They are an integral part of any graffiti hotline and database, they are effective educators about graffiti vandalism in neighborhoods and schools, and they are the ones that ultimately make the arrests.

More information about graffiti prevention and best practices for communities is available online at www.graffitihurts.org.

Source: Graffiti Hurts Program. Keep America Beautiful Inc. Reprinted by permission.

» Bratton (1996) defined community policing as the three *p*s: partnership, problem solving, and prevention.

» Rohe, Adams, Arcury, Memory, and Klopovic (1996) use three dimensions separating community policing from traditional policing: shared responsibility, prevention, and increased officer discretion.

» Roth and Johnson (1997) operationalized community as articulated by the COPS office using four dimensions: problem solving, community partnership building, preventive interventions, and organizational change.

» Maguire and Katz (1997) used four additive community policing indices measuring patrol officer activities, management activities, citizen activities, and organizational activities.

Clearly, just as there is no one definition of community policing that will satisfy everyone, there is no one way to look at how community policing is viewed in practice.

DEMOCRACY AND THE POLICE

According to Jones (2008, 2235): "Community policing is now so widely accepted that, no matter how the law is enforced within a jurisdiction, police departments are likely to have adopted this label. Just as dictatorships have the trappings of democratic elections, so too do autocratic police departments mimic community policing. Can police departments, hierarchical organizations with militaristic overtones (it's Sergeant Joe Friday, not Mr. Joe Friday), adapt to democratic norms like openness and equality? Is 'democratic policing' an attainable goal or an oxymoron?"

Many were skeptical of the durability of the community policing philosophy when the Office of Community Oriented Policing Services (COPS) was created more than 15 years ago. However, time has shown how practical and important this concept is to the mission of law enforcement in the United States, as will be demonstrated throughout the remaining chapters of this text.

COPS—*Not Just a Fad*

The COPS Office was created in 1994 as a component of the U.S. Justice Department. The mission of the Office is to advance the practice of community policing. The Office carries out its mission by providing grants and training to tribal, local, and state law enforcement agencies. The funding allows agencies to hire and train officers, to acquire technology, and to develop and test new policing strategies. It also provides community policing training and technical assistance, reaching not only law enforcement officers but state and local leaders and community members.

The Office also maintains an online Resource Information Center that offers publications and training materials on community policing topics.

The COPS Office continues to demonstrate its staying power and its significant financial investment in American law enforcement. Under the American Recovery and Reinvestment Act (ARRA) of 2009, the COPS Office is continuing to provide funding for agencies to hire additional police officers and sheriff's deputies.

The Fiscal Year (FY) 2012 COPS Hiring Program (CHP) made available approximately $111 million in funding to state, local, and tribal law enforcement agencies to hire new and/or rehire career law enforcement officers. To date, the COPS Office has funded the addition of nearly 123,000 officers to more than 12,000 state, local and tribal law enforcement agencies to advance community policing in small and large jurisdictions across the nation.

Source: COPS Web site: www.cops.usdoj.gov

SUMMARY

"Community policing is an organization-wide philosophy and management approach that promotes (1) community, government, and police partnerships; (2) proactive problem solving to prevent crime; and (3) community engagement to address the causes of crime, fear of crime, and other community issues" (Upper Midwest Community Policing Institute). Running through definitions of community policing are two basic themes: police–community partnerships and a proactive, problem-solving approach to the police function.

"Modern" policing began with the formation of the London Metropolitan Police, founded by Sir Robert Peel in 1829. Peel's principles emphasized the interdependence of the police and the public as well as the prevention of crime and disorder.

Policing in the United States has had three distinct paradigm shifts, or eras: political, reform, and community. During the political era the police sought an intimate relationship with the community. During the reform era the police relationship with the community they served was professionally remote. The professional model emphasized crime control by preventive automobile patrol coupled with rapid response to calls. During the community era the police sought to reestablish a close relationship with the community.

During the 1960s and 1970s relations between the police and the public were extremely strained. In an effort to improve relations, many police departments instituted public-relations programs whose goal was to improve the police image. Many departments also began crime prevention programs that enlisted the aid of citizens, including programs such as Operation Identification, neighborhood or block watches, and home and automobile security programs.

Cordner's four dimensions of community policing are the philosophical, strategic, tactical, and organizational dimensions.

DISCUSSION QUESTIONS

1. From the perspective of law enforcement, what are the strengths and weaknesses of each of the three eras of policing? Answer this question from the perspective of a citizen.

2. What lessons should community policing advocates learn from history?

3. Are any community policing strategies being used in your community? If so, which ones?

4. What advantages does community policing offer? Disadvantages?

5. How is the relationship between the police and the public usually portrayed in popular television programs and movies? In the news media?

6. How might the historical role of the police in enforcing slavery in the South and later segregation contribute to present-day police–minority relations?

7. Can you see any evidence of the patronage or spoils system of policing in the 21st century?

8. What is the relationship of community policing to problem-solving policing?

9. Is community policing being implemented in law enforcement agencies in the United States and to what extent?

10. Have you witnessed any examples of the "thin blue line"?

GALE EMERGENCY SERVICES DATABASE ASSIGNMENTS

ONLINE Database

- Use the Gale Emergency Services Database to help answer the Discussion Questions when appropriate.
  - Research and be prepared to discuss the origins of policing in the United States and how slave patrols influenced modern policing.
  - Research and write a brief report on the significance of the training offered to law enforcement officers by the Holocaust Museum in Washington, DC.

REFERENCES

Asirvatham, Sandy. 2000. "Good Cop, Bad Cop." *Baltimore City Paper*, May. http://www2.citypaper.com/columns/story.asp?id=1876

Bayley, David H. 1994. *Police for the Future.* New York: Oxford.

Bratton, William J. 1996 (Spring). "New Strategies for Combating Crime in New York City." *Fordham Urban Law Journal* 23: 781–795.

Burger, Warren E. 1991. "Introduction." *The Bench and Bar of Minnesota* (May/June): 26.

Community Policing Defined. 2009 (April 3). Washington, DC: U.S. Department of Justice, Office of Community Oriented Policing Services. http://cops.usdoj.gov/Publications/e030917193-CP-Defined.pdf

Community Policing: What Makes It Work? 2008 (August). Rand: Quality Policing Highlights.

Cordner, Gary W. 1999. "The Elements of Community Policing." In *Policing Perspectives: An Anthology*, edited by Larry K. Gaines and Gary W. Cordner, 137–149. Los Angeles: Roxbury.

del Carmen, Rolando V. and Jeffrey T. Walker. 2012. *Briefs of Leading Cases in Law Enforcement.* 8th edition. Waltham, MA: Anderson Publishing (Elsevier).

Dulaney, W. Marvin. 1996. *Black Police in America.* Bloomington, IN: Indiana University Press.

Foner, P. S. 1975. *History of Black Americans: From Africa to the Emergence of the Cotton Kingdom.* Westport, CT: Greenwood.

Ford, J. Kevin. 2007. "Building Capability throughout a Change Effort: Leading the Transformation of a Police Agency to Community Policing." *American Journal of Community Psychology* (39): 321–334.

Garmire, Bernard L., ed. 1989 (August). *Local Government Police Management.* Washington, DC: International City Management Association.

Graffiti Hurts®. http://www.graffitihurts.org/about.jsp

Hess, Kären M. and Christine H. Orthmann. 2012. *An Introduction to Law Enforcement and Criminal Justice.* 10th edition. Belmont, CA: Wadsworth, Cengage Learning.

Jones, E. T. 2008. "Democracy and the Police." *Choice* (August): 2235–2236.

Kelling, George L. 1994. "Defining Community Policing." *Subject to Debate* (April): 3.

Kelling, George L. 1988 (June). "Police and Communities: The Quiet Revolution." *Perspectives on Policing.* Washington, DC: U.S. Department of Justice, National Institute of Justice.

Kelling, George L. and Mark H. Moore. 1991. "From Political to Reform to Community: The Evolving Strategy of Police." In *Community Policing: Rhetoric or Reality?*, edited by Jack R. Greene and Stephen D. Mastrofski, 3–25. New York: Praeger.

Klockars, Carl B. 1983. *Thinking about Police: Contemporary Readings.* New York: McGraw-Hill.

Lord, Vivian B. and Paul C. Friday. 2008. "What Really Influences Officer Attitudes toward COP? The Importance of Context." *Police Quarterly* (June): 220–238.

Maguire, Edward R. and Charles M. Katz. 1997 (November). "Community Policing and Loose Coupling in American Police Agencies." Paper presented at the annual meeting of the American Society of Criminology, San Diego, CA.

Maguire, Edward R. and Stephen D. Mastrofski. 2000. "Patterns of Community Policing in the United States." *Police Quarterly* (March): 4–45.

Melekian, Bernard K. 2011. "The Office of Community Oriented Policing Services." *The Police Chief* (March): 14.

Mentel, Zoe. 2008. "Policing in a Democratic Society." *Community Policing Dispatch* (May).

Morabito, Melissa Schaefer. 2010. "Understanding Community Policing as an Innovation: Patterns of Adoption." *Crime & Delinquency* 56 (4): 564–587.

National Commission on Law Observance and Enforcement. 1931. *Report on Lawlessness in Law Enforcement.* Washington, DC: Government Printing Office.

Peak, Ken and Emmanuel P. Barthe. 2009. "Community Policing and CompStat: Merged, or Mutually Exclusive?" *The Police Chief* (December): 72, 73 ,74 ,76–78, 80–82, 84.

Peed, Carl R. 2008. "The Community Policing Umbrella." *FBI Law Enforcement Bulletin* (November): 22–25.

Reichel, Philip L. 1999. "Southern Slave Patrols as a Transitional Police Type." In *Policing Perspectives: An Anthology*, edited by Larry K. Gaines and Gary W. Cordner, 79–92. Los Angeles: Roxbury.

Retzlaff, Christine. 2012 (February 12). *Proactive Outreach to Hispanic Community Encourages Trust and Participation: Metropolitan Nashville Police Department's El Protector Program.* Local Initiatives Support Corporation's Community Safety Initiative, MetLife Foundation Community-Police Partnership Awards program. http://www.lisc.org/content/publication/detail/20015

Richardson, J. F. 1970. *The New York Police.* New York: Oxford University Press.

Rohe, W. M., R. E. Adams, T. A. Arcury, J. Memory, and J. Klopovic. 1996. *Community Oriented Policing: The North Carolina Experience.* Chapel Hill, NC: The Center for Urban and Regional Studies.

Rosenberg, Helen, et al. 2008. "Police Officer Attitudes toward Community Policing: A Case Study of the Racine, Wisconsin, Police Department." *Police Practice and Research* (September): 291–305.

Rosenthal, Arlen M., Lorie A. Fridell, Mark L. Dantzker, Gayle Fisher-Stewart, Pedro J. Saavedra, Tigran Markaryan, and Sadie Bennett. 2000 (September). *Community Policing: 1997 National Survey Update of Police and Sheriffs' Departments.* Washington, DC: National Institute of Justice. (NCJ 187693)

Roth, J. A. and C. C. Johnson. 1997 (November). "COPS Context and Community Policing." Paper presented at the annual meeting of the American Society of Criminology, San Diego, CA.

Simmons, R. C. 1976. *The American Colonies.* New York: McKay.

Skogan, Wesley G. 2004. "Community Policing: Common Impediments to Success." In *Community Policing: The Past, Present, and Future,* edited by Lorie Fridell and Mary Ann Wycoff, 159–168. Washington, DC: The Annie E. Casey Foundation and Police Executive Research Forum.

Skolnick, Jerome H. and David H. Bayley. 1988. "Theme and Variation in Community Policing." In *Crime and Justice: A Review of Research,* edited by M. Tonry and N. Morris, 1–37. Chicago: University of Chicago Press.

Sparrow, Malcolm K. 1998 (November). *Implementing Community Policing.* Washington, DC: U.S. Department of Justice, National Institute of Justice.

Trojanowicz, Robert and Bonnie Bucqueroux. 1990. *Community Policing: A Contemporary Perspective.* Cincinnati: Anderson.

Understanding Community Policing: A Framework for Action. 1994 (August). Washington, DC: Bureau of Justice Assistance.

Upper Midwest Community Policing Institute. n.d. "Community Policing Defined."

Vollmer, August. 1936. *The Police and Modern Society.* Berkeley: University of California Press.

Walker, Samuel. 1997. *Popular Justice: A History of American Criminal Justice.* 2nd ed. New York: Oxford University Press.

Walker, Samuel L. and Morgan Macdonald. 2009. "An Alternative Remedy for Police Misconduct: A Model State 'Pattern or Practice' Statute." *Civil Rights Law Journal* 19 (3): 479–552.

Williams, Hubert and Patrick V. Murphy. 1990 (January). *The Evolving Strategy of Police: A Minority View.* Washington, DC: National Institute of Justice, Perspectives on Policing, No. 13. (NCJ 121019)

Wilson, O. W. 1950. *Police Administration.* New York: McGraw-Hill.

Wilson, O. W. 1952. *Police Planning.* Springfield, IL: Thomas.

CASES CITED

Escobedo v. Illinois, 378 U.S. 478 (1964)
Gideon v. Wainwright, 372 U.S. 335 (1963)
Mapp v. Ohio, 367 U.S. 643 (1961)
Miranda v. Arizona, 384 U.S. 436 (1966)
Terry v. Ohio, 392 U.S. 1 (1968)
Weeks v. United States, 232 U.S. 383 (1914)

This available CourseMate has an interactive eBook and interactive learning tools, including flash cards, quizzes, and more. To learn more about this resource and access free demo CourseMate resources, go to **www.cengagebrain.com**, and search for this book. To access CourseMate materials that you have purchased, go to **login.cengagebrain.com**.

CHAPTER 2

Inside Police Agencies: Understanding Mission and Culture

> The strength of a democracy and the quality of life enjoyed by its citizens are determined in large measure by the ability of the police to discharge their duties.
>
> —*Herman Goldstein*

DO YOU KNOW ...

» What a mission statement is?

» What police spend the majority of their time doing?

» How the makeup of the police force has changed in recent years?

» What characteristics of the police culture may lead to a code of silence?

» Where the police image comes from?

» What a negative contact is?

» What the public expects of the police?

» What dilemma faces law enforcement?

» When agencies or officers exercise discretion?

» How discretion fits into the community policing philosophy?

» What ethics involves?

» What three ethics checks are?

CAN YOU DEFINE ...

discretion
Lucifer effect
mission statement
negative contacts
911 policing
police culture
selective enforcement

INTRODUCTION

Adhering to professional oaths and codes of conduct is an integral part of policing. One policy of the Commission for Accreditation of Law Enforcement Agencies (CALEA) states: "Any employee, prior to assuming sworn status, will take the oath of office to enforce the laws of the city and state government, and to uphold the Constitution of the United States and the Constitution of the state"

(CALEA 1.1.1, *Standards for Law Enforcement Agencies*, 2012). The Maryland oath of office is typical:

> I swear (or affirm) that I will support the Constitution of the United States, and that I will be faithful and bear true allegiance to the State of Maryland and support the Constitution and laws thereof; and that I will, to the best of my skill and judgment, diligently and faithfully, without partiality or prejudice, execute the office of police officer according to the Constitution and laws of this State.

Ramsey (n.d.) notes that he wants his officers to understand: "The oath of office stands for something ... something very sacred ... something they must never, ever violate, for when police officers violate their oath, there are indeed consequences. The Holocaust is probably the most extreme example of just how horrific and far-reaching those consequences may be. But even small ethical violations on the part of police officers can result in peoples' rights being denied, their confidence in the police being eroded, and their communities being made less safe."

Although "police officers" are the professionals entrusted with guarding the Constitution discussed in this chapter, the concepts explained apply equally to those with different titles such as deputies or sheriffs. And although the chapter focuses on police officers as professionals, always remember that police officers are first and foremost people—sons, daughters, mothers, fathers, brothers, sisters, aunts, uncles, neighbors, and friends. They may belong to community organizations, attend local churches, and be active in politics. Their individual attributes greatly influence who they are as police officers.

This chapter begins by discussing why we have police and how this is expressed through mission statements, including the two sometimes conflicting roles of law enforcement and service to the public. Next the chapter describes who the police are and some characteristics of their culture. This is followed by a discussion of the police image and public expectations of the police. Then the role of police discretion and use of force are discussed. The chapter concludes with an examination of ethics and policing.

THE POLICE MISSION

Why do law enforcement agencies exist? What is their mission? The answer is obvious to those who say the purpose is to catch "bad guys." Others believe the purpose is to prevent crime, maintain order, or protect the public. There are those who believe writing out a mission statement is baloney because it is just words. When one police chief was asked the question, "What is your mission statement?" he responded, "Look at our patch. It says to protect and serve. That's all the mission statement we need." This chief did not believe in a written mission statement. Nonetheless, articulating the reason for an agency's existence helps its members focus on the same goals and determine how to accomplish their purpose.

mission statement
A written declaration of purpose.

A **mission statement** is a written declaration of purpose.

According to DeLone (2007, 218): "Mission statements are instruments of organization communication. They have the ability to shape the attitudes and behavior of individuals in the organization. They also have the ability to shape the perceptions of the public." Mission statements are not necessarily constant or permanent. Many social changes such as the civil rights movement, the Vietnam antiwar demonstrations, the immigration of illegal aliens, and the like have influenced mission statements. DeLone (2007) studied the extent to which the terrorist attacks on September 11, 2001, influenced agencies' mission statements and found that all but one of the reviewed departments changed their mission statements in the wake of the attacks, making the argument that they all experienced forceful environmental incentives to change. He concludes: "One is left to wonder whether those critical of the importance of mission statements are correct" (2007, 231).

A mission statement is a "road map" that delineates how an agency will arrive at a desired destination. Without it, a law enforcement agency can wander, appearing inconsistent, inefficient, and purposeless. The mission statement defines what the agency's commitment is to the community it serves and how it views its relationship with the community. A mission statement can reveal rather accurately the state of police–community relations. The importance of mission statements is summarized eloquently by Lewis Carroll's Cheshire cat in *Alice in Wonderland:* "If you don't know where you're going, it doesn't matter which way you go."

A mission statement can also focus a police department's energies and resources. Will the department continue to be reactive, focused on fighting crimes that have already occurred, or proactive, focused on identifying problems and attacking them? As Wilson and Kelling (1989, 49) note, a community-oriented policing philosophy requires redefining the police mission: "To help the police become accustomed to fixing broken windows as well as arresting window-breakers requires doing things that are very hard for many administrators to do."

The Memphis (Tennessee) Police Department's mission statement embodies these goals: "Our purpose is to create and maintain public safety in the City of Memphis. We do so with focused attention on preventing and reducing crime, enforcing the law, and apprehending criminals." The Aurora (Illinois) Police Department's mission statement reads: "We will enhance the quality of life in Aurora through innovation, partnerships, and dedicated service to our community."

How are mission statements developed? A committee, composed of members of the community and police officers, assesses various police functions. Why would a law enforcement agency include input from the community when it develops its mission statement? Community input improves police–community relations and increases the likelihood of an agency accomplishing its missions. The public identifies the services it expects from its police department. If those expectations go unmet, the department generally suffers loss of financing and political support as well as increased interference in day-to-day operations.

A local police department's commitment to community policing can be, to some degree, measured at the management level by the presence of written objectives and policies. In 2007, 53 percent of all local law enforcement agencies, employing 81 percent of officers, had a written mission statement that included a community policing component, and 100 percent of agencies that served a population of 1 million or more maintained a mission statement with a community policing component (Reaves, 2010).

Developing a mission statement that reflects an agency's commitment to the community it serves can be the vehicle to positive, meaningful police–community relations as well as to a more effective police department. This mission statement in large part determines where the agency places its priorities.

Some departments also develop a vision statement, which is more philosophical and embodies the spirit of the department. The San Jose (California) Police Department has the following vision statement: "The San Jose Police Department is a dynamic, progressive, and professional organization dedicated to maintaining community partnerships which promote a high quality of life for the City's diverse population. The Department is committed to treating all people with dignity, fairness, and respect, protecting their rights and providing equal protection under the law" (San Jose, California, Police Department Web site, n.d.).

From the preceding examples, it is clear that such statements require thought and reflect how a department views itself. Closely related to the mission statement are the goals and objectives set by a department. Programs emphasizing a service philosophy may not sit well with some police officers. For example, in one police department, its Neighborhood-Oriented Policing (NOP) program was perceived as more social work than police work and was referred to as "Nobody on Patrol." To avoid such perceptions, top management should emphasize that the community policing philosophy enhances the ability to detect and apprehend law violators. In fact, community policing is tougher on crime than traditional policing because it relies on citizens helping the police and sharing responsibility for their neighborhood.

ON THE BEAT

Officers need to know the mission of their police department. Before an officer even considers submitting an employment application to a department, he or she needs to know what the city's mission is, as well as the department's mission. If the officer's professional values are not in line with those of a particular department, it will not be a good fit for the officer. The police mission I adhere to is in line with my own values. The piece that stands out most clearly for me is one simple goal: "active partnership with our community." I feel the police cannot, and should not, do their job alone. The police need to have partnerships within the community.

With programs such as Neighborhood Watch and Crime-Free Multi-Housing, the police and residents are able to work together to solve neighborhood issues. This is fundamentally how law enforcement can be effective in a community. Departments need to partner with community members in policing efforts. A few ways to do this include facilitating a Citizen Police Academy program, a Police Reserve Unit, or a number of other volunteer opportunities. All such efforts help strengthen bonds between the police and the citizens.

—Kim Czapar

Fighting Crime versus Service to the Public

Police departments are often divided on whether their emphasis should be proactive or reactive. Every department will have officers who are incident oriented (reactive) and believe their mission is to do **911 policing**—responding to calls—and may speak disparagingly of the community policing officers as "social workers."

911 policing
Incident-driven, reactive policing.

Is the best police officer the one who catches the most "bad guys"? Certainly police departments will continue to apprehend criminals. The crimes they target may, however, contribute to negative police–community relations. The police usually focus on certain kinds of crime, particularly common crimes such as burglary, robbery, assault, and auto theft. The police expect that offenders who commit these crimes might flee or try to avoid arrest in some other way. Police may need to use force to bring offenders to justice.

Police officers generally do not enforce white-collar crimes. They would not, for example, investigate or arrest a businessperson for insider trading, price fixing, or cheating on income taxes. White-collar crime involves those in business, the professions, or public life—those who tend to be relatively well-to-do, influential people.

Common crimes can conceivably be committed by anyone, rich or poor. The vast majority of these crimes, however, are committed by those from society's lower socioeconomic levels, and the population at or near the poverty level often includes a disproportionate number of minority citizens. As Klockars (1985, 57) notes, because the police officers' domain is the streets: "Those people who spend their time on the street will receive a disproportionate amount of police attention … particularly people who are too poor to have backyards, country clubs, summer homes, automobiles, air conditioning, or other advantages that are likely to take them out of the patrolman's sight."

These facts contribute to the impression that the police are focused solely on the kind of crime poor people and minorities commit and, therefore, that they are hostile to the poor or members of minority groups. This negative impression does little to foster good community relations.

Police work involves much more than catching criminals. It is a complex, demanding job requiring a wide range of abilities. Studies suggest that 80 percent of police officers' time is spent on nonenforcement activities. The vast majority of the problems police attend to are in response to citizen requests for service.

The majority of police actions have nothing to do with criminal law enforcement but involve service to the community.

Service to the community includes peacekeeping; preventing suicides; looking for lost or runaway children or vulnerable adults; protecting children and other vulnerable people; maintaining public safety; assisting motorists with disabled vehicles; dealing with emergencies and crisis situations, such as vehicle crashes and natural disasters; delivering death notifications; resolving conflicts; preventing crime; and educating the public.

Community policing emphasizes proactive strategies to help reduce social disorder and crime (Famega, Frank, and Mazerolle, 2005). Research has found that, on average, 75 percent of a typical police shift is unassigned, with officers spending the majority of unassigned time engaged in self-initiated routine patrol or offering backup rather than engaging in proactive policing activities (Famega, Frank, and Mazerolle, 2005). Furthermore, supervisors' directives often failed to accomplish the goals associated with proactive policing strategies. The researchers suggest that detailed directives based on valid crime analyses can improve patrol officer performance and promote positive outcomes in crime reduction (Famega, Frank, and Mazerolle, 2005).

Defining exactly what police work entails is almost impossible. Most would agree, however, that people have always called the police for help. They call not only about criminal matters but also about a variety of situations where they perceive a need for government intervention. The police respond to such calls and usually take whatever action is needed. It has been said that the police are the only social-service agency available 24/7, and they make house calls.

Neighborhood Cops or Special Ops?

The proactive or reactive controversy can be seen in the existence of two contradictory models in policing: community policing and special weapons and tactics (SWAT) teams. SWAT teams are by nature reactive. The number of SWAT units has grown rapidly, with the majority of departments serving cities with populations of more than 50,000 having SWAT units. In many emergency situations, such teams are indispensable and have saved lives. It is not a question of either–or.

Marcou (2009) contends that SWAT teams are not necessarily reactive and that community-oriented SWAT teams are becoming more proactive in their approach to problem solving. As part of a proactive approach, SWAT team

Police officers are often the first responders in emergencies. This police sergeant had to perform mouth-to-mouth resuscitation on the 2-year-old boy after the toddler was rescued from his burning home.

members are establishing partnerships with the community and learning that there are talents and resources outside of the agency at their disposal if needed (Marcou, 2009).

Recall from Chapter 1 the point emphasized by the Community Oriented Policing Services (COPS) Office: "The community policing model balances reactive responses to calls for service with proactive problem solving centered on the causes of crime and disorder."

WHO ARE THE POLICE?

Traditionally, police officers have been a fairly homogeneous group: White, male, with a high school education and a military background. Although the number of women and minorities going into law enforcement has increased over the past several decades, making the police a more heterogeneous group, officers are still primarily White males.

In 2007 approximately 1 in 4 full-time, sworn local police officers were members of a racial or ethnic minority, compared to 1 in 6 officers in 1987 ("Local Police," 2012). The percent of full-time, sworn law enforcement officers who were women also increased from 1987 to 2007, but the distribution varied by the size of the department:

> In 2007, women accounted for about 15 percent of the total sworn law enforcement officers in large local police departments. In large sheriffs' offices, female officers comprised about 13 percent of the total sworn officers. In contrast, local police departments with between 1 and 10 full-time sworn officers employed fewer than 2,000 female law enforcement officers nationwide (6%). Small sheriffs' offices across the country employed just over 200 total sworn officers who were women (4%) in 2007. (Langton, 2010, 2–3)

Despite some progress in recruiting, women remain significantly under-represented among the ranks of the police. Although college faculty may be seeing more women in their law enforcement classes, so far that increase has not been reflected in actual numbers hired. Possible reasons for the discrepancy are numerous. Some female law enforcement students become disillusioned by the bias against women in many departments; some conclude that police work does not fit with family life; some see the limited opportunity for promotion.

Hiring criteria in law enforcement have changed over the past 30 years. Where once new recruits were required to have only a high school diploma or less, today's officers are expected to have some college education. Many departments accept applicants with 2-year degrees, but increasingly more are seeking those with 4-year degrees. This evolving standard has, without question, changed the kind of officer getting hired because police officers have traditionally come from the working class and were less likely to have a college education. The majority of officers hired 30 years ago were military veterans, reinforcing the military model in departments. These officers followed rank, took orders without question, and were not encouraged or expected to "think for themselves." Today, most officers hired are not military veterans.

The advent of community policing has caused police departments to look for the type of people who are more likely to be successful at solving problems and building community relationships and who are more service oriented as opposed to adventure oriented. The COPS Office funded several demonstration sites at police departments to help redesign what these agencies were looking for in candidates:

> Some characteristics are commonly identified across sites and create a common core of service-oriented traits. They include integrity, courage, teamwork, people-oriented interpersonal skills that reflect an interest in and an awareness of others, strong communication skills, and a work ethic that demonstrates dedication and responsibility. They also include a measure of emotional health that was variably described as temperament, frustration tolerance, or ability to manage stress. Together, these traits appear to reflect a strong component of emotional intelligence, a dimension that is just now starting to emerge in the literature on the psychological screening of police applicants. (Scrivner, 2006, 67)

Of course, law enforcement candidates today are scrutinized as never before for signs of racial prejudice, drinking problems, drug issues, and other factors that could become liability issues down the road. The background investigations for midsize to larger departments are very rigorous, often to the depth of interviewing neighbors of a recruit's childhood residence, among other things.

Today police departments have more minority and female officers. The educational level of the officers is much higher, and fewer have military experience. More officers are also as interested in helping people as they are in fighting crime.

Such changes in the makeup of the police force are fundamental to the community policing philosophy. As police departments become more representative of the communities they serve, they will be better able to understand the problems they must address. As officers become better educated, they will be better equipped to devise solutions to community problems.

An obvious defining characteristic of the police—minority or nonminority, male or female, high school education or college degree—is that they have tremendous power over the citizens they serve and protect: "In American society, nothing is more sacred to us than our freedom. And, in an American society, only one segment of that society is given the authority, the power, and the responsibility to take that freedom away—the police. So, I say to you today that there is *no greater responsibility* than to be entrusted with the freedom of an entire free society" (Walls, 2003, 17).

In addition, police may face a life-threatening situation at any time. Their lives may depend on each other. They experience situations others would not be likely to understand. All of the preceding factors influence what has been called the police culture.

THE POLICE CULTURE

Police work is often unpleasant. Police frequently have to deal with ugly situations and antisocial behavior. Police are lied to, spit upon, and sworn at. They see unspeakable atrocities. Because of their shared experiences and unique exposure to their community, many police officers develop a fierce loyalty to each other. This unique conglomeration of organizational values, beliefs, and expectations that is passed on to newcomers in the department is known as the **police culture**.

Goldstein (1990, 29–30) observes:

> The strength of the subculture grows out of the peculiar characteristics and conflicting pressures of the job: the ever-present physical danger; the hostility directed at the police because of their controlling role; the vulnerability of police officers to allegations of wrongdoing; unreasonable demands and conflicting expectations; uncertainty as to the function and authority of officers; a prevalent feeling that the public does not really understand what the police have to "put up with" in dealing with citizens; a stifling working environment; the dependence that officers place on each other to get the job done and to provide for their personal safety; and the shared sense of awareness, within a police department, that it is not always possible to act in ways in which the public would expect one to act.

police culture

The informal values, beliefs, and expectations passed on to newcomers in the department; may be at odds with the formal rules, regulations, procedures, and role authority of managers.

Negative Perceptions of the Police Culture

Although the trend in American society is to celebrate diversity and embrace different cultures, the police culture has allowed itself to be painted in such a negative light that even some of its own members are calling for its abolishment (Oldham, 2006). This is due in part to researchers, many of whom have described a monolithic police culture focused on widely shared attitudes, values, and norms that help manage the strains created by the nature of police work and the punitive practices of police management and supervision (Paoline, 2004). These include a distrust and suspiciousness of citizens and a tendency to assess people and situations in terms of their potential threat (maintaining the edge), a lay-low or "cover-your-ass" orientation to police work, a strong emphasis on the law enforcement elements of the police role, a we-versus-them attitude toward citizens, and a norm of loyalty to their peer group (Paoline, 2004).

Skolnick's classic description, "A Sketch of the Policeman's 'Working Personality'" (1966), included such descriptors as social isolation, solidarity, and authority. Yet even four decades ago, he recognized the officer's desire to work with the community (117): "Although the policeman sees himself as a specialist in dealing with violence, he does not want to fight alone. He does not believe that his specialization relieves the general public of citizenship duties. Indeed, if possible, he would prefer to be the foreman rather than the workingman in the battle against criminals."

 Solidarity (loyalty) and secrecy within a police department can result in a code of silence.

The code of silence, the refusal of police officers to report any misconduct by other officers, has been written about extensively. The National Institute of Ethics conducted the most extensive research ever on the code of silence, involving 3,714 officers and recruits. The results: 70 percent said that a law enforcement code of silence exists and is fairly common throughout the country; 52 percent said that it did not really bother them. Excessive use of force was the most frequent situation in which the code occurred (Trautman, 2000).

To understand the power and persistence of the code, consider some observations made over the centuries regarding the nexus between truth, morality, and human action (or inaction):

"IT IS NECESSARY ONLY FOR THE GOOD MAN TO DO NOTHING FOR EVIL TO TRIUMPH."

—Edwin Burke (1729–1797)

"THE GREAT ENEMY OF TRUTH IS VERY OFTEN NOT THE LIE—DELIBERATE, CONTRIVED, AND DISHONEST—BUT THE MYTH—PERSISTENT, PERSUASIVE, AND REALISTIC."

—John F. Kennedy's Yale commencement speech, 1962

This code may result in a "culture of denial" (Futterman, Mather, and Miles, 2007, 3), with officers denying incidents of brutality or turning a blind eye to patterns of abuse and encouraging a culture of silence in the face of unethical behavior perpetuated by fellow officers.

Unfortunately, the code of silence, to whatever extent it exists in a department, is a reality in policing. While the code persists, presumably serving to protect officers and justify their conduct in their quest for justice, it causes irreparable damage to the public's perception of and faith in the police profession.

Positive Perceptions of the Police Culture

Although every profession, including law enforcement, will have "bad people," Oldham (2006, 18) asserts that "the law enforcement community is perhaps the best and quickest at culling these types of individuals from the ranks." This outlook suggests a different, positive view of the police culture, that it is "a wonderful thing. The concepts of duty, honor, dedication, and self-sacrifice are not lost on our 'people'" (Oldham, 2006, 18). He (21) concludes: "Our culture is about all of the things that are good in life. We are the ones who people call when they need help; we are the ones who run toward problems and we are the ones who keep our domestic enemies at bay."

Researching Police Officer Attitudes

Paoline's research (2004) has called into question the assumptions that have been made about a monolithic police culture. He has studied similarities and differences among contemporary police officer attitudes to locate some boundaries of the occupational culture of police, with the research examining officers' expectations about citizens, supervisors, procedural guidelines, law enforcement itself, order maintenance, community policing, aggressiveness, and selectivity. The results identified five analytically distinct groups or subcultures of officers that could be expected to form, as shown in Table 2.1.

This research has both positive and negative implications for community policing: "The bad news is that some patrol officers fail to embrace order

Table 2.1 Attitudinal Expectations for Group Formation

	Group 1: Tough Cops	Group 2: Clean-Beat Crime Fighters	Group 3: Avoiders	Group 4: Problem Solvers	Group 5: Professionals
Citizens	(−) citizens are hostile and uncooperative	(−) citizens are unappreciative	(−) citizens do not understand the police	(+) help citizens get to the root of problems	(+) maintain positive rapport with citizens
Supervisors	(−) supervisors are unsupportive	(−) supervisors are unsupportive	(−) or (+/−) pacify supervisors to keep out of trouble	(+) especially in more community policing departments	(+) value supervisory approval
Procedural guidelines	(−) they do more harm than anything	(1) value these due process safeguards	(−) viewed as obstacles	(−) too restrictive, impede efforts to solve problems	(+) accept the limitations placed on them
Law enforcement	(+) narrow role orientation that only includes law enforcement	(1) very rigid law enforcement orientation	(−) or (+/−) believe in only handling unavoidable (i.e., serious) crimes	(−) or (+/−) not the most important/defining function for an officer	(+) accept this role, though not rigid or inflexible
Order maintenance	(+) if handle, do so informally (not regarded as real police work)	(+) as long as they can handle them formally (i.e., ticket or arrest) as part of role	(−) would only create more work	(+) expansive role orientation in handling citizen problems	(+) value roles beyond crime fighting
Community policing	(−) not real policing	(−) may impede their efforts to fight street crime	(−) would only create more work	(+) expansive role orientation	(++) expansive role orientation
Aggressiveness	(+) believe in aggressive style of patrol, part of image	(+) believe in aggressive style of patrol in controlling all illegality	(+) only increases chances to get into trouble	(−) usually only results in negative consequences for citizens	(−) or (+/−) exception rather than the norm
Selectivity	(+) believe in handling only real (i.e., serious) violations formally	(+) believe in pursuing and handling all forms (i.e., minor and serious) of illegal behavior	(1) believe in handling only unavoidable serious offenses that, if not handled, would bring undue negative attention to them	(1) discretionary informal judgment (over strict law enforcement) valued in handling problems	(−) handle full range of offenses, though do not feel the need to handle all formally (i.e., ticket or arrest)

Note: (+/−) indicates neutral attitudes.

Source: Paoline, Eugene A. III. "Shedding Light on Police Culture: An Examination of Officers' Occupational Attitudes." *Police Quarterly*, June 2004, pp. 205–236, copyright © 2004 by *Police Quarterly*. Reprinted by permission of SAGE Publications.

maintenance and disorder objectives, which are commonly associated with community policing. … This is not too surprising given that many police reform efforts have met with similar resistance. The good news is that not all officers resist such policing. In fact, the most differentiating attitude across the groups, in terms of statistically significant mean differences, was community policing orientation" (Paoline, 2004, 231).

Having looked at some perspectives on police culture, let us now focus on how the public often views the police.

THE POLICE IMAGE

How does the public view the police?

» The handsome, relatively realistic cops of television and movies?
» Unselfish, fearless heroes who protect the weak and innocent?
» Dirty Harrys?
» Hard-hearted, brutal oppressors of the underclass?
» Corrupt abusers of power, who become part of the criminal world?

Our society has varied images of law enforcement professionals. As noted in Chapter 1, that image is greatly affected by how the public perceives the criminal justice system within which the police function. Many Americans believe in an ideal justice system in which fairness and equality are guiding principles, truth and justice prevail, and the accused is innocent until proven guilty. Law enforcement professionals are part of this idealized vision; many view police officers and sheriff's deputies as unselfish, fearless, compassionate protectors of the weak and defenseless, who can uncover the truth, bring the guilty to justice, and make things "right."

In contrast, others in our society see a criminal justice system that is neither fair nor just. Some individuals point out that the system primarily employs officers who are White, middle-class males. They also believe that some officers abuse their power and, in some cases, also abuse those with whom they come into contact in the line of duty.

Drawing from Gallup Polls conducted between 1977 and 2011, the Bureau of Justice Statistics compared the rating of law enforcement officers' honesty and ethical standards. In 1977, 8 percent of the polled American public rated the police "very high" and 29 percent rated them "high." In 2001, possibly as a result of 9/11, police were rated "very high" by 23 percent and "high" by 45 percent. In 2011, however, ratings had slipped back down, with police rated "very high" by 12 percent and "high" by 42 percent (*Sourcebook of Criminal Justice Statistics Online*, n.d.). The Gallup Poll also reported on responses to the question: "How much confidence do you have in the ability of the police to protect you from violent crime?" In 2006, the most recent time this question was asked in a poll, 20 percent responded "a great deal" and 41 percent responded "quite a lot" ("Crime," 2006).

Horowitz (2007, 8) notes: "Satisfaction with the police, while generally high, is unevenly distributed. Understanding why some people harbor negative views about police officers is the first and most important step in building a positive relationship with the community." Several National Institute of Justice (NIJ) studies examined the factors that influence citizen satisfaction with the police and found that public satisfaction is shaped by demographic variables, neighborhood crime conditions, and experiences with the police—whether firsthand or indirect. Race, interestingly, was not found in these studies to be directly related to satisfaction. Although police have no control over the first two factors, they have direct control over the third one: "Treating individuals respectfully and professionally during each encounter can establish, build, and maintain crucial support for the police within the community" (Horowitz, 2007, 9).

Horowitz (2007, 10) concludes: "The challenge for law enforcement officers is to treat each encounter—whether with a suspect, witness, or complainant—as if it is that person's first contact with police. If he or she believes that the officer was fair and professional, then that person is more likely to have positive impressions of the future encounters with police."

An individual's opinion of the police is based on many factors, possibly including television programs, movies, newspapers, magazines, books, the opinions of friends and family, level of education, neighborhood, economic status, disabilities, gender, minority group membership, and—most important—contacts with the criminal justice system.

 The police image is affected by individual backgrounds, the media, and citizens' personal experiences with the criminal justice system.

The media can greatly affect public opinion. The police image is affected by the manner in which television and newspaper stories present crime and law enforcement activities (Smith, 2011). The average citizen holds many mistaken beliefs about police work because of the proliferation of movies and television shows that "play fast and loose" with the truth, resulting in what is commonly called the *CSI effect*: "The popular crime show *CSI* and its spinoffs set in New York and Miami would have people believe that every police force has at its disposal high-tech gadgetry to solve every crime, as well as a team of experts to follow each case through to its quick and satisfying conclusion. Loyal TV viewers often expect the same from their local cops" (Basich, 2008, 55). Improving police–media relations is the focus of Chapter 8.

An additional source of the police image is the folklore surrounding citizen interactions with police. People tend to embellish stories of their contacts with the police. In addition, many stories people tell about contacts with the police are actually not theirs but those of a friend of a friend. Unfortunately, few if any of these stories can be traced to their origins, but in the meantime, police end up with a negative image. Further, police seldom participate in the same social circles in which the stories are recounted and therefore have no means of defending themselves, their co-workers, their departments, or their actions.

Yet another contributor is police work itself. Police officers are charged with some of society's most distasteful and dangerous tasks and are allowed to use reasonable force to effect arrests. They are even permitted, under strict circumstances, to use deadly force. This ability, however, creates a paradox for the police image—using force to achieve peace. Nonetheless, the nature of police work and the power they are legally permitted to use make the police extremely powerful and contribute to their image.

 The police image is also shaped by appearance and police actions.

The police image is further affected by the police uniform and equipment. The uniform most police officers wear is a visible reminder of the authority and power bestowed upon them. In fact, officers know that the uniform plays a major part in their ability to gain cooperation and compliance from the public. Much of their authority comes simply from what they are wearing. People recognize and react to visible symbols of authority. The police uniform conveys power and authority as well as the stereotypes about police officers. Citizens encountering a police officer in uniform usually cooperate more and curtail their illegal or deviant behaviors. The uniform and its trappings—patches, badges, medals, mace, nightsticks, handcuffs, and guns—can be intimidating and can evoke negative public responses. Reflective sunglasses and tie tacks with handcuffs or guns can add to this negative image.

Officers' behavior also has a direct impact on their image. One behavior that may negatively affect the police image is accepting gratuities, no matter how small, such as free coffee.

The manner in which police exercise their authority also has an impact on the police image. The attitude of law enforcement officers, their education, their personal image of policing, discipline, professionalism, and interaction with the community have an enormous impact on the public's perception of the police.

Seemingly innocent and humorous police novelty items have caused major confrontations between police and the communities they serve. Some police product companies produce calendars, posters, T-shirts, and mugs that support, encourage, and make light of police brutality. Almost always meant to be humorous, the public may not share the same sense of humor. Such items can be immensely destructive to police–community relations. Particularly offensive examples include slogans such as "Brutality, the fun part of police work" and takeoffs on the *Dirty Harry* line, "Go ahead, make my day."

A case in point: In the early 2000s an African American suspect died in police custody as the result of a carotid hold applied by police officers during a struggle. In response to the African American community's anger and concern, the chief of police issued an order prohibiting the carotid hold. Already in severe conflict with their chief over several other issues, two officers produced and sold T-shirts within the department that said, "Don't choke 'em, smoke 'em." The T-shirts went on sale the day of the suspect's funeral. It is not difficult to understand how destructive this was to the police image and community relations in that city as well as in other cities where the media reported these events. In 2007, 15 percent of all police departments nationwide authorized use of carotid holds, choke holds, or neck restraints; however, among those departments serving populations of 1,000,000 or more, 46 percent authorized this type of less-lethal use of force (Reaves, 2010).

In contrast to this unfortunate incident is the Hug-a-Bear Program that many departments now use. Plush teddy bears are used to calm traumatized children that officers encounter in the course of fulfilling their duties. The bears, sometimes donated to the department by community organizations, are often carried in patrol cars and have been invaluable at accident scenes, in child-abuse situations, and at the scene of fires. Programs such as this can reduce the effect of negative contacts people may have with the police.

Personal Contacts

Personal contact with the police is an important determinant of citizens' attitudes (Frank, Smith, and Novak, 2005). Results from a study of encounters between police and residents of Chicago have demonstrated the great importance of the quality of police–citizen encounters (Skogan, 2005). In 2008 an estimated 17 percent of U.S. residents age 16 or older had face-to-face contact with a police officer, a decline from the 19 percent who reported having face-to-face contact with police in 2005 (Eith and Durose, 2011). As with the results from the 2002 and 2005 surveys, the vast majority of citizens (89.7%) who reported having face-to-face police contact during 2008 felt that the officer or officers acted appropriately, and 91.8 percent reported that the police were respectful during the encounter (Eith and Durose, 2011).

One factor that contributes to a negative police image and difficulty in maintaining good community relations is what police commonly refer to as negative contacts.

Negative contacts are unpleasant interactions between the police and the public. They may or may not relate to criminal activity.

negative contacts
Unpleasant interactions between the police and the public; may or may not relate to criminal activity.

© Jack Dagley Photography/Shutterstock.com

Being arrested is without question one of the most negative contacts a citizen can have with police. Arrestees may be combative, verbally abusive, or try to bite, kick, spit on, or otherwise lash out at the arresting officer. Considering that many arrest situations are witnessed by curious onlookers, it is vital that officers maintain professionalism during these encounters—a negative contact with an individual citizen need not spread into a negative contact involving numerous bystanders as well.

Many people have police contact only when something goes wrong in their lives. Citizens commonly interact with the police when they receive a traffic citation, have an illegally parked vehicle towed, have a loud party terminated, have been victimized, discuss a child who is in trouble with the law, have a domestic "disagreement" broken up, are arrested for driving while intoxicated (DWI) or some other offense, or receive a death notification. Many more possible scenarios in which citizens become angry or disillusioned occur daily because of the actions police officers must take to perform their duties. And while officers have many opportunities to assist citizens and be a positive presence in the community, much of what they must do causes people unhappiness, a mix that leads the public to have a "love–hate relationship" with police:

> Not everyone has a positive view of law enforcement. And much of this feeling stems from the situations surrounding people's interactions with the police.…

> Even those who respect police officers might feel uneasy around them. Some are afraid that they could be treated unfairly because of stories they've heard. For others, the mystique surrounding the uniform and the badge, along with the requisite authority, is simply too foreign.…

> Immediately after 9/11, Americans had an exceptionally favorable opinion of police officers, seeing them as brave rescuers who risked life and limb to bring citizens to safety. Yet police were still second to firefighters in the outpouring of support. Now the 9/11 effect has long since faded from public memory, and most police officers have no illusions about their place in society. (Basich, 2008, 54)

For the most part, the police have no way to eliminate negative contacts and still perform their duties. A major challenge of law enforcement is to build good community relations despite the often adversarial nature of the job. The fact that many negative contacts take place between police and noncriminal individuals, the so-called average citizens, makes the task especially difficult.

More positive contacts are needed. For example, the Fremont (Nebraska) Police Department has put a new spin on the phrase "gotcha." In Fremont, officers observing young people doing something good (for example, wearing a bike helmet or picking up litter) give out tickets for soda and French fries at local fast-food restaurants. This works best for bike patrol officers.

Researchers Rosenbaum and colleagues (2005) studied the attitudes of African American, Hispanic, and White residents of Chicago before and after encounters with the police. They found that, contrary to previous research, direct contact with police during the past year did not change attitudes, but vicarious experience (hearing about someone else's good or bad encounter with the police) did predictably influence attitudes. This research found that people's initial attitudes about police play a "critical role" in shaping their judgments of subsequent direct and indirect experiences as well as their future attitudes: "Attitudes toward the police are relatively stable and not easily influenced by one or two police-initiated contacts" (359). The conclusion is that a negative attitudinal predisposition provokes a negative police response: "Consistent with prior research on police reactions to negative suspect demeanor—which is then accurately perceived by the respondent as a negative encounter" (Rosenbaum et al., 2005, 359).

Public Expectations

Skogan (2005) describes four expectations of citizens. First, they want to be able to explain their situation to the police. Second, they want the police to be unbiased, neutral, objective, evenhanded, and fair. Third, they want to be treated with dignity and respect and have their rights acknowledged. Fourth, they want the police to consider their needs and concerns about their well-being. Despite these findings, the reality is often different.

Otherwise law-abiding citizens who receive traffic tickets or who are arrested for a DWI episode often believe they should be excused and that the police should concentrate on "real" criminals. Many police officers feel that citizens want the law enforced to the letter except when it comes to themselves.

The public commonly demands that the police crack down on criminals, on drunk drivers, and even on traffic violators. For many police departments, the majority of their complaints involve traffic problems. Citizens often demand that police enforce speed laws near their homes. Inevitably, when the police respond by issuing citations to violators, some of those who want the laws to be strictly enforced are ticketed; they often feel betrayed and angry. Somehow they see their own violation of the speed law as different from that of teenagers or "outsiders," and they feel they deserve a break. Most police officers have been asked: "Why don't you spend your time catching real criminals instead of picking on citizens?"

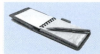 People expect the law to be enforced except when enforcement limits their own behavior.

Citizens become incensed when crime flourishes and hold the police responsible for combating crime. They hear it constantly referred to as a "war on crime" or "war on drugs," and since 9/11 a "war on terrorism," which demands an all-out attack by police on criminals and terrorists. Like American soldiers in Vietnam, however, the police are fighting a war they cannot win because it requires assuming social responsibilities that belong to politicians rather than to police.

 The police are placed in the dilemma of being expected to win the wars on crime, drugs, and terrorism but are given no control over the causes of these problems. The police cannot win these wars alone.

Klockars (1991, 244) also holds this view:

> The fact is that the "war on crime" is a war police not only cannot win, but cannot in any real sense fight. They cannot win it because it is simply not within their power to change those things—such as unemployment, the age distribution of the population, moral education, freedom, civil liberties, ambitions, and the social and economic opportunities to realize them—that influence the amount of crime in any society. Moreover, any kind of real war on crime is something no democratic society would be prepared to let its police fight. We would simply be unwilling to tolerate the kind of abuses to the civil liberties of innocent citizens—to us—that fighting any kind of a real war on crime would inevitably involve.

In addition, when citizens have a problem, they expect the police to help resolve it. In fact, police sociologist Egon Bittner (1974) states that we have police for just that reason—because "something-ought-not-to-be-happening-about-which-something-ought-to-be-done-NOW!" The NOW portion of Bittner's explanation refers to the police's unique ability to use force to correct a situation. Klockars (1985) notes that Bittner purposely did not refer to the situation as illegal because the police are called on in many situations that do not involve an illegality. Bittner left the purpose of police involvement wide open: Something ought to be done.

 People also expect the police to help them when they have a problem or when someone else is causing a problem.

What actions, if any, the police take in response to citizens' requests is usually up to the individual officer's discretion.

POLICE DISCRETION

discretion
Freedom to make choices among possible courses of action or inaction, for example, to arrest or not arrest.

The police have awesome discretionary power—to use force, to remove people's freedom by arresting and jailing them, and even to take someone's life. **Discretion** is the ability to act or decide a matter on one's own. Everett (2006, 10) defines *discretion* as using "professional judgment to choose from alternative courses of action."

Police use discretion because no set of policies and procedures can prescribe what to do in every circumstance. Indeed, as Chief Justice Warren Burger once acknowledged: "The officer working the beat makes more decisions and exercises broader discretion affecting the daily lives of people every day and to a greater extent than a judge will exercise in a week." The International Association of Chiefs of Police (IACP) "Police Code of Conduct" states: "A police officer will use responsibly the discretion vested in his position and exercise it within the law. The principle of reasonableness will guide the officer's determinations, and the officer will consider all surrounding circumstances in determining whether any legal action will be taken."

 Each agency exercises discretion when it establishes its mission, policies, and procedures. Each officer exercises discretion when deciding whether to issue citations or make arrests when laws are violated.

Officers make their choices based on a variety of reasons:

» Is there evidence to prove a violation in court?
» Will a good purpose be served by arrest or citation, or is police contact sufficient to end the violation?
» What type of crime and suspect are involved?
» What circumstances exist at the time?

Clearly, police agencies and officers have broad discretion in deciding which laws to enforce, under which circumstances, and against whom. Some believe the law should be enforced consistently and in every instance. Most officers, however, believe that such police action would soon be unacceptable, far too harsh, and virtually impossible. For example, officers would probably not arrest a stranded motorist in a blizzard who, in danger of freezing to death, breaks into an alarmed commercial building. Nor would they be likely to arrest a driver who develops chest pain and breathing difficulty and drives through a stop sign in an attempt to maneuver off the road. In these cases the value of police discretion, or **selective enforcement**, is apparent. It makes sense to most people not to enforce the letter of the law.

Police discretion may also pose a problem for police, however, because citizens know that officers can act subjectively. The person an officer tickets or arrests may feel discriminated against. The public is also concerned that discretion gives the police too much freedom to pick and choose when and against whom they will enforce the law. Citizens worry that discretion allows the police too much room to discriminate against some and overlook the violations of the wealthy and powerful. Martinelli (2011, 61) stresses: "Police discretion involves legal, educated decision-making processes. … Though there are many factors to consider regarding officer discretion, personal biases, prejudices, and values are not to be employed in this decision-making process."

Community policing functions well when officers have the discretion to make the decisions necessary to help solve community problems. Officers working in the community are usually more informed about the problems and community members and are often more connected and trusted by community members. However, the increased officer discretion necessary for community policing is a concern to many police administrators who fear loss of control of their officers.

The police are not the only players in the criminal justice system to exercise discretion. Prosecutors exercise discretion when determining priorities for prosecution and in plea negotiations. Judges exercise discretion in preliminary hearings, exclusionary rulings, and sentencing. Parole boards, parole officers, probation officers, corrections officials, and prison guards also exercise discretion.

selective enforcement
The use of police discretion, deciding to concentrate on specific crimes such as drug dealing and to downplay other crimes such as white-collar crime.

Reasons for Police Discretion

Police departments are bureaucracies subject to rules and regulations that may contribute to irrational and inappropriate behavior. Such regulations limit an officer's ability to use common sense or act in a humane way in certain situations. Such limitations subject the officer to critical media coverage and adverse public opinion. For example, the police strictly upheld the law and towed a car containing a crying and screaming girl who was paraplegic because the vehicle was parked 15 minutes too long in a restricted zone. Millions of Americans and Canadians viewed this episode on national television.

Discretion is necessary for a number of reasons. The statute books are filled with archaic or ambiguous laws. Some laws are almost never enforced, and no one expects them to be. There are not enough police to act on every violation. They must select which laws they will enforce. Police prioritize the offenses on which they act. Crime is of more concern than a violation of a regulation, and felonies are a greater threat than misdemeanors. The police act accordingly.

Discretion is important to maintaining good community relations. If the police were to enforce the letter of the law, community resentment would soon follow.

Changes in Police Discretion

Community standards influence how the police enforce laws. In most urban areas, significant changes have occurred over the past several decades regarding drunk driving, and law enforcement has responded to the increased public awareness of the dangers of drunk driving by routinely arresting and charging violators. Whereas driving under the influence was once given little attention by the public or the police, this violation is now rarely overlooked. Agencies and their officers have a mandate from the public to strictly enforce DWI laws. Thus, police discretion in this area is limited.

A similar change has occurred regarding public tolerance of domestic violence. Once among the laws the public knew police would not enforce, laws against spouse beating and the physical and sexual abuse of children are now strictly upheld, bringing again a significant change in police discretion. Community policing has also had a great impact on police discretion. Officers are trusted to use good judgment in everyday activities with fewer limits and restricting rules.

Community policing emphasizes wider use of officer discretion.

In *Terry v. Ohio* (1968), the Supreme Court recognized the role that discretion plays in policing. It granted police authority to stop and question people in field interrogations. Research has found this tactic to significantly reduce crime.

The Downside of Police Discretion

Officers usually work independently without direct supervision and have tremendous power to decide what action they will take, who they will arrest, and which laws they will enforce: "Police decisions not to invoke the criminal process largely determine the outer limit of law enforcement. … These police decisions, unlike their decision to invoke the law, are generally of extremely low visibility and consequently are seldom the subject of review. Yet an opportunity for review and appraisal of nonenforcement decisions is essential to the functioning of the rule of law in our system of criminal justice" (Goldstein, 2004, 77).

Discretion and the Police Image

Unless the police exercise their discretion with care, the community may complain about an actual or perceived abuse of power or discrimination in the way police enforce the law. If the community believes the police overlook violations committed by a certain segment of society or strictly enforce laws against another, severe community-relations problems will develop.

A police agency's policies, procedures, and priorities and the manner in which it equips and assigns its officers indicate how that agency will exercise discretion. Individual officers have the greatest amount of discretion. Police officers have wide discretion in matters of life and death, honor and dishonor in a tension-filled, often hostile, environment. In addition, within the police bureaucracy, discretion increases as one moves down the organizational hierarchy. Thus, patrol officers—the most numerous, lowest ranking, and newest to police work—have the greatest amount of discretion. All officers should be acutely aware of the power they wield and the immense impact the exercise of discretion has on the community and the police–community relationship.

Although officers often operate independently, it is important to remember that the community watches how officers perform their duties. The public notes how and when officers enforce the law. Citizens may form opinions about their police department and about all officers in that department based on an individual officer's actions. Perhaps the most critical discretionary decision an officer can make is when and how much force to use.

USE OF FORCE

Managing and applying force is one of the most important, complex, pressing issues in modern law enforcement: "The use of force—including deadly force—is at once *necessary* to achieve law enforcement goals and *contrary* to the core mission to protect life. … This awesome power to use force against the citizenry comes with a great responsibility to use it only when necessary and justified" (Ederheimer and Johnson, 2007, 1).

Police officers are trained and equipped to overcome the resistance they can expect to encounter as they perform their duties. Criminals are often likely to try to evade arrest and require the police to find and forcibly take them into custody. Police also deal with noncriminal situations that can require overcoming resistance, such as mentally ill individuals who are behaving dangerously and may require forceful intervention.

The use of force by the police encompasses a wide range of possible actions, from the officer's mere presence to the use of deadly force. The police presence affects a majority of citizens. The police uniform and squad cars are symbols of the officer's power to enforce the law and bring violators to justice—by the use of force if necessary. The visual image of power and authority created by the uniform and equipment facilitates the officer's ability to gain public compliance. The police image is also affected, either positively or negatively, by whether a department develops an authority-heavy image. Care must be taken not to develop such an intimidating image that it alienates the community.

Of the approximately 40 million people who reported a face-to-face contact with the police during 2008, an estimated 1.4 percent had force used or threatened against them during their most recent contact, which was not statistically different from the percentages in 2002 (1.5%) and 2005 (1.6%) (Eith and Durose, 2011). The majority (74.3%) of the people who had force used or threatened against them thought those actions were excessive, although an exact definition of *excessive* was not specified. There were also no differences found in the percentage of White, Black, and Hispanic individuals who described the incident as excessive (Eith and Durose, 2011).

Controversy on the use of force by police is almost always discussed in terms of police brutality, which is considered a problem by a large segment of the public. The extent of the problem is perceived differently among urban and suburban, rich and poor, and minority and majority populations. Valid reasons exist for why different people have different perceptions of the problem. One reason is that the job the police are required to do differs from community to community.

First recall that because the police must intervene in crimes where apprehension is likely to be resisted, most of their enforcement efforts are directed toward "common" criminals. In contrast, white-collar criminals are unlikely to flee or resist. They tend to see their situation as a legal dilemma to be won or lost in court. White-collar criminals are relatively wealthy and have a career and a place in the community; they have too much to lose to simply flee. Because police enforcement efforts focus on common criminals, who are frequently poor, use of force by the police will most commonly be directed against this part of the population.

Citizens in White suburban areas are more likely to see the police in more positive circumstances when they report a crime and have been victimized; when they need assistance after an automobile crash or in a medical emergency; when their child is lost or when their car has run out of gas; and when they have locked themselves out of a car or home—or want their home watched.

In each scenario the police are there to lend assistance. Citizens in suburban areas may never see a police officer use force. The most negative experience they are likely to have with a police officer is receiving a traffic ticket.

When people from these widely separated communities talk about the police, it seems as though they are speaking of entirely different entities. On the one hand, police may be referred to as brutal, racist aggressors, whereas on the other hand, they may be described as professional, helpful, efficient protectors. Which is the true picture of the police?

Although the public has many stereotypes of the police, those stereotypes are shattered or reinforced each time a citizen has personal contact with a police officer. Each individual police contact can have a positive or negative impact on police–community relations.

Most citizens understand and support law enforcement officers' obligations to enforce the law and to use appropriate force when necessary. All officers have a duty to the profession to encourage public support by professional behavior respectful of each citizen's rights. Sometimes, however, public support of the police does not exist in a community. Lack of support may be the result of the unique characteristics of coercion. Or it may be that the public does not feel that the actions of their police officers are ethical, or even feel that they are evil.

Wargo (2006) observes: "It is rare when a social scientist actually embraces theologically loaded words like 'good' or 'evil.' Yet this is exactly what Zimbardo explores." Philip Zimbardo has researched extensively the transformation of good people into evil, what he calls the **Lucifer effect**.[1] Zimbardo, who conducted the 1971 Stanford Prison Experiment, states: "We imagine a line between good and evil, and we like to believe that it's impermeable. We are good on this side. The bad guys, the bad women, they are on that side, and the bad people never will become good, and the good never will become bad. I'll say today that's nonsense. Because that line is ... permeable. Because sometimes, just like human cells, material flows in and out. And if it does, then it could allow some ordinary people like you to become perpetrators of evil" (Wargo, 2006). He also suggests that it can go beyond the individual to administrative evil, which describes a systemic culture of unethical behavior that is able to grow

Lucifer effect

The transformation of good people into evil.

---

[1] Lucifer was God's favorite angel who fell from grace and ultimately became Satan.

and persist within an organization when leaders allow corruption and immoral conduct to go unchecked.

ETHICAL POLICING

To maintain the public trust, police must be men and women of good character who hold foremost the ideals of fairness and justice. The manner in which police use their discretion to enforce the law and solve problems determines whether the public views the police as ethical.

The Building Blocks of Ethics

Borrello (2005, 65) describes the "building blocks of ethics": "Ethics are built upon a foundation of lesser but equally important individual components, each with their own unique well-defined meaning, and serve collectively as the framework that can offer a sweeping understanding of what ethics really are."

 Ethics involves integrity, honesty, values, standards, courage, and civility.

Integrity Ethics includes integrity, that is, doing right when no one is watching. Ethical integrity is paramount in a profession endowed with power, authority, and discretion, and thus, it is the most important value a law enforcement officer can have: "Everything in law enforcement works outward and upward from the foundation of integrity" (Lohner, 2011, 20). Police integrity can be defined as "the normative inclination among police to resist temptations to abuse the rights and privileges of their occupation" (*Enhancing Police Integrity,* 2005, 2).

Borrello explains integrity through the analogy of a balloon filled with all the preceding elements conjoined under ethics and then tightly tied. The balloon would be airtight, complete, uncompromised—it would have integrity. If that balloon were left unattended for a year, it might be half its original size, having lost its integrity. Unfortunately, even unnoticeably, this is what happens to some police officers over time (Borrello, 2005). Officers who start their careers with unimpaired integrity, if left alone or unsupervised, not held accountable, ignored, untrained, or unrewarded for ethical behavior, may lose their integrity. Integrity can become compromised in many ways: accepting a free meal, being part of the code of silence, calling in sick when healthy, failing to ticket a friend who is driving way over the speed limit. Whatever form it takes, compromising integrity is often the first step toward corruption.

Honesty Honesty is acutely similar to integrity, synonymous with credibility, and is the foundation on which to develop trust. Honesty is what keeps an officer from padding his or her expense account. It is what makes officers write truthful incident reports and testify accurately on the witness stand. Consider the case of a 3-year police officer in a large urban police department who came under investigation for logging out for an unauthorized coffee break during a follow-up investigation. When questioned, he denied taking the unauthorized break, not knowing another officer had seen him take it. Rather than facing minor disciplinary actions, he was terminated for his lie. Statistically, departments across the country are experiencing higher rates of termination for honesty issues than ever before (Sutton, 2005).

Values "A value is simply a belief or philosophy that is meaningful to us. Our values serve as a measure to determine what is important and this determination often controls our behavior" (Borrello, 2005, 66). If officers value the friendship of their peers more than they value honesty, and if a peer does something unethical, the code of silence is likely to flourish.

Standards Standards establish a baseline to guide officers as to what they should or should not do. Most police departments have set standards that officers are expected to meet. Policies and procedures are written standards officers are expected to meet or exceed. These are often used in evaluating officers' performance.

Courage Ethical courage is "being confronted with a difficult problem and making the right decision despite potentially adverse personal or professional consequences" (Borrello, 2005, 67–68). It is being willing to break the code of silence. It is being willing to speak up when a new policy seems not in the best interests of the community. Ethical survival requires officers to prepare their psyche with the same vigor they use to prepare for tactical survival (Sutton, 2005).

Civility Politeness and respect are vital attributes for police officers. One of the most common citizen complaints against police officers is that the officer was sarcastic, rude, or impatient. However: "The true test of civility for police officers is found in its application to those who don't seem to deserve it or who make it hard to be nice" (Borrello, 2005, 58).

Ethics in the Field

The ethical way to act is not always clear. Unfortunately, the police have often not been given appropriate guidance in ethical decision making. Given the complexities of enforcing the law in an increasingly diverse population, it is inadequate to teach rookie officers the technical skills of policing and then send them into the community under the assumption they will do the "right thing."

A move toward higher ethical standards is perhaps reflected by the decision of many police departments to require their police officers to have a college education. There is also an increasing need to begin a dialogue within the police community on ethics—what ethical behavior is and how to achieve it in the profession.

One simple adage, set forth several decades ago by Blanchard and Peale (1988, 9), might serve as a starting point for a discussion on ethics: "There is no right way to do a wrong thing." They (20) suggest three questions that can be used as personal "ethics checks."

Three ethics-check questions are:
- Is it legal?
- Is it balanced?
- How will it make me feel about myself?

The first question should pose little problem for most officers. The focus of the second question is whether the decision is fair to everyone involved, in the short and long term. Does the decision create a win–win situation? The third question is perhaps the most crucial. Would you mind seeing your decision published in the paper? Would you feel good if your friends and family knew about your decision? Ethical behavior by individual officers and by the department as a whole is indispensable to effective police–community partnerships.

Ethical Dilemmas

Ethical dilemmas are often rooted in the ends-versus-means controversy. If officers consider their mission to lock up the bad guys, whatever they have to do to obtain a conviction can be justified: excessive force to get a confession, planting evidence, lying in court—the ends justify the means used to accomplish them. Quinn (2005, 27) cautions that at some point in time officers are going to "walk with the devil" to get the job done:

> Every day is a new challenge, and ethical police conduct is often an uphill battle. Even the best of cops have days when they want to give up and do whatever it takes to put a child molester, baby murderer, or other lowlife in prison. When you sit inches away from these scum and they brag about the truly horrific things they have done to an innocent it's easy to abide by the Code—if that's what it takes. When the evidence isn't perfect, you just use a little creative report writing and this guy will never harm another person again. Illegal searches, physical abuse, or even perjury, you know you will be in the company of many good cops who have done the same. But are they really good cops? (13–14)

Sutton (2005, 64) describes how a police sergeant bolstered the strength of a case against a major narcotics trafficker by claiming in his report that narcotics found in the suspect's residence were discovered after a search warrant had been issued. The truth was that the evidence was discovered during a protective sweep before any warrant was issued. Sutton observes that the officer's motives were noble: "He wanted justice to prevail in a case where the suspect was clearly guilty—but by lying, he violated his oath of office." The ends do not justify the means.

Another source of ethical dilemmas is that police officers are often granted special privileges and allowed exceptions to the law. They can exceed speed limits and violate traffic laws to enforce the law. They can carry concealed weapons and own or have access to weapons that are restricted to citizens. Sometimes this leads new recruits to receive a message that says they are above the law.

Police Corruption

Closely related to unethical behavior, as a result of believing that the ends justify the means or that a police officer is above the law, is actual corrupt behavior. Since policing began, corruption in law enforcement has been a problem. It often begins with small, seemingly benign, actions that officers have little difficulty justifying, such as accepting free coffee. Figure 2.1 illustrates how such justifications can escalate, with loyalty overcoming integrity and then entitlement overcoming accountability.

Figure 2.1	The Continuum of Compromise

Honest Cop

1st Stop	*A perceived sense of victimization*—First development of "us vs. them" mentality and that the only people they can trust are other "real" cops, not administration.
2nd Stop	*Loyalty vs. integrity*—Early exposure to such statements as "How will the department find out about it if we all hang together?"
3rd Stop	*Entitlement vs. accountability*—Officers may develop a sense of entitlement, that they are above the law and "deserve special treatment," allowing both on- and off-duty officers to operate on the belief that many of the rules don't apply to them.
4th Stop	*Acts of omission*—When officers do not do things for which they are responsible. Can include selective nonproductivity (limiting traffic enforcement, ignoring certain criminal violations), avoidance of getting involved, and doing just enough to "get by." Can also allow officers to rationalize not reporting another officer's corrupt behavior.
5th Stop	*Administrative acts of commission*—Rather than just omitting duties and responsibilities, officers begin to commit administrative violations. Breaking small rules may lead to bigger violations, including carrying unauthorized equipment or weapons, engaging in prohibited pursuits, drinking on duty, or firing warning shots. For most officers, this is the extent of their journey down the compromise continuum with departmental sanctions the only risk they will face at this point.
6th Stop	*Criminal acts of commission*—Similar to administrative acts but consequences go beyond reprimands and suspension. The officer would be fired and criminally charged for these acts, such as throwing away evidence, embellishing payroll records, or purchasing equipment with money seized from a drug dealer. The officers justifies it with, "What the hell, we put our lives on the line, and they owe us." When stealing seized assets, the officer says, "It's not like real theft, where there's a real victim. Nobody is getting hurt but the dopers, so what's the big deal?"

Corrupt Cop

Source: Based on Kevin M. Gilmartin and John J. Harris, "The Continuum of Compromise," *The Police Chief* (January 1998): 25–28.

The continuum of compromise has sometimes been referred to as a "slippery slope." This parallels the broken windows theory of crime that if little signs of disorder are ignored, more serious indications of disorder and crime may flourish.

Research by Son and Rome (2004) found that nearly 70 percent of police officers in their study personally observed someone in their department accepting free coffee or food or speeding unnecessarily. They note that to most officers, such conduct probably constituted what they called "approved deviance." Nearly one-third of the officers reported seeing police officers displaying a badge to avoid a traffic citation while off duty and sleeping while on duty. These behaviors were also usually considered minor. More serious and clearly unacceptable forms of conduct were much less frequently observed.

Research has examined how approved deviance evolves among officers, in an effort to understand the forces and processes that pull rookies into a police subculture where ethically questionable conduct is accepted. Results of such studies have found that newer officers were more willing to admit to witnessing unethical acts committed by fellow officers than were those with more time on the job: "One conclusion would be that the [greater the] length of time an officer is exposed to this socialization process, the greater its impact. When this loyalty to the subculture becomes too strong, the solidarity that follows can adversely affect the ethical values of the officers. The typical 'us versus them' mentality creates an allegiance to the members stronger than that to the mission of the department or even the profession.... [C]onflicts can and will arise when personnel face a choice between what may be ethically right and their devotion to the other members" (Martin, 2011, 15). The importance of management and of ethical officers within the department in curbing corruption cannot be underestimated. Among the most important forms of corruption is adherence to the code of silence.

The scandals that rocked the Los Angeles Police Department illustrate the emphasis on ends over means and on the code of silence. Hundreds of criminal convictions may be questioned because of a police-corruption scandal involving allegations of officers framing innocent people, lying in court, and shooting unarmed suspects.

Investigative Commissions

Historically law enforcement administrators or local officials have responded to police corruption scandals by calling for investigative commissions, as discussed in Chapter 1. Many police chiefs or politicians convene an investigative commission or board of inquiry following a scandal. For example, the Knapp Commission, convened in 1972 by Mayor John Lindsay, was a response to alleged corruption in the New York City Police Department. This commission uncovered

---

Ideas in Practice

POLICE COMPLAINTS

The London Police Web site on making police complaints provides a good example of how to gain public trust by helping take the mystery out of making complaints against the police. The site lets people know how to complain, what will happen, and so on. The site also has a link for officers with information about what happens if someone complains about them.

In the United States, many departments are not very forthcoming about the complaint procedure. They make the complaining party work to find out how to complain; make it intimidating by insisting the complaints be made in person, rather than by phone or in writing; assert that complaints cannot be made on someone else's behalf; and so on. The result: Many people do not complain because they are frightened or intimidated about what will happen.

The Independent Police Complaints Commission (IPCC) became operational on April 1, 2004. It is a new nondepartmental public body funded by the Home Office, but by law entirely independent of the police, interest groups, and political parties, and whose decisions on cases are free from government involvement. The IPCC has a legal duty to oversee the whole of the police complaints system, created by the Police Reform Act of 2002. The IPCC's aim is to transform the way in which complaints against the police are handled, making sure that complaints against the police are dealt with effectively. The IPCC sets standards for the way the police handle complaints, and when something has

gone wrong, they help the police learn how to improve the way they work.

Complainants
This section tells complainants all they need to know about making a complaint against the police and the procedures that need to be followed. This page provides information on:
- Who can make a complaint.
- The different ways in which a complaint can be made.
- How to appeal to the IPCC if the person making the complaint is dissatisfied with the way the complaint was handled.

A downloadable complaint form is also available.

Information for Police
This section contains information for police officers and police staff who might be:
- Handling a complaint from a member of the public.
- The subject of a complaint.
- Making a complaint.

This page also explains the role and responsibility of police authorities and how the IPCC is working with different organizations to improve the police complaints system.

Source: Independent Police Complaints Commission (IPCC): http://www.ipcc.gov.uk/en/Pages/complaints.aspx

widespread corruption. However, 20 years later, the Mollen Commission found many of the same corruption issues had resurfaced.

The scandal involving the videotaped beating of Rodney King resulted in the Christopher Commission. A new chief was appointed who implemented many of the reforms recommended by the commission, but they were not institutionalized. Because these reforms were never made permanent, the corruption eventually returned in the form of the Rampart scandal, which led to formation of yet another commission, the Rampart Board of Inquiry.

The lesson to be learned from the investigative commissions is that too often implemented reforms are only temporary: Departments did not internalize the reforms so that with the passage of time, or once the chief left, the officers reverted to their "corrupt behavior."

Police corruption is an issue to be faced and dealt with. In a department where corruption is tolerated, the public trust will fade. "Ethics is our greatest training and leadership need today and into the next century. In addition to the fact that most departments do not conduct ethics training, nothing is more devastating to individual departments and our entire profession than uncovered scandals or discovered acts of officer misconduct and unethical behavior" (*Ethics Training in Law Enforcement*, n.d., 1).

SUMMARY

A mission statement is a written declaration of purpose. Departments must find in their mission a balance between fighting crime and providing service to the public. The majority of police actions have nothing to do with criminal law enforcement but involve service to the community.

Today police departments have more minority and female officers. The educational level of the officers is much higher, and fewer have military experience. More officers are also as interested in helping people as they are in fighting crime.

Solidarity (loyalty) and secrecy within a police department can result in a code of silence. Such a code has a negative impact on the police image. The police image is affected by individual backgrounds, the media, and citizens' personal experiences with the criminal justice system. The police image is also shaped by appearance and police actions. Negative contacts are unpleasant interactions between the police and the public. They may or may not involve criminal activity.

People expect the law to be enforced except when enforcement limits their own behavior. The police are placed in the dilemma of being expected to win the wars on crime, drugs, and terrorism but are given no control over the causes of these problems. The police cannot win these wars alone. People also expect the police to help them when they have a problem or when someone else is causing a problem.

Each agency exercises discretion when it establishes its mission, policies, and procedures. Each officer exercises discretion when deciding whether to issue citations or make arrests when laws are violated. Community policing emphasizes wider use of officer discretion. Police discretion and authority to use power are balanced by the responsibility to act ethically. Ethics involves integrity, honesty, values, standards, courage, and civility. Three ethics-check questions are: (1) Is it legal? (2) Is it balanced?, and (3) How will it make me feel about myself?

DISCUSSION QUESTIONS

1. What is the image of the police in your community? What factors are responsible for this image? Could the police image be made more positive?

2. What expectations do you have of law enforcement agencies?

3. Does police discretion frequently lead to abuse of alleged perpetrators?

4. Are police officers now more violent and less ethical than their predecessors?

5. Does the image of law enforcement affect officers' ability to get the job done?

6. How do you explain the development of the two contradictory models in policing: community-oriented policing (COP) and special weapons and tactics (SWAT) teams? Can they coexist?

7. What should be a department's ideal balance between fighting crime and service to the community?

8. Have you witnessed police exercise their discretion? How did it impress you?

9. Do you think mission statements are valuable for an organization, or are they only window dressing? How do they affect the organization? Compare the Los Angeles Police Department's mission statement with what appears to be the reality. Does this work?

10. What decisions commonly made by police officers involve ethical considerations?

GALE EMERGENCY SERVICES DATABASE ASSIGNMENTS

ONLINE Database

- Use the Gale Emergency Services Database to help answer the Discussion Questions when appropriate.
- Research and outline how law enforcement managers regulate:
  - Appearance of officers
  - Off-duty conduct of officers
  - Health and fitness of officers
- Research and be able to discuss the reasons behind written police policy and procedure manuals and why having officers use common sense, gut feelings, and luck would not be as effective.

REFERENCES

Basich, Melanie. 2008. "A Love-Hate Relationship." *Police* (April): 54–57.

Bittner, Egon. 1974. "Florence Nightingale in Pursuit of Willie Sutton: A Theory of Police." In *The Potential for Reform of Criminal Justice,* edited by H. Jacob, 17–44. Beverly Hills, CA: Sage, 1974.

Blanchard, Kenneth and Norman Vincent Peale. 1988. *The Power of Ethical Management.* New York: Fawcett Crest.

Borrello, Andrew. 2005. "Defining the Building Blocks of Ethics." *Law and Order* (January): 65–68.

Commission on Accreditation of Law Enforcement Agencies (CALEA). 2012. *Standards for Law Enforcement Agencies.* 5th ed. Fairfax, VA: Author.

"Complaints and Appeals." n.d. Independent Police Complaints Commission (IPCC). http://www.ipcc.gov.uk/en/Pages/complaints.aspx

"Crime." 2006 (October 9–12). The Gallup Poll. http://www.gallup.com/poll/1603/Crime.aspx#2

DeLone, Gregory J. 2007. "Law Enforcement Mission Statements Post-September 11." *Police Quarterly* (June): 218–235.

Ederheimer, Joshua and Will Johnson. 2007 (April). "Introduction." In *Strategies for Resolving and Minimizing Use of Force,* edited by Joshua A. Ederheimer, 1–11. Washington, DC: Police Executive Research Forum, Critical Issues in Policing Series.

Eith, Christine and Matthew R. Durose. 2011 (October). *Contacts between Police and the Public, 2008.* Washington, DC: U.S. Department of Justice, Bureau of Justice Statistics. (NCJ 234599)

Enhancing Police Integrity. 2005 (December). Washington, DC: National Institute of Justice.

Ethics Training in Law Enforcement. n.d. Report by the Ethics Training Subcommittee of the IACP Ad Hoc Committee on Police Image and Ethics, Ethics Toolkit. http://www.theiacp.org/PoliceServices/ProfessionalAssistance/Ethics/ReportsResources/EthicsTraininginLawEnforcement/tabid/194/Default.aspx

Everett, Bill. 2006. "Officer Discretion and Serving the Community." *Minnesota Police Chief* (Spring): 10–11.

Famega, Christine N., James Frank, and Lorraine Mazerolle. 2005. "Managing Police Patrol Time: The Role of Supervisor Directives." *Justice Quarterly* 22 (4): 540.

Frank, James, Brad W. Smith, and Kenneth J. Novak. 2005. "Exploring the Basis of Citizens' Attitudes toward the Police." *Police Quarterly* (June): 206–228.

Futterman, Craig, Melissa Mather, and Melanie Miles. 2007. "Report Says 'Culture of Denial' Allows Police Abuse in Chicago." *Criminal Justice Newsletter* (November 15): 3–4.

Gilmartin, Kevin M. and John J. Harris. 1998. "The Continuum of Compromise." *The Police Chief* 65 (1): 25–28.

Goldstein, Herman. 1990. *Problem-Oriented Policing.* New York: McGraw-Hill.

Goldstein, Joseph. 2004. "Police Discretion Not to Invoke the Criminal Process: Low-Visibility Decisions in the Administration of Justice." In *The Criminal Justice System: Politics and Policies,* 9th ed., edited by George F. Cole, Marc G. Gertz, and Amy Bunger, 77–95. Belmont, CA: Thomson Wadsworth.

Horowitz, Jake. 2007. "Making Every Encounter Count: Building Trust and Confidence in the Police." *NIJ Journal* (256): 8–11.

Klockars, Carl B. 1985. *The Idea of Police.* Newbury Park, CA: Sage.

Klockars, Carl B. 1991. "The Rhetoric of Community Policing." In *Community Policing: Rhetoric or Reality*, edited by Jack R. Greene and Stephen D. Mastrofski, 239–258. New York: Praeger.

Langton, Lynn. 2010 (June). *Women in Law Enforcement, 1987–2007*. Washington, DC: Bureau of Justice Statistics, Crime Data Brief. (NCJ 230521)

"Local Police." 2012 (May 10). Washington, DC: Bureau of Justice Statistics Online. http://bjs.ojp.usdoj.gov/index.cfm?ty=tp&tid=71

Lohner, Wyn. 2011. "What Does It Take to Excel?" *FBI Law Enforcement Bulletin* (August): 20–23.

Marcou, Dan. 2009 (February). "'Community Oriented' SWAT." *Police One*.

Martin, Rich. 2011. "Police Corruption: An Analytical Look into Police Ethics." *FBI Law Enforcement Bulletin* (May): 11–17.

Martinelli, Thomas J. 2011. "Noble Cause Corruption and Police Discretion." *The Police Chief* (March): 60–62.

Oldham, Scott. 2006. "Proud of the Police Culture." *Law and Order* (May): 18–21.

Paoline, Eugene A., III. 2004. "Shedding Light on Police Culture: An Examination of Officers' Occupational Attitudes." *Police Quarterly* (June 2004): 205–236.

Quinn, Michael W. 2005. *Walking with the Devil: The Police Code of Silence*. Minneapolis: Quinn and Associates.

Ramsey, Charles. n.d. "Law Enforcement and Society: Lessons of the Holocaust." Washington, DC: United States Holocaust Memorial Museum. http://www.ushmm.org/education/cpsite/lawenforcement/flyer.pdf

Reaves, Brian A. 2010 (December). *Local Police Departments, 2007*. Washington, DC: Bureau of Justice Statistics. (NCJ 231174)

Rosenbaum, Dennis P., Amie M. Schuck, Sandra K. Costello, Darnell F. Hawkins, and Marianne K. Ring. 2005. "Attitudes toward the Police: The Effects of Direct and Vicarious Experience." *Police Quarterly* (September): 343–365.

San Jose, California, Police Department. n.d. "Vision, Mission, and Values Statements." http://www.sjpd.org/COP/MissionStatement.html

Scrivner, Ellen. 2006. *Innovations in Police Recruitment and Hiring: Hiring in the Spirit of Service*. Washington, DC: U.S. Department of Justice, Office of Community Oriented Policing Services.

Skogan, Wesley G. 2005. "Citizen Satisfaction with Police Encounters." *Police Quarterly* (September): 295–321.

Skolnick, Jerome H. 1966. "A Sketch of the Policeman's 'Working Personality.'" In *Justice without Trial: Law Enforcement in a Democratic Society*, 42–62. New York: John Wiley & Sons, 1966. Reprinted in *The Criminal Justice System: Politics and Policies*, 9th ed., edited by George F. Cole, Marc G. Gertz and Amy Bunger, 109–126. Belmont, CA: Thomson Wadsworth, 2004.

Smith, Dave. 2011. "DVR Dreams." *Police* (August): 84.

Son, In Soo and Dennis M. Rome. 2004. "The Prevalence and Visibility of Police Misconduct: A Survey of Citizens and Police Officers." *Police Quarterly* (June): 179–204.

Sourcebook of Criminal Justice Statistics Online. n.d. Washington, DC: Bureau of Justice Statistics. http://www.albany.edu/sourcebook

Sutton, Randy. 2005. "Ethical Survival." *Law Officer Magazine* (March): 64–65.

Trautman, Neal. 2000. *Police Code of Silence Facts Revealed*. 2000 Conference Materials, Legal Officers Section, International Association of Chiefs of Police.

Walls, Kelly G. 2003. "Not a Token Effort." *FBI Law Enforcement Bulletin* (July): 16–17.

Wargo, Eric. 2006 (August). "Bad Apples or Bad Barrels? Zimbardo on 'The Lucifer Effect.'" *The Association for Psychological Science Observer* 19 (8). http://www.psychologicalscience.org/index.php/publications/observer/2006/august-06/bad-apples-or-bad-barrels-zimbardo-on-the-lucifer-effect.html

Wilson, James Q. and George L. Kelling. 1989. "Making Neighborhoods Safe." *Atlantic Monthly* (February): 46–52.

CASE CITED

Terry v. Ohio, 392 U.S. 1 (1968)

This available CourseMate has an interactive eBook and interactive learning tools, including flash cards, quizzes, and more. To learn more about this resource and access free demo CourseMate resources, go to **www.cengagebrain.com**, and search for this book. To access CourseMate materials that you have purchased, go to **login.cengagebrain.com**.

CHAPTER 3

Understanding and Involving the Community

I believe in the United States of America as a government of the people, by the people, for the people.

—*American Creed*

DO YOU KNOW ...

» How U.S. citizens established the "public peace"?

» What a social contract is?

» How to define *community*?

» How the decline in bowling leagues relates to crime?

» What the broken windows phenomenon refers to?

» What demographics includes?

» What role organizations and institutions play within a community?

» What power structures exist within a community?

» What issues in the criminal justice system affect police–community relations?

» What restorative justice is?

» How citizens and communities have been involved in community policing?

CAN YOU DEFINE ...

bifurcated society
bowling alone
broken windows phenomenon
community
community justice
demographics
displacement
diversion
formal power structure
ghetto
heterogeneous
homogeneous
incivilities
informal power structure
NIMBY syndrome
plea bargaining
privatization
restorative justice
social capital
social contract
syndrome of crime
tipping point
White flight

INTRODUCTION

The opening sentence of the American Creed, adopted by the House of Representatives on April 3, 1918, uses language attributed to Abraham Lincoln in his address at Gettysburg on November 19, 1863: "We here highly resolve that these dead shall not have died in vain; that this nation, under God, shall have a new birth of freedom; and that government of the people, by the people, and for the people, shall not perish from the earth." The philosophy implicit in the American Creed is central to the concept of "community" in the United States. Each community is part of a larger social order.

 The U.S. Constitution and Bill of Rights, as well as federal and state statutes and local ordinances, establish the "public peace" in the United States.

In the United States individual freedom and rights are balanced with the need to establish and maintain order. The United States was born out of desire for freedom. In fact, former President Jimmy Carter noted: "America did not invent human rights. In a very real sense, it is the other way around. Human rights invented America."

The importance of individual rights to all citizens is a central theme in the following discussion of community. Citizens have established a criminal justice system in an effort to live in "peace," free from fear, crime, and violence. As the gatekeepers to the criminal justice system, the police have an inherent link with the public, as expressed by Sir Robert Peel in 1829: "Police, at all times, should maintain a relationship with the public that gives reality to the historic tradition that the police are the public and the public are the police; the police being the only members of the public who are paid to give full-time attention to duties which are incumbent on every citizen in the interests of community welfare and existence." To ensure the peace, U.S. citizens have also entered into an unwritten social contract.

social contract

A legal theory that suggests that for everyone to receive justice, each person must relinquish some individual freedom.

 The **social contract** provides that for everyone to receive justice, each person must relinquish some freedom.

In civilized society, people cannot simply do as they please. They are expected to conform to federal and state laws as well as to local rules and regulations established by and for the community in which they live. Increased mobility and economic factors have weakened the informal social contract that once helped to keep the peace in our society. As a result, the police, as agents of social control, have had to fill the breach, increasing the need for law-abiding citizens to join with the police in making their communities free from fear, drugs, crime, and terrorism.

This chapter begins with definitions of community, social capital, and lack of community. This is followed by a look at crime and violence in our communities and an explanation of community demographics. Next the organizations and institutions, the public–private policing interaction, and the power structure within a community are described. Then the role of the criminal justice system in community policing and restorative justice is discussed. The chapter concludes with an explanation of citizen and community involvement in community policing.

COMMUNITY DEFINED

What does the word *community* bring to mind? To many people it conjures up images of their hometown. To others it may bring images of a specific block, a neighborhood, or an idyllic small town where everyone knows everyone and they all get along.

Community has also been defined as a group of people living in an area under the same government. In addition, community can refer to a social group or class having common interests. Community may even refer to society as a whole—the public. This text uses a specific meaning for community.

 **Community** refers to the specific geographic area served by a police department or law enforcement agency and the individuals, organizations, and agencies within that area.

community
The specific geographic area served by a police department or law enforcement agency and the individuals, organizations, and agencies within that area.

Police officers must understand and be a part of this defined community if they are to fulfill their mission. The community may cover a very small area and have a limited number of individuals, organizations, and agencies; it may be policed by a single officer. Or the community may cover a vast area and have thousands of individuals and hundreds of organizations and agencies and be policed by several hundred officers. Although police jurisdiction and delivery of services are based on geographic boundaries, a community is much more than a group of neighborhoods administered by a local government. The schools, businesses, public and private agencies, churches, and social groups are vital elements of the community. Also of importance are the individual values, concerns, and cultural principles of the people living and working in the community and the common interests they share with neighbors. Where integrated communities exist, people share a sense of ownership and pride in their environment. They also have a sense of what is acceptable behavior, which makes policing in such a community much easier.

 Community also refers to a feeling of belonging—a sense of integration, a sense of shared values, and a sense of "we-ness."

Research strongly suggests that a *sense of* community is the glue that binds communities to maintain order and provides the foundation for effective community action. It also suggests that shared values, participation in voluntary associations, spiritual or faith-based connectedness, and positive interaction with neighbors indicate a strong sense of community and correlate with participation in civic and government activities (Correia, 2000).

SOCIAL CAPITAL

Communities might also be looked at in terms of their **social capital**. Coleman (1990, 302) developed this concept, which he defined as: "A variety of different entities having two characteristics in common: They all consist of some aspect of a social structure, and they facilitate certain actions of individuals who are within the structure." Coleman saw the two most important elements in social capital as being trustworthiness—or citizens' trust of each other and their public institutions—and obligations—that is, expectation that service to each other will be reciprocated.

Social capital can be found at two levels: local and public. *Local social capital* is the bond among family members and their immediate, informal groups. *Public social capital* refers to the networks tying individuals to broader community institutions such as schools, civic organizations, churches, and the like as well as to networks linking individuals to various levels of government—including the police. According to Correia (2000, 53): "Taken together, the concepts of sense of community and social capital go a long way toward describing the strength of a community's social fabric."

Correia reports on a study using Community Action Support Teams (CASTs) and the community factors affecting social capital in six cities: Hayward, California; Davenport, Iowa; Ann Arbor, Michigan; Sioux City, Iowa; Pocatello, Idaho; and Ontario, California. Data came from self-administered mail surveys, direct observations, and interviews. Of the 22 hypotheses tested, 7 were supported by the data (Correia, 2000, 34–35):

1. Trust in others depends on the level of safety an individual feels in his or her environment. Therefore, the higher the levels of perceived safety, the higher the levels of local social capital will be.

2. The lower the levels of physical disorder, the higher the levels of perceived sense of safety will be.

3. Females will hold lower levels of perceived safety than males.

4. The higher the levels of public social capital, the higher the levels of collective action will be.

5. The more individuals trust one another, the more likely they will be to engage in collective activities. Consequently, the higher the level of local social capital, the higher the level of engagement in collective action will be.

6. The more individuals trust one another, the more likely they will be to interact. Therefore, the higher the levels of local social capital, the higher the levels of neighboring activity will be.

7. The higher the levels of civic activity, the higher the levels of public social capital will be.

However, sociologists have been describing for decades either the loss or the breakdown of "community" in modern, technological, industrial, urban societies such as ours.

LACK OF COMMUNITY

Community implies a group of people with a common history and understandings and a sense of themselves as "us" and outsiders as "them." Unfortunately, many communities lack this "we-ness." In such areas, the police and public may have a "them-versus-us" relationship. Areas requiring the most police attention are usually those with the fewest shared values and a limited sense of community. When citizens are unable to maintain informal social control, the result is social disorganization and a greater need for formal social control measures (i.e., the police). All entities within a community—individuals as well as organizations and agencies—must work together to keep that community healthy. Such partnerships are vital because a community cannot be healthy if unemployment and poverty are widespread; people are hungry; health care is inadequate; prejudice separates people; preschool children lack proper care and nutrition; senior citizens are allowed to atrophy; schools remain isolated and remote; social services are fragmented and disproportionate; and government lacks responsibility and accountability.

Bowling Alone

In 1995 Putnam explored social capital in America in an article entitled, "Bowling Alone." His article described a drastic decline in league bowling and proposed that this seemingly minor observation actually reflected a striking decline in social capital and civic engagement in the United States beginning in the 1960s. The article caused fierce academic debate and prompted Putnam to study the issue in depth. Extensive research supported his central thesis that in the past 40 years Americans have become increasingly isolated from family, friends, and neighbors.

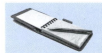 The **bowling alone** phenomenon refers to a striking decline in social capital and civic engagement in the United States.

bowling alone
A metaphor referring to a striking decline in social capital and civic engagement in the United States.

In 2000 Putnam's book *Bowling Alone* presented extensive evidence that America had lost much of its social capital, resulting in higher crime rates, lower educational performance, and more teen pregnancy, child suicide, low-birth-weight babies, and infant mortality. Analysis of nearly 500,000 interviews conducted over the last quarter century shows evidence that we sign fewer petitions, belong to fewer organizations that meet, know our neighbors less, meet with friends less frequently, and even socialize with our families less often (Putnam, 2000). Several possible reasons for this decline include changes in family structure (more people living alone); electronic entertainment; and, perhaps most important, generational change. The "civic" generation born in the first third of the 20th century is being replaced by baby boomers and Generation X-ers, who have been characterized as being much less civic minded.

Research by Correia, described earlier, supports Putnam's thesis that social capital is important and concludes:

> Effective community policing may be limited to those areas with high levels of social cohesion; most likely, these areas do not need community policing as badly as others. This suggests that communities lacking high levels of Putnam's social capital, yet with high levels of community policing activity, are possibly beyond repair; their stocks of social capital cannot be replenished without extraordinary effort, nor can their strained social cohesion be repaired exclusively by police efforts. Consequently, this method of law enforcement may in fact raise more expectations than it is able to satisfy. (Correia, 2000, 41)

In effect: "Social capital is a prerequisite to citizen engagement in community efforts" (Correia, 2000, 48). The implications of this significant finding are discussed in Chapter 5. Proponents of community policing in some areas may be missing a major sociologic reality—the absence of "community"—in the midst of all the optimism about police playing a greater role in encouraging it.

In some instances government policies may destroy social capital. Major freeways may physically divide neighborhoods. At the local level, budget cuts in schools may result in the elimination of sports or music programs, activities that have been shown to encourage civic engagement.

Putnam and others who propose that social capital is continuing to decline are not without their critics. Putnam explains: "Naturally all theories are open to question. … I've heard three broad complaints about social capital. First, it is theoretically sloppy; second, the evidence of causal direction is weak; and third, it has no policy levers" (Clarke, 2004). Putnam contends that sufficient hard evidence exists that social capital has value.

Another important theory of the causes of crime and neighborhood decline is the analogy used in Wilson and Kelling's "Broken Windows."

Broken Windows

In a classic article, "Broken Windows," Wilson and Kelling (1982, 31) contend:

> Social psychologists and police officers tend to agree that if a window in a building is broken and is left unrepaired, all the rest of the windows will soon be broken. This is as true in nice neighborhoods as in run-down ones. Window-breaking does not necessarily occur on a large scale because some areas are inhabited by determined window-breakers whereas others are populated by window-lovers; rather, one unrepaired broken window is a signal that no one cares, and so breaking more windows costs nothing. (It has always been fun.)

broken windows phenomenon

Suggests that if it appears no one cares about the community, as indicated by broken windows not being repaired, then disorder and crime will thrive.

 The **broken windows phenomenon** suggests that if it appears "no one cares," disorder and crime will thrive.

Wilson and Kelling based their broken windows theory, in part, on research done in 1969 by a Stanford psychologist, Philip Zimbardo. Zimbardo arranged to have a car without license plates parked with its hood up on a street in the Bronx and a comparable car parked on a street in Palo Alto, California. The car in the Bronx was attacked by vandals within 10 minutes, and within 24 hours it had been totally destroyed and stripped of anything of value. The car in Palo Alto sat untouched. After a week Zimbardo took a sledgehammer to it. People passing by soon joined in, and within a few hours that car was also totally destroyed. According to Wilson and Kelling (1982, 31): "Untended property becomes fair game for people out for fun or plunder, and even for people who ordinarily would not dream of doing such things and who probably consider themselves as law-abiding."

incivilities

Occur when social control mechanisms have eroded and include unmowed lawns, piles of accumulated trash, graffiti, public drunkenness, fighting, prostitution, abandoned buildings, and broken windows.

Broken windows and smashed cars are visible signs of people not caring about their community. Other less subtle signs include unmowed lawns, piles of accumulated trash, and graffiti, often referred to as **incivilities**. Incivilities

Wilson and Kelling's broken windows theory holds that signs of vandalism and general urban decay indicate that no one cares about a community and that this neighborhood will tolerate crime and disorder.

© Index Stock Imagery/Photolibrary

include rowdiness, drunkenness, fighting, prostitution, abandoned buildings, litter, broken windows, and graffiti.

Incivilities and social disorder occur when social control mechanisms have eroded. Increases in incivilities may increase the fear of crime and reduce citizens' sense of safety. Citizens may physically or psychologically withdraw, isolating themselves from their neighbors. Or increased incivilities and disorder may bring people together to "take back the neighborhood."

The real-world application to policing of the broken windows theory is often credited to William J. Bratton who, in the early 1980s, was in charge of the Boston transit police. Bratton referenced the broken windows theory when he declared that the primary responsibility of patrol was to keep order in a community and prevent offenses rather than simply responding to serious crimes after the fact. Crime on Bratton's watch dropped by 27 percent and, in 1993, Mayor Rudolph W. Giuliani hired Bratton as New York's police commissioner. Bratton focused on quality-of-life initiatives such as cracking down on panhandling, public drinking, street prostitution, and the like. In the 1990s New York City led the United States in a nationwide decline in serious crime, crediting "order maintenance."

In an interview with *Law Enforcement News,* Wilson explained: "Broken windows as a goal … is not about police officers going soft. … This can often mean being tough, but being tough about things that people care about. It also means being tough with respect to other city and county agencies, because many of the things people tell you need to be done in your community cannot be done by the police acting alone, and therefore, they must act with other government agencies" ("'Broken Windows,' 22 Years Later," 2005, 8).

Kelling, in this same interview, described how while working with Bratton in the Boston subway system, they had "this wonderful moment in the subway when we discovered while we were trying to enforce laws against fare-beating that in some of the stations, 7 or 8 out of 10 who were arrested either were wanted on a warrant or were carrying an illegal weapon" (6). Attending to minor infractions can result in the apprehension of criminals who commit major crimes.

In one study, researchers from Harvard and Suffolk universities worked with police in Lowell, Massachusetts, to identify crime hot spots. In half of the 34 locations identified, authorities cleared trash, fixed streetlights, and sent loiterers away. They secured abandoned buildings, forced businesses to meet codes, made more arrests for misdemeanors, and expanded mental health and homeless aid services. Normal policing and services continued in the remaining hot spots, which served as the "control" group. The results were striking: "A 20-percent plunge in calls to police from the parts of town that received extra attentions. It is seen as strong scientific evidence that the long-debated 'broken windows' theory really works—that disorderly conditions breed bad behavior, and that fixing them can help prevent crime" (Johnson, 2009). The Lowell experiment provides data and direction for other departments on which efforts seem to work best: "Cleaning up the physical environment was very effective; misdemeanor arrests less so, and boosting social services had no apparent impact." Such evidence-based policing is essential to ensure that policing efforts and resources are used most effectively.

Other Factors Negating a Sense of Community

The increasing diversity within our society can present a challenge to community policing. It is extremely difficult to implement community policing when the values of groups within a given area clash. For example, controversy may exist between gay communities and Orthodox Christian or Jewish communities in the same area. Do each of these communities deserve a different style of policing based on the "community value system"? Do "community" police officers ignore behavior in a community where the majority of residents approve of that behavior but enforce sanctions against the same behavior in enclaves where that behavior causes tension? These are difficult ethical questions.

Another factor that negates a sense of community is the prevalence of violence. We live in a violent society. The United States was born through a violent revolution. The media emphasize violence, constantly carrying news of murder, rape, and assault. The cartoons children watch contain more violence than most adults realize. Children learn that violence is acceptable and justified under some circumstances. Citizens expect the police to prevent violence, but the police cannot do it alone. Individuals must come together to help stop violence and in so doing can build a sense of community.

If the community is unresponsive, community policing cannot succeed, no matter how hard the police work:

Ironically, it is difficult to sustain community involvement in community policing. The community and the police may not have a history of getting along in poor neighborhoods. Organizations representing the interests of community members may not have a track record of cooperating with police, and poor and high-crime areas often are not well endowed with an infrastructure of organizations ready to get involved. Fear of retaliation by gangs and drug dealers can undermine public involvement. Finally, there may be no reason for residents of crime-ridden neighborhoods to think that community policing will turn out to be anything but another broken promise. Residents may be accustomed to seeing programs come and go in response to political and budgetary cycles that are out of their control. (Skogan, 2004, 166)

COMMUNITIES AND CRIME

Although traditional policing has most often dealt with high crime levels by stricter enforcement (zero tolerance), "get-tough" policies, and a higher police presence, police usually have little ability to change things for the better in the long run. Cracking down on crime often results in **displacement**, the relocation of crime and criminals to neighboring areas outside the enforcement zone. The community in which the crackdown occurs may be temporarily safer; however, forced by the increased police presence and increased likelihood of arrest, criminals usually just move their operations, often a few blocks or miles away, making adjacent communities less safe. Policing efforts can develop into an unending game of "cat and mouse."

displacement
The theory that successful implementation of a crime-reduction initiative does not really prevent crime; instead it just moves the crime to another area.

Traditional police tactics often fail because the causes of crime in communities are complicated and linked to a multitude of factors, including environmental design; housing age, type, and density; availability of jobs; residents' level of education; poverty level; family structure; demographics (average age of residents, ethnic and racial makeup of the community); mobility; and perhaps other unidentified factors. Such complicated underlying causes require creative solutions and partnerships. Police who form alliances with organizations and agencies associated with education, religion, health care, job training, family support, community leaders, and members can often affect the underlying factors in criminal behavior and community decay.

A theory called the ecology of crime explains how criminal opportunities are created in neighborhoods. Just like a natural ecosystem, a neighborhood can hold only a certain number of things. Add too many and the system will collapse. This is similar to the **tipping point**, the point at which an ordinary, stable phenomenon can turn into a crisis. For example, a health epidemic is nonlinear—that is, small changes can have huge effects and large changes can have small effects, in contrast to linear situations in which every extra increment of effort will produce a corresponding improvement in result.

tipping point
That point at which an ordinary, stable phenomenon can turn into a crisis.

This principle of nonlinearity is captured in the expression, "That's the straw that broke the camel's back." The principle can be applied to the phenomenon of **White flight**, the departure of White families from neighborhoods experiencing racial integration or from cities experiencing school desegregation. Depending on the racial views of White residents, one White neighborhood might empty out when minorities reach 5 percent of the neighborhood population, whereas another more racially tolerant White neighborhood might not tip until minorities make up 40 or 50 percent. Communities need to recognize when they are approaching the tipping point or the threshold in a given situation.

White flight
The departure of White families from neighborhoods experiencing racial integration or from cities experiencing school desegregation.

COMMUNITY DEMOGRAPHICS

In addition to understanding the complex concept of community, it is important to assess the demographics of the area. The term **demographics** refers to the characteristics of the individuals who live in a community.

demographics
The characteristics of a human population or community.

Demographics include a population's size, distribution, growth, density, employment rate, ethnic makeup, and vital statistics such as average age, education, and income.

Although people generally assume that the smaller the population of a community, the easier policing becomes, this is not necessarily true. Small communities generally have fewer resources. The demands of being the sole law enforcement person in a community—in effect, being on call 24 hours a day—may be difficult to manage. A major advantage of a smaller community is that people know each other. A sense of community is likely to be greater in such communities than in large cities such as Chicago or New York.

When assessing law enforcement's ability to police an area, density of population is an important variable. Studies have shown that as population becomes denser, people become more aggressive. In densely populated areas, people become more territorial and argue more frequently about "turf." Rapid population growth can invigorate a community, or it can drain its limited resources. Without effective planning and foresight, rapid population growth can result in serious problems for a community, especially if the population growth results from an influx of immigrants or members of an ethnic group different from the majority in that area.

The community's vital statistics are extremely important from a police–community partnership perspective. What is the average age of individuals within the community? Are there more young or elderly individuals? How many single-parent families are there? What is the divorce rate? What is the common level of education? How does the education of those in law enforcement compare? What is the school dropout rate? Do gangs operate in the community? What is the percentage of latchkey children? Such children may pose a significant challenge for police.

Income and income distribution are also important. Do great disparities exist? Would the community be described as affluent, moderately well off, or poor? How does the income of those in law enforcement compare to the average income? Closely related to income is the level of employment. What is the ratio of blue-collar to professional workers? How much unemployment exists? How do those who are unemployed exist? Are they on welfare? Do they commit crimes to survive? Are they homeless? Are there gangs?

homogeneous
Involving things (including people) that are basically similar, alike; the opposite of *heterogeneous*.

heterogeneous
Involving things (including people) that are unlike, dissimilar, different; the opposite of *homogeneous*.

The ethnic makeup of the community is another consideration. Is the community basically homogeneous? A **homogeneous** community is one in which people are all quite similar. A **heterogeneous** community, in contrast, is one in which individuals are quite different from each other. Most communities are heterogeneous. Establishing and maintaining good relations among the various subgroups making up the community is a challenge. Usually one ethnic subgroup will have the most power and control. It is helpful if police officers come from all groups, including the dominant one and smaller ones.

For example, the neighboring cities of Brooklyn Park and Brooklyn Center, Minnesota, experienced a 150-percent increase in foreign-born residents between 1990 and 2000, evolving rapidly from fairly homogenous communities to cities with populations reaching 40 to 50 percent diversity (Ankerfelt, Davis, and Futterer, 2011). By 2008 this area, often referred to as "the Brooklyns," had become home to what is estimated to be the largest population of Somali and Liberian civil war refugees in the United States. In addition, the prospect of affordable housing and job opportunities has drawn other African, Hispanic, Eastern European, and Asian refugees and immigrants to these cities, demographic changes which have prompted local law enforcement agencies to seek more ethnically diverse recruits: "The fact that the police departments have multicultural police cadets speaks volumes to community members whose race, background, and ethnic status may previously have been a cause for misunderstanding between them and the police. … To date, six diverse individuals representing a multitude of nationalities have been selected to enroll as police cadets. … [and] two Liberian and Hmong cadets have completed officer training" (Ankerfelt, Davis, and Futterer, 2011, 27).

The existence of ghettos in many major cities poses extreme challenges for law enforcement. A **ghetto** is an area of a city usually inhabited by individuals of the same race or ethnic background who live in poverty and, to outsiders, apparent social disorganization. Consequently, ghettos, minorities, and crime are frequently equated. Because ghettos are the focus of many anticrime efforts, this is often perceived as a clear bias by law enforcement against members of racial or ethnic minority groups.

ghetto
An area of a city usually inhabited by individuals of the same race or ethnic background who live in poverty and apparent social disorganization.

Poverty, unemployment, substandard housing, and inadequate education have all figured into theories on the causes of crime. They are often part of the underlying problems manifested in crime. In addition, our criminal justice system tends to focus on street crimes. Economic crimes such as those perpetrated by the CEOs of several large corporations in the past few years are not prosecuted as often and the penalties are seldom as severe.

A RAPIDLY CHANGING POPULATION

The 2010 Census reported 308.7 million people in the United States, a 9.7-percent increase from the Census 2000 population of 281.4 million (Mackun et al., 2011). This change was lower than the 13.2-percent increase for the 1990s and comparable to the growth during the 1980s of 9.8 percent. However, more than half of the total U.S. population growth between 2000 and 2010 was attributed to the increase in the Hispanic population, which grew from 35.3 million in 2000 to 50.5 million (16% of the U.S. population) in 2010 (Ennis, Rios-Vargas, and Albert, 2011). Between 2000 and 2010 the Hispanic population grew by 43 percent, which was four times the growth in the total population at 10 percent.

A report from the Pew Research Center projects that immigration will propel the population total to 438 million by 2050 and that the racial and ethnic profile of Americans will continue to shift—with non-Hispanic Whites losing their majority status in the second half of the 21st century (Haub, 2008). Indeed, communities have undergone tremendous changes in the past half-century. Consider that in 1950, the non-Hispanic White population made up 87 percent of the population. This population declined from 80 percent in 1980 to 66.4 percent in 2006.

According to 2010 Census data, the proportion of the total U.S. population self-identified as non-Hispanic White only was 64 percent.

Although the non-Hispanic White alone population is still numerically and proportionally the largest major race and ethnic group in the United States, it is also growing at the slowest rate. The Black population also experienced growth over the decade but grew at a slower rate than all other major race groups except for White. The Hispanic and Asian populations, on the other hand, have grown considerably, in part due to relatively higher levels of immigration. Figure 3.1 shows the racial and ethnic composition of the United States in 2000 and the projected composition in 2050.

In addition to a change in ethnic makeup, the United States is also experiencing a widening of the gap between those with wealth and those living in poverty. The middle class is shrinking, and the gap between the "haves" and the "have-nots" is widening, resulting in a **bifurcated society**.

The following trends in the United States are likely to continue: The minority population will increase, and White dominance will end; the number of legal and illegal immigrants will increase; and the elderly population will increase.

bifurcated society

The widening of the gap between those with wealth (the "haves") and those living in poverty (the "have-nots"), with a shrinking middle class.

Figure 3.1   The Racial and Ethnic Composition of the United States in 2000 and the Projected Composition for 2050

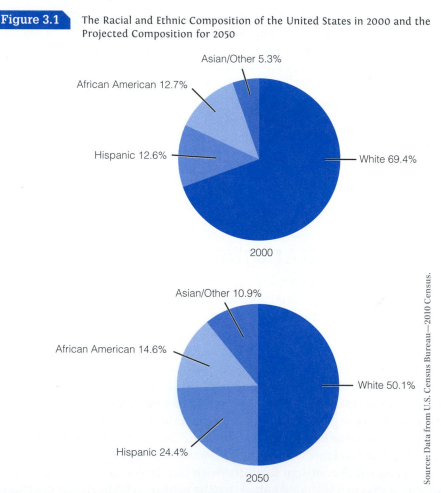

Source: Data from U.S. Census Bureau—2010 Census.

Note: White, Black, and Asian/Other categories exclude Hispanics, who may be of any race. The Asian/Other category includes American Indians, Eskimos, Aleuts, and Pacific Islanders. Totals may not add up to 100 because of rounding.

ORGANIZATIONS AND INSTITUTIONS

In addition to understanding the demographics of the community and being able to relate to a great variety of individuals, community policing officers must also be familiar with the various organizations and institutions within the community and establish effective relationships with them. A strong network of community organizations and institutions fosters cohesiveness and shared intolerance of criminal behavior and encourages citizens to cooperate in controlling crime, thereby increasing the likelihood that illegal acts will be detected and reported. These networks and partnerships are essential because no single organization or group is able to address all the problems and concerns of a community alone. All the organizations and groups working beyond their individual capacity are unable to do more than apply localized, specific band-aid solutions to all of the community problems.

 Organizations and institutions can play a key role in enhancing community safety and quality of life.

A good relationship between the schools in the community and the police is vital to maintaining order. Other organizations and institutions with which police officers should interact effectively include departments of human services, health care providers, emergency services providers, and any agencies working with youth. Communities may also have libraries, museums, and zoos that would welcome a good relationship with the police.

THE PUBLIC–PRIVATE POLICING INTERACTION

Historically, public and private security have seen themselves as being in competition, with private security usually coming out on the "short end of the stick." Police often view private security employees as poorly trained, poorly paid individuals who could not land a police job. Names such as "rent-a-cop" and "cop-in-a-box" add to this negative perception. However, private security plays a major role in safeguarding Americans and their property, with an estimated 85 percent of critical U.S. infrastructure protected by private security companies: "Many [officers] do not stop to realize that private security professionals in business places, at public gathering sites, and in corporate environments are truly first responders to every conceivable calamity from crimes to natural disasters" (Cooke and Hahn, 2006, 16).

The need for public and private police forces to establish good working relationships was recognized by the National Institute of Justice in the early 1980s when it began urging cooperation between the agencies and established the Joint Council of Law Enforcement and Private Security Association. The International Association of Chiefs of Police (IACP) has also recognized this need for cooperation by establishing a Private Sector Liaison Committee (PSLC). Indeed, many communities and police departments are using **privatization**, contracting with private security agencies or officers to provide services usually considered to be law enforcement functions.

privatization
Using private security officers or agencies to provide services typically considered to be law enforcement functions.

Carter (2007, 6) asserts: "The need for complex coordination, extra staffing, and special resources after a terror attack, coupled with the significant demands of crime prevention and response, requires boosting the level of partnership between public policing and private security. The benefits are clear. Law enforcement agencies possess legal powers and training not normally available to the general public. Private industry, with approximately triple the personnel resources of the law enforcement community, is more advanced in the use of technology to prevent and detect crime and is uniquely able to address certain crimes, such as workplace violence or computer crimes."[1]

Some areas of cooperation between police and private security are investigating internal theft and economic crimes, responding to burglar alarms, examining evidence from law enforcement in private crime labs, conducting background checks, protecting VIPs and executives, protecting crime scenes, transporting prisoners, moving hazardous materials, and controlling crowds and traffic at public events. Other likely areas for privatization include public building security, parking enforcement, public parks patrol, animal control, funeral escorts, public housing development patrol, applicant screening, and civilian fingerprinting.

An example of how the security industry can assist law enforcement is in responding to burglar alarms. The false alarm problem is of immense proportions: "The vast majority of alarm calls—between 94 and 98 percent (higher in some jurisdictions)—are false.... Nationwide, false alarms account for somewhere between 10 and 25 percent of *all* calls to police. For many U.S. police agencies, false burglar alarms constitute the highest-volume type of call for service" (Sampson, 2011, 7–8). Responding to false alarms may result in needless expense, inappropriate responses (complacency), and negative attitudes toward alarm systems. Partnering with the private sector to address the false alarm problem would benefit all concerned with the issue and relieve an estimated 35,000 officers from providing what is, essentially, a private service (Sampson, 2011).

The Office of Community Oriented Policing Services (COPS) is committed to promoting law enforcement–private security (LE–PS) partnerships and has sponsored several projects aimed at identifying and analyzing such collaborations. Operation Cooperation was one such study completed in 2000 in which roughly 60 LE–PS partnerships were identified nationwide. Operation Partnership, completed in 2007 and whose purposes were to identify LE–PS partnerships, explore successful practices and lessons learned, and analyze trends and challenges, found a substantial increase in the number of public–private policing partnerships throughout the country, identifying more than 450 such collaborative efforts:

> Private security and law enforcement professionals have been forming effective person-to-person liaisons and relationships for years. But changing crime patterns and increasingly difficult problems, whether in high-crime urban areas or high-tech venues like the Internet, necessitate different approaches and group activities, not just individual efforts. Further, the continuing threat

of terrorism demands greater collaboration to ensure maximum resources. To combat these threats effectively, both law enforcement and private security (LE–PS) must be involved in homeland security programs at the local, state, and national levels. Both private security and law enforcement must work jointly to protect the infrastructures on which society depends. These factors, as well as resource limitations, have fueled a desire to build more, more structured, and more lasting LE–PS partnerships.

Since the Operation Cooperation project was completed in 2000, thousands of private security and law enforcement executives and practitioners have come to consider, form, and enhance partnerships with one another. Private security is gaining recognition as an important partner in community policing. Law enforcement today has a greater awareness of private security's vast resources and increasing growth, and a better understanding of private security's need for crime and threat information. Numerous, diverse examples of successful partnerships show how obstacles can be overcome, and how results can be achieved that simply would not have been possible without collaboration. (Law Enforcement–Private Security Consortium, 2011, 109)

In addition to considering the role private security might play in community policing, the power structure within the community must be considered.

THE POWER STRUCTURE

Most communities have both a formal and an informal power structure.

The **formal power structure** includes divisions of society with wealth and political influence: federal, state, and local agencies and governments, commissions, and regulatory agencies.

formal power structure
Includes divisions of society with wealth and political influence such as federal, state, and local agencies and governments, commissions, and regulatory agencies.

The public can usually readily identify the formal power structure. Often policy decisions made at the federal and state levels directly affect local decisions. In addition, federal and state funding can directly influence local programs.

The **informal power structure** includes religious groups, wealthy subgroups, ethnic groups, political groups, and public interest groups.

informal power structure
Includes religious groups, wealthy subgroups, ethnic groups, political groups, and public interest groups.

The public cannot as readily identify the informal power structure, which includes banks, real estate companies, and other large and influential businesses in a community. The informal power structure is not merely a few people controlling the masses; rather, the control groups are entire subcultures that influence other subcultures. It has been alleged that 400 families control the wealth of the United States, affecting every other subculture. Awareness of the way informal groups, especially wealthy and political groups, exercise their ideologies is important. Knowing how informal group pressure is forced into an organization's formal structure is key to understanding why the community at large often conflicts with the criminal justice system.

Wilson and Kelling (1982, 34) suggest: "The essence of the police role in maintaining order is to reinforce the informal control mechanisms of the community itself. The police cannot, without committing extraordinary resources, provide a substitute for that informal control." Law enforcement personnel must understand the different subgroups within their jurisdiction and the power struggles that occur among them. They must also be aware of this reality: Democracy does not always ensure equality.

THE CRIMINAL JUSTICE SYSTEM

Many people equate policing or law enforcement with the criminal justice system when, in fact, it is only one part of this system. The other two components, courts and corrections, are much less visible in most communities. Because the police are the most visible component of the system, however, they often become "the criminal justice system" in the eyes of the community.

In the criminal justice process, the role of law enforcement is to prevent, detect, or act on reports of law violations, to apprehend suspects reasonably believed responsible for such violations, and to bring those suspects or defendants before a court of law. The court then assesses the charge and the evidence as presented by both the prosecution, for which the police officer may be a witness, and the defense to determine the defendant's guilt or innocence. If found guilty of the charge, the offender may be sentenced by the court to confinement in a correctional facility or be allowed to return to the community under supervision.

This three-part system provides a procedure of checks and balances intended to ensure that no person is accused of a crime and then deprived of freedom without every reasonable step being taken to guarantee fairness and equity throughout the process, guarantees consistent with the Fourteenth Amendment requirements of the "due process" and "equal protection" clauses. The courts are often criticized by the public as being the weak link in the criminal justice process, letting too many offenders "off easy" and allowing wealthy defendants to buy their way out of convictions. Those who criticize judges usually do so based on whether they agree with a judge's procedures and sentencing practices. Critics must remember, however, that the system is designed to work the way it does. After all, if we assumed that everyone arrested by the police is guilty of a crime, there would be no need for prosecutors, judges, juries, or courtrooms. The accused could be taken directly to prison.

Many people have a limited understanding of the role that the courts and corrections play in crime control. Indeed, at times various components of the criminal justice system seem to work against each other. When the perception or the reality is that criminals are not being convicted or are being released early from prison, some people demand more police and ask why they are not doing their job.

Members of the law enforcement community often become frustrated by such attitudes and incidents. Decisions made in court can discourage officers, who may become cynical and wonder why they work so hard to make arrests when they see cases dismissed or plea-bargained. Officers may also become frustrated when those who are convicted are given a light sentence or probation. Officers may be further aggravated by what they view as inadequacies of the corrections system, aware of the many career criminals whose behavior has not improved even after they have been through prison, probation, parole, halfway houses, and rehabilitation programs. Officers are not alone in their disappointment, however. The public, too, can be frustrated by the performance of the courts and corrections.

The public may have a negative opinion of the courts because of their failure to process cases promptly, their inconsistency in plea bargaining, and the long tenure accorded to judges. Many believe that the courts provide "assembly-line" justice and the legal process is filled with delays. Aspects of the correctional system that have impeded good public relations include failures to reform offenders, the early release of recidivists, and the growing prison population.

To help overcome negative opinions and improve public relations, agencies within the criminal justice system are now actively seeking partnerships with others in the community. Many communities now have community prosecution, community courts, community corrections, and even **community justice**. What constitutes good criminal justice administration is open to debate.

Numerous controversial issues related to the effectiveness of the criminal justice system affect police–community partnerships. Although many issues are outside police officers' appropriate sphere of action, they affect the system as a whole. Therefore, police officers need to be aware of these issues and their potential impact.

community justice
An ethic that transforms the aim of the justice system into enhancing community life or sustaining communities.

> Controversial issues in the criminal justice system that affect police–community partnerships include plea bargaining, diversion, sentencing, rehabilitation, community alternatives to prisons, victims' rights, and capital punishment.

Plea bargaining is a practice by which prosecutors charge a defendant with a less serious crime in exchange for a guilty plea, thus eliminating the time and expense of a trial. **Diversion** is a system operating in most states that removes juvenile status offenders and delinquents from the jurisdiction of the courts, when possible. This practice evolved because once offenders are labeled as juvenile delinquents, they may act out and perpetuate that negative role. Many individuals in the justice system consider this being "soft" on crime.

Within the courts, judges often have considerable discretion in sentencing. When the community perceives sentences as too lenient, it sparks controversy. Police officers often believe that sentences are too light for serious crimes. Issues within the corrections component of the criminal justice system include locating alternative correctional facilities within the community. These alternatives become especially controversial when a community must determine the location of the facilities. Citizens often have the **NIMBY syndrome**—that is, "not in my backyard."

plea bargaining
A practice in which prosecutors charge a defendant with a less serious crime in exchange for a guilty plea, thus eliminating the time and expense of a trial.

diversion
Turning youths away from the criminal justice system, rerouting them to another agency or program.

NIMBY syndrome
"Not in my backyard"; the idea that it is fine to have a halfway house—across town, not in my backyard.

A growing number of people are protesting the treatment of victims by the criminal justice system. The law enforcement community has responded to this protest in a number of ways, as discussed in Chapter 7. In addition, the debate continues on the merits and effectiveness of capital punishment as a deterrent to crime and a form of retribution.

Another controversial issue in the criminal justice system is that it has operated reactively, concentrating its efforts on fighting crime to keep the "public peace" and allowing police officers to function as armed social workers. Many believe the system has been shortsighted, focusing almost exclusively on detecting individual offenses and specific ways to eliminate each crime instead of concentrating on developing strategies to proactively attack the syndromes of crime. A **syndrome of crime** is a group of signs, causes, and symptoms that occur together to foster specific crimes. The syndromes of crime are central to problem-oriented policing, discussed in detail in Chapter 4.

syndrome of crime
A group of signs, causes, and symptoms that occur together to foster specific crimes.

As discussed earlier and in Chapter 1, some practitioners and academicians alike are advocating community involvement in all areas of criminal justice. Community justice has its roots in restorative justice.

RESTORATIVE JUSTICE

Restorative justice can be traced back to the code of Hammurabi in 2000 BCE. This type of justice holds offenders accountable to the victim and the victim's community rather than to the state. Rather than seeking retribution (punishment), it seeks restitution—to repair the damages as much as possible and to restore the victim, the community, and the offender. Under common law, criminals were often required to reimburse victims for their losses. Beginning in the 12th century, however, under William the Conqueror, crimes were considered offenses against the king's peace, with offenders ordered to pay fines to the state. This tradition was brought to the United States. In the 1970s, reformers began trying to change the emphasis of the criminal justice system from the offender back to the victim. The Victim Witness Protection Act of 1982 marked the reemergence of the victim in the criminal justice process.

restorative justice
Advocates a balanced approach to sentencing that involves offenders, victims, local communities, and government to alleviate crime and violence and obtain peaceful communities.

Restorative justice advocates a balanced approach to sentencing that involves offenders, victims, local communities, and government to alleviate crime and violence and maintain peaceful communities.

Table 3.1 summarizes the differences between the traditional retributive approach to justice and restorative justice.

The most common forms of restorative sentences include restitution (payments to victims) and community service. Other restorative justice practices include victim impact statements, family group conferences, sentencing circles, and citizen reparative boards.

Table 3.1   Paradigms of Justice—Old and New

Old Paradigm/Retributive Justice	New Paradigm/Restorative Justice
1. Crime defined as violation of the state	1. Crime defined as violation of one person by another
2. Focus on establishing blame, on guilt, on past (did he/she do it?)	2. Focus on problem solving, on liabilities and obligations, on future (what should be done?)
3. Adversarial relationships and process normative	3. Dialogue and negotiation normative
4. Imposition of pain to punish and deter/prevent	4. Restitution as a means of restoring both parties; reconciliation/restoration as goal
5. Justice defined by intent and by process; right rules	5. Justice defined as right relationships; judged by the outcome
6. Interpersonal, conflictual nature of crime obscured, repressed; conflict seen as individual vs. state	6. Crime recognized as interpersonal conflict; value of conflict recognized
7. One social injury replaced by another	7. Focus on repair of social injury
8. Community on sidelines, represented abstractly by state	8. Community as facilitator in restorative process
9. Encouragement of competitive, individualistic values	9. Encouragement of mutuality
10. Action directed from state to offender: • Victim ignored • Offender passive	10. Victim's and offender's roles recognized in both problem and solution: • Victim rights/needs recognized • Offender encouraged to take responsibility
11. Offender accountability defined as taking punishment	11. Offender accountability defined as understanding impact of action and helping decide how to make things right
12. Offense defined in purely legal terms, devoid of moral, social, economic, political dimensions	12. Offense understood in whole context—moral, social, economic, political
13. "Debt" owed to state and society in the abstract	13. Debt/liability to victim recognized
14. Response focused on offender's past behavior	14. Response focused on harmful consequences of offender's behavior
15. Stigma of crime unremovable	15. Stigma of crime removable through restorative action
16. No encouragement for repentance and forgiveness	16. Possibilities for repentance and forgiveness
17. Dependence on proxy professionals	17. Direct involvement by participants

Source: Howard Zehr. *Journal of Community Corrections* (formerly *IARCA Journal*) Volume 4 Number 4, March 1991, p. 7. © Civic Research Institute, Inc. Used by permission of Civic Research Institute, publisher of *Journal of Community Corrections*, official journal of the International Community Corrections Association, formerly the International Association of Residential and Community Alternatives.

CITIZEN INVOLVEMENT IN THE LAW ENFORCEMENT COMMUNITY

Once upon a time, when food resources in a village were seemingly gone, a creative individual—knowing that each person always has a little something in reserve—proposed that the community make stone soup. After setting to boil a single, simple, easy to find, albeit nutritionally void, ingredient—a stone—people in the community were asked if they had "just a little something" to improve the soup. One person found a carrot, another brought a few potatoes, another brought a bit of meat and so on. When the soup was finished, it was thick and nourishing. Such is the situation in our communities today. Because resources are stretched to the limit, people tend to hold on to their time, talent, or money. These self-protective actions leave most groups without enough resources to effectively handle community problems. Perhaps it is time to adopt the "stone soup" stance of cooperation.

Community members have a high interest level in their local police departments and have been involved in a variety of ways for many years. This involvement, although it establishes important contact, should not be mistaken for community policing. It usually does not involve the partnerships and problem-solving activities of community policing.

 Citizen involvement in the law enforcement community and in understanding policing has taken the form of civilian review boards, citizen patrols, citizen police academies, ride-alongs, and similar programs.

Civilian Review Boards

The movement for citizen review has been a major political struggle for more than 40 years and remains one of the most controversial issues in police work today; nonetheless, citizen oversight exists as an established feature within the world of U.S. policing: "By mid-2005 more than 100 oversight agencies covered the police departments in almost every large city in the United States (and consequently a substantial proportion of the population). Additionally, an increasing number of agencies covered county sheriff's departments and police departments in medium-sized cities. The growth of citizen oversight is not confined to the United States. External citizen oversight of the police is virtually universal in the rest of the English-speaking world and is spreading in Latin America, Asia, and continental Europe" (Walker, 2006, 1–2).

Supporters of civilian review boards believe it is impossible for the police to objectively review actions of their colleagues and emphasize that the police culture demands that police officers support each other, even if they know something illegal has occurred. Opponents of civilian review boards stress that civilians cannot possibly understand the complexities of the policing profession and that it is demeaning to be reviewed by an external source.

Currently, most departments handle officer discipline internally, with department personnel investigating complaints against officers and determining whether misconduct occurred.

In Favor of Civilian Oversight Citizens who demand to be involved in the review process maintain that internal police discipline is tantamount to allowing the "fox to investigate thefts in the chicken coop." According to these citizens, police protect each other and cover up improper or illegal conduct. Citizens believe that this perpetuates abuses and sends a message to brutal officers that their behavior will be shielded from public scrutiny.

In some larger cities, police have lost the power to investigate complaints against fellow officers. The trend is toward more openness and citizen involvement in these matters. Officers should assume they will be required to be more accountable for their actions. Officers may be held to a higher standard and will need to be prepared to justify their use of force in certain situations.

In Opposition to Civilian Oversight Theoretically, citizen review boards offer an efficient and effective means of identifying officer misdeeds and reconciling them to the satisfaction of the community at large. However, although civilian review boards may be good in theory, they are often poor in reality. They frequently fail to operate objectively, lack impartial or specialized agents to conduct essential investigations, and are devoid of any enforcement power needed to carry out their recommendations. Furthermore, some people who volunteer to serve on a board are not necessarily representative of the community and, in many cases, are "vocal rabble-rousers" who wish to impose their values on the community. Some boards require police officials to sit on them as members, which may cause the perception of impartiality. Opponents to civilian review boards cite such shortcomings as reasons to do without these ineffectual entities.

Police often maintain it would be unfair to allow those outside police work to judge their actions because only police officers understand the complexities of their job and, in particular, how and when they must use force. They stress that few citizens understand such concepts as "command presence" and "verbal force" which are so often necessary in high-risk encounters. As one police sergeant put it: "The public should walk a mile in our combat boots before they judge us."

Opponents also argue that police should have full responsibility for managing their own conduct just as other professionals such as physicians and lawyers do.

Striking a Balance Successful resolution of this issue requires that the concerns of both the community and the police be addressed. The desired outcome would be that the police maintain the ability to perform their duties without the fear that they will be second-guessed, disciplined, or sued by those who do not understand the difficulties of their job. Successful oversight agencies do not simply investigate complaints; they proactively seek the underlying causes of police misconduct or problems.

Citizen Patrol

Community policing is rooted in law enforcement's dependence on the public's eyes, ears, information, and influence to exert social control. In some communities citizens' attempts to be those eyes and ears have emerged in the form of citizen patrols. Some citizen patrols have formed as part of partnerships with the local police department, some independent of police partnerships, and some in the face of police opposition. It is difficult for citizen volunteers, especially those in citizen patrols formed in spite of police opposition, to win the respect, trust, and support of the police, who often have strong opinions about civilian involvement in what they consider police business or see citizens as critics of department efforts.

The Alliance of Guardian Angels, an organization that bills itself as serving communities, is controversial. Headed by a high-profile figure, Curtis Sliwa, the Angels go to communities having street crime problems and offer to patrol the streets and make citizen arrests. The members all wear red berets and are usually unarmed. Typically, citizens approve of the Guardian Angels, who they think are making their community safe. Local police, however, are not usually happy to have the Guardian Angels in their communities, often viewing them as untrained vigilantes who do not know the community, often provoke incidents, and sometimes use physical force.

Citizen patrols are not new. The sheriffs' posses that handled law enforcement in America's Wild West have evolved to present-day citizen patrols, reserve police programs, and neighborhood-watch groups. Many of the citizen patrols established throughout the country focus on the drug problem. For example, the Fairlawn Coalition in Washington, DC, established nightly patrol groups to walk the streets of Fairlawn and act as a deterrent to drug trafficking. Wearing bright orange hats, the citizen patrols drove drug dealers from their positions simply by standing out on the streets with them and later by bringing in video cameras, still cameras, and much publicity. The citizen group decided not to invite the Guardian Angels or Nation of Islam to help them, fearing their aggressive tactics could escalate into violence. They chose instead to include men and women aged 40 and older to create a presence on the street but to pose no threat to the physical well-being of dealers.

The Blockos in Manhattan, New York, used a similar approach. To combat street-level drug dealing in their middle-class neighborhood, residents held some meetings and decided to go out into the street as a group and stand near the dealers. They also had a graphic artist provide posters to announce their meetings, and a member persuaded the *New York Times* to publish a story on their efforts.

Another tactic was used in Manhattan by a group called 210 Stanton, referring to the address of a building that was headquarters of a major drug-selling operation. Community patrol officers guarded the entrances to the building, requiring all visitors to sign in. If the visitors were going to the apartment where the drug dealing was occurring, officers accompanied them. In addition, information provided by residents helped solidify the case against the resident of the apartment where most of the drug dealing was taking place. Search warrants were issued, charges filed, and the resident convicted.

In Arizona, ranchers near the Mexican border have formed the American Border Patrol (ABP), a citizens' patrol group whose goal is to help the official U.S. Border Patrol by finding and detaining illegal immigrants crossing into America from Mexico. They claim to have apprehended and turned over about 10,000 illegal immigrants to the Border Patrol in the past 5 years. Federal law enforcement agencies are not enthusiastic about the patrols. The U.S. Border Patrol does not comment on the matter but clearly is against any citizen activities beyond observing illegal activity and calling them for help.

Some citizen groups have exchange programs to reduce the chance of retribution by local drug retailers. Such exchange programs provide nearby neighborhoods with additional patrols while reducing the danger. Local dealers are less likely to recognize a vigil-keeper who lives in another neighborhood.

Citizen Police Academies

Another type of community involvement is through citizens' police academies (CPAs) designed to familiarize citizens with law enforcement and to keep the department in touch with the community. Police academies, which are popular with police departments and citizens, have the benefit of building community

Table 3.2	Typical Agenda of a Citizen Police Academy

EVANSTON, ILLINOIS, POLICE DEPARTMENT 12-WEEK COURSE OVERVIEW	
Independent	**Week 7**
• 4-Hour Ride-Along	• Use of Force
• 3-Hour Observation in 911 Communications Center	• Shoot/Don't Shoot
Week 1	**Week 8**
• History of the Police Department	• Drug Investigations
• Department Overview, Station Tour	• Gang Investigations
Week 2	**Week 9**
• Role of Prosecutor	• Juvenile Investigations
• Distinction between Civil and Criminal Law	• Drug Abuse Resistance Education (D.A.R.E.)
• Court System	**Week 10**
• Laws on Search and Seizure	• Community-Oriented Policing/Problem Solving/Community Strategies
• Citizens' Role in the Criminal Justice System	• Overview of Community Policing
• Mock Trial	• Problem-Solving Unit
Week 3	• Problem Solving
• Patrol Procedures	• Office of Professional Standards
• Concept of Preventive Patrol, Reactive vs. Proactive	**Week 11**
• Beat Boundaries, Motor and Foot Patrol	• Police Survival Skills
• Traffic Enforcement	• Martial Arts Demonstration
Week 4	**Week 12**
• Domestic Violence	• Welcome and Opening Remarks
• Youth Services	• Chief of Police Remarks
• Victim Services	• Keynote Speaker
Week 5	• Class Representative Speaker
• Evidence Technicians	• Presentation of Certificates, Class Photo, Distribution of Jackets
• Collection of Evidence	• Refreshments
• Demonstration of Crime Scene Processing	
• Fingerprinting Demonstration on Class Volunteers	
Week 6	
• Role of the Investigator	
• Major Case Investigation	
• The Use of Evidence	
• Crime Scene Processing	

Source: http://www.cityofevanston.org/police/citizen-police-academy/course-overview

support for law enforcement and of helping citizens understand the police. The typical agenda of a police academy is shown in Table 3.2.

In 1985 Orlando, Florida, hosted its first CPA and reports that it was an immediate success. Since that time more than 1,000 community-oriented citizens have graduated from the program. The program is free of charge and offered twice a year. The class lasts for 12 to 14 weeks and is held for 3 hours in the evening. Topics include uniformed patrol, special operations, criminal investigation, and youth/criminal law. The CPA also offers elective field trips to the jail and a ride-along with a uniformed patrol officer. In 2000 the department hosted its first CPA for senior citizens, held at one of the senior centers during the day.

The Arlington (Texas) Police Department began a CPA for Spanish-speaking residents in 1999 and has since developed an 8-week Asian CPA designed to teach Asian residents how the department functions. Detectives explain how investigations are conducted for homicides, robberies, wrecks, juvenile crimes, and gangs.

The Palm Beach (Florida) Police Department has a Teen Police Academy for students ages 13 to 16. The program includes classroom instruction, hands-on training, and field trips. Many departments around the country have developed similar programs.

In addition to regular CPAs and CPAs for seniors, teens, and specific ethnic groups, some departments have developed alumni CPAs. Any of these endeavors can result in a large pool of willing volunteers for police department projects.

Research by Brewster and colleagues (2005, 21) found that a CPA can improve the image of the police and increase the public's willingness to cooperate: "Overall, opinions about CPAs are favorable, and studies show that citizen participants and police personnel gain a number of benefits." A survey of 92 graduates from one CPA found that citizens were more educated about law enforcement, more realistic in their evaluation of media accounts, and more willing to volunteer for police projects.

ON THE BEAT

The community is involved in our police department in a number of ways. We have a Police Reserve program for which residents can volunteer to go out into the community and be extra sets of eyes and ears for the department. We also involve our community's youth by running a Police Explorer program. This gives juveniles an opportunity to learn firsthand what it is like to be a police officer. It is a healthy outlet for teens; they can practice discipline and learn responsibility along the way. We have a number of other programs as well that give citizens a chance to become involved. Some citizens sign up to be a block captain for their block and host Neighborhood Watch meetings. Some participate in our Police Advisory Commission. Others participate simply by giving input when they are asked to complete a neighborhood survey. All of these activities give community residents a chance to help. Engaged community residents will make healthier, safer communities. Police officers need to know the community's expectations in order to conduct effective policing strategies. If you do not get input from people within the community, you will not be able to effectively police that community. It is so important to listen to those you are there to serve.

—*Kim Czapar*

Citizen Volunteers

Volunteers supplement and enhance existing or envisioned functions, allowing law enforcement professionals to do their jobs more effectively (Kolb, 2005). Volunteers can provide numerous benefits to a department, including maximizing existing resources, enhancing public safety and services, and improving community relations. Other services that volunteers may provide include fingerprinting children, patrolling shopping centers, checking on homebound residents, and checking the security of vacationing residents' homes. Clerical and data support, special event planning, search and rescue assistance, grant writing, and transporting mail between substations also can be done by volunteers.

Volunteers in Police Service (VIPS) is one of five Citizen Corps partner programs. The International Association of Chiefs of Police (IACP) manages and implements the VIPS program in partnership with, and on behalf of, the White House Office of the USA Freedom Corps and the Bureau of Justice Assistance, Office of Justice Programs, U.S. Department of Justice. The VIPS program provides support and resources for agencies interested in developing or enhancing a volunteer program and for citizens who wish to volunteer their time and skills with a community law enforcement agency. The program's ultimate goal is to enhance the capacity of state and local law enforcement to utilize volunteers. Through this program, the VIPS staff seeks to:

» Learn about promising practices being used in existing VIPS programs and share this information with law enforcement agencies that want to expand their programs.

» Increase the use of volunteers in existing programs.

» Help citizens learn about and become involved in VIPS programs in their communities.

» Help agencies without volunteer programs get them started. (Volunteers in Police Service Web site, n.d.)

Use of volunteers is increasing in law enforcement departments across the country. Although establishing and maintaining a volunteer program is not cost free, the return on the investment can be substantial (Kolb, 2005). For example, the San Diego Police Department, in 2004, reportedly spent about $585,000 on the staffing, equipment, and management of its four volunteer programs but estimates the value of the hours contributed by volunteers at more than $2.65 million (Kolb, 2005). In another example, the Billings (Montana) Police Department was helped by volunteers doing computer work at what it estimated to be a billable value of $30,000 (Kingman, 2005).

It is important to note that citizen involvement in understanding and helping to police their communities is very important, but it, in itself, is not *community policing.* At the heart of the community policing philosophy is an emphasis on partnerships and on problem solving, the dual focus of the remainder of the text.

NATIONAL CRIME PREVENTION COUNCIL'S TEENS, CRIME, AND THE COMMUNITY (TCC)

Teens, Crime, and the Community is a program that believes smarter youth make safer communities. Through a combination of education and service learning, the Teens, Crime, and the Community (TCC) initiative has motivated more than one million young people to create safer schools and communities. TCC increases social responsibility in teens, educates them about the law, reduces their potential for victimization, and engages them in making their homes, schools, and communities safer.

Two programs are administered under the TCC initiative:

- *Community Works*, a comprehensive, law-related, crime-prevention curriculum
- *Youth Safety Corps*, the club component of the TCC initiative

Community Works educates students about the costs and consequences of crime, their rights and responsibilities as citizens, and their ability to bring about meaningful change through advocacy and service. Community Works' 11 core lessons teach students how to examine violence and law-related issues in the context of their schools and communities and apply what they learn to real-life circumstances. Twenty additional lessons tackle important youth-related issues including underage drinking, handguns and violence, substance abuse and drug trafficking, gangs, dating violence, conflict management, and police–youth relations.

Youth Safety Corps (YSC) provides youth interested in public safety and crime prevention (such as students who have completed a *Community Works* course) an opportunity to engage in ongoing, active participation in crime prevention. Young people partner with school resource officers, school personnel, and community volunteers to assess and analyze the safety and security issues within their schools and communities that contribute to youth violence and victimization. YSC teams then address those physical and social safety issues by implementing projects, such as painting over graffiti on the walls of a school, developing presentations to teach children about bullying, or surveying students about their attitudes toward underage drinking.

Source: © 2012 National Crime Prevention Council. http://www.ncpc.org/programs/teens-crime-and-the-community/about-tcc

SUMMARY

The U.S. Constitution and Bill of Rights, as well as federal and state statutes and local ordinances, establish the "public peace" in the United States. The social contract provides that for everyone to receive justice, each person must relinquish some freedom.

Community refers to the specific geographic area served by a police department or law enforcement agency and the individuals, organizations, and agencies within that area. Community also refers to a feeling of belonging—a sense of integration, a sense of shared values, and a sense of "we-ness." The *bowling alone* phenomenon refers to a striking decline in social capital and civic engagement in the United States. The broken windows phenomenon suggests that if it appears "no one cares," disorder and crime will thrive.

In order to understand a community, police must know about its demographics. Demographics include a population's size, distribution, growth, density, employment rate, ethnic makeup, and vital statistics such as average age, education, and income.

Organizations and institutions can play a key role in enhancing community safety and quality of life.

Operating within each community is a power structure that can enhance or endanger police–community relations. The formal power structure includes divisions of society with wealth and political influence: federal, state, and local agencies and governments, commissions, and regulatory agencies. The informal power structure includes religious groups, wealthy subgroups, ethnic groups, political groups, and public interest groups.

Controversial issues in the criminal justice system that affect police–community partnerships include plea bargaining, diversion, sentencing, rehabilitation, community alternatives to prisons, victims' rights, and capital punishment.

Restorative justice advocates a balanced approach to sentencing that involves offenders, victims, local communities, and government to alleviate crime and violence and maintain peaceful communities. Citizen involvement in the law enforcement community and in understanding policing has taken the form of civilian review boards, citizen patrols, citizen police academies, ride-alongs, and similar programs.

DISCUSSION QUESTIONS

1. How would you describe your community?
2. What instances of broken windows have you seen in your neighborhood? Other neighborhoods?
3. Can you give examples of the NIMBY syndrome?
4. What major changes have occurred in your community in the past 10 years? In your state?
5. Who is included in the power structure in your community?
6. What barriers hamper community involvement in poor neighborhoods?
7. How extensively are the services of private security used in your community? Do they cooperate with or compete against the local police?
8. Do you favor the use of civilian review boards? Why or why not?
9. Which seems more "just" to you: retributive justice or restorative justice?
10. What factors are most important in establishing a "sense of community"?

GALE EMERGENCY SERVICES DATABASE ASSIGNMENTS

ONLINE Database

- Use the Gale Emergency Services Database to help answer the Discussion Questions as appropriate.
- Select one of the following assignments to complete and share with the class.
  - Read about the Guardian Angels' activities. What are your views on the topic? Are they vigilantes or do they actually make the community safer?
  - Research and outline your findings on at least one of the following subjects: broken windows, ghettos, restorative justice, or social contract.
  - Read and outline one of the following articles:
    - "The Citizen Police Academy: Success through Community Partnerships" by Giant Abutalebi Aryani, Terry D. Garrett, and Carl L. Alsabrook
    - "Getting Along with Citizen Oversight" by Peter Finn
    - "A Medical Model for Community Policing" by Joseph A. Harpold

REFERENCES

Ankerfelt, Jeff, Michael Davis, and Logan Futterer. 2011. "The Brooklyn Park, Minnesota, Police's Joint Community-Police Partnership." *The Police Chief* 77 (3): 22–31.

Brewster, JoAnne, Michael L. Stoloff, and N. Sanders. 2005. "Effectiveness of Citizen Police Academies in Changing the Attitudes, Beliefs, and Behavior of Citizen Participants." *American Journal of Criminal Justice* (Fall): 21–34.

"'Broken Windows,' 22 Years Later." 2005. Interview with James Q. Wilson and George Kelling. *Law Enforcement News* (February): 8–9.

Carter, Joseph C. 2007. "Public–Private Partnerships: Vital Resources for Law Enforcement." *The Police Chief* (September): 6.

Clarke, Rory J. 2004. "Bowling Together." *Organization for Economic Co-operation and Development Observer* 242 (March).

Coleman, J. 1990. *Foundations of Social Theory*. Cambridge: Harvard University Press.

Cooke, Leonard G. and Lisa R. Hahn. 2006. "The Missing Link in Homeland Security." *The Police Chief* (November): 16–21.

Correia, Mark E. 2000. *Citizen Involvement: How Community Factors Affect Progressive Policing*. Washington, DC: Police Executive Research Forum.

Ennis, Sharon R., Merarys Rios-Vargas, and Nora G. Albert. 2011 (May). *The Hispanic Population: 2010. 2010 Census Briefs*. Washington, DC: U.S. Census Bureau. (C2010BR-04)

Haub, Carl. 2008. "U.S. Population Could Reach 438 Million by 2050, and Immigration Is Key." Washington, DC: Population Reference Bureau.

Johnson, Carolyn Y. 2009. "Breakthrough on 'Broken Windows.'" *Boston Globe*, February 8. http://www.dcvb-nc .com/cr/Broken_Windows-%20Lowell02-08-09.pdf

Kingman, Ken. 2005. "Volunteers: Three Ingredients for Success." *Community Links* (Winter): 4–5.

Kolb, Nancy. 2005. "Law Enforcement Volunteerism: Leveraging Resources to Enhance Public Safety." *The Police Chief* (June): 22–30.

Law Enforcement–Private Security Consortium. 2011 (August). *Operation Partnership: Trends and Practices in Law Enforcement and Private Security Collaborations.* Washington, DC: Office of Community Oriented Policing Services. (e08094224)

Mackun, Paul, Steven Wilson, Thomas Fischetti, and Justyna Goworowska. 2011 (March). *Population Distribution and Change: 2000 to 2010. 2010 Census Briefs.* Washington, DC: U.S. Census Bureau. (C2010BR-01)

National Crime Prevention Council. n.d. *About Teens, Crime, and the Community.* http://www.ncpc.org/programs/ teens-crime-and-the-community/about-tcc

Putnam, Robert D. 2000. *Bowling Alone: The Collapse and Revival of American Community.* New York: Simon and Schuster.

Sampson, Rana. 2011 (August). *False Burglar Alarms*, 2nd edition. Washington, DC: Center for Problem-Oriented Policing, Problem-Specific Guides Series, No. 5.

Skogan, Wesley G. 2004. "Community Policing: Common Impediments to Success." In *Community Policing: The Past, Present, and Future,* edited by Lorie Fridell and Mary Ann Wycoff, 159–168. Washington, DC: The Annie E. Casey Foundation and Police Executive Research Forum.

Volunteers in Police Service Program. n.d. "About VIPS." http://www.policevolunteers.org/about

Walker, Samuel. 2006 (May). "Chapter 1: The History of the Citizen Oversight." In *Citizen Oversight of Law Enforcement,* edited by Justine Cintron Perino, 1–10. Chicago, IL: American Bar Association.

Wilson, James Q. and George L. Kelling. 1982. "The Police and Neighborhood Safety: Broken Windows." *Atlantic Monthly* (March): 29–38.

Zehr, Howard. 1991. "Restorative Justice." *IARCA Journal* (March).

CHAPTER 4
Problem Solving: Proactive Policing

A problem well stated is a problem half solved.

—*Charles Kettering*

 DO YOU KNOW …

» How problem solving requires changes in the ways police treat incidents?

» How the magnet phenomenon occurs?

» How efficiency and effectiveness differ? Which one community policing emphasizes?

» What the first step in a problem-solving approach is?

» What four stages of problem solving are used in the SARA model?

» What three areas problem analysis considers?

» What the purpose and goal of the DOC model are?

» What crime-specific planning is?

» What the focus of crime mapping is?

CAN YOU DEFINE …

analysis (in SARA)
assessment (in SARA)
crime-specific planning
DOC model
effectiveness
efficiency
geographic information
    system (GIS)
geographic profiling
hot spots
impact evaluation
incident
least-effort principle
magnet phenomenon
mediation
problem-oriented policing (POP)
problem-solving approach
process evaluation
qualitative data
quantitative data
response (in SARA)
routine activity theory
scanning (in SARA)

INTRODUCTION

A **problem-solving approach** involves identifying problems and making decisions about how best to deal with them. A basic characteristic of community policing is that it is proactive rather than reactive, meaning it involves recognizing problems and seeking their underlying causes.

To illustrate, a man and his buddy, who could not swim, were fishing on a riverbank when a young boy floated past, struggling to stay afloat. The fisherman jumped in and pulled the young boy from the water. He resumed his fishing, but within a few minutes another person came floating by, again struggling to stay afloat. Again, the fisherman reacted by jumping in and pulling the person to safety. He then resumed his fishing and again, within minutes, another person came floating by. The fisherman got up and started heading upstream. His buddy called after him, "Where are you going?" To which the fisherman replied, "I'm going to find out who's pushing all these people into the river!"

It is usually more effective to get to the source of a problem rather than simply react to it. This chapter focuses on a problem-solving approach to policing, beginning with a definition of problem-oriented policing (POP) and a look at its basic unit—the "problem." Next efficiency and effectiveness are described, followed by an explanation of the importance of addressing substantive problems. Then the four-stage SARA model for problem solving is examined, including a look at problem analysis. This is followed by a discussion of making ethical decisions using the DOC (dilemmas–options–consequences) model and using mediation as a problem-solving tool. Then problem solving and crime-specific planning are discussed, as well as crime analysis. This is followed by a discussion of how technology is used for problem solving, including explanations of crime mapping, geographic information systems, and geographic profiling. Next common mistakes in problem solving are examined. The chapter concludes with a look at problem solving at work, describing several promising practices from the field.

Families living in poverty may find themselves trapped by their economic circumstances, unable to afford to move away from threatened neighborhoods. Although law enforcement cannot be expected to solve all of a community's problems, a proactive response to a neighborhood's social challenges, and an effort to partner with other community agencies, can help thwart future crime and disorder issues.

© AP Images/Gary Kazanjian

WHAT IS PROBLEM-ORIENTED POLICING?

Herman Goldstein, a pioneer of problem-oriented policing (POP), is credited with coining the term and describes it as follows:

> Problem-oriented policing is an approach to policing in which discrete pieces of police business (each consisting of a cluster of similar incidents, whether crimes or acts of disorder, that the police are expected to handle) are subject to *microscopic examination* (drawing on the especially honed skills of crime analysts and the accumulated experience of operating field personnel) in hopes that what is freshly learned about each problem will lead to discovering a *new and more effective strategy* for dealing with it. Problem-oriented policing places a high value on new responses that are *preventive* in nature, that are *not dependent on the use of the criminal justice system,* and that *engage other public agencies, the community, and the private sector* when their involvement has the potential for significantly contributing to the reduction of the problem. Problem-oriented policing carries a commitment to *implementing* the new strategy, rigorously *evaluating its effectiveness,* and, subsequently, *reporting the results* in ways that will benefit other police agencies and that will ultimately contribute to building a body of knowledge that supports the further professionalization of the police.[1] ("What Is POP?," n.d.)

Eck and Spelman (1987, XV) define **problem-oriented policing** more concisely as "a departmental-wide strategy aimed at solving persistent community problems. Police identify, analyze, and respond to the underlying circumstances that create incidents."

To fully understand problem-oriented policing, one must have a grasp of how a *problem* is defined.

problem-oriented policing (POP)
A department-wide strategy aimed at solving persistent community problems by grouping incidents to identify problems and to determine possible underlying causes.

Problem Defined

Goldstein (1990, 66) defines a problem as "a cluster of similar, related, or recurring incidents rather than a single incident, a substantive community concern, and a unit of police business." Identifying the problems in a community allows police to focus their efforts on addressing the possible causes of such problems.

A variation on this definition is that "a problem is a recurring set of related harmful events in a community that members of the public expect the police to address" (Clarke and Eck, 2005, 26). This definition draws attention to the six required elements of a problem captured by the acronym CHEERS: *c*ommunity, *h*arm, *e*xpectation, *e*vents, *r*ecurring, and *s*imilarity.

Community includes individuals, businesses, government agencies, and other groups. Only some community members need to experience the problem. *Harm* can involve property loss or damage, noise complaints, or serious crime. "Illegality is not a defining characteristic of problems" (Clarke and Eck, 2005, 26). *Expectation* should never be presumed but must be shown through such processes as citizen calls, press reports, or other means.

Events must be discrete, describable incidents. Most are brief. *Recurring* events—that is, events that happen more than a few times—may be symptomatic

---

[1] **Source: Reprinted by permission of the POP Center.**

of acute or chronic problems. An acute problem appears suddenly and may dissipate quickly, even if nothing is done. Or it may become a chronic problem, persisting for a long time if nothing is done. *Similarity* means the recurring events must have something in common—for example, the same type of victim, same location, same time, similar circumstances, or the like. Common crime classifications are usually not helpful.

From Incidents to Problems

Goldstein (1990, 20) was among the first to criticize the professional model of policing as being incident driven: "In the vast majority of police departments, the telephone, more than any policy decision by the community or by management, continues to dictate how police resources will be used." The primary work unit in the professional model is the **incident**—that is, an isolated event that requires a police response. The institution of the 911 emergency call system has greatly increased the demand for police services and the public's expectation that the police will respond quickly.

incident

An isolated event that requires a police response; the primary work unit in the professional model.

Goldstein (1990, 33) asserts: "Most policing is limited to ameliorating the overt, offensive symptoms of a problem." He suggests that police are more productive if they respond to incidents as symptoms of underlying community problems.

During the past quarter century, law enforcement agencies around the country have combined the operational strategies of community-oriented policing and problem solving to address crime and quality-of-life issues. Throughout this text, references to community policing infer that problem solving is involved.

 Problem-solving policing requires police to group incidents and identify the underlying causes of problems in the community.

Although problem solving may be the ideal, law enforcement cannot ignore specific incidents. When calls come in, most police departments respond as soon as possible. Problem solving has a dual focus. First, it requires that incidents be linked to problems. Second, time devoted to "preventive" patrol must be spent proactively, determining community problems and their underlying causes.

Regardless of whether police officers respond to incidents, seek symptoms of problems, or both, the public can help or hinder their efforts. Police and community members must discuss and agree to any community involvement program before it is adopted. At times well-meaning individuals and community groups, acting unilaterally, can actually interfere with a police effort and cause unnecessary destruction, injury, and even death.

The dual themes of this book are the manner in which police can form effective partnerships with the community to address the issues of crime and disorder and the necessity of a problem-solving approach to such issues. Like any response, the problem-solving process will not always result in success. In fact, mistakes should be expected and seen as learning opportunities. If no mistakes are made, then little problem solving is taking place.

Problem-Oriented Policing and Community Policing

Problem solving has been one of the three key components of community policing since it was introduced, but confusion between problem-oriented policing and community policing occasionally exists; some practitioners view the two as opposing approaches, while others equate community policing and problem solving. As Wilson and Kelling (1989, 49) note: "Community-oriented policing means changing the daily work of the police to include investigating problems as well as incidents. It means defining as a problem whatever a significant body of public opinion regards as a threat to community order. It means working with the good guys, and not just against the bad guys." Wilson and Kelling suggest

The POP Center

The mission of the Center for Problem-Oriented Policing is to advance the concept and practice of problem-oriented policing in open and democratic societies. It does so by making readily accessible information about ways in which police can more effectively address specific crime and disorder problems.

The Center for Problem-Oriented Policing is a non-profit organization comprising affiliated police practitioners, researchers, and universities dedicated to the advancement of problem-oriented policing.

Since the publication of the first POP Guide in 2001, over 900,000 copies of the POP guides and other POP Center publications have been distributed by the U.S. Department of Justice Office of Community Oriented Policing Services (COPS Office) to individuals and agencies throughout the world. POP Center materials are also widely used in police training and college courses.

Launched in 2003, the POP Center Web site has provided innovative learning experiences, curriculum guides, teaching aids, problem analysis tools, and an immense range of information to its users. Among the many ongoing accomplishments of the POP Center Web site are:

- Tens of thousands of visitors to the POP Center Web site read and download its content each month.
- The POP Center Web site was awarded the 2005 APEX Grand Award for Publication Excellence in Web & Intranet Sites. Wrote the judges: "Superbly researched and written reports clearly convey useful, actionable information in this easily-navigable, well-designed site."
- The POP Center Web site was awarded a League of American Communications Professional 2005 Spotlight Award for Web sites.

Source: Reprinted by permission of the POP Center.

that community policing requires the police mission to be redefined "to help the police become accustomed to fixing broken windows as well as arresting window-breakers."

The importance of problem-oriented policing to community policing is evidenced by the launching and funding of the Center for Problem-Oriented Policing (POP Center) by the COPS Office and its partners. The director of the POP Center, Michael Scott, believes all police can benefit from a POP approach, including those who embrace community policing: "The two approaches are compatible, though they emphasize different important aspects. Community policing develops a more harmonious working relationship between the police and the community. It emphasizes the community's role in addressing crime and disorder through its own actions. POP recognizes the value in those aspects, but it places the primary emphasis on finding fair and effective ways to control crime and disorder problems. The responses may or may not call for strong community engagement. It's seen as one means among many for achieving a particular public safety goal, not the ultimate goal itself" (Falk, 2005, 12).

Although Goldstein has suggested that community involvement is a positive development, he believes problem-oriented policing relies mostly on police participants. In addition, Goldstein's model emphasizes problem solving over partnerships. The differences between community policing and problem-oriented policing are summarized in Table 4.1.

Table 4.1 Selected Comparisons between Problem-Oriented Policing and Community Policing Principles

Principle	Problem-Oriented Policing	Community Policing
Primary emphasis	Substantive social problems within police mandate	Engaging the community in the policing process
When police and community collaborate	Determined on a problem-by-problem basis	Always or nearly always
Emphasis on problem analysis	Highest priority given to thorough analysis	Encouraged, but less important than community collaboration
Preference for responses	Strong preference that alternatives to criminal law enforcement be explored	Preference for collaborative response with community
Role for police in organizing and mobilizing community	Advocated only if warranted within the context of the specific problem being addressed	Emphasizes strong role for police
Importance of geographic decentralization of police and continuity of officer assignment to community	Preferred, but not essential	Essential
Degree to which police share decision-making authority with community	Strongly encourages input from community while preserving ultimate decision-making authority to police	Emphasizes sharing decision-making authority with community
Emphasis on officers' skills	Emphasizes intellectual and analytic skills	Emphasizes interpersonal skills
View of the role or mandate of police	Encourages broad, but not unlimited, role for police, stresses limited capacities of police, and guards against creating unrealistic expectations of police	Encourages expansive role for police to achieve ambitious social objectives

Source: Michael S. Scott. *Problem-Oriented Policing: Reflections on the First 20 Years*. Washington, DC: U.S. Department of Justice, Office of Community Oriented Policing Services, 2000, p. 99.

In Summary: The Key Elements of Problem-Oriented Policing

The following section is from the Center for Problem-Oriented Policing Web site.

» A problem, rather than a crime, a case, a call, or an incident, is the basic unit of police work.

» A problem is something that concerns or causes harm to citizens, not just the police. Things that concern only police officers are important, but they are not problems in this sense of the term.

» Addressing problems means more than quick fixes; it means dealing with conditions that create problems.

» Police officers must routinely and systematically analyze problems before trying to solve them, just as they routinely and systematically investigate crimes before making an arrest. Individual officers and the department as a whole must develop routines and systems for analyzing problems.

» The analysis of problems must be thorough but it may not need to be complicated. This principle is as true for problem analysis as it is for criminal investigation.

» Problems must be described precisely and accurately, and specific aspects of each problem must be identified. Problems often are not what they first appear to be.

» Problems must be understood in terms of the various interests at stake. Individuals and groups of people are affected in different ways by a problem and have different ideas about what should be done about the problem.

» The way the problem is currently being handled must be understood and the limits of effectiveness must be openly acknowledged in order to come up with a better response.

» Initially, any and all possible responses to a problem should be considered so as not to cut short potentially effective responses. Suggested responses should follow from what is learned during the analysis. They should not be limited to, nor rule out, the use of arrest.

» The police must proactively try to solve problems rather than just react to the harmful consequences of problems.

» The police department must increase police officers' freedom to make or participate in important decisions. At the same time, officers must be accountable for their decision making.

» The effectiveness of new responses must be evaluated so these results can be shared with other police officers and so the department can systematically learn what does and does not work.[2] ("Key Elements of Problem-Oriented Policing," n.d.)

---

[2] **Source: Reprinted by permission of the POP Center.**

BEING EFFICIENT AND EFFECTIVE

A problem-solving approach to policing was developed partially in response to concerns for efficiency and effectiveness. Wilson and Kelling (1989, 46) illustrate the consequences when emphasis is placed on efficiency:

> The police know from experience what research by Glenn Pierce, in Boston, and Lawrence Sherman, in Minneapolis, has established: Fewer than 10 percent of the addresses from which the police receive calls account for more than 60 percent of those calls. If each call is treated as a separate incident with neither a history nor a future, then each dispute will be handled by police officers anxious to pacify the complainants and get back on patrol as quickly as possible. ...

> A study of domestic homicides in Kansas City showed that in eight out of ten cases the police had been called to the incident address at least once before; in half the cases they had been called five times or more.

efficiency

Minimizing waste, expense, or unnecessary effort; results in a high ratio of output to input; doing things right.

Efficiency involves minimizing waste, expense, or unnecessary effort. Efficiency is doing things right. The police in the preceding studies were very efficient, responding promptly and dealing with the problem, usually to the citizen's satisfaction. But were they effective? And if they are not effective, efficiency does not really pay off. Making the same efficient responses to the same location is *not* really efficient. The response needs to be effective as well.

effectiveness

Producing the desired result or goal; doing the right things.

Effectiveness has to do with producing the desired result or goal. Effectiveness is doing the right thing. Ideally, both efficiency and effectiveness are present in policing. There can be effectiveness without efficiency, but there cannot be efficiency without effectiveness, because any effort that does not achieve the desired goal is wasted.

Police, along with other emergency services, face an inherent contradiction between effectiveness and efficiency. There must be enough staff available to respond to emergencies quickly at all times. Having this capacity, however, means that a number of personnel must have a substantial amount of slack time. Without slack time, all personnel may be busy when emergencies occur, reducing response effectiveness. Unfortunately, too often police departments have emphasized efficiency—for example, rapid response to calls, number of citations issued, and the like—rather than effectiveness, or what will produce the desired outcomes of the department.

Across the country, most police departments respond in a timely manner to every call for service. Just one example of this policy illustrates how efficiency can overshadow effectiveness as well as the magnet phenomenon.

magnet phenomenon

Occurs when a phone number or address is associated with a crime simply because it was a convenient number or address to use.

 The **magnet phenomenon** occurs when a phone number or address is associated with a crime simply because it was a convenient number or address to use.

For years, a convenience store across the street from a high school had been a magnet for high school students during the three lunch periods at the open-campus school. The store complained of disturbances, thefts, and intimidation of customers. Other businesses complained about "spillover" from student gatherings that affected their businesses. The grocery store experienced shoplifting; the dry cleaner had students smoking in the back of his building; and they all complained about drug sales at the bus stop at that intersection. Nearby residential neighbors complained about cigarette butts and empty soda cans littering their yards after lunch each day. Everyone disliked the loud music played on car stereos throughout the lunch periods. Every day one or more people called the police department to complain. And every day the police department dispatched one or two squad cars. Often the squads reported everything was quiet when they arrived. Lunchtime had ended, and the students had returned to school. Or if there was still a problem, the students scattered when they saw the police, and no action was necessary. Nearly every school day, for years, these same calls came into the police department. The police response was polite and quick. By police department standards, their response was efficient. By neighborhood standards, the police response was completely ineffective.

> Efficiency, doing things right, has been the traditional emphasis in law enforcement. Effectiveness, doing the right things, is the emphasis in community policing. Effectiveness should produce an increase in efficiency, because officers are proactively solving problems rather than simply reacting to them.

A focus on substantive problems (effectiveness) rather than on the smooth functioning of the organization (efficiency) is a radical change and difficult for some departments to make. Those departments that have made the shift in focus have achieved excellent results.

ADDRESSING SUBSTANTIVE PROBLEMS

Traditionally police have responded to incidents, handled them as effectively as possible, and then moved on to the next call. This fragmented approach to policing conceals patterns of incidents that may be symptomatic of deeper problems: "The first step in problem-oriented policing is to move beyond just handling incidents. It calls for recognizing that incidents are often merely overt symptoms of problems" (Goldstein, 1990, 33).

> The first step in problem solving is to group incidents as problems.

The basic elements in a problem-solving approach combine steps a police department can take and theoretical assumptions to make the steps work. Many departments have developed problem-solving approaches that incorporate these basic elements. One of the best known problem-solving approaches is the SARA model.

THE SARA MODEL: A FOUR-STAGE PROBLEM-SOLVING PROCESS

Eck and Spelman (1987) describe the four-stage problem-solving process used in the Newport News (Virginia) Police Department known as the SARA model.

 The four stages of the SARA problem-solving model are scanning, analysis, response, and assessment.

scanning (in SARA)

Refers to identifying recurring problems and prioritizing them to select one problem to address.

analysis (in SARA)

Examines the identified problem's causes, scope, and effects; includes determining how often the problem occurs and how long it has been occurring, as well as conditions that appear to create the problem.

response (in SARA)

Acting to alleviate the problem, that is, selecting the alternative solution or solutions.

assessment (in SARA)

Refers to evaluating how effective the intervention was; was the problem solved?

qualitative data

Examine the excellence (quality) of the response, that is, how satisfied were the officers and the citizens; most frequently determined by surveys, focus groups, or tracking complaints and compliments.

quantitative data

Examine the amount of change (quantity) as a result of the response; most frequently measured by before-and-after data.

Scanning refers to identifying recurring problems and prioritizing them to select one problem to address. The problems should be of concern to the public as well as the police. At this stage broad goals may be set.

Analysis examines the identified problem's causes, scope, and effects. It includes determining how often the problem occurs, how long it has been occurring, and what conditions appear to create the problem. Analysis also should include potential resources and partners who might assist in understanding and addressing the problem.

Response is acting to alleviate the problem—that is, selecting the alternative solution or solutions to try. This may include finding out what other communities with similar problems have tried and with what success and looking at whether any research on the problem exists. Focus groups might be used to brainstorm possible interventions. Experts might be enlisted. Several alternatives might be ranked and prioritized according to difficulty, expense, and the like. At this point goals are usually refined and interventions implemented.

Assessment refers to evaluating the effectiveness of the intervention. Was the problem solved? If not, why? Assessment should include both qualitative and quantitative data. **Qualitative data** examine the excellence (quality) of the response—that is, how satisfied were the officers and the citizens? This is most frequently determined by surveys, focus groups, or tracking complaints and compliments. **Quantitative data** examine the amount of change (quantity) as a result of the response. This is most frequently measured by before-and-after-response data.

The SARA model of problem solving stresses that there are no failures, only responses that do not provide the desired goal. When a response does not give the desired results, the partners involved in problem solving can examine the results and try a different response. Other communities might benefit from what was learned.

Scanning and Analysis

Scanning and analysis are integrally related. The sources for analyzing a community's problems provide the basis for analysis. Potential sources of information for identifying problems—beyond the internal sources of patrol, investigations, vice, communications, and records, the crime analysis unit, the chief's office, and other law enforcement agencies—include elected officials, local government agencies, community leaders, business groups, schools, neighborhood-watch groups, newspapers, and other media and community surveys. Comprehensively analyzing a problem is critical to the success of a problem-solving effort.

Effective, tailor-made responses cannot be developed unless one knows what is causing the problem (*Problem-Solving Tips,* 2011).

This step in the SARA model is often skipped for a variety of reasons. Sometimes it is because at first the nature of the problem seems obvious or because there is pressure to solve the problem immediately. Taking the time for analysis may be seen as too time consuming without producing tangible results, especially when responding to calls seems to preclude this type of activity. If not done, however, there is a chance of addressing a nonexistent problem or of applying ineffective solutions.

Problem-Solving Tips (2011, 14) suggests: "The first step in analysis is to determine what information is needed. This should be a broad inquiry, uninhibited by past perspectives. Questions should be asked whether or not answers can be obtained. The openness and persistent probing associated with such an inquiry are not unlike the approach that a seasoned and highly regarded detective would take to solve a puzzling crime: reaching out in all directions, digging deeply, asking the right questions."

The problem analysis triangle (sometimes called the crime triangle) illustrates how crime or disorder results when (1) likely offenders and (2) suitable targets come together in (3) time and space, in the absence of capable guardians (*Problem-Solving Tips*, 2011, 14). These three elements comprise the core of the triangle. Offenders can sometimes be controlled by other people, called handlers. Targets and victims can sometimes be protected by other people, called guardians. And places are usually controlled by certain people, called managers. These three control mechanisms comprise the outer perimeter of the crime triangle. Effective problem solving requires understanding how offenders, targets/victims, and places are or are not effectively controlled.

Problem solvers are advised to discover as much as possible about all three sides of the triangle as they relate to the problem by asking about each side: Who? What? When? Where? How? Why? and Why not?

Studies have shown that a small number of victims account for a large amount of crime and that effective interventions targeted at repeat victims can significantly reduce crime. Researchers in England found that victims of burglary, domestic violence, and other crimes are likely to be revictimized very soon after the first victimization—often within a month or two. Data from one study of residential burglary in West Yorkshire, England, showed that burglary victims were four times more likely than nonvictims to be victimized again, and the majority of repeat burglaries occurred within six weeks of the first (*Problem-Solving Tips*, 2011). To address this problem, the local police division tailored a three-tiered response to repeat burglary victims, based on the number of times their homes had been burglarized and, "according to initial reports, residential burglary has been reduced more than 20 percent since the project began, and they have experienced no displacement" (*Problem-Solving Tips*, 2011, 15).

Recall from Chapter 3 that displacement is the theory that successful implementation of a crime-reduction initiative does not really prevent crime. Instead it just moves the crime to the next block, neighborhood, or city. Police databases are not designed to track repeat victims, so police in the West Yorkshire project had some difficulty tracking repeat victims.

A Problem Analysis Guide To assist in problem analysis, the Newport News (Virginia) Police Department developed a problem analysis guide that lists topic headings police should consider in assessing problems. Their problem analysis guide highlights the complex interaction of individuals, incidents, and responses occurring within a social context and a physical setting. The problems that Newport News police identified and their ways of approaching them are discussed later in the chapter.

 Problem analysis considers the individuals involved, the incidents, and the responses.

Problem-solving experts Goldstein (1990) and Eck and Spelman (1987) suggest that effective problem solving involves these steps:

» Adopt a proactive stance.
» Focus on problems of concern to the public.
» Group incidents as problems.
» Focus on substantive problems as the heart of policing.
» Encourage a broad and uninhibited search for solutions.
» Capture and critique the current response.
» Make full use of the data in police files and the experience of police personnel.
» Avoid using overly broad labels in grouping incidents so separate problems can be identified.
» Seek effectiveness as the ultimate goal.
» Use systematic inquiry.
» Acknowledge the limits of the criminal justice system as a response to problems.
» Identify multiple interests in any one problem and weigh them when analyzing the value of different responses.
» Be committed to taking some risks in responding to problems.
» Strengthen the decision-making processes and increase accountability.
» Evaluate results of newly implemented responses.

Responses by Law Enforcement

"We know, from the numerous efforts to document police activity in the field, that the way in which different officers respond to the same type of incident varies tremendously. As for some problems, there may be as many ways to handle an incident as there are officers, and some methods may be very imaginative. On the other hand, many responses are highly routinized, reflecting a rather uniform pattern that has emerged on a shift, in a unit (like a precinct), or in an entire agency" (Goldstein and Susmilch, 1981, 29). The most prevalent law enforcement response to identified problems is generally increased use of conventional strategies such as enforcement and patrol (Bichler and Gaines, 2005).

Figure 4.1 The Problem-Solving Process and Evaluation

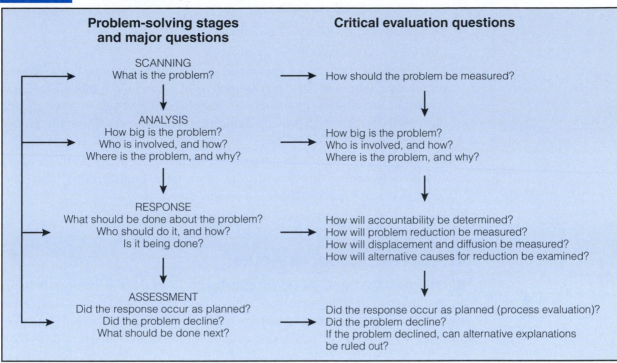

Source: John E. Eck, *Assessing Responses to Problems: An Introductory Guide for Police Problem-Solvers* (Washington, DC: Office of Community Oriented Policing Services, 2002), 6.

Assessing Responses to Problems

According to Eck (2002, 6): "You begin planning for an evaluation when you take on a problem. The evaluation builds throughout the SARA process, culminates during the assessment, and provides findings that help you determine if you should revisit earlier stages to improve the response." Figure 4.1 illustrates the problem-solving process and evaluation.

Two types of evaluations should be conducted: **Process evaluation** determines if the response was implemented as planned, and **impact evaluation** determines if the problem declined (Eck, 2002). Table 4.2 provides guidance in interpreting the results of process and impact evaluation.

process evaluation
Determines if the response was implemented as planned.

impact evaluation
Determines if the problem declined.

Table 4.2 Interpreting Results of Process and Impact Evaluations

		Process Evaluation Results	
		Response implemented as planned, or nearly so	Response not implemented, or implemented in a radically different manner than planned
	Problem declined	A. Evidence that the response caused the decline	C. Suggests that other factors may have caused the decline, or that the response was accidentally effective
Impact Evaluation Results	Problem did not decline	B. Evidence that the response was ineffective, and that a different response should be tried	D. Little is learned; perhaps if the response had been implemented as planned, the problem would have declined, but this is speculative

Source: John E. Eck, *Assessing Responses to Problems: An Introductory Guide for Police Problem-Solvers* (Washington, DC: Office of Community Oriented Policing Services, 2002), 10.

Several nontraditional measures will indicate if a problem has been affected by the interventions (Eck, 2002, 27):

» Reduced instances of repeat victimization

» Decreases in related crimes or incidents

» Neighborhood indicators: increased profits for legitimate businesses in target area, increased use of area/increased (or reduced) foot and vehicular traffic, increased property values, improved neighborhood appearance, increased occupancy in problem buildings, less loitering, fewer abandoned cars, less truancy

» Increased citizen satisfaction regarding the handling of the problem, which can be determined through surveys, interviews, focus groups, electronic bulletin boards, and the like

» Reduced citizen fear related to the problem

The SARA Model in Action

The Herman Goldstein Award for Excellence in Problem-Oriented Policing was established in 1993, honoring Professor Herman Goldstein for conceiving and developing the theory of problem-oriented policing. This award is given to innovative, effective POP projects that have demonstrated measurable success in reducing specific crime, disorder, or public safety problems. The Herman Goldstein Award is discussed in more detail later in this chapter.

The 1998 award winner was Operation Cease Fire, Boston Police Department (Brito and Allan, 1999, 328–339). This classic exemplary model has had a tremendous impact on police departments across the country, being replicated and adapted nationwide.

Scanning In 1987 Boston had 22 victims of youth homicide. In 1990 that figure had increased 230 percent to 73 victims. Police were responding to six or seven shootings every night and were becoming overwhelmed. For many of Boston's youths, the city had become a dangerous, even deadly, place. This situation led to the formation of a gun project working group.

The working group's line-level personnel believed the gun violence problem was a gang problem, because most victims and offenders were gang members and because the worst offenders in the cycle of fear, gun acquisition, and gun use were gang members. Another aspect of the problem identified was that many of the involved youths were not "bad" or inherently dangerous but were participating because gang membership had become a vital means of self-protection.

Analysis A team of Harvard University researchers framed the relevant issues in gun-market terms. Gun trafficking and other means of illegal firearm acquisition represented the supply side, whereas fear and other factors potentially driving illicit gun acquisition and use represented the demand side. Research techniques included geographic mapping of youth homicides, gathering of criminal histories of youth homicide victims and offenders, analyzing the gun market using Boston Police Department and Bureau of Alcohol, Tobacco, and Firearms gun recovery and tracing data, and collecting hospital emergency room data. Key findings of this research included the following:

» Most youth gun and knife homicides and woundings occurred in three specific neighborhoods.

» Of the 1,550 firearms recovered from youths, 52.1 percent were semiautomatic pistols.

» Trace analysis revealed that 34 percent of traceable firearms recovered from youths were first sold at retail establishments in Massachusetts.

» Of all traceable guns recovered from youths, 26 percent were less than 2 years old and, thus, almost certainly trafficked rather than stolen.

» Nearly 20 percent of all guns recovered from youths had obliterated serial numbers, suggesting they were relatively new "trafficked" guns.

» Of the 155 youth gun and knife homicide victims, 75 percent had been arraigned for at least one offense in Massachusetts courts.

» Boston had roughly 61 gangs with 1,300 members in the three high-risk neighborhoods previously identified. Although this represented less than 3 percent of the youths ages 14 to 24 in these neighborhoods, these gangs were responsible for at least 60 percent of Boston's youth homicides.

Response   The working group devised a two-pronged response known as Operation Cease Fire. The first prong involved mounting a direct law enforcement attack on illicit gun trafficking by (1) using trace information to identify gun traffickers and (2) systematically debriefing gang offenders facing serious charges for violent, drug, and other crimes.

The second, and perhaps more important, prong involved creating a powerful deterrent to gang-related violence by making clear to youths that future violence would result in a certain and severe crackdown on the gang and impose "costs" on the entire gang, not just the shooter. Such "costs" might include cash-flow problems caused by street-drug market disruption, arrests from outstanding warrants, the humiliation of strict probation enforcement, and possibly severe sanctions brought by federal involvement. The working group's familiarity with local gangs enabled them to link, with a high degree of accuracy, a particular act of violence to a certain gang relatively quickly and dispense sanctions swiftly. Operation Cease Fire transformed the police response to violence, turning uncertain, slow, and often mild responses into ones that were certain, rapid, and of whatever severity the working group deemed appropriate.

Assessment   In the first 2 years of Operation Cease Fire youth homicides dropped roughly 70 percent. Between 50 and 60 percent of the residents in the three identified high-risk neighborhoods felt satisfied the Boston Police Department was doing all it could to reduce area crime, and more than 33 percent of those residents reported a great deal of confidence in the department's ability to prevent crime (an increase from the 1995 average of 10 percent). Citywide, 76 percent of residents felt safe alone in their neighborhoods at night, compared with 55 percent in 1995. Perhaps the most significant result was that 88 percent of residents said they would be willing to work with each other and police to reduce and prevent crime—a noteworthy result because Operation Cease Fire not only achieved its goal but did so ethically.

MAKING ETHICAL DECISIONS

DOC model

Dilemmas–Options–Consequences challenges officers to carefully consider their decisions and the short- and long-term consequences of those decisions, with the goal of fusing problem solving and morality.

 The **DOC model** (dilemmas–options–consequences) challenges officers to carefully consider their decisions and the short- and long-term consequences of those decisions. The goal is to fuse problem solving and morality.

After a dilemma is identified, an action is needed, leading to the options phase and questions such as: What are my options? Am I considering all options? Am I being open-minded and creative? Do my options rely on only me, or could I use a resource or someone's help? Whose?

For each choice, officers must assess the consequences by asking: What happens because of my choice? What if I do nothing? Who is affected by what I do? How? Will I protect myself? Will I protect the quality of life and dignity of others? Will I preserve my moral and ethical integrity? What are the short-term effects? What are the long-term effects?

Ethical concerns can arise even in successful and popular police operations, such as stings. Sting operations and ethics are interconnected. Although sting operations have been used for over 40 years, artful deceptions and undercover operations have been used for as long as policing has existed (Newman, 2007). Since being introduced in the United States in the 1970s, modern sting operations have been justified as an effective, less forceful way to catch criminals as well as to collect evidence needed to convict them. The ethical challenge most often brought against sting operations is that stings are simply another form of lying, which is morally wrong, period (Newman, 2007). Detractors question whether such deception is ethically worse if the deceiver is a government official. Police defend stings with two arguments: (1) The benefits of a successful sting far exceed the ethical cost of using deception, and (2) Deception is "soft" coercion compared with other types police are authorized to use. Newman (2007, 30–31) contends:

The Government May Overreach

Is it the government's role to construct enticements and situations that encourage all citizens to commit a crime? The studies of selling stolen goods, for example, in bars and other places, have found a remarkably high proportion of ordinary people prepared to buy stolen articles, people who, had they not been provided the opportunity to do so, would not have committed the crime. Thus there is a very strong potential for the government to overreach. Indeed, there is a strong incentive to do so, given the positive publicity that is likely to follow the sting operation, even if no offenders were convicted.

There Are Entrapment Issues

Of all the negative features of sting operations, entrapment is by far the most widely cited. This is because many of the ethical issues described above come together to form the "entrapment defense," used by offenders to argue that the police tricked them into committing the crime. There are many legal tests for entrapment; and every U.S. state's law recognizes the defense. While we need not go into the legal technicalities, there are two legal tests of entrapment: the subjective and objective tests, both of which take as their starting point that the government encouraged or induced the offense in question. The subjective test asks whether the offender had a predisposition to commit the act, that is, it focuses on the offender's psychological state. The objective test asks whether the government's encouragement exceeded reasonable levels; thus, it focuses on the government's actions in constructing enticements—whether it went "too far." How each of these is assessed, of course, is the subject of legal wrangling, and may in the long run depend on a jury."

In addition to considering the ethics involved in problem solving, community policing officers often find they must rely on their skills in mediation as well.

MEDIATION AS A PROBLEM-SOLVING TOOL

Research shows that many calls for service involve landlord/tenant disputes, loud parties, rowdy teens, traffic complaints, and even domestic calls not requiring law enforcement intervention. But police traditionally use enforcement strategies such as rapid response and random patrol to address these problems.

Mediation, sometimes called alternative dispute resolution (ADR), is shared problem solving by parties in dispute guided by a neutral person:

mediation
The intervention of a third party into an interpersonal dispute, where the third party helps disputants reach a resolution; often termed alternative dispute resolution (ADR).

> Community mediation offers constructive processes for resolving differences and conflicts between individuals, groups, and organizations. It is an alternative to avoidance, destructive confrontation, prolonged litigation, or violence. It gives people in conflict an opportunity to take responsibility for the resolution of their dispute and control of the outcome. Community mediation is designed to preserve individual interests while strengthening relationships and building connections between people and groups, and to create processes that make communities work for all of us. ...
>
> Mediation is a process of dispute resolution in which one or more impartial third parties intervenes in a conflict with the consent of the disputants and assists them in negotiating a consensual and informed agreement. In mediation, the decision-making authority rests with the parties themselves. Recognizing variations in styles and cultural differences, the role of the mediator(s) involves assisting disputants in defining and clarifying issues, reducing obstacles to communication, exploring possible solutions, and reaching a mutually satisfactory agreement. Mediation presents the opportunity to peacefully express conflict and to "hear each other out" even when an agreement is not reached.[3] (National Association for Community Mediation, 2012)

In some instances the mediator might be a police officer. Changing roles from law enforcer authority to a partner in conflict resolution requires skills different from those many officers are accustomed to using. If a police officer is the mediator, mediation may provide a short-term solution, but this is often the result of the perceived coercive power of the mediating officer (resolve this, or else ...).

The community mediation program strategy, while not typically a police initiative, is one that can solve community problems and result in time savings

---

[3] **Source: Reprinted by permission of the National Association for Community Mediation.**

for the police. Community mediation provides an alternative to neighbors taking legal action against each other when minor issues arise. If they cannot settle a dispute between themselves, police are often called, and court action, lawsuits, and even relocation can follow. In rare cases, matters can escalate to include retaliation and violence. Mediation programs offer guidance from professionally trained and certified mediators to help conflicting parties reach agreement. Police involvement is often simply referral.

PROBLEM-SOLVING POLICING, CRIME-SPECIFIC PLANNING, AND CRIME ANALYSIS

To maintain effective police–community partnerships, police must also fulfill their crime-fighting role. Police can approach this role with many of the problem-solving skills just discussed, using crime-specific planning, a more precise strategy than POP in that it considers underlying problems categorized by type of offense. **Crime-specific planning** involves reviewing the following factors:

crime-specific planning

Uses the principles of problem solving to focus on identified crime problems.

» *The offense:* Seriousness, frequency of occurrence, susceptibility to control, whether a crime of opportunity or calculation, the modus operandi, and any violent characteristics present

» *The target:* Property taken or damaged, when attacked, how attacked, where located, number of potential targets in area, accessibility, transportation patterns surrounding the target

» *Impact:* On the community, public concern, drain on resources of the criminal justice system

» *Response:* Of the victim, the community, the criminal justice system

Traditionally, crime-specific planning involved only the first two factors. The last two factors have been added as a result of the community policing philosophy.

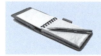 Crime-specific planning uses the principles of problem solving to focus on identified crime problems.

A careful analysis of these factors provides the basis for problem solving and deriving alternatives for approaching each specific crime problem.

Goldstein has argued that problem-oriented policing depends crucially on the availability of high-level analytic capacity in the department. Clarke and Eck (2005, 5), likewise, note: "A fully effective police agency must take advantage of the details of crime situations to reduce crime opportunities. Crime analysts have important roles in applying both elements—focusing with precision using their analytical methods, and helping to craft appropriate police tactics that fit the details of problems they have uncovered. This makes the 21st century the century of crime analysis in policing." White (2008, 1) describes the framework of crime analysis:

The theoretical framework of problem-oriented policing has evolved steadily over the past few decades and it has become increasingly clear how much the approach depends for its success on the careful analysis of data about crime problems. Indeed, problem-oriented policing and data analysis are highly interdependent. A framework for problem-oriented policing is of little use if good data are not available and, similarly, complex data about crime problems require a meaningful framework for analysis. In fact, methods of capturing and analyzing data about crime problems have rapidly developed at the same time as advances have been made in the theory of problem-oriented policing agenda. Computerized crime data and geographic information systems (GISs) are just two examples.

Assistance is available to agencies developing crime analysis units from the International Association of Crime Analysts (IACA), an advocacy group promoting professional standards, practical educational opportunities, and an international network for the standardization of analytic techniques. Also of assistance to crime analysis is computer software that provides probability assessments.

USING TECHNOLOGY FOR PROBLEM SOLVING

Technology has become an indispensable tool for law enforcement. Computers can greatly assist departments using the SARA model for problem solving. In the scanning phase, crime analysis can use information from the Records Management System (RMS) to identify problems. Computer Aided Dispatch (CAD) can identify locations getting repeat calls for police service. Likewise, databases, charts, graphs, and spreadsheets can identify similarities in incidents indicating a need for problem solving. Basic analysis can also be done with computerized data, including CompStat, crime mapping, geographic information systems (GISs), geospacial statistical analysis, and geographic profiling.

CompStat

CompStat, short for computer statistics or comparative statistics, originated in the New York City Police Department in 1994 under the leadership of then-commissioner William Bratton. CompStat is a progressive, goal-oriented, information-driven police management strategy based on four core components: (1) accurate and timely collection of crime data and intelligence analysis, (2) rapid deployment of personnel and other resources, (3) effective tactics and strategies to address crime and disorder problems, and (4) relentless follow-up, assessment, and accountability (Jang, Hoover, and Joo, 2010).

The crime control strategies that form the foundation of CompStat policing include hot-spot policing, problem-solving approaches, and broken windows enforcement (Jang, Hoover, and Joo, 2010). The CompStat model embraces the broken windows philosophy by taking a zero-tolerance approach to even minor infractions and offenses, under the premise that a police focus on improving social disorder and quality of life issues can ultimately impact and reduce serious crime. Research has found, however, that while the CompStat approach can be effective in reducing property crime and total index crime rates, it does not significantly reduce violent crime rates (Jang, Hoover, and Joo, 2010).

Serpas and Morley (2008, 60) assert: "There can be little debate that CompStat processes in police agencies across the United States have revolutionized crime fighting and made communities safer. For more than a decade, these innovations have brought about greatly enhanced accountability and empowerment to police officers at the neighborhood level." The Columbia (South Carolina) Police Department, for example, has successfully implemented CompStat, which "has created an air of openness, seamless communication, and enhanced teamwork in the department. It also improved relations with neighboring law enforcement agencies and community organizations. Most importantly, it has drastically reduced the incidents of crime within the city and increased the number of arrests" (Crisp and Hines, 2007, 48).

Wintersteen (2007, 56) provides additional support for CompStat, citing the results of its implementation in Paradise Valley, Arizona:

» Crime down 20 percent in 2005 compared with 2003
» Crime down 38 percent in 2006 compared with 2003
» Collisions down 16 percent in 2005 compared with 1997, despite increased traffic and more distraction factors

Not everyone finds CompStat effective and ethical, and care must be taken to ensure that this technology is not allowed to diminish the appropriate and necessary application of officer discretion or to form the basis for illegal productivity goals and quotas. For instance, some departments are facing harsh criticism for using CompStat to increase their numbers of summonses, stop-and-frisks, and arrests while constricting the ability of officers to make decisions and exercise discretion (Kates, 2012).

Crime Mapping

To answer the question, "What is crime mapping?" Rossmo (2005, 1) explains:

Crimes are human phenomena; therefore, their distribution across the landscape is not geographically random. For crimes to occur, offenders and their targets—the victims and/or property—must, for a period of time, exist at the same location. Several factors, from the lure of potential targets to simple geographic convenience for an offender, influence where people choose to break the law. Therefore, an understanding of where and why crimes occur can improve attempts to fight crime. Maps offer crime analysts graphic representations of such crime-related issues.

Mapping crime can help law enforcement protect citizens more effectively in the areas they serve. Simple maps that display the locations where crimes or concentrations of crimes have occurred can be used to help direct patrols to places they are most needed. Policy makers in police departments might use more complex maps to observe trends in criminal activity, and maps may prove invaluable in solving criminal cases. For example, detectives may use maps to better understand the hunting patterns of serial criminals and to hypothesize where these offenders might live.

Mapping crime has evolved from using color-coded pushpins to user-friendly mapping software, designed to examine and predict crime and criminal behavior. Traditional density mapping allows departments to visualize how crime is distributed throughout the jurisdiction and to detect patterns or trends along various corridors, within certain neighborhoods, or as associated with other geographical features. Such mapping allows departments to more readily identify **hot spots**, or areas where incidents of crime and disorder tend to cluster in close proximity to one another. Mapping can also reveal *hot dots*, or specific addresses of persistent calls for police service. These maps help law enforcement administrators direct patrols to areas where they are most needed—"putting cops on the dots."

hot spots
Areas where incidents of crime and disorder tend to cluster in close proximity to one another.

Crime mapping changes the focus from the criminal to the location of crimes—the hot spots where most crimes occur.

Given that prevention is one of the primary goals of proactive policing, hot spots enforcement may provide police with a new way to break the vicious cycle of crime: "Hot spots policing may be to the new millennium what problem-oriented policing was to the 1990s" (Wexler, 2008, 29). In 2005 and 2006 the Police Executive Research Forum (PERF) surveyed police to identify the most widely used antiviolence strategy and found that the highest-ranking program cited (63 percent of the respondents) was hot spot enforcement: "In general, hot spot enforcement refers to police efforts to identify the location—a residence, a store, a nightclub, or other particular address; a street corner; a city block; a neighborhood—that generates the most calls to 911 or other indicators of criminal activity. Then, police analyze the types of crimes being committed at each hot spot and devise ways of reducing the crime. ... [N]early 9 out of 10 agencies use hot spots enforcement efforts directed either at larger hot spot areas like neighborhoods, smaller hot spot places like intersections, or both" (*Violent Crime in America*, 2008, 3).

Several theories of crime and disorder concentration exist to explain different types of crime phenomena that occur at different geographic levels: "Crime theories are critical for useful crime mapping because they aid in the interpretation of data and provide guidance as to what actions are most appropriate" (Eck, 2005, 3).

Place theories deal with crimes that occur at the lowest level of analysis—specific places or *hot dots*—and explain why crime events occur at specific locations (Eck, 2005). These locations usually are represented on maps as dots. Police action at this level is very precise—for example, warrants.

Street theories look at hot spots at a slightly higher level such as streets or blocks—for example, a prostitution stroll. These hot spots are represented on maps as straight, bent, or curved lines. Police action is still quite precise—for example, they may focus on concentrated patrolling as well as changing traffic and street patterns.

Neighborhood theories deal with large areas such as square blocks, communities, and census tracts. Hot spots in these areas are represented by two-dimensional shapes such as ellipses, rectangles, and other polygons. Relevant police action might include engaging residents in collective action against crime and disorder.

| Table 4.3 | Hot Spot Concentrations, Evidence, Theory, and Causes |

Concentration	Hot Spot Depiction	Action Level	Action Examples
Place—at specific addresses, corners, or other places	Points	Place, corner	Nuisance abatement, hot spot patrols
Among victims	Points, lines, and areas depending on the nature of concentration	High-risk targets and potential victims	Developing networks among potential victims, repeat victimization programs
Street—along streets or block faces	Lines	Streets, highways	Concentrated patrolling of specific streets, traffic reengineering
Area—neighborhood areas	Ellipses, shaded areas, and gradients	Large areas	Community partnerships, neighborhood redevelopment

Source: Eck, John E. "Crime Hot Spots: What They Are, Why We Have Them, and How to Map Them." In *Mapping Crime: Understanding Hot Spots,* edited by John E. Eck, et al. Washington, DC: National Institute of Justice, August 2005, pp. 1–15. (NIJ 209393)

Other large area theories look at crime patterns on the city level, multijurisdictional level, or multistate level and, although interesting, are less useful for local police agencies. Table 4.3 provides more detail regarding hot spots and mapping.

Mapping in Practice

Mapping hot spots and using incident-based deployment has been used to address public safety issues such as traffic crashes. One jurisdiction with several miles of major interstate highway running through the city used mapping to identify the specific corridor of hot spot crash activity that was costing millions of dollars and several hundred injuries every year. Armed with that data, the department mobilized a unit for interstate traffic enforcement and crash reduction and was able to remedy a problem area in their community (Hoelzer and Gorman, 2011).

Recognizing that the majority of calls for police service—around 70 percent by some estimates—are for non-criminal matters, some departments have begun to use mapping to address, assess, and enhance the police response to other types of issues, such as locating lost children or elderly residents suffering from Alzheimer's disease, and improving surveillance and protection efforts around critical infrastructure in a post-9/11 era (Markovic and Scalisi, 2011). Many departments map field contacts in addition to locations at which officers provide services such as "well-being checks."

In addition to identifying hot spots, mapping is also routinely used to track registered sex offenders in communities. Information from mapping is often enhanced by geographic information systems (GIS).

Geographic Information Systems

geographic information system (GIS)

Creating, updating, and analyzing computerized maps.

A **geographic information system (GIS)** enhances traditional mapping by adding information from various other databases. For example, modern GIS software can generate maps that correlate crime with vacant housing units, parks, or schools; income level of a census tract; patterns of car thefts; and locations of chop shops.

ON THE BEAT

As a police officer, I can say from experience that problem solving is an essential skill in this line of work. Imagine for a moment that you have a job. Any job. Day after day, you do your job and you never seem to see any results. Would that be rewarding or even productive?

So often in a police officer's career he or she will take a police report, for instance, a burglary report, and will leave knowing they will more than likely take another report at that address in the future. The officer will notice flaws in the physical security or perhaps flaws in the victim's security habits. These flaws will alert the officer that this particular location is an "easy target." What can an officer do in this situation? There are many options. The officer can offer the victim information on home and business security, alarm systems, or a thorough premise survey of the property. An officer who is willing to take the time and offer crime prevention information is in many ways assisting the victim in stopping future revictimization. Often it just takes some extra time to educate the public on ways to actively contribute to their own crime prevention efforts.

An officer should take the time to look at the location (in this case, the scene of the burglary) and survey it with a critical eye. Look at the specifics of a situation, do some problem solving, and come up with possible solutions for that particular situation. The officer may notice that the lock is not functioning properly or that there should be a deadbolt lock on the door. These observations need to be communicated but are seldom found in a standard police report. The police officer must move out of the mindset of "I'm here only to take a report" and move toward a mindset focused on results and problem-solving resolutions.

—*Kim Czapar*

"Because police solutions to crime are necessarily about where crime takes place, the ability to visualize and analyze geographic patterns becomes paramount. ... Continuing improvements in GIS software have made it possible to better assemble, integrate, and create new ways of analyzing data. Not only can analysis, with the help of GIS software, assemble multiple and disparate sets of demographic, economic, and social data; they can also create new units of analysis that more accurately model human behavior" (Peed, Wilson, and Scalisi, 2008, 24).

Geospacial Statistical Analysis

Geospacial statistical analysis takes GIS technology a step further by allowing analysts to identify areas within the community that are statistically similar to locations where prior incidents have occurred and, thus, at increased risk for future incidents: "Geospacial statistical analysis... characterizes the locations associated with past events and creates a model that incorporates environmental factors statistically associated with past incidents. This model can then be used to identify similar locations where future incidents are likelier to occur. Ultimately, this approach enables law enforcement to act proactively to prevent crime and influence outcomes" (McCue, 2011, 4).

Drawing on environmental criminology and the principle set forth in the **routine activity theory**—that crime occurs at the intersection of a motivated offender, a suitable target, and an absent or ineffective guardian—geospacial statistical analysis seeks to help law enforcement understand and identify the specific jurisdictional characteristics associated with their local crime and disorder problems: "Certain environmental factors attract or enable crime, while other features may serve as deterrents. These factors can be ranked based on their relative contribution to the likelihood of future incidents and used for analysis. This factor analysis provides unique opportunities for information-based or 'tailor-made' crime prevention" (McCue, 2011, 5). This information-based response represents a game-changing shift in police operations by allowing law enforcement to create customized solutions to particular crime problems and, ultimately, keep their communities safer.

routine activity theory

Principle of environmental criminology that states crime occurs at the intersection of a motivated offender, a suitable target, and an absent or ineffective guardian.

Geographic Profiling

Geographic profiling takes crime-mapping technique and turns them inside out by using a complex mathematical algorithm and the locations of past crimes to calculate probabilities of a suspect's residence:

geographic profiling

A crime-mapping technique that takes the locations of past crimes and, using a complex mathematical algorithm, calculates probabilities of a suspect's residence.

> Geographic profiling is a technique that can help identify the likely area where a serial offender resides, or other place (e.g., work, girlfriend's place) that serves as an anchor point or base of operations. Several major software programs are being employed by police agencies to perform geographic profiling tasks, including Rigel®, CrimeStat, and Dragnet.
>
> Though there have been anecdotal successes with geographic profiling, there have also been several instances where geographic profiling has either been wrong on predicting where the offender lives/works or has been inappropriate as a model. Thus far, none of the geographic profiling software packages have been subject to rigorous, independent, or comparative tests to evaluate their accuracy, reliability, validity, utility, or appropriateness for various situations. ("Geographic Profiling," 2009)

Geographic profiling can help prioritize suspect lists, direct stakeouts, and conduct neighborhood canvasses. In March 2008 the Office of Community Oriented Policing Services (COPS) and the National Institute of Justice (NIJ) launched the first issue of *Geography and Public Safety*, dealing with applied geography for the study of crime and public safety, providing a valuable new resource for law enforcement in all capacities and ranks, from patrol to special investigations, from front-line officers to police chiefs.

A similar popular approach to geographic profiling is a psychological theory called the **least-effort principle**, which posits that criminals tend to commit crimes a safe distance away from their residence yet still within a zone where they feel comfortable and familiar: "With at least five or six incidents traceable back to the perpetrator, the search area for the criminal's residences is reduced by more than 90 percent. Key locations are weighted and then geocoded onto a map. The end process is known as a 'jeopardy surface,' a map that resembles a topographical map showing peaks and valleys color ramped to highlight the most likely area where the criminal resides" (Krish, 2003, 3).

least-effort principle

Concept proposing that criminals tend to commit acts of crimes within a comfort zone located near but not too close to their residence.

Dr. Kim Russmo, a former police detective from Vancouver, Canada, first proposed the concept of geoprofiling (or geographic profiling) in his doctoral thesis while at British Columbia's Simon Fraser University. His concept was eventually packaged commercially by Environmental Criminology Research, Inc., into a software program called Rigel® and has been used by police agencies worldwide, including the Federal Bureau of Investigation, the Bureau of Alcohol, Tobacco, Firearms, and Explosives and Scotland Yard.

Geographic profiling can be used as the basis for several investigative strategies, including suspect and tip prioritization, address-based searches of police record systems, patrol saturation and surveillance, neighborhood canvasses and searches, DNA screening prioritization, Department of Motor Vehicle searches, postal/zip code prioritization, and information-request mailings. It is important to stress that geographic profiling does not solve cases; rather, it provides a method for managing the large volume of information usually generated in major crime investigations. It should be regarded as one of several tools available to detectives and is best used in conjunction with other police methods. Geographic crime patterns are clues that, when properly decoded, can be used to point in the offender's direction.

Despite advances in technology, human intelligence and creativity are also still extremely important in problem solving. Consider next some of the most common mistakes that occur in problem solving.

COMMON MISTAKES IN PROBLEM SOLVING

Recall the statement made earlier in the chapter: The problem-solving process will not always result in success, and mistakes should be expected and seen as learning opportunities. If no mistakes are made, then little problem solving is taking place. Some mistakes, however, can and should be avoided because they signal procedural problems and inefficiencies that impede actual forward progress in solving a problem. For example, common mistakes in problem solving include spending too much energy on unimportant details, failing to resolve important issues, having a closed mind, being secretive about true feelings, and not expressing ideas (Hess and Orthmann, 2012). Other mistakes commonly made during problem solving include making multiple decisions about the same problem, finding the right decision for the wrong problem (that is, dealing with symptoms rather than causes), failing to consider the costs, delaying a decision, and making decisions while angry or excited. When evaluating a decision made during a problem-solving brainstorming session, ask: Is the decision consistent with the agency's mission, goals, and objectives? Is it a long-term solution? Is it cost-effective? Is it legal, ethical, and practical? Is it acceptable to those responsible for implementing it (Hess and Orthmann, 2012)?

PROBLEM SOLVING AT WORK

The theoretical foundation of problem solving in Newport News, Virginia, was discussed earlier. During the problem-identification process, several problems became evident (Eck and Spelman, 1987). The Newport News police categorized the problems so they could be analyzed. The way the department addressed the problem of commercial burglaries illustrates the problem-solving approach. The patrol officers surveyed the area and found that some major streets had been barricaded as a result of a major highway construction project. This resulted in limited vehicle traffic, limited police patrol at night, and a large increase in nighttime burglaries. To alleviate these problems, patrol officers were instructed to leave their squads and patrol the area on foot at night. The officers also persuaded the merchants to clean up the piles of trash and debris that could easily conceal the burglars' activities.

Besides dealing with the environment, Sergeant Quail, the officer in charge, also analyzed the specific problem (Eck and Spelman, 1987, 83). He collected reports of burglaries committed in the area and plotted them on a detailed map to identify geographic patterns. He also recorded a description of the suspects, time of commission, type of property taken, and similar information on a specially designed form to identify the modus operandi and repeat offender patterns. Finally, suspecting that some offenders were using vacant apartments located above some of the businesses to conceal stolen property, he began to investigate this possibility.

This resulted in the apprehension of several burglars and a decrease in the burglary rate. When construction was completed and the barriers removed, burglaries decreased further, so Sergeant Quail developed a policy on and procedure for allowing police and city agencies to communicate better about construction projects, street closings, and potential burglary problems.

Promising Practices from the Field

The Center for Problem-Oriented Policing provides on its Web site (www .popcenter.org) myriad examples of case studies and a variety of problem-specific guides to help police formulate effective responses to crime and disorder problems in their communities. The COPS Office Web site (www.cops.usdoj.gov) also contains numerous examples of promising practices in problem solving. Two examples follow.

San Diego, California—Prostitution

A business strip was plagued with a prostitution problem. The initial police response was to attempt undercover arrests of "johns" and prostitutes. Although they were able to take hundreds of johns into custody, few prostitutes were arrested because they knew the undercover detectives on sight.

The police decided to take a problem-solving approach to improve results. In examining the problem, officers learned many of the prostitutes were transients who would stay in the area only while it was profitable. To diminish profitability, the police obtained a temporary restraining order (TRO) prohibiting the defendants (prostitutes) from flagging down motorists, loitering on corners, or participating in other solicitation conduct within 100 yards of the plaintiffs (local business owners). Violation of the TRO meant an immediate 5 days in jail and a $1,000 fine.

One month after the TRO was obtained, the problem had been solved. Prostitutes abandoned the area, customers no longer cruised the business strip, and businesses reported increased revenues. The area has remained free of prostitution for more than 3 years (Jaus, 1994).

Mankato, Minnesota—Police Reclaimed Park for Use by Law-Abiding Citizens One area of a local park had become the gathering place for "Motorheads"—a group of car devotees—who would meet every day around noon to drink and socialize. Their parties would continue throughout the day and into the evening, so that by 10:00 A.M., the crowd had grown to between 300 and 400 people.

Problems linked to the Motorhead parties included the harassing of other park users, assaults, public urination, public and juvenile drinking, suspected drug dealing, and thousands of dollars in criminal property damage to the park. The initial police response included police park patrols, installation of floodlights in the area where the parties were occurring, and the scheduling of many nonparty events at the park. None of these approaches, however, were effective.

Taking a problem-solving approach, officers spent several weeks observing and interacting with the partygoers. During this time, they learned the Motorheads liked the spot because it was next to a large parking lot; had two exits; and, while being out of sight, still allowed them to see the police coming from a distance. Interviews with former park users revealed they had stopped visiting the park because they were intimidated by the partygoers. A community meeting was then held to solicit more information about the problem.

The officers partnered with the city parks director to develop a long-term solution to the problem. Aiming to reduce the appeal of the park to the partiers, park officials reduced the size of the large parking lot and restricted the flow of traffic to one way. Meanwhile, the officers had found an alternative site for the party group—an empty, highly visible downtown parking lot near the police department where activity could be easily monitored.

Once the Motorheads relocated downtown, young families and other former park attendees resumed use of the park. Although some Motorhead-related problems continued downtown (juvenile drinking, drug sales, reckless driving), immediate targeted enforcement efforts by the police convinced the Motorheads to "clean up their act" or risk losing access to the downtown lot (Sampson and Scott, 1999).

The Herman Goldstein Award Projects

Several award projects have been implemented to recognize individual agencies' and communities' efforts at curbing local crime and disorder through problem-oriented policing. Two of the better known awards are the Herman Goldstein Award and the Tilley Award.

Herman Goldstein Award First introduced in 1993, the Herman Goldstein Award recognizes outstanding police officers and police agencies—both in the United States and around the world—that engage in innovative and effective problem-solving efforts and achieve measurable success in reducing specific crime, disorder, and public safety problems. This international competition is named after the founder of POP, University of Wisconsin Professor Emeritus Herman Goldstein, and is administered by the Center for Problem-Oriented Policing. (The award program was administered by the Police Executive Research Forum, or PERF, from 1993 to 2003; www.policeforum.org.)

HALLOWEEN ON STATE STREET

One of the 2008 winners of the Herman Goldstein Award was the Madison (Wisconsin) Police Department's Halloween on State Street. In 2002 this traditional Halloween street event erupted into a riot involving disorderly behaviors, extensive criminal damage, assaults, injured officers, and looting of businesses. An annual problem-solving project was thereafter designed to prevent injury and property damage and instill peace. Repeated analysis of video clips, officer observations, and GIS analysis implicated problems with crowd movement; synthesis of arrest data showed the arrestees were 18- to 25-year-old males from Wisconsin and surrounding states, had university affiliation, and were disproportionately legally intoxicated. The response was guided by what had been used in other locations experiencing similar problems and by models of crowd behavior and theory. Stability was restored with policing responses, a fully gated event area with a fee assessed for admission, and entertainment on several stages. At the conclusion of the event, the fencing was adjusted and police were used to facilitate crowd movement away from problem areas. Halloween-related arrests decreased significantly over a 2-year period, most notably for alcohol and disorderly conduct. Crowd attendance stabilized to safe levels. Injuries to attendees and officers all but disappeared. In recent years, little or no property damage has occurred and the impact to the surrounding neighborhoods has been minimized.

Source: http://www.popcenter.org/library/awards/goldstein/2008/08-34(F).pdf

The Center for Problem-Oriented Policing has assembled a panel of seven judges, made up of experienced researchers and practitioners, who select a small number of finalists from among award submissions and, finally, the winner. Submissions usually come from the United States, Canada, the United Kingdom, and Australia. The judges consider a number of factors in their selections, including the depth of problem analysis, the development of clear and realistic response goals, the use of relevant measures of effectiveness, and the involvement of citizens and other community resources in problem resolution. Police agencies whose projects successfully resolve any type of recurring community problem that results in crime or disorder are eligible to compete for the award. The number of submissions is 50 to 70 per year, and of those roughly 5 to 10 per year are selected as finalists ("The Herman Goldstein Award Projects," 2012).[4]

Tilley Award   The Tilley Award was set up by the U.K. Home Office Policing and Reducing Crime Unit (now the Crime and Policing Group) in 1999 to encourage and recognize good practice in implementing POP. The award, funded by the Home Office, pays for winners to attend the Annual International Problem-Oriented Policing Conference in San Diego, and winners usually have the opportunity to present their projects at the conference. The prizes are presented at the annual U.K. National Problem-Oriented Policing Conference. The award is open to all U.K. police forces ("Tilley Award Projects, 2012").[5]

---

[4] Source: Reprinted by permission of the POP Center.
[5] Source: Reprinted by permission of the POP Center.

REDUCING CYCLE THEFT: A PARTNERSHIP APPROACH BETWEEN TRANSPORT FOR LONDON (TFL) AND THE METROPOLITAN POLICE SERVICE (MPS)

The 2011 Herman Goldstein Award went to the London Metropolitan Police Service (MPS) for their partnership with Transport for London (TfL) in an effort to promote cycling in the city while reducing a burgeoning cycle theft problem. Population projections required the city to look for ways to promote other transport options, such as cycling, to meet the future demands on London's transport system. Research, however, was showing that increasing cycle theft was acting as a barrier to cycling, and London's cycling community was becoming progressively discontent at the lack of action by politicians, police, and TfL commissioners. Thus a coordinated, multifaceted approach was undertaken.

Scanning

By 2031 there will be approximately 1.25 million *more* people in the capital. The provision of reliable and efficient transport, with the capacity and connectivity to accommodate this growth sustainability, is crucial to the continued success of the London and U.K. economies. This population growth will lead to an increasing demand on the already overstretched transport network.

Increasing the number of cycling trips in London is essential to ensuring that London can continue to operate effectively and successfully throughout this population growth. Furthermore, cycling can help reduce London's CO_2 emissions significantly. Therefore, it is imperative the people of London see cycling as an attractive and accessible transport option.

However, data show that 18,216 cycles were reported stolen during 2008/9, up 6 percent from the previous year. In 2009/10 cycle theft increased 28 percent to 23,317. Moreover, as cycle theft is presumed to be a highly underreported crime, estimates are that the "real" number of cycle thefts in London could be as high as 93,000. Cycle theft is attractive because it is a low-risk, high-reward crime that requires only inexpensive tools and little specialized knowledge. With research indicating that 25 percent of cyclists stopped cycling after being a victim of cycle theft, TfL concluded that cycle theft could seriously jeopardize their goal to increase cycling as a viable transportation option.

Analysis

Several sources were examined to obtain the most comprehensive picture possible surrounding the cycle theft problem, including data related to the victims/targets, offenders, locations, time and other factors. Among the factors identified as contributing to the problem were:

- Cyclists were not properly locking their bicycles.
- Cyclists did not keep bicycle records, making it difficult to prove ownership—more than three-fourths of cyclists surveyed had no record of their cycle frame number, and of those who did, less than half had registered this number online.
- The average offender was a White male, 16–25 years old, who operated in loose gangs, exploited opportunities to steal bicycles to trade for cash or goods, and showed a willingness to travel 3 or 4 miles to areas with a high concentration of unattended cycles. Ninety percent had history of offending prior to arrest.
- The high resale value, easy removability, and generally untraceable nature of cycles make them attractive targets.
- Online Web sites provide a legitimized avenue for resale—17 percent of cyclists surveyed recognized a stolen bike being sold on a Web site.
- Courts showed little understanding of the value of cycles and treated cycle theft as an entry-level offense, with punishment being diversionary and slight. Data indicated that, of the offenders proceeded against, 92 percent received a fine as the only punishment, and the average fine was considerably lower than the proceeds gained by one illegal sale.
- Low detection and clearance rates contributed to the perception of cycle theft as a low-risk offense. Ninety percent of bike theft victims did not have their cycle recovered, and 70 percent reported that the police made only a "token" effort to investigate the theft.

Response

As the analysis stage demonstrated the need for a co-coordinated, pan-London, partnership approach to address cycle theft, TfL partnered with the Mayor of London and London's policing agencies to develop and publish the Cycle Security Plan in 2010, detailing interventions planned to prevent and deter the risk of cycle theft. A dedicated working group was formed, including representatives from TfL, MPS, British Transport Police, City of

(continues)

(continued)

London Police, cycling interest groups, and the Greater London Authority (the strategic regional authority).

Specific response efforts were directed at victims, offenders, and locations and included:

- Target hardening—a campaign to improve levels of cycle marking and registration and to teach good cycle locking practices.
- Increasing the risks to offenders by engaging online sites to share information with police on suspicious activity and to put measures in place to make it harder for such sites to be used for the reselling of stolen cycles.
- Targeting hot spots for cycle theft as a way to crack down on cycle theft gangs.
- Encouraging the reporting of cycle theft.
- Engaging with magistrates to raise awareness about the impact of cycle crime and influence sentencing guidelines.

Assessment

During this first year of the project, the following results were observed:

- Reported cycle thefts decreased 5.4 percent from the previous year.
- More than 13,000 bikes have been properly marked and registered online by the MPS, and 130 stolen cycles have already been returned to their owners.
- The number of cycle journeys amongst London's cycling community has grown by 14 percent.
- The TfL's "Avoid Cycle Theft" Web page, which provides crime prevention advice, received 15,000 hits.
- Positive media stories about the working group's efforts to reduce cycle theft have helped improve public confidence in the response to cycle theft.

Source: http://www.popcenter.org/library/awards/goldstein/2011/11-54(W).pdf

SUMMARY

Problem-solving policing requires police to group incidents and identify the underlying causes of problems in the community. The magnet phenomenon occurs when a phone number or address is associated with a crime simply because it was a convenient number or address to use. One concern of a problem-solving approach is differentiating between efficiency and effectiveness. Efficiency, doing things right, has been the traditional emphasis in law enforcement. Effectiveness, doing the right things, is the emphasis in community policing. Effectiveness should produce an increase in efficiency, because officers are proactively solving problems rather than simply reacting to them.

The first step in problem solving is to group incidents as problems. The four stages of the SARA problem-solving model are scanning, analysis, response, and assessment. Problem analysis considers the individuals involved, the incidents, and the responses.

The DOC model (dilemmas–options–consequences) challenges officers to carefully consider their decisions and the short- and long-term consequences of those decisions. The goal is to fuse problem solving and morality.

Crime-specific planning uses the principles of problem solving to focus on identified crime problems. Crime mapping changes the focus from the criminal to the location of crimes—the hot spots where most crimes occur.

DISCUSSION QUESTIONS

1. How do you approach problems? Do you use a systematic approach?

2. Problem solving can take more time than the traditional approach to policing. Which is more effective? More efficient? More expensive? Explain your answers.

3. Does your department use problem solving? Is the department proactive or reactive?

4. Does your law enforcement agency employ anyone to specifically conduct crime analysis?

5. What difficulties can you foresee for a department that uses problem-solving techniques?

6. How do problem solving and crime-specific planning differ?

7. Some officers have resisted implementing problem-solving strategies. Why do you think that is?

8. In what kinds of problems do you think a problem-solving approach would be most effective?

9. What is the relationship between community-oriented policing and problem-oriented policing?

10. How might computers help police in their problem-solving efforts?

GALE EMERGENCY SERVICES DATABASE ASSIGNMENTS

ONLINE Database

- Use the Gale Emergency Services Database to help answer the Discussion Questions when applicable.

- Find an example of a police–community partnership that successfully used problem solving to deal with community issues. (You might also see the POP Center at www.popcenter.org; the Community Policing Consortium at www.communitypolicing.org; the Police Executive Research Forum at www.policeforum.org; or other community policing Web sites.)

- Explore ethical issues and examples of unethical decision making in law enforcement. Outline the issues in the following areas: police culture, use of force, racial profiling, and sting operations. Name the problems society sometimes sees with each and the law enforcement justification for their actions in these areas.

- Research and outline one of the following subjects and be prepared to share your work with the class: crime mapping, geographic profiling, or problem-oriented policing.

REFERENCES

Bichler, Gisela and Larry Gaines. 2005. "An Examination of Police Officers' Insights into Problem Identification and Problem Solving." *Crime and Delinquency* (January): 53–74.

Brito, Corina Sole and Tracy Allan, eds. 1999. *Problem-Oriented Policing.* 2nd vol. Washington, DC: Police Executive Research Forum.

Clarke, Ronald V. and John E. Eck. 2005 (August). *Crime Analysis for Problem Solvers in 60 Small Steps.* Washington, DC: Office of Community Oriented Policing Services. http://www.cops.usdoj.gov/pdf/CrimeAnalysis60Steps.pdf

Crisp, H. Dean and R. J. Hines. 2007. "The CompStat Process in Columbia." *The Police Chief* (February): 46–48.

Eck, John E. 2002. *Assessing Responses to Problems: An Introductory Guide for Police Problem-Solvers.* Washington, DC: Office of Community Oriented Policing Services.

Eck, John E. 2005 (August). "Crime Hot Spots: What They Are, Why We Have Them, and How to Map Them." In *Mapping Crime: Understanding Hot Spots,* edited by John E. Eck, et al., 1–15. Washington, DC: National Institute of Justice. (NIJ 209393)

Eck, John E. and William Spelman. 1987. *Problem-Solving: Problem-Oriented Policing in Newport News.* Washington, DC: The Police Executive Research Forum.

Falk, Kay. 2005. "Nothing New under the Sun." *Law Enforcement Technology* (September): 10–20.

"Geographic Profiling." 2009. Washington, DC: National Institute of Justice. http://www.nij.gov/maps/gp.htm

Goldstein, Herman. 1990. *Problem-Oriented Policing.* New York: McGraw-Hill.

Goldstein, Herman and Charles E. Susmilch. 1981 (March). *The Problem-Oriented Approach to Improving Police Service: A Description of the Project and an Elaboration of the Concept.* Madison, WI: Madison, Wisconsin Police Department and the Project on Development of a Problem-Oriented Approach to Improving Police Service at the Law School, University of Wisconsin—Madison.

"The Herman Goldstein Award Projects." 2012. Washington, DC: Center for Problem-Oriented Policing. http://www.popcenter.org/library/awards/goldstein

Hess, Kären M. and Christine H. Orthmann. 2012. *Management and Supervision in Law Enforcement.* 6th ed. Belmont, CA: Wadsworth.

Hoelzer, Gary and Jim Gorman. 2011. "Incorporating Hot-Spots Policing into Your Daily Patrol Plan." *FBI Law Enforcement Bulletin* (November): 10–15.

Jang, Hyunseok, Larry T. Hoover, and Hee-Jong Joo. 2010. "An Evaluation of CompStat's Effect on Crime: The Fort Worth Experience." *Police Quarterly* 13 (4): 387–412.

Jaus, Gary. 1994. "Temporary Restraining Order Keeps Prostitutes off Streets." *Problem-Solving Quarterly* 7 (314): 3, 10–11.

Kates, Graham. 2012 (May). "Cracking the 'Blue Wall of Silence.'" *The Crime Report.* New York: John Jay College of

Criminal Justice. http://www.thecrimereport.org/news/inside-criminal-justice/2012-05-cracking-the-blue-wall-of-silence

"The Key Elements of Problem-Oriented Policing." n.d. Washington, DC: Center for Problem-Oriented Policing. http://www.popcenter.org/about/?p=elements

Krish, Karthik. 2003. "Application of GIS in Crime Analysis and Geographic Profiling." Map India Conference, GISdevelopment.net. http://www.gisdevelopment.net/application/military/overview/pdf/146.pdf

Markovic, John and Nicole Scalisi. 2011. "Full Spectrum Use of GIS by Law Enforcement: It's Not Just about Mapping Crime." *Geography and Public Safety* 3 (1): 2–4.

McCue, Colleen. 2011. "Proactive Policing: Using Geographic Analysis to Fight Crime." *Geography and Public Safety* 2 (4): 3–5.

National Association for Community Mediation. 2012. "About NAFCM." Mesa, AZ: National Association for Community Mediation. http://www.nafcm.org/about/purpose

Newman, Graeme R., with Kelly Socia. 2007. *Sting Operations.* Washington, DC: Center for Problem-Oriented Policing, Response Guide No. 6.

Peed, Carl, Ronald E. Wilson, and Nicole J. Scalisi. 2008. "Making Smarter Decisions: Connecting Crime Analysis with City Officials." *The Police Chief* (September): 20–28.

Problem-Solving Tips: A Guide to Reducing Crime and Disorder through Problem-Solving Partnerships. 2011 (July). 2nd edition. Washington, DC: Office of Community Oriented Policing Services. (e050600069)

Rossmo, D. Kim. 2005 (July 1). *What Is Crime Mapping? Briefing Book.* Washington, DC: National Institute of Justice. http://www.cops.usdoj.gov/html/cd_rom/tech_docs/pubs/WhatIsCrimeMappingBriefingBook.pdf

Sampson, Rana and Michael S. Scott. 1999. *Tackling Crime and Other Public-Safety Problems: Case Studies in Problem-Solving.* Washington, DC: U.S. Department of Justice, Office of Community Oriented Policing Services.

Scott, Michael S. 2000. *Problem-Oriented Policing: Reflections on the First 20 Years.* Washington, DC: U.S. Department of Justice, Office of Community Oriented Policing Services.

Serpas, Ronald W. and Matthew Morley. 2008. "The Next Step in Accountability-Driven Leadership: 'CompStating' the CompStat Data." *The Police Chief* (May): 60–70.

"Tilley Award Projects." 2012. Washington, DC: Center for Problem-Oriented Policing. http://www.popcenter.org/library/awards/tilley

Violent Crime in America: What We Know about Hot Spots Enforcement. 2008 (May). Washington, DC: Police Executive Research Forum.

Wexler, Chuck. 2008 (May). "Conclusion." In *Violent Crime in America: What We Know about Hot Spots Enforcement,* 29–30. Washington, DC: Police Executive Research Forum.

"What Is POP?" n.d. Washington, DC: Center for Problem-Oriented Policing. http://www.popcenter.org/about/?p=whatiscpop

White, Matthew B. 2008 (February). *Enhancing the Problem-Solving Capacity of Crime Analysis Units.* Washington, DC: Center for Problem-Oriented Policing, Problem-Solving Tools Series, Guide No. 9. http://www.cops.usdoj.gov/Publications/e020827126.pdf

Wilson, James Q. and George L. Kelling. 1989. "Making Neighborhoods Safe." *Atlantic Monthly* (February): 46–52.

Wintersteen, John D. 2007. "CompStat and Crime Prevention in Paradise Valley." *The Police Chief* (February): 52–58.

CHAPTER 5
Implementing Community Policing

There is nothing more difficult to plan, more uncertain of success, or more dangerous to manage than the establishment of a new order, because the innovator has for enemies all those who have derived advantage from the old order and finds but lukewarm defenders among those who stand to gain from the new one.

—*Machiavelli*

DO YOU KNOW ...

» What basic changes are required in making the transition to community policing?

» What participatory leadership is?

» What a department's vision should include?

» Who should be included in a needs assessment?

» How law enforcement agencies have traditionally been organized?

» Which may be more important, targeting a "critical mass" of individuals or mobilizing the community at large?

» What a strategic plan includes?

» What the most important consideration in selecting strategies to implement community policing is?

» Whether training should be the spearhead of change?

» What the most important areas to cover in training are?

» What transition managers should anticipate and prepare for?

» What impediments to community policing may need to be overcome?

» What common pitfalls there are in making the transition to a community policing philosophy?

» When conducting evaluations, how failures should be viewed?

CAN YOU DEFINE ...

change management
critical mass
decentralization
empowered
flat organization
participatory leadership
strategic planning
vision

INTRODUCTION

You have looked at the philosophy of community policing and at the key players—politicians, business people, faith-based organizations, civic organizations, the schools, the community, and the police. You have also considered a basic component of community policing—problem solving. The challenge is to move from theories about using problem-solving techniques and partnerships to actual implementation.

This chapter begins with a consideration of the basic nature of change and how it influences implementing community policing and the changes needed to successfully make a transition. This is followed by a discussion of how the community policing philosophy should be reflected in the management style and the department's vision and mission statements, as well as the possible impact the philosophy may have on the entire police organization. Next is a look at needs assessment for both the department and the community, including an in-depth examination of how police are usually organized and managed. An explanation of strategic planning and ways to develop strategies is included, and the importance of hiring, promoting, and training is presented. Examples are given of how community policing has been implemented, including the benefits that might be achieved. Anticipating and preparing for resistance are covered, followed by impediments to overcome and pitfalls to avoid. The chapter concludes with ways to evaluate progress.

CHANGE

It has been said that nothing is constant except change. Nonetheless, police administrators, supervisors, and even line personnel frequently resist change in any form and prefer the status quo. Change is occurring, however, and will continue to occur. Police departments can resist, or they can accept the challenge and capitalize on the benefits that may result. Issues requiring departments to change include technological advances; demographic changes; fiscal constraints; shifting values; the need to do more with less; heightened media coverage of police misconduct; and citizen fear of crime, disorder, violence, gangs, and terrorism.

Change does take time. Traditions die hard. Most police officers will find proposed changes to their culture extremely threatening. The police culture is a tremendously strong force. However, when contemplating the challenges of change, one must remember that a huge ship can be turned by a small rudder. It just takes time and steadfast determination.

Efforts to implement significant changes in policing, of any kind, have encountered severe difficulties (Newburn, 2008). Frontline police services are "notoriously" resistant to change. Most officers usually are not seen as they perform their duties. In the field, they exercise discretion in applying whatever model of policing their department uses. They are also accustomed to changing fads, fancies, and directives from their superiors and so are often cynical about what the "dream factory" (headquarters) is asking from them. Unsympathetic officers will often comply as minimally as possible with such changes, ignoring "new-fangled" ideas and continuing to deliver the policing they feel appropriate, thus subverting new thinking from within. In addition, high rates of senior staff turnover, external political pressures, and traditional performance measurements can inhibit efforts to implement change (Newburn, 2008).

Five concerns that have most strongly influenced the development of problem-oriented policing and, by implication, community policing are (Goldstein, 1990, 14):

1. The police field is preoccupied with management, internal procedures, and efficiency to the exclusion of appropriate concern for effectiveness in dealing with substantive problems.

2. The police devote most of their resources to responding to calls from citizens, reserving too small a percentage of their time and energy for acting on their own initiative to prevent or reduce community problems.

3. The community is a major resource with an enormous potential, largely untapped, for reducing the number and magnitude of problems that otherwise become the business of the police.

4. Within their agencies, police have readily available to them another huge resource: their rank-and-file officers, whose time and talents have not been used effectively.

5. Efforts to improve policing have often failed because they have not been adequately related to the overall dynamics and complexity of the police organization. Adjustments in policies and organizational structure are required to accommodate and support change.

It is also helpful to be familiar with five categories of "adopters" to expect within any organization, as Figure 5.1 shows.

The *innovators* are risk takers. They embrace uncertainty and change. The *early adopters* are opinion leaders, the ones to whom others come for advice. The *early majority* accept new ideas slightly ahead of the majority. The *late majority* are more skeptical. They can be persuaded but usually require a great deal of peer pressure. The *late adopters* are the most difficult to convince. They tend to be suspicious of all innovations. Recognizing these individual characteristics may be helpful in developing strategies to "sell" community policing to the troops.

Some changes have already occurred within many departments that should make the transition to community policing easier, including better-educated police officers who are less inclined to accept orders unquestioningly; more diversity within the police ranks; and a shift in incentives with intrinsic, personal worth–type rewards becoming as important as extrinsic, monetary rewards. Other changes are needed to move from the traditional, reactive, incident-driven

Figure 5.1   Change Takes Time: The Five Categories of Adopters

mode of policing to the proactive, problem-solving, collaborative mode typical of community policing.

Before change to community policing can occur, management must know specifically what changes are needed.

NEEDED CHANGES

Some changes basic to implementing the community policing philosophy have already been briefly described in Chapter 2.

 Community policing will require a change in management style, mission statement, departmental organization, and the general approach to fighting crime.

How these changes fit into the transition from a philosophy to practice will become evident as the chapter progresses.

The Community Policing Consortium (CPC), a federally funded organization composed of the International Association of Chiefs of Police (IACP), National Organization of Black Law Enforcement Executives (NOBLE), National Sheriffs' Association (NSA), Police Executive Research Forum (PERF), and Police Foundation, has identified three core components of community policing, the first two of which—community partnerships and problem solving—have already been discussed. The third component—change management—requires departments to recognize that forging partnerships with the community and adopting a problem-solving approach will necessarily bring about a change in the organizational structure of policing. To be effective, this change must be properly managed, including recognizing the need for change, communicating a clear vision that change is possible and desirable, identifying the specific steps required for positive change to occur, developing an understanding of and embracing the benefits of change, and fostering an organization-wide commitment to change (Davis, 1998). Change management also requires recognizing the importance of organization-wide support for community policing, including support in terms of how calls for service are managed (McEwen et al., 2003). In essence, **change management** is the development of an overall strategy which examines the present state of the organization, envisions the future state of the organization, and devises the means of moving from one to the other.

Although the term *management* is pervasive in the literature seeking to guide departments in their move toward implementing community policing, the importance of *leadership* in this transition cannot be overlooked. A successful transition process requires the commitment of a leader who is open, willing to make change, and supports decisions with steadfastness and energy (Community Policing Consortium, 2000).

MANAGEMENT STYLES

Yet another change is that community policing usually requires a different management style. The traditional autocratic style effective during the industrial age will not have the same effect in the 21st century. One viable alternative to the autocratic style of management is participatory leadership.

change management

The development of an overall strategy to examine the present state of an organization, envision the future state of the organization, and devise a means of moving from one to the other.

In **participatory leadership** each individual has a voice in decisions, but top management still has the ultimate decision-making authority.

participatory leadership
A management style in which each individual has a voice in decisions, but top management still has the ultimate decision-making authority.

What is important is that everyone has an opportunity to express their views on a given issue or problem:

> Consultative, democratic, or participative leadership has been evolving since the 1930s and 1940s. Democratic leadership does not mean that every decision is made only after discussion and a vote. It means rather that management welcomes employees' ideas and input. Employees are encouraged to be innovative. Management development of a strong sense of individual achievement and responsibility is a necessary ingredient of participative or consultative leadership.

> Democratic or participative managers are interested in their subordinates and their problems and welfare. Management still makes the final decision but takes into account the input from employees. (Hess and Orthmann, 2012, 19)

Table 5.1 compares the authoritarian and participatory styles of management. The leader must also have a vision for the department and the community.

"As the lines of demarcation between leader and follower continue to blur, empowering strategies and inclusive decision-making styles will not just be recommended practices; they will be essential competencies of police leadership" (Wuestewald and Steinheider, 2006b, 32). Barriers to participative or shared leadership include a dysfunctional relationship between the administration and the union, apathy and nonparticipation, hidden agendas and informal leaders, lack of communication, and a power culture that will not let go of the status quo ("How to Implement Shared Leadership," 2006, 37). Wuestewald and Steinheider (2006a, 53) note: "Probably the most difficult aspect of undertaking a participative approach to management is for senior executives to make the personal commitment to accept the decisions of others."

Table 5.1   Old and New Styles of Leadership Compared

Authoritarian Style	Participatory Style
Response to incidents	Problem solving
Individual effort and competitiveness	Teamwork
Professional expertise	Community orientation; ask customers what they want
Go by the "book"; decisions by emotion	Use data-based decision making
Tell subordinates	Ask and listen to employees
Boss as patriarch and order giver	Boss as coach and teacher
Maintain status quo	Create, innovate, experiment
Control and watch employees	Trust employees
Reliance on scientific investigation and technology rather than people	Reliance on skilled employees—a better resource than machines
When things go wrong, blame employees	Errors mean failed systems/processes—improve them
Organization is closed to outsiders	Organization is open

Source: From HESS/ORTHMANN, *Management and Supervision in Law Enforcement*, 6E. © 2012 Cengage Learning.

CREATING VISION AND MISSION STATEMENTS

vision

Intelligent foresight; starts with a mental image that gradually evolves from abstract musings to a concrete series of mission statements, goals, and objectives.

Vision might be thought of as intelligent foresight. Examining the department's past for strengths and weaknesses, successes and failures is an important step in creating a vision for the future.

 This vision should include the essential elements of the community policing philosophy: problem solving, empowerment, forming community partnerships, and being proactive—making preventing crime as important as enforcing the law.

The vision for each department will be different. It must be tailored to reflect the personnel within the department and the community the department serves. A vision should be something that everyone involved can buy into and feel a part of. This means involving leaders from within the department and the community from the beginning of the transition. The CPC recommends the entire workforce be directly involved in the envisioning and planning processes; at the very least, a cross section of the workforce representing all ranks or grades and incorporating sworn, unsworn, and civilian personnel and their respective union representatives should be involved (*Changing Roles*, 2004).

Union support for community policing is absolutely necessary. Without it—or worse, with open opposition—the risk of failure is high. Union leadership has tremendous influence over its members, who will likely follow the lead of union officials. Unions are concerned about issues they perceive as affecting officers negatively, including the likelihood of permanent shifts and area assignments, concern that COP may negatively affect the union contract, the perceived increase of power and influence the community will have in department matters, the potential that citizen review boards may be formed under community policing, the perceived softening of the police image, officer safety concerns, and the concern of officers being held responsible for the crime that occurs in their assigned area.

Agencies with unions can take the opportunity to form partnerships within by inviting union leaders to participate in the process. Having been elected by their membership, they will have the advantage of not being seen as management's hand-selected few.

The CPC also recommends that those who have been identified as antagonistic to the change process be deliberately co-opted. They cannot be ignored because they will not go away. Actively seek ways to avert their antagonism (*Changing Roles*, 2004).

Once the vision is articulated, it should be translated into a mission statement, as discussed in Chapter 2. The development of a mission statement is important for any organization, but it is critical in developing and implementing community policing. Its importance cannot be overstated. Again, the mission statement must be something everyone can buy into and feel a part of. Once the vision and mission statements have been articulated, the next step is to conduct a needs assessment.

ASSESSING NEEDS

The needs assessment is critical to the successful implementation of community policing.

 A needs assessment should include not only the department but also the community of which it is a part.

Analyzing the Department

The first step in needs assessment is to analyze the department's organization.

 The traditional law enforcement organization design has been that of a pyramid-shaped hierarchy based on a military model. However, the pyramid might be inverted to implement community policing (Figure 5.2).

Under a traditional police management structure, command officers and supervisors have complete authority over subordinates, and they have little tolerance for ideas originating at the bottom of the pyramid. Communication flows downward through the bureaucratic chain of command. This bureaucratic organizational structure worked well for decades. Recently, however, it has been called into question, with many looking to corporate America as a more appropriate organizational model.

Figure 5.2 Typical Police Department Management Structure and an Inverted Pyramid

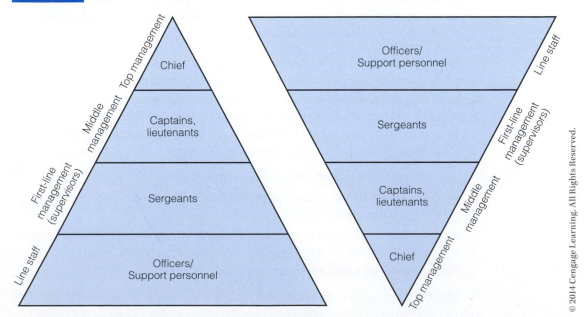

To remain competitive, business and industry are undergoing extensive changes in organization and management styles. Law enforcement agencies also face the need for change to meet the competition of private policing: "Private security is the nation's primary protective resource today, outspending public law enforcement by more than 73 percent and employing nearly three times the workforce" (Harr and Hess, 2010, 74). In addition, an estimated 85 percent of U.S. businesses and infrastructure are protected by private security.

Law enforcement agencies must compete not only with private police but also for the college graduates now entering the workforce. In addition, like business, many departments are turning to a **flat organization**: fewer lieutenants and captains, fewer staff departments, fewer staff assistants, more sergeants, and more patrol officers. Typical pyramid-organization charts will have the top pushed down and the sides expanded at the base.

flat organization

Unlike a typical pyramid organization chart, the top is pushed down and the sides are expanded at the base. In a police department, this means fewer lieutenants and captains, fewer staff departments, and fewer staff assistants but more sergeants and more patrol officers.

empowered

Granting authority and decision making to lower-level officers.

decentralization

An operating principle that encourages flattening of the organization and places decision-making authority and autonomy at the level where information is plentiful, usually at the level of the patrol officer.

Progressive businesses are restructuring top-heavy organizations, pushing authority and decision making as low as possible. Successful businesses concentrate on soliciting ideas from everyone in their organization about nearly every aspect of their operation. This approach can be applied to policing, especially in small departments. If officer retention is to be maintained and loyalty and morale preserved and heightened, officers must be **empowered**—that is, given authority and enabled to make decisions.

The operating principle of **decentralization** goes hand-in-hand with empowerment by pushing decision-making authority and autonomy as far down the management hierarchy as possible, to the rank where information is plentiful, typically at the level of the patrol officer:

> Decentralization is … closely linked to the implementation of community policing. … More responsibility for identifying and responding thoughtfully to community problems is delegated to individual patrol officers, who are encouraged to take the initiative in finding ways to deal with the problems of the communities in which they are operating. The consequence of this kind of decentralization is not only that the organization can become more proactive and more preventive, but also that it can respond to different sized problems. (National Research Council, 2004, 88)

Some ways to measure implementation of decentralization include participatory management initiatives, identification of community zones, use of bicycle and/or foot patrol, evaluation of policies and procedures, and improved citizen confidence in the patrol officers with whom they most often interact.

In summary, departments that have successfully implemented community policing have made several organizational changes:

» The bureaucracy is flattened and decentralized.

» Roles of those in management positions change to leaders and mentors rather than managers and supervisors.

» Patrol officers are given new responsibilities and empowered to make decisions and problem solve with their community partners.

» Permanent shifts and areas are assigned.

The department's organization should be carefully analyzed to identify barriers within the agency likely to impede the community policing initiative.

This needs assessment should also consider external constraints controlled by others outside the department such as finance and budgeting, hiring rules, and state-mandated training programs. In addition to analyzing the department, the community being served must also be analyzed.

Analyzing the Community

Law enforcement agencies can learn the views of their community and at the same time let citizens know that their opinions matter. Interviews of community leaders and focus groups can be useful, but they are limited to one segment of the community or a small group of people. Polls and surveys have also become popular ways to get a better idea of the views of a much larger segment of the population.

Skogan (2004b, 75) presents the three questions asked in a survey of Chicago residents regarding the quality of police service:

1. How responsive are the police in your neighborhood to community concerns? Do you think they are [very responsive to very unresponsive]?

2. How good a job are the police doing in dealing with the problems that really concern people in your neighborhood? Would you say they are doing a [very good job to poor job]?

3. How good a job are the police doing in working together with residents in your neighborhood to solve local problems? Would you say they are doing a [very good job to poor job]?

A community survey might also offer police an opportunity to find out how citizens perceive crime and disorder problems in their community, posing questions such as the following: How do you perceive crime in our community? Has crime affected you personally? Are you aware of any problems in your

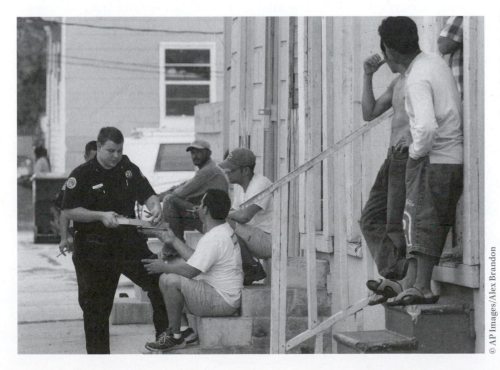

An officer conducts a neighborhood survey to learn of residents' needs and concerns, sending a clear message to community stakeholders that their opinions matter to the department.

© AP Images/Alex Brandon

neighborhood? Do you have any concerns about your safety while walking in your neighborhood?

At the heart of the community policing philosophy is the recognition that the police can no longer go it alone—if they ever could. They must use the eyes, ears, and voices of law-abiding citizens. A starting point is to analyze the community's demographics, as described in Chapter 3, including how much social capital is available for community policing efforts: "In communities with low levels of Putnam's social capital and high levels of COP activities, police officers may be perceived as facilitators who take responsibility for engaging citizens in alleviating complex social problems. On the other hand, in areas with high levels of Putnam's social capital and high levels of community policing, COP may be characterized as a partnership—that is, a collaborative effort featuring citizens and police working together to develop and implement effective problem-solving activities to enhance quality of life" (Correia, 2000, 54). Thus COP activity may be driven more by community factors than by factors internal to police organizations.

Police must develop a comprehensive picture of their community. They can do this through surveys and direct interactions with citizens. How community members respond when asked what problems they think the police should focus on and what solutions they would suggest can help the department meet the community's needs. Surveys ask for input from everyone instead of just the few citizens who are the most involved. Although usually a small number of leaders attend community meetings, the challenge is to reach beyond them to the average citizen. A survey is one answer; it offers some confirmation that community leaders are representing the needs and interests of their community.

It would be enlightening to conduct a similar survey with police officers and their managers. Such shared information could go far in building trust among line officers, managers, and citizens.

The Bureau of Justice Statistics (BJS) and the Office of Community Oriented Policing Services (COPS) have available for local law enforcement agencies a computer software package designed to help conduct public opinion surveys about how well the police are doing their jobs. While conducting needs assessments, attention should be paid to who might be community leaders to enlist in the community policing initiative.

According to Correia (2000, 56): "It appears that the number of participants actively engaged in a community policing program is not as important as the character of the individuals participating. A 'critical mass' of individuals with high levels of social engagement may be more effective in solving a community's problems than a large number of individuals with low levels of social cohesion." A critical mass in physics is the smallest amount of a fissionable material that will sustain a nuclear chain reaction. In the context of community policing efforts, a **critical mass** is the smallest number of citizens and organizations needed to support and sustain the community policing initiative.

critical mass

The smallest number of citizens and organizations needed to support and sustain the community policing initiative.

It may be more important and effective for COP agencies to target a critical mass of individuals—the smallest number of citizens and organizations needed to support and sustain the community policing initiative—than to try to mobilize the entire community.

Once the needs assessment has been conducted, the next step is to develop a blueprint—that is, to do some strategic planning.

STRATEGIC PLANNING

Strategic planning is long-term, large-scale, future-oriented planning. It begins with the vision and mission statements already discussed. It is grounded in those statements and guided by the findings of the needs assessment. From that point, specific goals and objectives and an accompanying implementation strategy and time line are developed. What looks like a straightforward process can turn extremely difficult as dilemmas arise and threaten the plan. Among the most predictable are the resistance to change and fear of the unknown that will be played out in the department and in the community. This resistance is also one of the most serious and difficult issues to be faced in a transition.

strategic planning
Long-term, large-scale, futuristic planning.

> The strategic plan should include community partnerships and problem solving as well as any needed cultural and organizational changes in the department. It should include a realistic time line and a way to assess progress. It must also be tied to the department's budget.

The strategic plan is long range. Departments do not successfully implement community policing in a year or two. It takes time—sometimes a decade or longer—for most departments to fully implement it. Again, all interested parties should be allowed input into the strategic plan.

The Durham (New Hampshire) Police Department used a 1-day planning session to develop its strategic plan (Kurz, 2006). The department wanted to reach the widest possible audience and at the same time limit the group to a reasonable size. They sent invitations to members of the town council, the chamber of commerce, the school board, the ecumenical council, the high school's student senate, district court judges, chairpersons of town boards, members of organizations with a history of community commitment (e.g., the Lions, the Rotary Club), area clergy, defense attorneys, business leaders, media representatives, and student senators and officials from the University of New Hampshire.

The eight long-term objectives (5-year plan) that came out of the planning session were: (1) reduce the incidence of crime, (2) increase quality of service and customer satisfaction, (3) increase availability of grants and alternative funding sources, (4) maintain status as a nationally accredited law enforcement agency, (5) implement a comprehensive equipment replacement program, (6) provide high-quality training for all agency personnel, (7) increase the diversity of agency personnel, and (8) maintain an acceptable workload for police officers (Kurz, 2006, 7–8). For each long-term objective, the plan identifies a performance indicator, target dates for achievement of a series of short-term goals, and a list of strategies the department will use to achieve the objective.

At the end of each year, progress toward accomplishing the vision, mission statement, goals, and objectives should be measured. This may require a change in how performance usually has been assessed. Historically police have measured their failures—the number of crimes committed—and successes—the number of arrests made. Such statistics are relatively easy to gather and to analyze. Assessing the effectiveness of crime prevention efforts, however, is much more difficult. How does a department measure reduced fear of crime or satisfaction with police service? Nonetheless, as the CPC notes: "What gets measured gets done."

In addition to having a realistic time line, the strategic plan must also be tied to the agency's budget. Without the resources to implement the activities outlined in the long-range plan, they are not likely to be accomplished. Again, the transition will take time and, in some instances, additional resources.

DEVELOPING STRATEGIES

Hundreds of strategies have been developed to implement community policing. Among the most common are use of foot, bike, and horse patrols; block watches; newsletters; community surveys; citizen volunteer programs; storefronts; special task units; and educational programs. Another common strategy is to assign officers to permanent beats and teach them community organizing and problem-solving skills. Some communities help teach landlords how to keep their properties crime free. Many communities encourage the development of neighborhood organizations, and some have formed teams (partnerships); for example, code and safety violations might be corrected by a team consisting of police, code enforcers, fire officials, and building code officers. Other communities have turned to the Internet to connect with their citizens.

The Los Angeles Police Department (LAPD) has added a blog (Web log) to its popular Web site that will give real-time, unfiltered information directly to the public ("LAPD Unveils Blog," 2006). Through the blog, the department can directly address rumors or misunderstandings that exist among the public or that are voiced by the media. The site also gives the department a chance to promote the good work of the officers and civilian employees, whose efforts often go unrecognized. The LAPD Web site registers about 1 million hits a day and 30 million a month. Naturally, smaller departments would not expect such impressive results, but even the smallest communities might find a computer expert to volunteer to set up and manage a Web site for the department.

"What works?" "Has somebody tried …?" "What can we do about …?" "Why can't we …?" Such questions are being asked by communities nationwide as they tackle the challenges of reducing violence, drugs, and other crimes and improving homeland security.

The most important consideration in selecting strategies to implement community policing is to ensure that the strategies fit a community's unique needs and resources.

Section III describes numerous strategies that have been used throughout the country as departments move toward community policing.

HIRING AND PROMOTING

Recruiting and selecting personnel are among the most important consider-ations in successfully implementing the community policing philosophy. Pick-ing suitable, adaptable, self-disciplined recruits from the start is far preferable to overhauling and training officers lacking these characteristics (Haberfeld, 2006). Goldstein believes police agencies that hold tight to the traditional "crime fighting" model of policing will have difficulty transitioning to new ways of doing the job, stating: "Of all the changes required, redefining the role of rank-and-file police officers is the most important and has the greatest implications for the future of policing" (*Recruitment and Selection for Community Policing,* n.d.). Officers for the 21st century working in a department that has made the transition to community policing will need different attitudes and skills than those used in the past:

> One frequently discussed way to boost organizational support for community policing over time is to recruit and train a "new breed" of officer. In addition to the skills and abilities traditionally associated with success in police work, community policing demands above-average skills in verbal and written com-munication, the ability to work closely with people from all walks of life, and a strong desire to develop skills in conflict resolution and creative problem solving through collaboration. The challenge for police departments is to reach out and attract individuals who might otherwise not think of police work, such as persons in education and social work fields. (Connors and Webster, 2001, 93)

In a characteristic-based job analysis of what recruits should look like to do community policing effectively, several core competencies were identi-fied, including (1) social competence, (2) teamwork, (3) adaptability/flexibility, (4) conscientiousness/dependability, (5) impulse control/attention to safety, (6) integrity/ethics, (7) emotional regulation and stress tolerance, (8) deci-sion making and judgment, (9) assertiveness/persuasiveness, (10) avoidance of substance abuse and other risk-taking behaviors, and (11) commitment to service/social concern (Scrivner, 2006). In addition to hiring officers who fit the community policing philosophy, departments are increasingly hiring for diversity. The International Association of Chiefs of Police (IACP) launched a Web-based recruiting site called DiscoverPolicing.org in November of 2008. In February 2009 the IACP won the Interactive Media Award's Best in Class for the Web site. The site was honored specifically for excellence in recruiting ("International Association of Chiefs of Police Wins," 2009). DiscoverPolicing .org is a central hiring place designed to recruit the right kind of officers who reflect community diversity. Military call-ups and limited budgets are making it increasingly difficult for agencies to find the officers they need. In addition, agencies need diversity on many levels. Today diversity refers not only to racial and ethnic groups and gender, but also includes religious beliefs, sexual orien-tation, and family background.

Agencies also seek candidates with the skills to complement their com-munity policing and intelligence-oriented policing styles. DiscoverPolicing .com seeks to correct the pervasive, completely inaccurate image of the law enforcement profession fostered by the media and popular culture. The site contains information on all aspects of law enforcement careers: benefits, kinds of agencies and job opportunities, skills and abilities needed, and information about hiring and training. The site also has links and contact information for agencies in all 50 states, allowing applicants to connect with hiring agencies (Kohlhepp and Phillips, 2009).

According to Goldstein, hiring minority officers so the department more closely resembles the community it serves will enhance community problem-oriented policing. Skills needed by officers in a problem-oriented policing environment include:

» Creativity
» Flexibility
» Imagination
» Intelligence
» Ability to function independently
» Problem-solving ability
» Critical reasoning ability
» Conflict mediation ability
» Capacity to relate to others
» Sensitivity to problems of urban life and community organization
» Considering the chief task of the job to be relating to people

In areas where the available pool of candidates is limited and force numbers need to be increased, some departments lower their standards, sacrificing quantity for quality.

TRAINING

Training is critical for a successful transition to community policing. However, "One important organizational function that often gets shortchanged is training. Training is expensive and officers have to be removed from the line—or paid overtime—to attend" (Skogan, 2004a, 163). The CPC recommends that departments embark on a training program for all personnel at all levels to explain the change process and reduce fear and resistance. Training should also explore the community policing philosophy and the planning process and encourage all stakeholders to participate. The consortium advises, however, that training should *not* be the spearhead of change.

 Do *not* make training the spearhead of change.

The consortium says that many efforts have been made to place training at the leading edge of change in both the public and private sectors. Much time and energy are expended in such efforts, but, no matter how effective the training, they will be neutralized if what is learned is at variance with practices and procedures occurring in the department. As the community policing philosophy takes hold in a department, officers will be more receptive to the training they will need to be effective community policing officers.

Among the most important areas to include in training are communication skills, problem-solving skills, and leadership skills.

Communication skills are the focus of Section II. Problem-solving skills were discussed in Chapter 4.

Once hired, new recruits are almost always trained by partnering them with seasoned officers for a few months. It is common for these training officers to influence recruits and their work for the rest of their careers. Most often, the influence includes strong pressure to adopt traditional policing methods and thinking. Recruits are frequently told to "forget what you learned in the academy." No matter what education and training the recruit had prior to hiring, it is frequently replaced with the methods and values of senior officers.

The COPS Office, in conjunction with the Reno (Nevada) Police Department and the Police Executive Research Forum (PERF), has developed a model Police Training Officer program that incorporates contemporary adult educational methods and a version of problem-based learning. The 15-week program begins with a 1-week integration period followed by four 3-week phases: nonemergency incident response, emergency incident response, patrol activities, and criminal investigation. A week between the second and third phase is devoted to midterm evaluation. The last week is devoted to final evaluation.

During each phase, journals (not part of the evaluation) are kept and neighborhood portfolio exercises are completed. The neighborhood portfolio exercises are designed to give trainees a sense of the community as well as to develop community contacts. Each phase also includes weekly coaching and training as well as problem-based learning exercises. According to *PTO: An Overview and Introduction* (n.d., 15): "The program has produced outstanding results. ... New officers enter the field with problem-solving skills that are rarely seen at that career level. New officers also display remarkable leadership and a willingness to work as partners with the local community to fight crime and disorder."

The COPS Office has also funded a network of Regional Community Policing Institutes (RCPIs) across the country to help local law enforcement agencies meet their community policing training needs. RCPIs train not only officers but citizens in the community as well, reaching more than 70,000 individuals each year and offering information on topics such as counterterrorism and homeland security, human trafficking, gangs, school safety, Internet predators, meth labs, domestic violence, cultural diversity, ethics and integrity, rural community policing, community partnerships, technology for community policing, and more ("Regional Community Policing Institutes," 2006).

AN EXAMPLE OF STRATEGIES USED TO IMPLEMENT COMMUNITY POLICING

The Portland (Oregon) Police Bureau's 2007 to 2012 Community Policing Strategic Plan (*Community Policing Strategic Plan*, 2008), shown in Figure 5.3, lists its mission, vision, values, and goals as well as initiatives, plan elements, and strategies (4–6). Although it is a 5-year plan, the bureau sees the plan as evolving each year and, as of mid-2012, was soliciting feedback for its 2012–2017 Strategic Plan.

Figure 5.3   The Portland, Oregon, Police Bureau's 2007 to 2012 Community Policing Strategic Plan

Mission: The mission of the Portland Police Bureau is to reduce crime and the fear of crime by working with all citizens to preserve life, maintain human rights, protect property and promote individual responsibility and community commitment.

Vision: The vision statement is a reflection of an ideal the bureau and community strive for: *Community policing recognizes a shared responsibility and connection between the police and community in making Portland a safer, more livable city. Community policing encourages a problem-solving partnership between citizens and police. This partnership jointly identifies community safety issues, determines resources and applies innovative strategies designed to create and sustain healthy, vital neighborhoods.*

Values: The values of the Portland Police Bureau, adopted in 2004, are commitments to the community and reflect the mission statement: *integrity, compassion, accountability, respect, excellence, service*

Goals:

Community goals

1. Focus efforts on repeat calls for service and chronic offenders

2. Enhance the community and police relationship

Organizational goals

1. Develop and encourage personnel

2. Continuously improve work processes

Initiatives, Plan Elements and Strategies:

The Portland Police Bureau is focusing on the following strategic initiatives that shape the way the police bureau functions:

- *Enhance community policing efforts* to build healthy productive relationships with all Portland communities, particularly with those communities that are underserved.

- *Improve accountability systems* by developing customer service standards for employees and establishing regular employee performance evaluations to provide feedback and mentorship and identify career development opportunities.

- *Recruitment and hiring priorities* to keep up with the retirement "bubble" that occurs every 25 years and to increase diversity.

- *Research new technology* to enhance the Police Bureau's communication tools to reach residents and other first responders.

- *Collaborate with regional and bureau partners* to identify resources and opportunities to improve efficiency in recruitment, hiring and training employees and other operational areas.

- *Design organizational systems and structures* that support efficiency and response.

- *Create a quartermaster unit* that organizes purchases of personnel equipment and uniforms, serves as a liaison to vendors and coordinates recycling equipment efforts.

Plan Elements:

The 2007 to 2012 Community Policing Strategic Plan is designed to incorporate elements of the bureau's annual work plan and tie it more concretely to the annual budget process. All of these reports should acknowledge and cross reference one another. The results will help the Police Bureau move forward and keep the communities we serve informed on our achievements and challenges.

Identifying initiatives, developing innovative strategies and recounting achievements are key elements in providing a successful plan to employees and the community. Other considerations of the plan include preparing for a loss of senior employees, both sworn and nonsworn, and the increasing need to upgrade to new technologies, internally and externally. The bureau needs to clearly and concisely prioritize our work to maximize results.

The structure of this strategic plan is intended to ensure that the 2007 to 2012 Community Policing Strategic Plan is simple to implement, easy to update and able to flex with the reality of day-to-day police work in Portland.

Source: *Community Policing Strategic Plan 2007–2012: A Five-Year Vision.* Portland (Oregon) Police Bureau. Reprinted with permission.

The plan (2008, 7–9) includes initiatives and detailed strategies for each of the bureau's branches. Some branch initiatives to be achieved during the 5-year period include:

» Implement new technology efficiencies
» Build a regional training center
» Establish emergency management capability
» Improve recruiting and hiring efforts
» Increase training capacity
» Improve internal and external communication
» Create an internal system to provide employee feedback and career development opportunities
» Increase new technology for detectives and investigators
» Build relationships with youth and the community
» Engage district officers in problem-solving efforts
» Develop and encourage personnel
» Target chronic locations and offenders

The Portland Police Bureau sought community involvement in developing the plan. They asked the public and bureau employees to comment on which programs were working, which needed improvement, and what strategies the bureau should focus on in the next 5 years. Community members and bureau employees participated in a joint strategic planning workshop and several budget planning workshops.

LESSONS LEARNED FROM TEAM POLICING

Scott (2000, 97) provides a look at team policing and its influence on community policing after some 20 years have passed:

> Team policing, a loose collection of ideas about how the police might more effectively serve the public, is, in hindsight, seen as the precursor to contemporary community policing methods. Several key people, like Patrick Murphy, who advocated team policing methods also would later advocate community policing. Many U.S. police agencies tested and implemented team policing in its various forms in the 1970s and 1980s. ... A number of large and medium-sized police agencies can today attribute geographic decentralization of their operations to team policing initiatives. The decentralization of *authority,* however, which was central to team policing's underlying theories, proved more threatening to many police executives, and did not survive as well as *geographic* decentralization.

> Few people today have declared team policing either an unqualified success or an unqualified failure (Walker, 1993). There is general consensus today that team policing might have been a bit ahead of its time but that many of its premises were and remain sound and that it had sufficient appeal both to the community and to rank-and-file police officers. Indeed, several core features of team policing, such as stability of geographic assignment, unity of command, interaction between police and community, geographic

decentralization of police operations, despecialization of police services, greater responsiveness to community concerns, some decentralization of internal decision making, and at least some shared decision making with the community, are in place in many of today's police agencies. Even when these features fall short of what some might consider optimal, most police managers generally consider them desirable almost 30 years after the advent of team policing.

Walker (1993) suggests that those implementing community policing should take some lessons from what was learned from the team policing programs instituted during the mid-1960s to mid-1970s. Both community policing and team policing had a neighborhood focus, decentralized decision making, community input, and a new police role. The basic goals of community policing differ radically from those of team policing, however, with community policing rejecting the crime-attack model in favor of an emphasis on order maintenance and quality-of-life problems. In addition, the team policing effort faced several major obstacles, including opposition from middle management, who feared losing their power of authority to officers of lower ranks; resentment by officers who felt the more nebulous "team" approach actually created disparate and unfair workloads; and shortcomings with communications technology, as dispatch was routinely unable to contact officers whose duties took them outside the boundaries of their team beat (Walker, 1993). Perhaps the most important lesson to be learned from team policing, however, was that unclear definitions of goals and roles held the greatest potential to thwart the successful implementation of community policing. Because community policing represents a radical redefinition of the traditional police role—from that of crime fighter to problem solver and public service provider—it requires resocializing not only the officers involved but also the public they serve (Walker, 1993).

The most important lesson to be learned from team policing, according to Walker (1993), was the problem associated with unclear definition of goals.

BENEFITS THAT MIGHT BE ACHIEVED FROM COMMUNITY POLICING

The benefits of implementing community policing are numerous, to the department, to individual officers, and to the community at large. Community policing brings police closer to the people, building relationships between police and community and among community members themselves. As police interaction with the community becomes more positive, productive partnerships are formed and community and officer leadership skills are developed. Citizens see that problems have solutions, and this gives citizens courage to tackle other community issues. As citizens feel more empowered to get involved, prevention and detection of crime increases, leading to reduced fear of crime in the community and improved quality of life. Reduced levels of crime allow more police resources to be allocated to services that have the greatest impact on the quality of community life. Making effective use of the talents and resources available within communities further extends severely strained police resources. Community policing also provides real challenges for officers, making them more

ON THE BEAT

Our department implemented the community policing model back in the mid-1990s. Because this model has been used by our department for more than a decade, many of our current officers never had to go through the transition to COP. Community policing is the only model they have ever known.

As an officer who works under this model, I see many community benefits, one being that communication between the police and community members is strengthened. Another benefit is that the quality of life for our citizens has improved because we take an active role in helping resolve many "livability" issues. Officers are often called to resolve a dispute between neighbors, and we take these concerns seriously. We are able to improve the quality of life for many residents by assisting

them in resolving their neighborhood problems. Finally, I see that COP fosters support and trust from the community. This is of utmost importance because it promotes satisfaction among residents, who then share the view that the police are partners with citizens rather than adversaries of them. These are just a few of the many benefits I see with the community policing model.

Communication, quality of life, satisfaction, and trust are all positive effects of policing with a proactive mindset. Gone are the days of showing up for a call and simply taking a police report. The community policing approach allows for creativity and empowers citizens and police to share in the responsibilities of keeping a community safe.

—*Kim Czapar*

than "order takers and report writers," which leads to increased job satisfaction among officers.

RESISTANCE TO COMMUNITY POLICING

Despite the many advantages and benefits presented by the community policing approach, resistance will be encountered and should be anticipated.

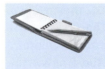

Managers should anticipate and prepare for resistance to the community policing philosophy and the changes that accompany the transition.

Consider the following analogy: A professional truck driver does not drive his 50-ton trailer-truck the same way he drives a sports car. In the truck, he corners more slowly and avoids braking sharply; otherwise, the trailer's momentum could cause the truck to overturn or jackknife. Police organizations also have considerable momentum, and many officers find a high degree of comfort in sticking to the status quo.

Kennedy (2006, 164) observes: "Law enforcement likes enforcing the law." And, as are most humans, police are creatures of habit. Law enforcement officers most readily accept change in small, incremental doses, including

Ideas in Practice

ALISON NEIGHBORHOOD INITIATIVE

(Category: Population over 250,000—Waterloo Regional Police Service, Ontario, Canada)

Population Served: 500,000

In 2006 when the chief of the Waterloo Regional Police Service (WRPS) received a letter from a Muslim resident titled, "Unrest in the Community," that described a crisis due to ethnic tensions in Cambridge, Ontario, Canada, a catalyst was launched. That catalyst inspired police and community members to overcome barriers and learn the power of collaboration and the value of small change. The police collaborated with Muslim community leaders, the Cambridge YMCA, Waterloo Regional Housing, and the City of Cambridge to create a long-term plan that aimed to develop relationships based on trust and inclusivity, to create training opportunities around cultural diversity, and to maintain a safe community.

The WRPS wanted the Muslim community to feel confident the police would respond to their concerns, would involve them in the investigative process, and would be sensitive to their cultural heritage. WRPS hoped to change the negative perception the community may have had about the police because of the way the police were perceived in their countries of origin. Because this initiative created an equal partner with the Muslim community, this initiative had support from the rest of the community.

In 2009, a collaborative event took place at the Islamic Center as a sign of the new partnership, the badging of new police recruits. At this event, two student winners presented their inspiring essays on "What Do Police Officers Bring to Our Community?" The news of this event brought such a stream of letters of support from the community that they were able to fund an outreach coordinator. WRPS realized that the police are not experts at everything, and there are many people with talents, skills, and connections that can be used when developing and implementing an action plan. However, the most important lesson WRPS learned was that they have a great deal more to learn from the community, and they will keep adapting their agency to the needs of the community.

Source: *IACP Community Policing Awards (Sponsored by Cisco): 2011 Winners and Finalists.* San Jose, CA: Cisco Systems, Inc. 2011. Retrieved June 1, 2012 from http://www.iacpcommunitypolicing.org/download/brochure_C02-690744_FINAL.pdf

"innovations that require the least radical departures from their hierarchical paramilitary organizational structures, continue incident-driven and reactive strategies, and maintain police sovereignty over crime issues. In its most basic form, hot spots policing simply concentrates traditional enforcement activity at high crime places" (Braga and Weisburd, 2007, 17). Other strategies, such as pulling levers or broken windows policing, also appeal to police because they permit officers to use mostly traditional tactics but deploy them in new ways that provide greater efficiency, effectiveness, and, consequently, better results: "It is not remarkable that the strategies that require the most radical changes to existing police practices and structures report the greatest difficulties in implementation. Nonetheless, the available evidence indicates a gradual transformation in police attitudes towards adopting these new strategies. In addition to the widespread reporting of innovative police practices across the United States, police officers' views towards the community and problem-oriented policing philosophy are becoming more positive" (Braga and Weisburd, 2007, 18).

If resistance to change is caused in part by concerns about community policing, these concerns may be somewhat allayed by changes in the communication process of the organization. Resistance can be reduced by positive communication from the chief or head of the agency, geared toward increasing readiness for change by providing information to reduce uncertainty and anxiety (Community Policing Consortium, 2000).

Impediments to COP implementation include:
- Organizational impediments—resistance from middle management, line officers, and unions; confusion about what COP is; problems in line-level accountability; officers' concerns that COP is "soft" on crime; lack of COP training
- Union impediments—resistance to change, fear of losing control to the community, resistance to increased officer responsibility and accountability, and fear that COP will lead to civilian review boards
- Community impediments—community resistance, community's concern that COP is "soft" on crime, civil service rules, pressure to demonstrate that COP reduces crime, and lack of support from local government
- Transition impediments—balancing increased foot patrol activities with maintaining emergency response time

PITFALLS TO AVOID

In making the transition to community policing, there are several pitfalls to avoid.

Common pitfalls in making the transition to community policing include unrealistic expectations and focusing on short-term instead of long-term results; adopting a task force approach; resisting the move toward community empowerment; taking advantage of the position; and misrepresenting an inadequate program as legitimate in order to receive funding.

Reconciling Expectations and Results

One pitfall is the common expectation that implementing a new strategy such as community policing, highly touted as an effective method of crime reduction, will have immediate and measurable results. It may have immediate results—but not the ones citizens were expecting. Ironically, increased citizen vigilance and reporting, although a desirable and positive outcome of successful community policing, may initially indicate an *increase* in crime and lead to disappointment and widespread skepticism regarding community policing's effectiveness. Such misunderstandings, generated by ambiguous promises, can sabotage a department's efforts to build the relationships with citizens necessary for community policing. Before making predictions and promises regarding community policing's long-term benefits, make sure everyone understands the possible short-term outcomes.

The Specialized Unit Approach

Another pitfall is management's inability to gain the commitment of the entire organization by encouraging officers to become specialists instead of generalists. This often occurs when an agency adopts a specialized unit approach, isolating acceptance of the philosophy to those in the community policing unit. As one reviewer commented: "Marginalizing COPPS [Community Oriented Policing and Problem Solving] in a separate unit or single district is essentially to doom the initiative to failure." Isolation has nearly always happened when specialized units have been formed. The area of crime prevention in agencies has almost always been the responsibility of specialized units. This usually resulted in a shift in thinking of officers, such that they felt preventing crime was the job of those few personnel assigned to the unit. It is not uncommon for an officer, when asked by a citizen how to prevent being burglarized, for example, to respond by telling the citizen to contact someone in the crime prevention unit.

There has also been a tendency for officers not assigned to specialized units to minimize such units' importance, claiming their own assignment was "real police work" and everything else was essentially unimportant. In some cases, officers assigned to special units became discounted and ignored by their colleagues as irrelevant and not part of the group.

Resisting the Move toward Community Empowerment

Lansing, Michigan, has had a citywide neighborhood-watch program in effect for more than 20 years with 151 watches serving more than 11,500 households. As part of a department reorganization designed to make officers "more accessible to the citizens they serve and enhance communication and problem-solving potential," the police department began working to strengthen neighborhood-watch groups in the southern part of the city, where they were less organized and active.

Problem-solving teams were formed that included a sergeant and officers from each shift as well as several watch coordinators from this part of the city. At team meetings, the sergeants explained the department reorganization to the coordinators and solicited feedback on the watch program and the department reorganization. The neighborhood-watch coordinators shared some of their concerns about the watch program. There was an information line, updated four times a week, with information on crimes occurring the previous day. Coordinators believed the information line was insufficient and not specific enough to be useful. After discussing how the information line could be improved, the teams developed an anonymous survey to gather information from the 91 coordinators in the southern part of the city.

The survey used a combination of Likert scales, dichotomous (yes/no) fill-in values, and open-ended questions. Surveys were mailed with a cover letter explaining the purpose, with self-addressed stamped envelopes for returning them to the police department. The teams had a response rate of 63 percent of completed surveys. The data were analyzed, and a committee of neighborhood-watch coordinators and a police sergeant reviewed the results and made recommendations for improving the program. The survey revealed that nearly half of the respondents (48%) rated the performance of their team as "unknown."

The results showed a correlation between a coordinator having contact with a team officer and the coordinator's positive feelings toward a team approach to problem solving. Conversely, a lack of communication between the police organization and the citizenry was shown to be a primary reason for lack of support by watch coordinators. The committee made several creative and useful recommendations for improving the neighborhood-watch program, including:

» That neighborhood-watch teams have a separate voice mailbox at the police department to provide specific crime information about each team area

» That coordinators attend the officers' monthly team meetings so that they could discuss neighborhood problems with team members and improve communication with the officers

» That coordinators "ride along" with their team officers to get a better idea of what the officers do every day

» That the department start a neighborhood-watch mentor program to assist in developing new watches

As a result, the police department continues to involve coordinators in the decision-making process to continue improving communications between officers and citizens.

According to Lansing Mayor David Hollister: "Decentralization of the police department is not being done as an end in itself; it is being done to help foster open and honest communication between the police officers and the citizens they serve." This kind of open communication often leads to identifying and solving problems.

ADVANTAGES AND DISADVANTAGES OF IMPLEMENTATION MODELS

Many agencies have numerous specialized units, so it is understandable that when they seek to implement community policing they do so by creating specialized community policing agencies (Scheider, 2008). Other agencies use community policing generalists, assigning responsibility for community policing to all officers, and still others use a combination of these two approaches (hybrid).

Community Policing Specialists

Having dedicated officers assigned full time to community policing has several advantages:

» Officers have sufficient time to devote to proactive problem-solving and partnership-building efforts.

» It is easier for agencies to develop the knowledge and skills needed to maximize efforts.

» The visibility of community policing activities both within the department and in the community is increased.

Specialized units, however, also have disadvantages, such as causing resentment among other officers who believe the units receive special treatment and their activities are not real police work (calling them "grin and wave squads"). Further, specialized units might lead the majority of officers to believe they are not responsible for developing partnerships, using problem-solving activities, or paying attention to community relations. Such units also limit the number of officers receiving community policing training, making it unlikely that community policing will grow beyond the special unit.

Community Policing Generalists

Community policing advocates (such as the COPS Office) generally support the agency-wide implementation of community policing, seeing community policing as a philosophy that should influence all aspects of police work. Adopting a community policing generalist model removes potential tension between a special unit and the other officers. This model also has other advantages: It emphasizes proactive problem solving and partnership development to all officers and builds these activities into their jobs.

» It applies community policing principles to all aspects of police business, including routine patrol, investigations, arrests, and traffic stops.

» It increases the potential scope and breadth of community policing efforts and facilitates its eventual institutionalization.

A disadvantage of the generalist model is that it can result in a watered-down version of community policing (more community relations than community policing), with officers devoting limited time to partnership building and problem solving. If officers do not see such activities as integrated into their current duties, they might see them as extra work and resist implementing them. In fact, officers often report they have insufficient time for community policing and will resist agency-wide implementation. Finally, it can be difficult for large agencies to provide adequate training to large enough numbers of officers to fully implement the community policing philosophy. To overcome concerns, some agencies have implemented a community policing model combining the specialized and generalist models.

Hybrid Approaches

Some agencies have formed special community policing units while encouraging all officers to participate in their efforts. For example, a special unit might engage in in-depth problem-solving efforts for a precinct or an entire city, but at the same time, agency leaders may make it clear that some problem-solving activities are expected of *all* officers focused on a specific neighborhood or even a single address. All officers are encouraged to rely on the special unit for help in implementing their own community policing efforts. Finally, all officers can receive appropriate training in community policing tailored to their positions.

EVALUATING PROGRESS

As the CPC warns, without specifying desired outcomes as part of the strategic plan, the community policing initiative could be reduced to another series of community relations exercises rather than the anticipated cultural, organizational, and structural changes achieved through community policing in partnership and problem solving. Recall from Chapter 4 that the SARA (scanning, analysis, response, and assessment) model of problem solving shows that there are no failures, only responses that do not provide the desired goal. Remember also from Chapter 4 the mental lock: "To err is wrong." Avoid this thinking trap by understanding that risk-taking is a necessary part of progress and that erring is wrong only if you fail to learn from your "mistake." Edison is quoted as saying he did not fail 25,000 times to make a storage battery. He simply knew 25,000 ways *not* to make one.

Evaluating progress can take many forms. It should have been built into the strategic plan in concrete form. Which goals and objectives have been met? Which have not? Why not? The evaluation might also consist of conducting a second needs assessment of both the department and the community a year later to determine whether needs are being better met. It can be done through additional surveys and interviews assessing reduced fear of crime and improved confidence in police. Are citizens making fewer complaints regarding police service? Are officers filing fewer grievances?

When evaluating, failures should be as important as successes—sometimes more important—because a department learns from what does not work.

Evaluating effectiveness is difficult. Police have long been able to evaluate their efficiency by looking at police activity—what police do rather than what effect it had. It is far easier to look at numbers—crime reports filed, arrests made, tickets issued, drugs seized—than to measure how problems have been solved. Measuring effectiveness requires that "performance indicators need to be carefully thought through and some pioneering undertaken to establish realistic and meaningful measures. These indicators need to be responsive to community concerns and reflect the accomplishments of the community policing philosophy and strategies. They involve devising new output measures reflecting police capability to adapt, to consult, to mobilize, to diagnose, and to solve problems" (Community Policing Consortium, 2000).

SUMMARY

Community policing will require a change in management style, mission statement, departmental organization, and the general approach to fighting crime. A department's vision should include the essential elements of the community policing philosophy: problem solving, empowerment, forming community partnerships, and being proactive—making preventing crime as important as enforcing the law.

A needs assessment should include not only the department but also the community of which it is a part. The traditional law enforcement organization design has been that of a pyramid-shaped hierarchy based on a military model. However, the pyramid might be inverted to implement community policing. Another change might occur in leadership style, with a preference for participatory leadership, where each individual has a voice in decisions but top management still has the ultimate decision-making authority.

It may be more important and effective for COP agencies to target a critical mass of individuals—the smallest number of citizens and organizations needed to support and sustain the community policing initiative—than to try to mobilize the entire community.

The strategic plan should include community partnerships and problem solving as well as any needed cultural and organizational changes in the department. It should also include a realistic time line and ways to assess progress. It must also be tied to the department's budget. The most important consideration in selecting strategies to implement community policing is to ensure that the strategies fit the community's unique needs and resources.

Training is also critical for a successful transition to community policing. However, do *not* make training the spearhead of change. Among the most important areas to include in training are communication skills, problem-solving skills, and leadership skills.

Managers should anticipate and prepare for resistance to the community policing philosophy and the changes that accompany the transition. They should also be aware of and try to avoid common pitfalls in making the transition to community policing, including unrealistic expectations and focusing on short-term instead of long-term results; adopting a task force approach; resisting the move toward community empowerment; taking advantage of the position; and misrepresenting an inadequate program as legitimate to receive funding.

Impediments to COP implementation include organizational, union, community, and transition impediments. Organization impediments may include resistance from middle management, line officers, and unions; confusion about what COP is; problems in line-level accountability; officers' concern that COP is soft on crime; and lack of COP training. Union impediments may include resistance to change, fear of losing control to the community, resistance to increased officer responsibility and accountability, and fear that COP will lead to civilian review boards. Community impediments may include community resistance, community's concern that COP is "soft" on crime, civil service rules, pressure to demonstrate COP reduces crime, and lack of support from local government. Transition impediments may include balancing increased foot patrol activities with maintaining emergency response time.

When evaluating, failures should be as important as successes—sometimes more important—because a department learns from what does not work.

DISCUSSION QUESTIONS

1. What do you consider the greatest obstacles to implementing community policing?
2. If you had to prioritize the changes needed to convert to community policing, what would your priorities be?
3. Find out what your police department's mission statement is. If it is not community policing focused, how would you revise it?
4. How would you determine whether community policing efforts are working?
5. Why might citizens not want to become involved in community policing efforts?
6. Why is a diverse law enforcement agency important? What ideas do you have for recruiting with this in mind?
7. How would you go about assessing your community's needs regarding efforts to reduce crime and violence?
8. Are there conflicting groups within your "community"? Does one group have more political power than another?
9. Can you explain why some police officers oppose community policing?
10. Name at least three attributes that would indicate a job candidate might be a good fit for a department engaged in community policing.

GALE EMERGENCY SERVICES DATABASE ASSIGNMENTS

ONLINE Database

- Use the Gale Emergency Services Database to help answer the Discussion Questions as appropriate.
- Find and outline two articles that discuss strategic planning. Do they suggest the same approach? If not, how do they differ?
- Research and take notes on how an administrator can build support within the department and the community.
- Outline two articles on leadership, one from a law enforcement journal and one from a business journal. Give the complete citation for each. Compare the contents of the two articles.

REFERENCES

Braga, Anthony A. and David L. Weisburd. 2007 (May). "Police Innovation and Crime Prevention: Lessons Learned from Police Research over the Past 20 Years." Unpublished paper presented at the National Institute of Justice (NIJ) Policing Research Workshop: Planning for the Future, Washington, DC. (Document No. 218585) https://www.ncjrs.gov/pdffiles1/nij/grants/218585.pdf

Broken Arrow Police Department Leadership Team. 2006. "How to Implement Shared Leadership." *The Police Chief* 73 (4): 34–37.

Changing Roles: Supervising Today's Community Police Officer. 2004 (September). (Course Manual). St. Petersburg, FL: Florida Regional Community Policing Institute and COPS. http://cop.spcollege.edu/training/supervising/chaningroles.pdf

Community Policing Consortium. 2000. *The Police Organization in Transition: Organization and Framework.* Washington, DC: Community Policing Consortium.

Community Policing Strategic Plan 2007–2012: A Five-Year Vision. 2008 (May). Portland (Oregon) Police Bureau. http://www.portlandonline.com/police/index.cfm?c=29866&a=196743

Connors, Edward and Barbara Webster. 2001 (January). *Transforming the Law Enforcement Organization to Community Policing.* (Final Monograph). Unpublished report prepared for the National Institute of Justice, Washington, DC. https://www.ncjrs.gov/pdffiles1/nij/grants/200610.pdf

Correia, Mark E. 2000. *Citizen Involvement: How Community Factors Affect Progressive Policing.* Washington, DC: Police Executive Research Forum.

Davis, Marcia. 1998 (March). *Community Policing and Law Enforcement.* Washington, DC: U.S. Department of Agriculture, Office of Community Development, OCD Technote 14.

Goldstein, Herman. 1990. *Problem-Oriented Policing.* Philadelphia: McGraw-Hill.

Haberfeld, M. R. 2006. *Police Leadership,* Upper Saddle River, NJ: Pearson/Prentice Hall.

Harr, J. Scott and Kären M. Hess. 2010. *Seeking Employment in Criminal Justice and Related Fields.* 6th ed. Belmont, CA: Wadsworth.

Hess, Kären M. and Christine H. Orthmann. 2012. *Management and Supervision in Law Enforcement.* 6th ed. Clifton Park, NY: Delmar Cengage Learning.

"International Association of Chiefs of Police Wins the 2008 Interactive Media Awards Best in Class for the Discover Policing Web Site." 2009 (February 25). Alexandria, VA: Matrix Group. http://www.matrixgroup.net/news-events/news/?fa=newsItem&articleId=286

Kennedy, David M. 2006. "Chapter 8: Old Wine in New Bottles: Policing and the Lessons of Pulling Levers." In *Police Innovation: Contrasting Perspectives,* edited by David L. Weisburd and Anthony A. Braga, 155–170. New York: Cambridge University Press.

Kohlhepp, Kim and Tracy Phillips. 2009. "DiscoverPolicing.org: A Nationwide Online Recruiting Resource for the Law Enforcement Profession." *The Police Chief* 76 (1).

Kurz, David L. 2006. "Strategic Planning: Building Police–Community Partnerships in Small Towns." *Big Ideas for Small Police Departments* (Summer): 1–9.

"Los Angeles Police Department News Release: LAPD Unveils Blog." 2006. *Los Angeles Times,* May 12. http://lapdonline.org/may_2006/news_view/29954

McEwen, Tom, Deborah Spence, Russell Wolff, Julie Wartell, and Barbara Webster. 2003 (July). *Call Management and Community Policing: A Guidebook for Law Enforcement.* Washington, DC: Office of Community Oriented Policing Services.

National Research Council. 2004. *Fairness and Effectiveness in Policing: The Evidence.* Committee to Review Research on Police Policy and Practices. Wesley Skogan and Kathleen Frydl, editors. Committee on Law and Justice, Division of Behavioral and Social Sciences and Education. Washington, DC: The National Academies Press, 2004.

Newburn, Tim. 2008. *Handbook of Policing.* Devon, UK: Willan.

PTO: An Overview and Introduction. n.d. Washington, DC: Police Executive Research Forum and the COPS Office. http://cops.usdoj.gov/CDROMs/PTO/pubs/CaseStudiesPDF3.pdf

Recruitment and Selection for Community Policing. n.d. (Monograph). Washington, DC: Community Policing Consortium.

"Regional Community Policing Institutes." 2006 (January 9). (Fact sheet.) Washington, DC: Office of Community Oriented Policing Services. http://www.cops.usdoj.gov/Publications/e01063526b.pdf

Scheider, Matthew. 2008. "Community Policing Nugget: Community Policing Specialists vs. Generalists." *Community Policing Dispatch* 1 (4).

Scott, Michael S. 2000 (October). *Problem-Oriented Policing: Reflections on the First 20 Years.* Washington, DC: Community Oriented Policing Services.

Scrivner, Ellen. 2006. *Innovations in Police Recruitment and Hiring: Hiring in the Spirit of Diversity.* Washington, DC: Office of Community Oriented Policing Services.

Skogan, Wesley G. 2004a. "Community Policing: Common Impediments to Success." In *Community Policing: The Past, Present, and Future*, edited by Lorie Fridell and Mary Ann Wycoff, 159–167. Washington, DC: The Annie E. Casey Foundation and the Police Executive Research Forum.

Skogan, Wesley G. 2004b. "Representing the Community in Community Policing." In *Community Policing (Can It Work?)*, edited by Wesley G. Skogan, 57–75. Belmont, CA: Wadsworth.

Walker, Samuel. 1993. "Does Anyone Remember Team Policing? Lessons of the Team Policing Experience for Community Policing." *American Journal of Police* 12 (1): 33–56.

Wuestewald, Todd and Brigitte Steinheider. 2006a. "Can Empowerment Work in Police Organizations?" *The Police Chief* 73 (1): 48–55.

Wuestewald, Todd and Brigitte Steinheider. 2006b. "The Changing Face of Police Leadership." *The Police Chief* 73 (4): 26–33.

ADDITIONAL RESOURCES

Community Policing Consortium
www.communitypolicing.org
COPS Office (Department of Justice)
www.cops.usdoj.gov
Justice Information Center
www.justiceinformationcenter.us
National Center for Community Policing
www.cj.msu.edu/~people/cp
Police Executive Research Forum
www.policeforum.org
Upper Midwest Community Policing Institute
www.umcpi.org

CourseMate

This available CourseMate has an interactive eBook and interactive learning tools, including flash cards, quizzes, and more. To learn more about this resource and access free demo CourseMate resources, go to **www.cengagebrain.com**, and search for this book. To access CourseMate materials that you have purchased, go to **login.cengagebrain.com**.

Building Relationships and Trust

CHAPTERS IN THIS SECTION

With the basic background supplied in Section I, you are ready to look at the interaction occurring between the police and the public they serve and protect. At the most basic level, police–community relations begin with one-on-one interaction between an officer and a citizen.

The section begins with a discussion of the communication skills needed to interact effectively with citizens, including with the increasingly diverse populace of the United States and with victims and witnesses (Chapter 6). Next, building partnerships with key stakeholders and selling the concept of community policing, both internally and externally, are explored (Chapter 7). The section concludes with a look at building partnerships with the media and how the media can also collaborate in selling the concept (Chapter 8).

Although these crucial components of community policing are discussed separately, overlap often exists.

© AP Photo/The Daily Oakland Press, Vaughn Gurganian

CHAPTER 6
Communicating with a Diverse Population

What we are communicates far more eloquently than anything we say or do. There are people we trust because we know their character. Whether they're eloquent or not, whether they have human-relations techniques or not, we trust them and work with them.

—Stephen R. Covey

DO YOU KNOW ...

» What the communication process consists of?

» What individual characteristics are important in the communication process?

» What two critical barriers to communication in a diverse society are?

» Why police officers may have more barriers to communication than other professionals, and what these barriers consist of?

» What dilemma law enforcement officers face when interacting with immigrants?

» What is needed to avoid discrimination?

» The difference between prejudice and discrimination?

» What disabilities police officers frequently encounter?

» What disabilities can mimic intoxication or a drug high?

» What special challenges are posed by persons suffering from Alzheimer's disease?

» What youths with special needs police officers should be familiar with?

» Why communicating effectively with victims of and witnesses to crime is essential?

CAN YOU DEFINE ...

acculturation
Alzheimer's disease (AD)
Americans with Disabilities Act (ADA)
assimilation
attention deficit hyperactivity disorder (ADHD)
bias
communication process
crack children
crisis behavior
EBD
ethnocentrism
fetal alcohol syndrome (FAS)
jargon
kinesics
nonverbal communication
posttraumatic stress disorder (PTSD)
poverty syndrome
racial profiling
stereotyping

INTRODUCTION

A woman executive at a shopping center discovered a minor theft of company property from her company car. The car had been parked outside a police office where several traffic officers took breaks between shifts. The office was not accessible to the public but had an identification sign on the locked door.

The woman knocked on the door and asked the sergeant who opened it who was responsible for watching the parking area. She also commented on the officers she could see sitting inside the room and suggested they were not doing their jobs. The officers in the room stopped talking with each other and turned their attention to the conversation at the office door.

The sergeant and the woman never got around to discussing the missing item. Instead he responded to her comments with questions. "What do you mean by that?" "What are you trying to say?" She left to tell her supervisor, refusing to file a police report. She soon returned, however, and encountered another officer just outside the office. Their conversation, later characterized as "heated" by witnesses, centered on the woman's suggestion that the officers should do more to prevent theft in the parking lot. She implied they were lazy and shirked their responsibilities.

At this point the woman asked to file a police report, and the officer asked her to enter the police office with him to do so. They entered the office, but when the officer suggested they enter a private office away from the hubbub of the break area, she refused to do so. She later said the officer intimidated her by slamming drawers, moving quickly, and ordering her into the room. She feared being alone with him.

The officer's perception of the incident was entirely different. He commented that the woman had a "chip on her shoulder" and an "attitude." She was demanding, and dealing with her was "impossible."

After refusing to enter the office to file the report, the woman sat down on a chair in the break area. She was told to either go into the other room and file the report or to leave. When she refused to do either, she was escorted from the office and left outside the locked doors. The woman filed a complaint against the police department.

With better communication, this problem and thousands like it could be avoided. Effective communication with the public is vital to good police–community relations. In fact, at the heart of police–community relations are the one-on-one interactions between an officer and a citizen: "Communication is essential to the development of partnerships that make community policing an effective strategy for ensuring public safety. Community policing programs, in which law enforcement officers partner with community members to identify and solve problems, cannot work well when officers and residents fail to understand each other" (Shah and Estrada, 2011, 5). Effective communication becomes even more challenging as our society becomes more diverse, requiring an understanding not only of the communication process but also of the differences among individuals that affect communication.

This chapter begins with a discussion of the communication process, including nonverbal communication and body language, communication barriers, and active listening. Then the discussion turns to community policing in a diverse society, beginning with a description of the multicultural diversity in the United States, including racial and ethnic diversity. Next, racism is discussed, including racial disparity, racial profiling, and strategies to overcome barriers based on racial or ethnic differences. Religious and socioeconomic diversities are examined briefly, with more extensive attention paid to persons in the lower socioeconomic class, the homeless, and the powerful and privileged. The discussion of diversity concludes with a consideration of the challenges facing police as they strive to "serve and protect" an increasingly diverse society. The third major area of discussion is communicating effectively with individuals with disabilities, including those with physical and mental disabilities, and interacting with elderly persons and youths. The final discussion focuses on communicating with victims of and witnesses to crime.

Keep in mind while reading this chapter that although various groups are presented separately to keep the discussion organized, in real life it is rare for individuals to be neatly compartmentalized. Americans embody every overlapping combination of diversity characteristics imaginable—from the young Hispanic girl who is deaf, to the middle-aged Jewish man who is homeless, to the elderly black woman with bipolar disorder.

THE COMMUNICATION PROCESS

Communication is basically the transfer of information.

communication process

Involves a sender, a message, a channel, a receiver, and, sometimes, feedback.

 The **communication process** involves a sender, a message, a channel, a receiver, and, sometimes, feedback.

Communication involves transferring thoughts from one person's mind to another's. The people involved, the accuracy of the message in expressing the sender's thoughts, and the channel used all affect communication. A simplified illustration of the process is shown in Figure 6.1.

Figure 6.1   The Communication Process

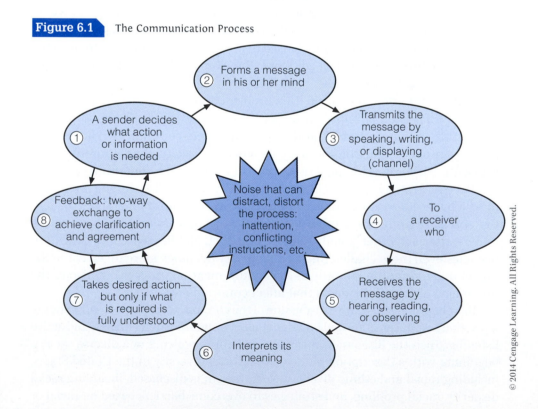

The sender encodes the message in words—spoken or written—and then transmits the message by phone, by texting, by fax, by letter, in person, or in some other way. The receiver decodes the message. The receiver may then provide the sender with some kind of feedback indicating the message has been received. Many factors will influence the message.

Important individual characteristics in communication include age, education, gender, values, emotional involvement, self-esteem, and language skills.

Surprisingly, police departments rarely train their officers in communication skills. They assume that the people they hire know how to communicate. It is an erroneous assumption. The Rand report, "Training the Twenty-First Century Police Officer: Redefining Police Professionalism for the Los Angeles Police Department," notes: "To communicate effectively is to be skilled in the overt and the subtle, to make one's intentions known whether the recipient is deaf, unable to understand English, mentally handicapped, enraged, under the influence of drugs or alcohol, or simply unfamiliar with normal police procedure" (Glenn et al., 2003, 120). Skilled officers can communicate effectively even when they are under tremendous stress. The skill is critical for successfully gaining compliance or cooperation from subjects and for managing situations where arrest, search and seizure, or use of force scenarios that are "intricately related" are required.

Nonetheless, "Tactical communications as currently taught are too limited in scope and poorly integrated with other instruction. Officers need to learn how, when, and with what type of person certain communication techniques are more effective. This is particularly important when deadly force might be applied. A person who does not understand English or a person with a mental illness might inadvertently send aggressive signals to the officer. The officer needs to be adept at selecting from and effectively applying various modes of communication, verbal and nonverbal, under conditions of extreme stress" (Glenn et al., 2003, 136).

The late Dr. George Thompson, the name behind the effective and popular police training company the Verbal Judo Institute, asserted that the use of courtesy and respect is the safest and most powerful way for police officers to interact with even dangerous or explosive members of the public (2009). Thompson, a college English professor who became a cop, called the technique *tactical civility*. According to Dr. Thompson, when officers respond to verbal attacks in kind, they give up their own personal and professional power and allow themselves to be controlled by others. A display of anger also reveals weakness and indecision, something most officers cannot afford to show in public. If officers react with rudeness or threatening comments, they put the other person on notice of pending attack, a tactical mistake.

Thompson recommended officers not give such an early warning but just remain civil, get tough if necessary, and return to civility. Politeness does not equal weakness, but the other person may mistake it for that, causing him or her to play into an officer's hands. An officer who can maintain a courteous manner, even in the face of extreme rudeness, will only benefit from such self-control, particularly down the road when an encounter may be brought into court or scrutinized by a supervisor or internal affairs (IA) division. Regardless of the temptation: "Don't use words that will betray you later" (Thompson, 2009).

Community policing can only work if officers handle people with dignity and respect. This mandate often becomes more challenging in those neighborhoods where residents live in fear of crime and are reluctant to "get involved" if they see something that requires a police response: "The people in affluent, successful America do not want a police presence, except indirectly. The people who *need* us bar their windows and hope for the best" (Thompson, 2006). The "gap" between the police and many areas in the community needs to be eliminated. If that gap can be closed, offenders have nowhere to commit their crimes. In communities where people see the police as protectors, they work in concert with the police to "take out the bad guys."

In a democracy, an effective police force requires the consent and cooperation of the citizens (Giles et al., 2005). When that consent and cooperation exist, witnesses to crimes willingly come forward with information; citizens are more likely to follow police directives in an emergency; and citizens are also more likely to support the police legislatively—for example, in increasing funding for police departments.

How can that consent and cooperation be achieved? Research has found that police are most likely to obtain cooperation if they engage in *process-oriented policing*—that is, they are attentive to the way they treat people, behaving in ways that positively influence the degree to which people perceive the procedures used as fair. Several elements influence people's judgments regarding fairness of procedures (Skogan and Frydl, 2004). One key element is participation; procedures are perceived as fairer if people are allowed to explain their situation. A second key element is neutrality. Evidence of evenhandedness and objectivity increases perceived fairness. Third, people value being treated with dignity and respect. Finally, people perceive procedures as being fairer when they trust the motives of decision makers.

Treating people fairly with dignity and respect involves not only the words officers speak but also their nonverbal messages.

Nonverbal Communication and Body Language

nonverbal communication

Includes everything other than the actual words spoken in a message, such as tone, pitch, and pacing.

Nonverbal communication includes everything except the actual words spoken in a message, such as tone, pitch, and pacing. Body language refers to messages conveyed by how a person moves. To test the power of body language, consider what the following actions say about a person:

» Walking—fast, slow, stomping
» Posture—rigid, relaxed
» Eye contact—direct, indirect, shifting
» Gestures—nod, shrug, finger point
» Physical spacing—close, distant

Police officers' nonverbal communication was discussed in Chapter 2. Officers communicate with the public most obviously through the uniforms they wear and the equipment they carry. Other forms of body language are equally important. How officers stand, how they look at those to whom they are talking, whether they smile or frown—all convey a message.

Eye contact is a powerful nonverbal communication tool. Eye contact inspires trust and shows confidence, even if it is merely the illusion of confidence. It can buy you time if you are caught off guard and need to form a response. Eye contact quietly keeps control while deftly wielding power.

Usually, police officers want to convey the impression that they "know their way around." However, this may actually interfere with effective communication. When interviewing a truthful witness, police officers may want to modify their body language and soften their language. A relaxed manner may result in more in-depth communication and better understanding.

In addition to understanding nonverbal messages, many police officers develop an ability to interpret body language, also called **kinesics**, to such an extent that they can tell when a person is lying or about to become aggressive or flee. This is what some call a "sixth sense," and it alerts officers when something is not as it appears or when someone is suspicious, untruthful, afraid or hesitant.

kinesics
The study of body movement or body language.

Criminals are often apprehended because an officer thought they looked suspicious or because something did not feel right about a traffic stop or other contact. Many law enforcement officers develop an uncanny ability to spot stolen cars in traffic based on a driver's actions and driving maneuvers. Officers also learn to read their own hunches. Acting on a hunch can save lives. Police officers can tell story after story of nagging and intuitive feelings on which they acted.

Barriers to Communication

Law enforcement officers must be aware of communication barriers that exist in the United States' increasingly diverse society.

 Two critical barriers to communication in a diverse society are language barriers and cultural barriers.

In the United States, more than 55 million people aged 5 and older—20 percent of the country's population—speak a language other than English at home, and for 62 percent of this group, that language is Spanish (Shin and Kominski, 2010). Approximately half of the individuals who speak another language at home report that they speak English "very well." The flip side to this is that the other half, or more than 25 million U.S. residents, need a degree of English assistance in some situations. An estimated 9 percent of the population is classified as limited-English proficient (LEP), meaning they have a limited ability to speak, read, write, or understand English (Shah and Estrada, 2011). The increasing numbers of LEP individuals living in the United States means that the majority of law enforcement agencies nationwide now have daily contact with people who do not speak English.

The implications for law enforcement are obvious, as the failure to communicate effectively can be disastrous in a variety of police functions from the routine to the deadly. It can compromise the integrity of the judicial process, interfere with crime control, and undermine the core purpose of police work (Venkatraman, 2006). In addition, federal law requires police departments to address the language barrier. Title VI of the Civil Rights Act of 1964

(42 U.S.C. § 2000d et seq.) and Executive Order 13166 mandate that all agencies that receive federal funding must provide meaningful access to people who have limited English proficiency. Failure to do so could constitute discrimination on the basis of national origin.

The spoken language is not the only barrier. Gestures can also be misinterpreted. For example, making the A-okay sign (a circle with the thumb and forefinger) is friendly in the United States, but it means "you're worth zero" in France, Belgium, and many Latin American countries. The thumbs-up gesture meaning "good going" in the United States is the equivalent of an upraised middle finger in some Islamic countries. The amount of eye contact also varies with different racial and ethnic groups. For example, in the United States, Caucasians maintain eye contact while speaking about 45 percent of the time, African Americans about 30 percent, Hispanics about 25 percent, and Asians about 18 percent.

Cultural differences can present numerous barriers and challenges to effective communication. Many new immigrants have a limited understanding of the role of police and how officers expect people to behave during routine encounters. For example, when police in El Salvador make a traffic stop, it is customary for the driver to get out of the car and approach the officer: "In the United States, this is exactly the wrong thing to do and can lead to law enforcement using force on the person. Similarly, it is common for Cambodian immigrants to keep their wallet in their socks. Consequently, when asked by a police officer for their driver's license, they might reach to their sock for the wallet, a gesture police officers—especially those not familiar with Cambodian habits—might interpret as reaching for a weapon. If a language barrier further impairs clear communication, the situation could escalate dangerously" (Lysakowski, Pearsall, and Pope, 2009, 5).

In some Asian cultures, only the oldest family member will deal with the police on behalf of the entire family. But older Asian immigrants are also the least likely in the family to speak English. The only way for officers to communicate, in many cases, is by using one of the elder's grandchildren as an interpreter, which the elder usually considers to be a loss of face.

Communication can also be hindered by the fear and distrust of government that immigrants may bring with them based on experiences with police in their homelands: "Many immigrants—refugees, especially—come from places where police are corrupt and abusive. In Lowell, Massachusetts, for example, many residents in the large Cambodian population fled the Khmer Rouge regime and genocide. People who have experienced civil war, genocide, and martial law may have difficulty trusting that the police are there to help" (Lysakowski, Pearsall, and Pope, 2009, 4). Immigrants may also be fearful that reporting any crime victimization to police may bring scrutiny to their immigration status, or the status of their family members or neighbors.

Police officers may have more barriers to communication because of the image they convey, their position of authority, and the nature of their work. Other barriers include lack of time, use of police jargon, lack of feedback, and a failure to listen.

Lack of time is another barrier to effective communication. Police officers and citizens are busy. Often, neither want to take the time to communicate fully and to establish high empathy. Bad timing can also interfere with communication. Police officers frequently are interrupted by calls for service and need to cut short conversations with others.

The use of **jargon**, the technical language of a profession, is another barrier to communication. Law enforcement has its own special terminology—for example, alleged perpetrator, modus operandi, and complainant. Officers should avoid using such terms when talking with the public.

jargon
The technical language of a profession.

Lack of feedback can also reduce effective communication. The old adage sums up this problem well: I know that you believe that you understand what you think I said, but I am not sure you realize that what you heard is not what I meant.

A failure to listen is one of the most common and most serious barriers to effective communication. Our educational system concentrates on the communication skills of reading and writing. Some time is devoted to speaking, but little or no time is devoted to listening. It is simply assumed that everyone knows how to listen.

Law enforcement officers need to receive information more than they need to give it. A major portion of their time is spent receiving information for forms and reports, taking action in arrests, eliciting information in interviews and interrogations, and many other duties requiring careful listening. As important as listening is, many people lack good listening skills.

Listening skills *can* be improved. The effective communicator is skilled not only at speaking (or writing) but also at listening (and reading). In addition, the effective communicator recognizes personal biases likely to occur in a society as diverse as the United States.

ETHNIC DIVERSITY: A NATION OF IMMIGRANTS

Dealing effectively with diversity is important to community policing because community outreach, communications, trust, and activism are all necessary to community partnerships, and none of these can be achieved without accepting—indeed, embracing—diversity: "Police officers and their agencies can accomplish much by working in partnership with citizens to implement the American vision of diverse and tolerant communities that offer freedom, safety, and dignity for all" (Turner, 1999).

Culture is a collection of artifacts, tools, ways of living, values, and language common to a group of people, all passed from one generation to the next. Diversity is most obvious and sometimes most problematic when groups with different "ways of living" coexist in the same community. The culture provides a framework or worldview, a cultural window through which events are interpreted. **Ethnocentrism** is the preference for one's own way of life over all others. People are naturally attracted to others who are similar to themselves because they feel less uncertain about how similar people will respond to them and more certain about the likelihood that similar people will agree with them. Ethnocentricity and segregation are consequences of a desire to avoid uncomfortable uncertainty.

ethnocentrism
The preference for one's own way of life over all others.

The sociologic literature on ethnic and racial diversity contains three theories on the consequences of two or more cultures inhabiting the same geographic area: assimilation, cultural pluralism, and cultural conflict. These are not mutually exclusive and may occur at the same time, creating problems for the transition to community policing.

assimilation

Occurs when a society takes in or assimilates various other cultures to become a "melting pot." Also called *acculturation*.

acculturation

Occurs when a society takes in or assimilates other cultures. Also called *assimilation*.

Assimilation theorists suggest that our society takes in or assimilates various cultures. Assimilation, also referred to as **acculturation**, was, indeed, what happened among the early colonists. Initially the colonists came from various countries with different religions. They settled in specific geographic areas and maintained their original culture—for example, the Pennsylvania Dutch.

Over time, the triple forces of continued immigration, urbanization, and industrialization turned the United States into a "melting pot" with diverse cultures from the various colonies merging. The melting pot was accomplished relatively painlessly because of the many similarities among the colonists. They looked quite similar physically; they valued religion and "morality"; most valued hard work; and, perhaps most important, there was plenty of land for everyone. The "homogenization" of the United States was fairly well accomplished by the mid-1800s. The formerly distinct cultures blended into what became known as the American culture, a White, male-dominated culture of European origin.

Unfortunately, the colonists excluded the Native Americans. Like animals, they were herded onto reservations. Native Americans have only recently begun to enter into the mainstream of American life. Some Native Americans do not want to be assimilated, seeking instead to maintain their culture and heritage. The same is true of many African Americans. Consequently, cultural diversity will continue to exist in the United States. Assimilation does not always occur.

An alternative to assimilation is *cultural pluralism,* with diverse cultures peacefully coexisting. One example of cultural pluralism is found in Native American culture. There are more than 450 recognized tribes and bands of Native Americans in this country, with populations ranging from less than 100 to more than 100,000. Before colonization of the United States, the tribes had distinct territories, languages, and cultures. Later, as the settlers took their lands, Native Americans joined together in self-defense. Today, Native Americans are often referred to as a single entity, although the individual tribes still maintain their unique identities.

Cultural pluralism is particularly noticeable when new immigrants arrive in the United States. Often, instead of attempting to assimilate into the mainstream of U.S. culture, immigrants seek out and live near others from their homelands, forming Chinatowns; Little Italys; Little Havanas; Little Greeces; and, most recently, Hmong and Somali communities. This has resulted in what is sometimes referred to as the *hyphenated American:* the Italian American, the Polish American, the African American, the Asian American, and so forth.

Cultural pluralism rests on the assumption that diverse cultures can coexist and prosper; but peaceful coexistence is not always the reality. The cultural conflict theory suggests that diverse cultures that share the same territory will compete with and attempt to exploit one another. Such cultural conflict was common between the early settlers and the Native American tribes. Conflict was also common between the White immigrants and the more than 6 million slaves imported from Africa between 1619 and 1860. The hostile treatment of Japanese Americans during World War II was rooted in cultural conflict. Following Japan's attack on Pearl Harbor, many U.S. citizens saw Japanese Americans as a national threat. More than 110,000 Japanese Americans, the great majority of whom were American-born citizens, were forced by the government to sell their homes and businesses and then were placed in internment camps.

Cultural conflict can currently be seen in growing tensions between specific ethnic groups as they compete for the limited remaining resources available. In Minnesota, for example, a controversial law permits only Native Americans to harvest wild rice or spear fish. The Mille Lacs band of Chippewa has sued the state of Minnesota, claiming treaty rights allow them to fish outside their reservation without state regulation. Native Americans are also lobbying to be allowed to take motorboats into wilderness areas to enhance their guide business.

The Immigration Issue

The words that appear at the base of the Statue of Liberty once reflected a welcoming philosophy of a country developed in large part by immigrants, primarily of European descent.

"GIVE ME YOUR TIRED, YOUR POOR,
YOUR HUDDLED MASSES YEARNING TO BREATHE FREE,
THE WRETCHED REFUSE OF YOUR TEEMING SHORE,
SEND THESE, THE HOMELESS, TEMPEST-TOST TO ME,
I LIFT MY LAMP BESIDE THE GOLDEN DOOR!"

—EMMA LAZARUS

Today the situation has changed.

Polls find that Americans are increasingly concerned about immigration, with a growing number of respondents believing immigrants are a burden to the country, taking jobs and housing and straining our health and educational systems. In 2010 nearly 40 million people living in the United States—13 percent of the total population—were foreign born (Grieco et al., 2012). It is not the numbers alone that alarm many Americans, however, but the fact that millions of immigrants are in the country illegally. The Department of Homeland Security (DHS) estimates that the number of unauthorized resident immigrants in the United States in January 2010 was 10.8 million, the same number as the previous year but less than the 11.8 million estimated in January 2007 (Hoefer, Rytina, and Baker, 2011). The DHS defines an unauthorized resident immigrant as a foreign-born non-citizen who is not a legal resident. Most unauthorized residents either entered the country without inspection or were admitted temporarily and stayed beyond the date they were required to leave.

DHS data indicate that the national unauthorized resident population grew by 27 percent between 2000 and 2010 and that, of all unauthorized immigrants residing in the United States in 2010, 62 percent had originally come from Mexico

(Hoefer, Rytina, and Baker, 2011). Increased efforts to secure our borders seem to be producing results, however, and the largest wave of immigration in history from a single country to the United States appears to have come to a standstill: "After four decades that brought 12 million current immigrants—most of whom came illegally—the net migration flow from Mexico to the United States has stopped and may have reversed" (Passel, Cohn, and Gonzalez-Barrera, 2012, 1). Public opinion polls reveal that while most citizens continue to support tightened border security and tough measures to crack down on illegal immigration, they also are increasingly supportive of creating better pathways to citizenship for those who are in the United States illegally (*Illegal Immigration,* 2011).

Communicating with New Immigrant Populations

Not since the early 20th century has the United States experienced such a large increase in immigration, and never in our country's history has the immigrant population been so diverse and geographically dispersed: "The new demography, combined with the threat of terrorism, has law enforcement agencies throughout the country examining and rethinking their relationships with hard-to-reach immigrant communities" (Khashu, Busch, and Latif, 2005, i). Police agencies nationwide are having unprecedented contact with immigrants—as victims, witnesses, suspects, and potential recruits—thus, building trust and rapport with these communities has become a vital task.

However, as already discussed, officers face numerous barriers to effective communication with new immigrants, including language and communication barriers, cultural misunderstandings, an imported distrust of police and judicial systems carried over from countries of origin, and fear that contact with police could lead to deportation. These barriers have prompted many agencies to examine and rethink how they police immigrant communities: "Gaining the trust of immigrant communities is particularly important among departments that incorporate community-oriented policing techniques. Community policing is an approach to law enforcement in which police engage communities in a working partnership to reduce crime and promote public safety, in part by identifying and eliminating the community conditions that foster crime. But generating this kind of involvement among new immigrant communities can be challenging" (Khashu, Busch, and Latif, 2005, 2). Promising practices undertaken by the Lexington (Kentucky) Division of Police to help bridge the language divide that often exists between officers and new immigrants included drawing upon the expertise of an academic institution to fine-tune its language learning programs and partnering with other law enforcement agencies to provide hands-on cultural training for officers: "The Lexington Division of Police has partnered with a local higher-learning institution—Murray State University, which houses the Kentucky Institute for International Studies—as well as two law enforcement agencies in Mexico—the city of Morelia Police Department and the Public Security Office of the State of Michoacán—for its Advanced Language Program (ALP). The academic institutions developed the agency's U.S.-based Spanish language curriculum. The Mexican law enforcement agencies host U.S. officers during a 5-week Spanish immersion program. Mexican officers take their U.S. counterparts with them on ride-alongs to facilitate their observation of local policing practices" (Shah and Estrada, 2009, 14).

Knowing another language can be a lifesaver. For example, in one incident, an officer in Washington, DC, conducting a late-night stop in a Spanish-speaking neighborhood, knew enough Spanish to understand when the driver instructed a passenger in Spanish to shoot the officer when he got close. The officer called for backup and ordered the occupants out of the car. When one suspect opened fire, the officer was prepared and shot back (Venkatraman, 2006).

In an effort to improve relations between new immigrant communities, the Vera Institute began working with the New York Police Department, organizing working groups with representatives from New York City's Arab, African, and emerging Latin American immigrant communities. A series of facilitated forums focused on such topics as the relationship between the police and the community; the community's crime, safety, and policing needs and concerns; and strategies for improving police–community relations. They also tested several initiatives, including developing fact sheets for police officers and coordinating public education and outreach campaigns on legal rights and responsibilities, reporting crimes, and police procedures. According to the institute, by cultivating alternative communication channels such as the police–immigrant working group forums, the project demonstrated new, more effective, more culturally sensitive ways to reach out to and serve New York City's immigrant communities.

Since September 11, 2001, some policing scholars and practitioners have encouraged local agencies to leverage their street-level position to become more involved in intelligence gathering and immigration enforcement, observing that in some jurisdictions local police have responded by embracing surveillance and intelligence gathering (Henderson et al., 2006).

 A dilemma facing law enforcement regarding the immigration issue is whether police can build trusting partnerships with immigrant communities if they are also to gather intelligence and enforce immigration law.

The 9/11 attacks sent "shock waves" through local and federal law enforcement agencies and Arab American communities alike. Law enforcement's role in immigration enforcement was stepped up, and their interactions with people of Arab descent became much more intense (Henderson et al., 2006). Before the attacks, Arab Americans were "largely unnoticed in the fabric of American life," but after the attacks, these persons found themselves at the center of attention that was mostly unwelcome. The Vera Institute tried to build relationships with Arab American communities and found that the number-one barrier, as perceived by community leaders, police personnel, and Federal Bureau of Investigation (FBI) personnel, was distrust of law enforcement. Among the top six solutions for overcoming barriers to working together, "improving or initiating communication and dialogue" was the most commonly suggested solution by police and FBI personnel. Improving or initiating communication and dialogue was the second most commonly suggested solution by community leaders, with cultural awareness training being the most commonly suggested (Henderson et al., 2006).

Some jurisdictions are tapping the cultural resources of their communities to tackle trust issues as well as communication barriers by encouraging citizens from diverse ethnicities to join the ranks of their reserve units. For example, in Dearborn, Michigan, where more than 30 percent of the residents are Arab American, the police department actively promotes and supports a reserve officer program in which 7 of the 33 volunteer reserves are from the Arab American community (Haddad, 2011). In addition, 8 of the 25 youth participants in the Dearborn Police Department's Explorer program are from the Arab American community. Such efforts have proven quite effective in helping the police build inroads and relationships with members of the increasingly diverse community (Haddad, 2011).

Communication is also a key factor in recognizing one's own and others' biases and prejudices.

Recognizing Prejudice and Discrimination

No one can be completely objective. Everyone, consciously or unconsciously, has certain preferences and prejudices.

 It is critical to recognize prejudices and stereotypes to avoid discrimination.

A *prejudice* is a negative judgment not based on fact; it is an irrational, preconceived negative opinion. Prejudices are often associated with a dislike of a particular group, race, or religion. They represent overgeneralizations and a failure to consider individual characteristics.

bias

A prejudice that inhibits objectivity; can evolve into hate.

Prejudice is also referred to as **bias**, a belief that inhibits objectivity. Taken to an extreme, a bias becomes hatred. It is important for law enforcement to understand bias and its extreme form—hate—to deal with bias and hate crimes, discussed in Chapter 14. Prejudices or biases are the result of overly general classification or stereotyping.

stereotyping

Assuming all people within a specific group are the same, lacking individuality.

Stereotyping assumes that all people within a specific group are the same and necessarily possess the same characteristics; they lack individuality.

Many people stereotype police officers based on what they see on television—scenes showing cops in car chases and shootouts. Officers are not shown standing on the street corner in late January directing traffic after a car crash or being tended to at the medical center because they were bitten on the arm by a prostitute who resisted arrest.

Police officers may also stereotype those with whom they come in contact. In the traditional mode of policing, officers spend a considerable amount of time dealing with criminals and their victims. Some officers may begin to categorize certain types of individuals as perpetrators. Police officers focus so much attention on crime that they may develop a distorted view of who the "bad guys" are. Generalizing from a few to the many is a serious problem for many police. It is a very natural tendency to stereotype people, but it is a tendency that can be fatal to effective communication.

Preconceived ideas about a person's truthfulness or "worth" can result in strained relationships with individuals and little or no interchange of ideas. The very language used to refer to others can interfere with communication. For example, would you rather be called a "cripple" or a "person with a disability"?

Prejudices may lead to discrimination, which can be manifested in two ways: (1) Some individuals or groups may be treated preferentially or (2) persons of equal stature may be treated unequally. Illegal unequal treatment may be based on race, religion, sex, or age.

 Prejudice is an attitude; discrimination is a behavior.

This difference between attitude and overt behavior was summed up by English Justice Cyril Salmon when he passed sentence on nine youths convicted of race rioting in 1958: "Think what you like … But once you translate your dark thoughts into savage acts, the law will punish you, and protect your victim." Unfortunately, prejudices may result in racism.

Racism   For the community policing philosophy to become a reality, racism, wherever it exists, must be recognized and faced. Racism is a belief that a human population having a distinct genetically transmitted characteristic is inferior. It also refers to discrimination or prejudice based on race. The racist idea that some groups (ethnic groups) are somehow genetically superior to others has no scientific basis.

The issue of racism as it relates to community policing is multifaceted and extremely emotionally charged. Furthermore, racism flows in both directions between the police and the citizens within the communities they serve. Some officers make the critical mistake of trying to achieve rapport by using terminology they hear members of a minority group using among themselves.

Racial Profiling   When police use certain racial characteristics, such as skin color, as indicators of criminal activity, the practice is commonly referred to as **racial profiling**. The contention that police single out subjects based solely on the color of their skin is a serious concern for any department engaged in such a practice and for the credibility of the police profession as a whole.

The *Sourcebook of Criminal Justice Statistics* (2004) states: "It has been reported that some police officers or security guards stop people of certain racial or ethnic groups because these officials believe that these groups are more likely than others to commit certain types of crimes." It then asks those surveyed if they believe such racial profiling is widespread in three specific circumstances: at motor vehicle stops, at airport security checkpoints, and in shopping malls (to prevent theft). Fifty-three percent believed racial profiling was widespread during motor vehicle stops; 49 percent believed it was widespread in shopping malls; and 42 percent believed it was widespread at airport security checkpoints. In all three circumstances, Blacks and Hispanics saw racial profiling as more widespread than Whites perceived it to be.

The "veil-of-darkness method" has been proposed as an innovative and low-cost approach to test for racial profiling in a department's traffic stop practices. This method uses changes in natural lighting to establish a benchmark for stop data, the basic premise being that during nighttime hours, traffic officers possess a degraded ability to discern motorists' race; therefore, stop patterns at night represent a presumptively race-neutral benchmark. The hypothesis is that if a comparison of daytime stops to nighttime stops reveals no statistically

racial profiling
A form of discrimination that singles out people of racial or ethnic groups because of a belief that these groups are more likely than others to commit certain types of crimes. Race-based enforcement is illegal.

significant difference regarding the race of the drivers involved, there is no racial bias by the traffic unit in determining which vehicles to pull over (Worden, McLean, and Wheeler, 2012).

Prior to the September 11, 2001, attacks on the World Trade Center and the Pentagon, the practice of racial profiling was being denounced by one police chief after another across the country. Suddenly, after the attacks, the debate was renewed, as police chiefs tried to decide if racial profiling was not only necessary but also the only sensible thing to do in view of the threat to the United States and its citizens. With the heightened threat of more terrorist attacks, people who appeared to be of Arab or Middle Eastern descent began reporting that they had been singled out for stops, questioning, searches, or arrests solely on the basis of their appearance. In some areas of the country, it seems that motorists of certain racial or ethnic groups are being stopped more frequently by police; oftentimes, the drivers claim, it is for no apparent reason.

However, profiles of certain serial crimes have been used for decades. Police have relied on profiles of drug couriers and serial rapists. Many practitioners argue that race is often part of a perpetrator's description and that to deny police this information because it might offend someone's sense of political correctness does a great disservice to law enforcement.

Racial Disparity in the Criminal Justice System

Closely related to the issue of racial profiling is the issue of whether our criminal justice system discriminates against racial minorities, resulting in a disproportionate number of members of minority groups being incarcerated. Although "Equal Justice under Law" is the foundation of our legal system and is carved on the front of the U.S. Supreme Court building, racial disparity is an unfortunate reality of the criminal justice system for both juveniles and adults. Although it is clear that minorities are overrepresented in the justice system, the more salient question is whether this represents racial discrimination.

Many discussions of racial discrimination are muddied because of failure to differentiate between *discrimination* and *disparity* (Walker, Spohn, and DeLone, 2007, 18). Whereas discrimination refers to unfair, differential treatment of a particular group, disparity refers simply to a difference and does not necessarily involve discrimination. In criminal justice the critical distinction is between legal and extralegal factors: "*Legal factors* include the seriousness of the offense, aggravating or mitigating circumstance, or an offender's prior criminal record. These are considered legitimate bases for decisions by most criminal justice officials because they relate to an individual's criminal behavior. *Extralegal factors* include race, ethnicity, gender, social class, and lifestyle" (Walker, Spohn, and DeLone, 2007, 18).

Disparity in the racial composition of individuals involved in the criminal justice system—either as victims or offenders—is likely a result of numerous factors related to socioeconomics, education, employment and other areas in which minorities are at a disadvantage. Controversy continues as to whether this is evidence of discrimination or disparity.

Strategies to Overcome Barriers Based on Racial and Ethnic Diversity

Various strategies have been proposed to help agencies attack bias and overcome racial or ethnic barriers between the police and the community. Some are very general, whereas others are quite specific.

One of the first steps to take is implementing a zero-tolerance policy for bias within police ranks and publicizing that philosophy. Another strategy is to develop an outreach effort to diverse communities to reduce victimization by teaching them practical crime prevention techniques. A critical part of this effort involves training and education for both police and citizens, as well as the formation of key partnerships between law enforcement and community groups.

Police must often rely on the services of translators, interpreters, community liaisons, religious leaders, and other trusted members of an ethnic community to develop an effective crime prevention program for that group. Schools can also assist by including crime prevention techniques in classroom instruction and special English as a Second Language classes.

Ethnic or racial diversity is usually visually obvious, but other forms of diversity within the United States may also pose a challenge to law enforcement and community policing, including religious and socioeconomic diversity.

RELIGIOUS DIVERSITY

Many of those who came to America in the 1600s did so to escape religious persecution, and the colonists' desire for religious freedom is evident in our Bill of Rights. The First Amendment protects, among other freedoms, freedom of religion. The First Amendment was drafted and adopted to protect the establishment and practice of different religious communities in the early colonies: Congregationalism in New England, Quakerism in Pennsylvania, and Catholicism in Maryland. Over the years, these distinctions have become much less important, with the term *Christian* taking on the meaning of a melting pot for people of similar religious beliefs. However, religious tension still exists between many Christians (the majority religious group) and those of Jewish faith (the minority religious group). Anti-Semitism is a problem in some communities and may result in hate crimes.

Religious diversity continues to increase, presenting unique challenges to community policing efforts aimed at enhancing citizens' levels of trust, communication, and activism. For example, in our post-9/11 society, Arab Americans have been increasingly discriminated against because of their religious beliefs, or their perceived beliefs. Although often considered a monolithic group, Arab Americans come from 22 different Arabic-speaking countries, and whereas the media and many non-Arabs usually associate them with Islam, in actuality an estimated two-thirds are Christian: "Prior to September 11, 2001, Arab Americans went largely unnoticed in the American mainstream. The relative scarcity of academic research on Arab Americans and the fact that the U.S. Census only began keeping information on people of Arab descent in 2000 are both evidence of their low profile" (Henderson et al., 2006, 5).

A national survey by the Pew Research Center shows that the public remains conflicted over Islam: "Favorable opinions of Islam have declined since 2005, but there has been virtually no change over the past year in the proportion of Americans saying that Islam is more likely than other religions to encourage violence. As was the case a year ago, slightly more people say the Islamic religion does not encourage violence more than other religions (42%) than say that it does (35%)" (*Public Remains Conflicted Over Islam*, 2010). Rituals undertaken during religious ceremonies may also present challenges to police, who must take care not to infringe on citizens' First Amendment right to freedom of religion. In Oregon a group lobbied for an exception to the general drug laws to make it legal for Native Americans to smoke peyote during their rituals. In this case, the Supreme Court ruled that such an exception need not be granted. Smoking peyote was illegal for all citizens; Native Americans had not been singled out as a special group. Cults may also pose special challenges to community policing efforts because they zealously advocate unorthodox beliefs.

SOCIOECONOMIC DIVERSITY

Even the casual observer recognizes social and economic differences in the United States. Sociologists usually divide individuals within the United States into three basic classes, based primarily on income and education: the lower, middle, and upper classes. These basic classes may be further subdivided. As noted, the middle class is shrinking, and the gap between the rich and the poor has become wider, resulting in tension.

The Lower Socioeconomic Class

Poor people have more frequent contact with the criminal justice system because they are on the streets and highly visible. A poor person who drives an old car may get a repair ticket, whereas a wealthier person is more likely to drive a newer car not requiring repairs. In addition, the repair ticket issued to the poor person is likely to be a much greater hardship for that person than a similar ticket would be to someone in the middle or upper classes.

Immigrants and certain races and ethnic groups are frequently equated with poverty and crime in an interaction described as the poverty syndrome. The **poverty syndrome** includes inadequate housing, inadequate education, inadequate jobs, and a resentment of those who control the social system.

poverty syndrome
Includes inadequate housing, education, and jobs and a resentment of those who control the social system.

The Homeless   Carrying their worldly goods and camping everywhere from laundry rooms to train and bus stations, the homeless pose a challenge for law enforcement: "Prior to the foreclosure crisis and economic recession, homelessness was already a national crisis, with 2.5 to 3.5 million men, women, and children experiencing homelessness each year, including a total of 1.35 million children and over a million people working full or part time—but unable to pay for housing. Since then, homelessness has increased dramatically" (National Law Center on Homelessness and Poverty, 2011, 6). In many cases, homelessness is temporary; people who are homeless one month may not be the following month. Thus, it is difficult to accurately measure the number of homeless on any given day.

Many of those who are homeless are women and children, veterans, alcoholics, drug addicts, and mentally impaired persons. Police need to balance the safety and other needs of the homeless with the need to protect the public from interference with its rights. The needs of the homeless are as varied as the people who comprise this group. Besides needing the obvious—a place to live and an income to support themselves—other needs include better nutrition; medical care; clothing; substance abuse and mental health treatment; and, especially for children, an education.

Officer Nicholas Godwin stops and talks to Michael Human, who is homeless and was begging on the street corner. Godwin, 28, has been with the Germantown (Tennessee) Police Department for seven years, having advanced from patrol officer to the SWAT team and then the Crisis Intervention Team (CIT), where he was named Crisis Intervention Officer of the year by the National Alliance on Mental Illness (NAMI). Officer Godwin says he enjoys helping people.

© Karen Pulfer Focht/The Commercial Appeal/ZUMAPRESS.com

In a study on homeless children, the National Center on Family Homelessness found that 1 in 45 children in America is homeless—a total of about 1.6 million youths (*America's Youngest Outcasts 2010*, 2011). For some children, the mental and physical stress of being homeless spawns a host of other difficulties:

> Children who are homeless are more likely to suffer from acute and chronic medical illnesses. They go hungry at twice the rate of other children. They have three times the rate of emotional and behavioral problems, such as anxiety, depression, sleep problems, withdrawal, and aggression. ...
>
> Given these circumstances, it is not surprising that children experiencing homelessness have difficulty in school. The level of fear and unpredictability in their lives is damaging to their growth and development, and ability to learn. ... They are four times more likely to have delayed development and twice as likely to have learning disabilities. They are 16 percent less proficient at reading and math than their peers. ... One-third of these children repeat a grade. ... The constant barrage of stressful and traumatic experiences has profound effects on their ability to learn, ultimately affecting their success in life.
>
> More than 40 percent of homeless children are younger than 6 years old and are dependent on their mothers for nurturance, protection, and support. But more than a third of homeless mothers have chronic physical health conditions, including higher rates of asthma, anemia, and hypertension than in the general population. ... Mothers also struggle with mental health and substance use. ... Rates of depression in homeless mothers are four to five times greater than for women overall. ... Although mothers' depression is very treatable, it is often not identified and may lead to adverse outcomes in their children. (*America's Youngest Outcasts 2010*, 2011, 10)

Although being homeless is not a crime, the activities of some homeless people do violate laws and local ordinances. Such activities include public drunkenness; public urination and defecation; loitering; trespassing; panhandling; littering; disorderly conduct; or more serious offenses such as vandalism, theft, and assault. Cities across the nation have tried numerous legislative and other tactical measures in their efforts to eliminate or minimize the problems presented by the homeless:

» Anticamping laws that make sleeping in public places illegal and in some cases make it illegal to possess camping equipment in the city
» Laws against soliciting employment in public places
» Removal of park benches
» Locking public restrooms
» Laws prohibiting providing food to homeless people
» Curfews for homeless people
» Laws against sitting, lying, or sleeping on sidewalks

"These common practices that criminalize homelessness do nothing to address the underlying causes of homelessness. Instead, they drastically exacerbate the problem. They frequently move people away from services. When homeless persons are arrested and charged under these ordinances, they may develop a criminal record, making it more difficult to obtain the employment and/or housing that could help them become self-sufficient" (*Homes Not Handcuffs,* 2009, 11).

More than a handful of communities across the country have enacted outright bans or placed extreme restrictions on providing food to the indigent and homeless. Lawsuits continue to be filed, with courts deciding in favor of cities in some cases and against them in other rulings. Thus no consensus can be found among court rulings to date regarding the constitutionality of feeding bans. Other criminalization measures, however, have been found to violate the civil rights of homeless persons.

In *Pottinger v. City of Miami* (1992), a U.S. district court judge found the city's practice of conducting "bum sweeps" (i.e., making minor arrests of transients and confiscating and destroying the property of the homeless) was a violation of their constitutional rights. The central question in this case was whether the government can lock up a person for being outside when that person has no place to go. Noting that there were roughly 6,000 homeless people in Miami but fewer than 700 shelter spaces, the court held that the criminalization of essential acts performed in public, when there was no alternative, violated the plaintiffs' rights to travel and due process under the Fourteenth Amendment, and the right to be free from cruel and unusual punishment under the Eighth Amendment.

In October 2005, the city of St. Louis, Missouri, agreed to settle a lawsuit filed against it by 25 homeless and impoverished people who claimed they were illegally "swept" from the downtown area and jailed prior to the city's Fourth of July celebration in 2004 (*Johnson v. Board of Police Commissioners,* 2004). The city, the police department, and the Downtown Partnership—all named defendants in the case—shared in paying a combined $80,000 in damages to the plaintiffs, $20,000 of which was to go toward meals and other services for the area's homeless. Following the settlement, the police department implemented several changes in the way it addressed the homeless issue, such as avoiding arresting homeless people or removing them from downtown areas without probable cause that a crime had been committed; instituting a policy where, under most circumstances, a summons to court is issued for "quality-of-life" violations rather than arrest; emphasizing to officers that an "individual's residential status (homeless or nonhomeless) is not to be considered in any of [their] decisions"; and affirming that begging is not a crime if it is not "aggressive" (*A Dream Denied,* 2006, 42).

Further complicating interactions with those who are homeless is the fact that they are often victims rather than perpetrators of crime. Between 1999 and 2010, hundreds of homeless people were attacked and killed, and many such attacks go undocumented: "Homeless people are treated so poorly by society that their attacks are often forgotten or unreported" (*Hate Crimes against the Homeless,* 2012, 11). In 2010 alone, 113 attacks on homeless individuals resulted in 24 deaths. And since 1999, the National Coalition for the Homeless has documented 1,184 acts of violence against the homeless, of which 312 led to the death of the victim (*Hate Crimes against the Homeless,* 2012).

As with other diversity issues, training for officers can be a valuable step toward improving relations with a community's homeless population. Unfortunately, many departments do not provide the means, training, or tools necessary for officers to successfully reach out to the community's homeless. However, in jurisdictions where police are trained and empowered to address the issue of homelessness, their intervention can benefit both the homeless and the neighborhood. A New York City police officer, Fran Kimkowski, developed an innovative approach to the homeless problem for a group of men who were homeless in the Long Island City section of Queens, New York. Assigned to calm the fears of residents when the Salvation Army opened a shelter for homeless veterans in the neighborhood, Kimkowski wanted to show the residents that the homeless men could and would contribute to the community if given a chance. She organized V-Cops, a group of homeless veterans who volunteer to help prevent crime in the neighborhoods. Partnerships to address the issue of homelessness are also discussed in Chapter 7.

The Powerful and Connected

At the opposite end of the socioeconomic scale are powerful, privileged, and politically connected people. In the traditional role of crime fighter, the police seldom interact with the upper class, but when they must, problems can arise. One of the most common issues occurs when officers provide accommodation and/or special treatment to powerful people in those rare circumstances when one might be arrested. Such special treatment often results in public outrage and bad press for the police department involved, and yet, it happens time and again. Much of the public assumes such actions to be the norm and imagines that many in this category are never arrested in the first place unless it is unavoidable.

In community policing, the personal and financial resources of those in the public eye and upper socioeconomic level can be invaluable. A population's socioeconomic profile can reveal much about the balance of power within a community.

FACING THE CHALLENGE OF DIVERSITY

Keeping the peace and serving and protecting a society as diverse as the one in the United States presents an extreme challenge to police officers. To meet the challenge, police might consider the following guidelines:

» Each person is, first and foremost, an individual.

» Each group, whether racial, ethnic, religious, or socioeconomic, consists of people who share certain values. Knowing what these values are can contribute greatly to effective police–community interactions.

» Each group can contribute to making the community safer.

» Communication skills are vital. Empathy, listening, and overcoming language barriers are crucial to implementing the community policing philosophy.

» An awareness of personal prejudices and biases can guard against discrimination. An awareness of the language used to talk about different groups is extremely important.

The term *minority,* for example, has subtle secondary, if not caste-status, implications that are the opposite of the implications of *majority,* which is frequently a polite code word for "White." *People of color* also places distance between those so designated and Caucasians. Officers should consider the terms they use and how they might be perceived by those being labeled. Of course, in an emergency, when officers need to communicate with each other rapidly, a descriptive term such as *Black* or *White* is appropriate and, indeed, necessary for a rapid response. It is important for officers to know when to use certain terms.

PERSONS WITH DISABILITIES

When people think of "cultural diversity," they typically think of racial, ethnic, religious, or socioeconomic differences among citizens. However, a significantly large "minority" group in the United States, an estimated 36 million noninstitutionalized people, consists of individuals with physical or mental disabilities. The U.S. Census Bureau estimates that about 12 percent of Americans have disabilities, a figure likely to rise as the population ages and baby boomers grow older. These are populations that provide even more diversity and challenge to community policing efforts.

Understanding Physical and Mental Disabilities and the Americans with Disabilities Act

A police officer asks a woman to perform some field sobriety tests. She cannot do so even though she is not under the influence of any drug, including alcohol. Another person ignores the direct order of a police officer to step back on the sidewalk. Yet another person approaches an officer and attempts to ask directions, but his speech is so slurred he is unintelligible. These common occurrences for police officers can often be misinterpreted. In each of the preceding instances, the individual interacting with the officer has a disability: a problem with balance, a hearing impairment, and a speech disability. A disability is a physical or mental impairment that substantially limits one or more of a person's major life functions. This includes people with mobility disabilities; mental illnesses; mental retardation; epilepsy or other seizure disorders; and speech, hearing, and vision disabilities.

Greater recognition of this "minority" came on July 26, 1990, when then-President Bush signed into law the **Americans with Disabilities Act (ADA)**, calling it "another Independence Day, one that is long overdue." The ADA guarantees that persons with disabilities will have equal access to any public facilities available to persons without disabilities.

In addition, the ADA affects virtually everything that law enforcement officers do—for example, receiving citizen complaints; interrogating witnesses; arresting, booking, and holding suspects; operating phone (911) emergency centers; providing emergency medical services; enforcing laws; and various other duties ("Justice Department Offers Local Police Guidance for Complying with ADA," 2006, 2). The ADA does not, however, grant special liberty to individuals with disabilities in matters of law, nor does it dictate that the police must take a "hands off" approach toward people with disabilities engaged in criminal conduct or those posing a direct threat to the health or safety of others or to him- or herself.

Because the ADA guarantees access to government services, it helps build partnerships for community policing. Under the ADA, all brochures and printed material must be available in Braille or on audiotape if requested. To include people with disabilities in community partnerships, the police must be able to communicate with them and should conduct their meetings in barrier-free places.

Many people in our communities have made treatment of those with disabilities a priority and are available and willing to work with law enforcement agencies to ensure that people with disabilities are treated respectfully and protected from those who would victimize them. The outcome of increased awareness and service in this area will not only make police officers' jobs easier when they encounter people with disabilities but will also help reduce their fear and vulnerability. The focus on those with disabilities will make the community a better and safer place for everyone and help to build police–community relations.

Americans with Disabilities Act (ADA)

Legislation signed in 1990 that guarantees that persons with disabilities will have equal access to any public facilities available to persons without disabilities.

ON THE BEAT

Police officers frequently encounter people with disabilities while working in the field. I recall one experience where I was on routine patrol on a busy stretch of roadway and saw a man in an electric wheelchair stopped in the middle of the sidewalk. The day was overcast, and rain was imminent. I glanced in my mirror and saw that the man in the wheelchair was not moving. I turned around and headed his way, parking my vehicle on the side of the road. When I approached him on foot, I asked him if everything was all right. The man began to speak slowly and softly. I could barely hear the words he was saying, so I leaned in closer. After several minutes, he was able to communicate to me that his wheelchair had broken down, and he wasn't sure what to do. I offered him a ride home and arranged for a pickup truck to take his wheelchair home. He got home safely that day, and he thanked me when he arrived.

It is important for officers to be tuned in to what is going on around them. In this case it was a man in a wheelchair who could have been overlooked had I not been paying attention and noticed that he was immobile.

—*Kim Czapar*

Frequently Encountered Disabilities

It is fairly common for on-duty police officers to encounter individuals who seem confused, are unable to communicate, or who otherwise exhibit behavior that is inappropriate to the time and/or place.

 Disabilities police officers frequently encounter include mobility impairment, vision impairment, hearing impairment, impairment as a result of epilepsy, and mental or emotional impairment.

Sometimes the cause of such behavior is intoxication or use of illegal drugs, but other times the behavior results from a medical condition. Some of these incidents occur when an individual is experiencing a seizure, either as a result of epilepsy, diabetes, or a consequence of drug use or some other medical problem. Regardless of the cause, a seizure is a disabling and involuntary condition that requires an appropriate police response, including the recognition that the individual involved is unable to make conscious decisions or respond to directions from a police officer (*Take Another Look*, 2010).

 An epileptic seizure may be mistaken for a drug- or alcohol-induced stupor because the person may have incoherent speech and a glassy-eyed stare and may be wandering aimlessly.

Individuals with mental or emotional disabilities, in contrast to the preceding disabilities, pose a significant challenge to community policing efforts.

Mental Disabilities

Historically, society institutionalized people who were mentally ill or mentally retarded. In the mid-1960s, however, treatment in the community replaced institutionalization. *Deinstitutionalization* refers to the release of thousands of individuals who were mentally disabled into society to be cared for by family or a special network of support services. This was the result of several factors, including development of medications to control mental illness; research showing that people who were institutionalized did not receive adequate treatment and could do better in the community; federal programs to build and operate mental health centers; and patients' rights litigation and state legislation.

Community-based mental health service rests on the premise that people have the right not to be isolated from the community simply because they are mentally disabled. This premise works only if a support system for them exists. Unfortunately, the network of support services has developed slowly. As a result, thousands of mentally disabled people are on the street and homeless and hundreds more are living with families that are ill equipped to provide the necessary care and assistance.

Mental Illness   Mental illness has been defined as a biopsychosocial brain disorder characterized by dysfunctional thoughts, feelings, and/or behaviors that meet diagnostic criteria (Cordner, 2006). It includes schizophrenia, major depression, and bipolar disorder; obsessive–compulsive disorder; and posttraumatic stress disorder. Mental illness is not, in and of itself, a police problem but rather a medical and social services problem. However, police officers frequently encounter people with mental illness—about 5 percent of U.S. residents have serious mental illness, and 10 to 15 percent of incarcerated individuals have severe mental illness (Cordner, 2006).

Problems associated with mental illness often become police problems, including crimes, suicides, disorderly behavior, and a variety of calls for service. Unfortunately, the traditional police response to people with mental illness has often been "ineffective and sometimes tragic" (Cordner, 2006).

Mental illness should not be confused with crisis behavior. **Crisis behavior** results when a person who is not mentally ill has a temporary breakdown in coping skills. Anyone can suffer from a crisis.

crisis behavior
Results when a person has a temporary breakdown in coping skills; not the same as mental illness.

The people that police encounter who are mentally ill frequently lack social support. They are difficult to manage and may have complications such as alcohol or drug abuse. Often people who feel threatened by the strange behavior of a person who is mentally ill may call the police to handle the problem. Officers become involved with people who are mentally ill because the police are the only responders who have around-the-clock, mobile emergency response capacity, as well as the authority to detain and arrest persons and use force when needed. When police are called to manage people who are mentally ill, the behaviors they most frequently encounter are bizarre, unusual, or strange conduct; confused thoughts or actions; aggressive actions; or destructive, assaultive, violent, or suicidal behavior. Suicide is the eleventh leading cause of death in the United States and the third leading cause of death among people age 15 to 24.

According to the National Institute of Mental Health (NIMH) more than 90 percent of people who kill themselves have a diagnosable mental disorder, most commonly a depressive disorder or a substance abuse disorder (*Suicide in the United States,* 2010).

Suicide by cop (SBC), a method in which a person engages in actual or apparent danger to others in an attempt to get oneself killed or injured by law enforcement, is a well-recognized phenomenon and a troubling trend. One study of officer-involved shootings (OIS) found that 36 percent of OIS incidents resulted from SBC situations, confirming the growing incidence of this method of suicide (Mohandie, Meloy, and Collins, 2009). Furthermore, of all SBC incidents examined during the study, the subject was killed 97 percent of the time. Even more troubling is data showing a one-in-three chance that someone other than the suicidal individual will be injured or killed during an SBC incident (Mohandie, Meloy, and Collins, 2009).

It is important to note that the California Court of Appeals ruled, in *Adams v. City of Fremont* (1998), that officers are not legally obligated to intervene on behalf of a suicidal individual if officers feel their own safety is in jeopardy: "We hold that police officers responding to a crisis involving a person threatening suicide with a loaded firearm have no legal duty under tort law that would expose them to liability if their conduct fails to prevent the threatened suicide from being carried out."

One natural outgrowth of a mental health system that withholds needed treatment until a person with a mental illness becomes dangerous is that police officers and sheriff's deputies are forced to become frontline mental health workers. The safety of both law enforcement officers and citizens is compromised when law enforcement responds to crises involving people with severe mental illnesses who are not being treated (*Law Enforcement and People with Severe Mental Illness,* 2006). Or, if they are being treated, Moore (2006, 134) suggests: "Most of the violent individuals with whom police deal are mental patients whose treatment plans have lapsed." Or they have simply stopped taking their medication.

Police in one city shot and killed a suspect who had just robbed a gas station. The suspect turned out to be a mentally disturbed female who they had dealt with often over the past year. After robbing the gas station, she ordered the clerk to call 911 and stayed there until he did. The confrontation and subsequent shooting seemed orchestrated, forced by the depressed, suicidal woman. She claimed to have a gun, threatened to shoot the officers, and advanced toward one with an object in her hand. The object turned out to be a comb. This is a tragic situation where a person who is suicidal arranges to die at the hands of the police.

Departments must train officers to deal with these types of crisis situations and make the necessary resources available (Scoville, 2010). Many departments are developing Crisis Intervention Teams (CIT) to improve their service and response to events and incidents involving unique populations such as the mentally ill (Dodge, 2005). The CIT model combines police officers with mental health professions and includes extensive training: "The purpose of a crisis intervention team (CIT) is to provide law enforcement officers with the skills they need to safely deescalate situations involving people with mental illness who are in crisis, *not* to turn officers into mental health workers" (Hill, Guill, and Ellis, 2004, 18).

Law enforcement members of a CIT team learn that people who are severely mentally ill need an entirely different approach; an entirely different voice tone, voice volume, and personal space; and both observational and questioning skills (*Tactical Response* Staff, 2006). Noting that the development of a CIT goes well beyond police training to focus, instead, on building relationships between law enforcement and the mental health community in an effort to improve the effectiveness of the response to mental health 911 calls, Anderson (2006, 14) asserts: "CIT is about humanizing people with mental illness and understanding that mental illness is first and foremost a health care problem."

Mental Retardation   Another challenging and frequently misunderstood mental disability that police encounter is mental retardation, which is often, and incorrectly, equated with mental illness. Mental retardation is the nation's fourth-ranking disabling condition, affecting 3 percent of the U.S. population. Mental retardation means that normal intellectual development fails to occur. Unlike mental illness, mental retardation is permanent. It is diagnosed when three criteria exist: (1) significant subaverage general intellectual functioning (as measured by IQ tests); (2) resulting in, or associated with, defects or impairments in adaptive behavior, such as personal independence and social responsibility; (3) with onset by age 18.

People who are mentally retarded are usually aware of their condition and may be adept at concealing it. Thus, it may be more difficult to recognize mental retardation than mental illness. Communication problems, interaction problems, inability to perform tasks, and personal history can help officers make this determination.

AGE DIVERSITY

Yet another communication challenge is posed when police officers must inter-act with those who are much older or much younger than they are. Law enforce-ment officers deal with individuals of all ages and must be able to communicate effectively with them. In 2010, nearly one-fifth (19.5 percent) of the U.S. popula-tion was younger than 5 or age 65 and older ("State and County QuickFacts," 2012). Although it is rare for most people in these age groups to be involved in criminal behavior, they are among the most vulnerable of our populations and, because of that, police officers will have considerable contact with them. Most contact will take the form of providing assistance and protecting their welfare.

The Elderly and Communication Challenges

"The aging of the baby-boom generation along with declining fertility rates is changing America's age structure. The number of people over age 65 will rise substantially beginning in 2011 as the oldest members of the baby-boom generation reach the 65-year mark" ("The Aging of America," 2012). The U.S. Census Bureau data indicate that in 2010, 38.6 million U.S. residents were 65 and older, 12.7 percent of the total U.S. population; population predictions are that by 2030, nearly one in five people (19.6%) will be age 65 or older and by 2050 that percentage will rise to 20.7 percent of the U.S. population—more than 86 million people age 65 and older.

Many individuals age 65 and older do *not* consider themselves elderly and, in fact, are in better physical and mental condition than other individuals much younger than they are. Police officers need to understand and empathize with the physical and emotional challenges of the aged so they may deliver the best possible service.

Older people tend to admire and respect authority and are often grateful for any help the police may offer. They are usually in contact with the police if they become victims of crime, are involved in an automobile crash, or are stopped for a traffic violation. Many older people have serious medical problems for which they may require emergency medical assistance. In fact, more than half of the U.S. population older than age 65 is disabled in some way.

Some older people suffer from **Alzheimer's disease (AD)**, a progressive, irreversible, and incurable disease of the brain that adversely affects behavior.

In 2012 an estimated 5.4 million Americans of all ages had Alzheimer's disease (AD). The vast majority (5.2 million) of those with AD are age 65 and older; however, approximately 200,000 people under age 65 have younger-onset Alzheimer's (*2012 Alzheimer's Disease Facts and Figures,* 2012). Nearly half (45 percent) of all people age 85 and older have developed AD, and considering that the number of Americans surviving to age 80 and beyond is expected to grow dramatically due to advances in medicine and medical technology, as well as social and environmental conditions, it is very likely that future police officers will encounter during their careers an increasing number of citizens with this type of dementia: "As the number of older Americans grows rapidly,

Alzheimer's disease (AD)

A progressive, irreversible, and incurable brain disease with no known cause that affects four million elderly Americans; the classic symptom is memory loss.

so too will the numbers of new and existing cases of Alzheimer's disease" (*2012 Alzheimer's Disease Facts and Figures,* 2012, 18).

Alzheimer's disease afflicts people of all social, economic, and racial groups. Officers should know the symptoms, the most classic of which is gradual loss of memory. Other symptoms include impaired judgment, disorientation, personality change, decline in ability to perform routine tasks, behavior change, difficulty in learning, loss of language skills, and decline in intellectual function. A number of behavior patterns common to patients with AD may bring them to the attention of police officers.

> People with AD may wander or become lost, engage in inappropriate sexual behavior, lose impulse control, shoplift, falsely accuse others, appear intoxicated, drive erratically, or become victims of crime. Many symptoms of AD and intoxication are identical: confusion and disorientation; problems with short-term memory, language, sight, and coordination; combativeness and extreme reactions; and loss of contact with reality.

Data indicate that an estimated 125,000 people with Alzheimer's disease or a similar condition wander from the safety of their home every year and are unable to find their way back (Schafer and McNiff, 2011). In addition to missing-person calls, other incidents that may bring Alzheimer's patients or those with general dementia into contact with the police include driving and traffic difficulties (getting lost, "losing" their car, running out of gas, causing crashes, or leaving the scene of a crash because they forgot it happened), false reports to 911, indecent exposure, shoplifting, cooking accidents, trespassing, overdoses, choking, homicide, suicide, abuse or neglect, and other types of victimization (Schafer and McNiff, 2011).

People afflicted with AD may become victims of crime because they are easy prey for con artists, robbers, and muggers. Also, police may become aware of patients with AD as a result of legal actions such as evictions, repossessions, and termination of utility service as a result of the patients' forgetfulness or inability to make payments.

The Helmsley Alzheimer's Alert Program, started in 1991, provides information on missing patients to public safety agencies. When a person with AD is reported missing, the Alzheimer's Association sends an alert with identifying information to a fax service that transmits it simultaneously to hundreds of locations, including police, hospital emergency rooms, and shelters. When the patient is found, another fax is sent to inform the agencies that the search is over.

The Young and Communication Challenges

A frequently overlooked segment of the population important to community policing implementation is youths. Just *who* is classified as a youth is established by state statutes and varies in age from 16 to 18 years. Because youths lack economic and political power, their problems and concerns may not receive the attention they deserve. But our nation's future depends on the values they form—they are the future decision makers of our country.

Most young people (95 percent, according to FBI statistics) have not been in trouble with the law. The overwhelming majority of "good kids" should not be forgotten in community policing efforts. They can be valuable as partners in problem solving and, if provided opportunities to become active in areas of interest to them, will most likely continue to be good citizens. And almost certainly some juveniles have been arrested multiple times, so that the actual percentage of youths who have been arrested is even lower than it appears at first glance. The youth who do have contact with police due to status offending, delinquency, or other antisocial conduct are discussed in greater detail in Chapter 12. Here the discussion focuses on youth with special needs, who may not necessarily come into police contact but are at a higher risk to do so because of their various disabilities or disorder—conditions that often present communication challenges to responding officers.

> Youths with special needs include those who are emotionally/behaviorally disturbed; who have specific learning disabilities; who have an attention deficit disorder; or who have behavior problems resulting from prenatal exposure to drugs, including alcohol, or to human immunodeficiency virus (HIV).

Emotionally/behaviorally disturbed children, often referred to as **EBD**, usually exhibit one or more of the following behavioral patterns: severely aggressive or impulsive behavior; severely withdrawn or anxious behavior such as pervasive unhappiness, depression, or wide mood swings; or severely disordered thought processes reflected in unusual behavior patterns, atypical communication styles, and distorted interpersonal relationships.

EBD
Emotionally/behaviorally disturbed.

Parents and teachers in some communities have expressed concerns that children labeled as EBD have fewer coping skills to deal with police contacts than other children and may be traumatized by such contacts. A large percentage of youths suspected of crimes are EBD, and that condition is one cause of their unlawful behavior. It is impossible, however, to arrange for an EBD specialist to be present at all police contacts because a majority of contacts are unplanned events that occur on the street.

Attention deficit hyperactivity disorder (ADHD) is one of the most common disruptive behavior disorders in youths, with an estimated 5 to 10 percent of all children having it. Occurring four times more often in boys than girls, ADHD is characterized by heightened motor activity (fidgeting and squirming), short attention span, distractibility, impulsiveness, and lack of self-control. (*Note:* The disorder of being easily distracted *without* the presence of hyperactivity is ADD, or simply attention deficit disorder. The two disorders, ADHD and ADD, are commonly confused and the terms used interchangeably; the absence of hyperactivity is the primary distinguishing feature between them.) Children with ADHD may do poorly in school and have low self-esteem. Although the condition often disappears by adulthood, by then those who had ADHD as children may have other behavior problems, including drug abuse, alcoholism, or personality disorders.

attention deficit hyperactivity disorder (ADHD)
A common disruptive behavior disorder characterized by heightened motor activity (fidgeting and squirming), short attention span, distractibility, impulsiveness, and lack of self-control.

Other children may present special challenges because of some form of specific learning disability (SLD), also known simply as a learning disability (LD), which is a disability category the federal government uses to define "a complex cluster of lifelong neurobiological disorders that can severely interfere with a person's ability to acquire competency in one or more of the following areas:

» Oral language (listening, speaking, understanding)
» Reading (decoding or phonics, word knowledge, comprehension)
» Written language (spelling and written expression)
» Mathematics (computation, problem solving)
» Executive functioning (planning, decision making, reasoning, organization, remembering, interpreting)
» Socialization (interpreting social situations, appropriate social interactions)."[1] ("About Specific Learning Disabilities," 2009)

The Association for Children with Learning Disabilities (ACLD) explains that SLDs, many of which occur before birth while the brain is forming, can severely interfere with a person's ability to interpret what is seen and heard or to process information, even though many people with SLDs possess the intellectual capacity to learn ("About Specific Learning Disabilities," 2009). SLDs do not include learning problems that result from visual, hearing, or motor handicaps, mental retardation, or emotional disturbance.

Data from the National Institutes of Health indicate that roughly 15 percent of the U.S. population—1 in 7 Americans—has some type of SLD. Common types of SLD include difficulty learning to read and spell, difficulty with handwriting, problems with mathematics, and difficulty understanding language despite normal hearing and vision ("About Specific Learning Disabilities," 2009). Symptoms of learning disabilities include short attention span; poor memory; difficulty following directions; disorganization; inadequate ability to discriminate between and among letters, numerals, or sounds; poor reading ability; eye–hand coordination problems; and difficulties with sequencing. Such children are often discipline problems, are labeled "underachievers," and are at great risk of becoming dropouts.

Although SLDs are usually discussed in an educational context, the effects of these deficits extend to all facets of life, including work. Characteristics that may bring a youth with a learning disability into conflict with the law include responding inappropriately to a situation; saying one thing and meaning another; forgetting easily; acting impulsively; needing immediate gratification; and feeling overly frustrated, which results in disruptive behavior. Those who interact with such children need to be patient and communicate effectively. Youths with learning disabilities look like their peers. Inwardly, however, most are very frustrated, have experienced failure after failure, and have extremely low self-esteem. When these types of disabilities go undiagnosed or are inappropriately treated, the consequences to the individual can be severe, greatly decreasing their ability to succeed in school, the workplace, and life in general.

crack children
Children who were exposed to cocaine while in the womb.

Prenatal exposure to drugs can also cause serious problems. The term **crack children** is sometimes used to refer to children exposed to cocaine while in the womb. They may exhibit social, emotional, and cognitive problems. Children

---

[1] **Source: ACLD, Inc. An Association for Children & Adults with Learning Disabilities, Greater Pittsburg, PA Region.**

who were exposed to drugs prenatally may also have poor coordination, low tolerance levels, and poor memory. Police officers should be aware of these symptoms and recognize that they reflect a condition over which the youth has limited or no control.

Another pressing problem is that of **fetal alcohol syndrome (FAS)**, the leading known cause of mental retardation in the Western world. FAS effects include impulsivity; inability to predict consequences or to use appropriate judgment in daily life; poor communication skills; and high levels of activity and distractibility in small children and frustration and depression in adolescents.

Yet another group of at-risk children who present special problems to law enforcement are children prenatally exposed to HIV. Such children may have mental retardation, language delays, gross- and fine-motor skill deficits, and reduced flexibility and muscle strength.

Children with special needs are likely to be in contact with the police, and many may become status offenders, committing offenses based on age such as underage smoking or drinking or violating curfews. Others may become more serious offenders, as discussed in Chapter 12. Youths with special needs may also be at greater risk for joining gangs, as discussed in Chapter 13.

fetal alcohol syndrome (FAS)

The leading known cause of mental retardation in the Western world; effects include impulsivity, inability to predict consequences or to use appropriate judgment in daily life, poor communication skills, high levels of activity, distractibility in small children, and frustration and depression in adolescents.

VICTIMS AND WITNESSES

A final population presenting communication challenges are victims of and witnesses to criminal acts.

"IF YOU HAVEN'T BEEN THERE, YOU DON'T KNOW THE FEELINGS OF EMPTINESS AND FEAR AND HOW IT CHANGES YOUR LIFE. I WAS IN A STATE OF SHOCK. I WALKED AROUND IN A DAZE FOR WEEKS. I WASN'T FUNCTIONING. NO ONE REALLY UNDERSTOOD HOW I FELT."

—Sherry Price, rape victim

Understanding others is particularly important in police work. Understanding others does not, however, mean that you sympathize with them or even that you agree with them. *Sympathy* is an involuntary sharing of another person's feelings of fear, grief, or anger. *Empathy* is an active process involving trying to *understand* another person's feelings. Empathy requires effective communication skills.

It is essential for law enforcement officers to communicate effectively with victims and witnesses because they are a major source of common crime information known to law enforcement.

Results of Being Victimized

People who become victims of crime often come out of the experience feeling victimized by both the perpetrator and the system. The entire criminal justice system is focused on the criminal. Victims are sometimes blamed for being victimized and many times are left in the dark about progress on their case. Perpetrators, on the other hand, have an attorney representing them every step of the way, ensuring that their rights are not violated. Many victims are shocked to learn that the prosecutor represents the state, not the victim. If the crime was a violent one, victims are often frightened, traumatized, and feel very much alone. They may suffer physical injury, financial and property losses, emotional distress, and psychological trauma. Some suffer from **posttraumatic stress disorder (PTSD)**, a persistent reexperiencing of a traumatic event through intrusive memories, dreams, and a variety of anxiety-related symptoms.

Nonreporting of Victimization

Many victims feel it is their civic duty to report victimization and hope doing so will bring offenders to justice. Others report crimes simply because they want to recover their property or file an insurance claim. In the absence of such motivators, however, a large percentage of robberies, aggravated assaults, burglaries, and rapes go unreported to the police. Victims may consider the matter private, feel ashamed, or believe the police will be unable to do anything. In the case of victims of sexual assault, they often feel they will not be believed and all too frequently, they are right.

When crime is underreported the police do not know there is a problem or may think it is only a minor problem. They do not have a true picture of the situation, which makes it difficult to problem-solve effectively.

Some victims and witnesses fear threats or retaliation from the offender(s). Many victims of violent crimes are warned by their attackers that going to the police will result in dire consequences for either the victims themselves or people they care about.

One reason gangs flourish is that they operate through intimidation, both inside and outside of court. Police must often deal with courtroom intimidation. Sometimes the court is packed with gang members who give threatening looks and suggestive signals to witnesses. Some departments counter this tactic by taking classes of police cadets into the courtroom. Confronted with this law enforcement presence, gang members usually give up and leave. It is important for law enforcement to encourage reporting crime by reassuring victims and witnesses they will be protected against threats, intimidation, or reprisals by the victimizers.

Assisting Victims

Society has made progress in assisting victims of crime. In 1981 then-President Ronald Reagan proclaimed National Victims of Crime Week, putting the full weight and influence of his office behind the victims' movement. Since then, a variety of organizations and programs have been created to help victims.

Organizations   Providing help to crime victims originated as a grassroots effort in the 1960s and 1970s to help battered women and victims of sexual assault. Organizations dedicated to helping victims include the National Organization for Victim Assistance (NOVA), founded in 1976; the Office for Victims of Crime (OVC), founded in 1984; and the National Victim Center, founded in 1985.

Other victim organizations have been formed, including Mothers against Drunk Driving, Students against Drunk Driving, Parents of Murdered Children, the National Organization of Victim Assistance, and Victims for Victims. In addition, victim compensation laws and victim advocacy and protection programs attempt to address what is widely perceived as the system's protection of the accused's rights to the victim's detriment.

Programs Implemented Numerous programs also have been implemented to help victims deal with the financial and emotional fallout of victimization. The two main types of programs provided for victims are victim compensation programs and victim/witness assistance programs. *Victim compensation programs* help crime victims cope with crime-related expenses such as medical costs, mental health counseling, lost wages, and funeral or burial costs. *Victim/ witness assistance programs* provide services such as crisis support, peer support, referrals to counseling, advocacy within the justice system, and, in some cases, emergency shelter.

Crime victim compensation programs have been established in every state. Programs are based on identified needs of victims and witnesses.

Victims' Bill of Rights Victims and witnesses have two basic rights: the right to obtain certain information from the criminal justice system and the right to be treated humanely by the system. Most victims' bills of rights include both informational and participatory rights. They commonly require the victim to be informed about available financial aid and social services, as well as the whereabouts of the accused; advised of case status and scheduling; protected from harassment and intimidation; provided with separate waiting areas during the trial; and granted a speedy disposition of the case and return of property held as evidence.

Police officers can help victims by letting them know their rights, including the right to become active in the case processing and to prepare a victim impact statement (VIS). They can also tell victims what services are available.

Some departments are using innovative approaches to reach out to victims and maintain lines of communication. For example, in some lower-income communities where few residents can afford telephone service, cellular phone links have been established to help crime victims reach the police. Cell phones have no lines to cut and can be preprogrammed with 911 and the general information number of the police department, but all other calling capability can be locked out. An example of how communications are maintained with prior victims is seen in Jefferson County, Kentucky, where the Victim Information and Notification Everyday (VINE™) system automatically alerts victims with a telephone call when an inmate is released from custody. VINE could serve as a national model for using technology.

Agencies That Can Assist

Agencies usually included in a victim/witness assistance referral network are community groups, day care centers, domestic violence programs, food stamp distribution centers, job counseling and training programs, mental health care programs, physical health care programs, private sector allies, private and community emergency organizations, rape crisis centers, unemployment services, victim assistance or advocacy organizations, victim compensation boards, volunteer groups, and welfare agencies.

The Direction of Victims' Rights and Services in the 21st Century

Examples of "promising practices" transforming victim services include children's advocacy centers; community criminal justice partnerships; crisis response teams; technologies to benefit crime victims (such as VINE); community police, prosecutors, and court programs; initiatives of allied professionals (such as partnerships between criminal justice agencies, schools, the medical and mental health communities, religious communities, and the business community); comprehensive victim service centers; and specialized programs for diverse crime victims (including disabled victims and victims of gang violence).

SUMMARY

The quality of police–community relations depends on effective communication. The communication process involves a sender, a message, a channel, a receiver, and, sometimes, feedback. Important individual characteristics in communication include age, education, gender, values, emotional involvement, self-esteem, and language skills. Two critical barriers to communication in a diverse society are language barriers and cultural barriers. Police officers may have more barriers to communication because of the image they convey, their position of authority, and the nature of their work. Other barriers include lack of time, use of police jargon, lack of feedback, and a failure to listen.

A dilemma facing law enforcement regarding the immigration issue is whether police can build trusting partnerships with immigrant communities if they are also to gather intelligence and enforce immigration law. One challenge facing our increasingly diverse society is discrimination. It is critical to recognize prejudices and stereotypes to avoid discrimination. Prejudice is an attitude; discrimination is a behavior.

Disabilities police officers frequently encounter include mobility impairment, vision impairment, hearing impairment, impairment as a result of epilepsy, and mental or emotional impairment. An epileptic seizure may be mistaken for a drug- or alcohol-induced stupor because the person may have incoherent speech and a glassy-eyed stare and may be wandering aimlessly. Another population the police encounter daily is the elderly, people age 65 and older, who may be victims of Alzheimer's disease (AD). People with AD may wander or become lost, engage in inappropriate sexual behavior, lose impulse control, shoplift, falsely accuse others, appear intoxicated, drive erratically, or become victims of crime. Many symptoms of AD and intoxication are identical: confusion and disorientation; problems with short-term memory, language, sight, and coordination; combativeness and extreme reactions; and loss of contact with reality.

Young people are a frequently overlooked segment of the population important to implementing community policing. Youths with special needs include those who are emotionally/behaviorally disturbed (EBD); who have specific learning disabilities; who have an attention deficit disorder; or who have behavior problems resulting from prenatal exposure to drugs, including alcohol, or to human immunodeficiency virus (HIV).

Finally, it is essential for law enforcement officers to communicate effectively with victims and witnesses because they are a major source of common crime information known to law enforcement.

DISCUSSION QUESTIONS

1. In what ways might a person become a victim and need assistance from the police?
2. What role do euphemisms ("soft" words) play in communication?
3. In what ways might the general public be perceived as "customers" of a police department? What implications does this have?
4. How diverse is your community?
5. Have you ever tried to communicate with someone who does not speak English? What was it like?

6. How would you describe the American culture?

7. Would you favor eliminating the word *minority* when talking about diversity? If so, what term would you use instead?

8. Do you consider yourself "culturally literate"? Why or why not?

9. Have you encountered instances of racism? Explain.

10. Have you or someone you know ever been a victim of crime? Was the crime reported to the police, and if not, why?

GALE EMERGENCY SERVICES DATABASE ASSIGNMENTS

ONLINE Database

- Use the Gale Emergency Services Database to help answer the Discussion Questions as appropriate.

- Research at least one of the following subjects and write a brief (three- to four-page) report of your findings: discrimination, Verbal Judo Institute, nonverbal communication, prejudices, or stereotypes.

- Research and report on at least one of the following subjects: cultural conflict, hate crime, homelessness, or racial profiling.

- Research how mental retardation affects the likelihood of criminal activity, conviction, incarceration, and rehabilitation. What systemic changes, if any, would you recommend based on your research?

- Research the police services that are available for mentally ill persons in your area.

REFERENCES

"The Aging of America." 2012. Washington, DC: Population Resource Center. Retrieved June 8, 2012 from http://www.prcdc.org/300million/The_Aging_of_America

America's Youngest Outcasts 2010. 2011. Needham, MA: The National Center on Family Homelessness.

Anderson, Mark. 2006. "The C.I.T. Model in Minnesota." *Minnesota Police Chief* (Spring): 13–14.

Association for Children with Learning Disabilities. 2009. "About Specific Learning Disabilities." Pittsburgh, PA: Association for Children with Learning Disabilities. Retrieved June 8, 2012 from http://www.acldonline.org/index.php?option=com_content&view=category&layout=blog&id=67&Itemid=111

Cordner, Gary. 2006 (May). *People with Mental Illness.* Problem-Oriented Guides for Police, Problem-Specific Guides Series, No. 40. Washington, DC: Office of Community Oriented Policing Services.

Dodge, Mary. 2005. "Reviewing the Year in Police, Law Enforcement, Crime Prevention." *Criminal Justice Research Reports* (July/August): 84–85.

A Dream Denied: The Criminalization of Homelessness in U.S. Cities. 2006 (January). A Report by the National Coalition for the Homeless and the National Law Center on Homelessness and Poverty.

Glenn, Russell W., Barbara R. Panitch, Dionne Barnes-Proby, Elizabeth Williams, John Christian, Matthew W. Lewis, Scott Gerwehr, and David W. Brannan. 2003. *Training the 21st Century Police Officer: Redefining Police Professionalism for the Los Angeles Police Department.* Santa Monica, CA: Rand Public Safety and Justice.

Giles, Howard, Jennifer Fortman, Rene Dailey, Valeria Barker, and Christopher Hajek. 2005. *Hate, Violence, and Death on Main Street USA: A Report on Hate Crimes and Violence against People Experiencing Homelessness, 2005.* Washington, DC: National Coalition for the Homeless.

Grieco, Elizabeth M., Yesenia D. Acosta, G. Patricia de la Cruz, Christine Gambino, Thomas Gryn, Luke J. Larsen, Edward N. Trevelyan, and Nathan P. Walters. 2012 (May). *The Foreign-Born Population in the United States: 2010.* Washington, DC: U.S. Census Bureau. (ACS-19)

Haddad, Ronald. 2011. "Building Trust, Driving Relationships with the Dearborn, Michigan, Arab American Community." *The Police Chief* 78 (3): 42–47.

Hate Crimes against the Homeless: Violence Hidden in Plain View. 2010 (January). Washington, DC: National Coalition for the Homeless.

Henderson, Nicole J., Christopher W, Ortiz, Naomi F. Sugie, and Joel Miller. 2006. *Law Enforcement and Arab American Community Relations after September 11, 2001: Engagement in a Time of Uncertainty.* New York, NY: Vera Institute of Justice.

Hill, Rodney, Guthrie Guill, and Kathryn Ellis. 2004. "The Montgomery County CIT Model: Interacting with People with Mental Illness." *FBI Law Enforcement Bulletin* 73(7): 18–25.

Hoefer, Michael, Nancy Rytina, and Bryan C. Baker. 2011 (February). *Estimates of Unauthorized Immigrant Population Residing in the United States: January 2010.* Washington, DC: Department of Homeland Security, Office of Immigration Statistics.

The Homeless Outreach Program (Ft. Lauderdale, Florida). 2008. Washington, DC: Center for Problem-Oriented Policing. Retrieved June 5, 2012 from http://www.popcenter.org/library/awards/goldstein/2008/08-07.pdf

Homes Not Handcuffs: The Criminalization of Homelessness in U.S. Cities. 2009 (July). Washington, DC: National Law Center on Homelessness & Poverty and the National Coalition for the Homeless.

Illegal Immigration: Gaps between and within Parties. 2011 (December 6). Washington, DC: Pew Research Center. Retrieved June 4, 2012 from http://www.people-press.org/files/legacy-pdf/12-6-11%20Immigration%20Release.pdf

"Justice Department Offers Local Police Guidance for Complying with ADA." 2006. *Criminal Justice Newsletter* (May 15): 1–3.

Khashu, Anita, Robin Busch, and Zainab Latif. 2005 (August). *Building Strong Police–Immigrant Community Relations:*

Lessons from a New York City Project. New York, NY: Vera Institute of Justice.

Law Enforcement and People with Severe Mental Illness. 2006. Arlington, VA: Treatment Advocacy Center.

Lysakowski, Matthew, Albert Anthony Pearsall III, and Jill Pope. 2009 (June). *Policing in New Immigrant Communities*. Washington, DC: Office of Community Oriented Policing Services. (e060924209)

Mohandie, Kris, J. Reid Meloy, and Peter I. Collins. 2009. "Suicide by Cop among Officer-Involved Shooting Cases." *Journal of Forensic Sciences* 54 (2): 456–462.

Moore, Carole. "Policing the Mentally Ill." 2006. *Law Enforcement Technology* 33(8): 134.

National Law Center on Homelessness and Poverty. 2011 (June). *"Simply Unacceptable": Homelessness and the Human Right to Housing in the United States 2011*. Washington, DC: The National Law Center on Homelessness and Poverty.

Passel, Jeffrey, D'Vera Cohn, and Ana Gonzalez-Barrera. 2012 (May 3). *Net Migration from Mexico Falls to Zero—and Perhaps Less*. Washington, DC: Pew Research Center. Retrieved June 3, 2012 from http://www.pewhispanic.org/2012/04/23/net-migration-from-mexico-falls-to-zero-and-perhaps-less

Public Remains Conflicted over Islam. 2010 (August 24). Washington, DC: Pew Research Center. Retrieved June 5, 2012 from http://www.pewforum.org/uploadedFiles/Topics/Religious_Affiliation/Muslim/Islam-mosque-full-report.pdf

Schaefer, Robert and Julie McNiff. 2011. "Awareness of Alzheimer's Disease." *FBI Law Enforcement Bulletin* 80 (10): 12–16.

Scoville, Dean. 2010. "Suicide by Cop." *Police* (April): 32–41.

Shah, Susan and Rodolfo Estrada. 2009 (February). *Bridging the Language Divide: Promising Practices for Law Enforcement*. New York, NY: Vera Institute of Justice, Center on Immigration and Justice.

Shin, Hyon B. and Robert A. Kominski. 2010 (April). *Language Use in the United States: 2007*. Washington, DC: U.S. Census Bureau. (ACS-12)

Skogan, Wesley and Kathleen Frydl, eds. 2004. *Fairness and Effectiveness in Policing: The Evidence*. Washington, DC: National Academies Press.

Sourcebook of Criminal Justice Statistics 2004. 2004. Washington, DC: Bureau of Justice Statistics. Retrieved June 5, 2012 from http://www.albany.edu/sourcebook/pdf/t226.pdf

"State and County QuickFacts." 2012. Washington, DC: U.S. Census Bureau. Retrieved June 8, 2012 from http://quickfacts.census.gov/qfd/states/00000.html

Suicide in the U.S.: Statistics and Prevention. 2010 (September 27). Bethesda, MD: National Institute of Mental Health. (NIH Publication No. 06-4594) Retrieved June 7, 2012 from http://www.nimh.nih.gov/health/publications/suicide-in-the-us-statistics-and-prevention/index.shtml

Tactical Response Staff. 2006. "Crisis Intervention Team." *Tactical Response* 4 (9): 54–59.

Take Another Look: Police Response to Seizures and Epilepsy. 2010. Landover, MD: Epilepsy Foundation of America and the Police Executive Research Forum. Retrieved June 7, 2012 from http://www.epilepsyfoundation.org/living-withepilepsy/firstresponders/policecurriculum.cfm

Thompson, George. 2006 (March 31). "Community Policing: The 'Gap' Theory." *PoliceOne.com*. Retrieved June 3, 2012 from http://www.correctionsone.com/corrections/articles/1841228-Community-Policing-The-gap-theory

Thompson, George. 2009 (March 27). "Tactical Civility: The Path of Power and Safety." *PoliceOne.com*. Retrieved June 3, 2012 from http://www.correctionsone.com/corrections-training/articles/1882989-Tactical-Civility-The-path-of-power-and-safety

Turner, Nancy. 1999. *Responding to Hate Crimes: A Police Officer's Guide to Investigation and Prevention*. Alexandria, VA: International Association of Chiefs of Police. Retrieved June 3, 2012 from http://www.theiacp.org/PublicationsGuides/LawEnforcementIssues/Hatecrimes/RespondingtoHateCrimesPoliceOfficersGuide/tabid/221/Default.aspx

2012 Alzheimer's Disease Facts and Figures. 2012. Chicago, IL: Alzheimer's Association.

Venkatraman, Bharathi A. 2006. "Lost in Translation: Limited English Proficient Populations and the Police." *The Police Chief* 73 (4): 40–50.

Walker, Samuel, Cassia Spohn, and Miriam DeLone. 2007. *The Color of Justice: Race, Ethnicity, and Crime in America*. 4th ed. Belmont, CA: Wadsworth.

Worden, Robert E., Sarah J. McLean, and Andrew P. Wheeler. 2012. "Testing for Racial Profiling with the Veil-of-Darkness Method." *Police Quarterly* 15 (1): 92–111.

CASES CITED

Adams v. City of Fremont, 80 Cal. Rptr. 2d 196 (1998)

Johnson v. Board of Police Commissioners, 351 F. Supp. 2d 929 (E.D. Mo. 2004)

Pottinger v. City of Miami, 76 F.3d 1154 (11th Cir. 1996)

CHAPTER 7
Building Partnerships: A Cornerstone of Community Policing

Problem solving without partnerships risks overlooking the most pressing community concerns. Thus, the partnership between police and the communities they service is essential for implementing a successful program in community policing.

—*Former Chief Darrel Stephens,*
Charlotte-Mecklenburg (North Carolina) Police Department

DO YOU KNOW ...

» Why police are asking the community to help them identify and prioritize crime concerns?

» What four dimensions of trust are?

» Whether beats and shifts should be permanent?

» What kind of beats community policing officers should be assigned to? Why?

» What may impede a shared vision and common goals?

» In addition to commonalities, what must be recognized when forming partnerships?

» What the common criticisms of community policing are?

» How these common criticisms can be addressed?

» How some cities are diverting nonemergency calls from 911?

» What purposes are served by citizen police academies?

» What key collaborators may be overlooked in community policing efforts?

» What some benefits of using citizens as volunteers are?

» Why it can be more difficult to build partnerships in a lower-income neighborhood?

CAN YOU DEFINE ...

call management
call stacking
collaboration
stakeholders
TRIAD
working in "silos"

INTRODUCTION

The Office of Community Oriented Policing says the following about partnerships:

> [Community partnerships are] collaborative partnerships between the law enforcement agency and the individuals and organizations they serve to develop solutions to problems and increase trust in police.

> Community policing, recognizing that police rarely can solve public safety problems alone, encourages interactive partnerships with relevant stakeholders. The range of potential partners is large and these partnerships can be used to accomplish the two interrelated goals of developing solutions to problems through collaborative problem solving and improving public trust. The public should play a role in prioritizing public safety problems. (*Community Policing Defined*, 2009, 5)

In community policing, the term *partnerships* refers to the collaboration that takes place between police officers, community members and groups, other government agencies, nonprofits, service providers, private businesses, the media, and other stakeholders: "The police become an integral part of the community culture, and the community assists in defining future priorities and in allocating resources. The difference is substantial and encompasses basic goals and commitments. Community partnership means adopting a policing perspective that exceeds the standard law enforcement emphasis. This broadened outlook recognizes the value of activities that contribute to the orderliness and well-being of a neighborhood" (*Understanding Community Policing,* 1994, 15).

This chapter begins with a discussion of why partnerships are important in community policing and the core components making up successful partnerships. This is followed by a discussion of the benefits of partnerships as well as some criticisms that have been raised. Next is a look at how departments can make time for partnerships through call management and how citizens can become educated partners through citizen academies. Some key partners are identified: criminal justice partners, including prosecutors, courts, and corrections; government agencies; the private security sector; victims; and volunteers. Community policing partnerships in diverse neighborhoods are discussed. The chapter concludes with a look at some effective partnerships in action.

WHY PARTNERSHIPS?

Community partnerships with various stakeholders are crucial for police agencies serious about community policing. Community policing cannot succeed without them. Traditional policing expected the community members to remain in the background. Crime and disorder were viewed as police matters, best left to professionals. That meant most citizen–police interactions were *negative contacts.* After all, people do not call the police when things are going well. A citizen's only opportunity to interact with officers was as a victim of crime, as an involved party in some other emergency situation, or as the subject of some enforcement action such as receiving a traffic ticket.

Some people may question why the police would consult the public about setting police priorities and why they would ask them to work with them to solve neighborhood problems. Some feel that the police are paid to deal with crime and disorder and should not expect communities to take any responsibility or do their job for them. The reality is that the police cannot effectively do the job we need them to do by themselves. Much of the information and resources they need lie in the communities they serve. Comparisons can be made to what we have learned from the medical profession. Most people understand that doctors cannot keep us well unless we take some responsibility for our own health by exercising, eating healthy, watching our weight, and avoiding tobacco. Just as we can have an impact on our own personal health and safety, we can have an impact on our community's health and safety.

 Partnerships usually result in a more effective solution to a problem because of the shared responsibilities, resources, and goals.

CORE COMPONENTS OF PARTNERSHIPS/ COLLABORATIONS

Partnerships are often referred to as collaborations. **Collaboration** occurs when several agencies and individuals commit to work together and contribute resources to obtain a common goal. Figure 7.1 illustrates the core components of a partnership or collaboration.

collaboration
Occurs when a number of agencies and individuals make a commitment to work together and contribute resources to obtain a common, long-term goal.

Figure 7.1   Core Components of a Successful Collaboration/Partnership

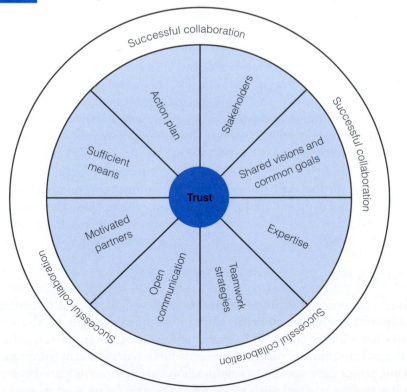

Source: Tammy A. Rinehart, Anna T. Laszlo, and Gwen O. Briscoe, *Collaboration Toolkit: How to Build, Fix and Sustain Productive Partnerships* (Washington, DC: U.S. Department of Justice, Office of Community Oriented Policing Services, 2001), 7.

Stakeholders

stakeholders

Those people who have an interest in what happens in a particular situation.

Partnerships are made up of **stakeholders,** those people who have an interest in what happens in a particular situation. This might include school board members, business leaders, elected officials, neighborhood-watch/block clubs, community activists, the attorney general, trade organizations, social service organizations, federal law enforcement agencies (e.g., Federal Bureau of Investigation, Drug Enforcement Administration, Bureau of Alcohol, Tobacco, Firearms and Explosives United States Citizenship and Immigration Services), the media, private foundations, and other charitable organizations. For example, a project to reduce thefts from cars on a college campus could involve stakeholders from several groups: students, administrators, teachers, the maintenance department, and police. Stakeholders will change depending on the problem being addressed, but when possible the collaboration should reflect the diversity of the community.

Active Community Involvement

Community policing relies on active community involvement, recognizing that such involvement gives new dimension to crime control activities. While police continue to handle crime fighting and law enforcement responsibilities, the police and community work together to modify conditions that can encourage criminal behavior. The resources available within communities allow for an expanded focus on crime prevention activities.

Patrol officers are the primary providers of police services and have the most extensive contact with community members. In community policing efforts, they provide the bulk of the community's daily policing needs and are assisted by immediate supervisors, other police units, and appropriate government and social agencies. Upper-level managers and command staff are responsible for ensuring that the entire organization backs the patrol officers' efforts.

Effective community policing depends on optimizing positive contact between patrol officers and community members. Patrol cars are only one method of conveying police services. Police departments may supplement automobile patrols with foot, bicycle, scooter, and horseback patrols and add mini-stations to bring police closer to the community. Regular community meetings and forums will afford police and community members an opportunity to air concerns and find ways to address them. Once the stakeholders are enlisted in partnerships, the focus becomes building trust among all collaborators.

Building Trust

Establishing and maintaining mutual trust is a central goal of community policing and community partnership. Police have recognized the need for cooperation with the community. In the fight against serious crime, police have encouraged community members to come forth with relevant information. In addition, police have spoken to neighborhood groups, participated in business and civic events, worked with social agencies, and taken part in educational and recreational programs for school children. Special units have provided a variety of crisis intervention services.

So then how do the cooperative efforts of community policing differ from the actions that have taken place previously? These actions include helping accident or crime victims, providing emergency medical services, helping resolve domestic and neighborhood conflicts (e.g., family violence, landlord–tenant disputes, or racial harassment), working with residents and local businesses to improve neighborhood conditions, controlling automobile and pedestrian traffic, providing emergency social services and referrals to those at risk (e.g., adolescent runaways, the homeless, the intoxicated, and the mentally ill), protecting the exercise of constitutional rights (e.g., guaranteeing a person's right to speak and protecting lawful assemblies from disruption), and providing a model of citizenship (helpfulness, respect for others, honesty and fairness). Although these are all services to the community, none are true partnerships, which require sharing of power and responsibility to identify and respond to problems.

Nonetheless, these services are important because they help develop trust between the police and the community. This trust will enable the police to gain greater access to valuable information from the community that could lead to the solution and prevention of crimes, will engender support for needed crime control measures, and will provide an opportunity for officers to establish a working relationship with the community. The entire police organization must be involved in enlisting community members' cooperation in promoting safety and security.

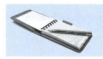
Four dimensions of trust are shared priorities, competency, dependability, and respect.

Building trust will not happen overnight; it will require ongoing effort. But trust must be achieved before police can assess community needs and construct the close ties needed to engender community support. The use of unnecessary force and arrogance, aloofness, or rudeness at any level of the agency will dampen the willingness of community members to ally themselves with the police. In addition, how officers have been traditionally assigned needs to be changed.

Changing Beat and Shift Assignments

Officers whose assignments continually change have no chance to develop the relationships and trust needed for community policing.

Traditional shift and beat *rotation* works to the detriment of building partnerships.

Communities also do not have the opportunity to get to recognize and know officers who work in their neighborhoods: "Having officers periodically rotate among the shifts impedes their ability to identify problems. It also discourages creative solutions to impact the problems, because the officers end up rotating away from the problems. Thus, a sense of responsibility to identify and resolve problems is lost. Likewise, management cannot hold the officers accountable to deal with problems if the officers are frequently rotated from one shift to another" (Oettmeier and Bieck, 1987, 12–13).

ON THE BEAT

Building trust with community members takes time and can occur in a variety of ways. One way is to have designated police districts. It is important that officers be assigned a particular geographic area so they can get to know the unique characteristics of that area. This creates ownership, in a sense. By working in the same area day after day, you begin to see patterns and develop a better understanding of the location's needs.

Our city is divided into four police districts. Officers bid to work in one district for an entire year. Some officers end up working in the same district for several years. Residents and businesses in your area get to know you and see you regularly. They learn who they can go to with an issue or concern. You begin to get a complete picture of what the needs are for the area and where your time is best spent.

An example of this is when you see many crimes occurring in a particular neighborhood. Based on what you see, you begin to do more directed patrols in the area—perhaps some foot or bike patrols. You are able to get others involved in problem solving and perhaps find people who are willing to report suspicious activity as it occurs. These conversations can happen when you are able to work in the same area for an extended period of time.

—Kim Czapar

The goal of community policing is to reduce crime and disorder by carefully examining the characteristics of problems in neighborhoods and then applying appropriate problem-solving remedies.

 The community (beat) for which a patrol officer is given responsibility should be a small, well-defined geographic area.

"Beats should be configured in a manner that preserves, as much as possible, the unique geographical and social characteristics of neighborhoods while still allowing efficient service" (*Understanding Community Policing*, 1994, 13). Officers who have permanent assignments become experts about their beats.

Beat officers know the community leaders, businesspeople, school personnel, and students. They know the crime patterns and problems and have the best chance to develop partnerships for problem solving. Community members will become accustomed to seeing the permanent beat officers working in the community.

This increased police presence is an initial move in establishing trust and serves to reduce fear of crime among community members, which, in turn, helps create neighborhood security. Fear must be reduced if community members are to participate actively in policing. People will not act if they feel that their actions will jeopardize their safety.

Police work proactively, often identifying and addressing issues before they become problems. They often collaborate with other agencies and community members to solve problems and identify potential trouble spots or situations and act on them instead of waiting for the radio calls that will surely come if the situation is ignored. They are able to respond to questions about crime in their area—for example, why burglaries or auto thefts have increased in a particular time period and what is going to be done about them. Of course, they still take all the enforcement action necessary and respond to calls as well. It is a far more challenging job and provides more job satisfaction because officers can see they are making a real difference. They are affecting a neighborhood, helping make it a safer, better place to live and work, and are building trust.

A Shared Vision and Common Goals

Although the delivery of police services is organized by geographic area, a community may encompass widely diverse cultures, values, and concerns, particularly in urban settings. A community consists of more than just the local government and the neighborhood residents. Churches, schools, hospitals, social groups, private and public agencies, and those who work in the area are also vital members of the community. In addition, those who visit for cultural or recreational purposes or provide services to the area are also concerned with the safety and security of the neighborhood. Including these "communities of interest" in efforts to address problems of crime and disorder can expand a community's resource base.

Concerns and priorities will vary within and among these communities of interest. Some communities of interest are long lasting and were formed around racial, ethnic, or occupational lines or a common history, church, or school. Others form and re-form as new problems are identified and addressed. Interest groups within communities can be in opposition to one another—sometimes in violent opposition. Intracommunity disputes have been common in large urban centers, especially in times of changing demographics and population migrations.

These multiple and sometimes *conflicting interests* require patrol officers to function not only as preservers of law and order but also as skillful mediators.

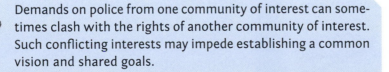

Demands on police from one community of interest can sometimes clash with the rights of another community of interest. Such conflicting interests may impede establishing a common vision and shared goals.

For example, a community group may oppose certain police tactics used to crack down on gang activity, which the group believes may result in discriminatory arrest practices. The police must not only protect the rights of the protesting group but must also work with all community members involved to find a way to preserve neighborhood peace. For this process to be effective, community members must communicate their views and suggestions and back up the negotiating efforts of the police. In this way, the entire community participates in the mediation process and helps preserve order. The police must encourage a spirit of cooperation that balances the collective interests of all citizens with the personal rights of individuals.

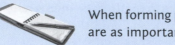

When forming partnerships, the conflicts within communities are as important to recognize as the commonalities.

The Remaining Core Components of Successful Collaboration and Partnerships

The remaining components, although vital, are not described, either because they are self-explanatory or because they have been discussed elsewhere in the text. With this understanding of the core components of partnerships, how can stakeholders be convinced to participate in collaborations? One way is to point out the personal benefits they might attain.

BENEFITS OF PARTNERSHIPS

This brings us back to the key question: Why partnerships? The benefits of participating in a partnership include:

» A sense of accomplishment from bettering the community
» Gaining recognition and respect
» Meeting other community members
» Learning new skills
» Fulfilling an obligation to contribute

Despite these benefits, partnerships have been criticized by some.

CRITICISMS OF PARTNERSHIPS

Partnerships are time consuming and therefore cost money. Most police agencies do not have extra personnel available for community policing–type projects. Many departments are 911 driven. Officers respond to one call after another and have a difficult time keeping up with the demand for service. When would they have the time to meet with stakeholders and develop plans to solve problems?

Criticism of the partnerships in community policing usually centers on time and money.

Working as partners with the community may take time and cost more in the short run, but continuing to treat the symptoms without solving the problem has its own long-term costs. It will mean responding again and again to the same calls, often involving the same people, and using temporary tactics to temporarily resolve problems. One way many departments free up time for officers to problem-solve with community members is to manage the volume of 911 calls and to ultimately reduce the number of calls through call management or call reduction.

MAKING TIME FOR PARTNERING AND PROBLEM SOLVING: CALL MANAGEMENT

In most departments, calls for service determine what police officers do from minute to minute on a shift. People call the police to report crime, ask for assistance, ask questions, get advice, and many other often unrelated requests. Police departments try to respond as quickly as possible, and most have a policy of sending an officer when requested.

 Departments might free up time for partnerships without expense through effective call management or call reduction.

When using **call management** or call reduction, departments take a fresh look at which calls for service require the response of one or more officers and, regardless of past practice, which do not. In call management, calls are prioritized based on the department's judgment about the emergency nature of the call (e.g., imminent harm to a person or a crime in progress), response time, need for backup, and other local factors. Priority schemes vary across the country, but many have four or five levels.

Call management usually involves **call stacking**. A computer-aided dispatch system is used to rank calls. Nonemergency, lower-priority calls are held (stacked), and higher-priority calls always receive attention and response ahead of the stacked calls. Using an officer to take telephone reports of nonemergency, low-priority calls is one change that has helped. Reports of minor thefts occurring days or even months in the past and made for insurance purposes are an example of incidents that could be handled completely by phone.

Similar results can be obtained by taking reports by appointment. If the reporting party is willing, an appointment can be set up to have an officer take a report at a time that is less busy for the department but still convenient for the caller. Many people find this method agreeable. Certain kinds of reports can be made on an agency's Web page, by mail, or by fax. Figure 7.2 illustrates the type of intake and response common in call management.

Another method of call management is to have civilian employees handle certain calls that do not involve dangerous situations, suspects, or investigative follow-up. These calls might include reports of abandoned vehicles, complaints about animals, bicycle stops, building checks, burglary, criminal mischief, funeral escorts, lost and found property, park patrol, parking issues, paperwork relays, runaways, subpoena service, theft, traffic crashes (with no injuries), traffic control, vandalism, and vehicle lockouts. However, police unions may take issue with such an approach unless reserve officers are used.

Call management may also involve dealing with the 911 system, which was set up for emergency calls for assistance. However, large numbers of callers, as many as 50 to 90 percent by some estimates, use 911 to ask for information or to report nonemergency situations (*311 for Non-Emergencies*, 2007). Most agencies field hundreds or even thousands of phone calls a year from citizens seeking information, often unrelated to police services. Keeping the public informed

call management

Calls are prioritized based on the department's judgment about the emergency nature of the call (e.g., imminent harm to a person or a crime in progress), response time, need for backup, and other local factors.

call stacking

A process performed by a computer-aided dispatch system in which nonemergency, lower-priority calls are ranked and held or "stacked" so the higher priorities are continually dispatched first.

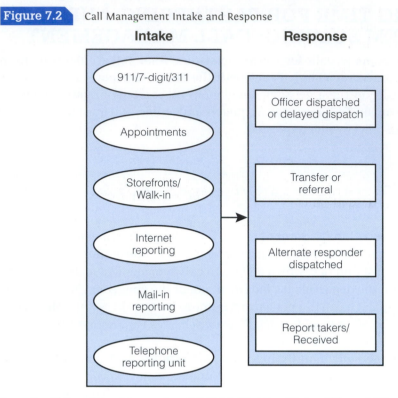

Figure 7.2 Call Management Intake and Response

Source: Tom McEwen, Deborah Spencer, Russell Wolff, Julie Wartell, and Barbara Webster, *Call Management and Community Policing: A Guidebook for Law Enforcement* (Washington, DC: U.S. Department of Justice, Office of Community Oriented Policing Services, February 2003), 12.

in other ways, such as on a Web site or through newspapers and newsletters, about city policies, services, and procedures and when and when not to call police can reduce the volume of calls.

People call the police for nonpolice matters for a variety of reasons: because they do not know who can help; because they believe the police know or should know the answers to all questions; because they know the phone number (911); and because, no matter what day of week or time of day it is, they know the phones will be answered. Every 911 call center fields calls asking why the electricity is out, what the weather conditions or driving conditions are, when the snowplows will start plowing, what time the shopping center opens, what time the neighborhood-watch meeting begins, what the driving directions are to a distant state, what the juvenile curfew hours are, where to pay a utility bill, and why there is no stop sign or semaphore at a certain location. Calls reporting pothole locations or complaining about raccoons, deer, and other wildlife—and even about noisy church bells—are clogging 911 lines across the country.

 Large cities have begun to implement 311 lines to divert non-emergency calls from 911.

A growing number of cities across the United States are implementing 311 call centers, at which trained employees field a wide range of questions from citizens or forward requests to an appropriate agency. The 311 system is increasingly viewed as a tool to enhance citizen access to government services and expand the original police nonemergency role. Three-one-one advances the community policing mission by providing an avenue through which citizens can share information with law enforcement and report quality-of-life issues before they escalate into more serious crime and disorder problems, taking a public service approach that reflects the nation's move toward community-oriented government (*311 for Non-Emergencies*, 2007).

Three-one-one systems are not without drawbacks. Disadvantages include high implementation costs, lack of caller ID or location identifiers for 311 as are provided by most 911 systems, failure to record information, underuse of neighborhood policing resources, and a common dispatch policy for both 311 and 911 (Mazerolle et al., 2005).

Results of a 311 Call System in Baltimore

Baltimore has implemented a 311 nonemergency call system to reduce the response burden on police and improve the quality of policing. Researchers note a 34-percent total reduction in calls to 911 (Table 7.1) and widespread community acceptance of 311 as an alternative number (Mazerolle et al., 2005, 3). Most low-priority calls have moved from 911 to 311. Certain types of calls in particular migrated from 911 to 311, such as reports of larceny, parking violations, and loud noise complaints.

Not all of the results of the study were positive, however. The number of priority 1 calls *increased* by more than 27 percent after the 311 system was introduced. Researchers believe this increase was unrelated to implementing the system, because their analysis showed that priority 1 calls for specific categories of serious crime had begun to increase several months before the 311 system was installed.

The large reduction in priority 5 calls to 911 was partly offset by an increase in nonemergency calls referred to other city agencies. Citizens may have stopped calling the police about priority 5 matters because the department stopped dispatching patrol cars in response to these calls after 311 was introduced.

Table 7.1   The Impact of 311 on Calls to the Police

	Pre-311 Implementation	Post-311 Implementation		
Call Priority	911 Only	911 Only	311 Only	911 + 311
1	417,728	470,263	62,534	532,797
2	902,565	633,706	184,931	818,637
3	415,133	177,967	138,722	316,689
4	201,043	66,169	103,878	170,047
5	111,500	375	50,454	50,829
Total	2,047,969	1,348,480	540,519	1,888,999

Note: Preintervention period was 730 days, from October 1, 1994, to October 1, 1996, excluding February 29, 1996 (leap year). Postintervention period was 730 days, from October 2, 1996, to October 1, 1998.

Source: Alberto R. Gonzales, Tracy A. Henke, Sarah V. Hart. *Managing Calls to the Police with 911/311 Systems.* Washington, DC: U.S. Department of Justice, Office of Justice Programs, February 2005, p.3. http://www.ncjrs.gov/pdffi lesl/nij/206256.pdf.

Unrecorded calls were estimated to be about 8 percent more frequent after the introduction of 311. This small but significant increase may have resulted from a greater inclination by 311 operators to handle calls about nonpolice matters without recording them.

Many elements of Baltimore's approach were successful—the overall burden on 911 was reduced, and citizen use of and satisfaction with calling 311 were high. The 311 system's impact on policing was muted because the department's response and dispatching protocols were not changed when the system was implemented. The research noted three key areas the 311 system was expected to have affected that actually showed little impact (Mazerolle et al., 2005, 4–5):

Response time for priority 1 calls to 911 was not lowered; rather, patrols were dispatched a bit more slowly following the introduction of 311. The increase in total number of priority 1 calls may account for this. Overall, after implementing 311, police responded to most categories of 911 calls in the same way as before.

Dispatch policy remained unchanged, with officers being dispatched, except on priority 5, whether 911 or 311. Either officers did not know or were indifferent about whether a call had been placed through 911 or 311.

Officer discretionary time increased only marginally. Almost two-thirds of the officers surveyed did not perceive a change in how much discretionary time they had available, most likely because time gains were spread out over shifts and obscured by the failure to dispatch 311 and 911 calls differently. Officer perceptions were about equally split on whether 311 implementation had changed their work routine. Sector managers, however, were certain 311 had decreased their patrol officers' 911 call response load.

Despite these mixed results, researchers concluded that linking 311 call technology with changes in policy and practice can advance a department's community-oriented policing agenda.

Online Reporting

Another way to make time for partnerships and problem solving is to have complainants report priority 5 calls online. A Web search of "citizen online reporting" will reveal the hundreds, if not thousands, of jurisdictions that make this reporting avenue available to local residents. Minneapolis, Minnesota, for example, has an e-report Web site. When people sign on, they are cautioned that the site is not monitored 24 hours a day and that, before they begin, they should make sure they do not need a police officer to take the report. The site also directs them to call 911 immediately if:

» A crime is in progress.
» Someone is hurt or threatened.
» They can provide information about someone who may have committed a crime.

The e-report site then asks specific questions such as who is reporting the incident, what happened, where it happened, and the like. Information from dispatch and online reports can be of great assistance in a department's problem-solving efforts.

| Table 7.2 | Percent of Departments Using Problem-Solving Measures |

Measures	Currently Doing	Plan to Do	No Plan to Do
Identifying top problem locations	92	7	1
Reporting/analyzing frequency of call types	84	13	3
Conducting "hot spot" analysis	66	23	12
Identifying repeat callers	65	17	18
Capturing and using premise history	61	27	12
Predicting emerging problem locations/areas	58	32	10
Assessing problem-solving efforts through change in number of calls	50	29	22
Determining which officers are performing problem-solving efforts	44	30	26
Assessing problem-solving efforts through displacement	32	28	40

* Totals may not equal 100 percent because of rounding.

Source: Tom McEwen, Deborah Spencer, Russell Wolff, Julie Wartell, and Barbara Webster, *Call Management and Community Policing: A Guidebook for Law Enforcement* (Washington, DC: U.S. Department of Justice, Office of Community Oriented Policing Services, February 2003), 104.

Calls for Service and Problem Solving

The data that departments obtain using computer-aided dispatch can be valuable in problem-solving efforts and can help identify top problem locations, hot spots, and repeat callers. The data can also help predict emerging problem locations. Table 7.2 shows the percent of departments using problem-solving measures or planning to do so using call-for-service data.

CITIZEN POLICE ACADEMIES

In addition to call management, many departments are finding they can improve citizens' participation in community policing and build trust through citizen police academies (CPAs), which were first introduced in Chapter 3.

A citizen police academy educates the public about the nature of police work and encourages public involvement in crime prevention and problem-solving efforts, making citizens more effective partners in community policing.

CPAs are popular among community members, with many agencies having waiting lists for admission to the next academy. Designed to give the participants a basic view of crime and policing in their community, many chiefs and sheriffs believe CPAs improve public relations and help build partnerships between the citizens and the police. Most academies include lectures, demonstrations, a ride-along with an officer, and an opportunity for participants to try their hand at some police technical skills. Numerous variations on the traditional CPA have been developed, including special academies for teens, older people, and limited English proficiency residents.

Norman, Oklahoma, has used CPAs to build trust among city residents and businesses in an effort to turn around its reputation for lawlessness and criminal

Two Somali teens "arrest" a Minneapolis (Minnesota) police officer during a mock traffic stop as part of a citizens' police academy. Local Somali youth participated in the 10-week course to learn more about the criminal justice system.

© AP Images/Minneapolis Police Dept/Jeanine Brudenell

activity. Police Chief Keith Humphrey tells the CPA participants, "You are the police department," and stresses that partnerships between the police, residents, and local merchants are the best way to produce permanent solutions to shared problems: "Officers who get to know the goings-on and the people within their beats will solve more crimes and drive the criminal element out of [the] city.... 'There will never be enough officers, so we need the eyes and ears of everyone who lives here,' [the chief] said" (Rieger, 2011).

A study of the Bowling Green (Kentucky) Police Department CPA indicates that, overall, opinions about CPAs are favorable, with data showing that citizen participants and police personnel gain a number of benefits (Pope et al., 2007). A preliminary survey found that participants began the program with generally positive attitudes toward police but with limited knowledge about the daily job of police officers and the department's programs. A survey taken after the CPA had ended showed that graduates left the program with increased positive attitudes and significantly increased knowledge about the job of officers and the department's programs (Pope et al., 2007).

The study also seemed to show that CPAs are designed to preach to the converted. CPAs reach a very small segment of the population, and that segment has little diversity. Stringent backgrounding of applicants keeps out any with past law violations. It might be helpful for CPAs to reach out to those who are neutral or even hostile toward the police. One way to increase diversity might be to move CPAs away from the police department, as some potential attendees may be unable to travel far due to lack of transportation.

KEY COLLABORATORS

In addition to offering CPAs, police departments might identify local key collaborators and be certain they are included in community policing efforts.

 Key collaborators who should not be overlooked include prosecutors, courts, corrections, other government agencies, private security providers, victims, the volunteers, and even such groups as taxi drivers.

The first group of collaborators discussed here are those within the justice system itself. The trend to involve the community is affecting all aspects of the system, with many researchers and practitioners advocating the move toward community justice. Three ways to measure the success of an idea are to (1) measure how rapidly an idea catches on, (2) measure the idea's staying power, and (3) measure how far the new concept travels: "By all three measures, community justice—the idea that the justice system should be more aggressive in engaging communities and more reflective about its impacts on neighborhoods—has been highly successful" (Wolf, 2006a, 4). The idea has spread to South Africa, England, Sweden, the Netherlands, Australia, British Columbia, and Scotland (Wolf, 2006a).

In the United States the community justice emphasis has influenced prosecutors, courts, and corrections.

Community Prosecutors

As community policing evolves, new collaborations continue to emerge. Including the prosecutor as a partner is one collaboration gaining popularity, and for good reason. Community members' concerns are often not murder or robbery but the types of things that contribute to neighborhood decline and fear of crime, such as abandoned buildings, heavy neighborhood traffic, or street-drug dealing. These neighborhood stability issues are frequently addressed by police, but prosecutors tend to see them as a low priority: "Community prosecution seeks to change the traditional orientation of prosecutors by more fully integrating them into the community and removing barriers between the office and those it is designed to serve" (Cunningham, Renauer, and Khalifa, 2006, 203).

Community prosecution builds on the 1980s' innovations of community policing and has steadily gained popularity throughout the country (Wolf, 2006b). Similar to community policing, community prosecution focuses not on specific cases but on community issues and problems, often involving quality-of-life-issues. The community prosecution philosophy calls on prosecutors to take a proactive approach and think of themselves as problem solvers "who seek not only to prosecute individual offenders but also develop lasting solutions to public-safety problems" (Campbell and Wolf, 2004, 1). When prosecutors become involved as partners in community policing, they attend neighborhood meetings, ride with officers on their beats, and get a completely different view

Table 7.3	Operational Elements of Community	
	Community Policing	**Community Prosecution**
Partnerships	The active enlistment of non-police individuals and agencies, public as well as private, in address[ing] community security programs	Partnerships between the prosecutor, law enforcement, public and private agencies, and the community
Problem-Solving	Remedying conditions that generate crime and insecurity, involving conditions-focused prevention at local levels	Varied prevention, intervention, and enforcement methods (e.g., use of tools other than criminal prosecution to address problems)
Community Involvement	Asking communities regularly and systematically what their security needs are and how the police might more effectively meet them	Inclusion of the community's input into the criminal justice system, including the courtroom

Source: Fanflik, Patricia L.; Budzilowicz, Lisa M.; and Nugent-Borakove, M. Elaine. *Managing Innovation: A Closer Look at Community Prosecution Management Issues.* Alexandria, VA: National District Attorneys Association, American Prosecutors Research Institute, October 2007.

of the issues and incidents that devastate communities and breed more crime and disorder. Three defining characteristics of community prosecution are:

» the development of partnerships with a variety of government agencies and community-based groups

» the use of varied enforcement methods, such as problem-solving techniques, to address crime and public safety issues

» the involvement of the community (Fanflik, Budzilowicz, and Nugent-Borakove, 2007)

Jansen and Dague (2006, 40) assert: "Forging a partnership with a community prosecutor can strengthen enforcement value and the services law enforcement provides." The similarities between community prosecution and community policing are many, and, as Table 7.3 illustrates, the operational elements of *community* are what enable community prosecution to work well in conjunction with community policing.

Many local district attorneys' offices report having adopted a "community prosecution" approach to crime control. Data from the Bureau of Justice Statistics indicate that, during 2005, two-thirds of all prosecutors' offices used tools other than traditional criminal prosecution to address community problems, and more than half sought input from the community to identify problem areas or information about crime (Perry, 2006). City attorneys' offices are also beginning to recognize the value of working with law enforcement and the community to develop creative solutions to livability issues. At the state level: "In 2005 nearly 40 percent of the prosecutors considered their office a community prosecution site actively involving law enforcement and the community to improve public safety" (Perry, 2006, 1). The nontraditional tools prosecutors are now aggressively using include nuisance abatement; drug-free and prostitute-free zones; landlord–tenant laws; truancy abatement; graffiti cleanup; and community courts, including several types of specialized courts (Wolf and Worrall, 2004, xi).

Community Courts

A recent alternative to the traditional courtroom is the community court, a neighborhood-focused court that offers an immediate, visible response to quality-of-life offenses that disrupt and degrade the community and provides an efficient way to process the most frequent types of complaints. With their origins in community policing and problem-oriented policing, community courts are a natural extension of the community justice movement and bridge the gap between the justice system and the local neighborhoods they serve by (1) bringing new resources from both inside and outside the justice system to bear on local crime and disorder issues and (2) applying problem-solving strategies to the complex issues that face state and local courts (Doniger, 2009).

The first community court was launched in 1993 in midtown Manhattan to target quality-of-life offenses such as graffiti, illegal vending, prostitution, fare beating, vandalism, and shoplifting. At the time, court dockets were overflowing with such misdemeanor cases, which limited the overburdened traditional court to either sentencing offenders to a few days of jail time or disposing of cases with no sentence at all—responses that communicated to the victims, community, and offenders that these offenses were not taken seriously. The Midtown Community Court, however, marked a "bold departure from 'business as usual' in the court system," by dispensing a combination of punishment and treatment, sentencing low-level offenders to pay back the neighborhood through visible community restitution projects while simultaneously providing services for issues such as substance abuse, addiction, unemployment, lack of job skills, and homelessness—problems commonly identified as the underlying sources of criminal behavior (Lang, 2011, 3). Data show the innovative approach has made a positive impact. For example, in 2009, only 50 percent of defendants processed through the traditional downtown criminal courts completed their community service mandates, whereas 87 percent of the Midtown-processed defendants completed their court-ordered mandates (Lang, 2011). Figure 7.3 illustrates case flow and interventions at the Midtown Community Court.

Community courts are as diverse as the communities they serve—some handle only criminal offenses such as stalking, auto theft, and assault, and others accept a wider variety of criminal and non-criminal offenses, from truant youth and landlord–tenant conflicts, to environmental code violations, drug addiction, chronic homelessness, shoplifting, vandalism, and sex trafficking (Lang, 2011). Despite their diversity, community courts share a common set of core principles and practices, including (Lang, 2011, 3–4):

» *Enhanced Information:* Using better staff training (about complex issues like drug addiction and mental illness) combined with better information (about defendants, victims, and the community context of crime) to help improve the decision making of judges, attorneys, and other justice officials

» *Community Engagement:* Engaging citizens to help the justice system identify, prioritize, and solve local problems

» *Collaboration:* Bringing together justice players (such as judges, prosecutors, defense attorneys, probation officers, and court managers) and potential stakeholders beyond the courthouse (such as social service providers, residents, victims groups, schools) to improve inter-agency communication, improve trust between citizens and government, and foster new responses to problems

» *Individualized Justice:* Using evidence-based risk and needs assessment instruments to link offenders to individually tailored community-based

Figure 7.3   Summary of Case Flow and Interventions at the Midtown Community Court

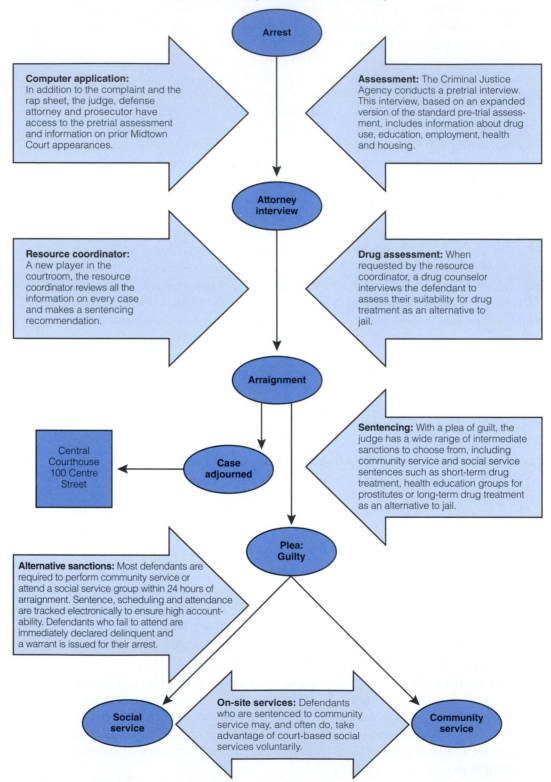

Midtown Community Court Case Flow Summary

Source: Eric Lee and Jimena Martinez. *How It Works: Summary of Case Flow and Interventions at the Midtown Community Court*. New York: Center for Court Innovation, 1998, p.4.

services (e.g., job training, drug treatment, safety planning, mental health counseling) where appropriate

» *Accountability:* Employing community restitution mandates and regular compliance monitoring—with clear consequences for non-compliance—to improve the accountability of offenders

» *Outcomes:* Collecting and analyzing data on an active and ongoing basis— measuring outcomes and process, costs, and benefits—to evaluate the effectiveness of operations and encourage continuous improvement

Although taking many forms, all community courts address neighborhood public safety issues through community collaboration, creative partnerships, and innovative programs. The goals community courts work toward are tangible—improved neighborhood safety, lower levels of public fear, decreased crime and disorder, greater accountability for low-level offenders, and increased public confidence in the justice system (Doniger, 2009). By year end 2010, 37 community courts were operating in jurisdictions throughout the country, and more communities were planning to install such courts (Lang, 2011). More information about community courts is available from the Center for Court Innovation at www.courtinnovation.org.

Community courts are a type of specialized court under the larger umbrella of *problem-solving courts,* which includes other specialized courts such as drug, domestic violence, gun, and mental health courts. Problem-solving courts subscribe to the philosophy that it is no longer sufficient for judges to simply process and adjudicate offenders, but that through their dispositions judges must also strive to ameliorate conditions conducive to crime and disorder, reduce recidivism, improve public confidence in the justice system, and prevent crime in the future (Wolf, 2007).

Several shared principles distinguish problem-solving courts from the conventional approach to case processing and case outcomes in state courts (Berman and Feinblatt, 2001, 131–132):

» *Case Outcome:* Problem-solving courts seek to achieve tangible outcomes for victims, for offenders, and for society, including reductions in recidivism, reduced stays in foster care for children, increased sobriety for addicts, and healthier communities.

» *System Change:* Problem-solving courts promote reform outside of the courthouse as well as within it. For example, family treatment courts that handle cases of child neglect have encouraged local child welfare agencies to adopt new staffing patterns and to improve case management practices.

» *Judicial Authority:* Problem-solving courts rely on the active use of judicial authority to solve problems and to change the behavior of litigants. Instead of passing off cases to other judges, to probation departments, or to community-based treatment programs, judges at problem-solving courts stay involved with each case throughout the post-adjudication process. Drug court judges, for example, closely supervise the performance of offenders in drug treatment, requiring them to return to court frequently for urine testing and courtroom progress reports.

» *Collaboration:* Problem-solving courts employ a collaborative approach, relying on both government and nonprofit partners (criminal justice agencies, social service providers, community groups, and others) to help achieve their goals. For example, many domestic violence courts have developed partnerships with batterers' programs and probation departments to help improve the monitoring of defendants.

» *Nontraditional Roles:* Some problem-solving courts have altered the dynamics of the courtroom, including, at times, certain features of the adversarial process. For example, at many drug courts, judges and attorneys (on both sides of the aisle) work together to craft systems of sanctions and rewards for offenders in drug treatment. And by using the institution's authority and prestige to coordinate the work of other agencies, problem-solving courts may engage judges in unfamiliar roles as conveners and brokers.

Community Corrections

The third component of the criminal justice system, corrections, also is an often-overlooked partner in the community policing effort. The movement toward community-based corrections has been growing steadily since the 1970s, when states, facing overcrowded correctional facilities strained beyond their intended capacities, began passing community corrections acts as ways to divert nonviolent, first-time offenders from the traditional path of incarceration. Community corrections, also called intermediate sanctions, usually has included a range of correctional alternatives existing along a continuum of increasing restriction and control—from day fines to forfeiture, restitution, community service, intensive supervision programs, house arrest, day reporting centers, and residential community centers—which are tougher than conventional probation but less restrictive and costly than imprisonment. Traditionally, the task of administering these correctional alternatives has fallen almost exclusively on those internal stakeholders within corrections—probation and parole officers.

Whereas it is one thing to conduct correctional activities outside the confines of barred institutions, it is quite another to actively draw the community and other external stakeholders into the corrections process. As with the overall movement of community justice, this has become the new paradigm in community corrections: "Community corrections includes any activities in the community aimed at helping offenders become law-abiding citizens and requires a complicated interplay among judicial and correctional personnel from related public and private agencies, citizen volunteers, and civic groups" (Hess and Orthmann, 2012, 561).

Probation is, by far, the most commonly imposed form of community corrections. Thus, partnerships between police and probation officers hold great potential to affect a large number of offenders within the criminal justice system and, ultimately, significantly affect public safety levels within a community. One type of partnership that has proved successful is that between individual patrol officers and probation officers in the same neighborhood. Probation officers who ride along with patrol officers can often spot probationers violating a condition of their probation, and the officer can make an immediate arrest. Or the probation officer can talk with the offending probationer, letting him or her know that the illegal activities will no longer go unnoticed.

For communities embattled in the gang–drug–gun issue, partnerships between police and corrections officers can prove beneficial. One effort to reduce gun crime across the country has been the Project Safe Neighborhoods (PSN) initiative, a task force idea based on the successful Operation Ceasefire implemented in Boston during the mid-1990s. Under Operation Ceasefire, police and probation and parole officers partnered to proactively search for individuals thought to be at high risk of illegal possession of firearms, jointly conducted nighttime home visits of these individuals, and gathered and shared intelligence to vigorously enforce the conditions of probation to ensure offender compliance. It is worth noting that the Supreme Court ruling in *United States v. Knights* (2001) upheld the constitutionality of warrantless searches of probationers' or parolees' homes based on "reasonable suspicion" or "reasonable grounds" by either probation or parole officers or the police. Police–probation partnerships may also include sharing probation or parole data for use in law enforcement geographic information systems (GIS) or CompStat databases to build criminal cases targeting serious offenders.

Philadelphia has forged a partnership between its Adult Probation and Parole Department and local police to address the growing violence in the city and attempt to gain control over increasing numbers of weapons violations. A unique feature of this effort is involving a research partner through the University of Pennsylvania's Department of Criminology: "A statistical model began to emerge from Penn's preliminary analysis of our data and from their mapping of the variables determined to be of interest. We named this model PROBE-Stat, articulating a mission statement to unite community supervision agencies and academic criminology in a data-driven partnership to prevent crime, especially serious violence, committed by and against offenders under court supervision in the community" (Malvestuto and Snyder, 2005, 2).

Other Government Agencies

Criminal justice agencies are not the only local government agencies responsible for responding to community problems. Partnering with other city and county departments and agencies is important to problem-solving success. Sometimes described as **working in "silos,"** local government agencies and departments have traditionally worked quite independently of each other. Under community policing, appropriate government departments and agencies are called on and recognized for their abilities to respond to and address crime and social disorder issues.

working in "silos"
Occurs when agencies with common interests work independently with no collaboration.

Fire departments, building inspections agencies, health departments, street departments, parks and recreation departments, and child welfare agencies frequently are appropriate and necessary stakeholders in problem-solving initiatives: "Elected officials have an important role to play in close coordination with their law enforcement executive, to make the community policing philosophy and the strategies it encourages work best and potentially expand beyond law enforcement" (Chapman and Scheider, 2006, 4).

Consolidation of Services The economic downturn that began in 2008 in the United States has had a widespread impact on society: "Unemployment rates have increased sharply, the stability of the housing market has collapsed, consumer spending has slowed, and city revenues have lessened. Law enforcement agencies are some of the hardest hit by the current economic climate, and they face a new reality in American policing—one that requires a shift in the methods they use to uphold levels of service while dealing with ever-shrinking budgets. The importance of maintaining and expanding community policing practices during this time of economic hardship is paramount" (*The Impact of the Economic Downturn*, 2011, 42).

Local governments across the nation have been forced to curb spending, and public safety operating budgets have not been immune to these cuts. In a 2010 survey by the National League of Cities, 75 percent of municipal officials reported that the overall economic and fiscal conditions within their cities had worsened over the past year. Nearly one-fourth of cities (22%) reported making cuts to public safety, the results of which were likely to impact activities essential to the quality of life and safety of their communities, such as crime prevention and service response times (McFarland, 2010).

With an increasing number of police departments throughout the country struggling to maintain their levels of service while losing personnel and other resources, many have chosen to consolidate efforts with neighboring agencies. Following are a few of various municipalities that have consolidated services (*The Impact of the Economic Downturn*, 2011, 30):

» Portage, Michigan, consolidated the police and fire departments, with the city's police chief taking on the role of public safety director and the responsibility for the overall management of both the fire and police departments.

» Berlin Township, Berlin Borough, and Waterford Township Police Departments in New Jersey combined their police detectives in a shared investigative bureau.

» Camden County, New Jersey, has regionalized some of their special services, such as a central detective bureau and SWAT.

» Marion County, Oregon, is consolidating dispatch services for local and county fire rescue and public safety, which is projected to save $370,000 yearly.

» Lansing, Michigan, plans to consolidate the north and south police precincts, saving the city more than $535,000 over several years in rent, utilities, and janitorial services.

» The cities of Greenfield and Soledad in California are merging police forces as part of a trend to regionalize public safety services, with projected savings to Greenfield of more than $158,000 in the first fiscal year of implementation.

Outsourcing Policing   Many smaller towns whose police departments consist of only a handful of officers hope to cut costs by eliminating their police department and contracting for services with county sheriff departments. Residents often resist this move, citing loss of local control, delayed response times, and impersonal police–community relationships, the result of having officers from distant jurisdictions, who are strangers to local residents, respond to several small towns with which they are not familiar. Objectors fear that sheriff's deputies will drive to their town on a call for service and leave when the call is completed. Most contract agencies seem to focus on emergency response and not on forming relationships, holding meetings, or engaging in problem-solving partnerships with local residents. In addition, contracting for services does not always cut costs and, in some cases, is actually more expensive.

Kelling and Bratton (2006, 4) point out that the radically decentralized law enforcement presence in the United States (i.e., more than 17,000 separate police departments) can be seen as both a strength and a weakness: "It is a great strength because the police are better attuned to their local communities and are directly accountable to their concerns. But it is also a terrible weakness in the post–September 11 world where information sharing is key."

State and Federal Agencies State and federal agencies may also be of assistance, including the Federal Bureau of Investigation (FBI), the Drug Enforcement Administration (DEA), the U.S. attorney in the region, the state attorney, the state criminal investigative agency, and the state highway department.

COPS and Homeland Security (2004) describes a partnership between the COPS Office, the FBI, and the Bureau of Justice Assistance (BJA) of the U.S. Department of Justice to enhance counterterrorism training and technical assistance to state, local, and tribal law enforcement. The FBI and COPS are delivering the BJA-funded State and Local Anti-Terrorism Training (SLATT) through the COPS network of local Regional Community Policing Institutes.

COPS has expanded its partnership with the FBI and BJA by developing counterterrorism roll call training programs for line officers, in which short segments on various aspects of counterterrorism are presented to officers during their roll calls.

Private Security Providers

Since September 11, 2001, law enforcement and private security organizations have been under pressure to not only provide traditional services but also to contribute to the national effort to protect the homeland from internal and external threats:

> Despite their similar interests in protecting the people of the United States, the two fields have rarely collaborated. In fact, through the practice of community policing, law enforcement agencies have collaborated extensively with practically every group but private security. By some estimates, 85 percent of the country's critical infrastructure is protected by private security. The need for complex coordination, extra staffing, and special resources after a terror attack, coupled with the significant demands of crime prevention and response, absolutely requires boosting the level of partnership between public policing and private security. (*Policy Paper: Private Security/Public Policing Partners,* 2004, 1)

Recognizing a need for collaboration between private policing and public policing, the International Association of Chiefs of Police held a summit in early 2004 to discuss possible collaborations between public and private police around the issue of terrorism. Their goal is to develop a national strategy to build such partnerships between federal, state, tribal, and local public sector police agencies and private security agencies. The focus of such partnerships will be terrorism prevention and response. The summit was supported by the COPS Office. The summit also looked at the differences in such collaborations, and some are significant, including differences in the screening, hiring, training, and responsibilities of private security and public police officers.

Some areas of cooperation are investigating internal theft and economic crimes, responding to burglar alarms, examining evidence from law enforcement in private crime labs, conducting background checks, protecting VIPs and executives, protecting crime scenes, transporting prisoners, moving hazardous materials, and controlling crowds and traffic at public events.

According to Dodge (2006, 84): "The proliferation of cybercrime and the need for specialized knowledge for crime investigation is driving the trend toward increased use of private policing." The expanding responsibilities of private security include surveillance, investigation, crowd control, prison escorts, court security, guarding and patrolling, proactive crime prevention, risk management and insurance assessment, weapons training, crime scene examination, and forensic evidence gathering.

Volunteers

Volunteer Programs (2010) notes that demands on law enforcement have greatly increased, especially since September 11, while budgets have shrunk and resources have become more limited. Volunteer programs can help leverage existing resources while simultaneously enhancing public safety. Volunteer programs not only allow agencies and officers to focus on policing and enforcement functions by providing supplemental and/or support services, they also create valuable ties between law enforcement and the community:

> Law enforcement volunteer programs are not designed to replace sworn or civilian personnel. Rather, volunteers are used to supplement and enhance existing or envisioned functions to allow law enforcement professionals to do their job in the most effective manner. Volunteers can provide innumerable benefits to a law enforcement agency. They can help enhance public safety and services, maximize existing resources, and create valuable ties between law enforcement and members of the community. Investing in a volunteer program can help sworn and civilian employees fulfill their primary functions and provide services that may not otherwise be offered. (Volunteers in Police Service, n.d.)

The use of citizen volunteers has significantly increased over the years. Data from the International Association of Chiefs of Police (IACP) shows that in 2004, approximately 75,000 citizen volunteers were used by police agencies throughout the United States but that by October 2010, the number of citizen volunteers serving law enforcement agencies had risen to roughly 240,000 (*The Impact of the Economic Downturn,* 2011).

Benefits to a police department that uses volunteers may include improved service delivery, increased cost effectiveness, relief of sworn personnel for other duties, improved public image, enhanced understanding of police functions, provision of new program opportunities, increased political support, restored community responsibility, reduced crime, and increased property values.

In addition, volunteers may benefit from reduced fear of crime, use of their skills and expertise, the opportunity to help others, enrichment of their daily lives, and a greater sense of belonging and worth. These benefits, compiled by the American Association of Retired Persons (AARP), are by no means exhaustive.

Profiles of Law Enforcement Volunteer Programs Countless volunteer programs in partnership with law enforcement agencies flourish across the country, many examples of which are described in the IACP's *Volunteer Programs* (2010). The IACP and Science Applications International Corporation (SAIC) co-sponsor an annual award to recognize excellence in leadership through the implementation of an effective, high quality volunteer program that successfully integrates volunteers into overall organizational operations and administration and to institutionalize the theories and practices of the Volunteers in Police Service (VIPS) Program. One winner of this award is the volunteer program at the Richardson (Texas) Police Department, where participants support more than 100 activities in five major categories of police operations and administration: communications, support services, investigations, special operations, and patrol:

> In these categories, volunteers provide services that support a myriad of projects and activities, including racial profiling statistical compilation, red light camera projects, planning and fiscal support, bicycle theft investigation and recovery program, crime scene searches, citizen fingerprinting services, Help End Auto Theft Registration, pawnshop recovery detail, translation services, accident investigation support, maintaining security for crime scene integrity, traffic surveys, commercial motor vehicle inspections, equipment and Quartermaster duties, crime prevention support, and Field Operations support. In addition, under the volunteer umbrella, the department also has a Police Chaplain Corps, an Explorer post, numerous neighborhood crime watch patrols, and a reserve officer program. (*Volunteer Programs,* 2010, 45)

The Denver (Colorado) Police Department has trained dozens of volunteers to serve on crime scene investigation (CSI) teams. These volunteers investigate automobile thefts, burglaries, and other property crimes that officers may not be able to respond to, and they are trained in evidence collection and crime scene photography. Volunteers must pass a background investigation, a polygraph test, and an interview, as well as receive final approval from the Director of the crime lab before they are admitted to the team (*Volunteer Programs,* 2010).

The Pasadena (California) Police Department has had a volunteer services program for more than 20 years. In 2006 the Pasadena Police Department received an award for their identity theft program—Community Response to Eradicate and Deter Identity Theft (C.R.E.D.I.T.)—from the IACP. In this innovative program, three volunteers assist the police department's Financial Crime Unit. Other endeavors volunteers are actively engaged in include the Chaplains Group, Citizens Assisting Pasadena Police Program, Equestrian Unit, Parade Watch, Safe Shopping Detail, Volunteer Translation Team, and Youth Accountability Board. Volunteers also help with traffic control and parking at local events, participate in National Night Out, and are required to complete the Citizens Police Academy prior to joining the department's volunteer group (*Volunteer Programs,* 2010).

Concerns about Using Volunteers Using volunteers may cause certain problems or concerns, such as the fact that volunteers often need to be supervised while working in the department; they may come into contact with sensitive or confidential material; they commonly lack awareness of the criminal justice system in general and specific agencies in particular; and they sometimes lack sensitivity to minorities. Because volunteers receive no pay, they cannot be docked or penalized for poor performance. Another criticism is that the use of volunteers by some departments has led to the failure of the local communities and politicians to take responsibility for solving the larger social problem and/or the refusal to hire adequate numbers of personnel or pay better wages.

One frequently expressed concern is that volunteers may do police officers' duties, thereby affecting future departmental hiring decisions. Some police unions have reacted negatively to volunteers, who are sometimes viewed as competitors for police jobs. Reserve officers, in particular, tend to cause patrol officers to feel their jobs are threatened by those willing to do police jobs for free or at greatly reduced pay. Officers should know that programs using volunteers are those that could not otherwise exist because of lack of personnel and funding.

Volunteer programs can be tailored to address most objections. Volunteers rarely perform actual police functions. They frequently work in programs the department could not otherwise afford to provide, such as fingerprinting children, distributing literature, maintaining equipment, entering computer data, organizing block groups, conducting department tours, and translating. Volunteers do, however, need supervision and recognition, and volunteer programs need a coordinator to handle those tasks. In some cases, a staff member can act as coordinator, or, when an extensive volunteer program is anticipated, a department may enlist a volunteer coordinator.

Older Volunteers with Law Enforcement Older persons make excellent volunteers. People in the boomer cohort (those born between 1943 and 1960) represent a great reservoir of talent and experience and possess a wealth of knowledge and background information to draw on (*Great Expectations,* n.d.). Older people tend to be dependable, experienced, stable, available, trainable, committed, skilled, conscientious, and service oriented. In addition, older volunteers have fewer accidents, are more careful of equipment than younger volunteers, use good judgment, follow directions, like to avoid trouble, have good attendance records, and tend to be team players.

Police departments across the country now staff innovative programs with older citizen volunteers, including neighborhood-watch clubs and anonymous reporting and court-watch programs. Some agencies tap the pool of experienced retired police officers to fill volunteer positions. One such agency is the Miami Police Department, whose Reserve and Auxiliary Officer Program is made up largely of ex-officers. These volunteers' law enforcement background and insight into local community concerns provides an invaluable resource to active duty officers regarding quality-of-life issues in the communities they patrol daily ("Community Involvement," 2011). The reserve and auxiliary officers are expected to participate in much of the same training as full-time officers to better enable the volunteers to supplement the agency's efforts in crime prevention and detection, response to emergency situations, and the general enforcement of laws while assigned specific police duties.

A joint resolution was adopted by the AARP, the International Association of Chiefs of Police (IACP), and the National Sheriffs' Association (NSA) to address criminal victimization of older people. The three organizations agreed to work together to design interjurisdictional approaches and partnerships to reduce victimization of older persons, assist those who have been victimized, and generally enhance law enforcement services to older adults and the community.

This three-way partnership, called **TRIAD**, provides specific information such as crime prevention materials (brochures, program guides, and audiovisual presentations on crime prevention and the elderly), policies, exemplary projects relating to the law enforcement response to the older community, and successful projects involving the formation of senior advisory councils to advise departments on the needs of seniors. TRIAD also trains police about aging, communication techniques with elderly citizens, victimization of the elderly, and management programs using older volunteers. TRIAD has been identified as a concrete example of community policing. Leadership is provided by an advisory group of older persons and those providing services to the elderly called Seniors and Law Enforcement Together (SALT).

TRIAD
A three-way partnership among the American Association of Retired Persons (AARP), the International Association of Chiefs of Police (IACP), and the National Sheriffs' Association (NSA) to address criminal victimization of older people.

BUILDING PARTNERSHIPS IN A VARIETY OF NEIGHBORHOODS

The effective mobilization of community support requires different approaches in different communities. Establishing trust and obtaining cooperation are often easier in middle-class and affluent communities than in poorer communities, where mistrust of police may have a long history.

 Building partnerships in lower-income neighborhoods may be more difficult because often there are fewer resources and less trust between the citizens and law enforcement.

Building bonds in some neighborhoods may involve supporting basic social institutions (e.g., families, churches, schools) that have been weakened by pervasive crime or disorder. The creation of viable communities is necessary if lasting alliances that nurture cooperative efforts are to be sustained. Under community policing, the police become both catalysts and facilitators in the development of these communities.

A PARTNERSHIP TO PREVENT STALKING

Data from the Bureau of Justice Statistics indicates that an estimated 14 in every 1,000 persons age 18 or older are victims of stalking during any given 12-month period. About half (46%) of stalking victims experience at least one unwanted contact per week, and 11 percent of victims said they had been stalked for 5 years or more. Approximately 1 in 4 stalking victims reported some form of cyberstalking, such as email (83%) or instant messaging, and 46 percent of stalking victims felt fear of not knowing what would happen next

(Baum et al., 2009). Many incidents of stalking are not reported to law enforcement because victims feel it is a private or personal matter, or they report it to another official (40.3%). The next most frequent reason for nonreporting is that the victim feels it is not important enough to report or that no crime has occurred (38.4%) (Baum et al., 2009).

Stalking is a complex and unique crime, making it more difficult to recognize, investigate, and prosecute. The factors that make stalking unique are, first, that the crime is committed repeatedly against the same victim. Second, these victims suffer extreme fear, and with good reason. Stalking victims are frequently severely injured, some fatally, by their stalkers. Stalkers, as a group, are highly motivated offenders, are especially determined to commit these crimes, and are difficult to deter. Protection orders, conviction, and even incarceration may not be sufficient to stop them, as some offenders are able to continue stalking, in some form, even from prison.

Like most police agencies in the United States at the end of the 20th century, the Philadelphia (Pennsylvania) Police Department (PPD) had no protocols or procedures for handling stalking cases. Acknowledging the need to increase officers' ability to recognize and respond to stalking crimes, the PPD agreed in 2000 to pilot test the National Center for Victims of Crime's Model Stalking Protocol (Velazquez, Garcia, and Joyce, 2009). With the goals of training the officers and developing a specific protocol on stalking, the PPD took a community policing approach to form key partnerships, beginning with a survey of the department's 7,000 officers. The survey found that officers were not knowledgeable about stalking, had not been trained in stalking, did not perceive it as a problem, and consequently were not providing the service victims deserved.

The department decided to process all stalking cases through one division during the pilot program. They first coordinated their efforts internally, and then they invited several community victim service agencies and the district attorney's office to serve as partners. All partners had representatives at the planning meetings.

The first step was training. The PPD developed a day-long training program and trained about 75 domestic violence detectives, victim assistance officers, victim assistance organizations, and the district attorney's office on stalking. All officers in the division attended a one-hour training session on how to recognize and respond to stalking. An invitation to attend was extended to all interested officers in the entire department, to signal how important the department viewed stalking offenses.

Project leaders then developed a stalking policy for the department, and in preparation for taking the project department-wide, they conducted train-the-trainer training. With funding from the U.S. Department of Justice's Office on Violence against Women, the PPD trained 700 first-line supervisors who, in turn, trained the officers they supervised. The training covered the interrelated crimes of domestic violence, sexual assault, and stalking. It also covered the new protocol in detail, including patrol procedures and individual officer responsibilities.

Although a formal program evaluation has not been done yet, the initiative has had positive effects, according to department leaders, who cite significant increases in the number of stalking and stalking-related investigations and in the quality of affidavits and arrest warrants. Training has eliminated many misconceptions officers held about the law, the process, and the willingness of prosecutors to pursue felony charges. Training has also resulted in the department being added to a judge's study group that reviews domestic violence–related cases and shares information that helps protect victims.

All partners in the initiative are now able to provide accurate and consistent information about stalking. The department provides officers with stalking tip cards to carry. In addition, the PPD has started a 24-hour hotline that is answered 7 days a week by partner agencies. With operators fluent in both English and Spanish, the hotline is able to assist victims of stalking, domestic assault, and sexual assault.

A new partnership with the probation department has also been developed. Police officers and probation officers make unscheduled visits to people who are on probation for domestic-related offenses. These unannounced visits are designed to check that offenders are not in violation of their probation and, in the case of those who have an order of protection against them, the visits provide an additional layer of security to victims.

The PPD, the fourth largest in the United States, with 7,000 officers, is a big ship to turn. Not every officer is on board yet with the idea that stalking is important or that the new protocol is useful, but department leaders believe that such buy-in will come as they continue to demonstrate their own steady, visible support of the importance of stalking and the protocol and procedures now in place (Velazquez, Garcia, and Joyce, 2009).

Ideas in Practice

CITYWIDE VANDALS TASK FORCE

Based in Brooklyn, with a satellite command in… Manhattan, the Citywide Vandals Task Force is charged with the responsibility of tracking and preventing vandalism in all boroughs. The unit is under the direction of Commanding Officer, Captain Elwood Selover. The unit falls under the direction of the Transit Bureau, and with good reason. "Though there are many vandals who do not 'tag' in the subways," explained Captain Selover, "[t]he transit system is still at the heart of the graffiti culture. We address this crime aggressively throughout the five boroughs, but effectively combating graffiti in the City means being able to do so in the subway system."

Part of battling graffiti is educating people; explaining how it hurts a community, and disabusing them of the idea that it is a victimless crime. Members of the Task Force regularly speak at Community Board meetings, schools, and other venues, about how the task of keeping parks, streets, and subways clear of graffiti goes a long way to cleaning up or outright preventing more serious and dangerous problems. Also on the syllabus is help in identifying signs that one's child maybe getting drawn into the graffiti culture. Parents sometimes dismiss their children's actions as normal adolescent behavior when they are in fact signs of more nefarious associations. The Task Force, in partnership with the Chief of Department's Office, and the Community Affairs Bureau, has put out a pamphlet to aid in this venture, and continues to look for new and better ways to incorporate every stake holder in the battle against graffiti.

The officers assigned to the Vandals Task Force possess a passion for their work that is matched only by the commitment of the Department to ensure that we are relentless in our efforts to battle graffiti. The majority of the unit functions in a patrol capacity; they have directed patrols and daily assignments. The Task Force members are dispatched in plainclothes, across the city, to target the areas hardest hit by vandals. They keep tabs on what is happening on the street, and parlay this information into arrests or more comprehensive investigations.

One of the subunits within the Task Force is the School Conditions Apprehension Team. They are specifically assigned to work with the myriad schools in the City to help identify and prevent graffiti vandalism. This reorganization has helped facilitate the more effective utilization of resources owing to the fact that the majority of those perpetrating this crime are youths.

(continues)

(continued)

Updating the Graffiti Offender Data Base and utilizing its myriad features to identify perpetrators and solidify cases are just some of the ways by which the Task Force accomplishes its mandate.

Tracking and nabbing the City's most industrious and destructive offenders has become a priority for the Task Force. Using conventional investigative skills, as well as a recently updated graffiti offender data base, officers can track and net those who wreak the most havoc on our City. The data bank allows officers from across the City to contribute to the effort. Offenders arrested for graffiti are brought to the attention of the Task Force and their arrest information is entered along with a mug shot and a photo of the damage caused. But an arrest is not required for the data bank to be utilized. A complaint made regarding graffiti is forwarded to the Citywide Vandals Task Force; that information is entered as well. This vigilance allows officers to match a number of identical "tags" to compile stronger cases against the offenders, to hold them responsible when they are eventually arrested.

"Tags" are like signatures, the vandals do them the same way each time. For them it is a matter of being recognized; they want people to know that each successive "tag" was made by the same person. Fortunately this enables the Task Force to work with the DA's office to compile cases and enhance arrests.

The Worst of the Worst book is constantly reviewed and Captain Selover is briefed on the updates enabling the Task Force to use the book as a key tool in its Anti-Graffiti offensive. Along with the database, the Task Force has put together a "Worst of the Worst" book, a sort of vade mecum of the 100 or so graffiti vandals that the Task Force has identified as the top menaces. This book is packed with information on each offender; detailing their area of operation, tags, pedigree information, and more. The Graffiti Coordinators in each patrol precinct have a copy and use [their copies] as tools to keep this crime in check. The Task Force is intent upon furthering the crime decline in the City and is, by far, one of the Department's best weapons in doing so. Their efforts have helped transform New York's reputation back into one [of] the preeminent travel destination[s] in the world.

Source: New York City Police Department. "Crime Prevention: Citywide Vandals Task Force," 2012. Retrieved June 17, 2012 from http://www .nyc.gov/html/nypd/html/crime_prevention/citywide_vandals_ taskforce.shtml

SUMMARY

Partnerships usually result in a more effective solution to a problem because of the shared responsibilities, resources, and goals. A partnership will only be successful, however, if trust exists between and among partners. Four dimensions of trust are shared priorities, competency, dependability, and respect.

Traditional shift and beat *rotation* works to the detriment of building partnerships. The community (beat) for which a patrol officer is given responsibility should be a small, well-defined geographic area.

Demands on police from one community of interest can sometimes clash with the rights of another community of interest. Such conflicting interests may impede establishing a common vision and shared goals. When forming partnerships, the conflicts within communities are as important to recognize as the commonalities.

Criticism of the partnerships in community policing usually centers on time and money.

Departments might free up time for partnerships without expense through effective call management or call reduction. Large cities have begun to implement 311 lines to divert nonemergency calls from the 911 system.

Departments might also enhance partnerships by providing citizen police academies (CPAs). A CPA educates the public about the nature of police work and encourages public involvement in crime prevention and problem-solving efforts, making citizens more effective partners in community policing. In addition, key collaborators who should not be overlooked include prosecutors, courts, corrections, other government agencies, private security providers, victims, the volunteers, and even such groups as taxi drivers. Benefits to a police department that uses volunteers may include improved service delivery, increased cost effectiveness, relief of sworn personnel for other duties, improved public image, enhanced understanding of police functions, provision of new program opportunities, increased political support, restored

community responsibility, reduced crime, and increased property values.

Building partnerships in lower-income neighborhoods may be more difficult because often there are fewer resources and less trust between the citizens and law enforcement.

DISCUSSION QUESTIONS

1. What are the most important factors that lead you to trust another person? To distrust someone?

2. Discuss the pros and cons of using volunteers in a law enforcement agency.

3. Select a campus problem you feel is important and describe the partners who might collaborate to address the problem.

4. Why are permanent shift and area assignments for officers important in community policing?

5. Why is trust an issue between police and residents of low-income neighborhoods?

6. What are the main criticisms or arguments against having police involved in community policing partnerships?

7. What strategies can help free up time for officers' involvement in partnerships?

8. Explain the difference between community courts and traditional courts.

GALE EMERGENCY SERVICES DATABASE ASSIGNMENTS

ONLINE Database

- Use the Gale Emergency Services Database to answer the Discussion Questions as appropriate.

- Select and research one of the following topics. Outline your findings and be prepared to discuss them with the class.

  - Citizen police academies
  - Future of private policing
  - Criminalizing homelessness

REFERENCES

Baum, Katrina, Shannan Catalano, Michael Rand, and Kristina Rose. 2009 (January). *Stalking Victimization in the United States*. Washington, DC: Bureau of Justice Statistics Special Report. (NCJ 224527)

Berman, Greg and John Feinblatt. 2001. "Problem-Solving Courts: A Brief Primer." *Law and Policy* 23 (2): 125–140.

Campbell, Nicole and Robert V. Wolf. 2004. *Beyond Big Cities: The Problem-Solving Innovations of Community Prosecutors in Smaller Jurisdictions*. New York, NY: Center for Court Innovation.

Chapman, Robert and Matthew Scheider. 2006. *Community Policing for Mayors: A Municipal Service Model for Policing and Beyond*. Washington, DC: Office of Community Oriented Policing Services.

"Community Involvement." 2011. Miami, FL: Miami Police Department. Retrieved June 17, 2012 from http://www.miami-police.org/community_involvement.html

Community Policing Defined. 2009 (April 3). Washington, DC: Office of Community Oriented Policing Services. (e030917193) Retrieved June 11, 2012 from http://cops.usdoj.gov/Publications/e030917193-CP-Defined.pdf

COPS and Homeland Security. 2004 (June 18). COPS Fact Sheet. Washington, DC: Office of Community Oriented Policing Services. Retrieved June 17, 2012 from http://www.cops.usdoj.gov/Publications/e06042393.pdf

Cunningham, William Scott, Brian C. Renauer, and Christy Khalifa. 2006. "Sharing the Keys to the Courthouse: Adoption of Community Prosecution by State Court Prosecutors." *Journal of Contemporary Criminal Justice* 22 (3): 202–219.

Dodge, Mary. 2006. "The State of Research on Policing and Crime Prevention: Expanding Roles and Responses." *Criminal Justice Research Reports* (July/August): 84–85.

Doniger, Kate. 2009 (February). "Inspiring the Judiciary: Community Courts Adapt Community Policing Principles." *Community Policing Dispatch*.

Fanflik, Patricia L., Lisa M. Budzilowicz, and M. Elaine Nugent-Borakove. 2007 (October). *Managing Innovation: A Closer Look at Community Prosecution Management Issues*. Alexandria, VA: National District Attorneys Association, American Prosecutors Research Institute.

Great Expectations: Boomers and the Future of Volunteering. n.d. San Francisco, CA: VolunteerMatch. Retrieved June 16, 2012 from http://cdn.volunteermatch.org/www/nonprofits/resources/greatexpectations/Great-Expectations_FullReport.pdf

Hess, Kären M. and Christine Hess Orthmann. 2012. *Introduction to Law Enforcement and Criminal Justice*. 10th ed. Clifton Park, NY: Delmar.

The Impact of the Economic Downturn on American Police Agencies. 2011(October). Washington, DC: Office of Community Oriented Policing Services.

Jansen, Steven and Ellen Dague. 2006. "Working with a Neighborhood Community Prosecutor." *The Police Chief* 73 (7): 40–44.

Kelling, George L. and William J. Bratton. 2006. "Policing Terrorism." *Civic Bulletin* 43 (September). Retrieved June 17, 2012 from http://www.manhattan-institute.org/html/cb_43.htm

Lang, Julius. 2011. *What Is a Community Court? How the Model Is Being Adapted across the United States.* New York, NY: Center for Court Innovation.

Lee, Eric and Jimena Martinez. 1998. *How It Works: Summary of Case Flow and Interventions at the Midtown Community Court.* New York: Center for Court Innovation.

Malvestuto, Robert J. and Frank M. Snyder. 2005. "Office of the Chief Probation Officers." In *2005 Annual Report.* Philadelphia, PA: Philadelphia Adult Probation and Parole Department. Retrieved June 15, 2012 from http://www.courts.phila.gov/pdf/report/2005appd.pdf

Mazerolle, Lorraine, Dennis Rogan, James Frank, Christine Famega, and John E. Eck. 2005 (February). *Managing Calls to the Police with 911/311 Systems.* Washington, DC: National Institute of Justice. (NCJ 206256)

McEwen, Tom, Deborah Spencer, Russell Wolff, Julie Wartell, and Barbara Webster. 2003 (February). *Call Management and Community Policing: A Guidebook for Law Enforcement.* Washington, DC: U.S. Department of Justice, Office of Community Oriented Policing Services.

McFarland, Christina. 2010. *State of America's Cities Survey on Jobs and the Economy.* Washington, DC: National League of Cities, Center for Research and Innovation.

New York City Police Department. 2012. "Crime Prevention: Citywide Vandals Task Force." Retrieved June 17, 2012 from http://www.nyc.gov/html/nypd/html/crime_prevention/citywide_vandals_taskforce.shtml

Oettmeier, Timothy N. and William H. Bieck. 1987. *Developing a Policing Style for Neighborhood Policing.* Houston, Houston Police Department.

Perry, Steven W. 2006 (July). *Prosecutors in State Courts, 2005.* Washington, DC: Bureau of Justice Statistics. (NCJ 213799)

Policy Paper: Private Security/Public Policing Partnerships. 2004. Washington, DC: Community Oriented Policing Services.

Pope, Jacqueline, Tena Jones, Shannon Cook, and Bill Waltrip. 2007. "Citizen's Police Academies: Beliefs and Perceptions Regarding the Program." *Applied Psychology in Criminal Justice* 3 (1): 42–53.

Rieger, Andy. 2011 (November 13). "Citizens Police Academy Participants Learn about Department." *The Norman Transcript.* Retrieved June 12, 2012 from http://norman-transcript.com/columns/x1267472220/Citizens-Police-Academy-participants-learn-about-department

Rinehart, Tammy A., Anna T. Laszlo, and Gwen O. Briscoe. 2001. *Collaboration Toolkit: How to Build, Fix, and Sustain Productive Partnerships.* Washington, DC: U.S. Department of Justice, Office of Community Oriented Policing Services.

311 for Non-Emergencies: Helping Communities One Call at a Time. 2007 (November 8). Fact Sheet. Washington, DC: Office of Community Oriented Policing Services. (e01060007)

Understanding Community Policing: A Framework for Action. 1994 (August). Monograph. Washington, DC: Bureau of Justice Assistance. (NCJ 148457) Retrieved June 11, 2012 from https://www.ncjrs.gov/pdffiles/commp.pdf

Velazquez, Sonia E., Michelle Garcia, and Elizabeth Joyce. 2009. "Mobilizing a Community Response to Stalking: The Philadelphia Story." *The Police Chief* 76 (1): 30–37.

Volunteer Programs: Enhancing Public Safety by Leveraging Resources. 2010. Alexandria, VA: International Association of Chiefs of Police, Volunteers in Police Service.

Volunteers in Police Service. n.d. *Enhancing Public Safety through Citizen Involvement.* Brochure. Alexandria, VA: International Association of Chiefs of Police. Retrieved June 15, 2012 from http://www.policevolunteers.org/pdf/New%20brochure_final.pdf

Wolf, Robert V. 2006a. "Community Justice around the Globe: An International Overview." *Crime & Justice International* 22 (93): 4–22.

Wolf, Robert V. 2006b. *How Do We Pay for That? Sustaining Community Prosecution on a Tight Budget.* New York: Center for Court Innovation.

Wolf, Robert V. 2007. *Principles of Problem-Solving Justice.* New York: Center for Court Innovation.

Wolf, Robert V. and John J. Worrall. 2004 (November). *Lessons from the Field: Ten Community Prosecution Leadership Profiles.* Alexandria, VA: American Prosecutors Research Institute.

CASE CITED

United States v. Knights, 534 U.S. 112 (2001)

CHAPTER 8

Forming Partnerships with the Media

> Police work is very much an "us-and-them" kind of thing. They are the beleaguered minority who are out there protecting the citizens from themselves, and the citizens are not smart enough to appreciate them. And the newsies are out there lying in wait, and the moment they screw up, we're there to jump down their throats and tell the world.
>
> —*Kevin Diaz*

DO YOU KNOW ...

» What the common goal of the police and the media is?

» Why the police–media relationship can be called symbiotic?

» What amendment protects freedom of the press?

» What amendment guides the police in their relationship with the media?

» What are some legitimate reasons for not giving information to the media?

» How to enhance the safety of members of the media during explosive situations?

» Whether conflict between the police and the media must be dysfunctional?

» Whether it is ever appropriate or justifiable to lie to the media?

» In a police–media relationship survey, what factor was found to most affect the relationship?

» Why reporters may foul up stories?

» How officers can improve relations with the media?

» Why partnerships with the media are critical to the successful implementation of community policing?

CAN YOU DEFINE ...

news media echo effect
perp walks
public information officer (PIO)
soundbites
symbiotic

INTRODUCTION

The media can be a powerful ally or a formidable opponent in implementing the community policing philosophy. Positive publicity can enhance both the image and the efforts of a department. Conversely, negative publicity can be extremely damaging. Therefore, police agencies can and should make every effort to build positive working partnerships with the media.

 The police and members of the media share the common goal of serving the public.

The public's fascination with crime is evident in the popularity of such reality shows as *America's Most Wanted, Cops, Vegas Strip,* and dozens of other criminal justice–themed broadcasts. In fact, some of these shows go beyond just reporting what the police are doing and actually get involved as crime-fighting extensions of law enforcement, engaging the television-viewing public by reenacting crime events and displaying suspects' faces on millions of screens across the world.

This chapter begins with a discussion of the mutual reliance of the police and the media and the inherent conflict between the guarantees of the First Amendment and the Sixth Amendment. This is followed by an examination of victims' privacy rights. Next is a discussion of the conflict between the media and the police, including the sources and the potential benefits of such conflict. General policies and protocols for media relations are presented, as well as recommendations on how to be professional when interviewed, whether police should ever lie to the media, the role of public information officers (PIOs), and how departments commonly address photographing and videotaping at crime scenes. Then suggestions for improving media relations and specific strategies for developing positive relationships with the media are discussed. The chapter concludes with a discussion of marketing community policing through the media.

MUTUAL RELIANCE OF THE POLICE AND THE MEDIA

Police departments and individual officers need the media. The media can shape public opinion, and most police agencies are concerned about their public image. Administrators know that crime and police activities are covered by the media regardless of whether the police provide reporters with information. Most police departments understand that the level of police cooperation will ultimately affect how the public views the police. At the same time, reporters rely on the police for information.

symbiotic
Describes a relationship of mutual dependence upon each other.

 The police and the media share a **symbiotic** relationship; they are mutually dependent on each other.

Understanding the relationship between the police and the media starts with being aware of what rights the media have, what their mission is, and why law enforcement does not always appear in a positive light in the media.

THE FIRST AMENDMENT AND FREEDOM OF THE PRESS

The First Amendment to the U.S. Constitution states: "Congress shall make no law … abridging the freedom of speech or of the press." The free flow of information is a fundamental right in our society.

 The First Amendment to the U.S. Constitution guarantees the public's right to know—that is, freedom of the press.

In fact, our society deems the public's right to know so important that the media operate without censorship but are subject to legal action if they publish untruths. The courts have usually stood behind journalists who act reasonably to get information, but they also have upheld the privacy protections fundamental under the Fourth Amendment.

Police beat reporters are often eager and aggressive in carrying out their duty to inform the public. Anxious to do well and to be the first with information, they gather and publicize police and crime news as much as they can. The police beat is a high-visibility beat, considered a prestigious assignment by many newspapers and television stations and is, therefore, sought by the experienced, aggressive reporters. Coverage of crime events also draws increased viewership and readership, prompting many news organizations to give "top billing" to such stories.

Although keeping the public informed about situations affecting their individual and community's safety is an important and valuable service, the priority and emphasis placed on these stories often confuse the public about the true extent of crime and inflate the general level of fear people feel regarding their chances of personal victimization. Mediascope, a nonprofit media research and policy organization, reports that stories of crime and violence increase newscasts' viewership and ratings, driving news directors to devote more coverage and airtime to crime-related stories ("Behind the Story," 2001).

THE SIXTH AMENDMENT, SUSPECTS' RIGHTS, AND CRIMINAL INVESTIGATIONS

The Sixth Amendment to the U.S. Constitution establishes that "in all criminal prosecutions, the accused shall enjoy the right to a speedy and public trial, by an impartial jury of the state and district wherein the crime shall have been committed."

 The Sixth Amendment guarantees suspects the right to a fair trial and protects defendants' rights.

In addition to ensuring these rights, police officers are also responsible for investigating the crimes that suspects are accused of committing. Law enforcement officers sometimes view reporters as an impediment to fulfilling their duties. Officers often try to protect information they deem imperative to keep out of the media and may, therefore, be at odds with reporters. Such conflicts arise when police try to prevent public disclosure of information that may tip off a criminal of impending arrest, make prosecution of a particular crime impossible, or compromise the privacy rights or safety of a victim or witness. Reporters are eager to do well on their assignments, whereas officers try to avoid weakening their case and getting reprimanded for being too open with the media. The parties' conflicting interests may result in antagonism.

Of special concern are information leaks from within the department. Sometimes those who leak information are showing off how much they know, but the results can devastate an investigation.

VICTIM PRIVACY RIGHTS

As explained later in this chapter, the Freedom of Information Act (FOIA) protects the privacy rights of some people, such as sex crime victims. However, amid the shock and confusion that often occur immediately after a crime, victims may easily be caught off guard by aggressive media personnel and may unwittingly put themselves or the investigation at risk by agreeing to an interview.

In addition, the Office of Victims of Crime (OVC) has created a new online Directory of Crime Victim Services, which links crime victims and victim service providers to contact information for assistance 24/7. Searchable by location, type of victimization, agency type, and available services, OVC's online directory is becoming the best resource for finding crime victim assistance (http://ovc.ncjrs.org/findvictimservices).

To help victims and witnesses protect their own rights, as well as safeguard the criminal investigation, some departments have begun distributing media relations advisory cards (see Figure 8.1). Such cards, however, have caused concern among some journalists, who contend the advisories will interfere with news gathering. Members of the Society of Professional Journalists (SPJ), a group that includes a wide range of media professionals, said the practice could negatively affect whether immigrants and those who do not know their rights decide to speak with reporters.

Not surprisingly, this opposing perspective often generates substantial conflict between the media and the police, which can contaminate an agency's efforts to fulfill its community policing mission. The Wisconsin Department of Justice, Crime Victim Services "Rights and Services for Crime Victims and Witnesses" (n.d.) brochure provides the following information for victims on dealing with the media:

> In high profile cases, dealing with the media can add stress to you and your family. Many victims and family members of victims have found it helpful to have one family member or a family friend assigned to handle all contacts with the media. No matter who responds to media requests, you should know that you can:
>
> » Decline an interview (even if you have given other interviews).
> » Agree to an interview, but refuse to answer certain questions.
> » Select a time and place for interviews. You may protect the privacy of your home by giving interviews elsewhere or providing your point of view through a spokesperson and/or a written statement.

Figure 8.1   Media Advisory Card for Crime Victims and Witnesses

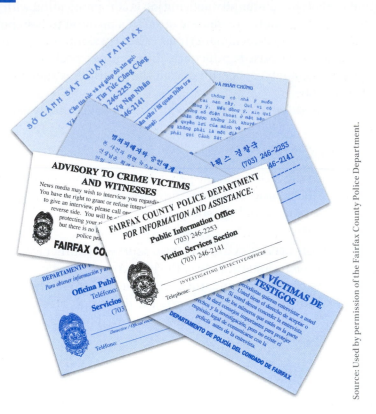

Source: Used by permission of the Fairfax County Police Department.

» Protect children from interviews. A child may be re-traumatized by having to talk to the media.

» Request offensive photos not be printed or aired.

» Grieve in private and ask reporters, photographers, or others to respect your privacy.

» Demand a retraction or correction of inaccurate reporting.

» Request to be treated with dignity and respect at all times.

CONFLICT BETWEEN THE MEDIA AND THE POLICE

The news media and the police are two powerful forces in our society that depend on one another but are often hostile toward and mistrust each other. A workshop held to bring law enforcement and media personnel together to air grievances, discuss issues of common concern, and generally get to know one another better so that the two groups could work more effectively together revealed their different perspectives. A major theme among media participants was their need to get information from law enforcement in a timely manner to keep the public informed, as the public has a right to know. One area of contention between the two groups, however, was *when* the public has the right to know, with the police commonly expressing that they were more interested in doing their job than in giving the media a story (Parrish, 2012). Nonetheless, an important part of the community policing job is communicating with the public through the media, and the media are often in a position to help police reach vital sources of information about crime within the community. Nonetheless, conflict continues because significantly different perspectives exist between the police and the media concerning what the priorities should be for officers in "doing their jobs."

In addition to differences in perspective, other sources may cause conflict.

Sources of Conflict

Conflict between the media and the police may arise from a variety of sources, but perhaps the most basic are competing objectives, contradictory approaches to dangerous situations, and stereotyping.

Competing Objectives
A fundamental source of conflict is the competing objectives of the media and the police. The First Amendment guarantee of freedom of the press is often incompatible with the Sixth Amendment guarantee of the right to a fair trial and protection of the defendant's rights. This leads to a basic conflict between the public's right to know and the individual's right to privacy and a fair trial.

Police may need to withhold information from the media until next of kin are notified, in the interest of public safety, or to protect the integrity of an investigation.

To do their job, members of the media need information from the police. Journalists say they have problems obtaining information they are entitled to because the police refuse to provide it. In some cases, reporters believe they have been singled out by the police for "punishment" in response to a negative story about the police. Reporters tell of police who restrict information, refuse requests for interviews, disregard reporters' deadlines, hang up the phone on reporters, provide inaccurate information, play dumb, or even blackball a particular reporter in retaliation for a story they did not like.

Indeed, some police agencies or officers who have had negative experiences with the media or believe they have been tricked into releasing information do react by becoming uncooperative, by not giving information to which the news media is entitled, by playing favorites among reporters, and even by lying. However, this behavior only aggravates an already difficult relationship.

Motivated by a desire to protect their case and the privacy of those involved, police complain that the media is critical and biased against the police; that reporting is often inaccurate; that journalists lack sensitivity, especially toward victims; and that the news media releases sensitive material and betrays the trust of officers.

One point of contention concerns "off the record" comments some public officials are inclined to make to reporters. Many have been unpleasantly surprised to find that they have been quoted in the next edition of the newspaper or online. Officers must learn to say only that which they can accept attribution for and are prepared to read or hear reported in the media. To speak to a reporter "off the record" does not guarantee the information will not be reported. It may, in fact, make it more likely to be reported. Because different reporters have different definitions of what it means to speak "off the record," an officer faced with such a situation should first ask the reporter, "What do you mean by that?"

In some cases, reporters promise to keep information "off the record" when they have no authority to do so. Although many media professionals do respect "off the record" information, they may misquote, which can cause significant problems and additional conflict. Law enforcement agencies should also be aware that the media may sometimes distort information received from the police department for a political purpose.

As discussed, the way the public views crime and the police depends in large part on what the media report. Although many police officers are keenly aware of the conflict between themselves and the media, they often do not understand how the need to withhold information contributes to the conflict and the resulting negative coverage or what they and their department can do to alleviate the problem. Officers must remember, however, that the media consist of businesses in fierce competition with each other for readers, listeners, and viewers. What officers may consider sensationalism, reporters might consider the competitive edge.

Contradictory Approaches to Dangerous Situations Another source of conflict between law enforcement and the media is the danger members of the media may expose themselves to in getting a story and the police's obligation to protect them. As with that of the general public, the safety of the media at crime scenes, riots, or potentially dangerous situations is important. Although most reporters and photographers will not cross yellow police tape lines, many are willing to risk a degree of personal safety to get close to the action.

If a situation is unfolding and the police and the media are both on the scene, officers should not order journalists to stay away—a red flag to most reporters. Instead, officers, better trained at reading dangerous situations, should urge reporters and photographers to leave an area if they deem it unsafe and tell them why, not just shout, "Get out of here!" This is especially true if citizens are allowed to be in the area but the media is moved away (Parrish, 2012).

Penny Parrish, at the time a television news director whose crew was attacked during a riot, talked with police after the incident. The officers said they knew their first responsibility was to secure the area and calm things down, but they also felt responsible for the safety of the media, and it angered them that the media were "stupid" enough to be in the middle of the riot. The crew was told to leave and was doing so when attacked. Despite their alleged dislike of the media, the officers did not want to see the media crew hurt.

One reporter who was injured so severely she was unable to walk for 2 months and eventually left the news business because she was so burdened by stress recalled after the attack: "We were there and they [the rioters] were angry. They saw us more as the arm of the law than as an unbiased journalist" (Krajicek, 2003, 4). She said the assault changed her perspective and she began to identify with victims. "We'd cover crime and show the video on the news and not take into consideration the victim's family watching that. I'd feel grief. I'd go home and cry myself to sleep at night." She now frequently shows video footage of her attack and its aftermath to journalism students. "I like to let young wanna-be reporters see what they are up against" (Krajicek, 2003, 4).

To avoid similar scenarios, police should meet with local media representatives to discuss rules of safety, so they might, together, develop a general policy. This should be done before an incident arises. It might boil down to deciding the media have the right to make decisions about their own well-being but that officers will issue warnings to try to ensure the safety of news crews.

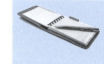 To help ensure the safety of media personnel at explosive situations, police should meet with media representatives to explain the safety rules *before* an incident arises.

The issue of media crew safety, and whether the police are responsible for that safety, remains a big issue. However, the International Association of Chiefs of Police's Model Media Policy states that the media cannot be kept from an area based *solely* out of concern for their safety (Parrish, 2012).

Most jurisdictions now differentiate between access at a crime scene and access at a natural disaster. Journalists are often given better access to areas ravaged by fires, storms, or floods. They help to inform the public regarding the disaster areas which they themselves cannot reach. In recent wildfires in Colorado, families relied on local television footage to find out whether or not their homes were still standing. Another important issue, according to Parrish (2012), is live media coverage of major incidents, such as hostage situations. Although police agencies should still urge the media to refrain from airing live pictures showing the location of officers at a scene, the greatest danger of live photos or video now comes from social media. Citizens with cell phones often capture incidents as they happen and post them immediately on social networking sites, actions that can endanger officers and citizens alike. Officers should be aware of the power of social media and how it impacts their jobs, incidents, and agencies, and all agencies should have a social media policy covering both on-duty and off-duty use (Parrish, 2012).

Stereotyping Stereotyping is a dangerous habit and can greatly impede good working relationships between law enforcement and members of the media. Although it happens to both the police and the media, by each other as well as by the general public, it is important for officers and reporters to see each other as individuals. Both work under the U.S. Constitution and, thus, need to open the lines of effective communication and work together for the public good.

Understanding differences in personality can help build effective relationships between individual police officers and individual media personnel and greatly reduce the barriers between the two professions. There can and must be a trust factor for this to be effective. For example, a radio newscaster who has the trust of the police department can be given confidential information, knowing that he or she will not release it until given the go-ahead. This one-on-one relationship can be of value to law enforcement and to the media.

Dissolving stereotypic views of each other is a significant step toward changing a dysfunctional conflict between the police and the media into a healthy, beneficial conflict.

Benefits of Conflict

Conflict between the police and the media is necessary because each must remain objective and able to constructively criticize the other when needed.

 Conflict need not be dysfunctional. In fact, healthy conflict between the media and the police is necessary and beneficial.

Conflict can stimulate people to grow and change. It can diffuse defensiveness if those in conflict recognize that their roles are, by definition, conflicting yet complementary. Better understanding of each other may lead to a cooperative effort to serve the public.

Most large law enforcement agencies recognize that a cooperative relationship with the media is to their benefit. Many have developed media policies that set forth for officers exactly what may and may not be released to the media, how information will be released, and by whom.

CRITICISM OF THE MEDIA

Journalists are sometimes criticized for giving fame to infamous criminals, such as the Columbine High School killers, while victims remain obscure. As Shakespeare wrote: "The evil that men do lives after them; the good is often interred with their bones."

Another criticism, according to some researchers, is that political leaders and law enforcement officials use the media to serve propaganda functions in the state's ideological machinery and to promote their "law-and-order" crime control agendas. They influence public perception of crime by filtering or screening the information provided to the media and, therefore, share responsibility with the media for the misleading depictions of crime and crime policy.

Phoenix (Arizona) police commander Kim Humphrey, center, answers reporters' questions following a news conference concerning the arrest of Mark Goudeau, Thursday, Sept. 7, 2006, in Phoenix. Police investigating eight deadly attacks blamed on the "Baseline Killer" have gathered forensic evidence connecting Goudeau, 42, to two sexual assaults that occurred on Sept. 20, 2005, and are related to the Baseline case, Phoenix Police Chief Jack Harris said.

© AP Images/Paul Connors

Such influence undermines the efforts of community policing by diminishing the importance of and need for partnerships between law enforcement and the community to effectively address crime. In addition to heavily influencing the public's perception of crime, the media also play a significant role in how the public views the criminal justice system, including law enforcement.

THE MEDIA'S IMPACT ON THE CRIMINAL JUSTICE SYSTEM

news media echo effect

The theory that the media have the power, through their coverage of isolated, high-profile cases, to influence the operations of the criminal justice system and even the disposition of individual cases.

Acknowledging the power of the media to shape public perception, some have also speculated that the media, through their coverage of isolated, high-profile cases, can influence the operations of the criminal justice system and even the disposition of individual cases, a phenomenon called the **news media echo effect**. Much like a pebble thrown into a pond, the impact of a highly publicized case has a rippling effect that spreads throughout the judicial system and affects the entire process—that is, defendants in a similar crime category as one recently publicized may be treated differently within the criminal justice system from the way they would have been treated had such a high-profile case not preceded theirs.

The media have been aided in their quest for newsworthy information through the passage of some legislation, including the Freedom of Information Act (FOIA), which establishes the presumption that the records of the agencies and departments of the U.S. government are accessible to the people. The "need to know" standard has been replaced by a "right to know" standard, with the government having to justify keeping certain records secret. Exceptions include when the national security is involved, if an investigation's integrity might be compromised, or when the privacy rights of individuals might be violated.

In addition, every state has a public records law that specifies what information a law enforcement agency must release, what information must not be released, and what is discretionary. Such laws are enacted to protect the rights of citizens under suspicion of breaking the law, as guaranteed by the Sixth Amendment.

GENERAL POLICIES AND PROTOCOL FOR MEDIA RELATIONS

Most agencies have developed written policies governing release of information to the media. These policies recognize the right of reporters to gather information and often direct officers to cooperate with the media. Parrish, one of the authors of the Model Media Policy of the International Association of Chiefs of Police, says policies are important to guarantee consistency in the manner in which information is disseminated to media (2012).

Being Professional When Interviewed

Officers who encounter and release information to the media are expected to display the highest level of professionalism because not only will their message be relayed to the public but so will their image and, by reflection, the image of their department. Consequently, many agencies have specific policies and protocols to guide officers during media interviews.

Parrish (2012) cautions that police often respond too quickly when they get a request for an interview, saying "yes" or "no" rather than buying some time and finding out just who will be doing the interviewing, what the subject(s) will be, and what the deadline is. Parrish notes that the closer the deadline is, the more frantic and pushy journalists may become. Although an interview should be a positive opportunity for the police to relay an important message to the community, such deadline pressure from the media can turn the situation into a negative, embarrassing, and potentially case-jeopardizing debacle for the unprepared interviewee.

Parrish (2012) suggests that officers who are interviewed should learn to speak in **soundbites**, very short sentences containing solid information. Most television interviews run only 7 to 12 seconds. The most important information should be put up front. However, this often requires telling a story in reverse, giving the conclusion before the background information leading up to it, an interview technique that usually requires practice to master. To develop a strong soundbite, the officer to be interviewed should write out the main points to be conveyed and then reverse the order of them, placing the "final," and usually most important, piece of information at the beginning to create "a perfect soundbite" (Donlon-Cotton, 2006, 22).

soundbites
Good, solid information stated briefly, that is, within 7 to 12 seconds.

Officers should also avoid using "no comment" and instead provide a truthful explanation of why they cannot respond. "No comment" implies there *is* a story. Alternatives to "no comment" might be, "This matter is currently under investigation, and it would be premature to discuss anything more at this point," or, "Making that information available at this time would jeopardize this active investigation," or simply, "I am not authorized to comment on that at this time."

The media knows that bad relations with the police can result in limited access to police information. Cooperation and mutual trust benefit both the media and the police.

Lying to the Media

Lying to the media is always a bad idea, as is making promises that you cannot keep or misleading reporters. Such actions usually haunt the individual officer or the agency in the form of negative press or lack of media cooperation when the police need help. It is better to honor commitments to the media and be straightforward when information is to be released.

Agencies and officers who deceive the media are at great risk of losing public confidence. On the very rare occasions when it becomes necessary to lie to the media, it must be followed at the earliest opportunity with an explanation for the deception.

If lying to the media might save a life or protect the public safety, after the need to lie has passed, the department should explain why lying was necessary and, perhaps, apologize.

Who Can Speak for the Department?

The nature of police business often requires the delicate handling and release (or retention) of information, and it is frequently difficult and time consuming, particularly for larger agencies, to keep all officers equally informed about which details of a case may be provided to the media.

Some police departments feel comfortable allowing any member to talk to the media and provide information. However, the trend, particularly for larger departments, is to designate a **public information officer (PIO)** to communicate with the media, as a PIO is trained in public relations and tasked with providing consistent, accurate information while controlling leaks of confidential or inaccurate details and managing controversial or negative situations to the department's benefit. Desirable traits of a PIO include strong community ties and the ability to communicate clearly in a way that promotes the agency's mission. It is not necessary that a PIO be a police officer, but it helps if the PIO has a solid understanding of police operations. Public speaking and writing skills are also important (Morley and Jacobson, 2007).

PIOs must be prepared to respond to three broad categories of questions the media typically asks during crises or other high-profile events, as illustrated in Figure 8.2.

public information officer (PIO)

An officer trained in public relations and assigned to disseminate information to the media, thereby providing accurate, consistent information while controlling leaks of confidential or inaccurate information and managing controversial or negative situations to the department's benefit.

Policies Regarding Photographing and Videotaping

They say a picture is worth a thousand words. Talking with reporters is one thing, but allowing the media to photograph or shoot video at crime scenes is something quite different because police must follow important Fourth

Figure 8.2   The PIO Triangle

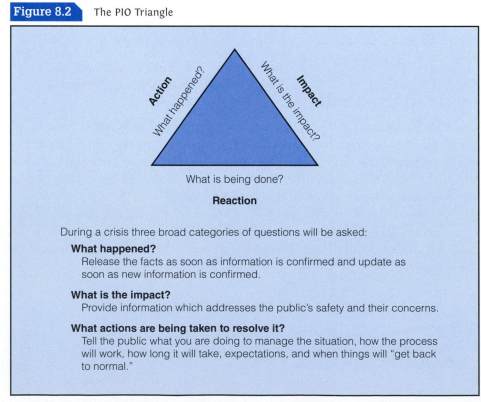

During a crisis three broad categories of questions will be asked:

What happened?
Release the facts as soon as information is confirmed and update as soon as new information is confirmed.

What is the impact?
Provide information which addresses the public's safety and their concerns.

What actions are being taken to resolve it?
Tell the public what you are doing to manage the situation, how the process will work, how long it will take, expectations, and when things will "get back to normal."

Source: Courtesy of Ronald G. Edmond, Group Manager, NSEMP/EMI.

TECHNOLOGY IN COMMUNITY POLICING: PIOs AND DIGITAL MEDIA

Advances in communications technology have brought both new capabilities and new challenges to PIOs and the law enforcement departments they work for. The rapid rise and spread of tools such as Facebook, Twitter, Nixle, RSS feeds, and YouTube have had a profound impact on the digital news environment, and today's PIOs must embrace and become proficient at using such technology to promote and control their messages or they risk becoming obsolete.

Source: Davis, Patrick. 2010. "The PIO and Today's Digital News Environment." *FBI Law Enforcement Bulletin* (July): 1–8.

Amendment constraints. Furthermore, although prohibiting cameras may give the impression that the police have something to hide, people not involved in an investigation must not be allowed to contaminate the crime scene. As a result, many departments have policies in place regarding the use of cameras at crime scenes.

Indeed, the popularity of television shows where camera crews ride along with officers as they patrol the community and respond to calls is evidence of the public's fascination with such activities.

Perp walks, another once-common police practice where suspects were paraded before the hungry eyes of the media, have also fallen on shaky legal ground. Although the public likes to see the "bad guys" apprehended and facing trial, if the perp walk is conducted before the trial, what happens to a core principle of the criminal justice system that a defendant is innocent until proven guilty?

This nearly century-old tradition may not see much action in the 21st century. As with media ride-alongs, courts have begun ruling that perp walks violate a suspect's right to privacy. Many jurisdictions have suspended the practice of perp walks, whereas others await rulings by the appellate courts.

Another problem with allowing cameras at crime or accident scenes is viewed not from the police perspective but from that of the victim or complainant, who might not want themselves, their family members, or their home to be on someone's video, documentary, or TV series. However, nobody has a right to expect privacy in a public place.

Police officers should also be aware of the news system called "file video" or "file photos," where pictures are kept indefinitely and can be reused at any time. For example, in one case a photographer arranged to go with a squad on a high-risk entry into a crack house. The police department let the reporter come along to get some video of how they were working to curb drug traffic in the city. The reporter did the story, and the police were pleased with the resulting public image. Two years later, one officer involved in the high-risk entry unit faced an indictment by a federal grand jury for police brutality. The reporter mentioned to his boss that they had video of this officer breaking into the home of some poor Black citizens on the north side. The editors decided that was just what they needed for the story, and the video the police had at one time encouraged the media to take was used against the officer.

perp walk
The police practice of parading suspects before the media, often simply for the publicity provided by news media coverage.

UNDERSTANDING AND IMPROVING RELATIONS WITH THE MEDIA

Police need to understand that the media are facing some of the same challenges law enforcement is facing, especially cutbacks and being asked to do more with less.

 A police–media relationship survey found that the factor most affecting this relationship was accessibility to police data and personnel.

The media also usually work under extreme time pressure and under the public eye. Seldom do journalists bungle a story intentionally. They are often uninformed about how their reporting may affect a case and are often also under extreme pressure to get the story submitted before a deadline.

 Reporters may bungle a story because of ignorance, oversimplification, or time constraints.

Reporters, particularly rookies or those new to the police beat, may be ignorant of law enforcement procedures and of Sixth Amendment requirements. Journalists must often fashion a complicated investigation or series of events into a paragraph-long news story or a 15- to 20-second story at the top of the hour. Furthermore, they commonly work under severe deadline pressure.

 To improve police–media relations, journalists should be informed of a department's policies and procedures regarding the media and crime scenes. Officers should avoid police jargon and technical terminology and respect reporters' deadlines by releasing information in a timely manner so the news media has a chance to fully understand the situation.

Inviting local newspaper and broadcast reporters to enroll in a citizens' police academy or participate in ride-along programs are ways to improve relationships and enhance the media's understanding of what police work involves. Conversely, police officers could benefit from learning more about the media and their mission and responsibilities. Officers must remember that reporting is a highly competitive business.

A good rapport with the media can also help the police department accomplish its mission because improved media relations lead to improving community relations. As stated earlier, the media are often the primary link between the law and the citizenry. To reach the community, the victims of crime, and possible witnesses, the police must first reach the media.

The media can also be of assistance in public education programs. For example, an agency in California wanted to increase the accuracy of citizens' reports of suspicious and criminal activities. They enlisted the aid of the local newspaper to run a public announcement about what to include in suspect and vehicle descriptions.

In Chicago, the police use the media in their crime prevention efforts. The Federal Communications Commission (FCC) requires all media to set aside airtime or publication space for community projects. This is another excellent avenue for law enforcement agencies to convey educational messages to the residents of their communities.

One tool that can help community policing achieve its mission through the media is the seasonal press release, designed to proactively address specific crime and disorder issues that routinely occur at certain times of the year. For example, when children are out of school on summer break, bicycle safety, water safety, and curfews become bigger issues than they are during the winter. Similarly, over the holidays, shoppers, who are often hurried and distracted, should be reminded how to stay safe in parking lots or how to keep their gift-laden homes from becoming the targets of thieves. Figure 8.3 provides some seasonal news release ideas.

Figure 8. 3   Seasonal News Release Ideas

Seasonal news release ideas

June/July/August
- Travel safety tips
- Teen curfew information
- Fireworks safety tips
- Bicycle safety
- Swimming safety
- Boating safety
- Drunk driving information
- Fishing and hunting laws and safety tips
- TV violence information
- Graffiti information and prevention

August
- Truancy sweeps
- Latchkey children safety tips

October
- Halloween safety tips

November/December/January
- Shopping safety
- Home invasion
- Drunk driving information and statistics

Anytime
- Car theft prevention (don't leave car keys in car, etc.)
- Phone safety
- Scams
- Safety at ATMs
- Internet safety tips
- Bioterrorism information
- Check and credit card fraud
- Babysitter tips
- Walking at night
- Car jacking prevention
- Parenting tips

Source: Christy Whitehead. "Seasonal Press Releases." *Law and Order,* June 2004, p. 21.

ON THE BEAT

The relationship between the police and the media is definitely a symbiotic one. They depend on each other time after time. It is important for police officers working the streets to keep this in mind. In many respects, when police and the media work together they can provide better results for the community at large than either could alone.

Crime alerts are one effort on which police and the media can work together. If a police department begins to see a pattern of criminal activity in a particular location, it is important to give as many citizens as possible the most accurate information possible about the situation. Obviously, the media can facilitate this need.

Another example of police and the media working together is in passing along crime prevention information to the community. Police can reach many more people by using media resources than by other means of communication. For instance, when summer rolls around and people start holding garage sales in their neighborhoods, I work with the local news channel to pass along tips on safe ways to hold a garage sale.

Ultimately, sharing as much information as possible and working together is the best approach. It's a good way to get everyone involved and is appreciated by everyone.

—Kim Czapar

STRATEGIES FOR DEVELOPING PARTNERSHIPS WITH THE MEDIA

Recall from Chapter 1 the definition of community policing: a philosophy that emphasizes working proactively with citizens to reduce fear, solve crime-related problems, and prevent crime. It is a collaborative effort founded on close, mutually beneficial ties between the police and the people. There is no more effective or efficient way for law enforcement to forge a relationship with the community than to partner with the media. Community leaders, key elected officials, church leaders, school boards, parent–teacher association members, philanthropists, and local celebrities often maintain contact with media sources. These people could be brought together through a police–media partnership to sponsor or support crime prevention activities in the community.

Parrish (2012) suggests that one of the most effective ways for police and media to better understand each other is to use a ride-along program:

Police managers should spend a shift riding with a reporter or a photographer—not as part of a story but as a way to get to know the individual and better understand the job of a journalist. Reverse ride-alongs are also important with police managers accompanying a reporter or photographer on a story.

Many police agencies allow the media to ride with officers for stories on topics such as DUI enforcement. The end result is that the public learns about police programs, and the media get to know officers as individuals.

Recently, some agencies are inviting the media to "embed" with officers on high-profile events such as protests. The Philadelphia, Miami, and Sacramento police departments are among the agencies who have tried this. The police often end up with pictures and video of arrests that can be used to show what really happened on the street. Many cases of police brutality went away when defendants saw the video.

Such partnerships with the media are not entirely new. For example, the McGruff "Take a Bite Out of Crime" national media campaign, created by the Ad Council for the National Crime Prevention Council, and other crime prevention public service announcements have existed for decades. (Using the media in crime prevention efforts is discussed again in Chapter 9.) However, local efforts to enjoin the media in the police effort to prevent crime have generally been lacking.

There are, of course, exceptions. For example, in Cleveland, Ohio, the mayor obtained sponsorship of a local television and radio station to publicize the city's gun exchange, violence reduction, and crime prevention initiatives. The television station not only helped to announce these very successful initiatives, it also operated the telephone banks for donations.

Law enforcement officials in San Antonio, Texas, invited prominent local media figures to participate in a city crime prevention commission. By involving the media in the panel's deliberations and programs, the department created a partnership that generated positive media coverage and provided free broadcast equipment and facilities for public service announcements and other programming.

The Utah Council for Crime Prevention also invited local media personnel to serve on the council's board, a collaboration resulting in locally produced television documentaries and public service announcements, as well as other activities raising public awareness of crime prevention throughout the state.

The Knoxville (Tennessee) Police Department (KPD) Public Information Office conducts periodic meetings with local media outlets to address concerns, answer questions, and get feedback on how to better serve the community through the release of pertinent public safety information. As part of this effort to enjoin the media in their mission to deliver quality community policing services to the residents of Knoxville, the KPD Public Information Office operates a Code-a-Phone system, a network of 30 mailboxes on a taped news line that is accessible to the media from any phone. KPD PIOs provide regular updates each day at 6:00 A.M. and then throughout the day as events warrant ("Knoxville Police Department Public Information Officer," 2012).

Although these collaborative efforts, and many others throughout the country, have generated a plethora of benefits for their respective communities, the strategy of developing partnerships with the media is not without obstacles: "No matter how good the working relationship with the media might be, it cannot overcome the constraints PIOs face. They must spend more time handling media inquiries about crime than doing anything else, which leaves them little time to invest in marketing community policing and similar initiatives" (Chermak and Weiss, 2003, 2). Despite such constraints, police departments should take every opportunity to forge creative, supportive, and respectful partnerships with the media.

 As police departments adopt the community policing philosophy and implement its strategies, public support is vital. The media can play an important role in obtaining that support—or in losing it.

MARKETING COMMUNITY POLICING

Chermak and Weiss (2006) not only studied the police–media relationship but also identified strategies law enforcement agencies can use to market community policing initiatives to the public, offering the following recommendations:

» Law enforcement agencies should implement and devise broad marketing strategies to increase public awareness and involvement in community policing activities.

» Law enforcement agencies will need to increase the amount of personnel and monetary resources to more effectively market community policing in the news and in the community.

» The media and community policing training curriculum will have to be broadened to include a discussion of more effective ways to market community policing.

» Research has to be conducted that can effectively evaluate whether implementing a broad marketing strategy is effective.

Among the options available to police departments are positive media stories (free advertising); a Web site sharing department information; social networking sites; blogs; email press releases; marketing alliances such as citizen police academies, a media academy, participation in committees, and community groups; poster campaigns; public service announcements; and addresses to community groups. All can help raise awareness of and interest in community policing.

Increasingly, police and fire departments are using social networking to disseminate information to the public. Hundreds of police departments across the country now maintain a presence on Facebook, with hundreds more subscribing to Twitter and other social media venues. Public safety officials are finding the use of sites to be not only speedy but also a convenient way to distribute news media releases, AMBER Alerts, road closings, and suspect descriptions. The Boca Raton (Florida) Police Department uses Facebook, MySpace, and Twitter to communicate with residents. When Lakeland (Florida) Police received a report of an explosive device on the roof of a city parking garage, they sent a squad to investigate and they posted a notice on Twitter. "We think the police department has an obligation to get information out to the community through whatever means or mechanisms we have at our disposal," said Lakeland Police Assistant Chief Bill LePere. "Traditional media releases, expecting the local print media to pick it up and run it in the newspaper tomorrow, is 24 hours too late" (France, 2009).

Probably the most well known police–media partnership is the one behind the hugely successful weekly television show *America's Most Wanted,* which began airing in 1988. Since the beginning, it has been hosted by John Walsh, whose son Adam was kidnapped and murdered in 1981. Walsh became a visible and tireless advocate for missing children, and the show's producers invited him to host the program. Four days after the first show aired, the first fugitive featured on the program was caught. In 2008 the show celebrated its 20th anniversary, and as of June 20, 2012, there had been 1,188 arrests of fugitives made because of the program. Fifteen of the fugitives caught were from the FBI's Top Ten Most

Wanted list. The show airs in countries all over the world, and 43 arrests have taken place outside the United States.

While law enforcement did not start the show, they are cooperative partners with Walsh and the show's producers. Police agencies submit so many cases every week for consideration on the show that only a very few of them can be aired. However, the show's Web site offers a relatively uncomplicated avenue by which agencies can post information on wanted fugitives.

A comprehensive discussion of marketing techniques available to police departments is beyond the scope of this text. Numerous resources in this area are available. Marketing community policing is important in efforts to make neighborhoods safe and to prevent or reduce crime. It is interesting that publicity about policing efforts has been shown to also have a deterrent effect on crime.

Past and present efforts to enlist the media in crime prevention and reduction efforts will be included throughout the next section of this text.

 ## SUMMARY

One important group with which the police interact is the media. The police and members of the media share the common goal of serving the public. They share a symbiotic relationship; they are mutually dependent on each other. The First Amendment to the U.S. Constitution guarantees the public's right to know—that is, freedom of the press. The Sixth Amendment guarantees suspects the right to a fair trial and protects defendant's rights. The differing objectives of these amendments may lead to conflict between the media and the police. Police may need to withhold information from the media until next of kin are notified, in the interest of public safety, or to protect the integrity of an investigation.

Another source of conflict between the media and the police is the danger in which members of the news media may place themselves when trying to obtain a story. To help ensure the safety of media personnel at explosive situations, police should meet with media representatives to explain the safety rules *before* an incident arises. Conflict need not be dysfunctional. In fact, healthy conflict between the media and the police

is necessary and beneficial. If lying to the media might save a life or protect the public safety, after the need to lie has passed, the department should explain why lying was necessary and, perhaps, apologize.

A step toward improved media relations is to recognize why reporters may foul up a story. Reporters may bungle a story because of ignorance, oversimplification, or time constraints. A police–media relationship survey found that the factor most affecting this relationship was accessibility to police data and personnel.

To improve police–media relations, journalists should be informed of a department's policies and procedures regarding the media and crime scenes. Officers should avoid police jargon and technical terminology and respect reporters' deadlines by releasing information in a timely manner so the news media has a chance to fully understand the situation.

As police departments adopt the community policing philosophy and implement its strategies, public support is vital. The media can play an important role in obtaining that support—or in losing it.

DISCUSSION QUESTIONS

1. What examples are you aware of where the police lied to the media? Were they justified in doing that?

2. Does your police department have a public information officer?

3. How fairly do you feel the media in your community report crime and violence? Collect three examples to support your position.

4. How fairly do you feel national media (radio, television, magazines, newspapers) cover crime and violence? Collect three examples to support your position.

5. What might make good topics for PIOs during crime prevention week?

6. Why is it important to remember that journalism is a for-profit business?

7. Do you feel the media are sometimes insensitive to victims and could also be part of the second injury of victimization? If so, can you give examples?

8. What media are available in your community to inform the public of police department operations?

9. Which media do you feel have the most impact on the public?

GALE EMERGENCY SERVICES DATABASE ASSIGNMENTS

ONLINE Database

- Use the Gale Emergency Services Database to help answer the Discussion Questions when appropriate.

- Find and outline an article on one of the following topics. Be prepared to share and discuss your outline with the class:

  - The goals a police agency expects a PIO to achieve
  - Treatment of victims in media reports
  - The difficult relationship between police and reporters

REFERENCES

Chermak, Steven and Alexander Weiss. 2006. "Community Policing in the News Media." *Police Quarterly* 9 (20): 135–160.

Chermak, Steven and Alexander Weiss. 2003 (July). *Marketing Community Policing in the News: A Missed Opportunity?* Washington, DC: National Institute of Justice Research for Practice. (NCJ 200473)

Davis, Patrick. 2010. "The PIO and Today's Digital News Environment." *FBI Law Enforcement Bulletin* (July): 1–8.

Donlon-Cotton, Cara. 2006. "TV Interview Tips." *Law and Order* (July): 20–22.

Edmond, Ronald G. n.d. "The PIO Triangle."

Fairfax County Police Department (Virginia). n.d. Media Advisory Cards. Fairfax, VA: Fairfax County Police, Victim Services Section.

France, Lisa Respers. 2009. "Police Departments Keeping Public Informed on Twitter." CNN.com, March 13. http://articles.cnn.com/2009-03-13/tech/police.social .networking_1_twitter-and-facebook-twitter-user-departments?_s=PM:TECH

"If It Bleeds, It Leads." 2001. In *Behind the Story,* LOCAL NEWS Online, Public Broadcasting Corporation. http://www .pbs.org/wnet/insidelocalnews/behind_leads.html

"Knoxville Police Department (KPD) Public Information Officer." 2012. Knoxville, TN: City of Knoxville Web site. http://www.cityofknoxville.org/kpd/publicinfoofficer .asp

Krajicek, David. 2003. "Chapter One: The Crime Beat." In *Covering Crime and Justice: A Guide for Journalists.* http:// www.justicejournalism.org/crimeguide

Morley, Edward M. and Martin J. Jacobson. 2007. "Building a Successful Public Information Program." *The Police Chief* 74 (12): 66–68.

Parrish, Penny (Parrish Institute of Law Enforcement and Media and retired media relations instructor, FBI Academy). 2012. Personal conversation with the author.

"Rights and Services for Crime Victims and Witnesses." n.d. Madison, WI: Wisconsin Department of Justice, Office of Crime Victim Services. http://www.doj.state.wi.us/ cvs/Victims_Rights/Rights_and_Services_Brochure.asp

Whitehead, Christy. 2004. "Seasonal Press Releases." *Law and Order* 52 (6): 21.

Community Policing in the Field: Collaborative Efforts

CHAPTERS IN THIS SECTION:

The Office of Community Oriented Policing Services (COPS) leads in the efforts to implement community policing throughout the country. The COPS Office defines community policing as "a policing philosophy that promotes and supports organizational strategies to address the causes and reduce the fear of crime and social disorder through problem-solving tactics and police–community partnerships."

The director of the COPS Office is Bernard K. Melekian, who was appointed by Attorney General Eric Holder on October 5, 2009. Director Melekian was the Police Chief for the City of Pasadena, California, for more than 13 years before assuming leadership of the COPS Office. He also served with the Santa Monica (California) Police Department for 23 years as well as the United States Army and the United States Coast Guard Reserve.

Community policing focuses on crime and social disorder through the delivery of police services that include aspects of traditional law enforcement, as well as prevention, problem solving, community engagement, and partnerships. The community policing model balances reactive responses to calls for service with proactive problem solving centered on the causes of crime and disorder.

© AP Images/Reed Saxon

Community policing requires police and citizens to join together as partners in the course of both identifying and effectively addressing these issues.

As explained in the previous section, communities consist of individuals, organizations, businesses, agencies, the media, citizen groups, schools, churches, and police departments. Effective interactions with the members of ethnic and cultural minorities, the disabled, the elderly, the young, crime victims and witnesses, and the media are critical to developing projects and programs to meet a community's needs.

This section begins by describing early experiments in crime prevention and community policing strategies (Chapter 9). It then looks at efforts to address crime, disorder, and fear concerns at the neighborhood level (Chapter 10). Next is a discussion of strategies to combat the drug problem (Chapter 11) and partnerships to involve youths and to make our nation's schools safer (Chapter 12). This is followed by discussions regarding the challenges presented by gangs (Chapter 13), strategies to understand and prevent violence (Chapter 14), and efforts to understand and prevent terrorism (Chapter 15). The section concludes with a look at what research reveals about the effectiveness of various strategies, including where efforts might be focused in the future (Chapter 16).

© AP Images/Gerry Broome

Early Experiments in Crime Prevention and the Evolution of Community Policing Strategies

> Don't be afraid to take a big step if one is indicated. You can't cross a chasm in two small jumps.
>
> —*David Lloyd George, former prime minister of England*

DO YOU KNOW ...

» What the most commonly implemented crime prevention programs have traditionally been?

» What types of special crime watches have been used?

» What organizations have concentrated their efforts on community crime prevention?

» How volunteers have been used in crime prevention?

» What traditional programs for youths have promoted positive police–community relations and enhanced crime prevention efforts?

» What a police–school liaison program is? What its dual goals are?

» What the most common strategies used in community policing have traditionally been?

» What was demonstrated in studies of community policing in Flint? Newark? Oakland? San Diego? Houston? Boston? Baltimore County?

» What was demonstrated in studies of community crime prevention programs in Seattle, Portland, and Hartford?

» What the CPTED Commercial Demonstration Project in Portland found?

» What components of the criminal justice system can help reduce the crime problem?

» What court-based approaches have proved effective?

» How successful the McGruff national campaign was?

» What characteristics of several exemplary police–community strategies are?

» What impediments might hinder implementing community policing?

CAN YOU DEFINE ...

CPTED
DARE
empirical study
Guardian Angels
PAL
police–school liaison program
PSAs
qualitative evaluations

INTRODUCTION

Community involvement with and assistance in accomplishing the mission of law enforcement is becoming widely accepted. The change toward community involvement is illustrated in a change in the Portland (Oregon) Police Department's mission statement. The old mission statement proclaimed:

> The Bureau of Police is responsible for the preservation of the public peace, protection of the rights of persons and property, the prevention of crime, and the enforcement of all Federal laws, Oregon state statutes, and city ordinances within the boundaries of the City of Portland.

The new mission, in contrast, is:

> To work with all citizens to preserve life, maintain human rights, protect property, and promote individual responsibility and community commitment.

The change from traditional policing to community involvement does require many chiefs of police and their officers to take risks. Are the results of the shift toward community policing worth the risks? This chapter reviews experiments conducted across the country to answer this question.

Although this chapter may appear somewhat dated, it is a necessary addition to document efforts during the past decades to improve crime prevention strategies and to involve citizens in such efforts. Many lessons were learned from the experiments of this time period.

The chapter begins with a look at traditional approaches to crime prevention and other effective initiatives, including traditional programs for youths. Next is a description of empirical studies in crime prevention conducted in the 1970s and 1980s, followed by a discussion of how community policing efforts may be enhanced through partnerships with the other elements of the criminal justice system—namely, the courts and corrections. Use of the media in crime prevention is discussed, as are lessons learned from previous decades. The chapter concludes with a discussion of qualitative evaluations and salient program features, impediments to community policing, and the important distinction of programs versus community policing.

TRADITIONAL APPROACHES TO CRIME PREVENTION

When crime prevention became popular in the late 1960s and early 1970s, many communities undertook similar types of programs. These programs have continued into the 21st century.

Among the most commonly implemented crime prevention programs have been street lighting projects; property marking projects; security survey projects; citizen patrol projects; and crime reporting, neighborhood-watch, or block projects.

Claims of success should be carefully examined. Critics often say that the evaluations are flawed. Indeed, research within communities is extremely difficult because:

» Measuring what did not happen is nearly impossible.

» Crime is usually underreported.

» A reduction in reported crime could be the result of the crime prevention program or because the responsible criminal or criminals left town, went to jail on some other charge, died, and so on.

» Crime can be influenced by everything from seasonal and weather changes, school truancy rates, and the flu, to road construction or even a change in a bus stop location. A drop in the crime rate does not necessarily mean a crime prevention program is working.

In addition, many of these programs are evaluated by people who have no training or experience in appropriate research methods; consequently, they sometimes produce flawed results.

Some also argue that crime is not prevented by programs like Neighborhood Watch; instead, they argue, crime is displaced to neighborhoods where the residents are not as likely to report suspicious activity to the police.

Use of crime data to evaluate crime prevention projects poses special problems. Crime data, obviously, are limited to reported crimes. Practitioners are aware of the dark side of crime—that is, the huge amount of crime that is unreported. When projects are instituted to enlist the community in preventing crime, the citizens' heightened awareness and involvement often result in an *increase* in reported crime, but this does not necessarily mean that crime itself has actually increased.

As you read this chapter, consider the difficulties in evaluating crime prevention projects or, indeed, any project involving many diverse individuals and problems.

Street Lighting Projects

Since ancient times, lighting has been one means to deter and detect crime. Street lighting projects aimed at crime prevention through environmental design (CPTED) are important elements in a community's crime suppression efforts. Most street lighting projects seek to improve not only the likelihood of deterring and detecting crime but also the safety of law-abiding citizens. Available research indicates that street lighting does not decrease the incidence of crime in participating target areas but that it is useful to reduce citizens' fear of crime and increase their feelings of security.

Property Identification Projects

Often referred to as "Operation Identification" or "O-I" projects, property identification aims to deter burglary and, when deterrence fails, return stolen property if it is recovered. Most property identification projects provide citizens with instructions, a marking tool, and a unique number to be applied to all valuable items within a household. Stickers are provided to homeowners to display on windows and doors warning possible burglars that the residents have marked their valuables and they are on record with the police. In addition to its deterrent effect, the property identification program also helps police track the source of stolen goods and return stolen property to its rightful owners.

It is sometimes difficult to get people to participate in such programs. In addition, although the burglary rate may drop for those enrolled in the program, it may not drop citywide. There is no evidence available to suggest a difference in the number of apprehended or convicted burglars in communities that do or do not participate in these types of programs.

Crime Prevention Security Surveys

Crime prevention user and security surveys are also usually an integral part of projects that focus on the environmental design of facilities and "target hardening" as a means to deter or prevent crime. Such surveys can reveal opportunities for improvement or indicate that people are afraid to visit a particular place because of high levels of victimization due to low lighting or because such locations are isolated, confining, or deserted. Surveys used to determine the effectiveness of the existing environmental design are usually conducted by police officers specially trained in this area. They perform comprehensive on-site inspection of homes, apartments, and businesses. Of particular interest are doors, windows, locks, lighting, and shrubbery that might be used to a burglar's advantage. The officer suggests specific ways to make a location more secure. Zahm (2007) explains the approach typically taken in CPTED:

CPTED

Crime Prevention through Environmental Design—altering the physical environment to enhance safety, reduce the incidence and fear of crime, and improve the quality of life.

Crime prevention through environmental design (**CPTED**) is an approach to problem solving that asks what is it about this location that places people at risk, or that results in opportunities for crime? In other words, *why here*? Three case examples will illustrate this point:

Case #1: Custodial workers routinely find evidence of smoking, drinking, and vandalism in a high school lavatory.

Why here? The lavatory is in an isolated area of the building, adjacent to a ticket booth and concession stand that are active only during athletic events. The school's open lunch policy allows students to eat anywhere on campus, while monitors are assigned only to the cafeteria.

CPTED response: A lock is installed on the lavatory door, and it remains locked unless there is an athletic event. The open lunch policy has been revised: Students are still allowed to leave the cafeteria but must eat in designated areas, and a faculty member is charged with patrolling these areas during lunch periods.

Case #2: The back wall of a building in an office center is repeatedly tagged with graffiti.

Why here? The taggers have selected an area that is out of the view of passers-by: a rear corner location where two buildings come together at the end of a poorly lit service lane. Visibility is further reduced by hedges at the site's perimeter. Businesses in the office center are open from 9 A.M. to 5 P.M. during the week; however, the tagged building is next to a roller skating rink where activity peaks at night and on weekends.

CPTED response: Hedges are trimmed and wall-mounted light fixtures installed along the service lane, with motion detection lighting in the problem area. The skating rink agrees to change to a "no re-admission" policy to keep skaters inside the building and away from the office property.

Case #3: ATM patrons at a bank are being robbed after dark.

Why here? The bank is situated along a commercial strip in a neighborhood with vacant properties and abandoned businesses. The ATM is in the front corner of the bank building, and the drive-through teller windows are at the side of the building, around the corner from the ATM. Robbers hide in the darkened drive-through teller area and attack unsuspecting ATM users after they complete a transaction.

CPTED response: The bank installs a fence at the corner of the building, creating a barrier between the ATM and the drive-through teller area.

In each of these case examples, asking *why here?* reveals that opportunities for crime and other problems arise out of a variety of environmental conditions related to the building, the site, and the location, and how the place is used. Solving a problem thus requires a detailed understanding of both crime and place, and the response should consider one of the three objectives of crime prevention through environmental design: control access, provide opportunities to see and be seen, or define ownership and encourage the maintenance of territory.... Crime Prevention through Environmental Design is an approach to problem solving that considers environmental conditions and the opportunities they offer for crime or other unintended and undesirable behaviors....

CPTED emerged out of research on the relationship between crime and place, theories known variously as environmental criminology, situational prevention, rational choice theory, or routine activities theory, among others. Each theoretical approach focuses on the crime event and how a criminal offender understands and uses the environment to commit a crime.

CPTED is unusual when compared with some police activities because it encourages prevention and considers design and place, while policing has traditionally valued an efficient and effective response to incidents, and identifying and arresting offenders.

Citizen Patrol Projects

Many variations of citizen patrol exist in the United States. Some are directed at a specific problem such as crack houses and the sale of drugs in a neighborhood. Others are aimed at general crime prevention and enhanced citizen safety. Citizen patrols may operate throughout a community or may be located within a specific building or complex of buildings such as tenement houses. The most successful patrols are affiliated with a larger community or neighborhood organization, sustain a working relationship with law enforcement, and are flexible enough to engage in non–crime prevention activities when patrolling is patently unnecessary.

One hazard of citizen patrols is the possibility of vigilantism, which has a long, often proud, history in the United States and, indeed, in the history of law enforcement and criminal justice. Now this hazard is quite serious because of the increase of readily available handguns in our country.

Probably the best-known citizen patrol is the **Guardian Angels**, a group of private citizens who seek to deter crime and to provide a positive role model for young children. A modern expansion of the Angels is the all-volunteer Internet Safety organization. Membership in this group unites more than 1,000 users from 32 countries who police the Internet through what they call Cyberspace Neighborhood Watch. Calling themselves CyberAngels, they focus on protecting children from online abuse by fighting child pornography and advising online victims about hate mail.

The largest online safety group is WiredSafety (www.wiredsafety.org), a non-profit organization with more than 9,000 volunteers worldwide. Calling itself a cyber-neighborhood watch, WiredSafety provides help for online victims of cybercrime and harassment and assists law enforcement anywhere in the world in preventing and investigating cybercrimes through its affiliate organization (www.wiredcops.org). Volunteers are trained how to patrol the Internet in search of child pornography, child molesters, and cyberstalkers.

Citizen Crime Reporting, Neighborhood, or Block Programs

Citizen crime reporting programs (CCRPs) help to organize neighborhoods as mutual aid societies and as the eyes and ears of the police. Thousands of neighborhood-watch programs exist throughout the United States, and many describe them as the backbone of the nation's community crime prevention effort as they serve to increase surveillance, reduce criminal opportunities, and enhance informal social control.

Usually local residents hold meetings of such programs in their homes or apartments. During the meetings, neighbors get to know each other and what is normal activity for their neighborhood. They receive educational information about crime prevention from the local police department and are told how to contact the police if they see something suspicious. Signs are posted throughout the neighborhood warning possible offenders of the program. Often the programs provide safe houses for children to use if they encounter danger on their way to or from school.

Some programs work to enhance citizens' reporting capability. Whistle Stop programs, for example, provide citizens with whistles, which they can blow if they are threatened or see something requiring police intervention. Anyone hearing the whistle is to immediately call the police. Whistle Stop programs are the modern-day version of the "hue and cry." Other programs have implemented special hotlines whereby citizens can call a specific number with crime information and perhaps receive a monetary reward.

Very few of the programs concentrate on only the "neighborhood watch." Crime prevention efforts such as Project Operation Identification and home security surveys are by far the most common activities of neighborhood-watch programs. Street lighting programs, crime tip hotlines, and measures to address physical environmental concerns are also quite common. Regardless of the activities incorporated, neighborhood-watch programs have been assessed through meta-analysis as being associated with reductions in crime (Holloway, Bennett, and Farrington, 2008).

FIGHTING FORECLOSURE PROBLEMS

Manhattan, Illinois

Following is an example of how police in one community tackled the problem of foreclosed properties. By encouraging frequent collaboration between stakeholders, engaging in problem-solving policing, and building trust with the community, local police were able to effectively monitor foreclosed properties with the goals of preserving property values and preventing the foreclosure-related crime that had affected nearby cities, thus preserving quality of life for their citizens.

Fighting Foreclosure Problems in Manhattan, Illinois

Problem properties create more than just an eyesore. They act as a drain on police resources, create hazardous environments, and lessen the quality of life for neighbors and community residents.

The Village of Manhattan, Illinois, is a residential community of about 6,897 people south of Chicago. It has more than doubled in size since 2000. With larger nearby towns facing serious foreclosure problems, Manhattan's police department and village administrators decided to take preventive action before their problem grew too large to control.

The village created a database, updated weekly, of all properties in the various stages of foreclosure.

Using the database as a guide, the police department, code compliance office, public works department, and finance department are responsible for a four-point approach to tracking and securing foreclosed structures: monitoring and securing the buildings; enforcing city codes; shutting off water service; and placing liens, if necessary, on delinquent accounts. Law enforcement officers regularly monitor the vacant houses, check for signs of vandalism, and conduct outreach to neighbors in adjacent properties through a Neighborhood Watch program.

Village officials and the Manhattan Police Department have considered these efforts a success. After checking all vacant structures, Manhattan police found that 27 percent of the area's vacant houses were not locked. They secured the houses and, using their monitoring system, identified additional potential problem properties. Since the initiative was put into place, one concerned neighbor alerted the authorities about a distressed homeowner who was illegally stripping his house and selling all valuable construction material and appliances on Craigslist.

Source: Zoe Mentel. "Shutting the Door on Foreclosure and Drug-Related Problem Properties: Two Communities Respond to Neighborhood Disorder." *Community Policing Dispatch, The e-Newsletter of the COPS Office,* July 2009, Vol. 2, Issue 7. Online: http://www.cops.usdoj.gov/html/dispatch/July_2009/communities_respond.htm

Special Crime Watch Programs

In addition to the traditional types of crime watch programs commonly implemented throughout the country, some communities have developed more specialized types of crime watch programs.

 Specialized crime watch programs include mobile crime watch, youth crime watch, business crime watch, apartment watch, realtor watch, and carrier alert.

Honolulu's mobile crime watch enlists the aid of motorists who have CBs, car phones, or cell phones. Volunteers attend a short orientation that trains them to observe and report suspicious activity. Participants also receive Mobile Watch decals for their vehicles. They are advised to call 911 if they hear screaming, gunshots, breaking glass, or loud explosive noises or if they see someone breaking into a house or car, a car driven dangerously or erratically, a person on the ground apparently unconscious, anyone brandishing a gun or knife, or an individual staggering or threatening others.

TECHNOLOGY IN COMMUNITY POLICING: iWATCH: NEIGHBORHOOD WATCH GOES HIGH TECH

iWatch is a new application (or "app") that allows citizens who are witnessing a criminal event unfold to use their iPhones, desktop or laptop computers, or virtually any mobile communication device to send a text, voicemail, or video—or any combination thereof—directly to the police to report that crime. The app, nicknamed "Community Policing 2.0," fits well with the national "See something, say something" campaign and is considered revolutionary, extending the power of the law right into citizens' hands and creating what one police chief describes as "an ongoing, 24/7, never off-duty, real-time, virtual block-watch."

Source: Tim Burke, "People Power Returns," *Public Safety IT* (January/February 2012), 38–40: http://www.ithinqware.org/pdf/public_safety_it.pdf

The volunteers are also trained to recognize and report other unusual behaviors such as children appearing lost; anyone being forced into a vehicle; cars cruising erratically and repetitively near schools, parks, and playgrounds; a person running and carrying something valuable; parked, occupied vehicles at unusual hours near potential robbery sites; heavier than normal traffic in and out of a house or commercial establishment; someone going door-to-door or passing through backyards; and persons loitering around schools, parks, or secluded areas or in the neighborhood.

Most successful community-based programs that focus on crime prevention or safety issues have a close partnership with law enforcement. The community and law enforcement have vital components to offer each other, making cooperation between the two highly desirable. It is difficult to imagine, for instance, an effective community-based crime watch program without input or cooperation from the local police agency. Crime watch programs are built on the premise of mutual aid—citizens and police working together.

OTHER EFFORTS TO ENHANCE CRIME PREVENTION

Continuing the community crime prevention momentum generated during the 1960s and 1970s, new programs were initiated during the 1980s and 1990s to encourage citizens to play an active role in reducing crime in their own neighborhoods. These initiatives have included National Night Out; the creation of organizations focused on crime prevention, such as Crime Stoppers and Mothers Against Drunk Driving (MADD); and the expanded use of volunteers.

National Night Out

National Night Out (NNO) is a program that originated in 1984 in Tempe, Arizona. Held annually on the first Tuesday of August, this nationwide program encourages residents to turn on their porch lights, go outside, and meet their neighbors in an effort to build stronger, more vigilant communities that are more resistant to crime and disorder. Neighborhood-watch programs are encouraged to plan a party or event during National Night Out.

Police officers, state police, and city officials meet on the Massachusetts Avenue Bridge to kick off National Night Out with a "Hands Across the River" event in Boston. Officers visit all 11 police districts in the Boston area to give Community Service Awards to residents who have helped fight crime in their neighborhoods.

Since 1984, when 2.5 million people in 23 states gathered for the first NNO, the event has grown significantly. In 2011 more than 37 million people in 15,325 communities from all 50 states, U.S. territories, Canadian cities, and military bases worldwide participated in NNO. In addition to the traditional "outside lights and front porch" vigils, many communities have expanded their NNO activities to include block parties, safety fairs, youth events, cookouts, parades, festivals, and visits from local law enforcement, fire/rescue personnel, and other local officials. Some neighborhoods also use NNO as an opportunity to collect food for the local food shelf or "gently worn" clothing for a local shelter for homeless people or battered women.

Organizations Focused on Crime Prevention

Community organizations encourage citizens to play an active role in reducing crime in various ways.

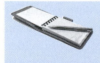 Among the most visible organizations focused on crime are citizen crime prevention associations, Crime Stoppers, and MADD.

Citizen Crime Prevention Associations The many activities undertaken by citizen crime prevention associations include paying for crime tips; funding for police and community crime prevention programs; supporting police canine programs; raising community awareness through crime prevention seminars, newsletters, cable TV shows, and booths; providing teddy bears for kids; raising money through sources such as business contributions, membership fees, charitable gambling, and sales of alarms and mace; and funding specific programs such as rewards to community members who call the hotline with crime information.

Crime Stoppers Crime Stoppers is a nonprofit program involving citizens, the media, and the police. Local programs offer anonymity and cash rewards to people who furnish police information that leads to the arrest and indictment of felony offenders. Each program is governed by a local board of directors made up of citizens from a cross-section of the community, the businesses of the community, and law enforcement. The reward money comes from tax-deductible donations and grants from local businesses, foundations, and individuals.

When a crime-related call is received by Crime Stoppers, it is logged in with the date, time, and a summary of the information given by the caller. Callers are given code numbers to be used on all subsequent calls by the same person regarding that particular case. Each week, one unsolved crime is selected for special treatment by the media. Over 1,000 programs throughout the United States, Canada, Australia, England, and West Africa are members of Crime Stoppers International. Statistics posted on the home page of the Crime Stoppers USA Web site (www.crimestoppersusa.com) indicate that as of July 1, 2012, the program has resulted in 617,847 arrests; 943,199 cases cleared; more than $94 million in rewards paid; more than $1.1 billion in property recovered; nearly $3 billion worth of drugs seized; and a total recovered property value of approximately $4.2 billion.

Mothers Against Drunk Driving MADD is a nonprofit, grassroots organization whose membership is open to anyone: victims, concerned citizens, law enforcement officers, safety workers, and health professionals. MADD was founded in California in 1980 after Candy Lightner's 13-year-old daughter was killed by a hit-and-run driver. The driver had been out of jail on bail for only 2 days for another hit-and-run drunk-driving crash. He had three previous drunk-driving arrests and two convictions, but he was allowed to plea bargain to vehicular manslaughter. His 2-year prison sentence was spent not in prison, but in a work camp and later a halfway house.

The most frequently committed violent crime in the United States is alcohol-impaired driving, which claimed more than 10,000 lives in 2010—an average of one every 51 minutes ("Impaired Driving," n.d.). Thus the mission of MADD is to stop drunk driving and to support victims of this violent crime. MADD seeks to raise public awareness through community programs such as Operation Prom/Graduation, their poster/essay contest, their "Tie One on for Safety" Project Red Ribbon campaign, and a Designated Driver program. Their national newsletter, "MADD in Action," is sent to members and supporters. MADD also promotes legislation to strengthen existing laws and adopt new ones. In addition, MADD provides victim services. Annual candlelight vigils are held nationwide to allow victims to share their grief with others who have suffered loss resulting from drunk driving.

Using Volunteers

Many police departments make extensive use of volunteers, as was discussed in Chapter 7.

Volunteers may serve in a crime prevention capacity as reserve officers, auxiliary patrol, or community service officers or on an as-needed basis.

ON THE BEAT

Many effective crime prevention programs are used by police departments across the United States. In our department, we have everything from the Neighborhood Watch program to Police Explorer and Reserve Officer programs. School liaison officers are placed in schools to develop positive police–youth relationships, and officers also go out into the community and help youth with their homework or play kickball or basketball with them. All of these components are important in reducing the incidence of crime and connecting with the community we serve.

Without engaging community members in police initiatives it can be next to impossible to have success with a program. For example, without *community* block captains to facilitate neighborhood watches, there would be no Neighborhood Watch program. Without *community* volunteers to be police reserve officers, there would not be a volunteer Police Reserve program. Without *citizen* interest in the daily efforts of police officers, there would not be a successful Citizen's Academy program. Volunteers from the community are an important asset to any police department, and crime prevention programs are much more effective when partnerships and collaborative efforts occur.

—Kim Czapar

Reserve officers, auxiliary patrol, or community service officers (CSOs) usually wear uniforms and badges but are unarmed. However, in some departments, reserve officers are armed and receive the same training as sworn officers. They are trained to perform specific functions that assist the uniformed patrol officers in crime prevention efforts, such as watching for suspicious activity and providing crime prevention education at neighborhood-watch meetings, civic groups, churches, and schools.

TRADITIONAL PROGRAMS FOR YOUTHS

Youths have traditionally been included in police–community relations efforts and crime prevention initiatives in several ways.

Common programs aimed at youths include the McGruff "Take a Bite Out of Crime" campaign, police athletic leagues (PALs), Officer Friendly, Police Explorers, police-school liaison programs, and the DARE program.

Other efforts have included school safety programs, bicycle safety programs, and programs to fingerprint young children. In different localities, police have developed variations of many of these programs. (Chapter 12 is devoted entirely to projects and programs aimed at youths.)

The McGruff "Take a Bite Out of Crime" Program

The traditional McGruff as a crime prevention spokesperson program, for example, has expanded in some areas to include McGruff Houses, which are safe havens for young children. Another expansion is the McGruff crime dog robot developed by Robotronics. Operated by remote control, the robot winks, blinks, moves his hands and arms, tips and turns his head, and has a two-way wireless voice system allowing the operator to talk and listen. The McGruff media campaign is discussed in greater detail later in this chapter.

Police Athletic Leagues

Police departments have also expanded on the National Police Athletic League—or **PAL** program—alternately called Police Activity Leagues. PAL, now more than 50 years old, was developed to provide opportunities for youths to interact with police officers in gyms or ballparks instead of in a juvenile detention hall.

Each PAL program is unique. For example, officers of the Portland (Oregon) Police Bureau joined with community members and civic leaders to start a PAL dedicated to encouraging and developing good citizenship through the provision of recreational, athletic, educational, and enrichment programs for at-risk youths (www.portlandonline.com). To accomplish their goals of reducing gang membership and youth violence in the community, reducing the street sale of drugs, and providing youth with prosocial opportunities, the department undertook several activities, including a weeklong Sport Quickness Day Camp for 600 at-risk youths. The camp kept the youths productively occupied for 8 hours a day in boxing, wrestling, football, soccer, martial arts, basketball, racquetball, track and field, volleyball, and speed and quickness training. The department also organized events in which officers could participate with PAL youths, including a 1-day fishing excursion and trips to Seattle Sea Hawks football games, and provided scholarships to summer camps.

Officer Friendly

Officer Friendly programs are designed for elementary school children and generally include a police officer who goes into classes to discuss good citizenship, responsibility, and general safety. The program uses coloring books and a special activity book that teachers can use with their regular social studies curriculum.

Police Explorers

The traditional Police Explorers program is affiliated with the Boy Scouts of America, but participants do not have to work their way up through the scouting program. Exploring is for teens (both males and females) to provide them an opportunity to "explore" a possible future career. Explorers usually are trained in various aspects of police work such as fingerprinting, identification techniques, first aid, and firearms safety. The minimum age for most programs is 15. Explorers usually have a 3- to 6-month probation, with full membership contingent on completing training and meeting proficiency standards as well as acceptable personal conduct.

Explorer programs have two purposes: positive community relations and early recruitment for police departments. Some departments, in fact, make even greater use of their Explorer programs. The Chandler (Arizona) Police Department, for example, used two 18-year-old Explorers in a sting operation involving a bar and liquor store's employees who sold alcohol to minors.

Many programs for juveniles involve the schools, which have historically been charged with instilling discipline in the students who attend.

Police–School Liaison Programs

In 1958 Flint, Michigan, developed a highly publicized delinquency prevention program involving joint efforts of school authorities, parents, businesses, social agencies, the juvenile court, and the police department. Known as a school liaison program, it became widely replicated across the country.

 A **police–school liaison program** places an officer in a school to work with school authorities, parents, and students to prevent crime and antisocial behavior and to improve police–youth relationships.

police–school liaison program
Places an officer in a school to work with school authorities, parents, and students to prevent crime and antisocial behavior and to improve police-youth relationships.

The goals of most police–school liaison programs are to reduce crime incidents involving school-age youths, to suppress by enforcement of the law any illegal threats that endanger the children's educational environment, and to improve the attitudes of school-age youths and the police toward one another.

Police–school liaison officers do not get involved in school politics or in enforcing school regulations. The school administrators are involved in these matters.

 The joint goals of most police–school liaison programs are to prevent juvenile delinquency and to improve police–youth relations.

The police–school liaison programs can also do much to promote better relations among the police, school administrators, and teachers. A number of organizations can focus attention on school–police relations and provide supportive programs both on the local and national levels—for example, the International Association of Chiefs of Police, the National Association of Secondary School Principals, and the National Association of School Boards.

Drug use is often a target of police educational programs. Frequently, officers work with schools to develop and promote programs aimed at preventing drug and alcohol abuse, one of the most popular of which is DARE.

The DARE Program

The Drug Abuse Resistance Education (**DARE**) program was developed jointly by the Los Angeles Police Department and the Los Angeles Unified School District. This controversial program is aimed at elementary school children and seeks to

DARE
Drug Abuse Resistance Education—a program aimed at elementary-age school children, seeking to teach them to "say no to drugs."

teach them to "say no to drugs," to resist peer pressure, and to find alternatives to drug use. The program uses a "self-esteem repair" approach.

The founder and president of DARE America concedes the program is not a "magic bullet," but believes it is a valuable part of the big picture and is confident it helps reduce drug use. Based on research findings, the program has been completely revised. In recent years, schools across the country have dropped DARE programs, although they still remain popular with parents, teachers, and some police officers. The current program is discussed in Chapter 11.

EARLY EMPIRICAL STUDIES OF COMMUNITY POLICING

empirical study

Research based on observation or practical experience.

During the 1980s many programs were adopted by departments moving toward community policing. Also during this time, many departments began experimenting with a variety of community policing strategies. As evidenced by numerous empirical studies, some strategies were successful; others were not. An **empirical study** is based on observation or practical experience. Greene and Taylor (1991, 206–221) describe studies of community policing in major cities throughout the country, including Flint, Newark, Oakland, San Diego, Houston, Boston, and Baltimore County.

> The most common strategies traditionally used in community policing were foot patrol, newsletters, and community organizing.

Flint, Michigan, Neighborhood Foot Patrol Program

The classic Neighborhood Foot Patrol Program of Flint, Michigan, was conducted from January 1979 to January 1982. It focused on 14 experimental neighborhoods to which 22 police officers and 3 supervisors were assigned. The officers were given great discretion in what they could do while on foot patrol, but communication with citizens was a primary objective.

> The Flint Neighborhood Foot Patrol Program appeared to decrease crime, increase general citizen satisfaction with the foot patrol program, reduce citizens' fear of crime, and create a positive perception of the foot patrol officers.

The Flint study tried to document what police did on foot patrol and how that differed from motorized patrol (Mastrofski, 1992, 24):

Looking at the department's daily report forms, the researchers found that foot officers reported many more self-initiated activities—such as home and business visits and security checks—than police in cars. Officers on foot averaged much higher levels of productivity across most of the standard performance measures: arrests, investigations, stopping of suspicious persons, parking citations, and value of recovered property. The only category in which motor patrol officers clearly outproduced their foot patrol counterparts was in providing miscellaneous services to citizens.

According to citizen surveys (Trojanowicz, 1986), 64 percent were satisfied with the project and 68 percent felt safer. When asked to compare foot patrol and motorized patrol officers, citizens rated the foot patrol officers higher by large margins in four of the six areas: preventing crime, encouraging citizen self-protection, working with juveniles, and following up on complaints. Motorized patrol officers were rated superior only in responding to complaints. In addition, in the foot patrol neighborhoods, crime rates were down markedly and calls for service were down more than 40 percent.

No statistical tests were done, however, and results across the 14 neighborhoods varied greatly. Therefore, the results should be interpreted with caution. In addition, problems were encountered in the Flint Foot Patrol Program. For example, because the program was loosely structured, some officers were not accountable, and their job performance was poor. Nonetheless, according to Skolnick and Bayley (1986, 216):

> Foot patrol... appears from our observations and other studies to generate four meritorious effects. (1) Since there is a concerned human presence on the street, foot patrol is more adaptable to street happenings, and thus may prevent crime before it begins. (2) Foot patrol officers may make arrests, but they are also around to give warnings either directly or indirectly, merely through their presence. (3) Properly carried out, foot patrol generates goodwill in the neighborhood, which has the derivative consequence of making other crime prevention tactics more effective. This effectiveness in turn tends to raise citizen morale and reduce their fear of crime. (4) Foot patrol seems to raise officer morale.

First Newark, New Jersey, Foot Patrol Experiment

The original Newark Foot Patrol Experiment was done between 1978 and 1979 and addressed the issues of untended property and untended behavior. This experiment used 12 patrol beats. Eight of the beats, identified as using foot patrol, were divided into pairs, matched by the number of residential and nonresidential units in each. One beat in each pair dropped foot patrol. An additional four beats that had not previously used foot patrol added foot patrol officers. As in the Flint experiment, officers had great flexibility in their job responsibilities while on foot patrol.

 In the first Newark Foot Patrol Experiment, residents reported positive results, whereas business owners reported negative results.

In areas where foot patrol was added, residents reported a decrease in the severity of crime and evaluated police performance more positively. Business owners, however, believed that street disorder and publicly visible crime increased and reported that the neighborhood had become worse. Pate (1986, 155) summarizes the results of the first experiment:

The addition of intensive foot patrol coverage to relatively short (8- to 16-block) commercial/residential strips during 5 evenings per week over a 1-year period can have considerable effects on the perceptions of residents concerning disorder problems, crime problems, the likelihood of crime, safety, and police service. Such additional patrol, however, appears to have no significant effect on victimization, recorded crime, or the likelihood of reporting a crime.

The elimination of foot patrol after years of maintenance, however, appears to produce few notable negative effects. Similarly, the retention of foot patrol does not prove to have notable beneficial effects.

Second Newark, New Jersey, Foot Patrol Experiment

A second foot patrol experiment was conducted in Newark in 1983 and 1984. This experiment used three neighborhoods and a control group (which received no "treatment").

The second Newark Foot Patrol Experiment included a coordinated foot patrol, a cleanup campaign, and distribution of a newsletter. Only the coordinated foot patrol appeared to reduce the perception of property crime and improve assessments of the police.

The cleanup effort and newsletter programs did not affect any of the outcome measures studied, nor did they reduce crime rates.

Oakland, California, Foot Patrol Program

In 1983 Oakland assigned 28 officers to foot patrol in its central business district. In addition, a Report Incidents Directly program was established whereby local businesspeople could talk directly to the patrol officers about any matters that concerned them. Mounted patrols and small vehicle patrols were also used.

The Oakland program, using foot patrol, mounted patrol, small vehicle patrol, and a Report Incidents Directly program, resulted in a substantial drop in the rate of crime against individuals and their property.

The crime rate dropped in the Oakland treatment area more than citywide declines, but again, no statistical tests were reported for this experiment.

San Diego, California, Community Profile Project

San Diego conducted a community profile project from 1973 to 1974 designed to improve police–community interactions. Twenty-four patrol officers and three supervisors were given 60 hours of community orientation training. The performance of these officers was compared with 24 other patrol officers who did not receive the training.

> The San Diego Community Profile Project provided patrol officers with extensive community-orientation training. These officers became more service oriented, increased their non–law enforcement contacts with citizens, and had a more positive attitude toward police–community relations.

The project did not consider the effect of community profiling on crime or on citizens' fear of crime.

Houston, Texas, Fear-Reduction Project

Like the second Newark experiment, Houston conducted a fear-reduction experiment between 1983 and 1984, testing five strategies: a victim recontact program following victimization, a community newsletter, a citizen contact patrol program, a police storefront office, and a program aimed to organize the community's interest in crime prevention.

> The victim recontact program and the newsletter of the Houston Fear-Reduction Project did not have positive results. In fact, the victim recontact program backfired, with Hispanics and Asians experiencing an increase in fear. Contact was primarily with White homeowners rather than minority renters. The citizen contact patrol and the police storefront office did, however, result in decreases in perceptions of social disorder, fear of personal victimization, and the level of personal and property crime.

The police storefront officers developed several programs, including monthly meetings, school programs, a fingerprinting program, a blood pressure program, a ride-along program, a park program, and an anticrime newsletter (Skogan and Wycoff, 1986).

Boston Foot Patrol Project

In 1983 Boston changed from predominantly two-officer motorized patrol to foot patrol and shifted the responsibilities of the foot patrol and motorized one-officer patrol to less serious crimes and noncrime service calls. The experiment studied 105 beats to determine whether high, medium, low, unstaffed, or no change in foot patrol affected calls for service by priority.

> The Boston Foot Patrol Project found no statistically significant relationship between changes in the level of foot patrol provided and the number of calls for service or the seriousness of the calls.

Violent crimes were not affected by increased or decreased foot patrol staffing. After the department shifted to foot patrol, the number of street robberies decreased but the number of commercial robberies increased.

Baltimore County Citizen Oriented Police Enforcement Project

The Baltimore Citizen Oriented Police Enforcement (COPE) Project, started in 1981, focused on the reduction of citizens' fear of crime. This problem-oriented project focused on solving the community problems of fear and disorder that lead to crime: "'Citizen Oriented Police Enforcement' officers would engage in intensive patrol, develop close contacts with citizens, conduct 'fear surveys' (door-to-door canvassing to identify concerns), and use any means within their power to quell fear" (Taft, 1986, 10).

Baltimore County's COPE Project reduced fear of crime by 10 percent and crime itself by 12 percent in target neighborhoods. It also reduced calls for service; increased citizen awareness of and satisfaction with the police; and improved police officer attitudes.

Summary and Implications of the Early Experiments

There is considerable inconsistency in findings across the preceding studies regarding both fear of crime and actual crime rates. Regarding fear of crime, the first Newark project observed a reduction and the second Newark project showed a reduction in the panel analysis (where the data were analyzed by individuals responding) but did not show a reduction in the cross-sectional analysis (where the data were analyzed by area rather than by individuals responding). The Houston study had the opposite results: a reduction in fear in the cross-sectional analysis but not in the panel analysis. In the Flint study, citizen perceptions of the seriousness of crime problems increased. In Baltimore County, fear of crime declined slightly. The San Diego, Oakland, and Boston programs did not consider fear of crime. Thus, the conclusion to be made at that time was that there was no consistent evidence to support the hypothesis that foot patrol reduces fear of crime (Greene and Taylor, 1991).

Inconsistent findings were also reported regarding crime rates. The Oakland study was the only one to demonstrate a reduction, but no statistical treatment was done. Again, the conclusion was: "Clearly, these studies do not point to decreases in crime or disorder as a consequence of community policing or foot patrol" (Greene and Taylor, 1991, 216).

Wycoff (1991), however, took an opposing view by stating that the fear-reduction studies conducted in Houston and Newark "provide evidence of the efficacy of what the authors referred to as 'community-oriented' policing strategies for reducing citizen fear, improving citizens' attitudes toward their neighborhoods and toward the police, and reducing crime."

Criticism has been leveled at these early experiments for their flawed research designs and lack of rigorous statistical analysis, with subsequent studies (discussed shortly) aiming to improve the methodology and empirical integrity of research efforts.

Fear-Reduction Strategies Experiments Compared

Wycoff (1991, 107–108) summarizes the seven strategies tested in the Newark and Houston experiments as follows:

Newsletters (Houston and Newark). These were tested with and without crime statistics. They were police produced and provided residents of the test area with information about crime prevention steps they could take, the police department, and police programs in their area.

Victim recontact (Houston). Patrol officers made telephone contact with victims to inform them of the status of their case, inquire whether they needed assistance, offer to send crime prevention information, and ask whether victims could provide additional information.

Police community station (Houston). A neighborhood storefront operation was conducted by patrol officers. The station provided a variety of services for the area.

Citizen contact patrol (Houston). Officers concentrated their patrol time within the target area where they made door-to-door contacts, introducing themselves to residents and businesspeople and asking whether there were any neighborhood problems citizens wished brought to the attention of the police.

Community organizing (Houston). Officers from the Community Services Division worked to organize block meetings attended by area patrol officers. They organized a neighborhood committee that met monthly with the district captain and developed special projects ("safe" houses for children, identifying property, and a cleanup campaign) for the area.

Signs of crime (Newark). This program focused on social disorder and conducted "random intensified enforcement and order maintenance operations" (e.g., foot patrol to enforce laws and maintain order on sidewalks and street corners, radar checks, bus checks to enforce ordinances and order, enforcement of disorderly conduct laws to move groups off the street corners, and road checks for DWI, improper licenses, or stolen vehicles). Addressing physical deterioration involved an intensification of city services and the use of juvenile offenders to conduct cleanup work in the target areas.

Coordinated community policing (Newark). This was the "kitchen sink" project that included a neighborhood community police center, a directed police–citizen contact program, a neighborhood police newsletter, intensified law enforcement and order maintenance, and a neighborhood cleanup.

Reducing Fear of Crime with Video Surveillance of Public Places

Many studies have tried to determine if closed-circuit television (CCTV) in public places reduces the fear of crime in those who use the areas. These studies looked at whether consumer buying increases in areas with CCTV systems; the basis was the belief that an area benefits from a positive economic impact when people feel safer. Although the findings are mixed, they generally show a somewhat reduced level of fear of crime among people in CCTV areas but *only* if those surveyed were aware they were in an area under surveillance. Most of the studies found that less than half of the interviewees were aware that they were in a CCTV area. Reduced fear of crime may increase the number of people using an area, and this, in turn, may increase the level of natural surveillance. It may also encourage people to be more security conscious (Ratcliffe, 2006). Because of this, relying on CCTV to reduce fear of crime may require a significant and ongoing publicity campaign (9).

One unintended consequence of using CCTV is the possibility of a negative public response to the cameras' existence (Ratcliffe, 2006, 5–6):

> In one survey, one-third of respondents felt that one purpose of CCTV was "to spy on people." In other surveys, some city managers were reluctant to advertise the cameras or have overt CCTV systems for fear they would make shoppers and consumers more fearful. In other words, it is hoped that most citizens will feel safer under the watchful eye of the cameras, but CCTV may have the reverse effect on some people.
>
> Remember that the primary crime prevention mechanism appears to work by increasing a perception of risk in the offender. With their reluctance to advertise the system, some city managers may be inadvertently reducing the cameras' effectiveness. By failing to advertise the cameras' presence, fewer offenders will be aware of the system and so will not perceive an increase in risk. On the whole, however, the public appears to be strongly in favor of a properly managed surveillance system for public areas.

OTHER CRIME PREVENTION PROGRAM STUDIES IN THE 1980s

Several communities conducted crime prevention studies in the 1980s. Studies in Seattle, Portland, and Hartford focused on citizen efforts to prevent residential crime; the study in Portland also focused on preventing crime in and around commercial establishments. Two studies examined the media and crime prevention: the McGruff national media campaign and the effectiveness of anticrime newsletters. Evaluations of these studies generally show positive results and support the conclusion that community crime prevention programs can be effective in reducing crime and fear of crime, improving citizens' quality of life, and enhancing the economic viability of urban neighborhoods and commercial locations (Heinzelmann, 1986).

The Seattle Program

The Citywide Crime Prevention Program (CCPP) of Seattle, described by Lindsay and McGillis (1986), focused on residential burglaries.

The Seattle Citywide Crime Prevention Program used property identification, home security checks, and neighborhood block watches to significantly reduce the residential burglary rate as well as the number of burglary-in-progress calls.

Fleissner, Fedan, and Klinger (1992, 9) note: "When citizens and police in South Seattle banded together to fight crime, quarterly crime statistics showed dramatic improvements in the quality of life. Citizen activity spread in the city's other three police precincts; now community policing is a going concern throughout Seattle—a citywide success."

Not only did the burglary rate drop significantly, "burglary-in-progress calls as a proportion of all burglary calls to police increased significantly in treated areas, and their quality was relatively high as measured by presentation of suspect information and the occurrence of subsequent arrests" (Lindsay and McGillis, 1986, 65).

The Portland Program

Portland also instituted a burglary prevention program, which included providing citizens with information about locks, alarms, outside lighting around entrances, removal or trimming of hedges, and precautions to take while on vacation (Schneider, 1986). The program also encouraged citizens to mark property with identification numbers. Door-to-door canvassing and a heavy emphasis on neighborhood rather than individual protection were important components of the program.

 The Portland antiburglary program succeeded in reducing the burglary rate for those who participated.

Data analysis revealed that Portland's higher crime areas went from a residential burglary rate that exceeded 20 percent annually—meaning more than one in five homes could expect to be burglarized at least once each year—to a burglary rate of approximately 8 percent for households participating in the prevention program (Schneider, 1986). There was also noted, however, a class bias in program participants, with those who attended meetings, engraved their property, and displayed the decals tending to be of a higher socioeconomic status (Schneider, 1986).

The Hartford Experiment

The Hartford Experiment used a three-pronged approach to reduce crime and the fear of crime: changing the physical environment, changing the delivery of police services, and organizing the citizens to improve their neighborhoods. This experiment centered on the interdependence of citizens, the police, and the environment: "The approach focuses on the interaction between human behavior and the (physically) built environment. It was hypothesized that the proper design and effective use of the built environment can lead to a reduction in crime and fear" (Fowler and Mangione, 1986, 80).

The program was based on four previous research efforts. First was that of Jacobs (1961), which found that neighborhoods that were relatively crime free had a mix of commercial and residential properties, resulting in many people on the streets and a great opportunity for police surveillance. In addition, a community with such mixed-use property tended to have residents who cared about the neighborhood and watched out for each other.

Angel (1968) described similar findings in his concept of "critical density," which states that if quite a few people are present on the most frequently used streets, they will serve as deterrents to burglary. In addition, Newman's classic work (1972) suggests that crime can be reduced by redesigning buildings to increase the number of doorways and other spaces that could be easily observed. Finally, Repetto (1974), like Newman, found that opportunities for surveillance could reduce crime and, like Jacobs, that neighborhood cohesiveness could have the same result.

Based on this research, the Hartford Experiment focused on Asylum Hill, a residential area a few blocks from the central business district of Hartford that was rapidly deteriorating. It was found that because of the high rate of vehicle traffic, residents did not use their yards and felt no ties to the neighborhood. The physical design of the neighborhood was changed to restrict through traffic and visually define the boundaries of the neighborhood. Cul-de-sacs were built at a few critical intersections, and some streets were made one way.

A second change in the neighborhood involved patrol officer assignments. Instead of rotating assignments within a centralized department, Hartford began using a decentralized team of officers assigned permanently to the Asylum Hill area.

Finally, the Hartford Experiment helped organize the neighborhood, including the establishment of block watch programs, recreational programs for youths, and improvements for a large neighborhood park.

As a result of these changes, "Residents used their neighborhood more, walked more often both during the day and evening hours, used the nearby park more often, and spent more days per week outside in front of their homes" (Fowler and Mangione, 1986, 96).

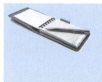

The Hartford Experiment restructured the neighborhood's physical environment, changed the way patrol officers were assigned, and organized the neighborhood in an effort to reduce crime and the fear of crime.

Researchers caution that these types of crime control programs must be tailored to fit the particular set of circumstances found in an individual neighborhood: "What one would want to derive from the Hartford Project is not a program design, but rather an approach to problem analysis and strategies to affect them" (Fowler and Mangione, 1986, 106).

LATER STUDIES OF FOOT PATROL PROGRAMS

As discussed, earlier studies of foot patrol programs were criticized because of various methodological shortcomings. Several recent studies have met with more encouraging results, as departments have begun to incorporate data analysis of crime types and locations into their foot patrol strategies (Craven, 2009).

San Francisco Police Department Foot Patrol Program

One such recent study of foot patrol was conducted at the San Francisco (California) Police Department (SFPD) and is reported on by Rosenfeld (2008). Among the key findings were:

» The SFPD committed significant resources to foot beat staffing. The number of hours dedicated to foot beats during the first 6 months of 2007 totaled 83,475, representing an 86 percent increase when compared to the same time period in 2006.

» Foot patrols increase the community's perception of safety. Eighty-two percent of those responding to the telephone survey and 73 percent of those responding to the written survey felt safer as a result of foot patrols.

» Both police staff and the community widely accept foot patrols. Seventy-nine percent of the SFPD respondents believe foot patrols are an effective tool for the department. Correspondingly, 90 percent of the community member respondents believe foot patrols are a necessary tool for the SFPD to use in addressing crime and quality of life issues.

Philadelphia Foot Patrol Experiment

The Philadelphia Foot Patrol Experiment has garnered attention lately for its focus on place-based policing, showing that when police resources are directed at hot spots, or those geographic locations where crime incidents tend to cluster, foot patrol can indeed have a net positive effect on reducing crime, particularly violent crime (Ratcliffe et al., 2011). The concept of spatial dosage, whether pertaining to the number of officers patrolling a certain area or the geographic extent of one patrol beat, was identified as a salient variable in whether foot patrol could effectively reduce violent crime.

COMMUNITY POLICING AND THE CRIMINAL JUSTICE SYSTEM

The criminal justice system includes law enforcement, the courts, and corrections. What happens in each component of the criminal justice system directly affects the other two components, and many of the trends that affect the criminal justice system as a whole directly affect the type of programs police departments should implement to improve community relations. Consequently, partnerships among the various entities within the criminal justice system are vital to achieving the community policing mission.

 A coordinated effort among law enforcement, courts, and corrections is required to effectively deal with the crime problem and to elicit the support of the community in doing so.

Effective efforts are those that partner various community institutions to address issues of housing, unemployment, illiteracy, lack of recreational opportunities for youths, and other social problems.

Community Policing and the Courts

The way courts address the accused has a direct impact on the crime problem and on community policing efforts. The National Symposium identified two model court programs: the Albany (New York) Community Dispute Resolution Centers and the Madison (Wisconsin) Deferred Prosecution/First Offenders Unit.

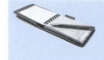 Model court programs also involving the police include community dispute resolution centers and a deferred prosecution/first offenders unit.

Community Dispute Resolution Centers (Albany) The 32 dispute resolution centers were independent, community-based, nonprofit organizations contracted by the Unified Court System of the State of New York, Albany, to (1) provide dispute resolution resources for local communities, (2) prevent escalation of disputes, (3) relieve the courts of matters not requiring judicial intervention, and (4) teach individuals to resolve their problems through mediation.

Police officers, probation officers, judges, district attorneys, and legal aid offices could refer cases to a local dispute resolution center, or individuals could be self-referred. The mediation, conciliation, or arbitration services were provided free. Mediation rather than law enforcement or court intervention was effective.

The Deferred Prosecution/First Offenders Unit (Madison) This program sought to prevent offenders' further involvements in crime by deferring prosecution on the condition that they satisfactorily complete appropriate treatment and rehabilitation programs. The program recognized the hazards of labeling individuals and the potential of treatment for first offenders who accept responsibility for their actions.

An offender's suitability for the program was based on several criteria: the nature of the offense, prior criminal record, admission of guilt, attitude, whether the offender was dangerous to self or community, likelihood of repeating the crime, and whether the offender would benefit from the treatment process.

The program used a large network of social service agencies and public and private organizations. Because a "substantial portion" of program participants was comprised of shoplifters, the staff conducted a 1-day Saturday workshop on retail theft. Another integral part of the program was voluntary community service, not as a means of punishment but as a way to repay the community for the crime committed and to change the offender's behavior patterns. The program conserved police, prosecutorial, judicial, and correctional resources. In addition, offenders' lives were minimally disrupted because they could continue to pursue their occupations and fulfill family obligations.

Community Policing and Corrections

Community-based corrections gained popularity in the 1990s but are still resisted by many neighborhoods. Sometimes referred to as intermediate sanctions, community corrections may take many forms, including halfway houses, prerelease centers, transition centers, work furlough and community work centers, community treatment centers, restitution centers, and a host of other innovative approaches to involving the community in efforts to reintegrate offenders into the community *without* danger to the citizens. Residents may live either part time or full time at such centers, depending on the other conditions set forth by the court.

Sharrock, Perry, and Phillips (2008) describe the grim corrections statistics in Kansas where, in 2006, two-thirds of the offenders entering Kansas prisons were guilty of parole violations, 90 percent of which were for technicalities such as missing meetings. One-third of all parole violations involved substance abuse, but fewer than half of the offenders got treatment in prison. Only 18 percent of offenders had completed job training. From 1985 to 2005 the state's spending on corrections increased fourfold. Werholtz, Kansas's secretary of corrections, was familiar with the "nothing works" theory based on a seminal study by sociologist Robert Martinson, which concluded: "With few and isolated exceptions, the rehabilitative efforts that have been reported so far have had no appreciable effect on recidivism" (Martinson, 1974, 25). But Werholtz hoped that a frequently overlooked caveat in the study—that perhaps nothing worked because the programs so far had been poorly designed or not implemented as intended—held credence and that the latest "buzz" at corrections conferences about reentry and reinvestment initiatives might be plausible solutions to the problem.

Werholtz believed targeting limited resources at helping the highest-risk offenders with job training, treatment, and counseling launched inside prison and continued on the outside might work on the reentry end. The reinvestment part was to channel the money saved by keeping offenders out of prison to the communities to which the offenders returned. Kansas was a prime candidate to test out the theory.

Starting in 2004, prisoners were given job training, treatment, and classes in life skills, including money management, parenting, and decision making. The year before they were to be released, efforts were made to secure for each prisoner a job, an apartment, and a connection to the right programs to stay within the law.

Although parole officers and social service workers were skeptical, by 2006, 401 fewer people were in prison in Kansas for violating parole than expected, saving $13.8 million in operating costs. Kansas used $2 million of that for community programs, including job training and drug treatment.

Mary Obregon, once a skeptical world-weary parole officer, lamented: "You see the same people over and over. You see these kids and their children's children. Show me that it works and then I will believe in it." However, after the program was implemented, Obregon became a convert to the newly designed reentry strategy. Noting that it is not a one-size-fits-all type of program, Obregon was impressed by the focus on getting to understand each client and their specific needs and tailoring the response to the individual risk factors. As a reentry case manager, Obregon spends her time building support networks for parolees to help them succeed at staying out of "the system," thereby filling the void that had previously allowed her clients to fall back into their old ways and end up returning to the system. These support networks often consist of potential employers and landlords, substance abuse and mental health counselors, parole and police officers, and community leaders (Sharrock, Perry, and Phillips, 2008).

One of Obregon's clients was a woman named Jeannette Brown, who enrolled in the reentry program in 2005. In anticipation of her release, Brown was tasked with creating a list of goals, which she identified as regaining custody of her children, keeping a job, getting a driver's license, and staying out of abusive relationships. To help prepare Brown for her reentry into society and achieve her stated goals, Obregon assembled a "release team" that included herself; substance abuse and corrections counselors; police and parole officers; mental health, housing, and job specialists; a business developer; a volunteer mentor; and the reentry program director. When Brown finally left prison in June 2007, she was met at the gates by four reentry staffers, who took her to her new apartment, where several parole officers helped her unpack. Obregon then took Brown to the local food shelf, set up a doctor's appointment, and helped Brown get an ID. The efforts and support of the "release team" have been transformative for Brown: "Instead of dreading her parole meetings, Brown stops by Obregon's office after work to say hello. 'Parole officers used to try to put me back in prison; now I feel like they are trying to keep me out.'" (Sharrock, Perry, and Phillips, 63).

EARLY EFFORTS USING THE MEDIA IN CRIME PREVENTION

Two different approaches to using the media have also been extensively studied: the "McGruff" media campaign and police–community anticrime newsletters.

The "McGruff" National Media Campaign

McGruff, the crime dog, is to law enforcement what Smokey the Bear is to the National Forest Service. The McGruff National Media campaign, also known as the "Take a Bite Out of Crime" campaign, is aimed at promoting citizen involvement in crime prevention activities through public service announcements, or **PSAs**.

PSAs
Public service announcements.

A press release from the National Crime Prevention Council describes the creation of McGruff and the campaign:

> The idea of a national public education campaign to teach Americans that they can prevent crime—and how to do so— was first conceived in 1978. The U.S. Department of Justice supported the plan, as did distinguished civic leaders and such organizations as the AFL-CIO, the FBI, the International Association of Chiefs of Police, and the National Sheriffs' Association. The Advertising Council, Inc., also agreed to support the campaign. Research and program development advisory groups helped formulate a strategy.... The first McGruff public service announcements (PSAs), developed in 1979, were premiered in February 1980....
>
> The campaign's objectives were clear: (1) to change unwarranted feelings and attitudes about crime and the criminal justice system, (2) to generate an individual sense of responsibility for crime prevention, (3) to initiate individual action toward preventing crime, (4) to mobilize additional resources for crime prevention efforts, and (5) to enhance existing crime prevention programs and projects conducted by national, state, and local organizations.

McGruff, the crime dog, helps teach citizens how to "take a bite out of crime."

Source: © National Crime Prevention Council. McGruff the Crime Dog® is a registered mark of the National Crime Prevention Council.

The McGruff program represents a successful early effort to engage citizens in crime prevention.

The public favorably received the "McGruff" format and content, and the campaign had a sizable impact on what people know and do about crime prevention.

Police–Community Anticrime Newsletters and Brochures

Barthe (2006, 30–31) describes how printed materials can help in crime prevention efforts:

> Ease of production and low distribution costs make fliers and leaflets favorites of police departments and other crime prevention agencies. Using readily available desktop publishing software, an agency can create a cost-effective publicity campaign. Police officers can deliver the material door-to-door or place it on car windshields.
>
> Mailings can also be an effective way to reach people with crime prevention messages. Some studies have shown newsletters and brochures to be effective

ways to spread crime prevention information, but such media do not always produce the intended result. In the early 1980s, the Houston Police Department failed to reduce residents' fear of crime by distributing newsletters containing local crime rates and prevention tips. In Newark, New Jersey, the police department used a similar strategy. While people liked receiving the newsletters, they rarely read them.

General publicity campaigns aimed at victims have had limited effectiveness. A 4-month national press and poster campaign tried to educate people about the importance of locking their parked cars, but it failed to change people's behavior. Another campaign used posters and television spots to remind people to lock their car doors, but it also proved ineffective. These studies demonstrate that people often pay little attention to crime prevention messages. A common reason given is that potential victims do not feel that it concerns them. For instance, domestic violence awareness campaigns have to compete with the possibility that women do not want to see themselves as victims.

QUALITATIVE EVALUATIONS AND SALIENT PROGRAM FEATURES

qualitative evaluations

Assessments that are more descriptive and less statistical than empirical studies; the opposite of quantitative evaluation.

Qualitative evaluations are more descriptive and less statistical than empirical studies. One large-scale qualitative evaluation, undertaken by the National Symposium on Community Institutions and Inner-City Crime Project, sought to identify model programs for reduction of inner-city crime. Almost 3,500 national organizations, criminal justice scholars, and federal, state, and local government agencies were asked to recommend outstanding local programs. The result was the identification of approximately 1,300 programs. Each was sent a request for detailed information, and 350 (27%) responded. From these, 18 were selected for site visits. Although each program was unique, they shared some common characteristics (Sulton, 1990).

Eighteen model programs shared the following characteristics. The programs:
- Focused on causes of crime.
- Built on community strengths.
- Incorporated natural support systems.
- Had an identifiable group of clients.
- Targeted those who were less affluent.
- Had clearly stated goals and well-defined procedures.
- Had sufficient resources.
- Had a strong leader.

Many of the programs focus on specific social problems of inner-city residents, problems that were "identified as correlates with, if not causes of, inner-city crime, such as emotional or family instability, lack of education, absence of vocational skills, unemployment, drug and alcohol abuse, juvenile gangs, and sexual abuse and exploitation" (Sulton, 1990, 10). The programs have a clear focus, a clear audience, and a clear idea of how to proceed.

On a much smaller scale, but equally instructive, is the Newport News (Virginia) Police Department's reliance on data to identify a problem and to evaluate a solution:

> Local hunters and other gun owners held target practice at an excavation pit. Officer Hendrickson found that between April and September one year, the department had been called 45 times to chase away shooters and that the problem had existed for at least 15 years. Most of the calls had come from a couple whose nearby home was bullet-riddled and who thought the police were doing a good job because each time they chased away the shooters.

> Officer Hendrickson interviewed shooters and learned that most were soldiers from nearby Fort Eustis; many others were sent to the pit by gun shop owners. The officer also determined the pit was close enough to a highway to make any firearms discharge there illegal. Deciding to use education backed by legal sanctions, he first photographed the damage and other evidence, which he used to persuade a judge to give anyone convicted once of illegal shooting a suspended sentence and a small fine; a second offense would result in confiscation of the weapon and a jail sentence. The officer obtained from the property owners permission to arrest on their property and the same from the C & O Railroad for shooters crossing the tracks to reach the pit. He also wrote a pamphlet defining the problem and the department's intended enforcement action, and distributed it to the military base and all area gun shops. Finally, he had "No Parking—Tow Zone" signs erected on the shoulder where most shooters parked.

> The results were simple. Officers issued 35 summonses to shooters in September, 15 in October, and the last on November 12. The pit soon became so overgrown that it was uninviting for target practice. (Adapted from Guyot, 1992, 321)

IMPEDIMENTS TO COMMUNITY POLICING REVISITED

Success in the preceding incident and others might indicate that community policing and problem-solving policing would be readily accepted by law enforcement officials and the communities they serve. Such acceptance is not, however, always the case because of several impediments (Skogan, 2004, 162–167):

» Making community policing an overtime program
» Making it a special unit
» Shortchanging the infrastructure
» Resistance in the ranks
» Resistance by police managers
» Resistance by police unions
» Resistance by special units
» Competing demands and expectations
» Lack of interagency cooperation
» Problems evaluating performance
» Unresponsive public
» Nasty misconduct
» Leadership transitions

Recall from Chapter 5 the challenges facing implementation of community policing:

» Resistance by police officers

» Difficulty involving other agencies and organizing the community

» Reluctance of average citizens to participate, either because of fear or cynicism

Resistance to change is common, especially in a tradition-oriented profession such as law enforcement: "Community policing is a fight for 'hearts and minds' of patrol officers and the public... involving a shift in the culture of policing" (Sadd and Grinc, 1996, 8).

Impediments to implementing innovative community-oriented policing include:
- The powerful pull of tradition.
- Substantial segments of the public not wanting the police to change.
- Unions that continue to be skeptical of innovation.
- The high cost of innovation.
- Lack of vision on the part of police executives.
- Police departments' inability to evaluate their own effectiveness (Skolnick and Bayley, 1986)

One challenge is that projects were usually established as special units that some saw as elite: "The perception of elitism is ironic because community policing is meant to close the gap between patrol and special units and to empower and value the rank-and-file patrol officer as the most important agent for police work" (Sadd and Grinc, 1996).

Another substantial impediment is how to respond to calls for service. A potential conflict exists between responding to calls for service and community policing efforts, because calls for service use much of the time needed for problem identification and resolution efforts. The unpredictability of calls for service presents management problems for agencies wanting to implement community policing strategies. Departments must set their priorities and determine how to balance calls for service (reactive) with a problem-oriented approach (proactive). As stressed throughout this text, the one-on-one interaction between police officers and the citizens they serve is critical.

Some simple services that police departments might provide for the community cost little and require limited personnel. For example, relatively inexpensive efforts to enhance community safety through crime prevention might include conducting monthly meetings, meeting with school administrators, conducting fingerprinting programs, participating in athletic contests, publishing newsletters, and providing ride-alongs. Other services, however, may be relatively expensive and require many officers.

Whatever the cost to implement, community policing appears to offer a realistic approach to reducing violence, crime, and the drug problem. The remaining chapters discuss several approaches to community policing and problem solving to address these issues.

A FINAL NOTE: THE IMPORTANT DISTINCTION BETWEEN PROGRAMS AND COMMUNITY POLICING

It must be stressed that programs identified throughout this chapter are not examples of community policing programs *per se*, although community policing may incorporate the use of these and other strategies. Too many police officials think that because they have a neighborhood-watch program or a ride-along program they are doing community policing. In fact, some police chiefs and sheriffs state with pride that they are deeply involved in community policing because they have a DARE program. Community policing is an overriding philosophy that affects every aspect of police operations; it is not a single program, or even a hundred programs. Such programs, particularly in isolation, are more community relations or even public relations, not community policing.

SUMMARY

Crime prevention became popular in the late 1960s and early 1970s, with many communities taking an active role. Among the most commonly implemented crime prevention programs have been street lighting projects; property marking projects; security survey projects; citizen patrol projects; and crime reporting, neighborhood-watch, or block projects. Specialized crime watch programs include mobile crime watch, youth crime watch, business crime watch, apartment watch, realtor watch, and carrier alert.

Continuing the community crime prevention momentum generated during the 1960s and 1970s, new programs and organizations were initiated during the 1980s and 1990s to encourage citizens to play an active role in reducing crime in their own neighborhoods. Among the most visible organizations focused on crime are citizen crime prevention associations, Crime Stoppers, and MADD. Many police departments also expanded their use of volunteers, who may serve in a crime prevention capacity as reserve officers, auxiliary patrol, or community service officers or on an as-needed basis.

Youths, who had traditionally been included in police–community relations efforts and crime prevention initiatives, were also addressed through programs including the McGruff "Take a Bite Out of Crime" campaign, police athletic leagues (PALs), Officer Friendly, Police Explorers, police–school liaison programs, and the DARE program. Many programs for juveniles involve the schools, which historically have been charged with instilling discipline in their students. For example, police–school liaison programs place an officer in a school to work with school authorities, parents, and students to prevent crime and antisocial behavior and to improve police–youth relationships. The joint goals of most police–school liaison programs are to prevent juvenile delinquency and to improve police–youth relations.

The most common components of community policing experiments have been foot patrol, newsletters, and community organizing. Several empirical studies in the 1980s assessed the effectiveness of community policing efforts. The Flint Neighborhood Foot Patrol Program appeared to produce a decrease in crime, an increase in general citizen satisfaction with the foot patrol program, a decline in the public's fear of crime, and a positive perception of the foot patrol officers.

In the first Newark Foot Patrol Experiment, residents reported positive results, whereas business owners reported negative results. The second Newark Foot Patrol Experiment included a coordinated foot patrol, a cleanup campaign, and distribution of a newsletter. Only the coordinated foot patrol was perceived to reduce property crime and improved assessments of the police.

The Oakland program, using foot patrol, mounted patrol, small vehicle patrol, and a Report Incidents Directly program, resulted in a substantial drop in the rate of crime against persons and their property. The San Diego Community Profile Project provided patrol officers with extensive community-orientation training. These officers became more service oriented, increased their non–law enforcement contacts with citizens, and had a more positive attitude toward police–community relations.

The victim recontact program and the newsletter of the Houston Fear-Reduction Project did not have positive results. In fact, the victim recontact program backfired, with Hispanics and Asians experiencing an increase in fear. Contact was primarily with White homeowners rather than minority renters. The citizen contact patrol and the police storefront office did, however, result in decreases in perceptions of social disorder, fear of personal victimization, and the level of personal and property crime.

The Boston Foot Patrol Project found no statistically significant relationship between changes in the level of foot patrol provided and the number of calls for service or the seriousness of the calls. Baltimore County's COPE Project reduced fear of crime by 10 percent and crime itself by 12 percent in target neighborhoods. It also reduced calls for service; increased citizen awareness of and satisfaction with the police; and improved police officer attitudes.

Other studies have reviewed the effectiveness of community crime prevention efforts. The Seattle Citywide Crime Prevention Program, using property identification, home security checks, and neighborhood block watches, significantly reduced the residential burglary rate as well as the number of burglary-in-progress calls. The Portland antiburglary program also succeeded in reducing the burglary rate for those who participated. The Hartford Experiment restructured the physical environment, changed the way patrol officers were assigned, and organized the neighborhood in an effort to reduce crime and the fear of crime.

The criminal justice system includes law enforcement, the courts, and corrections. What happens in each component of the criminal justice system directly affects the other two components. Consequently, a coordinated effort among law enforcement, courts, and corrections is required to effectively deal with the crime problem and to elicit the support of the community in doing so. Model court programs also involving the police include a community dispute resolution center and a deferred prosecution/first offenders unit.

The effectiveness of the media in assisting crime prevention efforts is another evaluation focus. The public favorably received the "McGruff" format and content, and the campaign had a sizable impact on what people know and do about crime prevention.

Eighteen model programs identified by the National Symposium on Community Institutions and Inner-City Crime Project shared the following characteristics: The programs (1) focused on causes of crime, (2) built on community strengths, (3) incorporated natural support systems, (4) had an identifiable group of clients, (5) targeted those who were less affluent, (6) had clearly stated goals and well-defined procedures, (7) had sufficient resources, and (8) had a strong leader.

Impediments to implementing innovative community-oriented policing include the powerful pull of tradition; substantial segments of the public who do not want the police to change; unions that continue to be skeptical of innovation; the cost of innovation; lack of vision on the part of police executives; and police departments' inability to evaluate their own effectiveness.

DISCUSSION QUESTIONS

1. Why is it difficult to conduct research on the effectiveness of community policing?

2. Which studies do you think have the most value for policing in the next few years? Which studies have the most promise?

3. Why would a police department want to reduce fear of crime rather than crime itself?

4. Which of the fear-reduction strategies do you believe holds the most promise?

5. What do you think are the most reasonable aspects of the crime prevention through environmental design (CPTED) approach?

6. Do you think that victims who ignored the CPTED approach to crime prevention are culpable?

7. Has your police department conducted any research on community policing or crime prevention efforts? If so, what were the results?

8. Does your police department have its own McGruff costume or robot? If so, how does the department use it?

9. What do you think are the most important questions regarding police–community relations that should be researched in the next few years?

10. How much of a police department's budget should be devoted to research? Which areas should be of highest priority?

GALE EMERGENCY SERVICES DATABASE ASSIGNMENTS

ONLINE Database

- Use the Gale Emergency Services Database to help answer the Discussion Questions as appropriate. Be prepared to share and discuss your outline with the class.

- Research and outline at least one of the following subjects: citizen crime reporting, CPTED, National Night Out, police athletic leagues.

REFERENCES

Angel, S. 1968. *Discouraging Crime through City Planning.* Berkeley, CA: University of California Press.

Barthe, Emmanuel. 2006 (June). *Crime Prevention Publicity Campaigns.* Washington, DC: U.S. Department of Justice, Office of Community Oriented Policing Services, Problem-Oriented Guides for Police, Response Guides Series, Guide No. 5.

Burke, Tim. 2012. "People Power Returns." *Public Safety IT* (January/February): 38–40. http://www.ithinqware.org/pdf/public_safety_it.pdf

Craven, Kym. 2009. "Foot Patrols: Crime Analysis and Community Engagement to Further the Commitment to Community Policing." *Community Policing Dispatch* 2 (2).

Fleissner, Dan, Nicholas Fedan, and David Klinger. 1992. "Community Policing in Seattle: A Model Partnership between Citizens and Police." *NIJ Journal* (August): 9–18.

Fowler, Floyd J., Jr. and Thomas W. Mangione. 1986. "A Three-Pronged Effort to Reduce Crime and Fear of Crime: The Hartford Experiment." In *Community Crime Prevention: Does It Work?,* edited by Dennis P. Rosenbaum, 87–108. Beverly Hills: Sage Publications.

Greene, Jack R. and Ralph B. Taylor. 1991. "Community-Based Policing and Foot Patrol: Issues of Theory and Evaluation." In *Community Policing: Rhetoric or Reality,* edited by Jack R. Greene and Stephen D. Mastrofski, 195–223. New York: Praeger Publishers.

Guyot, Dorothy. 1992 (May). "Problem-Oriented Policing Shines in the Stats." In *Source Book: Community-Oriented Policing: An Alternative Strategy,* edited by Bernard L. Garmire, 317–321. Washington, DC: International City/County Management Association (ICMA).

Heinzelmann, Fred. 1986. "Foreword." In *Community Crime Prevention: Does It Work?,* edited by Dennis P. Rosenbaum, 7–8. Newbury Park: Sage Publications.

Holloway, Katy, Trevor Bennett, and David P. Farrington. 2008 (April). *Crime Prevention Research Review No. 3: Does Neighborhood Watch Reduce Crime*? Washington, DC: Office of Community Oriented Policing Services.

"Impaired Driving." n.d. Washington, DC: National Highway Traffic Safety Administration. http://www.nhtsa.gov/Impaired

Jacobs, J. 1961. *The Death and Life of Great American Cities.* New York: Vintage.

Lindsay, Betsy and Daniel McGillis. 1986. "Citywide Community Crime Prevention: An Assessment of the Seattle Program." In *Community Crime Prevention: Does It Work?,* edited by Dennis P. Rosenbaum, 46–67. Beverly Hills: Sage Publications.

Martinson, Robert. 1974. "What Works?—Questions and Answers about Prison Reform." *The Public Interest* 35 (Spring): 22–54.

Mastrofski, Stephen D. 1992. "What Does Community Policing Mean for Daily Police Work?" *NIJ Journal* (August): 23–27.

Mentel, Zoe. 2009. "Shutting the Door on Foreclosure and Drug-Related Problem Properties: Two Communities Respond to Neighborhood Disorder." *Community Policing Dispatch, The e-Newsletter of the COPS Office* 2 (7).

Newman, O. 1972. *Defensible Space: Crime Prevention through Urban Design.* New York: Macmillan.

Pate, Anthony M. 1986. "Experimenting with Foot Patrol: The Newark Experience." In *Community Crime Prevention: Does It Work?,* edited by Dennis P. Rosenbaum, 137–156. Beverly Hills: Sage Publications.

Police Foundation. 1981. *The Newark Foot Patrol Experiment.* Washington, DC: The Police Foundation.

Ratcliffe, Jerry. 2006. *Video Surveillance of Public Places.* Washington, DC: Center for Problem-Oriented Policing.

Ratcliffe, Jerry H., Travis Taniguchi, Elizabeth R. Groff, and Jennifer D. Wood. 2011. "The Philadelphia Foot Patrol Experiment: A Randomized Controlled Trial of Police Patrol Effectiveness in Violent Crime Hotspots." *Criminology* 49 (3): 795–831.

Repetto, T. A. 1974. *Residential Crime.* Cambridge: Ballinger.

Rosenfeld, Ben. 2008 (April 8). "Letter to the Mayor of the City and County of San Francisco, the Members of the Board of Supervisors, and the Members of the San Francisco Police Commission." City and County of San Francisco, CA: Office of the Controller. http://sfcontroller .org/ftp/uploadedfiles/controller/reports/Foot%20 Patrol%20Final%20Report%20Transmittal%20Letter%20 (Final)%204-8-07.pdf

Sadd, Susan and Randolph M. Grinc. 1996 (February). *Implementation Challenges in Community Policing.* Washington, DC: National Institute of Justice Research in Brief.

Schneider, Anne L. 1986. "Neighborhood-Based Antiburglary Strategies: An Analysis of Public and Private Benefits from the Portland Program." In *Community Crime Prevention: Does It Work?*, edited by Dennis P. Rosenbaum, 68–86. Beverly Hills: Sage Publications.

Sharrock, Justine, Celia Perry, and Jen Phillips. 2008. "The Shawnee Redemption." *Mother Jones* (July/August): 61–63.

Skogan, Wesley G. 2004. "Community Policing: Common Impediments to Success." In *Community Policing: The Past, Present, and Future,* edited by Lorie Fridell and Mary Ann Wycoff, 159–168. Washington, DC: The Annie E. Casey Foundation and Police Executive Research Forum.

Skogan, Wesley G. and Mary Ann Wycoff. 1986. "Storefront Police Offices: The Houston Field Test." In *Community Crime Prevention: Does It Work?*, edited by Dennis P. Rosenbaum, 179–199. Beverly Hills: Sage Publications.

Skolnick, Jerome H. and David H. Bayley. 1986. *The New Blue Line: Innovation in Six American Cities.* New York: The Free Press.

Sulton, Anne Thomas. 1990. *Inner-City Crime Control: Can Community Institutions Contribute?* Washington, DC: The Police Foundation.

Taft, Philip B., Jr. 1986. *Fighting Fear: The Baltimore County C.O.P.E. Project.* Washington, DC: Police Executive Research Forum.

Trojanowicz, Robert C. 1986. "Evaluating a Neighborhood Foot Patrol Program: The Flint, Michigan, Project." In *Community Crime Prevention: Does It Work?*, edited by Dennis P. Rosenbaum, 157–178. Beverly Hills: Sage Publications.

Wycoff, Mary Ann. 1991. "The Benefits of Community Policing: Evidence and Conjecture." In *Community Policing: Rhetoric or Reality,* edited by Jack R. Greene and Stephen D. Mastrofski, 103–120. New York: Praeger Publishers.

Zahm, Diane. 2007. *Using Crime Prevention through Environmental Design in Problem Solving.* Washington, DC: Center for Problem-Oriented Policing.

ADDITIONAL RESOURCES

Every interest organization has a Web page on the Internet, including several federal agencies. A search using the terms *community policing* or *crime prevention* will yield a tremendous amount of current information. Many organizations offer expertise in building partnerships and provide a variety of publications, training, and services that can strengthen local efforts. A sampling follows.

Bureau of Justice Assistance Clearinghouse, Box 6000, Rockville, MD 20850; (800) 688–4252

Center for Community Change, 1000 Wisconsin Avenue NW, Washington, DC 20007; (202) 342–0519

Citizens Committee for New York City, 305 7th Avenue, 15th Floor, New York, NY 10001; (212) 989–0909

Community Policing Consortium, 1726 M Street NW, Suite 801, Washington, DC 20006; (202) 833–3305 or (800) 833–3085

National Center for Community Policing, School of Criminal Justice, Michigan State University, East Lansing, MI 48824; (517) 355–2322

National Crime Prevention Council, 1700 K Street NW, 2nd Floor, Washington, DC 20006-3817; (202) 466–6272

National Training and Information Center, 810 North Milwaukee Avenue, Chicago, IL 60622–4103; (312) 243–3035

Police Executive Research Forum, 2300 M Street NW, Suite 910, Washington, DC 20006; (202) 466–7820

This available CourseMate has an interactive eBook and interactive learning tools, including flash cards, quizzes, and more. To learn more about this resource and access free demo CourseMate resources, go to **www.cengagebrain.com**, and search for this book. To access CourseMate materials that you have purchased, go to **login.cengagebrain.com**.

CHAPTER 10
Safe Neighborhoods and Communities: From Traffic Problems to Crime

In the last analysis, the most promising and so the most important method of dealing with crime is by preventing it—by ameliorating the conditions of life that drive people to commit crime and that undermine the restraining rules and institutions erected by society against anti-social conduct.

—President's Commission on Law Enforcement and Administration of Justice, 1967

DO YOU KNOW ...

» What role crime prevention plays in community policing?

» What is usually at the top of the list of neighborhood concerns, and what behaviors are involved?

» What engineering and enforcement responses can address the problem of speeding in residential areas?

» How community policing has addressed citizens' fear of crime?

» What the three primary components of CPTED are?

» How CPTED directly supports community policing?

» What two side effects of place-focused opportunity blocking may be?

» What the risk factor prevention paradigm is?

» What three federal initiatives can assist communities in implementing community policing?

» What the Weed and Seed program does?

» What partnerships have been implemented to prevent or reduce crime and disorder?

CAN YOU DEFINE ...

cocoon neighborhood watch
contagion
diffusion
opportunity blocking
place
risk factor prevention paradigm
synergism
target hardening
traffic calming

INTRODUCTION

Community policing stresses using partnerships and problem solving to address making neighborhoods and communities safer, including looking at concerns related to traffic, at neighborhood disorder, at crime, and at the fear of crime. Many Americans, including many police, believe traffic problems and crime prevention are solely the responsibility of law enforcement. When crime surges in a community, the usual public response is to demand the hiring of more officers. Citizens often believe that a visible police presence will deter and reduce crime, even though most studies indicate this is not the case. For example, the classic Kansas City Preventive Patrol Experiment found overwhelming evidence that decreasing or increasing routine preventive patrol within the range tested had no effect on crime, citizen fear of crime, community attitudes toward the police on the delivery of police services, police response time, or traffic accidents. In 1975 the FBI's Uniform Crime Report noted:

> Criminal justice professionals readily and repeatedly admit that, in the absence of citizen assistance, neither more manpower, nor improved technology, nor additional money will enable law enforcement to shoulder the monumental burden of combating crime in America.

The advent of community policing and partnerships is often credited with the dramatic decrease in crime witnessed in the late 1990s (Rosen, 2006). Despite predictions that a significant crime wave would occur in the 1990s as a result of the increase in the population of youth and young adults (a "boom" that never materialized), the United States experienced the longest and deepest decline in crime since World War II. Some scholars have speculated that these drops in the crime rate may have resulted from modest improvements in policing. The New York Police Department (NYPD), for example, increased its workforce by 35 percent (13,000 people), changed its management style, and engaged in more aggressive police work, particularly in public-order offenses.

Other variables that may have contributed to a decrease in the crime rate are the booming economy, a drop in the high-risk (teens to young adult) population, and an increase in the number of people in prison. Research, however, has been unable to consistently demonstrate a clear correlation between these variables and the crime rate, as it is noted that the drop in the youth population and an increase in the incarceration rate also occurred in the 1980s when crime across the country soared.

Furthermore, and in contrast to what was happening in the United States, Canada experienced a 30-percent drop in violent crime during the 1990s at a time when the country's prison population was declining, there were fewer officers on the street, and the economic gains were moderate. Therefore, from these contrasting scenarios and societal variables, the difficulty in determining the causes of fluctuating crime rates becomes apparent.

In 2005 and 2006 it appeared that the downward trend in violent crime rates of the 1990s was over. Violent crime was growing at an alarming rate. The FBI reported the largest single-year-percentage increase in violent crime in 14 years. At the Police Executive Research Forum (PERF) National Violent Crime Summit in August 2006, 170 representatives—mayors, police chiefs, and public officials—from more than 50 cities met to discuss the gathering storm of violent crime sweeping through our nation's communities. The information they shared was sobering. Murder was up 27.5 percent in the first 6 months in Boston, 27 percent in Memphis, and 25 percent in Cincinnati. Robbery was up in even more startling numbers. Even communities with relatively low crime rates saw significant increases in 2005 and early 2006.

Police chiefs pointed to gangs, violent criminals returning from prisons, drug trafficking, and juveniles with easy access to guns as the forces behind the uptick in violent crime. Others, such as Mayor Douglas Palmer of Trenton, New Jersey, suggested that the focus on homeland security and fighting terrorism had taken resources away from hometown security and local crime prevention efforts (Rosen, 2006). Additional factors identified by PERF summit participants as contributing to the increasing violent crime trend included a decrease in police department staffing levels; decreased federal involvement in crime prevention and community policing; a strained social service community, educational system, and criminal justice system, particularly courts and corrections; the glamorization of violence and the "thug" pop culture; and the phenomenon of crime becoming "a sport" (Rosen, 2006, 9).

In discussing ways to stem the potential tide of increasing violent crime, participants in the summit were reminded of the crime wave that gripped the country during the late 1980s and early 1990s and how that situation was turned around. Los Angeles Police Chief William Bratton recalled the Omnibus Crime Bill of 1994, with its emphasis on community policing and problem solving, and how efforts then were focused on the holistic treatment of a community, an approach that, by all accounts, significantly helped reduce crime in the late 1990s (Rosen, 2006).

Then in 2007 violent crime rates once again began to trend downward across the country, with the biggest declines observed in the largest cities, suggesting that the rising rates of 2005 and 2006 were merely an anomaly. And while it may be hypothesized that big cities are doing better because they have more resources and more advanced policing methods, criminologists do not know for sure what factors have accounted for the differing rates.

In all, violent crime rates in 2007 fell 1.4 percent and property crime rates fell 2.1 percent. Declining crime rates have been reported each year since, and preliminary data for 2011 indicate a decrease from 2010 figures of 4.0 percent in violent crimes and 0.8 percent in property crimes (*Preliminary Annual Uniform Crime Report, January–December, 2011*).

In 2008 the United States entered a recession and a time when most experts expected crime to rise. However, for reasons that have yet to be identified or explained, crime has continued to fall at an even faster rate, with America's crime rate currently at its lowest level in nearly four decades. Once again, there are spikes in violent crime in certain cites. For example, in the first half of 2012, Chicago experienced a dramatic increase in gang-related homicides.

Whatever the reasons for the falling crime rate over the past two decades, the importance of getting the community involved in staving off local crime and disorder is clear. The broad nature of policing in the 1990s highlighted the critical contributions that citizens and community agencies and organizations can make to combat crime. For communities to thrive, citizens need to have a sense of neighborhood and work together as a team. The resulting synergism can accomplish much more than isolated individual efforts. **Synergism** occurs when

synergism
Occurs when individuals channel their energies toward a common purpose and accomplish what they could not accomplish alone.

individuals channel their energies toward a common purpose and accomplish together what they could not accomplish alone.

The technical definition of synergism is "the simultaneous actions of separate entities which together have greater total effect than the sum of their individual efforts." A precision marching band and a national basketball championship team are examples of synergism. Although there may be some outstanding solos and a few spectacular individual "dunks," it is the total team effort that produces the results.

The police and the citizens they serve must realize that their combined efforts are greater than the sum of their individual efforts on behalf of the community. When police take a problem-solving approach to community concerns and include the community, what they are doing often falls under "crime prevention."

 Crime prevention is a large part, in fact a cornerstone, of community policing.

Community policing and crime prevention are, however, distinct entities. Further, crime is usually not the greatest concern of a neighborhood—traffic-related problems are of greater concern because they affect all citizens daily.

This chapter begins with a discussion of the traffic concerns of neighborhoods and how community policing partnerships have addressed these concerns. This is followed by a look at how community policing addresses disorder concerns and citizen fear of crime. Next is a discussion of how advances in technology are used to fight crime, and a brief return to the topic of CPTED (crime prevention through environmental design), introduced in Chapter 9. The discussion then turns to the national focus on community policing and crime prevention and the assistance offered by Community Oriented Policing Services (COPS), the Community Policing Consortium, and the Weed and Seed program. This is followed by descriptions of partnerships and strategies to prevent or reduce crime and disorder in general and a look at specific strategies to prevent burglaries in public housing, burglaries at single-family construction sites, thefts of and from vehicles, robberies at automated teller machines (ATMs), witness intimidation, domestic violence, acquaintance rape, identity theft, street prostitution, human trafficking, assaults in and around bars, robbery of taxi drivers, violent confrontations with people with mental illness, and crimes against businesses. The chapter concludes with examples of partnerships to prevent crime.

A note: The discussion of domestic violence in this chapter is relatively brief. Domestic violence is most certainly a crime, but the discussion of community policing and domestic violence is placed later in the text (Chapter 14), where violence is discussed in depth.

TRAFFIC ENFORCEMENT AND SAFETY

The United States is a highly mobile nation, with motor vehicle travel being the primary means of transportation. Citizens consider it a *right* to drive their vehicles, although it really is a privilege, and they resent any limitations imposed on this "right." At the same time, however, they expect local and state governments to keep the roadways in good condition and the police to keep traffic moving: "Addressing traffic-related concerns is increasingly challenging because of dwindling municipal budgets, competing resources, and rising crime rates. [Yet t]he ease with which motorists can move about in a safe manner is an important attribute of a prosperous and livable community" (Maggard and Jung, 2009, 46). Mark Marshall, past president of the International Association of Chiefs of Police (IACP), put the importance of traffic enforcement and safety into perspective when he stated: "I believe that it is no exaggeration to say that few duties of the law enforcement community affect the quality of life of our citizens as significantly as the rendering of quality police traffic services" (Marshall, 2011, 6).

> Traffic problems top the list of concerns of most neighborhoods and communities. Concerns include speeding in residential areas, street racing, red-light running, impaired drivers, and nonuse of seat belts.

Speeding in Residential Areas

Studies have shown that traffic-related issues continue to top the list of citizens' complaints to police (Casstevens, 2008). Data from the National Highway Traffic Safety Administration (NHTSA) consistently shows that speeding is one of the most prevalent factors contributing to traffic crashes. In 2010 speeding was identified as a contributing factor in nearly one-third (32%) of all fatal crashes, and 86 percent of speeding-related fatalities in 2010 occurred on roads that were not Interstate highways (*Overview*, 2012).

Speeding in residential areas raises concern over the safety of children, pedestrians, and bicyclists and increases the risk of vehicle crashes as well as the seriousness of injuries to other drivers, passengers, pedestrians, and bicyclists struck by a vehicle.

> *Engineering responses* to speeding include using traffic calming, posting warning signs and signals, conducting anti-speeding public awareness campaigns, informing complainants about actual speeds, and providing realistic driver training.

In many cities, "traffic calming" has been the response. **Traffic calming** devices, such as speed bumps and traffic circles (roundabouts), are intended to slow traffic in residential areas and are popular in communities where residents believe the measures make children safer and neighborhoods quieter.

traffic calming
Describes a wide range of road and environmental design changes that either make it more difficult for a vehicle to speed or make drivers believe they should slow down for safety.

> *Enforcement responses* to reduce speeding include (1) enforcing speeding laws, (2) enforcing speeding laws with speed cameras or photo radar, (3) using speed display boards, (4) arresting the worst offenders, and (5) having citizen volunteers monitor speeding (Scott, 2001b).

Aggressive enforcement of speed limits may seem to run counter to community policing efforts to establish rapport with citizens. Nonetheless, NHTSA data indicate that of the 10,591 speeding-related traffic fatalities that occurred across the United States in 2009, 12 percent happened at speeds of less than 35 miles per hour (mph) and another 19 percent resulted from crashes occurring at speeds of 35–40 mph (*Speeding*, 2012). Such figures underscore the reality that speeds which are common in residential areas may still produce fatalities should a vehicle strike a pedestrian, bicyclist, or even another motorist.

Most speed-reduction enforcement efforts focus on highway or main thoroughfare speeding and aggressive driving, although broad public education campaigns can also have a positive effect on reducing speeding through residential areas. The Governors Highway Safety Association (GHSA) report *Speeding and Aggressive Driving* (2012, 4) highlights the continued role that speeding plays in traffic fatalities and makes several recommendations to the states and the NHTSA to address the problem:

» States should explore addressing speed concerns through aggressive driving enforcement since the driving public believes that aggressive driving is a serious threat to their safety.

» Speed concerns can also be addressed through targeted enforcement in school and work zones, which are additional enforcement strategies supported by the public.

» The National Highway Traffic Safety Administration (NHTSA) should sponsor a national high visibility enforcement campaign and support public awareness efforts to address the issues of speed and aggressive driving.

» NHTSA should promote best practices in automated enforcement strategies.

» NHTSA should sponsor a *National Forum on Speeding and Aggressive Driving*, similar to efforts undertaken in 2005, to bring together experts to review and update effective tools and strategies states can employ to reduce speed and aggressive driving.

Closely related to the challenge of preventing speeding is the challenge of preventing street racing.

Street Racing

Street racing of automobiles has been an American tradition since the early 1950s, and probably many years before. Although no national database currently tracks the number of lives lost every year to illegal street racing, an Internet search of "street racing crashes" provides ample evidence, stories, and images of the deadly results of these activities. Too often those injured or killed are innocent bystanders and other motorists who are at the wrong place at the wrong time. According to Domash (2006, 31): "Cops nationwide are working to deter drivers and spectators, while providing safer alternatives to illegal racing." In 2003 the Boise (Idaho) Police Athletic League started its own racing program with two donated cars, a Chevelle painted like a police car that reaches speeds of 138 mph and a Corvette that reaches approximately 100 mph in a quarter-mile run. The cars are fixtures at the local high school drag races put on at Firebird Raceway. The races are backed by donations that enable the officers to give out T-shirts and encourage youngsters to come to the track to race. Most of the street racing interdiction programs are affiliated with "Beat the Heat," an organization that began in 1984 in Jacksonville, Florida (Domash, 2006).

Red-Light Running

The Insurance Institute for Highway Safety (IIHS) reports that in 2009, red-light running killed 676 people and injured an estimated 113,000, and that approximately two-thirds of those killed were people other than the red-light-running drivers ("Red Light Running Kills," 2011).

In Phoenix, Arizona, a group of parents formed the Red Means Stop Coalition after their sons and daughters were hit by red-light runners. The group works alongside local police departments, the governor's highway safety office, and local corporations to elevate the issue of red-light running prevention in the press and among elected and public officials. Similar traffic safety groups across the United States complement the efforts of law enforcement officials by informing the public of the red-light running problem and focusing on driver behavior changes.

Civil liberties groups have expressed concern that the cameras could be used to spy on people and that privacy issues must be addressed (Samuels, 2006).

Use (or Nonuse) of Seat Belts

Recent data from the National Occupant Protection Use Survey (NOPUS), conducted annually by the National Center for Statistics and Analysis of the National Highway Traffic Safety Administration, indicates that an estimated 84 percent of Americans wear their seat belts while riding in or driving a vehicle, a number statistically unchanged from 85 percent in 2010 (*Seat Belt Use in 2011*, 2011). Seat belt use has increased steadily since 1994, when 58 percent of passenger

---

TECHNOLOGY IN COMMUNITY POLICING: RED-LIGHT CAMERAS

Automated red-light cameras are being used in many jurisdictions to address the problem of red-light running. Since the 1990s, when the technology was first introduced as a low-cost way to police intersections, red-light cameras have become increasingly popular and, as of July 2012, approximately 555 communities throughout the United States were using them ("Red Light Running Kills," 2011).

In June 2007, Springfield, Missouri, installed red-light cameras at selected intersections as part of their "respect red" drivers' education campaign. A vocal minority of residents were highly critical that such "Big Brother" technology was being used simply as a way to generate revenue from unsuspecting drivers—a complaint commonly heard among red-light camera opponents in other cities. However, nearly 3 years after the cameras were activated, the program was $33,000 in the red:

> Fortunately for the city, making money was never the goal. Improving safety was, and by that measure, the cameras were a success. City officials say their data show red-light running crashes decreased both at camera-equipped intersections and city-wide. Citations fell 36 percent to an average of 1.05 a day per camera.

> Springfield traffic engineer Jason Haynes says the fact that the program didn't make money helped to maintain community support.

Source: "City Uses Cameras as Safety Tool, not Moneymaker," *Red Light Running Kills, Status Report* (Publication by the Insurance Institute for Highway Safety), Vol.46, No.1, February 1, 2011, pp.1-2, 6-7.

vehicle occupants reportedly wore seat belts, and has been accompanied by a steady decline in the percentage of unrestrained passenger vehicle (PV) occupant fatalities during daytime. The 2011 NOPUS also found the following:

» Seat belt use for occupants in the West decreased significantly from 95 percent in 2010 to 93 percent in 2011.

» Seat belt use continued to be higher in the states in which vehicle occupants can be pulled over solely for not using seat belts ("primary law states") as compared with the states with weaker enforcement laws ("secondary law states") or without seat belt laws.

» Seat belt use for occupants traveling during weekday rush hours dropped to 83 percent in 2011 from 86 percent in 2010.

The NHTSA estimates that safety belt use at rates higher than the 90 percent level prevents 15,700 fatalities and 350,000 serious injuries each year. The country also saves about $67 billion in economic costs of fatalities and injuries from motor vehicle crashes.

Strategies used to encourage seat belt use vary from incentives for safe driving to mandatory use policies and fines for failure to buckle up. "Click It or Ticket," an annual nationwide, short-duration, high-visibility seat belt enforcement program, is an example of the latter. Officers in participating agencies are asked to focus on seat belt compliance and ticketing of violators. At the same time, federal funding pays for advertising that highlights the program and seat belt safety. The enforcement includes surveys that measure "before and after" seat belt use, seat belt checkpoints, saturation patrols, fixed patrols, and extensive media coverage. Agencies are encouraged to create partnerships with the media and other community organizations. These partners have conducted child/family vehicle check-up clinics, assisted at child seat checkpoints, attended the department's Click It or Ticket news conference, and assisted with public education. NHTSA points out that since the campaign began, seat belt use has climbed to its highest level ever, support for seat belt use laws and enforcement has improved, and child fatalities from traffic crashes have dropped substantially (Solomon et al., 2009).

Impaired Drivers

Decades ago, drunk driving was not considered the crime that it is today. Now, crashes caused by alcohol-impaired driving are treated as violent crimes. NHTSA data show that there were 10,228 alcohol-impaired-driving fatalities in 2010, which equates to 31 percent of all traffic fatalities that year (*Overview*, 2012). It is also recognized that driving under the influence of drugs, whether illegal or prescription, is also a form of impaired driving. In 2010 more than 1.4 million drivers were arrested for driving under the influence of alcohol or narcotics, an arrest rate of 1 out of every 149 licensed drivers in the United States (*Overview*, 2012).

Responses to address the drunk driving problem include legislation (lowering the legal limit for per se violations), strict enforcement by police, curtailing driving privileges, sanctioning convicted drunk drivers by requiring installation of electronic ignition locks that prevent intoxicated drivers from operating their vehicles, monitoring drunk drivers, providing public education, providing alternative transportation and environmental design, and locating licensed establishments in areas that reduce the need for patrons to drive. As of August 2005, laws setting a legal blood alcohol content (BAC) of .08 have taken effect in all 50 states, the District of Columbia, and Puerto Rico, an effort that took nearly 20 years of work by proponents.

Some of the most promising and potentially effective approaches to eliminating drunk driving have come through improvements in technology for monitoring a driver's BAC, such as ignition interlocks, passive alcohol sensors, and Secure Continuous Remote Alcohol Monitor (SCRAM) devices. Passive alcohol sensors (PASs) help agencies to work more effectively in enforcing driving while intoxicated (DWI) restrictions: "Research shows the use of passive alcohol sensors can increase detection of DWI by about 50 percent at checkpoints and about 10 percent on routine patrols" (Dewey-Kollen, 2006, 10–11). If all police officers used PAS technology, DWI arrests in the United States could increase by an estimated 140,000 to 700,000 (Dewey-Kollen, 2006).

Emerging technologies include infrared sensing that enforcement officers can use to help determine an offender's alcohol content level, devices that can detect subdural blood alcohol concentrations through a driver's hand placed on the steering wheel, and algorithms to detect a vehicle's weaving so an officer can determine if the driver is impaired. Another device still in the research phase is the Driver Alcohol Detection Systems for Safety (DADSS), which would prevent drunk drivers from starting their vehicles. "If the driver has a BAC of .08 or higher, the illegal level in all 50 states, the vehicle would not be operable by the driver. In fact, unless a driver is drunk, he or she won't know that the technology is even in the car," said Mothers against Drunk Driving (MADD) National President Jan Withers ("MADD President Calls for Summit," 2012). Withers added that the progress to date on the DADSS technology "is remarkable, yet more research and testing need to be done. This is truly game-changing technology."

Safe Communities

Nine agencies within the U.S. Department of Transportation (DOT) are working together to promote and implement a safer national transportation system by combining the best injury prevention practices into the Safe Communities approach to serve as a national model. The NHTSA defines a *safe community* as "a community that promotes injury prevention activities at the local level to solve local highway and traffic safety and other injury problems. It uses a 'bottom up' approach involving its citizens in addressing key injury problems" ("Best Practices for a Safe Community," n.d.). According to the Safe Communities Web site, safe communities have six elements. A safe community:

» Uses an integrated and comprehensive injury control system with prevention, acute care, and rehabilitation partners as active and essential participants in addressing community injury problems.

» Has a comprehensive, community-based coalition/task force with representation from citizens; law enforcement; public health, medical, injury prevention, education, business, civic, and service groups; public works offices; and traffic safety advocates that provides program input, direction, and involvement in the Safe Community program.

A patrol officer helps a girl through a bike safety course designed to teach children how to control their bikes, avoid obstacles, and properly use their brakes. Bicycle safety classes can significantly reduce incidents of child injury.

© AP Images/John Lovretta

» Conducts comprehensive problem identification and uses estimating techniques that determine the economic costs associated with traffic-related fatalities and injuries within the context of the total injury problem.

» Conducts program assessments from a "best practices" and a prevention perspective to determine gaps in highway and traffic safety and other injury activity.

» Implements a plan with specific strategies that addresses the problems and program deficiencies through prevention countermeasures and activities.

» Evaluates the program to determine the impact and cost benefit where possible.

In addition to traffic concerns, citizens are often more concerned about minor offenses (disorders) than they are about crime and violence in their communities.

ADDRESSING DISORDER CONCERNS

Neighborhood and business district improvements such as cleaning up trash, landscaping, and planting flowers can serve as a focus for community organizing and help residents take pride in their neighborhoods. Key partnerships in beautification projects include police departments, the public works staff, the business community, and residents. These partnerships can also be expanded to help fight crime and to reduce the fear of crime.

Addressing disorder goes far beyond beautification. Allowing neighborhood disorder to go unchecked creates "broken windows," an advertisement that no one in the area cares what happens. This condition attracts more disorder, crime, criminals, and other destructive elements. When communities begin to clean up the neighborhood, report crime, improve security, look out for each other, and work cooperatively, crime and disorder problems begin to disappear. Many of the topics in this chapter describe how *broken windows* get fixed and, as a result, how neighborhoods improve.

REDUCING THE FEAR OF CRIME

A major goal of community policing is to reduce the fear of crime in communities so that citizens will be willing to join together to prevent crime.

> Various community policing efforts to reduce citizens' fear of crime have included enhanced foot and vehicle patrol in high-crime neighborhoods, citizen patrols, neighborhood cleanup campaigns, community education and awareness programs, the placement of police substations in troubled neighborhoods, and the installation of closed-circuit video surveillance cameras.

An increasingly popular approach to reduce the fear of crime is video surveillance of public places.

Video Surveillance of Public Places

Video cameras connected to closed-circuit television (CCTV) can be used as a tool for "place management," for providing medical assistance, or for gathering information. Strategically placed cameras can be used to monitor traffic flow, public meetings, or demonstrations that may require additional police resources. The devices can also be a community safety feature, allowing camera operators to contact medical services if they see someone suffering from illness or injury as a result of criminal activity or noncrime medical emergencies. In addition, cameras can be used to gather intelligence and monitor known offenders' behavior in public places—for example, shoplifters in public retail areas (Ratcliffe, 2011).

According to the Center for Problem-Oriented Policing, use of CCTV can prevent crime by creating a deterrent to potential offenders who are aware of the cameras' presence (Ratcliffe, 2011). A key element in such prevention through deterrence, however, rests on adequate signage and recognition by the public that they are under surveillance. If offenders are unaware they are being watched, or if they are under the influence of drugs or alcohol and, thus, "altered" to the point where they do not care that they are being monitored, the deterrent value of CCTV is significantly diminished (Ratcliffe, 2011).

CCTV can also impact crime by helping police detect crimes in progress and provide visual identification of offenders for later arrest and prosecution. The value of this tool in this capacity is dependent, however, on how rapidly police can respond to incidents identified by camera operators: "Although there may be some initial crime reduction due to the installation and publicity of a new system, offenders may soon learn what types of incidents elicit a police response and the speed of that response. The availability of local resources is therefore a factor in the success of this mechanism" (Ratcliffe, 2011, 14).

Fake, or decoy, cameras are also used to create the illusion that people are being monitored. For example, the public transportation systems in some communities have installed both active and dummy cameras on board their bus fleet to enhance the public's perception of widespread surveillance capabilities. Augmenting the deterrent impact and crime prevention value through the use of such tactics is a concept referred to as a diffusion of benefits (Ratcliffe, 2011). Despite these numerous benefits, video surveillance can have unintended consequences.

Unintended Consequences of Video Surveillance

Among the unintended consequences of video surveillance are displacement, increased suspicion or fear of crime, and increased reported crime.

Displacement occurs when offenders, aware of the surveillance cameras, simply move their activity to another area out of camera sight. However, general crime prevention literature suggests that the amount of crime displaced rarely matches the amount of crime reduced. Video surveillance may also force offenders to be more imaginative and diversify operations.

Another concern is that the public may respond negatively to the cameras. Results of one survey showed that one-third of respondents felt one purpose of the cameras was to spy on people. Other surveys showed some city managers were reluctant to advertise the cameras or have the cameras very visible for fear they would make shoppers and consumers more fearful (Ratcliffe, 2011). Ironically, although it is hoped that most citizens would feel safer under the watchful eye of the cameras, the surveillance may have the reverse effect on some people.

A third concern is that reported crime rates will increase for some offenses with low reporting rates such as minor acts of violence, graffiti tagging, and drug offenses. The public needs to be prepared for the fact that the increase in recorded crime does not reflect an increase in actual crime. In addition to concerns about these potential unintended consequences, the public may be concerned about privacy issues.

Public Concerns Regarding Video Surveillance

As noted in the discussion of using cameras to detect red light runners, civil liberties unions often object to video surveillance, claiming it is an invasion of privacy and citing the Fourth Amendment's prohibition against unreasonable search and seizure. However, the Fourth Amendment protects *people*, **not** *places*. The Fourth Amendment does not protect people in clearly public places where there is no expectation of privacy. However, as Ratcliffe (2011, 34), points out: "The public is unlikely to support CCTV if there is a risk that video of them shopping on a public street when they should be at work will appear on the nightly news." He suggests that a policy be established covering when recorded images are to be released to the police, media, or other agencies in the criminal justice system. He further recommends that video footage not be released for any reason other than to enhance the criminal justice system.

Evaluation of Video Surveillance

Establishing whether video surveillance reduces crime is difficult because this problem-oriented solution is seldom implemented without incident or without other crime prevention measures being initiated simultaneously. In addition, as noted, use of video surveillance may inadvertently increase the crime rate, especially for offenses with low reporting rates.

Research results are mixed, with some studies finding video surveillance to be effective against property crime and less effective against personal crime and public order offenses. Other studies report mixed results regarding reducing fear of crime. Several studies produced inconclusive results. Ratcliffe (2011, 22–23) reports the following general findings:

» CCTV is more effective at combating property offenses than violent or public order crime (though there have been successes in this area).

» CCTV appears to work best in small, well-defined areas (such as public car parks).

» The individual context of each area and the way the system is used appear to be important.

» Achieving *statistically significant* reductions in crime can be difficult (i.e., crime reductions that clearly go beyond the level that might occur as a result of the normal fluctuations in the crime rate are difficult to prove).

» A close relationship with the police appears important in determining a successful system.

» There is an investigative benefit to CCTV once an offense has been committed.

» CCTV appears to be somewhat effective in reducing fear of crime but only among a subset of the population.

In addition to using video surveillance in public places, other advances in technology are also being used to fight and, in some instances, prevent crime.

USING ADVANCING TECHNOLOGY TO FIGHT CRIME

Numerous types of technology can be used effectively in crime fighting and prevention efforts. Although it is not new, crime mapping technology is often the first step in proactive policing to identify hot spots As discussed in Chapter 4, hot spots are areas where incidents of crime and disorder tend to cluster in close proximity to one another. Most veteran police officers are keenly aware of those areas in their beats that tend to be troublesome. However, in an effort to help the community formulate responses, law enforcement executives and crime analysts who are not on the streets patrolling beats can also identify hot spots by using maps and geographic information systems, and statistical tests ("How to Identify Hot Spots," 2010):

Maps and Geographic Information Systems

Analysts can create a variety of maps that visualize different aspects of a particular location. Density maps, for example, show where crimes occur without dividing a map into regions or blocks; areas with high concentrations of crime stand out.

Analysts use geographic information systems (GIS) to combine street maps, data about crime and public disorder, and data about other features such as schools, liquor stores, warehouses, and bus stops. The resulting multidimensional maps produce a visual display of the hot spots. The GIS places each crime within a grid system on a map and colors each cell based on how many incidents occurred in that area.

Although high-crime areas may often be defined as hot spots based on past experiences of officers or the characteristics of those areas, GIS allows law enforcement agencies to more accurately pinpoint hot spots to confirm trouble areas, identify the specific nature of the activity occurring within the hot spot, and then develop strategies to respond.

Statistical Tests

Analysts can use statistical software to determine whether an area with a high number of crimes is a hot spot or whether the clustering of those crimes is a random occurrence. CrimeStat III and GeoDa are two computer software programs for hot spot analysis.

» **CrimeStat III.** CrimeStat is a spatial statistical program used to analyze the locations of crime incidents and identify hot spots.

» **GeoDa.** The GeoDa Center for Geospatial Analysis and Computation at Arizona State University develops state-of-the-art methods for geospatial analysis, geovisualization, geosimulation, and spatial process modeling and implements them through software tools.

Biometric identification systems are also becoming more sophisticated, widely available, affordable, and useable. Biometrics can use one or more of several different physical and/or behavioral characteristics such as fingerprints and palmprints; hand and finger geometry; facial recognition; iris and

TECHNOLOGY IN COMMUNITY POLICING: MOBILE MULTIMODAL BIOMETRICS

In the decade since the 9/11 terrorist attacks, new emphasis has been placed on biometrics and priority given to making that technology more accessible to those on the front lines of national security efforts:

Very small, smartphone-based mobile devices with biometric capabilities are also in early development at this point. The familiar form factor of a handheld device is leading to increased acceptance by law enforcement for suspect identification in the field (early adoption at this point)…. The new mobile biometric devices allow first responders, police, military,

and criminal justice organizations to collect biometric data with a handheld device on a street corner or in a remote area and then wirelessly send it for comparison to other samples on watch lists and databases in near real-time. Identities can be determined quickly without having to take a subject to a central facility to collect his or her biometrics, which is not always practical.

Source: *The National Biometrics Challenge.* Washington, DC: National Science and Technology Council, Subcommittee on Biometrics and Identity Management, September 2011. Retrieved July 30, 2012 from http://www.biometrics.gov/Documents/BiometricsChallenge2011_protected.pdf

retinal scans; voice identification; and DNA analysis (*The National Biometrics Challenge*, 2011).

Following are examples of other technologies being used by police departments across the country (*How Are Innovations in Technology Transforming Policing?*, 2012):

» In Camden, New Jersey, gunshot detection technology is being used to immediately alert police to the exact location of shots being fired. Since installing the system in a location with the highest number of calls for service and crimes involving firearms, the department has learned that roughly one-third of the shootings in that area went unreported.

» In Minneapolis, Minnesota, police are testing video analytics, the automated analysis of video feeds that can trigger alerts based on criteria specified by the police. For example, the system can be programmed to monitor the feed from a camera at a train station and send an alert if an object resembling a backpack is abandoned on a platform.

A March 2011 survey of law enforcement agencies revealed (*How Are Innovations in Technology Transforming Policing?*, 2012):

» 71 percent of responding agencies reported having in-car video recording capability, and 25 percent of all the responding agencies have video cameras in *all* of their police cars.

» 23 percent of the responding agencies reported that they are able to stream video feeds from fixed surveillance cameras into police vehicles.

» 71 percent of the responding agencies said they use license plate readers (LPRs) that can automatically scan hundreds of vehicle tags per hour and trigger alerts—for example, when the device spots a stolen vehicle or a vehicle registered to a person who is the subject of an arrest warrant.

» 83 percent of responding agencies reported using global positioning system (GPS) devices to track the movements of criminal suspects, and 69 percent reported using GPS to determine the location of police vehicles. Tracking police vehicles can be useful for quickly dispatching officers who are closest to a crime scene, identifying the location of an officer who is injured and needs assistance, and managing officer deployments.

The survey also revealed that social media and Web sites are transforming the way law enforcement agencies communicate with the community, with 74 percent of surveyed agencies reporting they use Facebook, 57 percent use Twitter, 34 percent use YouTube, and 34 percent use Nixle (*How Are Innovations in Technology Transforming Policing?*, 2012). Social media not only helps police receive tips and other information from the public but can also help in criminal investigations; 89 percent of agencies reported monitoring social media to identify investigative leads, such as reviewing the Facebook or Twitter pages of known or suspected gang members for current photos and other incriminating information posted about illegal activity. Despite these notable benefits of social media to law enforcement, such technology has also presented challenges. For example, 57 percent of the responding agencies said they already have experienced disputes or controversies regarding officers' personal postings on social media sites (*How Are Innovations in Technology Transforming Policing?*, 2012).

ON THE BEAT

A big piece in the crime prevention puzzle centers around systems used by the police department for tracking crimes and neighborhood concerns. Geographic information system (GIS) crime mapping is a tool many departments use to map patterns of crime incidents; our department uses a mapping system to help determine where our greatest needs exist. Neighborhood concerns are entered into a system designed to track these issues and document officers' efforts.

Consider this example: John Doe, a local resident, calls the police department to report that people are constantly running a stop sign in the neighborhood. This stop sign is next to a city park frequently used by children and adults. Several other residents are reporting similar concerns. An officer takes the complaint and enters the information into the tracking system. From that point on, the information is passed along to a district officer to follow up on and track any police efforts at that location. The officer logs the date, time, and any action that was taken. The next time John Doe calls the police department and asks what is being done about the stop sign, the person taking the phone call can pull up the information on the computer and explain in detail what has been done. This system is great for tracking complaints and also police actions made in each particular case. It can be used for everything from traffic complaints to reports of suspicious drug activity. This is one example of a community policing strategy that seems to really work for both the police department and the community.

—Kim Czapar

Although new technologies continue to be developed and applied to policing, other crime prevention methods rely on more conventional, low-tech measures such as locks, lights, and community links—all common elements in CPTED.

CRIME PREVENTION THROUGH ENVIRONMENTAL DESIGN

CPTED has been a strategy for dealing with crime for decades and has had some proven successes.

 CPTED has three major components: target hardening, changes to the physical environment, and community building.

target hardening
Refers to making potential objectives of criminals more difficult to obtain through the use of improved locks, alarm systems, and security cameras.

Target hardening refers to making potential objectives of criminals more difficult to obtain. The three main devices used for target hardening are improved locks, alarm systems, and security cameras. Most people do not object to locks and alarm systems properly used, but some have "Big Brother" concerns about surveillance cameras.

Changes to the physical environment often include increased lighting, which has been a means of increasing security for centuries. Other changes usually involve removing items that give potential offenders the ability to hide—for example, dense vegetation, high shrubs, walls, and fences.

Community building, the third element of CPTED, can have the greatest impact on how individuals perceive the livability of their neighborhood. Community building seeks to increase residents' sense of ownership of the neighborhood and of who does and does not belong there. Community building techniques can include social events such as fairs or neighborhood beautification projects.

In addition to the trio of major components, CPTED is defined by five underlying principles: territoriality, natural surveillance, access management, physical maintenance, and order maintenance ("Using Environmental Design to Prevent School Violence," 2008). *Territoriality* establishes ownership and sends a clear message of who does and does not belong in a neighborhood. *Natural surveillance* allows potential victims a clear view of surroundings and inhibits crime. *Access control* delineates boundaries and areas where people do and do not belong (e.g., signs, clearly marked entrances and exits, limited access to certain areas). *Physical maintenance* includes timely repairs and upkeep of the physical space and removal of trash and graffiti. *Order maintenance* includes paying attention to unacceptable behavior and encouraging activities that are clearly acceptable. It may also include the presence of uniformed authority figures.

By emphasizing the systematic analysis of crime in a particular location, CPTED directly supports community policing by providing crime prevention strategies tailored to solve specific problems.

Glass doors or doors with windows right next to them present an easy access opportunity for burglars.

© Flying Colours Ltd/Getty Images

The Importance of Place

Eck (1997) has studied the importance of place to crime and disorder, noting that most places do not have crime while, conversely, most crime is concentrated in and around a small number of places. Eck's definition of **place** is specific: "A place is a very small area reserved for a narrow range of functions, often controlled by a single owner and separated from the surrounding area." This concept of place is similar to that of a hot spot.

Eck theorizes that preventing crime at these high-crime places can bring about a significant reduction in the total crime throughout the nation and suggests that **opportunity blocking**—changes to make crime more difficult, riskier, less rewarding, or less excusable—may have a greater direct effect on offenders than other crime prevention strategies. Eck notes two side effects from place-focused opportunity blocking efforts.

 Two side effects of place-focused opportunity blocking efforts are displacement of crime and diffusion of prevention benefits.

Displacement, in which offenders simply change the location of their crimes, has been discussed as a potential negative of prevention efforts. However, concern about displacement may cause a benefit of prevention efforts to be overlooked—that is, diffusion. **Diffusion** of prevention benefits occurs when criminals believe that the opportunity blocking of one type of criminal activity is also aimed at other types of criminal activity. For example, when magnetic tags were put in books in a university library, book theft declined, as did the theft of audiotapes and videotapes, which were not tagged. According to Eck (1997): "Diffusion is the flip side of the coin of crime contagion. **Contagion** [emphasis added] suggests that when offenders notice one criminal opportunity they often detect similar opportunities they have previously overlooked. Crime then spreads. The broken window theory is an example of a contagion theory. Thus under some circumstances offenders may be uncertain about the scope of prevention efforts and avoid both the blocked opportunities and similar unblocked opportunities. When this occurs, prevention may spread."

The Risk Factor Prevention Paradigm

Risk factors have been broadly defined as "those characteristics, variables, or hazards that, if present for a given individual, make it more likely that this individual, rather than someone selected from the general population, will develop a disorder" (Mrazek and Haggerty, 1994, 127). As Shader (2002, 1) explains:

> In recent years, the juvenile justice field has adopted an approach from the public health arena in an attempt to understand the causes of delinquency and work toward its prevention (Farrington, 2000). For example, the medical community's efforts to prevent cancer and heart disease have successfully targeted risk factors (Farrington). To evaluate a patient's risk of suffering a heart attack, a doctor commonly asks for the patient's medical history, family history, diet, weight, and exercise level because each of these variables has an effect on the patient's cardiac health. After this risk assessment, the doctor may suggest ways

---

place

A very small area reserved for a narrow range of functions, often controlled by a single owner and separated from the surrounding area.

opportunity blocking

Changes to make crime more difficult, risky, less rewarding, or less excusable; one of the oldest forms of crime prevention.

diffusion

Occurs when criminals believe that the opportunity blocking of one type of criminal activity is also aimed at other types of criminal activity.

contagion

Suggests that when offenders notice one criminal opportunity they often detect similar opportunities they have previously overlooked; crime then spreads; the broken window theory is an example.

for the patient to reduce his or her risk factors. Similarly, if a youth possesses certain risk factors, research indicates that these factors will increase his or her chance of becoming a delinquent. A risk assessment may aid in determining the type of intervention that will best suit the youth's needs and decrease his or her risk of offending. Farrington (2000) calls this recent movement toward the public health model the "risk factor paradigm," the basic idea of which is to "identify the key risk factors for offending and tool prevention methods designed to counteract them."

The **risk factor prevention paradigm** seeks to identify key risk factors for offending and then implement prevention methods designed to counteract them.

risk factor prevention paradigm
Seeks to identify key risk factors for offending and then implement prevention methods designed to counteract them.

Although community policing occurs on the local level, it often takes funding from the federal level to get programs off the ground and flying or to keep them going after they have become established. To encourage jurisdictions across the country to make the paradigm shift to community policing, several national organizations have been created that offer financial support, training opportunities, and other types of resources.

NATIONAL EMPHASIS ON COMMUNITY POLICING AND CRIME PREVENTION

Two federal programs established within the Department of Justice focus on community policing and crime prevention.

Federal initiatives to assist communities in implementing community policing are the COPS Office and the Community Policing Consortium.

The Office of Community Oriented Policing Services

The Violent Crime Control and Law Enforcement Act of 1994 authorized $8.8 billion over 6 years for grants to local police agencies to add 100,000 officers and promote community policing. To implement this law, Attorney General Janet Reno created the Office of Community Oriented Policing Services (or COPS) in the Department of Justice.

Although originally the COPS Office was designed to go out of business after 6 years, its success at increasing the numbers of police officers across the country and in raising awareness of community policing resulted in Congress extending the life of the agency.

COPS provides grants to tribal, state, and local law enforcement agencies to hire and train community policing professionals, acquire and deploy cutting-edge crime-fighting technologies, and develop and test innovative policing strategies. COPS-funded training helps advance community policing at all levels of law enforcement—from line officers to law enforcement executives—as well as others in the criminal justice field. Since 1994 COPS has invested $17.1 billion to add community policing officers to the nation's streets and schools, enhance crime-fighting technology, support crime prevention initiatives, and provide training and technical assistance to advance community policing: "The programs and initiatives developed have provided funding to more than 13,000 law enforcement agencies. By funding over 13,000 of the nation's 18,000 law enforcement agencies, the COPS Office has helped create a community policing infrastructure across the nation. Approximately 81 percent of the nation's population is served by law enforcement agencies practicing community policing" (*FY 2013 Performance Budget: Office of Community Oriented Policing Services*, 2012, 4). Because community policing is by definition inclusive, COPS training also reaches state and local government leaders and the citizens they serve. This broad range of programs helps COPS offer agencies support in virtually every aspect of law enforcement.

The Community Policing Consortium

Another organization that provides assistance is the Community Policing Consortium, a partnership of five police organizations: the International Association of Chiefs of Police (IACP), the National Organization of Black Law Enforcement Executives (NOBLE), the National Sheriffs' Association (NSA), the Police Executive Research Forum (PERF), and the Police Foundation (PF). The consortium, funded and administered by COPS within the Department of Justice, provides training throughout the United States, particularly to agencies that receive COPS grants. The training materials emphasize community policing from a local perspective, community partnerships, problem solving, strategic planning, and assessment. Their quick-read periodicals, *The Community Policing Exchange, Sheriff Times*, and the *Information Access Guide,* relate real-life experiences of community policing practitioners across the country.

THE WEED AND SEED PROGRAM

Until recently, a third federal initiative was the Weed and Seed program, launched in 1991 with three sites. Over its 20-year life span, the program grew to include 300 sites nationwide, ranging in size from several neighborhood blocks to several square miles, with populations ranging from 3,000 to 50,000. The program, which was not funded in 2012, strategically linked concentrated, enhanced law enforcement efforts to identify, arrest, and prosecute violent offenders, drug traffickers, and other criminals operating in the target areas and community policing (weeding) with human services—including after-school, weekend, and summer youth activities; adult literacy classes; and parental counseling—and neighborhood revitalization efforts to prevent and deter further crime (seeding).

The Weed and Seed program sought to identify, arrest, and prosecute offenders (weed) while simultaneously working with citizens to improve quality of life (seed).

The Weed and Seed Data Center noted that four fundamental principles underlie the Weed and Seed strategy: collaboration, coordination, community participation, and leveraging of resources. And although funding for the national program has been discontinued, countless Weed and Seed initiatives have taken hold in local jurisdictions across the country, many of which continue to be funded year after year as municipalities realize the benefit of such programming to the quality of life in their communities.

PARTNERSHIPS TO PREVENT OR REDUCE CRIME AND DISORDER

The specific needs of communities across the country, and the crime and disorder problems that plague them, are as diverse as the communities themselves. One strength of community policing is being able to adapt to these specific community needs and find creative solutions to each area's unique problems. The discussion now turns to examine various partnerships that have been formed to address specific crime and disorder problems experienced by jurisdictions throughout the United States.

> Partnerships to prevent or reduce crime and disorder include business anticrime groups, local government–community crime prevention coalitions, community coalitions, grassroots organizations, and landlords and residents in public housing using advances in technology and celebrating community successes.

ADDRESSING SPECIFIC PROBLEMS

As has been stressed throughout this text, problem solving is a key component of community policing. An invaluable resource for communities engaged in problem solving is the Center for Problem-Oriented Policing, a nonprofit organization comprising affiliated police practitioners, researchers, and universities dedicated to the advancement of problem-oriented policing. Its mission is to advance the concept and practice of problem-oriented policing in open and democratic societies. It does so by making readily accessible information about ways in which police can more effectively address specific crime and disorder problems.

Another invaluable resource is the COPS Office, introduced earlier. This office has published a series of problem-oriented guides, which focus on understanding and preventing specific community problems. Several of the most recent guides are cited in the following discussion. The COPS Office also provides funding for community policing initiatives and hiring and provides training through its regional community policing institutes.

Preventing Burglary in Public Housing

Eck (1997) notes: "Public housing complexes have become notorious for high crime rates in the United States." He suggests that restricting pedestrian access and movement is key to reducing burglary in such places. A second strategy is target hardening by providing locks and improved security to access points. A third approach is to make burglary targets unattractive to offenders. Eck suggests that focusing on residences with previous burglaries is effective, as is focusing on residences surrounding burgled dwellings. Focusing only on those living around at-risk places rather than an entire neighborhood is called **cocoon neighborhood watch**.

cocoon neighborhood watch

Focusing on only those living around at-risk places rather than an entire neighborhood.

Preventing Burglary at Single-Family House Construction Sites

Construction site burglary has been recognized as a significant problem in the United States and elsewhere in the world, with an estimated $1 billion to $4 billion worth of materials, tools, and construction equipment stolen every year in the United States alone (Boba and Santos, 2006). It is recommended that police establish cooperative working relationships with builders and that builders, in turn, share information about burglary problems and patterns, local building practices, and loss prevention efforts (Boba and Santos, 2006). If it can be established that certain houses are at high risk for victimization, response measures can be concentrated at those locations.

Specific responses to reduce construction site burglary include improving builder practices: limiting the number of construction sites supervised, coordinating delivery and installation, screening and training workers and subcontractors, limiting the hiring of subcontractors, having a tracking system for tools, encouraging hiring loss prevention personnel, hiring on-site private security patrols, and establishing an employee hotline to report crime.

Target hardening measures are also recommended, including improving lighting, installing and monitoring closed-circuit television, installing alarm systems, using portable storage units, installing fencing, marking property, installing global positioning satellite locater chips, and displaying crime prevention signage.

Preventing Theft of and from Vehicles

Thefts of and from vehicles might be prevented by hiring parking attendants, improving surveillance at deck and lot entrances and exits, hiring dedicated security patrols, installing and monitoring CCTV systems, improving the lighting, securing the perimeter, installing entrance barriers and electronic access, and arresting and prosecuting persistent offenders.

Many police departments furnish citizens with information on how to prevent auto theft. Information may be provided in the form of pamphlets, newspaper stories, public service announcements on television, or speeches to civic organizations. The two main messages of anti–car theft programs are to not leave the keys in the car ignition and to lock the car.

These messages are conveyed in a variety of ways, from stickers on dashboards to posters warning that leaving keys in the ignition is a violation of the law if the car is parked on public property. In addition, leaving one's keys in the ignition is an invitation to theft, could become a contributing cause of some innocent person's injury or death, and could raise the owner's insurance rates.

New York City has developed a voluntary anti–auto theft program that enlists the aid of motorists. The Combat Auto Theft (CAT) program allows the police to stop any car marked with a special decal between 1 A.M. and 5 A.M. Car owners sign a consent form affirming that they do not normally drive between 1 A.M. and 5 A.M., the peak auto theft hours. Those who participate in the program waive their rights to search and seizure protection.

Preventing Robberies at Automated Teller Machines

Automated teller machines, or ATMs, were first introduced in the late 1960s in the United States and now can be found almost everywhere. However, bank customers sometimes trade safety for convenience because the most recently available data show the overall rate of ATM-related crime is between one per 1 million and one per 3.5 million transactions (Scott, 2001a). Scott (2001a) presents the following general conclusions about ATM robbery:

» Most are committed by a lone offender, using some type of weapon, against a lone victim.

» Most occur at night, with the highest risk between midnight and 4 A.M.

» Most involve robbing people of cash after they have made a withdrawal.

» Robberies are somewhat more likely to occur at walk-up ATMs than at drive-through ATMs.

» About 15 percent of victims are injured. The average loss is between $100 and $200.

Specific responses to reduce ATM robberies include altering lighting, landscaping, and location; installing mirrors on ATMs; installing ATMs in police stations; providing ATM users with safety tips; installing CCTV; installing devices to allow victims to summon police during a robbery; and setting daily cash withdrawal limits (Scott, 2001a).

Preventing Witness Intimidation

People who are witnesses to or victims of crime are sometimes reluctant to report criminal offenses or to assist in their investigation. This reluctance may be in response to a perceived or actual threat of retaliation by the offender(s) or their associates. Dedel (2006) points out that historically witness intimidation is most closely associated with organized crime and domestic violence, but recently it has occurred in investigations of drug offenses, gang violence, and other types of crime.

An effective strategy to prevent witness intimidation usually requires multi-agency partnerships including the police, prosecutors, and other agencies such as public housing, public benefits, and social service agencies. The strategy should also consider how to limit liability should the witness actually be harmed. Dedel (2006) suggests liability can be limited in several ways:

» Taking reports of intimidation seriously and engaging in the defined process for protecting witnesses

» Promising only those security services that can reasonably be provided

» Documenting all offers of assistance and all efforts to protect witnesses, along with the acceptance or refusal of such assurance

» Making sure witnesses understand the circumstances under which protections will be withdrawn and documenting all decisions to withdraw security

Specific responses to reducing intimidation by protecting witnesses include minimizing the risk of identification witnesses face when reporting crime or offering statements; protecting the anonymity of witnesses; using alarms and other crime prevention devices; reducing the likelihood of contact between witnesses and offenders; transporting witnesses to and from work and school; supporting witnesses; keeping witnesses and defendants separated at the courthouse; and relocating witnesses, either temporarily, for a short term, or permanently through the Federal Witness Security Program (Dedel, 2006).

Strategies to deter intimidators include admonishing them and explaining the laws concerning intimidation, requesting high bail and no-contact orders, increasing penalties for intimidation, and prosecuting intimidators. Increasing patrols in a targeted area or compelling witnesses to testify is usually ineffective. Most states have material witness laws that allow the arrest and detention of a person who refuses to provide information in court. Dedel (2006, 32) recommends: "Because of concerns for the rights of victims and the lack of proof that compelling witnesses to testify is effective, this should be the option of last resort."

Addressing Domestic Violence

Domestic disputes are some of the most common calls for police service. Many domestic disputes do not involve violence, but the COPS Office has a guide discussing those that do (Sampson, 2007). The guide helps police analyze and respond to their local problem.

In the United States, domestic violence accounts for about 20 percent of the nonfatal violent crime women experience. Through the community policing philosophy and its practices, some law enforcement agencies are seeking to improve their effectiveness in dealing with the problem of domestic violence by forming police–community partnerships to enhance their response options. PERF, with funding from the COPS Office, explored the nature, function, and impact of such police–community partnerships. The research shows that partnerships between the police and community residents and agencies have improved the way agencies communicate with each other and the way they focus their energies on improving the safety of victims of domestic violence. This publication highlights such initiatives around the country that can be replicated to better address domestic violence.

Preventing Acquaintance Rape of College Students

Rape is one of the most common violent crimes on American college campuses today. Prevention has focused almost entirely on building security, escorts for students after dark, and workshops focusing on protection from dangerous strangers on campus. Unfortunately, these techniques are not very successful, because almost all sexual assaults occur between people who know each other and are part of the "legitimate" campus environment. The COPS Office has a problem-solving guide that can help police and campus public safety officers effectively prevent the problem (Sampson, 2003). The guide describes the problem and its scope, causes, and contributing factors; methods for analyzing the problem on a particular campus; tested responses; and measures for assessing response effectiveness.

Preventing Identity Theft

Americans worry more about becoming a victim of identity theft than they do about any other crime, including terrorism and murder (*Sourcebook of Criminal Justice Statistics Online*, 2011). According to the Federal Trade Commission (FTC), the top consumer complaint in 2011, for the 12th year in a row, was identity theft ("FTC Releases Top Complaint Categories for 2011," 2012). In 2010 approximately 8.6 million U.S. households—7.0% of all households in the nation—had at least one member age 12 or older who experienced one or more types of identity theft victimization (Langton, 2011). Although this percentage was similar to the percentage of households that experienced identity theft in 2009, it represented a significant increase from the 5.5% of households, or 6.4 million households, that were victims of one or more types of identity theft in 2005. The increase in reported identity theft victimization between 2005 and 2010 was attributed largely to an increase in the misuse or attempted misuse of existing credit card accounts (Langton, 2011).

Four commonly recognized types of identity theft are described in Figure 10.1. Congressional hearings on identity theft in the 1990s found that police generally did not regard identity theft victims as "true victims" because the credit card companies that absorbed the financial loss typically did not report the loss to local police. Studies also showed that victims seldom reported the loss or theft of a credit card to police, because they believed the card company would cover the loss: "However, because the repeated use of a victim's identity caused serious

Figure 10.1   The Four Types of Identity Theft

	Financial Gain	**Concealment**
High Commitment (lots of planning)	*Organized:* A fraud ring systematically steals personal information and uses it to generate bank accounts, obtain credit cards, etc. *Individual:* The offender sets up a look-alike Internet Web site for a major company; spams consumers, luring them to the site by saying their account information is needed to clear up a serious problem; steals the personal/financial information the consumer provides; and uses it to commit identity theft.	*Organized:* Terrorists obtain false visas and passports to avoid being traced after committing terrorist acts.* *Individual:* The offender assumes another's name to cover up past crimes or avoid capture over many years.
Opportunistic (low commitment)	An apartment manager uses personal information from rental applications to open credit card accounts.	The offender uses another's name and ID when stopped or arrested by police.

*An Algerian national facing U.S. charges of identity theft allegedly stole the identities of 21 members of a Cambridge, Massachusetts, health club and transferred the identities to one of the people convicted in the failed 1999 plot to bomb the Los Angeles International Airport.

Source: Graeme Newman. *Identity Theft*. Washington, DC: Community Oriented Policing Services Office, 2004.

disruption and emotional damage, more victims began to report the offense....
Credit-reporting agencies now require that victims do so as part of an 'identity
theft affidavit'" (Newman, 2004, 2).

Until recently, victims had great difficulty in getting reports of identity
theft from the police. However, in response to growing media coverage and
congressional testimony concerning identity theft, the IACP adopted a resolution in 2000 urging all police departments to provide incident reports
and other assistance to identity theft victims. In fact, the FTC has issued a
memorandum to all police officers stating that, under the federal Fair Credit
Reporting Act (FCRA), a detailed police report is required before victims of
identity theft can claim certain rights under the law ("The Importance of the
Police Report," n.d.). By law, a victim can only assert his or her rights if the
police report specifies which accounts and information on the credit report
resulted from the identity theft. The FTC has made available online an ID
Theft Complaint form to help police gather all of the victim's information
required by law.

Preventing Street Prostitution

Street prostitution is a sign of neighborhood disorder and attracts strangers,
drug dealers, pimps, and other criminals into a neighborhood. Prostitutes,
often addicted to drugs and/or infected with the human immunodeficiency
virus (HIV), wait on street corners for customers from more orderly and affluent
neighborhoods, who cruise the streets and frequently assume any females they
see to be prostitutes. Women residents of the neighborhood become afraid to
wait for a bus or walk to a store. Parents do not want their children exposed to
the problem and worry about the dangerous trash (used condoms and needles)
left on public and private property. Whereas prostitution has often been a low
priority for police, it is a high-priority issue for affected neighborhoods (Scott
and Dedel, 2006b).

Traditional responses have been largely ineffective. Basically consisting
of arrest and prosecution, they include neighborhood "sweeps," in which as
many prostitutes as possible are arrested and sporadic arrests of "johns" are
conducted. Community policing has spawned a multitude of other responses,
many of which have proved more effective. Some responses include establishing a very visible police presence; holding public protests against prostitution;
educating and warning prostitutes and clients; targeting the worst offenders;
obtaining restraining orders against prostitutes; suspending government aid
to prostitutes; imposing curfews on prostitutes; exposing clients to humiliat-
ing publicity; notifying those with influence over a client's conduct (employers,
spouses, etc.); restricting a client's ability to drive by vehicle confiscation or
drivers license revocation; helping prostitutes to quit; encouraging prostitutes
to report serious crime; providing prostitutes with information about known
dangerous clients; diverting traffic by closing alleys, streets, and parking lots;
providing enhanced lighting; securing abandoned buildings; and holding property owners responsible when their property is being used for prostitution (Scott
and Dedel, 2006b).

As more and more police departments develop their own Web sites, many
are posting online photos of johns and others involved in the prostitution trade.

For example, the Canton (Ohio) Police Department's Web site posts numerous photos, preceded by this statement:

> The following individuals were arrested by the Canton Police Department and convicted in Canton Municipal Court for either soliciting for prostitution or patronizing prostitution. This service is provided as a deterrent to prostitution in Canton, Ohio. Our citizens deserve an environment that promotes health, safety, and stability.

A related problem often involving prostitution is that of human trafficking.

Preventing Human Trafficking

The term "human trafficking" is used to describe many forms of exploitation of human beings. Human trafficking crimes are defined in Title 18, Chapter 77, of the U.S. Criminal Code and focus on "the act of compelling or coercing a person's labor, services, or commercial sex acts. The coercion can be subtle or overt, physical or psychological, but it must be used to coerce a victim into performing labor, services, or commercial sex acts. Because these statutes are rooted in the prohibition against slavery and involuntary servitude guaranteed by the Thirteenth Amendment to the United States Constitution, the Civil Rights Division [of the U.S. Department of Justice] plays a paramount role in enforcing these statutes," in partnership with the United States Attorneys' offices (USAOs) and law enforcement agencies ("Human Trafficking Prosecution Unit: Overview," 2011).

Human trafficking victims have been found in agricultural fields, sweatshops, suburban mansions, brothels, escort services, bars, and strip clubs. Many victims of human trafficking speak limited or no English and are fearful of strangers and the police: "While undocumented migrants can be particularly vulnerable to coercion because of their fear of authorities, traffickers have demonstrated their ability to exploit other vulnerable populations and have preyed just as aggressively on documented guest workers and U.S. citizen children. Indeed, because of the vulnerability of minors, where minors are offered for commercial sex the statutes do not require proof of force, fraud, or coercion" ("Human Trafficking Prosecution Unit: Overview," 2011).

The problem of human sex trafficking has become particularly acute, comprising the fastest-growing business among organized crime groups and the third largest criminal enterprise worldwide (Walker-Rodriguez and Hill, 2011). While data is limited regarding the exact number of children who are sex trafficked in the United States, an estimated 293,000 youths are currently at risk for such victimization in this country, the majority of whom are runaways or thrownaways and come from a background of abuse and neglect (Walker-Rodriguez and Hill, 2011).

In June 2012 the FBI initiated a three-day law enforcement action called Operation Cross Country—the sixth iteration of its kind—which resulted in the recovery of 79 children and the arrest of 104 pimps on various prostitution-related charges. The operation partnered hundreds of FBI special agents with thousands of local police officers, deputy sheriffs, state troopers, and other law enforcement personnel throughout the United States to find and arrest those responsible for exploiting underage children through prostitution ("Nearly 80 Juveniles Recovered," 2012):

> Operation Cross Country is part of the Innocence Lost National Initiative that was created in 2003 by the FBI's Criminal Investigative Division, in partnership with the Department of Justice and National Center for Missing & Exploited Children (NCMEC), to address the growing problem of domestic child sex trafficking in the United States. …

> To date, the 47 Innocence Lost Task Forces and Working Groups have recovered more than 2,200 children from the streets. The investigations and subsequent 1,017 convictions have resulted in lengthy sentences, including eight life terms and the seizure of more than $3.1 million in assets.

Because of enhanced criminal statutes, victim-protection provisions, and public awareness programs introduced by the Trafficking Victims Protection Act of 2000, the numbers of trafficking investigations and prosecutions have increased dramatically in recent years, as demonstrated by a 360-percent increase in convictions for the fiscal years 2001–2007 as compared to the previous 7-year period ("Human Trafficking Prosecution Unit: Overview," 2011). Unfortunately, however, research has found that most police departments still do not consider human trafficking a high priority, and that although some local law enforcement agencies are aware of the nature and seriousness of the crime, few have engaged in proactive endeavors to address the problem (Wilson, Walsh, and Kleuber, 2006). Police officers and citizens alike must be made more aware of suspicious activities to watch for, such as avoiding strangers, never leaving the place of employment, and showing fear of authorities.

Preventing Assaults in and around Bars

Assaults in and around bars are a frequent problem in large cities as well as small towns. Most of these assaults are alcohol-related, but some are not. The majority occur on weekend nights at a relatively small number of places (Scott and Dedel, 2006a).

In addition to alcohol, factors that contribute to aggression and violence in bars include the type of establishment, the concentration of bars, the closing time, aggressive bouncers, a high proportion of young male strangers, price discounting of drinks, continued service to drunken patrons, crowding and lack of comfort, competitive situations, a low ratio of staff to patrons, lack of good entertainment, unattractive décor and dim lighting, tolerance for disorderly conduct, availability of weapons, and low levels of police enforcement and regulation.

An effective strategy to address the problem of violence in and around bars requires a broad-based coalition incorporating the interests of the community, the bars, and the government (Scott and Dedel, 2006a). In addition, any response strategy should address as many identified risk factors as possible, such as the practices of serving and patterns of consumption, the physical comfort of the environment, the overall permissiveness of the environment, and the availability of public transportation to disperse crowds after bars have closed. Scott and Dedel (2006a) recommend combining two groups of responses to address the problem: (1) responses to reduce how much alcohol patrons drink and (2) responses to make the bar safer.

Reducing Alcohol Consumption   Alcohol consumption can be reduced by establishing responsible beverage service programs including monitoring drinking to prevent drunkenness, promoting slower drinking rates, prohibiting underage drinking, providing reduced-alcohol or nonalcoholic beverages, requiring or encouraging food services with alcohol services, and discouraging alcohol price discounts. Additional measures include establishing and enforcing server liability laws and reducing the concentration and/or number of bars (Scott and Dedel, 2006a).

Making Bars Safer   Bars can be made safer by training staff to handle patrons nonviolently; establishing adequate transportation; relaxing or staggering bar closing times; controlling bar entrances, exits, and immediate surroundings; maintaining an attractive, comfortable, entertaining atmosphere; establishing and enforcing clear rules of conduct for bar patrons; reducing potential weapons and other sources of injury; communicating about incidents as they occur; and banning known troublemakers from bars.

Preventing Robbery of Taxi Drivers

A barrier to understanding the problem of taxi driver robbery is a lack of data collected on the crime. Much of what is known about taxi robbery is included in records on assaults and homicides by occupation. These data consistently show that taxi drivers have the highest or one of the highest risks of job-related homicides and nonfatal assaults (Smith, 2005). Several risk factors increase taxi drivers' chances of becoming robbery victims: They have contact with a large number of strangers; they often work in high-crime areas; they usually carry cash in an unsecured manner and handle money as payment; they usually work alone, often to (or through) isolated locations; and they often work late at night or early in the morning (Smith, 2005).

Among the strategies used to prevent taxi driver robberies are separating drivers from passengers, recording activity with security cameras, having a radio or alarm to call for help, keeping track of taxi locations with automatic vehicle location (AVL) systems, putting trunk latches on the inside of vehicle trunks and near drivers, and disabling vehicles. Other strategies focus on limiting the availability of cash, including eliminating cash payments, dropping cash off, keeping cash locked up or out of sight, and minimizing expectations about the amount of money present (Smith, 2005).

Some strategies focus on other driver practices such as controlling who gets into the taxi, directing passengers to particular seats in the cab, finding out the destination before moving, sharing destination information with others, putting additional people in the cab, setting rules and asking those who do not meet them to get out, trying not to provoke passengers, knowing where to go for help late at night, allowing others to see inside the cab, limiting where the cab will make a drop off, staying in the cab unless it is safe to get out, and limiting injury when a robbery occurs by simply handing over the money and not fighting back (Smith, 2005).

Police practices might also help to prevent taxi driver robberies, including targeting repeat offenders and authorizing police stops without reasonable suspicion or probable cause if the drivers have signed an authorization to do so.

Finally, industry rules, regulations, and practices might include controlling the environment around taxi stands, eliminating passenger and driver conflict over money, setting driver competency standards, running driver safety training programs, screening passengers by the dispatching company, and exempting drivers from seat belt use.

Preventing Violent Confrontations with People with Mental Illness

The importance of communicating effectively with individuals who are mentally ill and partnering with mental health professionals was discussed in Chapter 6. Among the most important partners in working with violent individuals who are mentally ill is the mental health community, including emergency hospitals to which police may take those in crisis. It is widely recognized that traditional police responses to violent individuals are often not effective with those who are mentally ill. Among the responses suggested are training generalist police officers; providing more information to patrol officers; using less-lethal weapons; deploying specialized police officers as members of a crisis intervention team (CIT); or deploying specialized nonpolice responders. Whichever approach is selected, training of police officers is a crucial element in achieving a successful response and is most effective when it includes consultation with mental health professionals and other social service providers (Tucker et al., 2011).

A partnership approach to dealing effectively with violent individuals who are mentally ill should involve stakeholders—for example, initiating assisted outpatient treatment, establishing crisis response sites, establishing jail-based diversion, and establishing mental health courts.

Preventing Crimes against Businesses

The annual cost of crime against business is in the billions of dollars. Such victimization hurts business owners, employees, neighbors, customers, and the general public (Chamard, 2006). One way to address the problem of crimes against businesses is to develop police–business partnerships. Such partnerships can take a variety of forms, ranging from an individual business working with the police to address a specific problem to an area-wide partnership including businesses from a particular geographic location. The partnerships can also be issue specific or business specific. One of the most common police–individual business partnerships involves police assisting retailers in preventing shoplifting.

Police–Individual Business Partnerships to Prevent Shoplifting

Shoplifting might be prevented by improving store layout and displays, upgrading security, establishing early warning systems (to notify other stores about shoplifters), banning known shoplifters, installing and monitoring CCTV systems, using electronic article surveillance (EAS), and attaching ink tags to merchandise.

With EAS a tag is attached to each piece of merchandise. When a person pays for an article, the tag is deactivated and removed by a checkout clerk. Tags that have not been removed or deactivated are detected at store exit gates, and an alarm is sounded. Ink tags, rather than setting off an alarm if not removed, ruin the merchandise to which they are attached when the offender tries to remove them.

Area-Specific Police Business Partnerships One approach to area-specific police–business partnerships is the business improvement district (BID), a consortium of property and business owners who voluntarily pay a special assessment in addition to their regular taxes. The funds from the special assessment are spent on beautification, security, marketing, or whatever the membership decides is needed to enhance the viability of the area. Goals usually include raising the standards of public spaces; reducing crime, social disorder, and the fear of victimization; improving public transportation; generating sales and revenues for area businesses; and increasing the number of local jobs. The United States has an estimated 2,000 BIDs (Chamard, 2006). Although no solid research has been conducted, anecdotal evidence suggests this approach holds promise.

Issue-Specific Police–Business Partnerships Issue-specific partnerships focus on a certain type of crime or a particular situation, often a public order problem such as public drinking or panhandling that has reached the point where intervention is required (Chamard, 2006). Such partnerships need not last after the specific problem has been solved.

Business-Specific Police–Business Partnerships Business-specific partnerships are often formed in response to an outbreak of crimes targeting a particular type of business such as robberies of banks or convenience stores (Chamard, 2006). Others are formed to address specific chronic problems such as safety in public parking lots and garages.

Ideas in Practice

IDENTITY THEFT AND FRAUD PREVENTION PROGRAM

Beaverton, Oregon, Police Department Wins Webber Seavey Award

The Webber Seavey Award recognizes innovative police programs from around the world and is co-sponsored by the International Association of Chiefs of Police (IACP) and Motorola, Inc.

The Beaverton, Oregon, Police Department began its identity theft and fraud prevention program in 2003, after analyzing the increasing case load they were seeing. Identity theft and fraud cases were up 54 percent over the previous 4 years, similar to what police departments all over the country were experiencing. Beaverton police applied for and won a $238,375 federal grant from the Department of Justice to tackle the community's identity theft problem. They formed a planning committee, which decided to direct their efforts toward enhanced investigations, helping victims, and educating the public on protecting themselves from these crimes.

"The department formed a Special Enforcement Unit and during its first 2 years, members of the unit made 494 fraud-related arrests, prevented the loss of more than $701,000 from citizens and businesses, and recovered $33,170," said Michelle Harrold, a management analyst with the Beaverton police.

Partnerships for this initiative also included a banking industry group to help police solve a case involving more than $126,450, and a marketing firm to assist in outreach.

(continues)

(continued)

Careful to make their efforts proactive, the department provided targeted training to officers and volunteers to enable them to assist victims of identity theft and fraud. They also developed identity theft and fraud prevention literature that officers gave out to residents and local businesses, and they posted prevention information and tips on their Web site. "The team really hit the streets and worked with our local retailers to try to change habits that put their businesses at risk," Harrold said.

The police department conducted free workshops and educational seminars for the community. Some seminars were designed especially for the business community in an effort to make them more aware of business practices that put them and their customers at risk.

Because thieves often search recycling and garbage for personal identifying information of potential victims, community members were informed that shredding sensitive documents with a cross-cut shredder is a good preventative practice. The department recommended shredding paper containing personal information such as credit card statements, financial statements, preapproved credit card offers, old tax documents, checks, and household bills.

Going a step further, the police department provided free document shredding events for the public at which a commercial-sized shredding truck was available. Participants were allowed to bring up to three boxes of documents, per vehicle, to be shredded and were encouraged, at the same time, to bring canned food to donate to the Oregon Food Bank.

"We need to compliment the community for working with us. The key to our success is it's an ongoing program," said Beaverton Police Chief David Bishop.

Sources: The Bureau of Justice Statistics; the International Association of Chiefs of Police (IACP) Web site (http://www.theiacp.org/About/Awards/WebberSeaveyAwardforQualityinLawEnforcement/tabid/310/Default.aspx); Christina Lent, "Police ID Theft Work Earns International Recognition," *Beaverton Valley Times*, October 26, 2006; David G. Bishop, "Identity Theft and Fraud Prevention Program," *The Police Chief*, May 2007.

PARTNERSHIPS IN ACTION AGAINST CRIME AND DISORDER

Partnerships across the country are working on reducing crime and disorder, some focusing on one specific area, and others taking more comprehensive approaches.

Norfolk, Virginia, cut homicides by more than 10 percent and has reduced overall crime rates citywide by 26 percent and in some neighborhoods by as much as 40 percent. A good share of the credit goes to Police Assisted Community Enforcement (PACE), a crime prevention initiative that works neighborhood by neighborhood in conjunction with teams of social, health, and family services agencies (the Family Assistance Services Team, or FAST) and public works and environmental agencies (Neighborhood Environmental Assistance Teams, or NEAT) to cut through red tape and help residents reclaim their neighborhoods (*350 Tested Strategies to Prevent Crime*, 1995).

The Minnesota Crime Prevention Association enlisted the support of families, public officials, and 45 statewide and local organizations, including schools and churches, to wage a campaign against youth violence. Actions ranged from encouraging children and parents to turn off violent television shows to providing classroom training in violence prevention (*350 Tested Strategies to Prevent Crime*, 1995).

In Trenton, New Jersey, a partnership of schools, parents, city leaders, and others led to a Safe Haven program in which the schools in the neighborhood became multipurpose centers after school hours for youth activities including sports, crafts, and tutoring. Children have flocked to the centers as a positive alternative to being at home alone after school or being at risk on the streets (*350 Tested Strategies to Prevent Crime*, 1995).

Crime near a college campus in Columbus, Ohio, became an opportunity for a partnership formed by the City of Columbus, the State of Ohio, Ohio State University, the Franklin County Sheriff, and the Columbus Police. The Community Crime Patrol puts two-person, radio-equipped teams of observers into the neighborhoods near the campus during potential high-crime hours. A number of these paid, part-time observers are college students interested in careers in law enforcement (*350 Tested Strategies to Prevent Crime*, 1995).

In Danville, Virginia, a partnership approach to working with public housing residents resulted in a 53-percent reduction in calls about fights, a 50-percent reduction in domestic violence calls, and a 9-percent reduction in disturbance calls. The Virginia Crime Prevention Association worked with the Danville Housing Authority to bring public housing residents, local law enforcement, social services, and other public agencies together into an effective, problem-solving group. Residents were at the heart of the group, identifying problems that were causing high rates of aggravated assault in the community and working to provide remedies such as positive alternatives for youths and social services and counseling for adults and children. Residents developed a code of conduct for the community, spelling out expectations for the behavior of those who live there (*350 Tested Strategies to Prevent Crime*, 1995).

Boston's Neighborhood Justice Network, in partnership with the Council of Elders, the Jewish Memorial Hospital, the Boston Police Department, the Department of Public Health, and the Commission on Affairs of the Elderly, created a program to help reduce violence and other crimes against older people. It provides basic personal and home crime prevention education, assistance in dealing with city agencies, training in nonconfrontational tactics to avert street crime, and other helpful services that reduce both victimization and fear among the city's older residents (*350 Tested Strategies to Prevent Crime*, 1995).

These are just a few of a wide range of programs designed by community groups that have changed the quality of life in small towns and large cities, in neighborhoods and housing complexes, in schools and on playgrounds. These groups have proved that there is strength in numbers and that partnerships can provide the community basis for correcting the problems and conditions that can lead to crime. They achieved success because the people involved developed the skills to work together effectively.

SUMMARY

Synergism occurs when individuals channel their energies toward a common purpose and accomplish together what they could not accomplish alone. It can greatly enhance community policing efforts to prevent or reduce crime and disorder. Crime prevention is a large part, and in fact a cornerstone, of community policing.

Traffic problems top the list of concerns of most neighborhoods and communities.

Concerns include speeding in residential areas, street racing, red-light running, impaired drivers, and nonuse of seat belts. Engineering responses to speeding include using traffic calming, posting warning signs and signals, conducting anti-speeding public awareness campaigns, informing complainants about actual speeds, and providing realistic driver training. Enforcement responses to speeding include

(1) enforcing speeding laws, (2) enforcing speeding laws with speed cameras or photo radar, (3) using speed display boards, (4) arresting the worst offenders, and (5) having citizen volunteers monitor speeding.

Various community policing efforts to reduce citizens' fear of crime have included enhanced foot and vehicle patrol in high-crime neighborhoods, citizen patrols, neighborhood cleanup campaigns, community education and awareness programs, the placement of police substations in troubled neighborhoods, and the installation of closed-circuit video surveillance cameras.

One frequently used strategy is crime prevention through environmental design. CPTED has three major components: target hardening, changes to the physical environment, and community building. By emphasizing the systematic analysis of crime in a particular location, CPTED directly supports community policing by providing crime prevention strategies tailored to solve specific problems. Another approach to crime prevention is focusing on place. Two side effects of place-focused opportunity blocking efforts are displacement of crime and diffusion of prevention benefits.

The risk factor prevention paradigm seeks to identify key risk factors for offending and then implement prevention methods designed to counteract them. It is useful in identifying strategies that might be effective for a specific community.

Three federal initiatives to assist communities in implementing community policing are the Community Oriented Policing Services Office, the Community Policing Consortium, and the Weed and Seed program. The Weed and Seed program sought to identify, arrest, and prosecute offenders (weed) while simultaneously working with citizens to improve quality of life (seed).

Partnerships to prevent or reduce crime and disorder include business anticrime groups, local government–community crime prevention coalitions, community coalitions, cooperation with grassroots organizations, and landlords and residents in public housing using advances in technology and celebrating community successes.

DISCUSSION QUESTIONS

1. What examples of synergy have you been a part of or witnessed?

2. What crime prevention programs are in your community? Have you participated in any of them?

3. Traffic calming techniques have gained wide support from some drivers but, at the same time, the anger of other drivers. What accounts for the differing perspectives?

4. How does CCTV work to prevent crime and reduce fear?

5. What could be the explanation for some CCTV applications not having the desired effect?

6. Name and explain the five principles underlying CPTED.

7. Because taxes pay for police to combat crime, why should citizens get involved?

8. Why is it so difficult to know the reason for rises and declines in crime?

9. What is it about human trafficking that makes it difficult to detect or even understand the scope of the problem?

10. Which do you feel merits the most attention from community policing: concerns about disorder, fear of crime, or crime itself?

GALE EMERGENCY SERVICES DATABASE ASSIGNMENTS

 ONLINE Database

- Use the Gale Emergency Services Database to help answer the Discussion Questions as appropriate.

- One of the most effective and least expensive security initiatives is to design and build safety from crime and fear of crime into a structure. Research CPTED and discuss how the following can affect crime and/or fear of crime: smell and sound, parking garages, maintenance, color, mix of activities, restrooms, signage, vehicle–pedestrian conflicts, loitering, and "hanging out."

REFERENCES

"Best Practices for a Safe Community." n.d. Washington, DC: National Highway Traffic Safety Administration. http://www.nhtsa.gov/Driving+Safety/Safe+Communities/Best+Practices+for+a+Safe+Community

Bishop, David G. 2007. "Identity Theft and Fraud Prevention Program." *The Police Chief* (74) 5: 36–38, 41.

Boba, Rachel and Roberto Santos. 2006 (August). *Burglary at Single-Family House Construction Sites.* Washington, DC: Office of Community Oriented Policing Services, Problem-Oriented Guides for Police, Problem-Specific Guides Series, Guide No. 43.

Casstevens, Steven. 2008. "Traffic Enforcement Is Real Police Work." *Law and Order* (August): 44–46.

Chamard, Sharon. 2006 (April). *Partnering with Businesses to Address Public Safety Problems.* Washington, DC: Office of Community Oriented Policing Services, Problem-Oriented Guides for Police, Problem-Specific Guides Series, Guide No. 5.

"City Uses Cameras as Safety Tool, not Moneymaker." 2011 (February 1). *Status Report* (Publication by the Insurance Institute for Highway Safety) 46 (1): 1–2, 6–7.

Dedel, Kelly. 2006 (July). *Witness Intimidation.* Washington, DC: Office of Community Oriented Policing Services, Problem-Oriented Guides for Police, Problem-Specific Guides Series, Guide No. 42.

Dewey-Kollen, Janet. 2006. "Ten Ways to Improve DUI Enforcement." *Law and Order* (September): 10–17.

Domash, Shelly Feuer. 2006. "How to Crack Down on Street Racing." *Police* (June 1): 30–35.

Eck, John E. 1997. "Preventing Crime at Places." In *Preventing Crime: What Works, What Doesn't, What's Promising,* edited by the University of Maryland, Department of Criminology and Criminal Justice. Washington, DC: Office of Justice Programs, U.S. Department of Justice.

Farrington, David P. 2000. "Explaining and Preventing Crime: The Globalization of Knowledge—The American Society of Criminology 1999 Presidential Address." *Criminology* 38 (1): 1–24.

"FTC Releases Top Complaint Categories for 2011." 2012 (February 28). Press release. Washington, DC: Federal Trade Commission. http://ftc.gov/opa/2012/02/2011complaints.shtm

FY 2013 Performance Budget: Office of Community Oriented Policing Services. 2012 (February 8). Congressional justification. Washington, DC: U.S. Department of Justice. http://www.justice.gov/jmd/2013justification/pdf/fy13-cops-justification.pdf

How Are Innovations in Technology Transforming Policing? 2012 (January). Washington, DC: Police Executive Research Forum, Critical Issues in Policing.

"How to Identify Hot Spots." 2010 (May 25). Washington, DC: National Institute of Justice. http://www.nij.gov/topics/law-enforcement/strategies/hot-spot-policing/identifying.htm

"Human Trafficking Prosecution Unit: Overview." 2011. Washington, DC: U.S. Department of Justice. http://www.justice.gov/crt/about/crm/htpu.php

"The Importance of the Police Report." n.d. Memorandum. Washington, DC: Federal Trade Commission. http://www.idtheft.gov/probono/docs/D.7.%20Memorandum%20to%20Police%20on%20Importance%20of%20Taking%20Police%20Reports%20for%20Identity%20Theft.pdf

Langton, Lynn. 2011 (November). *Identity Theft Reported by Households, 2005–2010.* Washington, DC: Bureau of Justice Statistics. (NCJ 236245)

Lent, Christina. 2006. "Police ID Theft Work Earns International Recognition." *Beaverton Valley Times,* October 26.

"MADD President Calls for Summit of Traffic Safety Leaders to Renew Focus on Proven Solutions." 2012 (June 14). Press release. Irving, TX: MADD National Office. http://www.madd.org/media-center/press-releases/2012/lifesavers2012.html

Maggard, David L. and Daniel Jung. 2009. "Irvine's Area Traffic Officer Program." *The Police Chief* 77 (3): 46–50.

Marshall, Mark A. 2011. "'The Greatest Threat' to Public Safety." *The Police Chief* 78 (7): 6.

Mrazek, P. J. and R. J. Haggerty, editors. 1994. *Reducing Risks for Mental Disorders: Frontiers for Preventative Intervention Research.* Washington, DC: National Academy Press.

The National Biometrics Challenge. 2011 (September). Washington, DC: National Science and Technology Council, Subcommittee on Biometrics and Identity Management. http://www.biometrics.gov/Documents/BiometricsChallenge2011_protected.pdf

"Nearly 80 Juveniles Recovered in Nationwide Operation Targeting Underage Prostitution." 2012 (June 25). Press release. Washington, DC: Federal Bureau of Investigation.

http://www.fbi.gov/news/pressrel/press-releases/nearly-80-juveniles-recovered-in-nationwide-operation-targeting-underage-prostitution

Newman, Graeme R. 2004 (June). *Identity Theft.* Washington, DC: Office of Community Oriented Policing Services, Problem-Oriented Guides for Police, Problem-Specific Guides Series, Guide No. 25.

Overview (Traffic Safety Facts: 2010 Data). 2012 (June). Washington, DC: National Highway Traffic Safety Administration. (DOT HS 811 630)

Preliminary Annual Uniform Crime Report, January–December, 2011. 2012. Washington, DC: Federal Bureau of Investigation. http://www.fbi.gov/about-us/cjis/ucr/crime-in-the-u.s/2011/preliminary-annual-ucr-jan-dec-2011

Ratcliffe, Jerry. 2011 (August). *Video Surveillance of Public Places.* Washington, DC: Office of Community Oriented Policing Services, Problem-Oriented Guides for Police, Problem-Specific Guides Series, Guide No. 4.

"Red Light Running Kills." 2011 (February). *Status Report* (Publication by the Insurance Institute for Highway Safety) 46 (1): 1–2, 6–7.

Rosen, Marie Simonetti. 2006 (October). *Chief Concerns: A Gathering Storm—Violent Crime in America.* Washington, DC: Police Executive Research Forum.

Sampson, Rana. 2003 (August). *Acquaintance Rape of College Students.* Washington, DC: Office of Community Oriented Policing Services, Problem-Oriented Guides for Police, Problem-Specific Guides Series, Guide No. 17.

Sampson, Rana. 2007 (January). *Domestic Violence.* Washington, DC: Office of Community Oriented Policing Services, Problem-Oriented Guides for Police, Problem-Specific Guides Series, Guide No. 45.

Samuels, Adrienne. 2006. "It Could Be a Snap to Catch Red-Light Runners but Camera Idea Raises Privacy Issue." *The Boston Globe,* October 4.

Scott, Michael S. 2001a (September 14). *Robbery at Automated Teller Machines.* Washington, DC: Office of Community Oriented Policing Services, Problem-Oriented Guides for Police, Problem-Specific Guides Series, Guide No. 8.

Scott, Michael S. 2001b (August 14). *Speeding in Residential Areas.* Washington, DC: Office of Community Oriented Policing Services, Problem-Oriented Guides for Police, Problem-Specific Guides Series, Guide No. 3.

Scott, Michael S. and Kelly Dedel. 2006a (August). *Assaults in and around Bars.* 2nd ed. Washington, DC: Office of Community Oriented Policing Services, Problem-Oriented Guides for Police, Problem-Specific Guides Series, Guide No. 1.

Scott, Michael S. and Kelly Dedel. 2006b (August 6). *Street Prostitution.* 2nd ed. Washington, DC: Office of Community Oriented Policing Services, Problem-Oriented Guide for Police, Problem-Specific Guides Series, Guide No. 2.

Shader, Michael. 2002. *Risk Factors for Delinquency: An Overview.* Washington, DC: Office of Juvenile and Delinquency Prevention.

Smith, Martha J. 2005 (March). *Robbery of Taxi Drivers.* Washington, DC: Office of Community Oriented Policing Services, Problem-Oriented Guides for Police, Problem-Specific Guides Series, Guide No. 34.

Solomon, Mark G., David F. Preusser, Julie Tison, and Neil K. Chaudhary. 2009 (December). *Evaluation of the May 2007 "Click It or Ticket" Mobilization.* Washington, DC: National Highway Traffic Safety Administration. (DOT HS 811 239)

Sourcebook of Criminal Justice Statistics Online. 2011. http://www.albany.edu/sourcebook/pdf/t2392011.pdf

Speeding (Traffic Safety Facts: 2009 Data). 2012 (May). Washington, DC: National Highway Traffic Safety Administration. (DOT HS 811 397)

Speeding and Aggressive Driving. 2012 (March 1). Washington, DC: Governors Highway Safety Association.

350 Tested Strategies to Prevent Crime: A Resource for Municipal Agencies and Community Groups. 1995. Washington, DC: National Crime Prevention Council.

Tucker, Abigail S., Vincent B. Van Hasselt, Gregory M. Vecchi, and Samuel L. Browning. 2011. "Responding to Persons with Mental Illness." *FBI Law Enforcement Bulletin* (October): 1–6.

"Using Environmental Design to Prevent School Violence." 2008 (June 23). Atlanta, GA: Centers for Disease Control.

Walker-Rodriguez, Amanda and Rodney Hill. 2011. "Human Sex Trafficking." *FBI Law Enforcement Bulletin* (March): 1–9.

Wilson, Deborah G., William F. Walsh, and Sherilyn Kleuber. 2006. "Trafficking in Human Beings: Training and Services among U.S. Law Enforcement Agencies." *Police Practice and Research* 7 (2): 149.

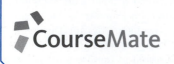

CHAPTER 11
Community Policing and Drugs

Imagine a world without drugs ... where teens are not fooled into taking death pills disguised as harmless fun ... where children can play in their neighborhoods without fear of drug violence ... where we don't have to spend millions of dollars a year and put our agents' and officers' lives on the line arresting drug traffickers ... and one where we don't have to experience the agony of loved ones suffering from a tragic addiction. Our mission at the DEA is to do everything possible to make that world a reality.

—*Michele Leonhart, Administrator of the Drug Enforcement Administration, 2008*

DO YOU KNOW ...

» Whether crime and drugs are linked?

» What the most commonly abused drug at all ages is?

» What the three core components of the national drug control policy are?

» What strategies have been implemented to combat the drug problem in neighborhoods?

» What type of drug market poses the greatest threat in apartment complexes?

» What two general approaches to address rave parties are?

» What Lead On America is?

» What federal grant programs aimed specifically at the drug problem are available?

» If crime, drugs, and the American Dream are related?

» How the conservative and liberal crime control strategies differ?

CAN YOU DEFINE ...

binge drinking
closed drug market
conservative crime control
gateway theory
liberal crime control
open drug market
rave

INTRODUCTION

The correlation between drugs and crime is well established: "Fifty-three percent of State and 45 percent of Federal prisoners met the DSM–IV criteria for drug dependence or abuse" (Mumola and Karberg, 2007, 1). Drug users often commit crimes to support their habit. Drug dealers fight territorial wars over the drug market, making neighborhoods hazardous for all residents. Roughly half (51%) of federal inmates in 2010 were serving time for drug offenses and about 18 percent of those in state prisons were serving time for drug offenses (Guerino, Harrison, and Sabol, 2012). Data also indicates that approximately 25 percent of federal inmates and 33 percent of state inmates committed the offense for which they were currently serving time while under the influence of drugs (Mumola and Karberg, 2007).

 Crime and drugs are clearly linked.

Any efforts to reduce the drug problem are likely to also reduce crime and disorder in a neighborhood and community. One study of the relationship between serious crime, drug arrests, and nuisance abatement seizures in New York between the years 1995 and 2001 tested the broken windows theory and found that the rate of marijuana arrest and the closing of drug locations through nuisance abatement statutes were inversely related to the crime rate and that the rate of controlled substance arrest was directly related to a reduced crime rate (McCabe, 2008).

This chapter begins with a discussion of the current extent of the drug problem in the United States, the "war on drugs," and the National Drug Control Strategy. This is followed by strategies for prevention—stopping drug use before it starts, including a discussion of the DARE program. Then treatment efforts are described, followed by a description of law enforcement strategies for dealing with a drug problem. Addressing specific drug-related problems is examined next, followed by a look at legislation as a tool in the war on substance abuse. Next is a discussion of collaborative efforts to combat drug dealing; examples of comprehensive, coordinated community approaches; and the federal grants that are available to help combat the drug problem. The chapter concludes by examining the relationship between crime, drugs, and the American Dream and providing another example of a successful problem-solving partnership in action.

THE CURRENT DRUG PROBLEM

The extent of the current drug problem is difficult to accurately pinpoint, although several survey tools have been designed to conduct annual assessments in an effort to gain insight into the situation. The Substance Abuse and Mental Health Services Administration (SAMHSA) *2010 National Survey on Drug Use and Health* (NSDUH) (2011b) estimated that 22.6 million Americans aged 12 or older—8.9 percent of the population over age 11—were current (past month) illicit drug users, meaning they had used an illicit drug during the month prior to the survey interview. Illicit drugs include marijuana/hashish, cocaine (including crack), heroin, hallucinogens, inhalants, or prescription-type psychotherapeutics used nonmedically.

One of the most reliable sources of information on the drug problem is *Monitoring the Future* (*MTF*), a national survey of drug use divided into two volumes—Volume I addresses drug use among secondary school students, and Volume II covers drug use among college students and adults ages 19–50. *MTF* now spans a 37-year interval, having been launched in 1975. It is funded by the National Institute on Drug Abuse (NIDA), one of the National Institutes of Health, under a series of investigator-initiated, competitive research grants made to the University of Michigan.

Among the more important findings from the 2011 *MTF*, which help put into perspective the magnitude and variety of substance-use problems that currently exist among American youth, are the following (Johnston et al., 2012, 41):

» About a quarter (26%) of today's 8th graders has tried an *illicit drug* (if inhalants are included as an illicit drug), and about a half (52%) of 12th graders has done so.

» By their late 20s, nearly 3 of 5 (59%) of today's young adults have tried an *illicit drug*, and a third (33%) has tried some *illicit drug other than marijuana*, usually in addition to marijuana. (These figures do not include inhalants.)

» Today, about 1 in 8 young adults (13% in 2011) has tried *cocaine*, and 5.2 percent have tried it by their senior year of high school, when they are 17 or 18 years old. One in every 53 12th graders (1.9%) has tried *crack*. Among young adults 29–30 years of age, 1 in 22 (4.5%) has tried crack.

» One in every 15 12th graders (6.6%) in 2011 smoked *marijuana daily*. Among young adults ages 19 to 28, the percentage is about the same (6.1%) and slightly above the recent peak level. Among those same 12th graders in 2011, one in every six (17%) had been a daily marijuana smoker at some time for at least a month, and among young adults the comparable figure is 17 percent, also about 1 in 6.

» About 1 in 5 12th graders (22%) had *five or more drinks in a row* on at least one occasion in the 2 weeks prior to the survey, and we know that such behavior tends to increase among young adults 1 to 4 years past high school—that is, in the peak college years. Indeed, 43 percent of all male college students report such binge drinking.

» Even with considerable improvements in smoking rates among American adolescents since the late 1990s, about one-fifth (19%) of 12th graders in 2011 currently smokes *cigarettes*, and 1 in 10 (10%) is already a current *daily smoker*. In addition, we know from studying previous cohorts that many young adults increase their rates of smoking within a year or so after they leave high school.

Illicit drug use is highest among people aged 18 to 28. In 2011 the rank order by age group for annual prevalence of using any illicit drug was 12th graders (40%), college students (36%), 19- to 28-year-olds (35%), 10th graders (31%), and 8th graders (15%) (Johnston et al., 2012). Data from the 2010 NSDUH (SAMHSA, 2011b) shows that the rate of illicit drug use among 18- to 25-year-olds is currently on the rise, from 19.6 percent in 2008 to 21.2 percent in 2009, to 21.5 percent in 2010, a trend driven largely by an increase in marijuana use. Among young adults aged 18 to 25, the rate of current nonmedical use of prescription-type drugs in 2010 was 5.9 percent, similar to the rate in the years from 2002 to 2009 (SAMHSA, 2011b). Drug abuse is not strictly a problem for America's youth. The baby boomer generation is also contributing to the higher numbers of illicit drug use. Among adults aged 50 to 59, the rate of illicit drug use increased from 2.7 percent in 2002 to 5.8 percent in 2010, a trend partially reflecting the aging into these age groups of members of the baby boom cohort, whose rates of illicit drug use have been higher than those of older cohorts (Han, Gfroerer, and Colliver, 2009). The baby boom cohort refers to persons born in the United States after World War II between 1946 and 1964.

Drug use becomes increasingly problematic when the users get behind the wheel. In 2010, 10.6 million persons (4.2%) of the population aged 12 or older reported driving under the influence of illicit drugs during the past year, a rate unchanged from that in 2009 but lower than the rate in 2002 (4.7%) (SAMSHA, 2011b). Across age groups, the rate of driving under the influence of illicit drugs in 2010 was highest among young adults aged 18 to 25 (12.7%).

There is some encouraging news, however, as *MTF* indicates signs of decreased use in 2011 of inhalants, cocaine powder, crack cocaine, the narcotic drug Vicodin, the amphetamine Adderall, sedatives, tranquilizers, and over-the-counter cough and cold medicines used to get high (Johnston et al., 2012).

Marijuana

Marijuana is the most commonly used illicit drug. In 2010 there were 17.4 million past-month users, a substantial increase over the 2007 number of 14.4 million users (SAMHSA, 2011). *MTF* reports that one in three 10th graders and half of 12th graders reported using marijuana at least once in their lifetime (Johnston et al., 2012).

 Marijuana is the most commonly abused illicit drug at all ages.

Marijuana use among teens rose in 2011 for the fourth straight year—a sharp contrast to the considerable decline that had occurred in the preceding decade. Daily marijuana use currently exceeds daily alcohol use among high school students and is at a 30-year peak level among high school seniors (Johnston et al., 2012).

Overall, marijuana is the most prevalent illegal drug detected in impaired drivers, fatally injured drivers, and motor vehicle crash victims (DrugFacts: What Is Drugged Driving?, 2010). Each day thousands of new driver's licenses are issued to 16- and 17-year-olds nationwide, the very same age group at greatest risk for marijuana use. It is a disturbing fact that one in five (19.9%) teen drivers reports having driven under the influence of marijuana, and more than one-third (36%) of these teens believe the drug presents no distraction to their driving ("Hazy Logic," 2012).

In fact, marijuana influence is significantly more prevalent among teen drivers than alcohol, as compared to the 13 percent of teens surveyed who report that they have driven after drinking.

Marijuana has often been considered a gateway to drug abuse and addiction, and many drug policies are structured around such a **gateway theory**—that use of milder drugs leads to experimentation with and, consequently, addiction to harder drugs.

Critics of the gateway theory assert that most drug users begin using drugs in their teens or young adult years and suggest that most people who try any drug, even heroin, use it only experimentally or continue use moderately and without ill effects. Research aimed at shedding light on the veracity of this theory is limited, but what evidence does exist suggests that the "gateway" pattern is more likely the product of combined common influences and variables such as drug availability, favorable attitudes toward drug use, and the involvement of friends in drug use than it is indicative of causal effects of specific earlier drug use that promote progression to "harder" drugs (Degenhardt et al., 2010). The policy implications of such findings are that any efforts to prevent use of specific "gateway" drugs may not, in themselves, successfully reduce the use of later drugs. Nonetheless, marijuana retains its "gateway" status not because it *will* inevitably lead to addiction but that it *can* lead to addiction (Caulkins et al., 2005).

The results of the November 2012 election, in which voters in two states won their bid to legalize the recreational use of marijuana, present an interesting dilemma, as the federal government continues to regard the drug, even for medical use, as an illegal substance. A relatively new threat is the emergence of synthentic marijuana, also called spice, K2, or fake weed ("DrugFacts: Spice," 2012). Resembling potpourri and often marketed as "natural herbal incense," synthetic marijuana is a mixture of herbs and spices that is typically sprayed with JWH-018, a synthetic compound chemically similar to tetrahydrocannabinol, or THC, the psychoactive ingredient in marijuana. Spice has become increasingly popular among youth, in part because it is easily available and relatively inexpensive. In fact, synthetic marijuana was added to the *MTF* survey in 2011 and was found to be the second most commonly used illicit drug by 12th graders, after natural marijuana (Johnston et al., 2012).

Another reason for spice's growing popularity is the misperception that its "natural" ingredients make this drug harmless. However, across the country, incidents in emergency rooms and calls to police tell a different story, with statistics indicating that emergency room visits nationwide due to synthetic marijuana use went from 13 in 2009 to more than 500 in the first half of 2010 alone (Macher, Burke, and Owen, 2012). In March 2011 the Drug Enforcement Administration (DEA) placed JWH-018 and four other similar compounds used to make synthetic marijuana into Schedule I of the Controlled Substances Act amidst concern over the chemicals' potential for harm, abuse, and addiction and their lack of accepted medical use. Designation as a Schedule I controlled substance makes spice illegal to sell, buy, or possess. Canada, Britain, Germany, France, and Poland have also banned synthetic marijuana (Macher, Burke, and Owen, 2012).

gateway theory
Teaches that milder illicit drugs—such as marijuana—lead directly to experimentation with and an addiction to hard drugs such as crack cocaine and heroin.

The Methamphetamine Problem

Methamphetamine (meth) has become a significant problem across the country. The 2010 NSDUH (SAMHSA, 2011b) reveals that the number of new meth users aged 12 and older (referred to in the literature as *initiates*) was an estimated 105,000 in 2010. Although this estimate is significantly lower than the initiate estimate in 2007 (157,000) and only about one-third of the initiate estimate in 2002 (299,000), the number of active meth users remains higher, as approximately 353,000 (SAMHSA, 2011b). According to the *National Drug Threat Assessment 2011* (32):

> High levels of production in Mexico along with an increase in the number of domestic manufacturing operations have combined to make methamphetamine readily available throughout the United States. Methamphetamine production in Mexico is robust and stable, as evidenced by recent law enforcement reporting, laboratory seizure data, an increasing flow from Mexico, and a sustained upward trend in Mexican methamphetamine availability in U.S. markets. Law enforcement and intelligence reporting, as well as seizure, price, and purity data, indicate that the availability of methamphetamine in general is increasing in markets in every region of the country.

Methamphetamine (meth) abuse is concentrated in certain parts of the United States. Hawaii, California, Arizona, and Montana all have high methamphetamine abuse problems, while the states in the eastern part of the United States have lower use of methamphetamine ("Methamphetamine Use Estimated to Cost the U.S. about $23 Billion in 2005," 2009). Methamphetamine has also become a serious problem for Native American communities. According to a survey of 150 Native American law enforcement agencies nationwide by the Bureau of Indian Affairs, 74 percent of the respondents said methamphetamine is the greatest threat on reservations. Only 11 percent thought marijuana was the greatest threat. Crack cocaine and powder cocaine, heroin, and pharmaceutical drugs all claimed small percentages (*National Methamphetamine Initiative Survey*, 2006). On some rural Indian reservations, meth abuse rates have reached an estimated 30 percent, and in some Indian communities nearly two-thirds of all documented child abuse and neglect cases involve parental involvement with methamphetamine (Van Dam, 2012).

The Combat Methamphetamine Epidemic Act, enacted in 2006, put tough restrictions on the sale of the chemical precursors used to manufacture methamphetamine. In 2007 the Methamphetamine Remediation Research Act was passed to assist state and local governments in the environmentally sound cleanup of illegal methamphetamine "labs" shut down by law enforcement. It calls for establishing voluntary guidelines to remediate former labs, establishes a research program to develop new meth detections, and mandates research on the effects of exposure to meth labs on first responders (Greene, 2008, 6).

After a 34-percent drop in lab seizures in 2007, domestic methamphetamine production began increasing again in 2008. Although nowhere near the peak years of 2003 and 2004, when 10,249 labs were seized, the first ten and a half months of 2008 (from January 1 through November 13) saw the seizure of 2,584 labs. According to the National Drug Intelligence Center (NDIC), the increase is primarily due to a rise in small-capacity labs, many of which circumvent the precursor restriction laws by a technique called "smurfing." A smurfing operation consists of a group of individuals—documented sizes have ranged from 30 to 100 individuals—who travel throughout a region using multiple false identifications to purchase large quantities of the access-restricted ingredients need to manufacture meth, including pseudoephedrine (*National Drug Threat Assessment 2011*).

Underage Drinking

According to the NSDUH, there were an estimated 10.0 million underage (aged 12 to 20) drinkers in the United States in 2010 (SAMHSA, 2011b). Despite the fact that it is illegal for all secondary school students and most college students to purchase alcoholic beverages, surveys indicate they have considerable experience with alcohol—33 percent of 8th graders, 56 percent of 10th graders, 70 percent of 12th graders, and 81 percent of college students, many of whom are under 21 years old, have tried alcohol (Johnston et al., 2012).

The University of Maryland's Center for Substance Abuse Research reports that 47 percent of youths who began drinking before age 14 were alcohol dependent at some point in their lifetime, compared to just 9 percent of those who began drinking after age 20. According to another study, individuals who become alcohol dependent before age 25 are less likely to seek treatment than those who become alcohol dependent after age 30 ("Study Underscores Need to Address Early Onset of Alcohol Dependency," 2006).

A growing concern is **binge drinking**, or having five or more drinks in a row at least once in the past 2 weeks. In 2011 this type of occasional heavy drinking was reported by 6 percent of 8th graders, 15 percent of 10th graders, 22 percent of 12th graders, and 36 percent of college students (Johnston et al., 2012). The NSDUH reports an estimated 6.5 million underage binge drinkers in 2010 (SAMHSA, 2011b). Heavy drinking peaks in the early 20s and recedes with age after that.

binge drinking
Five or more drinks in a row during the previous 2 weeks.

The Cost of Substance Abuse

The Office of National Drug Control Policy (ONDCP) estimates the cost of illicit drug use in the United States to be $193 billion, a cost that includes the use of resources to address health and crime consequences as well as the lost productivity from disability, death, and withdrawal from the work force (*National Drug Control Strategy*, 2012).

In 2009 the Rand Corporation issued results of a study that examined the cost of the methamphetamine problem alone in the United States. According to the study, which was commissioned by the Meth Project Foundation with support from the National Institute on Drug Abuse, the cost of the meth problem in 2005 was about $23.4 billion, a figure that included the "burden of addiction," drug treatment costs, premature death (900 premature deaths among users in 2005), resulting crime, costs of arresting and incarcerating drug offenders, lost productivity, expense of removing children from homes of methamphetamine users and paying for foster care, cost resulting from the production of methamphetamine (fires, explosions, etc.) and the injuries to emergency personnel and other victims, and the cost of cleaning up the hazardous waste resulting from the production process ("Methamphetamine Use Estimated to Cost," 2009).

There is no doubt drug use exacts an increasingly high toll on communities throughout the United States, despite efforts to legislate the problem. Laws aimed at curbing drug use, abuse, and related crime are nothing new. In fact, the United States is approaching the century mark regarding its first official attempt at controlling drug use through law.

THE "WAR ON DRUGS" AND THE NATIONAL DRUG CONTROL STRATEGY

In 1914 the Harrison Act made buying, selling, or using certain drugs illegal. Initially, trafficking in and/or using illicit drugs did not receive much attention. Then in 1973 President Nixon declared "war" on drugs. Since that time, federal spending on this war against drug smugglers, users, and sellers has increased more than 60-fold—from $420 million in 1973 to $26.2 billion in 2012 (*National Drug Control Budget—FY 2012 Funding Highlights*, 2012). Drug arrests have nearly tripled since 1980, when the federal drug policy shifted to arresting and incarcerating users, and in 2010, an estimated 1,638,846 arrests were made for drug abuse violations (*Crime in the United States*, 2010).

The White House Office of National Drug Control Policy (ONDCP), a component of the Executive Office of the President, was established by the Anti-Drug Abuse Act of 1988. The principal purpose of ONDCP is to establish policies, priorities, and objectives for the nation's drug control program. The goals of the program are to reduce illicit drug use, manufacturing, and trafficking; drug-related crime and violence; and drug-related health consequences. To achieve these goals, the director of ONDCP is charged with producing the National Drug Control Strategy, a strategy that directs the nation's antidrug efforts and establishes a program, a budget, and guidelines for cooperation among federal, state, and local entities.

By law, the Director of ONDCP also evaluates, coordinates, and oversees both the international and domestic antidrug efforts of executive branch agencies and ensures that such efforts sustain and complement state and local antidrug activities. The director advises the president regarding changes in the organization, management, budgeting, and personnel of federal agencies that could affect the nation's antidrug efforts, and regarding federal agency compliance with their obligations under the strategy.

Since the first national drug control strategy was published in 1989, variation has been seen in the strategy's goals. The initial strategy focused on reducing the overall level of drug use as well as reducing initiation and use at every level of intensity from casual use to total addiction. Other official objectives have included reduction in hospital emergency room drug-associated admissions, in the import availability and the domestic production of drugs, and in adolescents' approval of drug use. During the 1990s the goals were simplified to reducing drug use and drug-related consequences (Caulkins et al., 2005).

The three core components of the national drug control strategy are (1) stopping drug use before it starts—prevention, (2) healing America's drug users—treatment, and (3) disrupting the market—law enforcement efforts.

The *2012 National Drug Control Strategy* aims to reduce drug use and its consequences through innovative and evidence-based public health and safety approaches. The new *Strategy* outlines 113 specific action items to be undertaken throughout the federal government to reform U.S. drug policy, with the overall *Strategy* being guided by three facts: addiction is a disease that can be treated; people with substance-use disorders can recover; and innovative new criminal justice reforms can stop the revolving door of drug use, crime, incarceration, and rearrest ("Obama Administration Releases 21st-Century Drug Policy Strategy," 2012). Director of the ONDCP, Gil Kerlikowski, stated: "Outdated policies like the mass incarceration of nonviolent drug offenders are relics of the past that ignore the need for a balanced public health and safety approach to our drug problem. The policy alternatives contained in our new *Strategy* support mainstream reforms based on the proven facts that drug addiction is a disease of the brain that can be prevented and treated and that we cannot simply arrest our way out of the drug problem" ("Obama Administration Releases 21st-Century Drug Policy Strategy," 2012).

The administration's Synthetic Drug Control Strategy is a companion to the national strategy, focusing on methamphetamine and prescription drug abuse. It follows the main principles set out in the national strategy: that supply and demand are the ultimate drivers in all illicit drug markets and that a balanced approach incorporating prevention, treatment, and market disruption initiatives is the best way to reduce the supply of, and demand for, illicit drugs (*Synthetic Drug Control Strategy,* 2006). In June 2012 Congress passed S. 3187 which will classify 26 synthetic chemicals, including those used to make spice and bath salts, as Schedule I substances. Substances classified as Schedule I have a high potential for abuse, no medical use in the United States, and lack acceptable safety levels for use.

The first core principle, stopping drug use before it starts, stresses education and benefits from community policing efforts.

PREVENTION: STOPPING DRUG USE BEFORE IT STARTS

Prevention has been a focus of the National Drug Control Strategy since its inception. However, the FY 2012 budget designates only 6.4 percent of the $26.2 billion total to prevention.

Despite the Supreme Court's approval, most public schools do not randomly test youths involved in extracurricular activities. In 2005, the most recently available data, only 55 of the country's 14,000 school districts received financing for drug testing programs. These 55 districts oversee only 152 of the country's 23,000 public high schools (Katel, 2006).

"Myth vs. Fact" (2007) states that it is a myth that random drug testing of qualifying students is unnecessary if a school already has a policy of testing students based on reasonable suspicion of drug use. The fact is: "Testing based on reasonable suspicion is designed to confirm drug-using behavior, rather than deter it.... The goal of random student drug testing (RSDT) is to prevent drug use and to halt the pipeline to addiction by identifying students in the early stages of drug use, before use becomes readily apparent or a dependency begins."

The DARE Program

One key to preventing drug use is education. Probably the most evaluated program is DARE— the Drug Awareness Resistance Education program developed in Los Angeles in 1983. A report on DARE issued by the government's General Accounting Office in the early 2000s concluded that the program had no statistically significant long-term preventive effect on youths' attitudes toward illicit drug use when compared to children who had not been exposed to the program. In 2001 the U.S. Surgeon General categorized it as an "ineffective program."

Based on the shortcomings of the DARE program revealed by extensive research, the curriculum has been completely revised thanks to a $15-million research grant given to the University of Akron by the Robert Wood Johnson Foundation, the largest health philanthropic organization in the world. The new curriculum is undergoing extensive evaluation, and the results are not yet available.

A Reality-Based Approach to Drug Education

Many programs use the terms *drug use* and *drug abuse* interchangeably, but teenagers know there is a difference. The gateway theory, a drug education mainstay, argues that using marijuana leads to using "harder" drugs, but there is no evidence of this. Again, teenagers believe they are being told "untruths."

The Safety First reality-based alternative rests on three assumptions: (1) teenagers can make responsible decisions if given honest, science-based drug education; (2) total abstinence may not be a realistic alternative for all teenagers; and (3) use of mind-altering substances does not necessarily constitute abuse.

Life Skills Training

Another approach to preventing substance abuse is to provide students with skills needed to avoid drugs: "Programs that teach middle-school students how to resist peer pressure, to become more assertive, and to make better decisions are the most successful kind of drug use prevention programs in schools" ("Best School Drug Prevention Programs Teach Life Skills, Studies Find," 2005). One such program is LifeSkills Training (LST), a research-validated substance abuse program proven to reduce the risks of alcohol, tobacco, and drug abuse and violence. The program reports that students completing the program have cut marijuana use by 75 percent and alcohol use by up to 60 percent. Rather than simply teaching information about drugs, the LifeSkills program consists of three major components covering critical skills dealing with drug resistance, personal self-management and general social competencies that make it less likely that students will engage in a wide variety of high-risk behaviors ("Botvin's Life Skills Training," 2010).

LifeSkills Training has been cited for prevention excellence by the National Institute on Drug Abuse, the White House Office of National Drug Control Policy, the U.S. Department of Education, the American Medical Association, the Centers for Disease Control and Prevention, the Center for Substance Abuse Prevention, Blueprints for Violence Prevention, the Coalition for Evidence-Based Policy, and the U.S. Department of Justice's Office of Juvenile Justice and Delinquency Prevention.

When prevention efforts fail, other strategies come into play.

TREATMENT: HEALING AMERICA'S
DRUG USERS

In 2010 an estimated 22.1 million persons aged 12 or older had been classified with substance dependence or abuse over the past year (8.7% of the population aged 12 or older). Of those, 2.9 million were classified with dependence or abuse of both alcohol and illicit drugs, 4.2 million had dependence or abuse of illicit drugs but not alcohol, and 15.0 million had dependence or abuse of alcohol but not illicit drugs (SAMHSA, 2011b).

The government's willingness to spend billions of dollars attacking the drug supply, many critics argue, is a costly and ineffective approach to the drug war; the focus, instead, should be on funding drug *treatment* programs (Katel, 2006). The National Drug Control Budget for FY 2012 designates $8,982,100, or 34.3 percent of the total budget, to treatment—significantly more than is allocated for prevention yet less than the 36.3 percent apportioned for domestic law enforcement efforts (*The National Drug Control Budget—FY 2012 Funding Highlights*, 2012).

Empirical evidence supports the argument that substance abuse treatment is a sound public investment. For example, one study reported a 7:1 cost offset, meaning that every dollar spent on treatment yielded an average of seven dollars in costs savings, mostly through reduced criminal justice system involvement and increased employment earnings by users who were successfully treated (*National Drug Control Strategy*, 2012). Another study found that substance abuse treatment was associated with a net savings of $2,500 per person per year in Medicaid costs. A study by the State of Washington found that drug abuse treatment yielded an estimated $252 per person per month in cost reductions associated with medical care and state and community psychiatric hospitalizations (*National Drug Control Strategy*, 2012).

Effective treatment of drug abusers can also produce significant reductions in the number of offenders cycling through the criminal justice system: "Far too many offenders return to drug use and reenter the criminal justice system. Among state prisoners with substance use disorders, 53 percent had at least three prior sentences to probation or incarceration, compared to 32 percent of other inmates. Drug dependent or abusing state prisoners (48%) were also more likely than other inmates (37%) to have been on probation or parole supervision at the time of their arrest" (*National Drug Control Strategy*, 2012, 19).

In 2010, 4.1 million persons aged 12 or older (1.6% of the population) received substance abuse treatment (SAMHSA, 2011b). Among those, 1.7 million were treated at a rehabilitation facility as an outpatient, 1.0 million received outpatient treatment at a mental health center, 2.3 million received treatment at a self-help group, 1.0 million received treatment at a rehabilitation facility as an inpatient, 731,000 were treated at a hospital as an inpatient, 653,000 were treated at a private doctor's office, 467,000 received treatment at an emergency room, and 342,000 received treatment at a prison or jail. The total numbers treated exceeds 4.1 million because some people received treatment at more than one type of facility. None of these estimates changed significantly between 2009 and 2010 or between 2002 and 2010 (SAMHSA, 2011b).

A one-day snapshot of people in drug treatment is provided by the *National Survey of Substance Abuse Treatment Services* (N-SSATS), which reports there were 1,175,462 clients receiving substance abuse treatment in facilities across the nation on March 31, 2010, a rate of 462 clients per 100,000 population aged 18 and over (SAMHSA, 2011a). The rate was highest for persons with both alcohol and drug abuse (194 per 100,000 population), followed by drug abuse only (182 per 100,000 population) and alcohol abuse only (86 per 100,000 population). In 2010, during their most recent treatment in the past year, 2.6 million persons aged 12 or older reported receiving treatment for alcohol use, and 1.0 million persons reported receiving treatment for marijuana use (SAMHSA, 2011b). Estimates on receiving treatment for the use of other drugs were 754,000 persons for pain relievers, 699,000 for cocaine, 417,000 for heroin, 350,000 for tranquilizers, 343,000 for stimulants, and 333,000 for hallucinogens (SAMHSA, 2011b).

In light of the fact that a high number of defendants entering (and re-entering) the juvenile and criminal justice systems have as their only offense drug possession, drug courts have become an increasingly popular alternative for processing these offenders, the goal being to connect these substance abusers with the treatment needed to keep them from repeated drug use and a return to the justice system. The first drug court, established in 1989 in Miami, Florida, to handle adult drug offenders, had the multiple goals of reducing substance abuse and the related criminal behavior while freeing up the criminal court and corrections to handle other more serious nondrug-related cases (Myers, 2007). The popularity of drug courts, combined with promising research results, led to the application of drug court principles in juvenile drug cases. The philosophy behind the creation of juvenile drug courts is that children and adolescents are different from adults and that the root causes of drug use among young people are found in developmental and family-based risk factors (Myers, 2007).

The ONDCP reports there are more than 2,500 drug courts operating in the United States (*Drug Courts: A Smart Approach to Criminal Justice*, 2011). A growing body of research serves to document the benefits of drug courts in terms of reduced recidivism and cost-effectiveness. Five separate meta-analyses have found that drug courts significantly reduce crime by an average of 8 to 26 percentage points and that well-administered drug courts reduce crime rates by as much as 35 percent, when compared to traditional case dispositions (*Drug Courts*, 2011). Furthermore, a cost-effectiveness analysis conducted by The Urban Institute found that drug courts yielded $2.21 in benefits to the criminal justice system for every $1 invested and that expanding the program to all at-risk arrestees raises the average return on investment to $3.36 for every $1 spent (*Drug Courts*, 2011).

Drug courts are even more effective when partnered with law enforcement, as stressed by the ONDCP (*Drug Courts*, 2011, 3-4):

> A strong partnership with local law enforcement is a critical component of a successful drug court. Street-level enforcement officers provide a unique perspective and benefit to drug court teams. Law enforcement can improve referrals to the court and extend the connection of the drug court team into the community for further information gathering and monitoring of participants. Law enforcement personnel play important roles not only in the day-to-day operations of the drug court, but also in showing other government and community leaders the public safety efficacy of these courts.

A comprehensive study of the key attributes of successful drug courts reinforces the importance of this relationship. In the 18 adult drug courts studied, researchers found that:

> » Having a member from law enforcement on the team was associated with higher graduation rates, compared to teams without a law enforcement member (57% versus 46%).

> » Drug court teams that included law enforcement personnel reduced costs an additional 36 percent over the reductions achieved by traditional drug courts.

LAW ENFORCEMENT: DISRUPTING THE MARKET

A comprehensive approach to the drug problem includes not only prevention and treatment but also efforts at stopping drug sale and use, the third core component of the national drug control strategy.

 Law enforcement strategies to deal with the drug problem include drug raids, surveillance, undercover operations, arresting sellers and buyers, and improving intelligence.

Drug Raids

During the 1980s, drug raids made frequent headlines. Tank-like vehicles, SWAT teams, and sophisticated weaponry all have been involved in drug raids, which can be highly successful when used properly.

An Internet search of *drug raid* produced nearly 25 million results, highlighting the magnitude of the drug problem in our society. Many of the search results were newspaper stories of such raids carried out in communities across the country. For example, a two-day raid across the New York metro area in June 2012 netted 98 people, including 3 medical practitioners, involved in the illegal sale of prescription painkillers (Mian, 2012). In another June 2012 raid, DEA agents raided a home in Olathe, Kansas, as part of a federal sweep to extinguish a marijuana ring that spanned from the heartland of America to California. The alleged drug dealer lived in the home with his wife and two children (Townsend, 2012). Hundreds more such stories exist, illustrating how the drug market permeates neighborhoods of all sizes and often involves persons regarded as "upstanding" members of the community.

Surveillance

The purpose of surveillance is to gather information about people and their activities and associates that may help solve a crime. Surveillance can be designed to serve several functions, including gathering information required for building a criminal complaint, verifying a witness's statement about a crime, gaining information required for obtaining a search or arrest warrant, identifying a suspect's associates, observing criminal activities in progress, apprehending a criminal in the act of committing a crime, and making a legal arrest.

A common type of surveillance is the stakeout, a stationary surveillance in which officers set up an observation post and monitor it continuously. Other types of surveillance include aerial surveillance and audio surveillance, wiretapping, video surveillance, and a host of rapidly developing technologies. Before a judge will approve an application for electronic surveillance, those requesting it must show why surveillance is necessary—for example, standard techniques have been tried and have failed.

Previous editions of this text noted how GPS was increasingly being used as a surveillance tool to catch not only drug dealers but also thieves, robbers, sexual predators, and killers, often without a warrant or court order. After all, it is easy for police to attach a GPS device to a car without the driver ever knowing about it. However, the unsanctioned ability of police to use this method of surveillance was brought to a halt in *United States v. Jones* (2012), when the Supreme Court held that using a GPS device to surveil a person constituted a search within the meaning of the Fourth Amendment and, as such, required a warrant. In *Jones*, federal investigators surreptitiously attached a GPS device to suspected drug trafficker Jones's vehicle as a way to monitor the vehicle's movements on public streets. Although a warrant had been obtained, the device was used beyond the approved scope of the warrant. (The warrant authorized installation of the GPS device in the District of Columbia and within 10 days, but agents installed it on the 11th day and in Maryland, and then proceeded to track the vehicle for 28 days.) Investigators used the GPS data to have Jones indicted for drug trafficking conspiracy, and Jones was convicted in the district court, which ruled that the defendant held no expectation of privacy while driving on public streets. Jones appealed, and the DC circuit court reversed, concluding that the warrantless use of the GPS device did, in fact, violate the Fourth Amendment. The U.S. Supreme Court affirmed, with Justice Scalia delivering the opinion of the Court:

> The Fourth Amendment provides in relevant part that, "The right of the people to be secure in their persons, houses, papers, and effects, against unreasonable searches and seizures, shall not be violated." It is beyond dispute that a vehicle is an "effect" as that term is used in the Amendment. ... We hold that the Government's installation of a GPS device on a target's vehicle, and its use of that device to monitor the vehicle's movements, constitutes a "search."

> It is important to be clear about what occurred in this case: The Government physically occupied private property for the purpose of obtaining information. We have no doubt that such a physical intrusion would have been considered a "search" within the meaning of the Fourth Amendment when it was adopted.

This ruling does not mean police cannot use GPS in their investigations, but it does make clear the need for officers to obtain a warrant before applying such surveillance technology. Indeed, a 2011 Police Executive Research Forum (PERF) survey found that most of responding law enforcement agencies (83%) use global positioning system (GPS) technology to track the movements of criminal suspects ("PERF Survey Shows Widespread Use," 2012).

Undercover Assignments

Most undercover assignments are used to obtain information and evidence about illegal activity when it can be obtained in no other way. *Light cover* involves deception, but the officer usually goes home at the end of the shift. An example is an assignment where an officer poses as a utility worker or repair person to obtain access to a suspect's home. Often an officer poses as a drug addict to make a drug buy, obtaining evidence to make an arrest. *Deep cover* is much more dangerous but can be very effective. In deep cover an officer lives an assumed identity to infiltrate a group or organization. No identification other than the cover identification is carried. Communication with the police department is carefully planned.

Regardless of whether the cover used is light or deep, such work requires a "carefully crafted persona and unrelenting self-discipline" (Grossi, 2009, 24). The DEA recommends that undercover officers keep their real first names in case they are greeted by someone on the street who does not know they are working undercover. It is also advisable for UC officers to keep their real birth date so it comes naturally if asked for it.

Some police departments have used *sting operations* during which undercover police agents sell drugs and then arrest those who buy them. These operations have sometimes been criticized as unethical or even an illegal form of entrapment. Police must exercise extreme care if they use such operations as a strategy to reduce the drug problem.

Arresting Dealers

The traditional response to users and sellers has been to arrest them when possible. The current antidrug campaign has increasingly focused on a law enforcement model attacking the supply side (traffickers, smugglers, and users) rather than prevention and treatment (Katel, 2006).

Most law enforcement agencies focus efforts on enforcing laws against dealing drugs and increasing prosecution of drug dealers. In addition to being concerned with those who deal in drugs, police officers need to be prepared to manage those who use them.

Arresting Drug Users

Arresting users is not without its critics. Hubert Williams, former president of the Police Foundation, suggests: "If we want to use the standard of the number of people we arrest—about 1.7 million people get busted every year—these numbers deal [only] with quantity, not quality. We're busting people for use—not trafficking. We need a new strategy that doesn't focus on the ghetto and the inner city … [one] that brings together intelligence and analyses on the big gangs" (Katel, 2006). Efforts to address the gang problem are the focus of Chapter 13.

Improving Intelligence

If police can enlist citizens to provide information about drug dealing to the police, much can be accomplished. Most public housing residents know where drug deals are made. Many also believe, however, that the police either do not care or are actually corrupt because they arrest few dealers. When dealers are arrested, they are often back on the street within hours. Residents should be educated about the difficulties of prosecuting drug dealers and the need for evidence.

Some departments conduct *community surveys* in low-income neighborhoods to learn about how residents view the drug problem. Some departments have established tip lines where residents can provide information anonymously.

Improved reporting can be accomplished in a number of ways, and intelligence can be increased by unusual procedures. Police have been known to interview arrestees to obtain inside information on how certain criminal activities are conducted. In some agencies, arrestees have been interviewed in jail with a jail debriefing form. This information is useful as police continue to document the link between drugs and criminal activity.

Intelligence information can also be improved by facilitating the communication between narcotics investigators and patrol officers. For example, in Atlanta, Georgia, a narcotics supervisor recognized that patrol and narcotics

Ideas in Practice

CHARLOTTE, NORTH CAROLINA, BELMONT NEIGHBORHOOD VIOLENCE REDUCTION PROJECT

The Belmont Neighborhood Violence Reduction Project was an effort to reduce the violence associated with drug markets in the northeast section of the Belmont neighborhood in Charlotte, North Carolina. The Belmont neighborhood, in the heart of Charlotte's inner city, experienced an increase in violence in 1999. Neighborhood residents contended that many of the people involved in drugs and the associated violent activity did not live in the Belmont neighborhood. A preliminary review of offense reports showed that many of the victims of violent crime did not live there but were traveling through the neighborhood to purchase drugs.

Officers identified all known drug sales markets in the Belmont neighborhood and had them geocoded by crime analysts. Analysts then mapped the addresses of offenders arrested for drug activity in Belmont and found that over 80 percent of the drug arrests in the northeast corner of Belmont were of individuals who did not live in Belmont. Officers assumed that this was due, in large part, to the distinct travel routes through the neighborhood that facilitated drug activity.

Officers suggested the installation of traffic barriers on two Belmont streets, Umstead and Parson, at their intersection with Kennon Street. The barricades would be strategically located in the northeast corner of the neighborhood, an area associated with its greatest density of crime and drug arrests over an extended period of time. Officers felt that disrupting the easy access to the drug markets would reduce the number of people coming into the area specifically to buy drugs, consequently reducing the associated violence. Officers partnered with the City Department of Transportation to install the barricades and worked extensively with neighborhood residents to gain acceptance for the barricades to be installed for a trial period.

The overall impact of the barricades, in comparing 5 years of prebarricade and postbarricade data, reveals extensive reductions in all categories evaluated: violent crime, crime in general, arrests and drug arrests, violence to victims who live inside Belmont and elsewhere, and drug arrests of offenders who live inside Belmont and elsewhere. An analysis of 5 years of before-and-after data shows that violent crime in the study area decreased by 46 percent, overall arrests decreased by 51.8 percent, and arrests for violence decreased by 57 percent. The data demonstrate that the environmental change associated with the barricades was the variable responsible for the decrease in violent crime and overall crime. The 48-percent decrease in violence to victims living outside the Belmont neighborhood and the reduction in drug arrests for individuals living outside the neighborhood suggest that the barricades achieved the desired effect of closing drug markets by disrupting the external traffic flow through the area.

When considered as a whole, it is clear that the installation of the barricades was an appropriate response to a chronic drug and violence problem in the Belmont community.

This project illustrates the Charlotte–Mecklenburg Police Department's willingness to partner with neighborhoods in finding mutually acceptable solutions to their concerns. It also demonstrates the extensive use of data to assess the quality of the results of our problem-solving efforts.

Source: Charlotte, NC, Police Department. Reprinted by permission.

had historically used a different radio frequency and were unable to communicate. The problem was quickly corrected.

Combating Street-Level Narcotics Sales

Citizens know where drug dealing is taking place. If they can be encouraged to report these locations, police can concentrate their efforts on locations receiving the most complaints. Often police officers want to go higher than the street pusher, but they should avoid this temptation. If information regarding someone higher up is obtained, it should be given to the narcotics unit for follow-up. The main purpose of the street-level raids is to respond to citizen complaints and to let them see their complaints being acted on—that is, arrests being made. Officers should know where to search a person being detained on suspicion of possession of drugs. The variety of hiding places for illegal drugs is limited only by the violators' ingenuity. Common hiding places include body orifices, boots, chewing gum packages, cigarettes, coat linings, cuffs, false heels, hair, hatbands, inside ties, lighters, pants, pens and pencils, seams, shoes, shoulder pads, sleeves and waistbands.

Mazerolle, Soole, and Rombouts (2007, 22) summarize the findings from rigorous academic studies evaluating a range of street-level drug law enforcement interventions and conclude: "Police partnerships with a variety of entities (regulators, inspectors, business owners, and local councils) that are community-wide or geographically focused policing approaches to tackling street-level drug market problems are more productive for reducing drug problems than law-enforcement-only approaches focused on hot spots."

Public Housing and the Drug Problem

Various specific strategies have been used to tackle the drug problem in public housing. Often efforts focus on improving the physical environment, limiting entrances, improving lighting, erecting fences, requiring a pass card to gain entrance to the housing, and keeping trash collected.

Another strategy for dealing with the drug problem in public housing projects is for police officers to acquire an understanding of the workings of the local public housing authorities or agencies (PHAs) that manage these complexes. Officers need to work at establishing a relationship with the PHAs and at overcoming the occasional disbelief of management and residents that the police truly want to help. Once this is accomplished, a fact-finding mission should identify key players, provide information about each organization, and determine what programs exist and the participation level.

Next the specific problem and who is impacted should be identified: What drug or drugs are involved? For whom is this a problem—police, residents, housing personnel, the mayor? Does one problem mask another problem? Then a dialogue should be undertaken with key players to enlist support and mobilize the housing project's residents. Next a strategy should be developed, including goals, objectives, and tactics that might be used. The strategy should then be implemented, coordinating all available resources, specifying roles for each key player, and determining a time frame. The final step is to evaluate progress. Was the problem improved or changed?

Addressing Drug Dealing in Privately Owned Apartment Complexes

open drug market

Dealers sell to all potential customers, eliminating only those suspected of being police or some other threat.

Apartment complexes can harbor open or closed drug markets. In an **open drug market**, dealers sell to all potential customers, eliminating only those suspected of being police or some other threat. In a **closed drug market**, dealers sell only to people they know or who are vouched for by other buyers.

closed drug market

Dealers sell only to people they know or who are vouched for by other buyers.

In apartment complexes, open drug markets pose a greater threat than closed drug markets.

Methamphetamine Labs

Methamphetamine (meth) labs have three main dangers associated with them: (1) injury from explosions, fires, chemical burns, and toxic fumes; (2) environmental hazards; and (3) child endangerment (Scott and Dedel, 2006):

Physical Injury from Explosions, Fires, Chemical Burns, and Toxic Fumes

Mixing chemicals in clandestine methamphetamine labs creates substantial risks of explosions, fires, chemical burns, and toxic fume inhalation. Those who mix the chemicals (known as "cooks" or "cookers") and their assistants, emergency responders, hazardous material cleanup crews, neighbors, and future property occupants are all at risk from chemical exposure. The long-term health risks such exposure poses are not yet fully known, but one must assume they are significant (2).

Many lab cooks do not take basic lab safety precautions. Using heat to process chemicals poses a higher risk of explosion, although indirect heat in the processing

A member of the Michigan State Police Methamphetamine Response Team looks over evidence suspected to be meth-making supplies. The items were removed from an apartment within a large apartment complex. Meth labs can pose considerable hazards to neighboring residents as well as to law enforcement agents responding to calls at such locations.

© REX LARSEN/Grand Rapids Press/Landov

area—such as from smoking, electrical switches, or even equipment-generated friction—can also trigger explosions. In addition, police-forced entry into labs can cause explosions—some accidental and some triggered by booby traps set by lab operators. (The published literature commonly reports that lab operators are often well armed, but how many shootings occur during lab seizures is unknown.) Despite a decrease in the number of reported fires and explosions over the past few years, the number of police injured when responding to methamphetamine labs increased during that time. Poor lab ventilation increases the risks both of explosions and of toxic fume inhalation. On the other hand, good ventilation spreads toxic fumes outside, where they put other people at risk. Heating the chemical red phosphorous can create phosphine, a deadly gas (3).

About three to six people working in clandestine U.S. methamphetamine labs die each year from explosions, fires, or toxic fumes. One out of every five or six labs discovered is found because of an explosion or fire. A survey of those who cook methamphetamine revealed one-quarter had experienced a fire while cooking and, in one-fifth of these, no emergency services were called. Those present tended to leave the premises without warning others, which is particularly dangerous in multiunit buildings (4).

Environmental Hazards

Each pound of manufactured methamphetamine produces about 5 to 6 pounds of hazardous waste. Clandestine drug lab operators commonly bury or burn the waste on or near the site, or dump the waste along the road or into streams or rivers. Others pour waste down the drain, place it in household or commercial trash, or store it on the property. Dumping toxic waste into trash cans and commercial dumpsters puts sanitation workers at risk. The water used to put out lab fires can also wash toxic chemicals into sewers. In addition, toxic waste can be transferred from surfaces and equipment onto the body and clothing of those in contact with the lab, and can subsequently contaminate other locations. More research is needed to understand this toxic dumping's long-term environmental effects. Residual contamination of the ground, water supplies, buildings, and furniture may last for years (4).

Child Endangerment

Many jurisdictions are now finding that children are commonly exposed to the hazards of clandestine methamphetamine labs. ... Young children frequently put their hands in their mouths, have higher metabolic and respiratory rates than adults, and have developing central nervous systems, all leaving them vulnerable to harm from inhaling, absorbing, or ingesting toxins from chemicals. About two-thirds of children found at labs seized by police tested positive for toxic levels of chemicals in their bodies. Others suffer burns to their lungs or skin from chemicals or fire. Some have died in explosions and fires. Many are badly neglected or abused by parents suffering from drug abuse's effects. (Senior citizens whose caretakers are lab operators are similarly vulnerable. Pets, including guard dogs, can also be harmed.) When police agencies start targeting labs for investigation and seizure, social service agencies and family courts should be prepared for increased workloads as well (5).

The Center for Problem-Oriented Policing cautions law enforcement agencies that it is critical that responses be tailored to local circumstances and that each response be based on reliable analysis. In most cases, an effective strategy will involve implementing several different responses. Law enforcement responses alone are seldom effective in reducing or solving the problem. The POP Center (www.popcenter.org) publishes a guide for dealing with meth labs.

Combating Prescription Drug Diversion

Teens are turning away from street drugs and using prescription drugs to get high. New users of prescription drugs have caught up with new users of marijuana. These drugs are easy to get and are often free because the youth usually get them from friends or relatives. Teens believe the myth that these drugs provide a medically safe high. However, unintentional overdose deaths involving prescription opioids have quadrupled since 1999 and now outnumber those from heroin and cocaine combined ("Topics in Brief: Prescription Drug Abuse," 2011).

According to the National Institute on Drug Abuse, an estimated 7.0 million people (2.7% of the U.S. population) used psychotherapeutic drugs nonmedically in 2010, an estimate similar to that in 2009 ("Topics in Brief: Prescription Drug Abuse," 2011). This class of drugs is broadly described as those targeting the central nervous system, including drugs used to treat psychiatric disorders. The medications most commonly abused are:

» Pain relievers: 5.1 million users
» Tranquilizers: 2.2 million users
» Stimulants: 1.1 million users
» Sedatives: 0.4 million users

Among adolescents, prescription and over-the-counter medications account for most of the commonly abused illicit drugs by high school seniors. When asked how they obtained prescription narcotics, 70 percent of 12th graders said the drugs were given to them by a friend or relative. The number of students obtaining them over the Internet was negligible ("Topics in Brief: Prescription Drug Abuse," 2011).

Two organizations available to help law enforcement tackle this problem are the RxPATROL (Pattern Analysis Tracking Robberies and Other Losses) and the National Association of Drug Diversion Investigation (NADDI). RxPATROL maintains a national computer database to help law enforcement solve pharmacy robberies, burglaries, and other major crimes committed in health care facilities. NADDI is a nonprofit organization that provides prescription drug abuse education to law enforcement, regulatory agents, and health care professionals.

Strategies to Combat Underage Drinking

Mantel (2006) reports that one in three postsecondary schools now bans alcohol on campus for all students, regardless of age, and more than 40 percent restrict alcohol use at athletic contests, homecoming, tailgate parties, dances, concerts, and other events. Critics say such policies merely drive student drinking off campus. Indeed research data indicates the alcohol crackdowns as practiced

TECHNOLOGY IN COMMUNITY POLICING: IDENTIFYING PHARMACY ROBBERS

In the ever-evolving effort to deal with drug-related crime, law enforcement is now collaborating with different national organizations, drug companies, and partners in their own jurisdiction to develop innovative ways to try to deter potential pharmacy robbers and to catch those who do commit such robberies. One innovative, low-cost technology being used in Long Island, New York, is a DNA tracking system developed by Applied DNA Sciences of Stony Brook. With this technology, a pharmacy employee activates a device that sprays a mist at a suspect as he or she exits the pharmacy after a robbery. The colorless, odorless mist is unnoticeable to the suspect but contains plant DNA that is visible under a special light. The presence of this DNA provides strong physical evidence linking a suspect to a crime scene and, thus, makes convicting a suspect much easier.

Source: Jabeen, Amber. 2012. "Using Technology to Combat Pharmacy Robberies." *Community Policing Dispatch* 5 (4). http://cops.usdoj.gov/html/dispatch/04-2012/technology-andpharmacy-robberies.asp

merely displace the location of drinking without having any effect on the drinking behavior (Mantel, 2006).

Mantel (2006) also suggests that advertisements that include people drinking alcoholic beverages appear to correlate with youths' drinking. Mantel cites a survey that presented statistically significant evidence that youths who saw more alcohol advertising drank more. Others contend that local marketing by bars and liquor stores may have more of an impact on underage drinking.

The City of New Britain, Connecticut, developed a collaborative community response program to combat the underage drinking problem experienced by neighborhoods adjacent to a local university, with complaints ranging from loud, late night parties to fighting; drinking and driving; excessive traffic and speeding; public urination; broken glass; vandalism (littering, public vomit, parking on lawns); blockage of homeowners' driveways by illegally parked cars; drunken students intimidating and disrespecting neighbors; and occupancy issues related to overcrowded apartment units (*Combating Underage Drinking through a Collaborative Community Response Program*, 2009, 3):

> City departments, neighborhood residents, law abiding students, and University officials [had] had increasing difficulty in recent years combating the multiple problems associated with off-campus underage drinking. Underage drinking has led to problem house parties and drinking and driving, in addition to significantly disrupting the local neighborhood surrounding the university. Pervasive underage drinking and associated behaviors have undermined confidence in the police, led to a decline in the quality of life in the neighborhood, and has [con]tributed to the perceived decline in the market value of homes. The intent of the project is to engage the multiple stakeholders in problem solving, to reduce the incidence of aberrant behavior, to promote health and safety by encouraging healthy habits on the part of students, and to restore order in the Belvidere neighborhood surrounding Central Connecticut State University.[1]

---

[1] **Reprinted by permission of the New Britain, CT, Police Department.**

A task force coalition was formed comprised of community stakeholders—residents, students, businesses, the media, campus officials, campus police, and local police—with empowerment from both the Mayor of the City of New Britain and the President of Central Connecticut State University (CCSU). A "mutual aid agreement" was drafted to resolve jurisdictional issues between campus and local police that had previously impeded response efforts, and officers from both departments received updated training and education regarding applicable underage drinking laws and party interdiction tactics. House party patrols and DUI checkpoints increased. Educational resources were distributed to CCSU students regarding high-risk versus low-risk drinking, consistent late-night alternative activities, and consistent, constructive late-night activities were made available as an alternative to off-campus drinking parties. Enforcement efforts were stepped up regarding off-campus student misconduct that posed a threat to the health and safety of others. And a federal grant was obtained to cover police overtime (*Combating Underage Drinking through a Collaborative Community Response Program*, 2009).

The collaborative community response achieved positive results, including a 50-percent decrease in campus judicial misconduct cases; a 10-percent reduction in off-campus vandalism and a 60-percent reduction in on-campus vandalism; a decrease in student binge drinking; a 74-percent reduction in hospitalizations related to alcohol intoxication; and positive feedback from residents confirming the significant improvement in quality-of-life in their neighborhood: "Viewing underage drinking as a 'community problem' has led to an overall enhanced sense of responsibility in the Belvidere neighborhood. Such prevention strategies have . . . lowered [students'] overall 'risk profile,' helping to ensure academic success while promoting health and safety on campus and in the surrounding community. These strategies have also helped restore confidence in government services" (*Combating Underage Drinking through a Collaborative Community Response Program*, 2009, 21).

The Challenge of Rave Parties

rave

A dance party with fast-paced electronic music, light shows, and use of a wide variety of drugs and alcohol.

A **rave** is a dance party with fast-paced electronic music, light shows, and use of a wide variety of drugs and alcohol both to enhance users' sensory perceptions and increase their energy levels. Scott (2004, 1–2) contends:

Dealing appropriately with raves is difficult for police. On the one hand, police often face substantial pressure from mainstream society to put an end to raves, usually through aggressive law enforcement. On the other hand, raves are enormously popular among a significant minority of teenagers and young adults, most of whom are generally law-abiding and responsible. Strict enforcement efforts can alienate a key segment of this population from government in general, and the police in particular. To be sure, raves can pose genuine risks, but those risks are frequently exaggerated in the public's mind. It is important that police recognize that most rave-related harms happen to the ravers themselves, and while ravers are not wholly responsible for those harms, they willingly assume much of the risk for them. Accordingly, rave party problems are at least as much public health problems as they are crime and disorder problems. It is critical that you establish a solid base of facts about rave-related harms in your community, facts from which you can intelligently develop local policies and responses.

The principal rave-related concerns for police are:

> » Drug overdoses and associated medical hazards.
> » Drug trafficking and the potential for violence associated with it.
> » Noise (from rave music, crowds, and traffic).
> » Driving under the influence.
> » Traffic control and parking congestion.

Two general approaches to addressing rave party problems are *prohibition*—strictly enforcing all drug laws and banning raves (either directly or through intensive regulation)—and *harm reduction*—acknowledging that some illegal drug use and raves are inevitable and trying to minimize the harms that can occur to drug users and ravers (Scott, 2004).

 The two general approaches to addressing rave party problems are prohibition and harm reduction.

Many jurisdictions blend enforcement with harm reduction approaches. Whatever approach is adopted should be coherent and consistent. For example, if harm reduction is emphasized, it would be inconsistent to then use rave operators' adoption of harm reduction strategies, such as hiring private emergency medical staff, stocking bottled water, or establishing rest areas ("chill out" areas), as evidence that they are condoning and promoting illicit drug use. Conversely, if a strict drug prohibition approach is used, it would be inconsistent to permit, for example, anonymous drug testing at raves (Scott, 2004). Local public and political attitudes, as well as police policies regarding similar problems, will influence the general stance an agency takes.

LEGISLATION AS A TOOL IN THE WAR ON SUBSTANCE ABUSE

The government has the power to finance the war on drugs by seizing drug traffickers' illegally obtained assets, including cars, weapons, and cash. Among items that have been seized are airplanes, vehicles, radio transmitters with scanners, telephone scramblers, paper shredders, electronic currency counters, assault rifles, and electronic stun guns.

Legislation such as drug abatement statutes is also helping in the war on drugs. Such legislation makes it much easier to shut down crack houses and clandestine drug laboratories. Other legislation is aimed at regulating the sale of cold tablets containing pseudoephedrine, a key ingredient in methamphetamine. Such cold tablets must be locked up, and their sale requires identification and a signature.

In addition to individual counseling approaches that have been demonstrated in numerous experimental studies to reduce alcohol problems, states can play an important role in deterring underage and excessive drinking by passing laws, enforcing compliance, and providing guidance to local communities. Actions states have taken include:

» Enforcement of the legal drinking age of 21 years and laws making it illegal to drive after any drinking if one is under 21 (the law in every state and the District of Columbia).

» Administrative license revocation (the law in 41 states and the District of Columbia).

» Lowering the legal blood alcohol limit to 0.08 percent (the law in every state and the District of Columbia).

» Mandatory screening and treatment of persons convicted of driving under the influence of alcohol (the law in 23 states).

» Primary enforcement of safety belt laws (the law in 32 states and the District of Columbia).

The National Highway Traffic Safety Administration (NHTSA) contends that laws raising the drinking age to 21 led to an immediate decline in crashes of roughly 15 percent, or nearly 1,000 lives saved per year. However, the number of laws, the level of enforcement, and the severity of penalties vary from state to state and, as might be expected, so does the level of drinking. Slightly more than 33 percent of college students binge drink in states with four or more laws restricting promotion and sales of high volumes of alcohol, but in states with fewer laws, the binge-drinking rate was just more than 48 percent (Mantel, 2006).

COLLABORATIVE EFFORTS

Dealing with the substance-abuse problem requires the collaborative efforts of the police, public housing authorities, other agencies, and, most important, the residents themselves.

Empowering Residents

Many police agencies have focused on the broader needs of residents of low-income housing. In Tulsa, Oklahoma, for example, officers believed that limited job opportunities were a problem for youths living in public housing. The officers now steer youths into Job Corps, a training and job service program that is an alternative to the traditional high school. Residents can also be empowered in other ways—for example, by forming associations or holding rallies.

In 2001 a Snohomish County (Washington) deputy introduced Tina Hagget and Susan York to each other. Both lived in neighborhoods plagued by car prowling, speeding, and frenzied traffic associated with drug dealing. The women compared notes and realized the same cars were operating in both neighborhoods, about 5 miles apart. They agreed to partner with law enforcement to stop the drug market in their neighborhood. They learned deputies' names and schedules and contacted them with information, limiting the need to repeatedly explain the problem.

Soon Hagget and York became the unofficial community link between Snohomish County deputies and other neighborhoods struggling against drug crime, sharing their stories, giving advice on what to report to their local authorities, and saving deputies hours of explanations to angry, frustrated residents.

In January 2002 the women attended a Meth Summit sponsored by Snohomish County and volunteered with 10 other citizens and police officers to work on a law enforcement task force exploring options to reduce drug activity in their communities. The result of the task force was Lead On America.

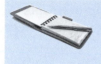 Lead On America is a citizen coalition that helps instruct and mobilize communities to partner with law enforcement throughout the country to combat drug problems.

The group has published a guide that includes a neighborhood activity log in which residents can describe suspicious vehicles and visitors to the suspect drug house, as well as the signs of a drug house. Figure 11.1 illustrates a portion of the log.

Improving the Physical Environment

Improving indoor and exterior lighting has been successfully used in some projects. Cleanup efforts in trash-strewn lots, which provide easy hiding places for drugs, have also been successful. Some housing projects have developed identification cards for their residents so that outsiders can be readily observed. Others have limited access by reducing the number of entrances and exits. Crime prevention through environmental design (CPTED), as described in Chapter 10, is clearly applicable here.

Just as one of the underlying causes of violence in this country is believed to be the ready availability of guns, another cause commonly acknowledged is the ready availability of drugs, and communities across the country are rallying to stop that flow. In Minneapolis, Minnesota, police and property owners are using black and gold "No Trespassing" signs in inner-city neighborhoods. The signs are part of a program intended to improve residents' security and deter street-level drug dealing by telling officers that they can enter the properties to question loiterers without a call from the property owner. This expands the power of the

 Figure 11.1   Neighborhood Activity Log

Neighborhood Activity Log

Never place yourself in any danger trying to gather information. Always call 911 if there is any reason to believe you or someone else is in danger or that there is an in-progress crime being committed.

Date	Start Time	Activity Description	License Number	Vehicle Description	# of Persons	Name or Description of Each Person	End Time	Other	Initial
/ /	: □ AM □ PM						: □ AM □ PM		
/ /	: □ AM □ PM						: □ AM □ PM		
/ /	: □ AM □ PM						: □ AM □ PM		

Source: Cindi Sinnema. "Residents Learn Ways to Best Serve Sheriff's Office in Fight against Meth." *Community Links*, May 2003, 12. Department of Justice.

police greatly and removes from landlords the sometimes-threatening responsibility of signing a citizen's arrest form before the police can act.

The city of St. Paul, Minnesota, also enlisted the aid of residents to forge an alliance to fight drug dealers. The program, called FORCE (Focusing Our Resources on Community Empowerment), centered on getting longtime residents to permit narcotics officers to use their homes to monitor drug sales in the neighborhood. The FORCE team worked with a network of block club leaders to target drug dealers and to force the removal of, or improvements to, ramshackle drug houses. Ramsey County provided child protection services for youths found in drug houses.

Another very successful crime prevention program was developed in Wilson, North Carolina. Their program, "Operation Broken Window," was rooted in the broken window philosophy discussed earlier in this book. One specific block—an open-air drug market widely known as a place where drugs could be easily bought and where undercover police operations had been unsuccessful in reducing the problem—was selected as their "broken window." The Wilson Police Department, using problem-oriented policing as a possible solution, formulated a four-pronged attack: undercover operations; increased uniform police presence with more officers and a satellite police station in the target area; two K-9 units assigned to drug interdiction at the local bus station; and attention to social and environmental conditions. They identified conditions that facilitated drug sales in the target area, cut grass, removed trash, and installed, repaired, or replaced street lights. They inspected buildings for code violations and notified owners to correct the problems. They also boarded up abandoned buildings frequented by drug users. Operation Broken Window was a success. The drug dealers left, and crime rates went down.

In Rialto, California, a successful Operation Clean Sweep was conducted. The department used the SARA model to identify the problem. Their first step was to develop a target list of drug hot spots and dealers. Meetings were held with patrol officers, detectives, and neighborhood-watch groups, which provided valuable, up-to-the-minute insight into activity on the street. This project used small video cameras to record dozens of transactions made by undercover officers in unmarked patrol cars. The drug dealers "sauntered away" after completing their deals, not realizing the drugs they had sold would be taken to the crime lab for evidentiary analysis. The project also involved establishing liaisons with the district attorney and other agencies. Knowing the project would need a multiagency effort to "sweep" those involved in the 89 separate videotaped hand-to-hand narcotics buys, an arrest plan was made including 15 other agencies. For three days these agencies and the California Highway Patrol helped serve arrest warrants.

In Ocean City, Maryland, a swelling tourist population and inexperienced servers and wait staff led to a major problem for the Ocean City Police Department (OCPD). Underage drinking resulted in crime, injury, and even death for vacationing teenagers, and adults served past the point of intoxication were also a concern. The OCPD created Teaching Effective Alcohol Management (TEAM) to educate seasonal servers and wait staff on examining identification and dealing with intoxicated customers. TEAM incorporated the support of a state alcohol service training agency, the county's licensed beverage association, the local high school Students Against Drunk Driving group, and the Hotel–Motel Restaurant Association.

COMPREHENSIVE, COORDINATED COMMUNITY APPROACHES

The Des Moines (Iowa) Police Department has a community involvement handbook, developed jointly by the police department, the United Way, and more than 35 neighborhood groups. The handbook serves as a source of information as well as a guide for action and is intended to help neighborhood groups become active and start making a difference. Called the "municipal approach," the program has four prongs: community involvement, enforcement, prevention/education, and treatment. Portions of the handbook have been translated into Spanish, Vietnamese, Cambodian, and Laotian. The handbook covers topics such as knowing when to call the police; improving street lighting and residential security lighting; removing trash and litter; cutting down shrubbery; working with landlords and businesses in the area; boarding up abandoned houses; forming neighborhood associations; conducting neighborhood block walks, rallies, and marches; occupying parks and streets; and writing newsletters.

The handbook contains an extensive list of suspicious activity and common indicators of residential drug trafficking that could be of much help to communities seeking to tackle this problem (Figure 11.2).

Figure 11.2 Suspicious Activity and Common Indicators of Residential Drug Trafficking

1. A high volume of foot and/or vehicle traffic to and from a residence at late or unusual hours.

2. Periodic visitors who stay at the residence for very brief periods of time.

3. Alterations of property by the tenants, including the following:

   a. Covering windows and patio doors with materials other than curtains or drapes;

   b. Barricading windows or doors;

   c. Placing dead bolt locks on interior doors; and

   d. Disconnecting fire alarms.

4. Consistent payment of rent and security deposits with U.S. currency, especially small denominations of cash. (Large amounts of 20 dollar bills are commonly seized from drug dealers.)

5. The presence of drug paraphernalia in or around the residence, including, but not limited to, glass pipes, syringes, propane torches, paper or tinfoil bundles, folded shiny-slick paper (snow seals), large quantities of plastic baggies, scales, money wrappers and small glass vials.

6. The presence of unusual odors coming from the interior of the residence, especially the odor of pungent chemical substances and/or burning materials.

7. The presence of firearms, other than sporting firearms, including fully automatic weapons, assault weapons, sawed-off shotguns, machine pistols, handguns, and related ammunition and holsters.

8. The presence of a tenant's possessions and furnishings which are inconsistent with the known income level of the tenant. This would include, but is not limited to, the following:

   a. New and/or expensive vehicles;

   b. Expensive jewelry and clothing; and

   c. Expensive household furnishings, stereo systems and other large entertainment systems.

9. Tenants who are overly nervous and apprehensive about the landlord visiting the residence.

Any of the indicators, by itself, may not be reason to suspect drug trafficking. However, when combined with other indicators, they may be reason to suspect drug trafficking. If you suspect drug trafficking in your neighborhood, please contact the police department.

Source: Des Moines Police. *Drugs: A Municipal Approach, A Community Handbook*, p. 26. Reprinted by permission.

This practical guide might serve as a model for other police departments that wish to involve the community in the fight not only against drugs but also against crime and violence.

Groups that can benefit from a partnership with law enforcement include home/school organizations such as parent–teacher associations; neighborhood associations; tenants' groups; fraternal, social, and veterans' groups; community service clubs (such as Lions, Kiwanis, Jaycees, Rotary); religiously affiliated groups; and associations of homeowners, merchants, or taxpayers.

A Drug Problem in New York City

The following description is from the COPS Web site:

> The Clinton Hill neighborhood had tremendous assets: landmark-worthy brownstone houses, an attractive park, nearby commercial strips, and a hardworking, racially diverse population. A local college added a dependable stream of young consumers to the community's economy. Public signs and well-tended gardens indicated the existence of many block associations and of other civic activism.
>
> The residents' commitment to the community was strong, despite the abandoned and poorly kept rental buildings and high levels of car thefts and break-ins, muggings, and drug activity. As drug dealing increased along a commercial corridor, resident anger at apparent police inaction grew. It took a tragedy to catalyze change.
>
> A local convenience-store owner was murdered in his store, and neighborhood block leaders organized a mass meeting to find out what the police were doing. Unfortunately, residents did not think the police were prepared, and the meeting went poorly. As patrol officers stood in the back of the meeting hall, a yelling match ensued between residents and police department spokespeople. Relations between the two groups were at their worst.
>
> Block leaders reached out to the Neighborhood Anti-Crime Center of the Citizens Committee for New York City, due to its reputation for helping citizens and police get together to take back their neighborhoods. The Citizens Committee dedicated a staff organizer's time to helping the community go through a collaborative problem-solving process. A problem-analysis meeting was scheduled.
>
> Block leaders prepared for the meeting by discreetly inviting a small, core group of concerned residents and identifying specific problem locations, offensive conditions, and past efforts to solve the problems. Due to the rancor between residents and police, residents were urged to conduct this first meeting with limited police presence, so that issues could be aired and strategies developed to improve relations.
>
> The meeting itself was the first positive outcome. Residents invited a couple of trusted community-oriented patrol officers, who helped to discern the nature of the problem. The meeting revealed that there were multiple privately owned, and a few city-owned, problem properties housing drug operations and/or addicts. One multifamily structure was identified as a major drug-dealing center, impervious to enforcement action for over two decades. It was a fortified drug house. However, much necessary information remained unknown.

The Citizens Committee trained the residents to conduct property research (identifying landlords), and then linked them up with key guardians: the district attorney's narcotics eviction unit; legal technical assistance; the city's housing agency representative, who could work on drug-infested property; and trusted police narcotics investigators, who had good information about specific locations. The Citizens Committee also designed an inside-building survey form and introduced the resident leaders to a Muslim patrol organization, which was invited to visit problem locations in an effort to get more accurate information about the narcotics trade and landlord–tenant issues.

The resident leaders asked these guardians to join them in a collaborative planning meeting, which the Citizens Committee organizer facilitated. The pieces of the puzzle were now assembled, revealing that the police had never been able to get into the significant locations, especially the fortified one, because the landlords either colluded with the dealers or were unresponsive to police department contacts. A combined enforcement and legal strategy was hatched, and subsequent meetings kept everyone informed and on target with follow-up.

The block leaders committed to continued outreach and pressure on those landlords, such as the city itself, who were poorly managing their buildings but not allied with the dealers. And residents continued to provide information.

District Attorney Charles Hynes's office committed to pressing civil charges against landlords if they failed to secure their property appropriately after notification of problems and/or criminal activity. In addition, the community activists recruited a law firm (pro bono) to discuss whether, if criminal enforcement did not pan out, bringing a civil lawsuit for money damages was the best approach—similar to the Oakland Drug Abatement Institute strategy.

As a direct result of the collaborative analysis and meetings, the police received help from other city code-enforcement agencies to execute a new warrant at the most egregious location. Coordination continued between all parties after the search warrant revealed how extensive the drug-dealing operation was at the vacant, privately owned building.

Community members and police attended a housing court hearing and alerted the judge that the landlord's track record of failing to maintain the building warranted a case disposition that would serve community interests. The Clinton Hills neighborhood won. The judge legally bound the landlord to secure the property and maintain it crime-free, and authorized the police to have keys to the premises and check up on the landlord.

The landlord agreed to comply in court but failed to do so. Residents, the police, and the district attorney took the landlord back to court, where the judge ruled against the landlord and granted the police permanent access to the premises for safety inspections. Illegal activity has never resumed at this vacant, and formerly fortified, building.

The community sought to build on this victory to publicize the value of working with the police and others, and to encourage efforts to clean up remaining problem locations. A media event was organized, celebrating everyone's hard work. The first court win proved to be just the beginning, as more buildings were successfully targeted and block leaders and police communicated more openly and consistently.[2]

Editors' note: The Neighborhood Anti-Crime Center of the Citizens Committee for New York City builds community capacity to tackle neighborhood crime problems. In this case, they helped the community collect information from the police, residents, and government agencies and helped the community through a civil-court process. Closing the property made a huge difference in building the community's capacity to take on other problem buildings. This project offers insight into the citizens' perspective on neighborhood crime problems. Citizens sometimes think that if a highly visible crime problem exists in the neighborhood, the police must be allowing it to grow and fester. They may misconstrue police inability to solve a crime problem as collusion in it. This distrust in police must be addressed and worked through for collaborative work between the community and the police to proceed. Oftentimes, in the initial meeting between the community and the police concerning a particular problem, time must be devoted to airing and discussing the community's distrust.

GRANTS TO ASSIST IN IMPLEMENTING SELECTED STRATEGIES

The numerous federal grants available to law enforcement agencies to fund illegal and dangerous drug prevention and abatement efforts have been reduced in recent years, and future funding of other programs is in question. Yet several grants are still available.

Federal assistance specifically aimed at the drug program is available through the Byrne Justice Assistance Grant, the Drug-Free Communities program, and the Community Oriented Policing program. The Weed and Seed program has been defunded.

The Drug-Free Communities (DFC) Support Program is directed by the White House ONDCP in partnership with the Substance Abuse and Mental Health Services Administration (SAMHSA). In 2011 the ONDCP awarded $12.3 million in new DFC grants to 87 communities and 20 new DFC Mentoring grants across the country. The awards were in addition to nearly $76 million in Continuation grants to 607 already funded DFC coalitions and twelve DFC Mentoring Continuation coalitions. These grants provide community coalitions needed support to prevent and reduce youth substance use ("FY 2011 DFC New and Continuation Grants," 2011).

Before leaving the subject of community policing and substance abuse, it is appropriate to briefly consider the American Dream.

---

[2] Narrative prepared by Felice Kirby of the Citizens Committee for New York City, submitted to Rana Kirby as part of an NIJ-sponsored problem-solving project and reprinted—with minor editorial changes—with Kirby's permission.

CRIME, DRUGS, AND THE AMERICAN DREAM

The American Dream has been described as a national ethos of the United States—an established ideal that through hard work and diligence, success and prosperity, are available to all.

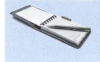 Crime, drugs, and the American Dream are integrally related. In fact, a drug problem may be the result of the American Dream for many people.

Messner and Rosenfeld (2007, x) draw a very distinct correlation between crime and the American Dream: "The American Dream contributes to crime directly by encouraging people to employ illegal means to achieve goals that are culturally approved. It also exerts an indirect effect on crime through its inter-connections with the institutional balance of power in society." They suggest:

> **Conservative crime control** [emphasis added] policies are draped explicitly in the metaphors of war. We have declared war on crime and on drugs, which are presumed to promote crime. Criminals, according to this view, have taken the streets, blocks, and sometimes entire neighborhoods from law-abiding citizens. The function of crime control policy is to recapture the streets from criminals to make them safe for the rest of us (104). …
>
> In contrast to conservative crackdowns on criminals, the **liberal crime control** [emphasis added] approach emphasizes correctional policies and broader social reforms intended to expand opportunities for those "locked out" of the American Dream (107).

conservative crime control

Comes down hard on crime; wages "war" on crime and drugs.

liberal crime control

Emphasizes correctional policies and broader social reforms intended to expand opportunities for those "locked out" of the American Dream; wages "war" on poverty and inequality of opportunity.

 The conservative camp traditionally wages war on crime and drugs; the liberal camp wages war on poverty and inequality of opportunity.

These competing interests need to be considered in any strategies used to combat the drug problem in a given neighborhood or community. Messner and Rosenfeld (2007, 101) suggest that what is needed is crime reduction through social reorganization: "Crime reductions would follow from policies and social changes that vitalize families, schools, and the political system, thereby enhancing the 'drawing power' of the distinctive goals associated with institutions and strengthening their capacity to exercise social control."

A Problem-Solving Partnership in Action—Rocky Pomerance Excellence in Policing Award: Ocala Police Department (Ocala, Florida)

The Rocky Pomerance Law Enforcement Excellence Award—named in honor of the late Rocky Pomerance, former police chief of Miami Beach, Florida, and past president of the International Association of Chiefs of Police, who has been recognized as exemplifying the image of an innovative and visionary leader—provides a mechanism for the Florida Police Chiefs Association to recognize member agencies for developing and implementing an innovative approach to policing. In 2010 the Ocala (Florida) Police Department (OPD) was a recipient of this award for its innovative and effective community policing response to the negative impact of open-air drug markets on the local community. The problem-solving strategy implemented by the OPD was the Drug Market Intervention (DMI) Initiative developed by Professor David Kennedy of the John Jay College of Criminal Justice in New York, which proved an effective response to illegal drug markets and their associated crime, violence, and disorder. The following account of the program is adapted from an article (Taylor, *Rocky Pomerance Excellence in Policing Award*, 2011) posted on the National Network for Safe Communities (NNSC) Web site.

Problem Identification and Analysis

Drug markets both reflect and exacerbate breakdown in community social control characterized by disorder, crime, and fear of crime. In certain neighborhoods in Ocala, drug dealers and drug buyers had taken over the streets, forcing residents to withdraw.

Many community problems, including the most severe problems with violence and disorder, associated with "the drug problem" are a function of drug *markets*, and particular *forms* of drug markets, rather than with drugs as such. These problems included crime hot spots created by street sales and drug houses; unusable public spaces, for example, sidewalks, parks, and stores; enabling markets for prostitutes and drive-through sex buyers, transients whose presence drives out longtime residents; reduced property values; failed or displaced businesses; eased entry into criminality for young people; and facilitated drug use and addiction. Overt drug markets are areas in which a stranger can readily purchase drugs on the street, in drug houses, from apartments, and the like. Typically, overt markets are located in poorer communities and have clearly defined geographical boundaries.

Unfortunately, these overt markets created strong self-sustaining dynamics. Buyers knew that they could buy in a particular area and sellers know that they could sell there; both continued in the same place despite the risks (i.e. arrest, injury, etc.) associated with their illegal behavior. Enforcement and prevention efforts rarely shut down entire markets, which continue to provide attractive venues for new dealers and users returning from jail or prison. The experience of law enforcement is that overt markets, once established, are fiercely resistant to even heavy and sustained attention. Routine drug enforcement is often intrusive with high levels of street stops, vehicle stops, and warrants served on residents, and frequently leads to high levels of arrest, conviction, probation, incarceration, and parole, especially for younger men. In some neighborhoods, a substantial majority of young men end up with criminal records and histories of incarceration or court supervision. Communities frequently resent police practices and the unintended harm that often flows from drug enforcement: criminal records that inhibit people from finishing school, taking entry-level jobs, and pursuing higher education; the sense among young men that arrest and imprisonment are normal or even a rite of passage; parents taken away from the children and families.

Implementation

Rather than focusing on individual drug users and sellers, Drug Market Intervention (DMI) focuses on shutting down drug markets utilizing a multiple-step process:

» **The Identification of Drug Markets:** This was accomplished by mapping drug arrests, Part I crimes, weapons, sexual, and prostitution offenses; reviewing serious crimes within hot spots for a drug connection; and analyzing information from patrol officers, vice/narcotics investigators, informants, and crime tip lines. Six neighborhoods were identified as major overt markets.

» **Identification of Dealers Operating in the Drug Markets:** "Tipping" the market to a closed condition and addressing the small-group/network dynamics that supported offending required identifying and taking out all street-level dealers. To develop the list, vice/narcotics detectives surveyed patrol officers, probation officers, street narcotics officers, and community members; reviewed every arrest report, incident report, and field interview associated with possible dealers; reviewed all known associates; checked suspects' current activities; and generated a list. It was found that only a small number of offenders were driving the problem.

» **Create Deterrence by Banking Cases:** For each drug market, police used ordinary investigative techniques to make cases against each dealer. Undercover officers or confidential informants made buys using digital audio and video surveillance equipment. Volume dealers or violent offenders (those with records of violent or gun crimes, or who were otherwise known to be violent), or those facing a probation or parole revocation or an upcoming court date, were arrested and prosecuted. The cases for low-level dealers without a history of violence were "banked"; that is, taken to the point where a warrant could be signed, and held there. This allowed police to tell dealers that if they continued dealing, they would be arrested immediately and without further investigation, but if they stopped dealing, nothing need happen to them. Banking a case meant that the dealers knew to a certainty ahead of time that they faced whatever inconvenience, expense, and formal penalties their arrests would precipitate. With the charge hanging over their heads, they faced the consequences not just for the single drug transaction (or few drug transactions) for which they could be arrested at the moment, but for *all* transactions they might contemplate while the charge was banked.

» **Identifying "Influentials":** The hope was to enlist those close to the offenders—parents, grandparents, guardians, older members of the communities, ministers, ex-offenders—to create and reinforce positive norms and expectations. The "influentials" were identified in what was, in effect, a parallel investigative phase of the initiative. One or several "influentials" were identified for each dealer—primarily mothers and grandmothers.

» **Organizing Services:** Agencies, volunteer groups, and others that could provide social services and assistance in core areas such as education, housing, employment, food and clothing, drug and alcohol treatment, transportation, and the like were identified and recruited to assist. Resources were reprogrammed, primarily from existing efforts, to support the drug market initiative.

» **Home Visits**—Just weeks prior to the first DMI "Call-In," teams consisting of an Ocala police officer, a service provider, and a respected community leader visited the homes of the identified dealers and their "influentials." They were told that the police had made undercover buys from the dealer; that probable cause existed for an arrest; and that an opportunity to avoid prosecution and an offer of assistance would be discussed at an upcoming meeting that family members and others were encouraged to attend. The offenders received a letter from the police chief inviting them to the meeting with a promise that no one would be arrested that night. Most of these visits went surprisingly well, given the concerns the team had about whether the "influentials" would be receptive to the plan.

» **The Call-In:** The key operational moment in the strategy was the call-in at which law enforcement, community members, and service providers delivered a unified message to dealers in the company of their "influentials." On November 9, 2009, six local drug dealers voluntarily walked into a room amongst a crowd of police and prosecutors, service providers, and community members and were presented with an ultimatum: quit selling drugs or go to prison.

Confronted with photographs, video clips, and binders full of evidence gathered during the course of a long-term undercover operation, the drug dealers were promised they would not be arrested, prosecuted, or jailed if they walked away from the drug dealing life-style. And, if they were willing, job training, educational opportunities, and chemical-dependency treatment would be offered to them. Should they squander the second chance and return to drug dealing anywhere in Marion County, the dealers were told they would feel the full force of the law.

This initiative helped mend broken bridges that existed between law enforcement in Ocala and the community. Law enforcement's willingness not to act on existing cases seemed to make a profound impression on the dealers' families and other community members. Dealers' mothers and families cheered both the community's and law enforcement's messages. Dealers were given an opportunity to immediately meet the service providers following the call-in meeting for the purpose of assessing their various needs and arranging services.

The success of DMI, and ultimately the transformation of neighborhoods in Ocala, rested on the ability to arrange a variety of services, to include drug/alcohol/substance abuse treatment, education, job training, pathways to gainful employment, family counseling, transportation, and ex-offender mentoring. The strategy brings together drug dealers, their families, law enforcement and criminal justice officials, service providers, and community leaders to eliminate overt community drug markets; arrests and prosecutes violent drug dealers; offers non-violent, first-time drug dealers opportunities for education, job training, and other assistance; and establishes clear, predictable, and meaningful consequences for those who return to dealing.

Improvement Process, Results, and Conclusion

After the first year, in one of the six identified drug market neighborhoods, calls for police service dropped 10 percent, police presence increased 104 percent, violent crime decreased 47 percent, and community drug tips increased 16 percent. In another neighborhood, calls for police service dropped 11 percent, police presence increased 62 percent, violent crime decreased 16 percent, and community drug tips increased 40 percent.

The most important benefit of this work is the reconciliation that emerges from the dialogue between the community and police. While numbers are often utilized to gauge change, the true measure of positive change is demonstrated by the "new life" visible in both of these neighborhoods.[3]

SUMMARY

Crime and drugs are clearly linked. The most commonly abused drug at all ages is marijuana. The three core components of the national drug control strategy are (1) stopping drug use before it starts—prevention, (2) healing America's drug users—treatment, and (3) disrupting the market—law enforcement efforts. Law enforcement strategies to deal with the drug problem include drug raids, surveillance, undercover operations, arresting sellers and users, and improving intelligence.

In apartment complexes, open drug markets pose a greater threat than closed drug markets. The two general approaches to addressing rave party problems are prohibition and harm reduction.

One source of assistance is Lead On America, a citizen coalition that helps instruct and mobilize communities to partner with law enforcement throughout the country to combat drug problems. Federal assistance specifically aimed at the drug problem is available through the Byrne Justice Assistance Grant, the Drug-Free Communities program, and the Community Oriented Policing program. The Weed and Seed program has been defunded.

Crime, drugs, and the American Dream are integrally related. In fact, the drug problem may be the result of the American Dream for many people. How to approach the drug problem is often political. The conservative camp traditionally wages war on crime and drugs; the liberal camp wages war on poverty and inequality of opportunity.

---

[3] Reprinted by permission of the Ocala, Florida, Police Department.

DISCUSSION QUESTIONS

1. What do you see as the relationship between drugs and the American Dream?

2. What programs in your community are directed at the drug problem?

3. Which of the programs discussed in this chapter seem most exemplary to you? Why?

4. Explain how lease enforcement reduces criminal activity in public housing.

5. Some rave party strategies used by police have been criticized as racist. Discuss why some law enforcement responses might be considered racist.

6. Did you receive DARE training as a child? What were your impressions? Do you believe it had any effect on your attitudes and actions regarding drugs?

7. Explain the strategy behind improving the physical environment of a neighborhood or apartment complex. What does that have to do with illegal drug activity?

8. What are the three core principles of the National Drug Control Strategy? Which do you believe to be the most effective? The least?

9. Explain the "gateway" theory of drug use. What is your opinion of the theory?

10. What bar marketing promotions are you aware of that encourage irresponsible drinking?

GALE EMERGENCY SERVICES DATABASE ASSIGNMENTS

ONLINE Database

- Use the Gale Emergency Services Database to help answer the Discussion Questions as appropriate.

- Read and outline two articles that address the pros and cons of zero-tolerance policies. Be prepared to share and discuss your outlines with the class.

REFERENCES

"Belmont Neighborhood Violence Reduction Project." 2005 Goldstein Award Finalist. http://www.popcenter.org/library/awards/goldstein/2005/05-04(F).pdf

"Best School Drug Prevention Programs Teach Life Skills, Studies Find." 2005. *Medical Studies/Trials,* April 19.

"Botvin's Life Skills Training." 2010. Waltham, MA: National Center for Mental Health Promotion and Youth Violence Prevention, Education Development Center. http://www.promoteprevent.org/publications/ebi-factsheets/botvins-life-skills-training-lst

Caulkins, Jonathan P., Peter Reuter, Martin Y. Iguchi, and James Chiesa. 2005. *How Goes the "War on Drugs?" An Assessment of U.S. Drug Problems and Policy.* Occasional paper. Santa Monica, CA: The Rand Corporation.

Combating Underage Drinking through a Collaborative Community Response Program. 2009. City of New Britain, CT: Central Connecticut State University (CCSU) Police Department and New Britain Police Department, Herman Goldstein Award Submission. http://www.popcenter.org/library/awards/goldstein/2009/09-32.pdf

Crime in the United States, 2010. 2010. Washington, DC: Federal Bureau of Investigation, Uniform Crime Reports. http://www.fbi.gov/about-us/cjis/ucr/crime-in-the-u.s/2010/crime-in-the-u.s.-2010/persons-arrested

Degenhardt, L., L. Dierker, W. T. Chiu, M. E. Medina-Mora, Y. Neumark, N. Sampson, J. Alonso, M. Angermeyer, J. C. Anthony, R. Bruffaerts, G. de Girolamo, R. de Graaf, O. Gureje, A. N. Karam, S. Kostyuchenko, S. Lee, J. P. Lépine, D. Levinson, Y. Nakamura, J. Posada-Villa, D. Stein, J. E. Wells, and R. C. Kessler. 2010. "Evaluating the Drug Use 'Gateway' Theory Using Cross-National Data: Consistency and Associations of the Order of Initiation of Drug Use among Participants in the WHO World Mental Health Surveys." *Drug and Alcohol Dependence* 108 (1–2): 84–97.

Des Moines (Iowa) Police Department. 1990. *Drugs: A "Municipal Approach."* Des Moines, IA: Des Moines Police Department.

Drug Courts: A Smart Approach to Criminal Justice. 2011 (May). Washington, DC: Office of National Drug Control Policy. http://www.whitehouse.gov/sites/default/files/ondcp/Fact_Sheets/drug_courts_fact_sheet_5-31-11.pdf

"DrugFacts: What Is Drugged Driving?" 2010 (December). Bethesda, MD: National Institutes of Health, National Institute on Drug Abuse. http://www.drugabuse.gov/publications/drugfacts/drugged-driving

"DrugFacts: Spice (Synthetic Marijuana)." 2012 (May). Bethesda, MD: National Institutes of Health, National Institute on Drug Abuse. http://www.drugabuse.gov/publications/drugfacts/spice-synthetic-marijuana

"FY 2011 DFC New and Continuation Grants." 2011. Washington, DC: Office of National Drug Control Policy. http://www.whitehouse.gov/ondcp/fy-2011-new-grants

Greene, Kevin E. 2008. "2007 Legislative Year in Review." *Subject to Debate* 22 (1): 6.

Grossi, Dave. 2009. "Going Under." *Law Officer Magazine* (April): 24–28.

Guerino, Paul, Paige M. Harrison, and William J. Sabol. 2012 (January 9). *Prisoners in 2010.* Washington, DC: Bureau of Justice Statistics. (NCJ 236096)

Han, Beth, Joseph Gfroerer, and James Colliver. 2009 (August). *An Examination of Trends in Illicit Drug Use among Adults Aged 50 to 59 in the United States: An OAS Data Review.* Rockville, MD: U.S. Department of Health and Human Services, Substance Abuse and Mental Health Services Administration, Office of Applied Studies.

"Hazy Logic: Liberty Mutual Insurance/SADD Study Finds Driving under the Influence of Marijuana a Greater

Threat to Teen Drivers Than Alcohol." 2012 (February 22). Press release. *PRNewswire*. http://www.prnewswire.com/news-releases/hazy-logic-liberty-mutual-insurancesadd-study-finds-driving-under-the-influence-of-marijuana-a-greater-threat-to-teen-drivers-than-alcohol-139973393.html

Jabeen, Amber. 2012. "Using Technology to Combat Pharmacy Robberies." *Community Policing Dispatch* 5 (4). http://cops.usdoj.gov/html/dispatch/04-2012/technology-and-pharmacy-robberies.asp

Johnston, Lloyd D., Patrick M. O'Malley, Jerald G. Bachman, and John E. Schulenberg. 2012 (June). *Monitoring the Future: National Survey Results on Drug Use, 1975–2011.* Ann Arbor, MI: The University of Michigan Institute for Social Research.

Katel, Peter. 2006. "War on Drugs." *CQ Researcher Online* 16 (21): 481–504.

Leonhart, Michele. 2008 (October). "Target America: Opening Eyes to the Damage Drugs Cause." Paper presented at the California Science Center, Los Angeles, CA.

Macher, Roland, Tod W. Burke, and Stephen S. Owen. 2012. "Synthetic Marijuana." *FBI Law Enforcement Bulletin* (May): 17–22.

Mantel, Barbara. 2006. "Drinking on Campus." *CQ Researcher* (16): 649–672.

Mazerolle, Lorraine, David W. Soole, and Sacha Rombouts. 2007 (July 22). *Crime Prevention Research Reviews No. 1: Disrupting Street-Level Drug Markets.* Washington, DC: Office of Community Oriented Policing Services.

McCabe, James E. 2008. "What Works in Policing? The Relationship between Drug Enforcement and Serious Crime." *Police Quarterly* 11 (3): 289–314.

Messner, Steven F. and Richard Rosenfeld. 2007. *Crime and the American Dream.* 4th ed. Belmont, CA: Wadsworth Thomson Learning.

"Methamphetamine Use Estimated to Cost the U.S. about $23 Billion in 2005." 2009 (February 4). Press release. Santa Monica, CA: The Rand Corporation.

Mian, Rashed. 2012. "LI Doctors among 98 Arrested in Drug Raid." *Long Island Press.com*, June 6. http://www.longislandpress.com/2012/06/06/li-doctors-among-98-arrested-in-drug-raid

Mumola, Christopher J. and Jenifer C. Karberg. 2007 (January 19). *Drug Use and Dependence, State and Federal Prisoners, 2004.* Special report. Washington, DC: Bureau of Justice Statistics. (NCJ 213530)

Myers, David L. 2007. "Assessing the Implementation and Effectiveness of Juvenile Drug Courts." *Criminal Justice Research Reports* 8 (6): 89–90.

"Myth vs. Fact." 2007. *Strategies for Success: New Pathways to Drug Abuse Prevention* 2 (1): 12.

The National Drug Control Budget—FY 2012 Funding Highlights. 2012. Washington, DC: Office of National Drug Control Policy. http://www.whitehouse.gov/sites/default/files/ondcp/policy-and-research/fy12highlight_exec_sum.pdf

The National Drug Control Strategy, 2012 Annual Report. 2012. Washington, DC: Office of National Drug Control Policy.

National Drug Threat Assessment 2011. 2011 (August). Washington, DC: U.S. Department of Justice, National Drug Intelligence Center.

New Mexico Investigative Support Center. 2006 (April 12). *National Methamphetamine Initiative Survey: The Status of the Methamphetamine Threat and Impact on Indian Lands.* Analysis prepared for the Bureau of Indian Affairs Law Enforcement Services.

"Obama Administration Releases 21st-Century Drug Policy Strategy." 2012 (April 17). Press release. Washington, DC: White House, Office of National Drug Control Policy. http://www.whitehouse.gov/ondcp/news-releases-remarks/obama-administration-releases-21st-century-drug-policy-strategy

"PERF Survey Shows Widespread Use of Many Technologies in Policing." 2012 (January). In *How Are Innovations in Technology Transforming Policing?*, 1–3. Washington, DC: Police Executive Research Forum, Critical Issues in Policing Series.

Scott, Michael S. 2004 (August). *Rave Parties.* Washington, DC: Office of Community Oriented Policing Services, Problem-Oriented Guides for Police, Problem-Specific Guides Series, Guide No. 14.

Scott, Michael S. and Kelly Dedel. 2006. *Clandestine Methamphetamine Labs.* 2nd ed. Washington, DC: Office of Community Oriented Policing Services, Problem-Oriented Guides for Police, Problem-Specific Guides Series, Guide No. 16.

Sinnema, Cindi. 2003. "Residents Learn Ways to Best Serve Sheriff's Office in Fight against Meth" *Community Links* (May): 10–12.

"Study Underscores Need to Address Early Onset of Alcohol Dependency." 2006. *Juvenile Justice*, September 12.

Substance Abuse and Mental Health Services Administration. 2011a (September). *National Survey of Substance Abuse Treatment Services (N-SSATS): 2010. Data on Substance Abuse Treatment Facilities.* Rockville, MD: Substance Abuse and Mental Health Services Administration. DASIS Series S-59, HHS Publication No. (SMA) 11-4665.

Substance Abuse and Mental Health Services Administration. 2011b (September). *Results from the 2010 National Survey on Drug Use and Health: Summary of National Findings.* Rockville, MD: Substance Abuse and Mental Health Services Administration. NSDUH Series H-41, HHS Publication No. (SMA) 11-4658.

Synthetic Drug Control Strategy: A Focus on Methamphetamine and Prescription Drug Abuse. 2006 (May). Washington, DC: Office of National Drug Control Policy.

Taylor, Corey M. 2011 (February 1). *Rocky Pomerance Excellence in Policing Award.* Ocala, FL: Ocala Florida Police Department. http://www.nnscommunities.org/Rocky_Pomerance_Excellence_in_Policing_Award.pdf

"Topics in Brief: Prescription Drug Abuse." 2011 (December). Bethesda, MD: National Institutes of Health, National Institute on Drug Abuse. http://www.drugabuse.gov/publications/topics-in-brief/prescription-drug-abuse

Townsend, Robert. 2012. "Neighbors Stunned by Drug Raid at Olathe Home." *Fox 4 News Kansas City* online, June 13. http://fox4kc.com/2012/06/13/neighbors-stunned-by-drug-raid-at-olathe-home

Van Dam, Andrew. 2012 (June 19). "Meth and Other Drugs Overwhelm Reservations." *Covering Health.* Blog maintained by the Association of Health Care Journalists. http://www.healthjournalism.org/blog/2012/06/page/2

What Americans Need to Know about Marijuana. 2003 (October). Washington, DC: Office of National Drug Control Policy.

"White House Drug Czar Awards $72 Million to Drug-Free Community Coalitions." 2006 (August 31). Press release. Washington, DC: Office of National Drug Control Policy.

CASE CITED

United States v. Jones, 565 U.S. _____ 132 S.Ct. 945 (2012)

CHAPTER 12
Bringing Youths into Community Policing

Children are likely to live up to what you believe of them.

—*Lady Bird Johnson*

To see youth as problem solvers, rather than as problems to be solved …
—*New York State Regional Youth Voice Forums: An Exercise in Positive Youth Development*

DO YOU KNOW …

» What important group is often overlooked when implementing the community policing philosophy?

» How negative attitudes toward the police can be changed?

» What the developmental asset approach to children involves?

» What federal initiatives are aimed at protecting our nation's youths?

» What many consider to be the cornerstone of the community?

» How schools should be viewed?

» Why it is important to build students' sense of community in school?

» At minimum, what links the school should have with the community?

» What bullying is more accurately termed?

» How bullying has been viewed, and the result of this view?

» What the "tell or tattle" dilemma is?

» How threats might be classified?

» What the FBI's four-pronged threat assessment consists of?

» What most violent students do before they commit acts of violence?

» What two highly successful programs to build safe schools are?

» What the seven prongs in effective school security are?

» Whether zero tolerance is an effective deterrent to nonconforming behavior?

CAN YOU DEFINE …

bullying
conditional threat
developmental assets
direct threat
indirect threat
leakage
peer child abuse
protective factor
risk factor
tattling
veiled threat
zero tolerance

345

INTRODUCTION

A relatively small percentage of youth engage in criminal behavior but many more become victims of crime: "In 2009 youth ages 12 to 24 had the highest rate of victimization. … More than one in four children (25.3%) witnessed an act of violence within [a] one-year period, and 38 percent witnessed an act of violence sometime during their childhood. Over the course of their childhood, 71 percent of youth ages 14 to 17 in the United States had been assaulted, 28 percent had been sexually victimized, 32 percent had been abused or neglected, and 53 percent had experienced a property victimization (including robbery)" (*Outreach to Underserved Teen Victims of Crime*, 2012, 3). Teens and young adults are also more likely than people of other ages to be murdered with a gun, and over a three-decade period (from 1976 to 2005), 77 percent of homicide victims ages 15–17 died from gun-related injuries ("Who Is Most Affected by Gun Violence?," 2010).

If community policing is to succeed, it is imperative that the important youth segment of the community not be forgotten. If youths can come to feel a part of their community and their school early on, many future problems might be eliminated. Unfortunately, the violence so prevalent within our society has found its way into our schools, as the school shootings in the past few years have dramatically shown. In addition some youths turn to gangs for the support and feelings of self-worth they cannot find at home or school, as discussed in the next chapter.

This chapter begins with a discussion of the importance of involving youths in community policing and some strategies for building positive relationships between law enforcement and youths, as well as some strategies aimed at engaging them in community policing efforts. Then the importance of involving parents in community policing efforts to prevent youth delinquency and violence is discussed. Next the role of the school in promoting healthy growth and development is described, followed by the problems of crime, bullying, violence, and shootings in schools. This is followed by a discussion of after-school programs, creating safe schools, crisis planning, and the importance of early intervention.

YOUTHS AND COMMUNITY POLICING

Forman (2004, 2) contends that community policing has not reached its full potential because a critical group—youths and young adults—has largely been left out of the policing model: "Leaving young people out of [the] model of community policing has tremendous implications. Public safety turns, to a great extent, on what the young do and what is done to them. This is the group most likely to engage in criminal conduct, to be victims of crime, and to be targeted by police." Rather than leaving young people out of community policing effects, youth should be placed alongside other community members and officers in "trust-engendering deliberations regarding matters of community safety" (Forman, 2004, 3). Forman (48) concludes: "It is possible to build on existing community policing models to develop an approach that would, for the first time in modern policing, fundamentally alter the relationship between police and the young … allowing us to see the young as the potential assets they are."

POLICE MAGNET SCHOOLS

New York, New York

Police magnet schools involve youth in police agencies, develop bonds between youth and police officers, and encourage youth to view law enforcement as a rewarding career path. The COPS Office has worked with community organizations in New York City and Los Angeles to develop police magnet schools that build bonds of respect and admiration between law enforcement and youth, giving young people strong role models in the community. Additionally, it is expected that these programs will expand the overall pool of prospective police applicants and, in doing so, increase the numbers of minorities and women applying for law enforcement positions.

Magnet schools allow youth who have experienced trouble fitting into the traditional academic environment to belong to a smaller educational community that connects their academic studies directly with career aspirations and goals, and develops strong relationships between students and professional entities. These projects harness the promise that magnet schools have shown in other career fields for the benefit of law enforcement and the community in general.

East Brooklyn Congregations/East New York High School for Public Safety and Law

In 1999 a magnet school for public safety and law was established in several largely Hispanic and African American neighborhoods of East Brooklyn. The college-track high school program prepares ninth- to twelfth-grade students to meet the New Standards and Regents requirements, while also exposing them to a wide array of public safety, security, and law courses, developed in partnership with the John Jay College of Criminal Justice. The curriculum emphasizes performance-based assessment, study skills, and research. Graduating students are academically prepared to continue their education as well as to pursue careers in public safety, law, forensics, and corrections.

This program was developed as a partnership between the COPS Office, the New York City Police Department (NYPD), and the East Brooklyn Congregations—a not-for-profit umbrella organization of congregations and associations working in East Brooklyn. This program also partnered with a variety of local and national educational institutions, including the John Jay College of Criminal Justice; the National Partnership for Careers in Public Safety, Law, and Security; the Teachers College/Columbia College; Middle College Charter High School; the Justice Resource Center (funded by the New York City Council); and the national organization Educators for Social Responsibility.

Entrance requirements and enrollment standards are exacting and require the full commitment of students. The curriculum includes all of the required academic courses leading to a diploma, as identified by the State of New York and the New York City Board of Education. However, the regular academic courses are infused with concepts related to public safety and law. To augment the classroom instructions, teachers organize special activities involving law and public safety locations, including field trips to courts, penal institutions, and law offices; participation in the NYPD Citizens Committee (a 16-week workshop); mock trials and "youth court"; internships; workshops facilitated by NYPD personnel; and student trips to the FBI Training Academy in Quantico, Virginia.

The John Jay College of Criminal Justice supports the magnet school by providing law-related curricula, guest speakers, and college entrance preparatory classes. Administrators are exploring the possibility of awarding college credits for advanced classes. The successes of the academy are widely recognized. For example:

- In the first year of operation, 45 students who were previously seen to be in danger of failing have raised their grades to above average.
- Attendance has steadily improved to almost 79 percent, and 99 percent of incoming ninth graders have been retained.
- Only one superintendent suspension took place during the first year, which was far below the annual performance benchmark.
- Academically, the benchmarks set for passing the Regents tests were exceeded across all academic subjects.
- Retention and attendance rates in the first 2 years have exceeded those of the rest of the city.

Additionally, youth previously viewed as "at risk" now interact with law enforcement officers on a daily basis and are developing personal relationships with them. Research shows involvement of adult role models with at-risk youth can reduce delinquency.

Source: Dylan Presman, Robert Chapman, and Linda Rosen. *Creative Partnerships: Supporting Youth, Building Communities.* Washington, DC: Office of Community Oriented Policing Services, September 11, 2002 (e03021471).

Children and teenagers are an important segment of the community often overlooked when implementing the community policing philosophy.

One example of an effort to strengthen youth–police relations is occurring within the at-risk teen community in Houston, Texas. The Houston Police Department, in partnership with the University of Houston–Clear Lake (UHCL), Texas Southern University, and the Beechnut Academy, launched the Teen and Police Service Academy (T.A.P.S.) in January 2012. Funded by a federal grant from the COPS Office, the goal of T.A.P.S. is to increase teens' trust in law enforcement by having police officers mentor at-risk youth ("HPD's T.A.P.S. Academy," 2012).

BUILDING PERSONAL RELATIONSHIPS

Departments across the country have developed programs to allow youngsters and police officers to get to know and understand each other better.

To counteract negative perceptions of police held by children and youths, many departments have programs aimed at fostering positive relations with them.

The Kops 'n' Kids program, endorsed by the International Association of Chiefs of Police (IACP), brings together children and officers to have fun rather than to deliver antidrug or anticrime speeches. Officers come with their motorcycles and their K-9s for demonstrations; they share lunch; they form running clubs; they do whatever helps present police as positive role models and build trust with the children.

The LaGrange Park (Illinois) Police Department sponsors an Adopt-a-Cop Program. Each participating elementary grade school level "adopts" an officer, who then serves as their liaison for the entire school year.

Many police departments across the United States hold an annual Shop with a Cop day in December. One of the largest events takes place in San Diego County, where local, state, and federal law enforcement personnel raise $30,000 every year to give underprivileged children a fun day and a brighter holiday season. In 2008 the program was able to provide holiday gifts to 338 children ("Mission Statement," 2009). The San Diego Shop with a Cop is a nonprofit organization, funded by grants and corporate donations. Other police departments treat seriously ill or homeless children to special events, and at least one also gives the parents a $75 grocery gift card.

PARTNERSHIPS THAT CONNECT YOUTHS AND THE COMMUNITY

Partnerships should include youths at all levels of activity, with their roles considered as important as those of adults. A potential obstacle is the attitude of some adult policymakers and leaders that youths are the source of the community's violence problems rather than part of the solution. Forums where youths can present their views can help overcome this bias.

Royal Canadian Mounted Patrol's National Youth Strategy

One program that invites young people to the table in full partnership has been developed by the Royal Canadian Mounted Police (RCMP)—the National Youth Strategy. The RCMP's National Youth Officer Program teaches front-line officers about the causes of youth crime and how to effectively partner with young people to help prevent youthful offending and victimization ("National Youth Strategy," 2012). Additional tools and instructional materials are available to officers through the Youth Officer Resource Center.

Oakland, California's Teens on Target (TNT)

In the late 1980s gun violence was on the rise in Oakland, California, and an increasing number of youth homicides were occurring as the result of heightened gang activity, drug dealing, and racial tensions in the schools and on the streets. In 1989 the nonprofit youth development agency, YouthALIVE!, created the Teens on Target (TNT) initiative, the mission of which was to reduce youth injuries and deaths through peer education, peer intervention, mentoring, and leadership development (Sheppard, 1999). The program is still in operation, training urban youth who live in neighborhoods with the highest rates of violence how to become active advocates for violence prevention: "The program provides positive roles for youth to portray in schools, at conferences, at public hearings, and in the media that show low-income urban youth as leaders and spokespersons in preventing violence. The program seeks to demonstrate that violence is not an inevitable part of urban youth's lives" (Sheppard, 1999, 189). The TNT program trains high school students and young adults to be Peer Educators, whose role it is to present interactive violence prevention workshops to middle and high school students and to work with community leaders and policy makers to develop solutions to violence. Some of the Peer Educators have suffered serious physical injury and are in wheelchairs from being shot, and most have firsthand experience with violence. Results presented on the TNT Web site speak to the program's success:

» Almost 100 percent of TNT Peer Educators graduate from high schools that have graduation rates of only 40 percent.
» Twice as many Peer Educators said they could talk a friend out of carrying a gun after participating in the program, compared to before.
» 79 percent of TNT workshop audience members stated that they would not be safer if they joined a gang.
» 92 percent of middle school audience members thought that TNT members were positive role models. (Lack of positive peer role models is a risk factor for violence.)[1]

To date, more than 900 young people have been trained to be Peer Educators who have, as a group, presented workshops to over 45,000 students, teaching

[1] Reprinted by permission of Youth ALIVE!

them how to be active players in making their own lives, neighborhoods, and communities healthier and safer ("Teens on Target," 2010).

Metropolitan (DC) Police Department's Youth Advisory Council (YAC)

The Metropolitan Police Department (MPD) in the District of Columbia started a School Security Division Youth Advisory Council (YAC) in fall of 2002 as a way to include the area youth in community policing and the problem-solving process as well as enable the department to develop partnerships with area youth ("Youth Advisory Council," n.d.). The YAC engages public school students ages 14–18 throughout DC in activities that focus on three basic objectives:

» To expose students to the variety of career paths available

» To provide access to mentors, role models, and internships that can serve as springboards for future career choices

» To offer the opportunity to gain the tools and skills necessary to become successful adults

Monthly meetings include social and educational events and field trips, educational seminars, basic career planning, and special guest speakers who interact with the youth to encourage positive change. Good citizenship is a common topic of discussion among YAC participants, and the citizenship theme changes from year to year. During meetings students also participate in group-related activities, such as holding elections, planning group activities, problem solving, or a combination thereof. Examples of past activities include ("Youth Advisory Council," n.d.):

» **Beat the Street Program:** A citywide program targeting high crime areas that conducts community awareness activities, provides informational handouts to residents, and coordinates youth activities

» **Police Ride-Alongs and MPD Site Visits:** Allows YAC participants to get a comprehensive look at law enforcement as a possible career path

» **Trip to the Newseum:** Another career path opportunity with a structured itinerary to give YAC students insight into different news-related professions, such as journalism, news reporting, and public speaking

» **College Tours:** Lead YAC participants through a series of college tours, including local institutions and those along the east coast. Before the tour, students attend a college readiness workshop to learn how to stay on track for higher education and employment. During the tour to various colleges, MPD School Resource Officers speak to students about college admission requirements, the application process, financial aid, SAT testing, grade point averages, and housing options.

developmental assets

Forty ideals, experiences, and qualities established by the Search Institute to "help young people make wise decisions, choose positive paths, and grow up competent, caring, and responsible."

THE DEVELOPMENTAL ASSET APPROACH

"The Asset Approach: Giving Kids What They Need to Succeed" was developed by the Search Institute in Minneapolis, Minnesota. The Search Institute promotes establishing 40 ideals, experiences, and qualities—**developmental assets**—that are associated with reduced high-risk behaviors and increased thriving behaviors (Mannes, Roehlkepartain, and Benson, 2005). These 40 developmental assets are grouped into eight categories.

> The developmental asset approach promotes (1) support, (2) empowerment, (3) boundaries and expectations, (4) constructive use of time, (5) commitment to learning, (6) positive values, (7) social competence, and (8) positive identity to help youngsters succeed in school and in life.

Mannes, Roehlkepartain, and Benson (2005, 237) contend: "Developmental assets appear to play an important role in the healthy development of young people across varied life circumstances and in the face of multiple challenges, yet too few youths report experiencing enough of these assets. Young people report having, on average, 19 of the 40 assets." In the communities surveyed, 15 percent of young people had zero to 10 of the 40 assets; 41 percent had 11 to 20 assets; 35 percent had 21 to 30 assets; and only 8 percent had 31 to 40 assets (Mannes, Roehlkepartain, and Benson, 2005). Research found that "experiencing fewer than 10 assets was two to five times as powerful in predicting high-risk behaviors as was poverty" (Mannes, Roehlkepartain, and Benson, 2005, 239), supporting the conclusion that the greater the number of developmental assets youth possess, the greater the likelihood they will demonstrate adaptive behaviors such as valuing diversity, maintaining good health, and resisting danger (Mannes, Roehlkepartain, and Benson, 2005).

RECOGNIZING RISK AND PROTECTIVE FACTORS

Communities that seek to include youths in their community policing efforts must be aware of the myriad risk and protective factors that play a role in victimization and delinquency. Various definitions of risk factors exist, but in the context of juvenile justice, a working definition of a **risk factor** is a condition, characteristic, or variable that increases the likelihood that a child will become delinquent. Exposure to multiple risk factors can have a cumulative effect, and the relative impact any risk factor has on a child may be either augmented or diminished by the developmental state of that child (Shader, 2002). Conversely, the existence of certain protective factors can work to offset the risk factors and keep a child headed toward a law-abiding adulthood. In general, a **protective factor**, often the opposite of a risk factor, is a condition, characteristic, or variable that increases the likelihood that a child will avoid delinquency. For example, if poor parental supervision is a risk factor, then a high degree of parental monitoring is a protective factor. Truancy is a risk factor; staying in school is a protective factor. Low IQ is a risk factor, high IQ, a protective factor.

Researchers have identified hundreds, if not thousands, of risk factors related to delinquency and have grouped them into five basic domains: individual, family, school, peers, and community. Protective factors also relate to individual characteristics, family, school, peers, and community. The most significant individual risk factor for predicting later delinquency is early antisocial behavior, specifically aggression.

risk factor
A condition, characteristic, or variable that increases the likelihood that a child will become delinquent; often the opposite of a *protective factor*.

protective factor
A condition, characteristic, or variable that increases the likelihood that a child will avoid delinquency; often the opposite of a *risk factor*.

In 2005 the Rand Corporation released a research report, *Stopping Violence before It Starts: Identifying Early Predictors of Adolescent Violence*, which identified several early predictors of middle school students becoming perpetrators of violence in high school. The study showed that the presence of three characteristics in 7th graders made it more likely that a student would frequently resort to overall violence 5 years later: (1) having poor grades, (2) having experienced frequent moves between elementary schools, and (3) exhibiting early deviant behavior. Although these general findings held true for both boys and girls, there were differences. Having low self-esteem and living in a poor neighborhood were additional risk factors for girls, and just being born a boy and going to a school with high drug use were additional risk factors for boys. In addition, boys were more affected than girls by elementary school mobility.

Additional research has found gender-specific risk factors for girls to include early puberty coupled with stressors such as conflict with parents and involvement with delinquent, and often older, male peers (Zahn et al., 2010). The implications of such findings allow practitioners to tailor victimization, delinquency, and violence prevention programs to specific at-risk children. For example, programs may target girls with low self-esteem or boys who move frequently during the elementary school years, as evidence shows these populations may be especially vulnerable to developmental disruptions linked to later delinquency and violence (*Stopping Violence before It Starts*, 2005).

KEY INDICATORS OF CHILDREN'S WELL-BEING

In 1994 the Office of Management and Budget (OMB) joined with six other federal agencies to create the Federal Interagency Forum on Child and Family Statistics. Today the Forum is a collection of 22 federal government agencies involved in research and activities related to children and families. The Forum's annual report, *America's Children: Key National Indicators of Well-Being*, provides a comprehensive summary of 3 demographic background measures and 41 selected indicators to describe our nation's population of children and depict both the promises and the challenges affecting child well-being in the areas of family and social environment, economic circumstances, health care, physical environment and safety, behavior, education, and health. Additionally, the Forum monitors and reports changes in these indicators over time. Some of the highlights of the 2011 report include (Federal Interagency Forum on Child and Family Statistics, 2011):

> » In 2010, there were 74.2 million children ages 0–17 in the United States, or 24 percent of the population. By 2050, 39 percent of U.S. children are projected to be Hispanic and 38 percent are projected to be White, non-Hispanic.

> » In 2010, 66 percent of children ages 0–17 lived with two married parents, down from 67 percent in 2009 and 77 percent in 1980. In 2010, 23 percent of children lived with only their mothers, 3 percent lived with only their fathers, and 4 percent lived with neither of their parents.

> » About 6 percent of school-age children spoke a language other than English at home.

» In 2009, the adolescent birth rate was 20.1 per 1,000 adolescents ages 15–17, lower than the 2008 rate of 21.7 and the 2007 rate of 22.1 per 1,000.

» In 2009, 21 percent of all children ages 0–17 (15.5 million) lived in poverty. This is up from the low of 16 percent in 2000 and 2001.

» In 2009, 90 percent of children had health insurance coverage at some point during the year, a percentage not statistically different from 2008. The number of children without health insurance at any time during 2009 was 7.5 million (10 percent of all children).

» In 2009, 59 percent of children lived in counties in which one or more air pollutants were above allowable levels of the Primary National Ambient Air Quality Standards, compared with 69 percent in 2008.

» Younger children are more frequently victims of child maltreatment than are older children.

» In 2009, substantiated reports of maltreatment of children ages 0–17 were 10.1 per 1,000, down from 10.3 per 1,000 in 2008.

» In 2009, 10 per 1,000 children were victims of serious violent crime, down from 2008 when it was 12 per 1,000 children.

» In an average week during the 2010 school year, 9 percent of youth ages 16–19 were neither enrolled in school nor working.

» In 2009, 90 percent of young adults ages 18–24 had completed high school with a diploma or an alternative credential such as a General Educational Development (GED) certificate.[2]

FEDERAL INITIATIVES

Clearly, the news is not all bad regarding our nation's youth. However, areas of concern do exist, and several federal initiatives have been directed at protecting our country's young people.

Federal initiatives to protect our nation's youths include passage of the Adam Walsh Child Protection and Safety Act, America's Promise Alliance, Project Safe Childhood, and the Safe Start Initiative.

The Adam Walsh Child Protection and Safety Act

The Adam Walsh[3] Child Protection and Safety Act, also known as the Sex Offender Registration and Notification Act (SORNA), went into effect in 2006 and strengthens the national standards for sex offender registration and notification

---

[2] Source: Federal Interagency Forum on Child and Family Statistics. America's Children: Key National Indicators of Well-Being, 2011. Washington, DC: U.S. Government Printing Office, 2011.

[3] Adam Walsh was 6 years old in 1981 when he was abducted from a store and brutally murdered. His parents have worked relentlessly since that time to pass this law to protect children from sexual predators. John Walsh, Adam's father, is host of the popular television show *America's Most Wanted*.

as well as provides statutory authorization for Project Safe Childhood, described later in this chapter. Of the hundreds of thousands of registered sex offenders nationally, the whereabouts of a large number—approaching 20 percent by some estimates—are currently unknown. The Adam Walsh Act creates stricter requirements for sex offender registration—to prevent offenders from slipping through the cracks and harming children.

Although SORNA did not create a federal sex offender registry, it did create a new federal felony offense for failing to register as a sex offender and established a baseline sex offender registry standard for all jurisdictions to achieve, while allowing states to enact more stringent requirements if they so desired (McPherson, 2007). The legislation also calls for stricter prison sentences for offenders who fail to register and keep their information current. The offender will be assigned to one of three tiers; the worst offenders will have to check in more frequently, and all offenders have to register in person. In addition, the Act:

» Makes registration as a sex offender a mandatory condition of probation and supervised release.

» Eliminates the statute of limitations for prosecutions of child abduction and felony sex offenses against children.

» Directs the Attorney General to provide technical assistance to jurisdictions to help identify and locate sex offenders relocated due to a major disaster.

All states were required to comply with the Adam Walsh Act by July 2011. However, as of January 2012, only 15 states had substantially complied with SORNA requirements. Some states, including Texas and New York, have officially declined to comply with the Act, even though failure to comply means the loss of 10 percent of their federal Byrne grants. Hurdles to compliance include the high cost of implementation and objections to the juvenile registration requirement, which requires offenders as young as 14 who are adjudicated in juvenile court with a serious sex offense to be listed on law enforcement registers for 25 years. Critics of this SORNA requirement point to the growing body of empirical evidence that shows fewer than 10 percent of youth who commit sex offenses recidivate ("The Adam Walsh Act," 2012).

America's Promise Alliance

Another federal initiative is America's Promise Alliance. Established in 1997 with General Colin Powell as the founding chairman, America's Promise Alliance is the nation's largest partnership dedicated to improving the lives of youth, consisting of more than 400 corporations, nonprofits, communities, faith-based organizations, advocacy groups, educators, and policy makers. The Alliance's mission, as stated on its Web site, is to forge a "strong and effective partnership … committed to seeing that children experience the fundamental resources they need to succeed—the Five Promises (Caring Adults, Safe Places, A Healthy Start, Effective Education, and Opportunities to Help Others)—at home, in school, and out in the community. Together with our partner organizations, we know the success of our children is grounded in experiencing these Promises" ("Mission and Purpose," 2011). The America's Promise Alliance believes what research tells us, that if every child receives these five fundamental resources, he or she is 5 to 10 times more likely to stay in school, avoid drugs and alcohol, not get in trouble with the law, and grow up to be an engaged citizen in his or her community.

Noting that one student drops out of high school every 26 seconds, the Alliance has made a top priority of ending the high school dropout crisis: "We cannot afford to lose one out of four young people to the dropout crisis. A high school diploma is an important step in preparing a young person to live an independent, secure, and happy life and to contribute to America's economic competitiveness as part of an educated, innovative workforce" ("Our Work," 2011).

A 2009 Gallup Student Poll revealed that more than one-third of students surveyed in grades 5–12 were struggling or suffering in school, and half were not hopeful about their future educational and employment prospects ("First-Ever Gallup Student Poll," 2009). Referencing the poll results, Alma Powell, co-founder and current chair of the Alliance (and wife of Colin Powell), stated: "When more than 1.2 million young people drop out of high school every year, everyone needs to work together to address the crisis—educators, parents, business and community leaders.... For too long the voice of youth has been missing from the national dialogue. This poll gives insights into the daily experiences, challenges, and aspirations of our young people, so that we can better identify ways to meet their needs and help them be successful" ("First-Ever Gallup Student Poll," 2009). Powell also commented on the nexus between the children's well-being and the nation's economic health, citing statistics that showed that dropouts from just the class of 2007 will cost the nation $329 billion in lost wages, taxes, and revenue over their lifetimes ("America's Promise Alliance Chair," 2009).

Project Safe Childhood

Project Safe Childhood was launched in 2006 by the Department of Justice to combat the proliferation of technology-facilitated crimes involving the sexual exploitation of children. Using a network of federal, state, and local law enforcement agencies and advocacy organizations, Project Safe Childhood aims to protect children by investigating and prosecuting offenders involved in child sexual exploitation. In May 2011, Project Safe Childhood was expanded to encompass all federal crimes involving the sexual exploitation of a minor, including sex trafficking of a minor and crimes against children committed in Indian country. Failure to register as a sex offender is now an offense that also falls within the reach of Project Safe Childhood (*Fact Sheet: Project Safe Childhood,* 2012).

Safe Start Initiative

The Safe Start Initiative, funded by the Office of Juvenile Justice and Delinquency Prevention (OJJDP), was developed to prevent and reduce the impact of family and community violence on young children (primarily from birth to age 6) and their families in response to emerging statistics and research on the prevalence and effects of children's exposure to violence. The program also seeks to broaden the knowledge of and promote community investment in evidence-based strategies for reducing the impact of children's exposure to violence ("About Safe Start," 2012).

Safe Start is designed to expand current partnerships among service providers in key areas such as early childhood education/development, health, mental health, child welfare, family support, substance abuse prevention/intervention, domestic violence/crisis intervention, law enforcement, the courts, and legal services. The project's goal is to create a comprehensive service-delivery system that will meet the needs of children and their families at any point of entry into the system by expanding, enhancing, coordinating, and integrating services and support to families. This comprehensive system should improve the accessibility, delivery, and quality of services for young children who have been exposed to violence or are at high risk for exposure.

Ten sites across the country were funded in 2010 to provide evidence-based or theory-based interventions to children and youths between the ages of 0 and 17 who have been exposed to violence in their homes and communities ("About Safe Start," 2012). Figure 12.1 illustrates the Safe Start National Framework.

Figure 12.1   Safe Start National Framework

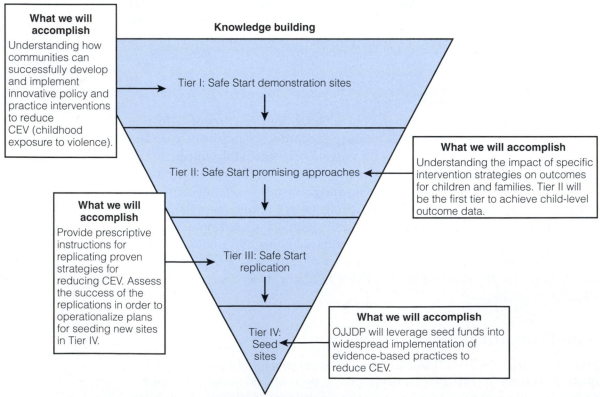

Source: Office of Juvenile Justice and Delinquency Prevention (OJJDP), Office of Justice Programs, U.S. Department of Justice. Retrieved on August 17, 2012 from http://www.safestartcenter.org.

A PARTNERSHIP TO PREVENT JUVENILE DELINQUENCY

An alliance in Livermore, California, has Horizons Family Counseling operating out of the police department. The program began in 1973 when the city received a grant for a juvenile delinquency program. When it was learned that the activities funded by the program were not having any effect on youthful offenders, the state Office of Criminal Justice Planning asked the Livermore Police Department to oversee the program. The program focus became high-risk youths who were running away, truant, having school behavior problems, or beyond parental control, with Horizons brought in to provide counseling ("Horizons Family Counseling," 2012).

Horizons is an alliance based on interface and interdependence. Horizons Family Counseling and the Livermore Police Department literally work "shoulder to shoulder" because the counseling service is located inside the police department. Families of first-time youth offenders arrested for a minor offense have a "unique opportunity: three family sessions will change the arrest to a nonarrest." Police officers and counselors have different roles with these first-time offenders:

» Officers making the arrest interact with the family when emotions are running high.

» When families arrive for counseling after police have been at their home, they have had some time for reflection.

» Counselors have more permission to explore family members' lives.

» Counselors help weave emotional reconnections for a family.

» Families can then take responsibility for "inviting" a police intervention.

In moving from incident-driven policing to solution-focused policing, the department recognizes that outreach to young people and their families is important to community health and safety.

THE IMPORTANCE OF PARENTAL INVOLVEMENT

Findings released by the OJJDP suggest that violent acts of delinquency are less likely to be committed by youths who have adult supervision after school than by those who are unsupervised one or more days a week. Even more important than actual adult supervision is whether parents know where their children are after school.

 The family is viewed by many as the cornerstone of the community.

In many American families, the traditional bonds of discipline and respect between parent and child have loosened considerably, if not unraveled completely. If the integration process between parents and children is deficient, the children may fail to learn appropriate behaviors: "Ask a guidance counselor, teacher, or law enforcement officer the greatest problem they face when it comes to juvenile crime, and the answer is unanimous—parents" (Garrett, 2005, 6).

A survey of educators identified "emotionally immature" parents as the most crucial problem facing schools: "Discipline and violence problems in schools can be directly traced back to parenting problems in our society" (Yeager et al., 2006). Such parents detach from their children academically and developmentally and often defend their children's bad behavior. Thus, what begins as a family problem becomes a school and community problem as these children grow older.

THE IMPORTANCE OF SCHOOLS

Schools play an important role in the lives of children and in their social development.

 A school should be viewed as a community, not as an institution.

The Child Development Project (CDP) is a comprehensive, whole-school improvement program designed by the Developmental Studies Center in Oakland, California. This project fosters children's cognitive, ethical, and social growth by providing all students with engaging, challenging learning opportunities and creating a strong sense of community among students, teachers, and parents.

 Research suggests that students' academic motivation, commitment to democratic values, and resistance to problem behaviors depend on their experience of the school as a community.

CDP research suggests that increases in children's sense of community are linked to their later development of intrinsic academic motivation, concern for others, democratic values, skill and inclination to resolve conflicts equitably, intrinsic prosocial motivation, enjoyment of helping others learn, inclusive attitudes toward out-groups, and positive interpersonal behavior in class. In addition to building a sense of community within the school, schools should also partner with the community of which they are a part.

 At a minimum schools need to link with parents and with local law enforcement departments to teach students about the dangers of crime.

Students whose families are involved in their growth both inside and outside of school are more likely to experience school success and less likely to become involved in antisocial activities. School staff, students, and families should be involved in developing, discussing, and implementing fair rules. In addition, law enforcement can be brought into the school to get to know students and through select police–school programs can help students become mentors, peacekeepers, and problem solvers.

School Teams

Some schools have developed teams to watch for signs of trouble and to step in to prevent problems. In California, Butte County's Safe Schools teams are one example. These teams are a partnership of the Chico (California) Police Department, which assigns a full-time youth services officer to each school in the program; the Butte County Probation Department, which redefined its case-loads to correspond to specific schools; and the Chico Unified School District, which provides office space and equipment and integrates its referral services with those of the police and probation department.

The officers monitor *all* students' behavior but focus on those on probation. They conduct safety checks, perform searches, and enforce curfew and atten-dance policies. The team also makes a point of supporting youths working hard to "stay on track" by attending sporting events, graduations, and other activities in which youths are taking part.

Another way the team is proactive is in forging relationships with gang members, their peers, and others "in the know." Students alert team members when they think something is "going down."

The School Resource Officer

School resource officers (SROs) function as an integral connection between the school and the community. In the accepted school resource officer model, SROs engage in three types of activities: law enforcement, teaching, and mentoring (Finn, 2006). The emphasis devoted to each duty varies considerably from school to school. Often efforts start with a focus on law enforcement but evolve into a more balanced approach. In a teaching capacity, an SRO can educate students about their legal rights and responsibilities. They can also assist in efforts to teach conflict management and peer mediation skills.

© Jim Commentucci/Syracuse Newspapers/The Image Works

More than 17,000 school resource officers (SROs) exist in schools nationwide, serving as advisers to and positive role models for students and faculty. Partnerships with local law enforcement are an important element of safe and effective schools.

Finn (2006, 2) reports: "Interest has grown in placing sworn law enforcement personnel in schools to improve school safety and relations between officers and young people." Finn's research found four main benefits of an SRO program: reducing the workload of patrol officers or road deputies, improving the image of officers among juveniles, creating and maintaining better relationships with the schools, and enhancing the agency's reputation in the community. In addition to saving patrol officers' time, SROs can also reduce frustration and stress.

Funding for SRO programs is usually shared by the police department and the school district. Law enforcement agencies can use three main features of an SRO program to convince school districts to share expenses: improved school safety, increased perception of safety, and increased response time. Increased response time is especially important if a crime is committed on school grounds.

CRIME AND VIOLENCE IN OUR SCHOOLS

According to the *Indicators of School Crime and Safety: 2011* (Robers et al., 2012), an estimated 55.3 million children (pre-kindergarten through grade 12) were enrolled in schools in the United States in the 2009–2010 school year. Of the 33 student, staff, and nonstudent school-associated violent deaths occurring between July 1, 2009, and June 30, 2010, 25 were homicides, 5 were suicides, and 3 were legal interventions. During this time period, 17 of the homicides and 1 suicide involved school-age youth (ages 5–18) at school (Robers et al., 2012). Other key indicators of school crime and safety include the following (Robers et al., 2012, iii–iiv):

> » About 828,000 million students between the ages of 12 and 18 were victims of nonfatal crimes at school. This includes violent crimes and theft.

> » In 2009, 10 percent of male students in grades 9 through 12 reported being threatened or assaulted with a weapon on school property. Girl students were victimized half as often.

> » Teachers were threatened with injury or actually assaulted more often in public and urban schools than in private or suburban, town, or rural schools. Four times as many public school teachers as private school teachers reported being assaulted.

> » In 2009, about 20 percent of students ages 12–18 reported that there were gangs present at their schools.

> » The percentage of students in grades 9–12 who reported that drugs were offered, sold, or given to them decreased from 32 percent in 1995 to 23 percent in 2009.

> » In 2009, about 9 percent of students ages 12–18 reported being targets of hate-related words at school.

> » In 2009, about 28 percent of 12- to 18-year-old students reported having been bullied at school during the school year and 6 percent reported having been cyber-bullied.

> » In 2009, about 27 percent of males carried a weapon anywhere, compared to 7 percent of females, and 8 percent of males carried a weapon on school property, compared to 3 percent of females.

There is some concern that the government school crime reports do not tell the whole story. Unlike the FBI, which collects Uniform Crime Reports based upon actual reported crimes to law enforcement, federal education reports are based only on limited academic research surveys, not a comprehensive collection of actual reported crimes to law enforcement nationwide. Even if the *Indicators of School Crime* cited actual reported crimes, it would still underestimate the true level of offending and victimization because K–12 schools have no federal mandate requiring them to report crime; in contrast, colleges and universities are mandated to report such crimes ("School Crime Reporting and School Crime Underreporting," 2012). Although some states require reporting, there is no real auditing or enforcement to require compliance. Also, where inaccuracies have surfaced in local newspaper investigations, schools blame clerical orders or "a lack of understanding of the law and guidelines" for reporting. Consequently, the "persistently dangerous school" label that schools can be saddled with under the No Child Left Behind law creates pressure on local school administrators to underreport school crime. Many administrators worry about being seen as incompetent if crime and serious discipline problems become public or that talking about crime and security issues will alarm parents ("School Crime Reporting and School Crime Underreporting," 2012).

Because children are sometimes victimized on the way to or from school, programs that address this critical time period can be of great help. The University of Southern California (USC) has established a successful partnership with

ON THE BEAT

Community policing in the schools starts with building police–youth partnerships. The first step is having police personnel who are dedicated to working with youth in the community. In our city, we have three School Liaison Officers. One liaison is assigned to the high school, one to the junior high school, and one to the elementary schools throughout the city. These officers get to know students and are able to work with the school staff to solve problems that arise.

Liaison officers are often able to curtail violence before it happens; for instance, if they hear rumors of an upcoming fight at a local park, they can get information out to other officers to be in the area to stop the violence before it starts. If officers see problematic behaviors in a student, they can work with school staff to resolve some of those issues.

As everyone knows all too well, school shootings have taken place across the United States. Every school official and liaison officer should have a plan in place in the event that a violent act occurs at a school. Police departments work hard to train for the unlikely and unfortunate event that something traumatic happens. In our city, we conduct a full-scale practical training exercise involving the police and other agencies, city officials, and school officials. This enables everyone to work together to plan for the unlikely event of a school shooting. Agencies must collaborate with others in the community to better prepare themselves for an act of violence and develop appropriate responses.

—*Kim Czapar*

area schools and residents to keep students safe. The Kid Watch Program—a partnership between USC, the Los Angeles Unified School District, and the Los Angeles Police Department—recruits volunteers to watch over students on their way to and from school and to provide safe houses for kids who feel threatened or otherwise unsafe on the streets. Volunteers are vetted by the university and police department, free of charge, and safe houses are marked with a yellow sticker shaped like a house with stick figures of a boy and girl inside. In 2009 more than 1,000 neighbors watched over 9,000 children as they walked to and from school ("Kid Watch," 2010).

School Vandalism and Break-ins

The Center for Problem-Oriented Policing has studied the problem of school vandalism and break-ins, and their Problem-Oriented Guide for Police on the topic defines *school vandalism* as "willful or malicious damage to school grounds and buildings or furnishings and equipment," such as breaking windows, spraying graffiti, or generally destroying property (Dedel, 2005, 1). *A school break-in* is defined as "an unauthorized entry into a school building when the school is closed (e.g., after hours, on weekends, on school holidays)" (Dedel, 2005, 1). School break-ins typically fall into one of three categories (Dedel, 2005, 2):

» *Nuisance break-ins*, in which youth break into a school building, seemingly as an end in itself. They cause little serious damage and usually take nothing of value.

» *Professional break-ins*, in which offenders use a high level of skill to enter the school, break into storage rooms containing expensive equipment, and remove bulky items from the scene. They commit little incidental damage and may receive a lot of money for the stolen goods.

» *Malicious break-ins* entail significant damage to the school's interior and may include arson. Offenders sometimes destroy rather than steal items of value.

According to the POP Guide, although individual acts of school vandalism and break-ins are often trivial incidents, taken as a whole they pose a serious problem for schools and communities and for those charged with protecting them. For example, many school fires originate as arson or during an act of vandalism, having significant potential to harm students and staff. In the United Kingdom in 2000, about one-third of school arson fires occurred during school hours, when students were present.

Over the past 20 years, concerns about school violence, weapons, drugs, and gangs have eclipsed concern about school vandalism, its causes, and its possible responses. However, vandalism and break-ins continue to occur regularly and affect a significant number of U.S. schools. Although many education associations and national organizations routinely gather data on school-related violence, weapons, and gang activity, they do not gather data on school vandalism and break-ins. This may be because schools have different definitions of vandalism depending on what their insurance policies state or because school administrators may hesitate to report all cases of vandalism, break-ins, or arson, viewing some as trivial or fearing that such incidents will reflect poorly on their management skills. The failure to report vandalism and break-ins, however, may result in few perpetrators being apprehended and even fewer being prosecuted, thus allowing the problem to perpetuate (Dedel, 2005).

The lack of consistency in reporting school vandalism and break-ins also leads to imprecise cost estimates (Dedel, 2005). Such costs usually result from many small incidents rather than just a few more serious incidents. However, several estimates reveal that the costs of school vandalism are high and are increasing. In addition to the financial consequences of having to repair or replace damaged or stolen property and having to pay higher insurance premiums if property has not been self-insured, there may be difficulties in finding temporary accommodations in which to conduct classes and there may be negative effects on student, staff, and community morale.

The POP Guide (Dedel, 2005, 32–34) highlights 28 effective responses, including the following community-focused responses:

» **Providing rewards for information concerning vandalism or break-ins:** Offender-focused responses require that vandals and intruders be identified and apprehended. Police investigations of vandalism incidents can be enhanced by high-quality information provided by students and community residents. As seen with traditional "Crime Stoppers" programs, setting up telephone or Internet-based tip lines, offering rewards for information, and guaranteeing anonymity encourage students and residents to come forward with specific information. The most effective programs actively involve students in collecting and synthesizing information for police, and in determining payout amounts in the event of apprehension.

» **Creating "School Watch" programs:** Similar to "Neighborhood Watch" efforts, community residents can conduct citizen patrols of school property during evenings and weekends. Membership and regular participation in voluntary patrols increase when some form of prestige is offered to volunteers. Effective practices include:

  » Patrolling regularly, but at unpredictable times.

  » Equipping volunteers with cell phones for prompt communication with police or other emergency services.

  » Engaging in passive surveillance only, and not interacting with potential vandals or intruders in any way.

  » Publicizing activities and outcomes among students and residents through school-based and local media outlets.

  In response to a specific problem or rash of incidents, School Watch has produced short-term reductions in vandalism. However, community watch programs are difficult to sustain, have not been shown to reduce crime over the long term, and may actually increase the fear of crime.

» **Evaluating public use of school facilities after hours:** There is no consensus on how effective after-hours use of school facilities is in deterring vandalism and break-ins. On the one hand, making facilities and amenities available to residents increases the opportunities for natural surveillance to protect school buildings and property. Such access is also in keeping with the spirit of schools as hubs of community activity. However, residents who use the facilities after hours may not always have innocent intentions. If this response is adopted, rules and boundaries should be made very clear to participants, and only those areas required for the activities should be accessible, with other areas of the school secured by movable gates and locking partitions.

Responses with Limited Effectiveness

» **Controlling the sale of vandalism tools:** Some jurisdictions have attempted to control the various implements used for vandalism—for graffiti, in particular. Age-specific bans on the sale of spray paint or wide-tipped markers are designed to limit youth access to them. These bans are particularly difficult to implement and enforce because they require extensive cooperation from merchants.

» **Increasing penalties:** Responding to school vandalism and break-ins with excessively punitive criminal justice sanctions or harsh administrative punishments (for example, expulsion) has been found to increase the incidence of vandalism.

Further, legal deterrents are generally ineffective when victim reporting and offender apprehension are not consistent, as is the case with school vandalism. Finally, most acts of vandalism are relatively minor, and thus are not serious enough to warrant severe consequences.

Bullying in Schools

bullying

Name calling, fistfights, purposeful ostracism, extortion, character assassination, repeated physical attacks, and sexual harassment; also called *peer child abuse*.

peer child abuse

Another term for *bullying*—name calling, fistfights, purposeful ostracism, extortion, character assassination, repeated physical attacks, and sexual harassment.

Bullying—name calling, fistfights, purposeful ostracism, extortion, character assassination, repeated physical attacks, and sexual harassment—has been a common behavior in schools since they first opened their doors. Its occurrence is often taken lightly, with the belief that "kids will be kids."

 Bullying is more accurately termed **peer child abuse**.

The Virginia Youth Violence Project reports that bullying seems to have increased in recent years, although it is not clear if the increase reflects more bullying incidents or perhaps greater awareness of bullying as a problem ("Bullying," n.d.). According to this project, student bullying is one of the most frequently reported discipline problems in schools, with 26 percent of elementary schools, 43 percent of middle schools, and 25 percent of high schools reporting problems with bullying.

Bullying is greatly underreported for many reasons, including the fact that most children and adults view reporting as tattling. Other reasons for underreporting include feelings of shame, fear of retaliation, and youngsters' belief that adults will not intervene even if they report the bullying. In that belief, they are often right.

 Bullying has been seen as a rite of passage and has resulted in schools where violence is accepted.

Results of one study revealed that verbal bullying was the most prevalent form of bullying (53.6%), followed by relational (51.4%), physical (20.8%), and electronic (13.6%) (Wang, Iannotti, and Nansel, 2009). Gender differences in bullying involvement were also noted, with boys more involved in the physical and verbal forms of bullying and girls more involved in the relational form. With regard to cyberbullying, boys were more likely to be perpetrators and girls more like to be victims. A rather expected result of this study was the association between higher parental support and lower juvenile involvement across all forms and classifications of bullying. An interesting finding was the relationship between the number of friends a juvenile has and their involvement in bullying: "Having more friends was associated with more bullying and less victimization for the physical, verbal, and relational forms but was not associated with cyberbullying" (Wang, Iannotti, and Nansel, 2009, 368).

Several studies emphasizing the link between bullying and criminal behavior have led police and educators to re-examine their attitudes and responses to bullying: "Approximately 60 percent of boys identified as bullies were convicted of a crime by the age of 24, and an astonishing 40 percent of bullies had three or more convictions by age 24" (*Developing an Anti-bullying Program,* 2006). Research has found that men who reported bullying their childhood peers in school were at a significantly increased risk of committing intimate partner violence as adults (Falb et al., 2011). One implication of this finding is that programs seeking to reduce childhood bullying may also have potential to reduce later domestic violence.

The detrimental effects of bullying are widespread and include fear of going to school, interference with school achievement, loneliness, humiliation, insecurity, hindered ability to develop prosocial skills or make friends, difficulty making emotional or social adjustments, and diminishing overall psychological well-being of both victims and perpetrators (Ericson, 2001; Wang, Iannotti, and Nansel, 2009). Types of antisocial behavior linked to bullying behavior include vandalism, shoplifting, truancy, dropping out of school, and substance abuse (Ericson, 2001).

Strategies to Mediate Bullying Strategies to mediate bullying include clear rules against such behavior applied consistently with appropriate sanctions for violation of the rules; a buddy system to pair younger students with older students; peer mediation; and close monitoring of cafeterias, playgrounds, and hot spots where bullying is likely to occur away from direct adult supervision.

A Johnson Institute program gives teachers step-by-step guidelines on how to teach students the difference between telling and tattling. Children, teenagers, and adults need to learn that **tattling** is something done to get someone in trouble, but telling or reporting is done to keep someone safe.

tattling
Something done to get someone in trouble, in contrast to telling or reporting to keep someone safe.

 The "tell or tattle" dilemma occurs when students hesitate to tell anyone that they are being bullied because it is seen as tattling—something they have been taught not to do.

Dr. Olweus of the University of Bergen, Norway, has been named "the world's leading authority" on bullying by *The Times* newspaper of London. His Olweus

Bullying Prevention Program, used worldwide, is a multilevel, multicomponent school-based program designed to prevent or reduce bullying in elementary, middle, and junior high schools (students 6 to 15 years old).

A basic tenet is intervention by teachers when they see bullying behavior. Olweus recommends seven strategies: (1) adult supervision at recess, (2) strict enforcement of clear rules for student behavior, (3) consistent, nonphysical punishment of students who misbehave, (4) assistance to bullying victims that helps them to assert themselves, (5) parental encouragement that helps students develop and maintain friendships, (6) clear and positive communication between parents and school officials, and (7) clear and swift reaction to persistent physical or verbal bullying. Schools that implemented the program found a 40- to 50-percent reduction rate in bullying behavior within the first 2 years (*The Olweus Bullying Prevention Program*, 2006). The Olweus Bullying Prevention Program has proven results:

» A 30-percent reduction in student reports of being bullied and bullying others; results are largely parallel with peer ratings and teacher ratings

» Significant reductions in student reports of general antisocial behavior—for example, vandalism, fighting, theft, and truancy

» Significant improvements in classroom order and discipline

» More positive attitude toward schoolwork and school

A Partnership to Prevent Bullying

In December 2011, the Royal Canadian Mounted Police (RCMP) and researchers from the University of Victoria formed a partnership to address the issues of youth bullying and suicide. The effort draws on the evidence-based WITS Program to create communities that are responsive to the prevention of peer victimization and bullying. WITS stands for **W**alk away, **I**gnore, **T**alk it out, and **S**eek help—skills children can use to deal with bullying. Trained RCMP youth officers will partner with school staff, parents, and community leaders to take a unified approach to reducing bullying in their communities ("RCMP to Pilot WITS Bullying Prevention Program," 2012).

The Chula Vista Bullying Prevention Project

The Chula Vista (California) Police Department (CVPD) has implemented a successful bullying prevention program using the Olweus antibullying model. The program was funded by a School Community Policing Partnership grant for school districts, law enforcement, and community agencies to collaborate in reducing juvenile violence.

The project began by conducting annual surveys of students in three schools to determine the frequency, location, and types of bullying. Then a CVPD public safety analyst created a training curriculum to educate SROs on the different types of bullying, bullying's long- and short-term effects, and the best practices in intervening with this behavior. Each school that participated in the program organized a Bullying Prevention Committee, consisting of teachers, administrators, parents, campus staff, SROs, and family resource coordinators. Each committee developed a consistent message about bullying and delivered it to parents, educators, and students, thereby preventing students from getting mixed messages.

The SROs were a driving force behind the expansion of the project. When they responded to a bullying call at a school, they advised the administration about proactive steps that could be taken to reduce bullying. The Chula Vista Bullying Prevention Project has been adopted by nine schools and recognized with a 2005 Helen Putnam Award from the League of California Cities. According to the continuing surveys, the following results have been achieved (*Developing an Anti-bullying Program,* 2006):

» Name calling has been reduced 17 percent, and racial name calling has decreased 2 percent

» Exclusion from groups decreased by 9 percent

» Hitting and kicking decreased by 18 percent

» False rumors dropped by 13 percent

» Threats decreased by 21 percent

» Bullying has been reduced

　　» 23 percent in bathrooms

　　» 27 percent in gym classes

　　» 11 percent in lunchrooms

» More students (12%) were willing to intervene when witnessing bullying

» The vast majority of parents (82%) agreed that the school was treating bullying more seriously

Addressing bullying promises measurable returns in terms of crime prevention, violence reduction, and investment of scarce police resources. Unfortunately, bullying is not the only form of violence found in our schools.

School Shootings

Pearl, Mississippi; West Paducah, Kentucky; Jonesboro, Arkansas; Fayetteville, Tennessee; Springfield, Oregon; Richmond, Virginia; Littleton, Colorado; Conyers, Georgia; Santee, California; Red Lake, Minnesota; Chardon, Ohio—these cities house schools that come to mind when school violence is mentioned. While such shootings are, statistically, relatively rare events, "Each attack has a terrible and lasting effect on the students, school, and surrounding community—and on the nation as a whole" (Schuster, 2009, 42). Consider the 1999 tragedy at Columbine High School in Littleton, Colorado, where two shooters killed a dozen students and a teacher and wounded 23 others before turning their guns on themselves. Further investigation revealed the shooters had been plotting for a year to kill at least 500 and blow up their school.

One resource that details school shootings and other violent deaths occurring within the nation's schools is the National School Safety Center's *School Associated Violent Deaths* (SAVD) report. According to this report, the vast majority (74.7%) of school-associated violent deaths that occurred between 1992 and 2010 were caused by shootings, 77.4 percent of fatally injured victims were male, and 66.5 percent of deaths occurred at high schools (*School Associated Violent Deaths,* 2010).

School Shooters "I hate being laughed at. But they won't laugh after they're scraping parts of their parents, sisters, brothers, and friends from the wall of my hate." These words were written in the journal of 15-year-old Kip Kinkel before he killed both parents and then moved into his Springfield, Oregon, high school and shot more than two dozen students, two fatally (Piazza, 2001).

A study by the FBI's National Center for the Analysis of Violent Crime (NCAVC), *The School Shooter: A Threat Assessment Perspective*, declares: "All threats are not created equal" (O'Toole, 2000, 5). This study describes four categories of threats (O'Toole, 2000, 7):

direct threat

Identifies a specific act against a specific target and is delivered in a straightforward, clear, and explicit manner.

A **direct threat** identifies a specific act against a specific target and is delivered in a straightforward, clear, and explicit manner: "I am going to place a bomb in the school's gym."

indirect threat

Tends to be vague, unclear, and ambiguous; the plan, the intended victim, the motivation, and other aspects of the threat are masked or equivocal.

An **indirect threat** tends to be vague, unclear, and ambiguous. The plan, the intended victim, the motivation, and other aspects of the threat are masked or equivocal: "If I wanted to, I could kill everyone at this school!" …

veiled threat

One that strongly implies but does not explicitly threaten violence.

A **veiled threat** is one that strongly implies but does not explicitly threaten violence. "We would be better off without you around anymore" clearly hints at a possible violent act, but leaves it to the potential victim to interpret the message and give a definite meaning to the threat.

conditional threat

The type of threat often seen in extortion cases; warns that a violent act will happen unless certain demands or terms are met.

A **conditional threat** is the type of threat often seen in extortion cases. It warns that a violent act will happen unless certain demands or terms are met: "If you don't pay me one million dollars, I will place a bomb in the school."

 Threats may be classified as direct, indirect, veiled, and conditional.

The School Shooter (O'Toole, 2000, 26) stresses: "It is especially important that a school not deal with threats by simply kicking the problem out the door. Expelling or suspending a student for making a threat must not be a substitute for careful threat assessment and a considered, consistent policy of intervention. Disciplinary action alone, unaccompanied by any effort to evaluate the threat or the student's intent, may actually exacerbate the danger—for example, if a student feels unfairly or arbitrarily treated and becomes even angrier and more bent on carrying out a violent act."

The study (O'Toole, 2000, 10) describes an innovative model designed to assess someone who has made a threat and evaluate the likelihood that the threat will actually be carried out.

 The FBI's four-pronged assessment evaluates four major areas making up the "totality of the circumstances": (1) personality of the student, (2) family dynamics, (3) school dynamics and the student's role in those dynamics, and (4) social dynamics.

leakage

Occurs when a student intentionally or unintentionally reveals clues to feelings, thoughts, fantasies, attitudes, or intentions that may signal an impending violent act.

The first behavior listed as being associated with violence is leakage. **Leakage** occurs when a student intentionally or unintentionally reveals clues to feelings, thoughts, fantasies, attitudes, or intentions that may signal an impending violent act. These clues can take the forms of subtle threats, boasts, innuendos, predictions, or ultimatums. They may be spoken or conveyed in stories, diary entries, essays, poems, letters, songs, drawings, doodles, tattoos, or videos.

Data indicate that nearly half of school homicide perpetrators show some type of leakage, including making a verbal threat or leaving a written note (Booth, Van Hasselt, and Vecchi, 2011).

Leakage can be a cry for help, a sign of inner conflict, or boasts that may look empty but actually express a serious threat. Leakage is considered to be one of the most important clues that may precede an adolescent's violent act.

 Most students who are violent "leak" their feelings and intentions in the weeks and months before committing the violent act. Such messages should never be ignored.

The School Shooter: A Threat Assessment Perspective states that children who commit violent acts in school typically do not have a moment at which they "snap" from nonviolence into violence, but rather evolve gradually toward violence, with signposts along the way (O'Toole, 2000). The report stresses that the task for law enforcement agencies and school officials is to learn how to interpret the "leakage" and accurately assess whether a particular student poses a real threat to others or is merely having a bad day or "blowing off steam."

An extensive list of other personality traits and behaviors is presented (O'Toole, 2000, 17–21): low tolerance for frustration, poor coping skills, lack of resiliency, failed love relationship, "injustice collector," signs of depression, narcissism (self-centered), alienation, dehumanizes others, lack of empathy, exaggerated sense of entitlement, attitude of superiority, exaggerated or pathological need for attention, externalizes blame, masks low self-esteem, anger management problems, intolerance, inappropriate humor, manipulative, distrustful, closed social group, change of behavior, rigid and opinionated, unusual interest in sensational violence, fascination with violence-filled entertainment, negative role models, or behavior appears relevant to carrying out a threat.

The report (O'Toole, 2000, 15) stresses: "It should be strongly emphasized that this list is not intended as a checklist to predict future violent behavior by a student who has not acted violently or threatened violence. Rather, the list should be considered only *after* a student has made some type of threat and an assessment has been developed using the four-pronged model." It also cautions (15): "No one or two traits or characteristics should be considered in isolation or given more weight than the others. … Behavior is an expression of personality, but one bad day may not reflect a student's real personality or usual behavior patterns."

In addition, as Piazza (2001, 68) reports: "A study by the Secret Service National Threat Assessment center that looked at 37 school shootings found that in more than two-thirds of the attacks, the attackers felt persecuted, bullied, threatened, attacked, or injured by others." Factors associated with the family and violent behavior include a turbulent parent–child relationship, acceptance of pathological behavior, access to weapons, lack of intimacy, and the student "rules the roost" and there are no limits or monitoring of television and the Internet (O'Toole, 2000, 21–22).

According to *The School Shooter* (O'Toole, 2000, 22): "If an act of violence occurs at a school, the school becomes the scene of the crime. As in any violent crime, it is necessary to understand what it is about the school which might have influenced the student's decision to offend there rather than someplace else ... from the *student's perspective*. Factors to consider include the student's attachment to school, tolerance for disrespectful behavior, inequitable discipline, inflexible culture, pecking order among students, code of silence, and unsupervised computer access."

"Social dynamics," according to O'Toole (2000, 13), "are patterns of behavior, thinking, beliefs, customs, traditions, and roles that exist in the larger community where students live." Factors to consider include easy, unmonitored access to media, entertainment, and technology; peer groups; drugs and alcohol; outside interests; and the copycat effect. The study (O'Toole, 2000, 24) reports that copycat behavior is common and that everyone in the school should be more vigilant in noting disturbing student behavior in the days, weeks, and even months following a heavily publicized incident somewhere else in the country.

In 40 cases of school violence in the past 20 years, the Secret Service's National Threat Assessment found that teenagers often told someone before they did the deed. Most of these kids were White and they preferred (and somehow acquired) semiautomatics. Almost half had shown some evidence of mental disturbance, including delusions and hallucinations.

School officials want to know if there are any clear signs to watch for and to tell parents about. They know they must be especially careful because any action they take has the potential of landing them in court. The problem is that few school psychologists have received training on this issue, so they are not sure what to do or what to look for. As with all dangerousness assessments, the most telling factor in what a child might do is what a child has already done. In other words, a history of violent actions or words is the best indicator of future violence potential.

Any pattern of behavior that persists over time tends to intensify. This does not necessarily mean that a bully will become a school killer, but it means that kids who develop an obsession with weapons or violent games and who tend to threaten violence are more likely to eventually act out than those who do not. Some of the behaviors to be especially concerned about include an increase in lying, blaming others, avoiding responsibility, avoiding effort to achieve goals, using deception or force or intimidation to control others, showing lack of empathy for others, exploiting others' weaknesses, or engaging in petty crimes like theft or damage to property.

Other behaviors are getting involved in gang behavior, having a pattern of overreacting, having a history of criminal acts without a motive, experiencing continual family discord, having a history of criminality in the family, having a history of running away from home, showing a pattern of anger, and being depressed or withdrawn. Other behaviors include showing inconsistencies, such as a sudden uncharacteristic interest in guns; developing an intense dislike of school; complaining about classmates treating him or her badly; having excessive television or video game habits (three or more hours a day); carrying weapons such as a knife; complaining of feeling lonely; and showing intense resentment.

Preventing School Shootings and Other Targeted Attacks

In the wake of several highly publicized school shootings during the 1990s, most notably the massacre at Columbine High School in Littleton, Colorado, on April 20, 1999, the U.S. Secret Service and the U.S. Department of Education formed the Safe School Initiative (SSI) to study incidents of violence occurring in the nation's schools. One particular focus of examination by the SSI was whether past school-based attacks were planned, or *targeted*, and how such attacker preparations could be detected in an effort to prevent future attacks.

One of the most salient findings from the SSI was that in most attacks, other people knew beforehand about the perpetrators' plans (Vossekuil et al., 2002). In fact, in 81 percent of the incidents, at least one other person had some type of prior knowledge of the attacker's plan, and in 59 percent of the incidents, more than one person had such knowledge (Vossekuil et al., 2002). The overwhelming majority (93%) of those who knew of the plan in advance were the attacker's peers—friends, classmates, and siblings.

Many found it troubling that, despite advance knowledge about a planned attack at a school, the attacks still occurred. Thus, a follow-up study was conducted to explore how *bystanders*—those with some type of prior knowledge about planned school violence—decided what to do, if anything, after learning about the plan and to identify ways to encourage more students to share with an adult any information they learn about potential targeted school-based violence (Pollack, Modzeleski, and Rooney, 2008). One of the primary findings of the subsequent study was that the relationships between the bystanders and the attackers varied, as did the means by which bystanders came upon the information regarding the planned attacks (Pollack, Modzeleski, and Rooney, 2008, 6):

» 34 percent of bystanders were friends with the attacker
» 29 percent of bystanders were acquaintances, co-workers, or schoolmates
» 6 percent of bystanders were family members
» In 31 percent of the cases, the relationship was of another type or unknown
» 82 percent of the bystanders received information directly from the attacker
» 13 percent of bystanders were told secondhand
» In a majority of cases, bystanders received the information more than a day before the attack:
  » 59 percent were told days or weeks in advance
  » 22 percent were told months or years prior
  » Only 19 percent were told a few hours or less before the attack

Other notable findings from the study were (Pollack, Modzeleski, and Rooney, 2008):

» Bystanders shared information related to a threat along a continuum that ranged from bystanders who took no action to those who actively conveyed the information (6).
» School climate affected whether bystanders came forward with information related to the threats (7).
» Some bystanders disbelieved that the attacks would occur and thus did not report them (7).
» Bystanders often misjudged the likelihood and immediacy of the planned attack (7).
» In some situations, parents and parental figures influenced whether the bystander reported the information related to the potential attack to school staff or other adults in positions of authority (7).

AFTER-SCHOOL PROGRAMS

For many students, the closing bell at the end of the school day does not necessarily mean it is time to go home. For some of these youths, the hours after school present the most dangerous time of day. After-school programs are often touted as one means to keep youths out of trouble and to help them succeed in school. Data has consistently shown that on school days, juvenile crime and delinquency peaks in the hours immediately after school, when youths are more likely to be unsupervised. Research also links after-school programs to increased school-day attendance and improved graduation rates (Lee, 2010).

A Justice-Based After-School (JBAS) Program has been piloted by the COPS Office, which asserts: "Without supervision between the hours of 2 and 10 P.M., children are more likely to be victimized and to engage in risk-taking behavior" (*Justice-Based After-School Program,* 2002, 1). The JBAS program encourages law enforcement officers to work in partnership with community organizations, especially in high-crime neighborhoods, to develop a preventive approach to juvenile crime and victimization. In Minneapolis, Minnesota, for example, COPS funds have been used to expand an existing Police Athletic League (PAL) project in one school and to start programs in two other schools.

A poll of 1,200 youths between the ages of 13 and 18 found that 55.3 percent do not attend after-school programs other than sports because of lack of interest. Among the teens who do participate, 62.1 percent do so at school, 18.1 percent at a church, and 8.6 percent in a traditional after-school setting such as a YMCA. When asked what would increase their interest, 94.3 percent said they would like programs that offer opportunities for college scholarships; 92.1 percent said they would be interested if the programs offered an opportunity to earn college credit ("Teens Not Interested in After-School Programs," 2006).

TECHNOLOGY IN COMMUNITY POLICING: PREVENTING LOITERING AND VANDALISM WITH THE MOSQUITO

When youth are unsupervised and lack structured activity, their idle minds and hands may turn to mischief. Sometimes that mischief manifests as nuisance behavior, such as loitering around businesses, and may escalate into delinquent or criminal behavior, including vandalism. While many businesses, such as gas station convenience stores, have successfully kept loitering youths at bay by playing classical or chill-out music over their outside speakers, new technology is providing a more subtle way to deter loitering and prevent vandalism.

The Mosquito is one such device capable of emitting a high-frequency sound audible only to people under a certain age. It has been marketed to cities, municipalities, school districts, and parks boards throughout North America as a loitering and vandalism prevention tool. The patented Mosquito uses a small speaker to produce a high-frequency sound similar to the buzzing of the insect it is named after. The latest version of the Mosquito—the MK4 Multi-Age—has two different settings: the 17 KHz setting can be heard only by young people approximately 13 to 25 years of age, whereas the 8 KHz setting is audible to persons of all ages.

Source: "The Mosquito Device," Moving Sound Tech, 2012: http://www .movingsoundtech.com

Research on whether such programs are effective is mixed. In 2008 the Rand Corporation published results of a study of youth programs, including after-school programs (Beckett, 2008). The study concluded that some programs had positive effects whereas others did not. One after-school program was a low-cost program, open to all students. Participation in this program was found to have an overall *negative* effect on the participants themselves: "In the second year, participants were more likely to be suspended from school and to have been disciplined in school (e.g., missed recess or were sent out to the hall), and their teachers were more likely to have called parents about behavioral problems. Participation had no effects on academic outcomes, on social outcomes, on being supervised afterschool (by a parent, other adult, or older sibling), or on homework completion" (Beckett, 2008, 18). After-school programs that targeted at-risk youth, however, tended to be more research-based and have a longer history of careful program assessment and evaluation. Thus, for either or both of these reasons, more-convincing evidence of positive behavioral impacts was found among targeted (specialized) programs (Beckett, 2008).

Another report by Miller (2003) found differently. After examining the results of research studies conducted over two decades regarding a broad range of after-school programs, Miller concludes that the evidence supports a link between after-school program participation and educational success. With school resources becoming more limited, the debate over whether to provide after-school programs is likely to continue.

CREATING SAFE SCHOOLS

Figure 12.2 illustrates the strategic process in designing a safe school.

Figure 12.2   Strategic Process in Developing a Safe School

1. Develop school/community partnerships.
2. Conduct comprehensive needs assessment.
3. Develop comprehensive school plan.
4. Identify strategies and implement programs.
5. Conduct evaluation.
6. Share outcomes and make adjustments.

Source: Ira Pollack and Carlos Sundermann. "Creating Safe Schools: A Comprehensive Approach." *Juvenile Justice*, June 2001, p. 15.

New Jersey schools are using an iris recognition program to enhance security. The system, nicknamed T–PASS (Teacher–Parent Authorization Security System), links eye-scanning cameras with computers to identify people who have been preauthorized to enter the schools and, once their identity is confirmed, lets them in by unlocking the door. A review of the system noted: "Of the more than 9,400 times someone attempted to enter the schools using the iris scanner, there were no known false positives or other misidentifications" (Cohn, 2006, 14). The system appeared to make parents, teachers, and staff members feel safer in the school. A significant loophole in the system occurs, however, when someone who is authorized to enter, having passed the eye-scan check, holds the door open for others, who are then able to access the school without being scanned and authenticated.

 Two highly successful programs to help build safe schools are Student Crime Stoppers and PeaceBuilders®.

Student Crime Stoppers, like the adult program, offers youth tools to stand up against crime and violence without reprisal or peer pressure through an anonymous tip line to get the information to those who can stop the crime or violence. Those with information about solving crimes on school property or at school events can qualify for cash awards up to $100. The first Student Crime Stoppers program was started in a Boulder, Colorado, high school in 1983. Today, more than 2,000 programs exist in middle and high schools, community colleges, and colleges throughout the country.

PeaceBuilders® is a long-term, community-based, violence reduction or prevention program designed to help create an environment that reduces violence and establishes more peaceful ways of behaving, living, and working in families, schools, organizations, and communities. Schools may send up to four people to attend a 2 1/2-day training session to become site trainers. These site trainers then provide 4-hour PeaceBuilders® Staff Implementation Workshops at their schools or in their own districts. Up to 60 people may attend this workshop.

Safe schools depend not only on programs such as these but also on a comprehensive approach to safety.

 A seven-pronged approach is needed for effective school security: (1) school/law enforcement/community partnerships, (2) education about nonviolence, (3) problem-solving training, (4) mediation and anger management training, (5) clear policies on accepted behavior with consequences for nonconformity, (6) security procedures and technology, and (7) crisis planning.

The COPS Office has a long-standing and proven commitment to school safety, having invested more than $913 million in America's schools through programs like Secure Our Schools (SOS), COPS in Schools, School-based Partnerships, and the Safe Schools Initiative. In fiscal year 2011 more than $13 million in SOS grant funding was awarded to law enforcement agencies to help schools respond to growing school safety and security concerns ("Secure Our Schools," 2011).

School/Law Enforcement/Community Partnerships

The differences between traditional policing in the schools and community policing in the schools parallel those in the community, as summarized in Table 12.1.

> The IACP has published a *Guide for Preventing and Responding to School Violence* (2nd edition, 2009), which includes as one topic developing partnerships with schools. One of the oldest and most commonly used partnerships is assigning police officers to schools—the school resource officer (SRO).

Education about Nonviolence

Many school systems have successfully relied on counselors, nurses, and other specialists to supplement teachers' efforts to teach nonviolence, giving students a sense of a supportive network of adults available to help them resolve problems nonviolently.

Mediation and Anger Management Training

When a dispute occurs on school grounds, the involved parties seek out a teacher or the program's adult coordinator. The coordinator assigns peer mediators to intervene and attempt to resolve the dispute peacefully through the parties' mutual agreement and commitment to a contract with set

Table 12.1   Comparison between Traditional and Community Policing in Schools

Traditional Policing in Schools	Community Policing in Schools
Reactive response to 911 calls	Law enforcement officer assigned to the school "community"
Incident driven	Problem oriented
Minimal school–law enforcement interaction, often characterized by an "us versus them" mentality	Ongoing school–law enforcement partnership to address problems of concern to educators, students, and parents
Police role limited to law enforcement	Police role extended beyond law enforcement to include prevention and early intervention activities
Police viewed as source of the solution	Educators, students, and parents are active partners in developing solutions
Educators and law enforcement officers reluctant to share information	Partners value information sharing as an important problem-solving tool
Criminal incidents subject to inadequate response; criminal consequences imposed only when incidents reported to police	Consistent responses to incidents are ensured—administrative and criminal, as appropriate
Law enforcement presence viewed as indicator of failure	Law enforcement presence viewed as taking a positive, proactive step to create orderly, safe, and secure schools
Police effectiveness measured by arrest rates, response times, calls for service, etc.	Policing effectiveness measured by the absence of crime and disorder

Source: From "Guide 5: Fostering School–Law Enforcement Partnerships." Reprinted by permission of Education Northwest (formerly Northwest Regional Educational Laboratory).

standards for conduct. Such mediation may substitute for detention or suspension of youths involved in fights, verbal threats, or intimidation of others on school grounds.

Potential obstacles to this strategy include lack of funds for staff to train students and faculty and coordinate mediator assignments. In addition, convincing students that violence can be prevented can be difficult.

Clear Policies on Accepted Behavior with Consequences for Nonconformity

Clear policies should be established for tardiness, absenteeism/class cutting, physical conflicts among students, student tobacco use, verbal abuse of teachers, drug use, vandalism of school property, alcohol use, robbery or theft, gangs, racial tensions, possession of weapons, physical abuse of teachers, and sale of drugs on school grounds.

zero tolerance

A policy of punishing all offenses severely, no matter how minor an offense may be.

Many schools have adopted **zero tolerance** toward possession of guns, drugs, or alcohol in schools—that is, no matter what the underlying circumstances, a student bringing a weapon, drugs, or alcohol to school will be suspended or expelled.

No data suggest that zero-tolerance policies reduce school violence. Such policies result in sometimes unreasonable suspensions and expulsions.

Crisis Planning

The final prong in effective security is preparation—planning and practice. A crisis preparedness team might be formed to look at what technologies are available and the procedures that should be followed in a crisis.

THE CURRENT STATUS OF SCHOOL SAFETY IN THE UNITED STATES

Although concerns about school safety have never been greater than they are today, federal funding for programs has been on a steady decline since 2002.

At the federal level, funding was cut by one-third between 2002 and 2009. The Cops in Schools program was eliminated in 2008. States are cutting funding for school security, too, and local school districts are using funding they received for school security on textbooks. Antiviolence, bullying, and conflict resolution programs are disappearing. "Ten Years after Columbine" (2009, 1) states flatly: "Ten years and $10 billion dollars later, school are not significantly safer." The Executive Summary of this report explains (2009, 1):

> In the weeks following Columbine, national leaders expressed outrage and communities vowed to make schools safer for all children. "Zero Tolerance" laws regarding school violence were passed in over 28 states. At least 19 states passed antibullying laws. Over $10 billion has been spent nationwide on "airport-like"

security, such as cameras, metal detectors, fences, and security personnel. Despite these measures, there is very little evidence that Zero Tolerance, antibullying legislation, or increased spending on security has led to significantly safer schools.

While there has been some success in improving school safety, on average, the results are disappointing and point to the need for a more comprehensive approach. Violence-prevention efforts, to date, have had limited success for four primary reasons:

1. While high levels of federal funding were allocated to school violence prevention immediately following Columbine, in recent years, funding has been cut dramatically.

2. There has been an overemphasis by schools on an "outside-in" approach that focuses heavily on security, crisis management, and punitive measures.

3. There has not been enough emphasis on a complementary, "inside-out" approach that focuses on strengthening relationships and actively empowering young people to improve the school climate and change the social norms so that bullying and violence are no longer condoned.

4. There has been a failure to integrate violence-prevention strategies and social-emotional skills development programs and curricula into the schools' larger goals, culture, and climate.[4]

On overall violence prevention, the "Ten Years after Columbine" report gives our nation's schools a collective grade of D+.

HOPE FOR THE FUTURE

Despite the lack of progress in some areas, the outlook is not as bleak as some would paint it. Law enforcement agencies, particularly those embracing community policing, are part of the entire juvenile justice system, and that system appears to be changing. In introducing *The Future of American Children*, Steinberg (2008, 3) states: "American juvenile justice policy is in a period of transition.... State legislatures across the country have reconsidered punitive statutes they enacted with enthusiasm not so many years go. What we may be seeing now is a pendulum that has reached its apex and is slowly beginning to swing back toward more moderate policies, as politicians and the public come to regret the high economic costs and ineffectiveness of the punitive reforms and the harshness of the sanctions."

Combining this changing perspective with the focus of community policing on involving youths in partnerships and problem-solving efforts, the future for our youths can be more positive. In the words of James Baldwin: "For these are all our children. We will all profit by, or pay for, whatever they become."

---

[4] **Reprinted by permission of Community Matters.**

URBAN HIGH SCHOOL DISORDER REDUCTION PROJECT: THE IACP 2011 COMMUNITY POLICING AWARD IN THE 100,001 TO 250,000 POPULATION CATEGORY

Over a 6-year period, Belmont High School in Dayton, Ohio, was the scene of a reported 145 violent crimes. Responding to calls for service in and around the school had led to a significant decline in patrol officer efficiency in the affected district, and a growing number of complaints from residents and businesses indicated that the problem had spread beyond the school grounds. In response, the Dayton Police Department (DPD) partnered with Dayton Public Schools, the Montgomery County Juvenile Court, and the Juvenile Division of the Montgomery County Prosecutor's Office to create the Urban High School Disorder Reduction Project, the goal of which was to implement community-policing strategies, such as crime prevention through environmental design (CPTED) and the engagement of community stakeholders, to deny youths the opportunities for crime and disorder:

The project committee and stakeholders agreed on the following strategies:

1. Continuously communicating with all community partners
2. Identifying students requiring special intervention through arrest records
3. Reassigning classrooms to group students by grade level
4. Emphasizing a no-tolerance policy for violations and crimes
5. Assigning school staff members to monitor the lunch period, the school grounds, and nearby hot spots (alleyways, bus stops, bathrooms, hallways)
6. Assigning patrol officers to assist with monitoring hot spots and addressing violations
7. Establishing clear rules for student behavior
8. Reinforcing rules by making arrests, issuing citations, and subjecting students off school grounds to discipline

The project was successful on many levels. The number of crimes and calls for service were drastically reduced; there was a 76.6-percent drop in reported crime in the area, and a 92-percent decrease in the number of assaults (from 51 to 4). Educational goals were also enhanced, with the 9th grade graduation rate increasing 54 percent and the 10th grade rate increasing 38 percent. The number of 11th graders taking the ACT college entrance exam increased from just 8 percent during the 2008–2009 school year to 80 percent in the 2010–2011 school year. Finally, a safer environment was achieved for students and neighborhood residents. However, as the Dayton Police Department note, the work is far from over:

> Continued monitoring of the project is essential, as well as continued communication with Belmont High School's staff, students, and parents. DPD continues to improve those relationships by holding periodic in-school trainings like Prom DUI prevention. DPD also continues to monitor the school during monthly meetings with CAPERS (crime analysis police enforcement and response strategies), command staff, and other city agencies.

Source: "Urban High School Disorder Reduction Project." *IACP Community Policing Award: 2011 Winners and Finalists.* San Jose, CA: Cisco Systems, Inc., pp. 5–6. Retrieved August 17, 2012 from http://www.cisco.com/web/strategy/docs/gov/IACP_brochure.dpf

SUMMARY

Children and teenagers are an important segment of the community often overlooked when implementing the community policing philosophy. To counteract negative perceptions of police held by children and youths, many departments have programs aimed at fostering positive relations with them.

The developmental asset approach promotes (1) support, (2) empowerment, (3) boundaries and expectations, (4) constructive use of time, (5) commitment to learning, (6) positive values, (7) social competence, and (8) positive identity to help youngsters succeed in school and in life. Federal initiatives to protect our nation's youths include passage of the Adam Walsh Child Protection and Safety Act, America's Promise Alliance, Project Safe Childhood, and the Safe Start Initiative.

The family is viewed by many as the cornerstone of the community and should be included in community policing efforts focused on youths. Likewise, a school should be viewed as a community, not as an institution. Research suggests that students' academic motivation, commitment to democratic values, and resistance to problem behaviors depend on their experience of the school as a community. At a minimum, schools need to link with parents and with local law enforcement departments to teach students about the dangers of crime.

A precursor to school violence is bullying. Bullying is more accurately termed *peer child abuse.* Bullying has been seen as a rite of passage and has resulted in schools where violence is accepted. The "tell or tattle" dilemma occurs when students hesitate to tell anyone that they

are being bullied because it is seen as tattling—something they have been taught not to do.

Threats may be classified as direct, indirect, veiled, and conditional. The FBI's four-pronged assessment evaluates four major areas making up the "totality of the circumstances": (1) personality of the student, (2) family dynamics, (3) school dynamics and the student's role in those dynamics, and (4) social dynamics. Most students who are violent "leak" their feelings and intentions in the weeks and months before committing the violent act. Such messages should never be ignored.

Two highly successful programs to build safe schools are Student Crime Stoppers and Peace-Builders. In addition, a seven-pronged approach is needed for effective school security: (1) school/law enforcement/community partnerships, (2) education about violence, (3) problem-solving training, (4) mediation and anger management training, (5) clear policies on accepted behavior with consequences for nonconformity, (6) security procedures and technology, and (7) crisis planning. The IACP has published a *Guide for Preventing and Responding to School Violence* (2nd edition, 2009), which includes as one topic developing partnerships with schools. One of the oldest and most commonly used partnerships is assigning police officers to schools—the school resource officer (SRO).

One of the most popular strategies to promote safe schools is a zero-tolerance policy against violence, guns, and drugs in school. However, no data suggest that zero-tolerance policies reduce school violence. Such policies result in sometimes unreasonable suspensions and expulsions.

DISCUSSION QUESTIONS

1. Which of the programs for youths do you feel are the most effective?

2. Why do school administrators not consider drugs a security or crime problem?

3. What major differences in philosophy often exist between school administrators and police?

4. On which age group do you think police–school programs should focus? Why?

5. Was violence a problem in the high school you attended? If yes, what was the major problem?

6. What are the advantages and disadvantages of expelling disruptive students from school?

7. Is zero tolerance for violence, drugs, and weapons in school a workable policy? Why or why not?

8. How did you feel about the police when you were a child? Did that attitude change as you grew older? Why or why not? If so, how?

9. Do you think bullying is a serious problem? Did bullying occur in your school?

10. What risk factors for delinquent behavior do you think are most important?

GALE EMERGENCY SERVICES DATABASE ASSIGNMENTS

ONLINE Database

- Use the Gale Emergency Services Database to help answer the Discussion Questions as appropriate.

- Research either bullying or zero-tolerance policies. Outline your findings. Be prepared to share and discuss your outlines with the class.

- Read and outline "Scholastic Crime Stoppers: A Cost-Benefit Perspective" by Giant Abutalebi Aryani, Carl L. Alsabrook, and Terry D. Garrett. Be prepared to share and discuss your outline with the class.

REFERENCES

"About Safe Start." 2012. Washington, DC: Office of Juvenile Justice and Delinquency. http://www.safestartcenter .org/about/communities.php

"The Adam Walsh Act: The Cost of Compliance and the Danger to Juveniles in the Justice System." 2012 (January 17). Washington, DC: National Juvenile Justice Network. http://www.njjn.org/article/the-adam-walsh-act–the-cost-of-compliance-and-the-danger-to-juveniles-in-the-justice-system

"America's Promise Alliance Chair Alma Powell Says Reducing High School Dropout Rate and Elevating Young People on National Agenda Are Critical to Economic Growth." 2009 (April 1). Press release. Washington, DC: America's Promise Alliance. http://www.americaspromise.org/About-the-Alliance/Press-Room/Press-Releases/2009/2009-April-1--Americas-Promise-Alliance-Chair-Alma-Powell.aspx

Atkinson, Anne J. 2002 (September). *Fostering School–Law Enforcement Partnerships.* Naperville, IL: Northwest Regional Educational Laboratory.

Beckett, Megan K. 2008. *Current-Generation Youth Programs: What Works, What Doesn't, and at What Cost?* Santa Monica, CA: The Rand Corporation.

Booth, Brandi, Vincent B. Van Hasselt, and Gregory M. Vecchi. 2011. "Addressing School Violence." *FBI Law Enforcement Bulletin* (May): 1–9.

"Bullying." n.d. Charlottesville, VA: University of Virginia, Virginia Youth Violence Project. http://youthviolence .edschool.virginia.edu/bullying/home.html

Cohn, Jeffrey P. 2006. "Keeping an Eye on School Security: The Iris Recognition Project in New Jersey." *NIJ Journal* 254: 12–15.

Dedel, Kelly. 2005 (August). *School Vandalism and Break-ins.* Washington, DC: Office of Community Oriented Policing Services Problem-Oriented Guides for Police, Problem-Specific Guides Series, Guide No. 35.

Developing an Anti-bullying Program: Increasing Safety, Reducing Violence. 2006 (May). Arlington, VA: International Association of Chiefs of Police. http://www.theiacp.org/LinkClick.aspx?fileticket=RrzWMyZjLA0%3d&tabid=151

Ericson, Nils. 2001 (June). *Addressing the Problem of Juvenile Bullying.* Washington, DC: Office of Juvenile Justice and Delinquency Prevention, Fact Sheet #27.

Fact Sheet: Project Safe Childhood. 2012. Washington, DC: Department of Justice. http://www.justice.gov/psc/docs/psc-fact-sheet_2-21-12_.pdf

Falb, Kathryn L., Heather L. McCauley, Michele R. Decker, Jhumka Gupta, Anita Raj, and Jay G. Silverman. 2011. "School Bullying Perpetration and Other Childhood Risk Factors as Predictors of Adult Intimate Partner Violence Perpetration." *Archives of Pediatric and Adolescent Medicine* 165 (10): 890–894.

Federal Interagency Forum on Child and Family Statistics. 2011. *America's Children: Key National Indicators of Well-Being, 2011.* Washington, DC: U.S. Government Printing Office.

Finn, Peter. 2006. "School Resource Officer Programs: Finding the Funding, Reaping the Benefits." *FBI Law Enforcement Bulletin* (August): 1–7.

"First-Ever Gallup Student Poll Shows That One-Third of America's Young People Are Struggling or Suffering." 2009 (May 5). Press release. Gallup, America's Promise Alliance, and the American Association of School Administrators. http://www.aasa.org/content.aspx?id=1540

Forman, James, Jr. 2004. "Community Policing and Youth as Assets." *Journal of Criminal Law and Criminology* 95 (1): 1–48.

Garrett, Ronnie. 2005. "Kids Today..." *Law Enforcement Technology* 325 (5): 6.

Guide for Preventing and Responding to School Violence. 2009. 2nd edition. Alexandria, VA: The International Association of Chiefs of Police. http://www.theiacp .org/LinkClick.aspx?fileticket=MwvD03yXrnE%3D&ta bid=392

"Horizons Family Counseling." 2012. Livermore, CA: Livermore Police Department. http://www.cityoflivermore .net/citygov/horizons/default.asp

"HPD's T.A.P.S. Academy Receives National Recognition." 2012 (March 9). Press release. Houston, Texas: Houston Police Department. http://www.houstontx.gov/police/nr/2012/ mar/nr030912-1.htm

Justice-Based After-School Program. 2002 (October). Fact sheet. Washington, DC: Office of Community Oriented Policing Services.

"Kid Watch." 2010. Los Angeles, CA: University of Southern California. http://communities.usc.edu/neighbors/ kid_watch.html

Lee, Brian. 2010. *California's After-School Commitment: Keeping Kids on Track and out of Trouble.* San Francisco, CA: Fight Crime: Invest in Kids California.

Mannes, Marc, Eugene C. Roehlkepartain, and Peter L. Benson. 2005. *Unleashing the Power of Community to Strengthen the Well-Being of Children, Youths, and Families: An Asset-Building Approach.* Washington, DC: Child Welfare League of America.

McPherson, Lori. 2007. "Practitioner's Guide to the Adam Walsh Act." *Update* (published by the American Prosecutors Research Institute's National Center for Prosecution of Child Abuse) 20 (9–10).

Miller, Beth M. 2003 (May). *Critical Hours: After-School Programs and Educational Success.* Quincy, MA: Nellie Mae Education Foundation. http://www.nmefoundation .org/getmedia/08b6e87b-69ff-4865-b44e-ad42f2596381/ Critical-Hours?ext=.pdf

"Mission and Purpose." 2011. Washington, DC: America's Promise Alliance. http://www.americaspromise.org/ About-the-Alliance/Mission.aspx

"Mission Statement." 2009. San Diego, CA: Shop with a Cop San Diego. http://www.shopwithacopsandiego.com/ about.php

"The Mosquito Device." 2012. Moving Sound Tech. http:// www.movingsoundtech.com

"National Youth Strategy." 2012 (October 12). Ottawa, ON: Royal Canadian Mounted Police. http://www.rcmp-grc .gc.ca/yorc-crpe/nys-snj-eng.htm

The Olweus Bullying Prevention Program. 2006. Washington, DC: Substance Abuse and Mental Health Services Administration.

O'Toole, Mary Ellen. 2000. *The School Shooter: A Threat Assessment Perspective.* Washington, DC: Federal Bureau of Investigation. http://www.fbi.gov/stats-services/publi cations/school-shooter

"Our Work." 2011. Washington, DC: America's Promise Alliance. http://www.americaspromise.org/Our-Work.aspx

Outreach to Underserved Teen Victims of Crime: Chart a Course for Expanding Victim Services to Youth. 2012. Arlington, VA: National Crime Prevention Council and the National Center for Victims of Crime. http://www.ncpc.org/ resources/files/pdf/utvi/Outreach%20to%20Under served%20Teen%20Victims%20of%20Crime-DRAFT%20 Ciarlante-2%2028%2012.pdf

Piazza, Peter. 2001. "Scourge of the Schoolyard: Technology Alone Isn't Enough." *Security Management* (November 1): 68–73.

Pollack, Ira and Carlos Sundermann. 2011. "Creating Safe Schools: A Comprehensive Approach," *Juvenile Justice* 8 (1): 13–20.

Pollack, William S., William Modzeleski, and Georgeann Rooney. 2008 (May). *Prior Knowledge of Potential School-Based Violence: Information Students Learn May Prevent a Targeted Attack.* Washington, DC: U.S. Secret Service and U.S. Department of Education.

Presman, Dylan, Robert Chapman, and Linda Rosen. 2011 (September 11). *Creative Partnerships: Supporting Youth, Building Communities.* Washington, DC: Office of Community Oriented Policing Services. (e03021471)

"RCMP to Pilot WITS Bullying Prevention Program." 2011 (December 8). Ottawa, ON: Royal Canadian Mounted Police. http://www.rcmp-grc.gc.ca/news-nouvelles/2011/12-08-wits-eng.htm

Regional Youth Voice Forums. n.d. Washington, DC: Office of Youth Development.

Robers, Simone, Jijun Zhang, Jennifer Truman, and Thomas D. Snyder. 2012. *Indicators of School Crime and Safety: 2011.* Washington, DC: National Center for Education Statistics, U.S. Department of Education, and Bureau of Justice Statistics, Office of Justice Programs, U.S. Department of Justice. (NCES 2012-002/NCJ 236021)

School Associated Violent Deaths. 2010. Westlake Village, CA: National School Safety Center. https://docs.google.com/ viewer?a=v&pid=sites&srcid=c2Nob29sc2FmZXR5LnVz fG5zc2N8Z3g6NWFlZDdjZjBjMGY1Yjc3Mw

"School Crime Reporting and School Crime Underreporting." 2012. Cleveland, OH: National School Safety and Security Services. http://www.schoolsecurity.org/trends/ school_crime_reporting.html

Schuster, Beth. 2009. "Preventing, Preparing for Critical Incidents in Schools." *NIJ Journal* 262: 42–46. (NCJ 225765)

"Secure Our Schools." 2011 (September). Fact sheet. Washington, DC: Office of Community Oriented Policing Services. http://www.cops.usdoj.gov/pdf/2011AwardDocs/CSPP-SOS-CHP/2011-SOS-Post-FactSheet.pdf

Shader, Michael. 2002. *Risk Factors for Delinquency: An Overview.* Washington, DC: Office of Juvenile Justice and Delinquency Prevention. https://www.ncjrs.gov/ pdffiles1/ojjdp/frd030127.pdf

Sheppard, David. 1999 (February). *Promising Strategies to Reduce Gun Violence.* Washington, DC: Office of Juvenile Justice and Delinquency Prevention. (NCJ 173950)

Steinberg, Laurence. 2008. "Introducing the Issue." *Juvenile Justice: The Future of Children* 18 (2): 3–14.

Stopping Violence Before It Starts: Identifying Early Predictors of Adolescent Violence. 2005. Santa Monica, CA: The Rand Corporation.

"Teens Not Interested in After-School Programs." 2006. *American School Board Journal* 193 (9): 74–75.

"Teens on Target." 2010. Oakland, CA: YouthAlive! http://www.youthalive.org/teens-on-target

"Ten Years after Columbine: A Report Card on School Violence Prevention." 2009. Santa Rosa, CA: Community Matters. http://www.community-matters.org/downloads/ColumbineSchoolViolenceReportCardExecutiveSummary.pdf

"Urban High School Disorder Reduction Project." 2011. In *IACP Community Policing Award: 2011 Winners and Finalists*, 5–6. San Jose, CA: Cisco Systems. http://www.cisco.com/web/strategy/docs/gov/IACP_brochure.pdf

Vossekuil, Bryan, Robert Fein, Marisa Reddy, Randy Borum, and William Modzeleski. 2002. *The Final Report and Findings of the Safe School Initiative: Implications for the Prevention of School Attacks in the United States.* Washington, DC: U.S. Department of Education, Office of Elementary and Secondary Education, Safe and Drug-Free Schools Program, and U.S. Secret Service, National Threat Assessment Center.

Wang, Jing, Ronald J. Iannotti, and Tonja R. Nansel. 2009. "School Bullying among U.S. Adolescents: Physical, Verbal, Relational, and Cyber." *Journal of Adolescent Health* 45 (4): 368–375.

"Who Is Most Affected by Gun Violence?" 2010 (May 19). Washington, DC: National Institute of Justice. http://www.nij.gov/nij/topics/crime/gun-violence/affected.htm

Yeager, Dale, Sam Sulliman, Andreas Demidont, and Dane Brandenberger. 2006. *The State of School Safety in American Schools, 2004–2006.* Publically released version of a report prepared for Congress. Southeastern, PA: SERAPH Research Team.

"Youth Advisory Council." n.d. Washington, DC: Metropolitan Police Department. http://mpdc.dc.gov/page/youth-advisory-council-yac

Zahn, Margaret A., Robert Agnew, Diana Fishbein, Shari Miller, Donna-Marie Winn, Gayle Dakoff, Candace Kruttschnitt, Peggy Giordano, Denise Gottfredson, Allison A. Payne, Barry C. Feld, and Meda Chesney-Lind. 2010 (April). *Causes and Correlates of Girls' Delinquency.* Washington, DC: Office of Juvenile Justice and Delinquency Prevention. (NCJ 226358)

CHAPTER 13

The Challenge of Gangs: Controlling Their Destructive Force

Gangs are the master predators of the urban landscape. Their ability to instill fear into the people of a community knows no bounds. They will kill indiscriminately to make their point. This fear percolates through the community.

—Wesley D. McBride

DO YOU KNOW …

» How prevalent gangs are?

» What needs are served by gangs?

» What implications for preventing youths from joining gangs are suggested by the Seattle study?

» What the GREAT program is? The GRIP program?

» What indicators of gang activity are?

» What indicators of gang membership are?

» What strategies have been used to address the gang problem? Which has been found to be most effective?

» What OJJDP initiatives are available to help communities address a gang problem?

» What National Youth Gang Center publications are available to help communities address a gang problem?

» What strategies are currently being used to address the gang problem?

» Why a community might be ambivalent toward gangs?

CAN YOU DEFINE …

community mobilization
gang
graffiti
moniker
organizational development
pulling levers
representing
social intervention
social opportunities
street gang
suppression
turf
youth gang

INTRODUCTION

To underscore the important role community policing plays in addressing the challenge of gangs, renowned gang researcher Malcolm Klein has asserted: "The gang is, first and foremost, a community problem. It is the community's kids who decide whether or not to form or join gangs, and it is the community's residents, institutions, and businesses that are most victimized by gang activity" (2007, 84–85). Without question, law enforcement has a part to play in responding to gangs, but in the absence of partnerships with an engaged community, any policing efforts will be futile. According to the *2011 National Gang Threat Assessment* (2011, 9):

> Gangs are expanding, evolving, and posing an increasing threat to U.S. communities nationwide. Many gangs are sophisticated criminal networks with members who are violent, distribute wholesale quantities of drugs, and develop and maintain close working relationships with members and associates of transnational criminal/drug trafficking organizations. Gangs are becoming more violent while engaging in less typical and lower-risk crime, such as prostitution and white-collar crime. Gangs are more adaptable, organized, sophisticated, and opportunistic, exploiting new and advanced technology as a means to recruit, communicate discretely, target their rivals, and perpetuate their criminal activity.

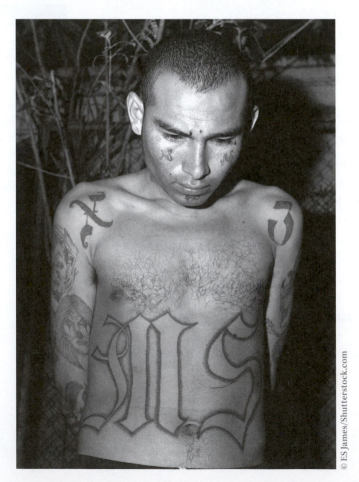

© ES James/Shutterstock.com

A gang member displays the many tattoos that identify him as belonging to the Mara Salvatrucha-13 (MS-13) gang.

This chapter begins with a discussion of understanding gangs and gang members, including definitions of gangs, types of gangs, the demographics of gangs, their subculture, and activities, including trends. Next is a look at why youths join gangs and how this might be prevented. This is followed by a discussion of recognizing the presence of gangs and identifying gang members. Then the traditional police response is described, followed by specific strategies to engage the community in addressing the problem. The chapter ends with examples of alternatives to gangs and other problem-solving partnerships in action.

UNDERSTANDING GANGS AND GANG MEMBERS

Gangs have spread through our country like a plague and now exist in rural, suburban, and inner cities—in every metropolitan area. Some analogize the gang problem to a societal cancer, where street gangs prey on the community like a malignant growth, eating away at its host until only a wasted shell remains. They use harassment, intimidation, extortion, and fear to control their territory. Daily, countless news stories depict the tragedy of gang violence. The following examples document only the tip of the problem:

» A gang fight at a crowded park results in a 7-year-old girl being shot in the head while picnicking with her family.

» Shotgun blasts from a passing car, intended for a rival gang member, strike a child.

» A shoot-out between rival gangs kills a high school athlete as he jogs around the school track.

The 2010 National Youth Gang Survey (NYGS) reports:

Nationally, violent crime and property crime rates have declined dramatically over the past decade. An enduring concern for many jurisdictions, however, is the continued presence of gangs and gang activity, which are often associated with violence and serious crimes. Despite the overall decline in crime, gang violence continues at high levels in some cities. . . .

The 15-year trend [in reported gang activity], marked by decreasing prevalence rates in the 1990s and increasing prevalence rates in the early 2000s, is statistically unchanged in the past 5 survey years. The overall estimate of gang activity in the study population remained stable from 2009 (34.5%) to 2010 (34.1%). Larger cities consistently reported greater rates of gang presence and seriousness of gang crime during the 15-year period.

Based on law enforcement responses to the NYGS, it is estimated that in 2010, there were 29,400 gangs and 756,000 gang members throughout 3,500 jurisdictions in the United States. Each estimate represents less than a 5-percent change from 2009, and although this change is not statistically significant, these numbers underscore the seriousness of the continuing national gang problem. (Egley and Howell, 2012, 1–2)

Table 13.1	Law Enforcement Reports of Gang Activity, 2005–2009	
Area Type	Gang Activity Reported in 2009	Gang Activity Consistently Reported, 2005–2009
Larger cities	86.3%	79.8%
Suburban counties	51.8	38.9
Smaller cities	32.9	23.8
Rural counties	17.0	11.0

Source: Arlen Egley, Jr. and James C. Howell. *Highlights of the 2009 National Youth Gang Survey*. Washington, DC: Office of Juvenile Justice and Delinquency Prevention, June 2011. p. 2.

Table 13.1 shows how the reported prevalence of gang activity varies by jurisdiction size.

 An estimated 756,000 gang members are active in more than 29,000 gangs nationwide.

The National Gang Threat Assessment is an annual intelligence evaluation of the threat posed to the United States by criminal gangs. The assessment is prepared by the National Gang Intelligence Center (NGIC) and is based on information from federal, state, and local law enforcement and supplemented with information retrieved from open sources. Key findings from the *2011 National Gang Threat Assessment* include the following (2011, 9–10):

» There are approximately 1.4 million active street, prison, and outlaw motorcycle gang members comprising more than 33,000 gangs in the United States.

» Gang membership increased most significantly in the Northeast and Southeast regions, although the West and Great Lakes regions boast the highest number of gang members. Neighborhood-based gangs, hybrid gang members, and national-level gangs such as the Sureños are rapidly expanding in many jurisdictions. Many communities are also experiencing an increase in ethnic-based gangs such as African, Asian, Caribbean, and Eurasian gangs.

» Gangs are increasingly engaging in non-traditional gang-related crime, such as alien smuggling, human trafficking, and prostitution. Gangs are also engaging in white collar crime such as counterfeiting, identity theft, and mortgage fraud, primarily due to the high profitability and much lower visibility and risk of detection and punishment than drug and weapons trafficking.

» Many gang members continue to engage in gang activity while incarcerated.

» Gangs encourage members, associates, and relatives to obtain law enforcement, judiciary, or legal employment in order to gather information on rival gangs and law enforcement operations. Gang infiltration of the military continues to pose a significant criminal threat, as members of at least 53 gangs have been identified on both domestic and international military installations.

» Gang members are acquiring high-powered, military-style weapons and equipment which poses a significant threat because of the potential to engage in lethal encounters with law enforcement officers and civilians. Gang members also target military and law enforcement officials, facilities, and vehicles to obtain weapons, ammunition, body armor, police gear, badges, uniforms, and official identification.

» Gangs on Indian Reservations often emulate national-level gangs and adopt names and identifiers from nationally recognized urban gangs.

» Gangs are becoming increasingly adaptable and sophisticated, employing new and advanced technology to facilitate criminal activity discreetly, enhance their criminal operations, and connect with other gang members, criminal organizations, and potential recruits nationwide and even worldwide.

Note that the National Gang Threat Assessment estimates given in the first bullet pertaining to gangs and gang membership differ substantially from those provided by the *2009 National Youth Gang Survey*. One explanation for this discrepancy is that no single, agreed-upon definition has been developed to apply to gangs; thus, estimates as to their magnitude and prevalence can vary significantly. Also, outlaw motorcycle gangs (OMGs) rarely include juveniles, and a significant number of prison gang members are adults, so membership counts that focus on youth gangs are likely to underestimate the scope of national gang involvement and activity.

Gangs Defined

Defining a gang is not always a simple, straightforward task. Some definitions emphasize criminal activity whereas others stress territoriality. A working group of American and European gang researchers, an assembly that has come to be known as the Eurogang program, defines a street gang as "any durable, street-oriented youth group whose own identity includes involvement in illegal activity" (Klein, 2007, 18). The National Youth Gang Center (NYGC) defines a youth gang as "a self-formed association of peers having the following characteristics: three or more members, generally ages 12 to 24; a name and some sense of identity, generally indicated by such symbols as style of clothing, graffiti, and hand signs; some degree of permanence and organization; and an elevated level of involvement in delinquent or criminal activity" (Howell and Egley, 2008, 1). The current federal law (18 USC § 521 (a)) defines a criminal street gang as "an ongoing group, club, organization, or association of five or more persons: (A) that has as one of its primary purposes the commission of one or more of the criminal offenses described in subsection (c); (B) the members of which engage, or have engaged within the past 5 years, in a continuing series of offenses described in subsection (c); and (C) the activities of which affect interstate or foreign commerce."

Adding to the challenge of defining a gang is the diversity observed among such groups: "There is no *one* form of street gang. Gangs can be large or small, long term or short term, more or less territorial, more or less criminally involved, and so on. If one treats all gangs as being the same, then the treatment will often be wrong, perhaps even making things worse. . . . It is the fact of gang diversity itself that should make us cautious about generalizing too quickly about their

gang

An ongoing group of people that form an allegiance for a common purpose and engage in unlawful or criminal activity. See also *street gang* and *youth gang*.

turf

Territory occupied by a gang, often marked by graffiti.

street gang

A group of people whose allegiance is based on social needs, who have an identifiable leadership, who claim control over a specific territory in the community, and who engage in acts injurious to the public; the preferred term of most local law enforcement agencies.

youth gang

A subgroup of a street gang; may refer to a juvenile clique within a gang.

nature" (Klein, 2007, 54). For the purposes of this discussion, a **gang** will be defined as an ongoing group of people that form an allegiance for a common purpose and engage in unlawful or criminal activity. Gangs are identified by a name, **turf** (territory) concerns, symbols, special dress, and colors. A gang is recognized by both its own members and by others.

A **street gang** is a group of people whose allegiance is based on social needs, who have an identifiable leadership, who claim control over a specific territory in the community, and who engage in acts injurious to the public. Members of street gangs engage in an organized, continuous course of criminality, either individually or collectively, creating an atmosphere of fear and intimidation in a community. Most local law enforcement agencies prefer the term *street gang* because it includes juveniles and adults and designates the location of the gang and most of its criminal behavior. For criminal justice policy purposes, a **youth gang** is a subgroup of a street gang. It may refer to a juvenile clique within a gang.

Types of Gangs

Gangs vary extensively in membership, structure, age, and ethnicity, but three basic types of gangs have been identified and defined by gang investigators: street gangs, prison gangs, and outlaw motorcycle gangs (OMGs) (*National Gang Threat Assessment*, 2011). One Percenter OMGs and neighborhood/local gangs are considered subsets of OMGs and street gangs, respectively (*National Gang Threat Assessment*, 2011, 7):

> **Street gangs** [emphasis added] are criminal organizations formed on the street operating throughout the United States . . . . Street gangs are involved in a host of violent criminal activities, including assault, drug trafficking, extortion, firearms offenses, home invasion robberies, homicide, intimidation, shootings, and weapons trafficking . . . . Gang control over drug distribution and disputes over drug territory has increased, which may be responsible for the increase in violence in many areas. Conflict between gangs, gang migration into rival gang territory, and the release of incarcerated gang members back into the community has also resulted in an increase in gang-related crime and violence in many jurisdictions.

> **Prison gangs** [emphasis added] are criminal organizations that originated within the penal system and operate within correctional facilities throughout the United States, although released members may be operating on the street. Prison gangs are also self-perpetuating criminal entities that can continue their criminal operations outside the confines of the penal system.

> **Outlaw Motorcycle gangs (OMGs)** [emphasis added] are organizations whose members use their motorcycle clubs as conduits for criminal enterprises. Although some law enforcement agencies regard only One Percenters as OMGs, the NGIC, for the purpose of this assessment, covers all OMG criminal organizations, including OMG support and puppet clubs.

> **One Percenter OMGs** [emphasis added] [The Bureau of Alcohol, Tobacco, Firearms, and Explosives] (ATF) defines *One Percenters* as any group of motorcyclists who have voluntarily made a commitment to band together to abide by their organization's rules enforced by violence and who engage in activities that

bring them and their club into repeated and serious conflict with society and the law. The group must be an ongoing organization, [an] association of three (3) or more persons who have a common interest and/or activity characterized by the commission of or involvement in a pattern of criminal or delinquent conduct. ATF estimates there are approximately 300 One Percenter OMGs in the United States.

Neighborhood or **Local street gangs** [emphasis added] are confined to specific neighborhoods and jurisdictions and often imitate larger, more powerful national gangs. The primary purpose for many neighborhood gangs is drug distribution and sales.

Demographics—Profile of Gang Members

The National Gang Center's *National Youth Gang Survey Analysis* (n.d.) provides demographic information about our country's gang population, including data about gang members' age, gender, and race/ethnicity.

Between 1998 and 2008, law enforcement agencies consistently reported a greater percentage of adult (age 18 and older) gang members compared with juvenile (under age 18) gang members. In 2008, the most recent year for which survey data is available, approximately three out of every five gang members were adults (*National Youth Gang Survey Analysis*, n.d.). Large cities and suburban areas, which generally have longer-standing gang problems, were more likely to report a higher ratio of adult to juvenile gang members, whereas smaller cities and rural counties—those areas where gang problems are relatively more recent—were more likely to report a higher percentage of juvenile gang members (*National Youth Gang Survey Analysis*, n.d.).

The overwhelming majority of gang members are male. However, nearly 25 percent of law enforcement agencies surveyed lacked data regarding the prevalence of female membership within their jurisdiction's gangs, a finding that suggests this issue is of secondary or lesser significance for law enforcement (*National Youth Gang Survey Analysis*, n.d.). And despite a growing concern about females joining gangs, there has been no significant change observed in the past decade in terms of the percentage of female gang members—reported percentages have held fairly steady between 7 and 8 percent of total gang membership (*National Youth Gang Survey Analysis*, n.d.).

A common misconception about gang demographics has been that they are comprised almost exclusively of racial or ethnic minorities (Howell, 2007). One explanation for the perpetuation of this fallacy is that most gang research has focused on high-risk neighborhoods in large cities—areas characterized by high rates of poverty, welfare dependency, single-parent households, and residential mobility. These highly socially disorganized communities, which tend to draw the attention of researchers, are also disproportionately inhabited by racial and ethnic minorities. Consequently, the assessment of the overall ethnic or racial composition of gangs becomes skewed (Howell, 2007). Nonetheless, law enforcement agencies do report a greater percentage of Hispanic/Latino and African American/Black gang members than other races or ethnicities, with the most recent data indicating an estimated 50 percent of gang members are Hispanic/Latino, 32 percent are African American/Black, 10 percent are White, and 8 percent are another race or ethnicity (*National Youth Gang Survey Analysis*, n.d.).

Table 13.2	Average Race/Ethnicity of Gang Members by Area Type, 2005–2008			
	Larger Cities	**Suburban Counties**	**Smaller Cities**	**Rural Counties**
Black or African American	35.6%	32.3%	29.6%	41.3%
Hispanic or Latino	48.1	43.8	49.7	30.2
White	9.3	14.5	15.3	18.9
Other	6.9	9.3	5.1	9.6

Source: *National Youth Gang Survey Analysis.* Washington, DC: National Gang Center, no date. Retrieved August 20, 2012 from http://www.nationalgangcenter.gov/Survey-Analysis/Demographics

Table 13.2 shows the average race/ethnicity of gang members in jurisdictions of varying sizes from survey years 2005 to 2008.

Although many, if not most, gangs are organized around race or ethnicity and are highly homogeneous with respect to this variable, some street gangs are more racially or ethnically heterogeneous in their membership. Such mixed-race or mixed-ethnicity gangs are known as hybrid gangs, a term that originally referred to a gang's ethnic or racial composition. More recently, however, hybrid gangs have come to include a more diverse group of gangs, including those in which membership is comprised of both males and females.

In the least populous areas—communities with populations of fewer than 50,000—gangs tend to be much smaller (Howell, 2006, 1). In these areas a youth gang problem may dissipate as quickly as it develops. This is especially true of communities with a population fewer than 25,000 and in rural counties. In the smallest areas (less than 25,000), only 10 percent of the localities report persistent gang problems.

In contrast, in cities and suburban areas with populations of 50,000 and greater, gang problems are more formidable. In areas with populations between 60,000 and 99,999, 58 percent of the communities report persistent gang problems. Of the next largest population group, 85 percent reported persistent gang problems, and 100 percent of the largest cities (populations of 250,000 and more) report persistent gang problems. In short: "The impact of gangs is notably worse in the more densely populated areas" (Howell, 2006, 2).

Los Angeles, the second-largest city in America, has one of the biggest gang problems, with approximately 45,000 gang members in 450 gangs threatening to overwhelm the city. Many of these gangs have existed for more than 50 years. Between 2009 and 2012, there were over 16,398 verified violent crimes in the City of Los Angeles, including 491 homicides, 98 rapes, more than 7,000 felony assaults, and approximately 5,500 robberies ("Gangs," 2012).

The Gang Subculture

A gang member's lifestyle is narrow and limited primarily to the gang and its activities. Members develop fierce loyalty to their respective gang and become locked into the gang's lifestyle, values, attitudes, and behavior, often making it difficult for a member to later break away from a gang.

A gang member may receive a new identity by taking on a nickname, or **moniker**, which others in the gang world would recognize. Monikers affirm a youth's commitment to gang life and may become their sole identity, the only way they see themselves and the only name they go by. They may no longer acknowledge their birth name, rejecting any previous identity or life outside the realm of the gang.

moniker
A nickname, often of a gang member.

GANG ACTIVITIES AND THEIR IMPACT ON COMMUNITIES

Gangs have different characteristics based on the activities in which they engage. Some gangs are violent; others focus on crime commission with violence as a by-product. The same is true with a gang's relationship to drugs. Some focus on the drug business; others engage in business to meet their own drug needs.

Females are used by gangs in a variety of ways, often because they arouse less suspicion than male adults. Females may serve as lookouts for crimes in progress, conceal stolen property or tools used to commit crimes, carry weapons for males who do not want to be caught with them, carry information in and out of prison, and provide sexual favors (they are often drug dependent and physically abused).

Gangs use children to commit shoplifting, burglaries, armed robberies, and drug sales in schools. Their youthful appearance is an advantage because they often do not arouse suspicion. Furthermore, if they are caught, the juvenile justice system generally deals more leniently with them than with adults.

Most youths who join gangs are already involved in delinquency and drug use, but once in a gang, they usually become more actively involved in delinquency, drug use, and violence—and are more likely to be victimized themselves. Gang involvement dramatically alters youths' life chances, particularly if they remain active in the gang. The street-life cycle of many gang members involves going from a community to detention, to juvenile corrections, to adult prisons, and back into a community. Howell (2006, 3) contends: "Gang members were more likely than nonmembers to be arrested, were rearrested more quickly following release from prison, were rearrested more frequently, and were more likely to be arrested for violent and drug offenses than were nongang members."

Research consistently demonstrates that youths are significantly more criminally active during periods of gang membership, particularly in serious and violent offenses. Furthermore, gang members commit more serious crimes. In general, gang members' violent offense rates are up to seven times higher than those of nongang members. Studies comparing the criminal behavior of gang members with nongang members show that gang members living in high-crime areas are responsible for far more than their share of all self-reported violent offenses committed by the entire sample (Howell, 2006). The NGIC indicates that gang members are responsible for an average of 48 percent of violent crime in jurisdictions across the nation and may be responsible for as much as 90 percent or more of violent crime in some areas (*National Gang Threat Assessment*, 2011). Gangs are also estimated to be responsible for 17 to 24 percent of all homicides occurring throughout the United States each year.

In some large cities, youth gangs and drug gangs have taken over a number of public-housing developments: "Fear of crime and gangs was an 'immediate,' daily experience for people who lived in lower-income neighborhoods where gangs were more prevalent and dangerous. But for people in other areas, fear was generally an abstract concern about the future that became immediate only when they entered certain pockets of the county" (Howell, 2006, 3).

When they have a "substantial presence," youth gangs are linked with serious delinquency problems in elementary and secondary schools in the United States. A strong correlation exists between gangs in schools and both guns and availability of drugs in school. The presence of gangs at school more than doubles the likelihood of violent victimization at school. And while the economic impact of gang crimes cannot be estimated because most law enforcement agencies do not record such data, clearly there is a high social cost associated with gangs' presence in a community.

Analysis of gang activity, past and present, has led the NGIC to form the following outlook regarding gangs in the United States (*National Gang Threat Assessment*, 2011, 46):

» Gangs will increasingly seek to diversify both their membership and their criminal activities in recognition of potential financial gain. New alliances between rival gangs will likely form as gangs suspend their former racial ideologies in pursuit of mutual profit. Gangs will continue to evolve and adapt to current conditions and law enforcement tactics, diversify their criminal activity, and employ new strategies and technology to enhance their criminal operations, while facilitating lower-risk and more profitable schemes, such as white collar crime.

» The expansion of communication networks, especially in wireless communications and the Internet, will allow gang members to form associations and alliances with other gangs and criminal organizations—both domestically and internationally—and enable gang members to better facilitate criminal activity and enhance their criminal operations discreetly without the physical interfacing once necessary to conduct these activities.

» Changes in immigrant populations, which are susceptible to victimization and recruitment by gangs, may have the most profound effect on street gang membership.

» Continued drug trafficking-related violence along the U.S. Southwest border could trigger increased migration of Mexicans and Central Americans into the United States and, as such, provide a greater pool of victims, recruits, and criminal opportunities for street gangs as they seek to profit from the illegal drug trade, alien smuggling, and weapons trafficking.

» Street gang activity and violence may also increase as more dangerous gang members are released early from prison and re-establish their roles armed with new knowledge and improved techniques.

» Gang members armed with high-powered weapons and knowledge and expertise acquired from employment in law enforcement, corrections, or the military may pose an increasing nationwide threat, as they employ these tactics and weapons against law enforcement officials, rival gang members, and civilians.

» Stagnant or poor economic conditions in the United States, including budget cuts in law enforcement, may undercut gang dismantlement efforts and encourage gang expansion as police agencies redirect their resources and disband gang units and taskforces, as reported by a large number of law enforcement agencies.

WHY YOUTHS JOIN GANGS

Gangs have strong appeal for many children who live in communities where gangs thrive. Gangs can fulfill the need to belong or the need for attention. Children with low self-esteem can gain identity in the gang culture (Krohn et al., 2011). Gang membership also can provide friendship and the emotional and psychological support lacking in a child's home (Miller, Barnes, and Hartley, 2011). Additional reasons youths may join gangs include the potential to make "easy money," to engage in exciting activities, and to express defiance by rebelling against parents and other authority figures. Additionally, to children living in crime-ridden neighborhoods with heavy gang activity, joining a gang may give them the only way they know to feel safe. They join to gain protection from violence and attack from rival gangs or because they are forced into membership by a gang's violent recruitment methods. And some children are simply following family tradition.

Shelden, Tracy, and Brown (2004, 175) report: "There is a general consensus in the research literature that girls become involved in gang life for generally the same reasons as their male counterparts—namely, to meet basic human needs, such as belonging, self-esteem, protection, and a feeling of being a member of a family. The backgrounds of these young women are about the same as those of male gang members—poverty, single-parent families, minority status, and so on." They also note: "The case studies of girl gang members in many different parts of the country reveal the common circumstances in their lives. The crimes that they commit are for the most part attempts to survive in an environment that has never given them much of a chance in life. Most face the hardships that correspond to three major barriers: being a member of the underclass, being a woman, and being a minority. The gang, while not a total solution, seems to them a reasonable solution to their collective problems."

Youths seeking protection, security, status, an identity, a sense of belonging, and economic security can fulfill all of these needs through gang membership.

Gangs often fulfill survival functions for youths in low-income, socially isolated ghetto or barrio communities and in transitional areas with newly settled populations. In the text by Shelden and colleagues, an entire chapter is devoted to inequality in American society and concludes: "Unemployment, poverty, and general despair lead young people to seek out economic opportunities in the growing illegal marketplace, often done within the context of gangs" (Shelden, Tracy, and Brown, 2004, 191). It must be emphasized, however, that despite the numerous enticements, the vast majority of youths living in gang-ridden areas never join a gang.

PREVENTING GANG MEMBERSHIP

Common sense suggests that preventing a gang problem in the first place is preferable to finding strategies to deal with such a problem after it surfaces. Research has identified risk factors associated with gang membership, with implications for developing effective, targeted prevention and intervention methods.

Early Precursors of Gang Membership and Implications for Prevention

The Seattle Social Development Project (SSDP) is a long-term study that looks at the development of positive and problem behaviors among adolescents and young adults. The study began in 1981 to test strategies for reducing childhood risk factors for school failure, drug abuse, and delinquency. This project identified childhood risk factors that predict whether a youth is likely to join a gang and the duration of the membership.

Findings from the SSDP study have three implications for efforts to prevent youths from joining gangs (Hill, Lui, and Hawkins, 2001, 4):

 Prevention efforts should (1) begin early, (2) target youths exposed to multiple risk factors, and (3) address all facets of youths' lives.

Prevention Efforts Should Begin Early   Although research indicates that the peak age for joining a gang was 15, this does not mean that prevention efforts should be aimed only at 14-year-olds. Instead, prevention efforts should begin well before the peak age for joining a gang, around ages 10 to 12, according to the study (Hill, Lui, and Hawkins, 2001).

Prevention Efforts Should Target Youths Exposed to Multiple Risk Factors   As with risk factors for generalized delinquency and youth victimization, risk factors for joining a gang fall into five broad categories: individual, family, peer groups, school, and neighborhood/community (Hill, Lui, and Hawkins, 2001). The more risk factors present in a youth's environment, the higher his or her odds are of joining a gang. Compared with youths who experienced none or only 1 of the 21 risk factors, youths who experienced 7 or more were 13 times more likely to join a gang.

Prevention Efforts Should Address All Facets of Youths' Lives   Efforts to prevent youths from becoming gang members must address the different aspects of their lives. No single solution or "magic bullet" will prevent youths from joining gangs.

The GREAT Program

One program aimed at preventing gang membership is the Gang Resistance Education and Training (GREAT) program, a nationally used program with some proven success.

The Gang Resistance Education and Training (GREAT) program is aimed at stopping gang membership.

The GREAT program is a proactive approach to deter violence before it begins. The program builds a foundation focused on teaching children the life skills they need to avoid violence and gang membership. A study supported by the National Institute of Justice (NIJ) documented the program benefits in a cross-sectional evaluation. The study showed that students who graduated from the GREAT course showed lower levels of delinquency, impulsive behavior, risk-taking behavior, and approval of violence. The study also found that students demonstrated higher levels of self-esteem, parental attachment, commitment to positive peers, antigang attitudes, perceived educational opportunities, and positive school environments.

The GRIP Program

Another prevention program with some proven effectiveness is the Gang Resistance Is Paramount (GRIP) program developed by the city of Paramount, California, after it recognized in the early 1980s that it had a severe gang problem and that its efforts to dismantle established gangs had little success. Paramount decided the key to approaching their problem was prevention.

The Gang Resistance Is Paramount (GRIP) program seeks to prevent youths from joining gangs through education.

The GRIP program teaches second-, fifth-, and ninth-grade students about gangs and territory, gangs and vandalism, peer pressure, drugs, alcohol, gangs and family, self-esteem, gang violence, gangs and the police, and alternatives to gang membership. A University of Southern California research team evaluated 20 years of experience with GRIP and found a significant decrease in the activity of major gangs, gang members, and the ratio of gang members to residents in Paramount since the program began in 1982 (Solis, Schwartz, and Hinton, 2003). A survey of 735 ninth-grade students found that those who had experienced the GRIP program were less likely to report involvement with gang activity than nonparticipating students, were more likely to have negative perceptions of gang activities, and were more likely to believe that drugs and alcohol are a big part of gang life (Solis, Schwartz, and Hinton, 2003).

Connecting with Youths—*Cops and Kids*

Just as many departments are connecting with youths to combat the drug problem, many departments seek to connect with youths to prevent their involvement in gangs. One initiative aimed at improving the youth–police connection is *Cops and Kids*, a professional development training program created by the Pittsburgh-based Fred Rogers Company (producers of the well-known public television program *Mr. Rogers' Neighborhood*). The training is intended to increase officer effectiveness in encounters and interactions with youth by

(1) raising officers' awareness of the tremendous impact their presence has on children and (2) showing how basic knowledge of children's development can enhance an officer's impact, safety, and ability to achieve law enforcement goals ("Nationwide Rollout of 'Cops and Kids' Trainings Begin," 2011). The program's success in the Pittsburgh area led to its receiving a COPS Office grant to conduct workshops in other cities throughout the country: "This training program gives officers the tools they need to build trust among children and families in the communities they serve; increases their safety and effectiveness while on patrol; helps them promote greater cooperation and reporting of criminal activity; strengthens partnerships with social service agencies that provide protective services to children; and enhances officers' ability to improve public safety ("Nationwide Rollout of 'Cops and Kids,'" 2011). Efforts such as this can go far in equipping police with the skills they need to effectively connect with their community's teens and help steer them away from the destructive forces of gangs.

When prevention efforts fail, it is important that communities recognize the presence of a gang or gangs in their neighborhoods and take steps to address the problem.

RECOGNIZING THE PRESENCE OF GANGS (OR A GANG PROBLEM)

Within the school, gangs can thrive on anonymity, denial, and lack of awareness by school personnel. The gang member whose notebook graffiti goes unaddressed today may likely be involved in initiations, assaults, and drug sales in school in the near future.

The condition that makes the school environment most ripe for gang activity is *denial* because public officials who are more focused on image concerns for their organizations have misplaced their efforts, which should be on dealing with the problem. The longer the denial continues, the more entrenched the problem becomes, and in the end, the worse the image will be. Even when school and community officials come out of denial and acknowledge a gang presence, they tend to downplay it and give a "qualified admittance" of the problem, underestimating its extent. This tactic only leads to a more serious gang problem in the end.

The flip side of the issue is that a gang problem in a school or community should not be *overstated,* making people unnecessarily fearful or giving the gang more credit and status. The majority of students in any given school are not in a gang and do not want gang activity in their institutions. The problem, however, is that a small number of gang members, along with their associates outside the school, can account for a significant amount of violence in a short time if their activities go unaddressed: "Both denial of gang problems and overreaction to them are detrimental to the development of effective community responses to gangs. Denial that gang problems exist precludes early intervention efforts. Overreaction in the form of excessive police force and publicizing of gangs may inadvertently serve to increase a gang's cohesion, facilitate its expansion, and lead to more crimes" (Howell, 2006, 53).

School officials and community leaders can prevent such occurrences—or at least reduce the risks and impact of those that do occur—by training their staff on gang identification, behavior, prevention and intervention strategies, and related school security issues.

 Indicators of gang activity include graffiti, drive-by shootings, intimidation assaults, murders, and the open sale of drugs.

Once a community recognizes a gang problem, the next step is to identify the gang members.

IDENTIFYING GANG MEMBERS

Often people think of "colors" or tattoos as indicating membership in a gang. However, as the National School Safety and Security Services suggests, gang membership indicators can be quite subtle, especially when school officials, law enforcement, parents, and other adults become increasingly aware of a gang's presence ("Gangs and School Safety," 2012). Gang identifiers can vary but may include:

» *Colors*: clothing in a particular color; also includes wearing of a specific brand of clothing or jewelry, or wearing a specific style of haircut

» *Tattoos*

» *Lit* (gang literature): often found in notebooks and depicting gang signs and symbols; gang-related poems, prayers, procedures, etc.

» *Initiations*: injuries caused by "jumping in"–type initiation rituals

» *Hand signs*

» *Behavior*

Gang allegiance may also be indicated by **representing**, a manner of dress that uses an imaginary line drawn vertically through the body. Anything to the left of the line represents "dress left" and vice versa. An example of right dress would be a hat cocked to the right side, right pants leg rolled up, a bandanna in gang colors tied around the right arm, one glove worn on the right hand, right-side pocket turned inside out and sometimes dyed gang colors, shoes or laces of the right shoe in gang colors, belt buckle worn loose on the right side, earrings worn in the right ear, and two fingernails on the right hand painted in gang colors.

representing
A manner of dress to show allegiance or opposition to a gang; uses an imaginary line drawn vertically through the body.

 Indicators of gang membership include colors, tattoos, hand signs, and behavior.

One or several of these identifiers may indicate gang affiliation. It is important to remember, however, that identifiers help recognize gang affiliation, but a focus on behavior is especially important.

According to Howell (2006, 27): "Determining a particular individual's gang involvement is as difficult as identifying true youth gangs. In many instances, a youth may associate occasionally with a gang, participate episodically in the activities of a gang, or desire gang membership without actually being a member. Likewise, many youths leave gangs by drifting out, gradually dissociating

Girlfriends of gang members flash their gang signs at the Mexican Day Parade in New York City.

© Joel Gordon

themselves. Because severe criminal sanctions can be applied to gang membership in certain jurisdictions, a valid determination is important." The following criteria (any one of which qualifies the individual) might be used to determine whether a youth is a gang member:

» The individual admits membership in a gang (i.e., self-reported)

» A law enforcement agency or reliable informant identifies an individual as a gang member

» An informant of previously untested reliability identifies an individual as a gang member, and this information is corroborated by an independent source

» The individual resides in or frequents a particular gang's area and adopts its style of dress, use of hand signs, symbols, or tattoos; maintains ongoing relationships with known gang members; and has been arrested several times in the company of identified gang members for offenses consistent with usual gang activity

» There is reasonable suspicion that the individual is involved in a gang-related criminal activity or enterprise

THE POLICE RESPONSE

Often, police chiefs in cities where gangs have recently arrived are slow to recognize the threat. If police chiefs deny a gang problem despite mounting evidence, the gang problem may become unmanageable. However, if police publicly acknowledge the existence of gangs, this places the police administrator in a catch-22 situation. Publicly acknowledging gangs validates them and provides notoriety.

An important task in most police departments is gathering information or intelligence on gangs and their members. Intelligence is knowing what gangs are out there, where they are, the names of the individual gang members and their gang affiliation, where they have been seen, and who they have been seen with. Howell (2006, 53) recommends: "Each city's gang program should be supported by a gang information system that provides sound and current crime incident data that can be linked to gang members and used to enhance police and other agency interventions. At a minimum, law enforcement agencies must ensure that gang crimes are coded separately from nongang crimes so that these events can be tracked, studied, and analyzed to support more efficient and effective antigang strategies."

A computerized Gang Intelligence System (GANGIS), including comprehensive gang profile data such as monikers and vehicle information, can be an effective crime-fighting tool.

National networks of gang intelligence databases can greatly enhance a department's effort to understand and respond to gang activities in their jurisdiction. The Regional Information Sharing System (RISS) network links six regional intelligence databases, including a gang database, RISS-GANGS. Another computer technology used for tracking gangs is the General Reporting, Evaluation, and Tracking (GREAT) system—a combination hot sheet, mug book, and file cabinet. This system is not to be confused with the GREAT program used in schools to teach children about resisting gangs, discussed earlier in the chapter.

The proliferation of gang problems in jurisdictions of all sizes—urban, suburban, and rural—over the past two decades led to the development of a comprehensive, coordinated response to the nation's gang problem by the Office of Juvenile Justice and Delinquency Prevention (OJJDP), which has long supported a combination of activities, including research, evaluation, training and technical assistance, and demonstration programs, aimed at combating youth gangs. However, upon recognizing that street gang activities transcend the ages of gang members, the Office of Justice Programs merged its existing resources in October 2009 to create a new National Gang Center (NGC), to create a comprehensive approach to reduce gang involvement and levels of gang crime. The reinvigorated NGC is a single, more efficient entity, responsive to the needs of researchers, practitioners, and the public. The NGC Web site (www.nationalgangcenter .gov) features the latest research about gangs; descriptions of evidence-based, antigang programs; and links to tools, databases, and other resources to assist in developing and implementing effective community-based gang prevention, intervention, and suppression strategies. The site also posts data analysis of the findings from nearly 15 years of data collected by the annual National Youth Gang Survey (NYGS) of 2,500 U.S. law enforcement agencies.

EVOLUTION OF STRATEGIES FOR DEALING WITH THE GANG PROBLEM

The Office of Juvenile Justice and Delinquency Prevention (OJJDP) reports a distinct difference in the approach used in the 1950s and 1960s compared to that used in more recent years. In the 1950s and 1960s law enforcement used a social services approach toward gangs. During more recent years the focus has been on suppression. Neither approach is clearly superior. Some communities have adopted a comprehensive approach combining social services intervention and suppression strategies (National Gang Center, 2010).

suppression

Strategy to address the gang problem that includes tactics such as prevention, arrest, imprisonment, supervision, and surveillance.

social intervention

Strategy to address the gang problem that includes crisis intervention, treatment for youths and their families, outreach, and referral to social services.

social opportunities

Strategy to address the gang problem that includes providing basic or remedial education, training, work incentives, and jobs for gang members.

community mobilization

Strategy to address the gang problem that includes improved communication and joint policy and program development among justice, community-based, and grassroots organizations.

organizational development

A law enforcement strategy to address the gang problem that includes special police units and special youth agency crisis programs.

 According to the OJJDP, law enforcement has used five strategies to address the gang problem: suppression, social intervention, social opportunities, community mobilization, and organizational development.

Suppression includes tactics such as prevention, arrest, imprisonment, supervision, and surveillance. **Social intervention** includes crisis intervention, treatment for youths and their families, outreach, and referral to social services. **Social opportunities** include providing basic or remedial education, training, work incentives, and jobs for gang members. **Community mobilization** includes improved communication and joint policy and program development among justice, community-based, and grassroots organizations. **Organizational development** includes special police units and special youth agency crisis programs.

 The OJJDP found community mobilization to be the most effective strategy to address the gang problem.

According to Howell (2006, 5):

Communities that begin with suppression as their main response generally discover later that cooperation and collaboration between public and private community agencies and citizens are necessary for an effective solution. Considerable advantage accrues from involving the entire community from the onset, beginning with a comprehensive and systematic assessment of the presumed youth gang problem. Key community leaders must mobilize the resources of the entire community, guided by a consensus on definitions, program targets, and interrelated strategies. Comprehensive programs that incorporate prevention, intervention, and enforcement components are most likely to be effective.

Suppression—The Traditional Police Response

Howell (2006, 53) reports: "Law enforcement agents view suppression tactics (e.g., street sweeps, intensified surveillance, hot spot targeting, and caravanning), crime prevention activities, and community collaboration—in that order—as most effective in preventing and controlling gang crime. Targeting specific gang crimes, locations, gangs, and gang members appears to be the most effective suppression tactic; therefore, police increasingly adhere to the mantra: 'Investigate the crime; not the culture.'"

The *suppression component* involves collaboration between police, probation, and prosecution, targeting the most active gang members and leaders. The *intervention component* would help gang members who want to get out of the gang and help them immediately. They might be referred to a community program, given the chance to finish high school or obtain a GED, have tattoos removed, or find employment. The *prevention component* would give young children the tools to handle the pressures involved in living in a gang neighborhood or attending a school with a gang problem.

A valuable partner to law enforcement in gang suppression efforts is corrections: To enhance suppression efforts, many departments have established gang units or task forces.

Gang Units

To combat the gang problem a full-service gang unit uses the components of prevention, suppression, and intervention. Respondents to the National Youth Gang Survey provided information regarding operation of a gang unit in their agency, defined in the survey as "a specialized unit with at least two officers primarily assigned to handle matters related to youth gangs." The survey found (*National Youth Gang Survey Analysis*, n.d.):

» Approximately 4 in 10 law enforcement agencies with a gang problem operated a gang unit in 2006, including 54 percent of larger cities.

» With the exception of smaller cities, the percentage of agencies operating a gang unit increased yearly and was highest in 2006.

» In 2006, 31 percent of law enforcement agencies with a gang problem that did not operate a gang unit reported that one or more officers were assigned to handle gang problems exclusively.

Weisel and Shelley (2004) studied specialized gang units and their function in community policing. They found that between 1980 and the mid-1990s, the number of specialized gang units increased substantially, an increase coinciding with the unprecedented adoption of community policing. In many ways, the increase in gang units seems in conflict with the move to community policing and its emphasis on decentralization and despecialization within law enforcement agencies.

Instead of preventing gangs from forming, the gang units in this study focused primarily on both preventing and controlling criminal activity related to gangs. These preventive and control strategies were not focused on indiscriminate enforcement tactics but reflected a range of strategies, including (Weisel and Shelley, 2004, ii–iii):

» Using techniques of natural surveillance—drawing on information provided by informants, citizens, and patrol officers—to monitor and identify emerging problems and subsequently strengthen formal surveillance, thus increasing perceptions of risk to potential offenders

» Reducing anonymity associated with gang behavior, by obtaining photographs and detailed information about the routine activities of individual gang members—their associates, hangout locations, and vehicles—through recurring contacts

» Using "specific deterrence" by identifying, investigating, and clearing gang-related offenses and subjecting case dispositions to enhanced penalties

» Intensifying "specific deterrence" through the strategic use of civil injunctions for turf-based gangs when less coercive measures had not been successful

» Developing sets of strategies that address unique characteristics of different types of gangs—using truancy initiatives for juvenile gangs, graffiti abatement for tagger gangs, enterprise investigations for well-organized gangs, and civil injunctions for turf-based gangs

» Reducing provocation and opportunity for gang violence by monitoring and dispersing troublemakers; monitoring contact between rival gangs, such as at sporting or musical events; monitoring potential conflict by examining challenges conveyed by graffiti; and reducing notoriety or prestige and avoiding retaliatory violence by suppressing gang names in media coverage

» Improving police effectiveness by prioritizing violent or chronic offenders and/or prioritizing violent gangs

» Monitoring recurring and responding to local-based information about emerging problem locations

These prevention and control strategies represent a major improvement over general deterrence tactics such as zero tolerance, sweeps, and crackdowns—broad tactics that are largely indiscriminate in target selection and independent of empirical information and that serve primarily to randomly and temporarily inconvenience gang members, expose police to claims of racial profiling, and create incentives for police corruption and excessive force.

FEDERAL EFFORTS TO ADDRESS THE GANG THREAT

Although there is no national strategy to address violent street gangs and the challenges they present to communities across the country—despite the fact many scholars and practitioners have been calling for such a plan—several approaches have been developed by various agencies and entities at the federal level.

The Federal Bureau of Investigation (FBI) Safe Streets Violent Crime Initiative

The Federal Bureau of Investigation's Safe Streets Violent Crime Initiative began in 1992 and was designed to allow each field office to address violent street gangs and drug-related violence through the establishment of FBI-sponsored, long-term, proactive task forces that focused on violent gangs, violent crime, and the apprehension of violent fugitives. The Violent Gang Safe Streets Task Force became the vehicle through which law enforcement agencies at all levels—local, state, and federal—could join together to address the gang-related violent crime plaguing their communities. The FBI's Safe Streets and Gang Unit administers 160 Violent Gang Safe Streets Task Forces nationwide.

The FBI also leads the National Gang Intelligence Center (NGIC), a multiagency effort that integrates the gang intelligence assets of federal, state, and local law enforcement departments and serves as a centralized intelligence resource for gang information and analytical support. The mission of NGIC is to allow timely and accurate information sharing between law enforcement agencies and to facilitate strategic and tactical analysis of intelligence regarding the growth, migration, criminal activity, and association of gangs that pose a significant threat to communities throughout the United States. The NGIC is not connected with the National Gang Center, which is an OJJDP project.

Other FBI antigang initiatives and partnerships include:

» Central American Intelligence Program
» Central American Law Enforcement Exchange
» MS-13 National Gang Task Force
» San Salvador Legal Attaché
» Transnational Anti-Gang Initiative

The National Crime Prevention Council (NCPC) Anti-Gang Initiative

In February of 2006 the Department of Justice announced a twofold strategy to combat gang violence. First, it recommended prioritizing prevention programs to provide America's youth and offenders returning to the community with opportunities that help them resist gang involvement. Second, it recommended ensuring robust enforcement policies when gang-related violence does occur. The cornerstones of this initiative were an expansion of the established Project Safe Neighborhoods (PSN) programs and included new and enhanced antigang efforts in six cities with significant gang problems ("Anti-Gang Initiative Announced," 2006). This program addressed the full range of personal, family, and community factors that contribute to juvenile delinquency and gang activity, combining prevention, enforcement, and reentry efforts to address gang membership and gang violence.

The six target areas were Los Angeles; Tampa, Florida; Cleveland, Ohio; the "222 Corridor" that stretches from Easton to Lancaster, Pennsylvania (near Philadelphia); the Dallas/Fort Worth metroplex; and Milwaukee, Wisconsin. Supported by $2.5 million in grant funds per site, this new initiative incorporated prevention and enforcement efforts, as well as programs to assist released prisoners as they reenter society. By integrating prevention, enforcement, and prisoner reentry, this new initiative aims to address gang membership and gang violence at every stage.

The Office of Juvenile Justice and Delinquency Prevention (OJJDP) Comprehensive Gang Model

The OJJDP's Gang Reduction Program, launched in 2003, was a multimillion-dollar initiative designed to reduce gang crime in targeted neighborhoods by incorporating research-based interventions to address individual, family, and community factors that contribute to juvenile delinquency and gang activity. The program leveraged local, state, and federal resources in support of community partnerships that implement progressive practices in prevention, intervention, suppression, and reentry (National Gang Center, 2010).

The foundation of the program is the Comprehensive Gang Model, developed by Dr. Irving Spergel and colleagues at the University of Chicago. This model, the product of decades of OJJDP-funded gang research, holds that two factors largely account for a community's youth gang problem: the lack of social opportunities available to gang members younger than 22 years old and the degree of social disorganization present in a community (National Gang Center, 2010). The model also suggests other contributing factors, including poverty, institutional racism, deficiencies in social policies, and a lack of or misdirected social controls. The model includes five strategies: mobilizing communities, providing youth opportunities, suppressing gang violence, providing social interventions and street outreach, and facilitating organizational change and development. According to Howell (2006, 7): "Based on research and community experience, the model is multifaceted and multilayered and involves individual youths, families, the gang structure, agencies, and the community."

The success of the model has led to its replication in sites nationwide. The Rural Gang Initiative funds adaptation of the Comprehensive Gang Model at four rural sites and funds evaluation, training, and technical assistance for these efforts.

The *Gang-Free Schools and Communities Initiative* (2000), also a replication of the OJJDP's Comprehensive Gang Model, was launched in 2000 to address and reduce youth gang crime and violence in schools and communities throughout the nation. Four sites were selected (East Cleveland, Ohio; Houston, Texas; Miami/Dade County, Florida; and Pittsburgh, Pennsylvania). In phase one, sites assembled steering committees and assessment teams, drawing on the wide range of stakeholders in each community. Sites then assessed gang problems extensively by using multiple sources of information, including school and law enforcement records, community leaders, students, parents, teachers, and youth gang members. Applying their assessment findings, sites developed strategic plans for implementing OJJDP's Comprehensive Gang Model. Implementation plans included designs for gang prevention, intervention, and suppression at the community level, with an emphasis on school involvement. In phase two, sites are now implementing their strategic plans and delivering services and antigang activities in schools and across the communities. Specific activities vary across sites, but all sites follow the five broad strategies outlined in the Comprehensive Gang Model.

The Gang Reduction Program is designed to reduce gang activity in targeted neighborhoods by incorporating a broad spectrum of research-based interventions to address the range of personal, family, and community factors that contribute to juvenile delinquency and gang activity. The program integrates local, state, and federal resources to incorporate state-of-the-art practices in prevention, intervention, and suppression in program activities and resources to enhance prosocial influences in the community. Pilot communities identify and coordinate current resources, programs, and services that address known risk factors in the community and use grant funding to fill gaps to address risk factors for delinquency across the broadest possible age spectrum. The program design includes a framework for coordinating a wide range of activities that have demonstrated effectiveness in reducing gang activity and delinquency.

The Gang Prevention through Targeted Outreach Program enables local boys' and girls' clubs to prevent youths from entering gangs, intervene with gang members early in their involvement, and divert youths from gang life into more constructive activities. In addition, the OJJDP provides publications, funding opportunities, training, and technical assistance.

LOCAL STRATEGIES TO ADDRESS A GANG PROBLEM AND GANG VIOLENCE

Several strategies have been implemented to address gang problems and gang violence on the local level.

> Current strategies to address the gang problem include establishing behavior codes, obtaining civil injunctions, establishing drug-free zones (DFZs) around schools, implementing conflict prevention strategies, applying community pressure, and instituting graffiti removal programs.

Behavior codes should be established and firmly, consistently enforced. These codes may include dress codes and bans on showing gang colors or using hand signals. On the positive side, schools should promote and reward friendliness and cooperation.

Another way to address the gang problem is through *civil injunctions.* This strategy was used by the Redondo Beach (California) Police Department in an award-winning experiment. The department obtained an injunction against the gang members who had essentially taken over a city park. The department sued them and won. The injunction resulted from a partnership between the community and the police department and exemplifies an innovative,

pulling levers

Refers to a multiagency law enforcement team imposing all available sanctions on gang members who violate established standards for behavior.

Ideas in Practice

PULLING LEVERS IN BOSTON

Pulling levers refers to a multiagency law enforcement team imposing all available sanctions on gang members who violate established standards for behavior. This strategy was used in Boston, Massachusetts, with a small group of youths who had extensive involvement in the justice system and who accounted for a majority of youth homicides. Boston's pulling levers program, Operation Ceasefire, was initiated by a multiagency law enforcement team convening a series of meetings with the chronic gang offenders where law enforcement communicated new standards for behavior. Violence will no longer be tolerated.

The program sent a message to gang members that *all* members of the gang would suffer consequences if any *one* gang member committed a crime involving a gun. Consequences included saturation patrols in the gang's neighborhood, crackdowns on probation and parole violations and outstanding arrest warrants and even stringent enforcement of child support orders, public housing rules and other controls that might apply to gang members.

When the standards were violated, the multiagency law enforcement team responded by imposing all available sanctions. Since Boston implemented the strategy in 1996, youth homicides have decreased by two-thirds.

Source: David M. Kennedy, Anthony A. Braga, and Anne M. Piehl, "Developing and Implementing Operation Ceasefire." In *Reducing Gun Violence: The Boston Gun Project's Operation Ceasefire.* (Washington, DC: National Institute of Justice, September 2001), 1–53. (NCJ 188741)

proactive approach to ensuring public safety. The injunction restricted the following actions:

» Possessing, or remaining in the company of anyone with, dangerous weapons, including clubs, bats, knives, screwdrivers, BB guns, and so on

» Entering private property of another without prior written permission of the owner

» Intimidating, provoking, threatening, confronting, challenging, or carrying out any acts of retaliation

» Forbidding a gang member younger than 18 years of age to be in a public place after 8 P.M. unless going to a legitimate business, a meeting, or an entertainment activity

» Disallowing gang members to associate or congregate in groups of three or more in the park or within 10 yards of the outside fence surrounding the park

The constitutionality of such an approach needs to be considered by any community wishing to implement this innovative strategy.

Establishing *drug-free zones (DFZs) around schools* is another commonly used strategy. This may include rewiring any pay phones so that only outgoing calls can be made.

Conflict prevention strategies are also important to address the gang problem. Teachers should be trained to recognize and deal with gang members in nonconfrontational ways. Staff should identify all known gang members and try to build self-esteem and promote academic success for all students, including gang members.

Community pressure is also needed to effectively reduce and prevent gang activity. Parents and the general public should be made aware of gangs operating in the community, as well as of popular heavy metal and punk bands that may be having a negative influence on youths. They should be encouraged to apply pressure to television and radio stations and to book and video stores to put an age limit on material that promotes use of alcohol, drugs, promiscuity, devil worship, or violence. This may raise constitutionality or censorship issues, but as long as it is private citizens who apply the pressure, it should not present a problem.

graffiti

Painting or writing on buildings, walls, bridges, bus stops, and other available public surfaces; used by gangs to mark their turf.

Graffiti removal programs should be put in place calling for the prompt removal of graffiti anywhere it appears. **Graffiti**, unauthorized writing or drawing on a public surface, is not only unattractive but is also the written language of the gang, allowing gang members to advertise their turf and authority. No longer limited to inner cities, graffiti has become universal. Beyond its unsightliness, graffiti damage is very expensive, now costing the American public more than $4 billion a year. In some instances photographs of the graffiti may aid certain police investigations. School officials should give to the police remaining paint cans and paint brushes that might be used as evidence. As an alternative to graffiti, students might be encouraged to design and paint murals in locations where graffiti is most likely to occur.

The Beaverton (Oregon) Police Department's graffiti removal program targets taggers because tagger graffiti is the majority of what they experience ("Graffiti Removal Program," 2012). A tagger takes on a nickname (or "tag") and then writes it on public and private property. Tagger graffiti is not territorial because the taggers are determined to place as many tags as possible throughout an area to seek recognition among their peers. Tagger vandals may operate as a crew. Most crew graffiti shows the tag name and the tag crew. A tag crew can be identified by the initials scrawled somewhere in the tag. Usually there are three initials, but sometimes two or four are used.

The Beaverton "Graffiti Removal Program" (2012) enlisted the cooperation of parents, teachers, community members, and businesses. The program alerts *parents* that taggers may proudly sport samples of their "art" on books or notebooks. Some even carry tagging scrapbooks, complete with samples of their writing. Taggers may also carry copies of magazines that support the tagging trade. Parents should check their children's fingers for paint and should also be aware that taggers often wear baggy pants and loose shirts so as to easily hide cans of spray paint. *Teachers* should take notice of graffiti on notebooks, desks, homework, and in lockers and should watch for students with paint on their fingers. Any tagging should be immediately reported to school security staff ("Graffiti Removal Program," 2012).

The *community* has a responsibility to maintain their neighborhoods and keep them graffiti-free. When an area is hit repeatedly by graffiti, citizens may feel the area is unsafe and in a condition that may serve as a welcome to more serious crime. To defeat the vandals and keep neighborhoods safe, everyone must continually monitor the problem. Citizens should paint over

ON THE BEAT

Gang activity is prevalent in many large cities and often can spill over into smaller communities. Although the community I work in is a first-ring suburb of Minneapolis, Minnesota, we do not see the gang activity that other suburban communities see. A big deterrent, in my mind, has been a crackdown on graffiti. We have seen our share of graffiti. Although much of the damage to property has been caused by local juveniles, it can still breed blight and cause fear in residents. Our city leaders understand the "broken windows theory" and, because of this, we were able to crack down on graffiti in a way that has really made a difference in the last few years.

In 2007 our city began to take the issue of graffiti vandalism seriously. We proactively began to find, photograph, and clean up the different graffiti tags in the community. We began to prosecute those responsible for the damage. This approach was extremely different from our previous response, which was primarily to take citizen complaints first and then take action. We even began to track information through an Internet-accessible database containing suspect information, photographs of the different graffiti tags, and a map showing where incidents occurred. This database has expanded into a tool that agencies in many surrounding communities have found beneficial as well. This collaboration and information sharing has allowed us to help one another and coordinate crime information. Graffiti rates in our community have declined over the past few years thanks to this approach.

—*Kim Czapar*

graffiti on their property as soon as it appears. Not only is fresh graffiti easier to clean, but prompt removal discourages future tags, as taggers seek visibility. A quick cover-up of their work denies them this visibility, thus deterring future attacks. *Businesses* also can participate by taking part in the police department's Responsible Retailer Program, keeping spray paint out of the hands of minors and immediately removing any graffiti that appears on their property.

THE GANG'S PLACE WITHIN THE COMMUNITY

Despite a gang's desire for autonomy and rejection of outside authority, a relationship must still be maintained with the neighborhood and larger community. Four factors that motivate gangs to make concerted efforts to establish ties with the community are: (1) the gang's need for a "safe haven" and a place to exist; (2) the need for a recruitment pool from which to draw its membership; (3) the community's ability to provide important information such as details concerning other gang activity within the city; and (4) psychological reasons (Sanchez-Jankowski, 1991). Regarding this final factor, Sanchez-Jankowski (1991, 201) explains: "A bonding occurs between the gang and the community that builds a social adhesive that often takes a significant amount of time to completely dissolve."

These bonds may present a challenge to the dissipation and eradication of local gang activity and can hinder law enforcement's efforts to rally a community against the presence of such gangs.

"Community ambivalence toward gangs exists because many of the gang members are children of residents, the gangs often provide protection for residents, residents identify with gangs because of their own or relatives' prior involvement, and the gangs in some instances have become community institutions" (Sanchez-Jankowski, 1991).

A COMMUNITY APPROACH TO A GANG PROBLEM

Gangs are not only a law enforcement problem, they are the entire community's problem. To effectively tackle a gang problem, all affected parties—law enforcement, schools, parents, youths, businesses, religious groups, and social service organizations—must be engaged in finding a solution. Shelden and colleagues (2004, 223) explain: "The community approach, as the name suggests, reaches out to include a broad spectrum of individuals, groups, and organizations. The community itself makes it clear that certain unhealthy behaviors are unacceptable and will not be tolerated. This approach takes advantage of existing community resources in the broadest sense and pools them to develop a community-wide strategy. The mobilization process involves four specific steps: (1) involving key community leaders, (2) forming a community board or task force, (3) conducting a community risk and resource assessment, and (4) planning the program and deciding on evaluation methods."

Howell (2006, 53) stresses: "Community responses to gangs must begin with a thorough assessment of the specific characteristics of the gangs themselves, crimes they commit, other problems they present, and localities they affect. To conduct a thorough assessment, communities should look at community perceptions and available data. Data from law enforcement sources such as local gang and general crime data are critical. Other data should be collected from probation officers, schools, community-based youth agencies, prosecutors, and community residents."

PROVIDING ALTERNATIVES TO GANGS

Many gang experts stress the need to provide alternatives for youths who may be drawn to a gang or who may already be in a gang but are becoming disenchanted. Following are several examples of successful programs offering alternatives to gangs, many involving parents and building a sense of family.

Homeboy Industries: Jobs for the Future

In 1992, responding to the civil unrest in Los Angeles, Father Gregory Boyle formed Homeboy Industries and its Jobs for a Future project to create businesses that provide counseling, training, work experience, and many other services (including free tattoo removal)—opportunities that allow at-risk youth to plan their futures, not their funerals. In providing employment services, Homeboy Industries targets and focuses on that segment of the community that finds it most difficult to secure employment on their own—former gang members, parolees, and at-risk youth. According to the Homeboy Web site, no organization in Los Angeles serves a greater number of gang-involved men and women, offering a much-needed intervention to those who deserve a second chance at life. Most importantly, Jobs for a Future provides the opportunity for rival gang members to work side by side.

The guiding principle of Homeboy Industries' Jobs for a Future project is both purposeful and pragmatic: "Nothing stops a bullet like a job." Located in the gang-afflicted East Los Angeles community of Boyle Heights, Homeboy Industries offers gang-involved and at-risk youth the opportunity to become productive members of society through a variety of employment-centered services.

Several economic development enterprises have been created since Homeboy Bakery, the first venture, was started: Homeboy Silkscreen, Homeboy/Homegirl Merchandise, Homeboy Graffiti Removal, Homeboy Diner, Homeboy Farmer's Market, and Homegirl Café and Catering. Homeboy Industries is supported by the OJJDP's Gang Reduction Program.

Jobs for a Future is, today, a nationally recognized center that assists 1,000 people a month in redirecting their lives. For many of the former gang members in the program, this is their first real job. Receiving a paycheck and developing meaningful skills count as tangible benefits of the program, but it is the intangibles—altered perspectives and fresh hopes—that may most affect participants' lives.

Pierce County, Washington: Safe Streets Campaign

Safe Streets is a community resource that helps individuals, families, communities, and organizations develop strategies to reduce gang violence and drug use. Programs for youths include the Interagency Gang Task Force, which unites the schools, the health department, local law enforcement, the prosecutor's office, and a children's commission to identify gang-involved youths and prevent the cycle of youth violence. The "Youth Leading Change" program engages area youth in leadership activities, working to promote healthier choices among their peers. Founded in 1996, the program has grown into and reaches out to high school aged youth around Pierce County ("About the Safe Streets Campaign," n.d.).

Los Angeles, California: Summer Night Lights

Summer Night Lights (SNL) is an antigang initiative that targets park facilities in Los Angeles's Gang Reduction and Youth Development (GRYD) zones—areas where rates of violent gang-related crime are at least 400 percent higher than in other parts of the city. SNL offers expanded programming, after-school activities, athletic leagues, art initiatives, family programs, and free food, with the hope that by keeping parks open after dark—during the peak hours for gang activity—at-risk youth will have a safe place to spend the summer ("Gang Reduction Program: Summer Night Lights," 2012). Since 2008 the SNL program has grown from 8 parks to 24 citywide. In 2010 the number of shots fired in SNL neighborhoods dropped 55 percent and the number of gang-related homicides decreased by 57 percent. An estimated 710,000 people participated in SNL during 2010, a significant increase from the approximately 270,000 participants in 2009; 382,000 meals were served; and 1,000 jobs were created ("Summer Night Lights," 2012).

PROBLEM-SOLVING PARTNERSHIPS TO ADDRESS GANG CRIME AND GANG PROBLEMS

One national partnership aimed at reducing gang-related crime and attendant problems is Project Safe Neighborhoods (PSN), a networking initiative that connects existing local programs that target gun and gang crime and provides these programs with additional tools necessary to be successful: "Since its inception in 2001, approximately $2 billion has been committed to this initiative. This funding is being used to hire new federal and state prosecutors, support investigators, provide training, distribute gun-lock safety kits, deter juvenile gun crime, and develop and promote community outreach efforts as well as to support other gun and gang violence reduction strategies" ("Project Safe Neighborhoods," 2012).

Local partnerships coordinated through the 94 U.S. Attorneys' Offices across the United States integrate five elements from successful gun crime reduction programs such as the Boston Operation Ceasefire Program and the Department of Justice's Strategic Approaches to Community Safety Initiative. The five elements are partnerships, strategic planning, training, outreach, and accountability.

SUMMARY

An estimated 756,000 gang members are active in more than 29,000 gangs nationwide. Youths seeking protection, security, status, an identity, a sense of belonging, and economic security can fulfill all of these needs through gang membership.

Prevention efforts should (1) begin early, (2) target youths exposed to multiple risk factors, and (3) address all facets of youths' lives. The Gang Resistance Education and Training (GREAT) program is aimed at stopping gang membership. The Gang Resistance Is Paramount (GRIP) program seeks to prevent youths from joining gangs through education.

Indicators of gang activity include graffiti, drive-by shootings, intimidation assaults, murders, and the open sale of drugs. Indicators of gang membership include colors, tattoos, hand signs, and behavior.

A computerized Gang Intelligence System (GANGIS), including comprehensive gang profile data such as monikers and vehicle information, can be an effective crime-fighting tool.

According to the OJJDP, law enforcement has used five strategies to address the gang problem: suppression, social intervention, social opportunities, community mobilization, and organizational development. The OJJDP found community mobilization to be the most effective strategy to address the gang problem.

Current strategies to address the gang problem include establishing behavior codes, obtaining civil injunctions, establishing drug-free zones (DFZs) around schools, implementing conflict prevention strategies, applying community pressure, and instituting graffiti removal programs.

Community ambivalence toward gangs exists because many of the gang members are children of residents, the gangs often provide protection for residents, residents identify with gangs because of their own or relatives' prior involvement, and the gangs in some instances have become community institutions.

DISCUSSION QUESTIONS

1. What do you think are the main reasons individuals join gangs?
2. How does a street gang member differ from other juvenile delinquents?
3. What are the advantages and disadvantages of expelling disruptive gang members from school?
4. Were gangs present in your high school? How did you know? If they were, did they present a threat?
5. Are there efforts in your community to combat the gang problem?
6. Why is a uniform definition of gangs important for the law enforcement profession and what has prevented it from being established?
7. Why do schools and policing agencies sometimes deny or downplay the presence of gangs?
8. Explain the consequences of denying the existence of gangs.
9. In your opinion, is it possible to prevent youngsters from joining gangs?
10. Explain community ambivalence toward gangs.

GALE EMERGENCY SERVICES DATABASE ASSIGNMENTS

ONLINE Database

- Use the Gale Emergency Service Database to help answer the Discussion Questions as appropriate.

- Injunctions against gangs have been a highly successful strategy in some cities and states. Research the controversy surrounding the constitutionality of using injunctions in this way.

- The city of Boston, using community policing strategies, won an Innovations in American Government Award for its program Operation Ceasefire. Research this much-replicated program and explain why it was considered innovative and how it affected gang violence and teenage deaths by handguns.

REFERENCES

"About the Safe Streets Campaign." n.d. Tacoma, WA: Safe Streets Web site. http://www.safest.org/en/about

"Anti-Gang Initiative Announced." 2006 (May). *Catalyst Newsletter* (National Crime Prevention Council). http://www.ncpc.org/programs/catalyst-newsletter/catalyst-newsletter/archives/may-2006-catalyst/anti-gang-initiative-announced

Egley, Arlen, Jr., and James C. Howell. 2011 (June). *Highlights of the 2009 National Youth Gang Survey.* Fact sheet. Washington, DC: Office of Juvenile Justice and Delinquency Prevention.

Egley, Arlen, Jr., and James C. Howell. 2012 (April). *Highlights of the 2010 National Youth Gang Survey.* Fact sheet. Washington, DC: Office of Juvenile Justice and Delinquency Prevention.

Gang-Free Schools and Communities Initiative. 2000. Washington, DC: Office of Juvenile Justice and Delinquency Prevention. (SL000427)

"Gang Reduction Initiative of Denver." 2012. Denver, CO: City and County of Denver Web site. http://www.denvergov.org/safecity/GangReductionInitiativeofDenverGRID/tabid/434422/Default.aspx

"Gang Reduction Program: Summer Night Lights." 2012. Los Angeles, CA: City of Los Angeles Mayor's Web page. http://mayor.lacity.org/Issues/GangReduction/SummerNightLights/index.htm

"Gangs." 2012. Los Angeles, CA: Los Angeles Police Department Web site. http://www.lapdonline.org/get_informed/content_basic_view/1396

"Gangs and School Safety." 2012. Cleveland, OH: National School Safety and Security Services. http://www.schoolsecurity.org/trends/gangs.html

"Graffiti Removal Program." 2012. Beaverton, OR: Beaverton Police Department Web site. http://www.beavertonoregon.gov/index.aspx?nid=767

Hill, Karl G., Christina Lui, and J. David Hawkins. 2001 (December). *Early Precursors of Gang Membership: A Study of Seattle Youth.* Washington, DC: Office of Juvenile Justice and Delinquency Prevention. (NCJ 190106)

Howell, James C. 2006 (August). *The Impact of Gangs on Communities.* Washington, DC: Office of Juvenile Justice Delinquency Prevention, National Youth Gang Center.

Howell, James C. 2007. "Menacing or Mimicking? Realities of Youth Gangs." *Juvenile and Family Court Journal* 58 (2): 39–50.

Howell, James C. and Arlen Egley, Jr. 2008. *Frequently Asked Questions Regarding Gangs.* Tallahassee, FL: Institute for Intergovernmental Research.

Kennedy, David M., Anthony A. Braga, and Anne M. Piehl. 2001 (September). "Developing and Implementing Operation Ceasefire." In *Reducing Gun Violence: The Boston Gun Project's Operation Ceasefire*, 1–53. Washington, DC: National Institute of Justice. (NCJ 188741)

Klein, Malcolm W. 2007. *Chasing after Street Gangs: A Forty-Year Journey.* Upper Saddle River, NJ: Pearson Prentice-Hall.

Krohn, Marvin D., Nicole M. Schmidt, Alan J. Lizotte, and Julie M. Baldwin. 2011. "The Impact of Multiple Marginality on Gang Membership and Delinquent Behavior for Hispanic, African American, and White Male Adolescents." *Journal of Contemporary Criminal Justice* 27 (1): 18–42.

Miller, Holly V., J. C. Barnes, and Richard D. Hartley. 2011. "Reconsidering Hispanic Gang Membership and Acculturation in a Multivariate Context." *Crime and Delinquency* 57 (3): 331–355.

National Gang Center. 2010 (October). *Best Practices to Address Community Gang Problems: OJJDP's Comprehensive Gang Model.* 2nd edition. Washington, DC: Office of Juvenile Justice and Delinquency Prevention. (NCJ 231200)

National Youth Gang Survey Analysis. n.d. Washington, DC: National Gang Center. http://www.nationalgangcenter.gov/Survey-Analysis

"Nationwide Rollout of 'Cops and Kids' Trainings Begin." 2011 (July/August). *Neighborhood News* (COPS Office). http://www.fredrogers.org/e-newsletters/july-2011/cops.html

"Project Safe Neighborhoods (PSN)." 2012. Washington, DC: Bureau of Justice Assistance. https://www.bja.gov/programdetails.aspx?program_id=74

Sanchez-Jankowski, Martin S. 1991. *Islands in the Street: Gangs and American Urban Society.* Berkeley, CA: University of California Press.

Seattle Social Development Project. 2009. Seattle, WA: Seattle Social Development Project Web site. http://www.ssdp-tip.org/SSDP/index.html

Shelden, Randall G., Sharon K. Tracy, and William B. Brown. 2004. *Youth Gangs in American Society.* 3rd edition. Belmont, CA: Wadsworth.

Solis, Angelica, Wendy Schwartz, and Tamika Hinton. 2003 (October 1). *Gang Resistance Is Paramount (GRIP) Program Evaluation: Final Report.* Los Angeles, CA: University of Southern California. http://www.usc.edu/schools/price/ced/GRIP_Evaluation.pdf

2011 National Gang Threat Assessment: Emerging Trends. 2011. Washington, DC: National Gang Intelligence Center. http://www.fbi.gov/stats-services/publications/2011-national-gang-threat-assessment/2011-national-gang-threat-assessment-emerging-trends

Weisel, Deborah Lamm and Tara O'Connor Shelley. 2004 (October). *Specialized Gang Units: Form and Function in Community Policing.* Washington, DC: U.S. Department of Justice.

ADDITIONAL RESOURCES

Following are Web sites recommended for the study of gangs.

Gangs and Security Threat Group Awareness
www.dc.state.fl.us/pub/gangs/index.html
This Florida Department of Corrections Web site contains information on, photographs of, and descriptions of a wide variety of gang types, including Chicago- and Los Angeles-based gangs, prison gangs, nations, sets, and supremacy groups.

Gangs OR Us
www.gangsorus.com
This site offers a broad range of information, including a state-by-state listing of all available gang laws, gang identities, and behaviors applicable to all areas of the United States, and links to other sites that provide information for law enforcement, parents, and teachers.

Southeastern Connecticut Gang Activities Group (SEGAG)
www.segag.org
This coalition of law enforcement and criminal justice agencies from southeastern Connecticut and New England provides information on warning signs that parents and teachers often observe first, along with a large number of resources and other working groups that are part of nationwide efforts to contain gang violence.

This available CourseMate has an interactive eBook and interactive learning tools, including flash cards, quizzes, and more. To learn more about this resource and access free demo CourseMate resources, go to **www.cengagebrain.com**, and search for this book. To access CourseMate materials that you have purchased, go to **login.cengagebrain.com**.

CHAPTER 14

Understanding and Preventing Violence

> Violence is one of the most pressing social problems and important public health issues in American society.
>
> —*National Crime Prevention Council (NCPC)*

DO YOU KNOW ...

» What causes violence?

» What a problem-solving approach to preventing violence must attempt to do?

» What developing effective violence prevention tactics will require?

» What strategies are suggested for general violence prevention?

» How hate can be classified?

» How to describe the majority of hate crimes?

» What the three phases in the gun violence continuum are?

» What strategy for each phase is suggested by the National Crime Prevention Council?

» Who the Office of Juvenile Justice and Delinquency Prevention has identified as potential partners in efforts to combat gun violence?

» Whether animal abuse is linked to domestic violence?

» What cultural diversity issue must be addressed when forming partnerships to prevent domestic abuse?

» What three risks children face in violent homes?

» What the CD–CP model emphasizes?

» What common motivations behind workplace violence are?

» What characteristics are common to workplace violence and school violence?

CAN YOU DEFINE ...

bias crime
bias incident
cycle of violence
gun interdiction
hate crime
intimate partner violence (IPV)
process mapping
straw purchasers

INTRODUCTION

Our nation was born in the violence of the Revolutionary War. The Union remained intact after a bloody Civil War that pitted brother against brother. Since then America has been willing to fight for freedom. It also cherishes the peace and freedom at home, however, that others fought to secure. But violence continues to exist, as shown in Figure 14.1.

Violent crime is composed of four offenses: murder and nonnegligent manslaughter, forcible rape, robbery, and aggravated assault. According to the Federal Bureau of Investigation's (FBI) Uniform Crime Reports *Crime in the United States 2010*, an estimated 1,246,248 violent crimes occurred nationwide, a decrease of 6.0 percent from the 2009 estimate. There were an estimated 403.6 violent crimes per 100,000 inhabitants in 2010 (*Crime in the United States 2010*):

» When considering 5- and 10-year trends, the 2010 estimated violent crime total was 13.2 percent below the 2006 level and 13.4 percent below the 2001 level.

» Aggravated assaults accounted for the highest number of violent crimes reported to law enforcement at 62.5 percent. Robbery comprised 29.5 percent of violent crimes, forcible rape accounted for 6.8 percent, and murder accounted for 1.2 percent of estimated violent crimes in 2010.

» An estimated 14,748 persons were murdered nationwide in 2010. This was a 4.2-percent decrease from the 2009 estimate, a 14.8-percent decrease from the 2006 figure, and an 8.0-percent decrease from the 2001 estimate.

Figure 14.1 2010 Crime Clock

2010 Crime Clock

One violent crime every	**25.3 seconds**
One murder every	35.6 minutes
One forcible rape every	6.2 minutes
One robbery every	1.4 minutes
One aggravated assault every	40.5 seconds
One property crime every	**3.5 seconds**
One burglary every	14.6 seconds
One larceny-theft every	5.1 seconds
One motor vehicle theft every	42.8 seconds

Source: http://www.fbi.gov/about-us/cjis/ucr/crime-in-the-u.s/2010/crime-in-the-u.s.-2010/offenses-known-to-law-enforcement/crime-clock

» Nearly 44 percent (43.8%) of murders were reported in the South, the most populous region, with 20.6 percent reported in the West, 19.9 percent reported in the Midwest, and 15.6 percent reported in the Northeast.

Crime rates are not evenly distributed, and the actual rate and risk of being victimized depends greatly on the region of the country, the city, and the neighborhood within the city. There also appears to be a strong correlation between crime rates and median household income. New England, the wealthiest region, has the lowest crime rates and the lowest homicide rates in the country. New York and New Jersey, though densely populated, have crime rates below the national average. The South historically has the highest crime rates in the country and the lowest median household income.

The most current data on criminal victimization rates from the National Crime Victimization Survey (NCVS), the FBI, and other sources are available on the Bureau of Justice Statistics (BJS) Web site at bjs.ojp.usdoj.gov.

Violence occurs on our streets as road rage, in our schools and workplaces as shooting sprees, and behind closed doors as domestic abuse. It permeates and weakens our social fabric. This chapter begins with a look at data that reveal trends in violent crime, followed by a discussion on the causes of violence and general guidelines on its prevention. Next is a discussion of bias or hate crimes, followed by an examination of gun violence and comprehensive gun reduction strategies. Next domestic violence is examined, including partner abuse and child abuse, and the law enforcement response to domestic violence is also discussed. The chapter concludes with a discussion of workplace violence and a final look at a problem-solving partnership in action.

VIOLENT CRIME RATE COMPARISONS

The United States has a very high violent crime rate compared with many other countries. In 2010 the United States (population approximately 308.7 million) had an estimated 14,748 homicides, a rate of 4.8 homicides per 100,000 citizens (*Crime in the United States 2010*). In contrast, England and Wales had 636 homicides in 2010 among a population of approximately 55.2 million, for a homicide rate of 1.15 per 100,000. Similarly, Canada, with a population of approximately 34 million, had 554 homicides in 2010, for a homicide rate of 1.6 per 100,000 (Brennan and Dauvergne, 2011). The risk of being murdered depends on many factors, the most important being the location of residence (region of the county, city, and neighborhood), age, and participation in a risky life style (drug use, criminal associations, etc.).

After years of declining crime rates, law enforcement leaders grew alarmed when, in 2006, violent crime rates began to increase. Police chiefs from across the country suggested several plausible reasons: significant increases in gang activity; the movement of former gang members from New Orleans to other cities; release of offenders who were incarcerated at high rates during the 1990s; displacement of crime from cities where some crime-infested public housing units were dismantled; the changing nature of the drug market; and petty fights that escalated into major violent crimes.

Concern that these violent crime increases represented the front end of a tipping point of an epidemic of violence not seen for years, representatives from more than 50 cities—170 mayors, police chiefs, and public officials—met in August 2006 at the Police Executive Research Forum (PERF) National Violent

Crime Summit to examine violent crime across the country and determine the nature and extent of the problem (Rosen, 2006). City after city reported that much of the violence was hitting the nation's minority communities hardest, both as victims and perpetrators of violent crime (Rosen, 2006, 8). Comments from participants included the following:

» "What is particularly frustrating about our homicides is that they occur for no apparent rhyme or reason. They come up over the smallest issue—someone feels disrespected." Chris Magnus, Richmond (Virgina) Police Chief (4)

» "A big part of the problem is too many kids having kids and too many kids raising themselves." R. T. Rybak, Minneapolis (Minnesota) Mayor (4)

» "A small segment of our youth has become a 'throwaway' generation. Nobody cares for them. They lack parental, educational, or social support." George Gascon, Mesa (Arizona) Police Chief (8)

» "All the people we put in jail 10 years ago are now back. They come out of the system more hard core than when they went in." Richard Pennington, Atlanta (Georgia) Police Chief (9)

» "We are sacrificing hometown security for homeland security. Local police departments cannot be effective homeland security partners if they are overwhelmed by their core mission responsibilities." Douglas Palmer, Trenton (New Jersey) Mayor (12)

© AP Images/Lee Celano

Children and adults parade down a busy street during a peace march against violence in South Central Los Angeles. Nearly two dozen organizations took part in the event. Citizens are key stakeholders in violence prevention partnerships.

The report on the summit concludes: "In 2006, American law enforcement finds itself once again facing a tipping point in violence on its streets, and it is spreading from city to city. While the nation has understandably focused on homeland security, it must recognize that there is a gathering storm of violent crime that threatens to erode the considerable crime reductions of the past" (Rosen, 2006, 14).

Despite the dire predictions, in the following year violent crime resumed the downward trend of previous years and, as this text goes to print, have continued to drop.

CAUSES OF VIOLENCE

The causes of violence are as difficult to pinpoint as the causes of crime. Many suggest that the ready availability and lethal nature of guns, especially handguns, are major factors. In colonial America, however, every household had guns—survival depended on them—yet children did not shoot each other in their one-room schoolhouses. Nonetheless, the gun factor must be considered.

Another major cause of violence may be desensitization to violence. Violence permeates our television programs and movies, our video games and DVDs. Violence on our streets is graphically portrayed by the media.

> Causes of violence may include ready availability of guns, drugs, and alcohol; a desensitization to violence; disintegration of the family and community; social and economic deprivation; and increased numbers of children growing up in violent families.

Researchers Stretesky, Schuck, and Hogan (2004, 817) examined 236 cities to determine if a relationship existed between poverty clustering and violent crime rates. They found that "disadvantage" has a much stronger relationship to homicide in cities with high levels of poverty clustering.

> A problem-solving approach to preventing violence must attempt to identify the underlying causes of specific violent situations that threaten a community before solutions can be devised.

PREVENTING VIOLENCE

Violence prevention should be addressed by the community as a whole.

> Developing effective prevention tactics will require long-term collaborations between criminal justice and juvenile justice practitioners and other social service agencies. It also requires involvement of the entire community of which these agencies are a part.

Prevention should include strategies directed toward children and their caregivers, especially those children at risk of becoming delinquent, as well as at areas with high levels of poverty and single-parent families. Efforts should also be directed at situations or locations where violent events cluster, such as illegal drug markets, certain places where alcohol and firearms are readily available, and physical locations conducive to crime.

 Strategies for general violence prevention include public dialogue and community mediation, and addressing violence as a public health problem.

Key partnerships in a *public dialogue and community mediation* strategy include schools, police, probation agencies, area courts, community organizations, and individual citizens, including youths. In addition, community newspapers and grassroots word-of-mouth networks help publicize the community dialogue and mediation services. A potential obstacle to the service is that it may be difficult to finance.

Another strategy is to *address violence as a public health problem.* A successful public health campaign against violence requires violence prevention curricula, community partnerships, public awareness involving the mass media, and clinical education and training. Community groups, the clergy, business leaders, schools, and parents can all contribute to a network of services. In addition, physicians, nurses, and other health care providers can be trained in violence prevention techniques, including counseling and teaching patients anger management.

The Boston City Department of Health and Hospitals initiated the Boston Violence Prevention Project in 1982 to prevent youth violence. It began in high school classrooms with lessons presenting violence statistics and addressing ways to avert violence and expanded into a comprehensive effort to reach the entire community.

This nationally known program also incorporates education and training for youth-serving agencies and has trained thousands of people and hundreds of agencies. The program also spurred development of the "Friends for Life, Friends Don't Let Friends Fight" media campaign and "Increase the Peace" weeks.

Chapter 3 discussed the concept of community and its social capital. Some researchers suggest that communities with limited social capital will be a harder "sell" for community policing efforts. Others suggest that communities consisting largely of minority members will be a harder "sell."

HATE CRIMES

Some people feel threatened by simply coming into contact with those who are culturally different. No other nation is as culturally diverse as the United States, thrusting people of different customs, languages, lifestyles, and beliefs together and hoping they can coexist peacefully. Unfortunately, this does not always happen, and severe tension can result between cultural groups when their members are poorly informed and suspicious of cultures and lifestyles outside their own. What people do not understand, they tend to fear, and what they fear, they often hate.

 Hate can be classified into two categories: rational and irrational.

hate/bias crime
A criminal offense committed against a person, property, or society that is motivated, in whole or in part, by an offender's bias against an individual's or group's race, religion, ethnic/national origin, gender, age, disability, or sexual orientation. *Hate crime* and *bias crime* are considered synonymous.

A **hate** or **bias crime** is "a traditional offense like murder, arson, or vandalism with an added element of bias" ("Hate Crime—Overview," n.d.). For data collection purposes, Congress has defined a hate crime as a "criminal offense against a person or property motivated in whole or in part by an offender's bias against a race, religion, disability, ethnic origin, or sexual orientation. Hate itself is not a crime—and the FBI is mindful of protecting freedom of speech and other civil liberties" ("Hate Crime—Overview," n.d.). FBI investigations of hate crimes date as far back as the 1920s, but the protection of civil rights was considered to be a local rather than a federal concern. The murders of three African American civil rights workers in Mississippi, in June 1964, provided the impetus for a visible and sustained federal effort to protect and foster civil rights for all Americans and led to the passage of the Civil Rights Act in July 1964, which increased the role of the FBI in protecting civil rights. The Mississippi Burning (MIBURN) case became the largest federal investigation ever conducted in Mississippi. On October 20, 1967, seven men were convicted of conspiring to violate the constitutional rights of the slain civil rights workers and were sentenced to prison terms ranging from 3 to 10 years ("Hate Crime—Overview," n.d.).

Hate crimes include any act, or attempted act, to cause physical injury, emotional suffering, or property damage through intimidation, harassment, racial or ethnic slurs and bigoted epithets, vandalism, force, or the threat of force. The majority of hate crimes are against the person, including assault (the most common), harassment, menacing/reckless endangerment, and robbery. Crimes against property include vandalism/criminal mischief (most common), arson/cross burning, and burglary.

As discussed, cultural tension commonly occurs in this country from an intolerance of racial and ethnic diversity. Although many would like to believe the intense racial hatred and slaughter of minorities is a relatively distant part of our nation's history and that we have come a long way from the "lynching era" of the late 1800s and early 1900s, events in the 1990s indicate otherwise.

» In 1998 James Byrd, Jr., a Black man, was hitchhiking home when a truck pulled up. Byrd was kidnapped, taken to a wooden area, beaten to unconsciousness, chained to the back of the truck, and then dragged for several miles. His head and right arm were torn from his body during the dragging. His assailants were three White men with links to racist groups.

» Also in 1998, openly gay college student Matthew Shepard was beaten with a pistol and then tied to a fence on the edge of town and left to die.

» In 2000 Jose Padilla was on a work break, sitting at a picnic table with two friends who worked at the adjoining business. The men were speaking Spanish. His friends' boss struck Padilla with a wooden two-by-four, telling him, "We don't speak Spanish here." Padilla suffered a fractured skull and permanent brain damage. The assailant went to prison.

Hate Crimes and Hate Groups by the Numbers

National Crime Victimization Survey (NCVS) data show an annual average of 195,000 hate crime victimizations from 2003 through 2009, with the majority of these victims suspecting racial bias as the offender's motivation (Langton and Planty, 2011). From 2003 to 2009 the rate of violent hate crime victimizations in the United States decreased from 0.8 per 1,000 persons age 12 or older to 0.5 per 1,000. In almost all hate crimes (98%), the offender used hate-related language against the victim. The vast majority (nearly 87%) of all hate crimes involved violence, and about 23 percent were serious violent crimes (rape/sexual assault, robbery, or aggravated assault), yet the police were notified in fewer than half (45%) of all hate crime victimizations (Langton and Planty, 2011).

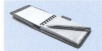 The majority of hate crimes are motivated by racial bias and involve violence.

According to the Southern Poverty Law Center (SPLC), the number of hate groups in the United States increased by 69 percent from 2000 to 2011, with 1,018 active hate groups operating within the country during 2011 ("Hate and Extremism," 2012). All hate groups have beliefs or practices that attack or malign an entire class of people, typically for their immutable characteristics. The dramatic increase in such groups has been fueled by anger and fear over the nation's ailing economy, the influx of non-White immigrants, and the diminishing White majority. These factors have also fed a powerful resurgence of the antigovernment "Patriot" movement, including the formation of armed militias, which grew by 755 percent during the first 3 years of the Obama administration. Hate groups known to be active during 2011 included neo-Nazis, Klansmen, White nationalists, neo-Confederates, racist skinheads, Black separatists, and border vigilantes ("Hate and Extremism," 2012).

Most states have passed mandatory reporting laws requiring police departments to keep statistics on the occurrence of bias and hate crimes. In 1990 the Federal Hate Crime Statistics Act was passed, mandating the justice department to secure data on crimes related to religion, race, sexual orientation, or ethnicity. Although the laws vary considerably, the most common elements are (1) enhanced penalties for common law crimes against persons or property motivated by bias based on race, ethnicity, religion, gender, or sexual orientation; (2) criminal penalties for vandalism of religious institutions; and (3) collection of data on bias crimes.

Using bigoted language does not violate hate crime laws and is frequently classified as a **bias incident**. However, hate crime laws apply when words threaten violence and when bias-motivated graffiti damages or destroys property.

bias incident
Use of bigoted and prejudiced language; does not in itself violate hate crime laws.

Addressing and Preventing Hate Crimes

If a community ignores "minor" incidents, they may grow into a major and potentially deadly situation (Figure 14.2). In fact, an appropriate analogy is given in the likening of racism to carbon monoxide—it may be silent, you may not see or hear it, but uncontrolled, it can kill. Groups whose language

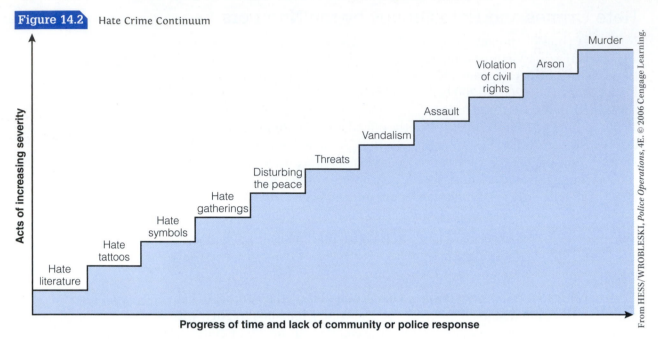

Figure 14.2 Hate Crime Continuum

Acts of increasing severity

Murder
Arson
Violation of civil rights
Assault
Vandalism
Threats
Disturbing the peace
Hate gatherings
Hate symbols
Hate tattoos
Hate literature

Progress of time and lack of community or police response

From HESS/WROBLESKI, *Police Operations*, 4E. © 2006 Cengage Learning.

or literature targets groups of individuals for discrimination and abuse can create an atmosphere that breeds more aggressive acts. A community that shows indifference to hate-oriented groups sends the message that the police and community tolerate this behavior (Bune, 2004).

Many colleges and universities have responded to hate crimes on campus with broad-based public condemnation of bias, prejudice, and violence, including an open letter from the president or dean to the campus community and meetings open to the entire campus community. Several schools have implemented peer diversity education groups that promote understanding of diversity on campus. The Center for the Prevention of Hate Violence at the University of Southern Maine has initiated the Campus Civility Project to address bias, prejudice, and harassment.

Bune (2004, 41) outlines several external actions a police department can take to direct the community's energy into constructive actions, including:

» Establish clearly that the department has "zero tolerance" for any form of hate crime, regardless of apparent seriousness

» Participate in or sponsor community events and activities promoting diversity, tolerance, bias reduction, and conflict resolution

» Collaborate with community organizations, schools, and other public agencies to develop coordinated approaches to hate crime prevention and response

» Engage the media as partners in restoring victimized communities and preventing bias-motivated incidents and crimes

Law enforcement can forge partnerships with local businesses and institutions to better understand and tackle hate crimes. In addition, the National Crime Prevention Council (NCPC) suggests various strategies for preventing the occurrence of bias crimes in a community, such as diversity and tolerance education in schools, ongoing police–cultural organization service partnerships, rapid response to reported incidents, media campaigns about community standards for tolerance, counseling for offenders involved in hate groups, and community-based dispute mediation services. Creating a strong and unified voice condemning the proliferation of hate is what is needed to stamp out bias and keep it from jeopardizing public safety.

Working with the families, friends, neighbors, and communities that surround a hate/bias incident becomes as important as working with the victim. Secondary victimization induces blame, outrage, or fear in a family, group of friends, or community. These groups may be motivated to act in response to a hate/bias crime and retaliate in their own ways unless they are educated and provided other options for response or healing. Training victims and communities to cooperate with law enforcement and other community programs takes the control out of the perpetrator's hands, instills confidence in the victim and community, and prevents future crimes.

GUN VIOLENCE

Other violence prevention programs are aimed at gun violence, which often manifests itself in specific types of violence that can be addressed through community policing strategies. According to the FBI's Uniform Crime Reports (*Crime in the United States 2010*), of those homicides committed in 2010 for which weapons data was known, most (67.5%) involved the use of firearms. Of all murders and nonnegligent manslaughters committed in 2010 with a firearm, handguns were the weapon used in 68.5 percent of the cases.

Gun violence may be considered as a three-phase continuum: (1) the illegal acquisition of firearms; (2) the illegal possession and carrying of firearms; and (3) the illegal, improper, or careless use of firearms.

Effective gun control strategies focus on one, two, or all three of these points of intervention. These strategies and programs focus on three points of intervention: (1) interrupting sources of illegal guns, (2) determining illegal possession and carrying of guns, and (3) responding to illegal gun use.

Strategies to Interrupt Sources of Illegal Guns

The strategies to interrupt sources of illegal guns include law enforcement initiatives that disrupt the illegal flow of firearms by using intelligence gathered through crime gun tracing and regulatory inspections or undercover operations involving suspected illegal gun dealers. Comprehensive crime gun tracing facilitates both the reconstruction of the sales history of firearms associated with crime and the identification of patterns of illegal gun trafficking. Similarly, focusing criminal and regulatory enforcement on suspect dealers allows law enforcement to efficiently focus limited resources. Suspect dealers include those at the greatest risk of selling firearms to **straw purchasers**—that is, purchasers fronting for people linked to illegal gun trafficking.

straw purchasers
Weapons buyers fronting for people linked to illegal gun trafficking.

Initiated in 1994, the Boston Gun Project—Operation Ceasefire—includes gun trafficking interdiction as one component in their broad strategy to stop gun violence. Partners in the project include the Bureau of Alcohol, Tobacco, Firearms, and Explosives (ATF); the Boston Police Department (BPD); the Suffolk County District Attorney's Office; and the U.S. Attorney's Office. A seasoned violent crime coordinator was assigned by ATF to pursue federal firearm arrests. Six ATF agents were also assigned to collaborate with ballistics and crime laboratories at BPD to trace recovered handguns and match them to other crimes.

Based on the ATF tracing data set, the working group established priorities for disrupting the illegal gun market. First, the group prioritized investigating every trace that showed a gun with a time-to-crime of less than 30 months. Priority was also given to certain types of guns popular with youths—for example, semiautomatic handguns, those with restored obliterated serial numbers, those found in high-risk neighborhoods, and those associated with gang members or territories. Priority was also given to swift federal prosecution for gun trafficking (Kennedy, Braga, and Piehl, 2001).

The project was evaluated by the Kennedy School of Government at Harvard University and found to be successful. Based on this demonstrated success, ATF launched the Youth Crime Gun Interdiction Initiative in 17 demonstration cities in 1996.

 The National Crime Prevention Council suggests that regulations and ordinances on gun licensing may interrupt sources of illegal guns.

Municipal ordinances may affect the first two phases of gun violence simultaneously. Interrupting the sale of illegal firearms also reduces the number of people possessing and carrying guns illegally.

Strategies to Deter Illegal Gun Possession and Carrying

Strategies to deter illegal gun possession and carrying include municipal gun ordinances; weapons hotlines; directed police patrols; focusing on hot spots where disproportionate amounts of crime and violence occur; and focusing on individuals most likely to possess and carry firearms illegally, including gang members and probationers.

A 1992 report by the Violence Policy Center showed that the United States had more licensed gun dealerships than it had gas stations—280,000. In response the ATF implemented stiffer licensing requirements and raised the licensing fee from $30 to $200. Applicants were now to be fingerprinted and to undergo more extensive background checks aimed at weeding out unscrupulous dealers. The tougher laws and stricter enforcement cost nearly 200,000 U.S. gun dealers their licenses since the mid-1990s. Since 1994 the number of federally licensed firearms dealers has decreased 79 percent nationwide (Doyle, 2007).

This same strategy can be implemented locally if stakeholders work together to get legislation passed. For example, the East Bay Gun Violence Prevention Project was initiated by the East Bay Public Safety Corridor Partnership, a regional coordinating body formed to reduce crime and violence in response to an alarming level of gun violence among cities in the East Bay Corridor.

 Gun interdictions may be an effective deterrent to illegal gun possessing and carrying.

A **gun interdiction** is a law enforcement–led strategy whereby local police direct intensive patrols to specific geographic areas with high rates of gun-related incidents of violence. Proactive patrols focus on traffic stops and other mechanisms to detect illegal or illegally concealed weapons and seize them. Community support for the interdiction strategy is vital because such searches and seizures can raise controversy. Community input should be sought in identifying the targeted areas to reduce the chance of charges of racial discrimination should the hot spot be inhabited by members of a minority group. Gun interdictions also affect the third phase of the gun violence continuum.

gun interdiction
Local police direct intensive patrols to specific geographic areas with high rates of gun-related incidents of violence.

The COPS Guidelines for Responding to Drive-by Shootings

The Problem-Oriented Policing Center has published a problem-solving guide for police to help them prevent drive-by shootings (Dedel, 2007). Dedel (2007) describes drive-by shootings in detail:

A drive-by shooting refers to an incident when someone fires a gun from a vehicle at another vehicle, a person, a structure, or another stationary object. Many drive-by shootings involve multiple suspects and multiple victims (2).

The specifics of a drive-by shooting—in which the shooter is aiming a gun out the window of a moving vehicle at a moving target, and is often inexperienced in handling a gun—mean that shots often go wild and injure people or damage property that was not the intended target. There are no national data on the volume of drive-by shootings. National statistical databases such as the Uniform Crime Reports record the outcome (e.g., homicide, aggravated assault, weapons law violations) rather than the method (i.e., drive-by shooting) (3).

Although gang membership is certainly not a prerequisite to being involved in a drive-by shooting, studies have shown that larger proportions of gang members reported being involved in drive-by shootings than at-risk youth who were not gang-involved (4).

Motivations: At the most basic level, the aggressors must have access to both a vehicle and a gun, but beyond that, these events appear to be rather unpredictable. Drive-by shootings that occur as an extreme form of road rage often occur in reaction to seemingly trivial events (e.g., another driver is driving "too slow," won't let another driver pass, is tailgating, fails to signal before turning) (6).

Analyzing the local problem carefully is vital to designing an effective response strategy. The first step in such an analysis is to identify the stakeholders. In addition to criminal justice agencies, stakeholders might include local hospitals and emergency services, city public works agencies (e.g., parking, streets, transportation, utilities), federal law enforcement agencies (e.g., Drug Enforcement Administration [DEA]; ATF), probation and parole agencies, corrections departments, bar and nightclub owners and managers, social service providers, gang members, and members of other neighborhood "groups" and neighborhood associations (Dedel, 2007).

Effective Response Strategies

The following response strategies, drawn from a variety of research studies and police reports, provide a foundation of ideas that localities can tailor to address their unique drive-by shooting problems. In most cases, an effective approach involves implementing several different responses, including what police can do to involve the community in solving the problem.

A problem-focused approach would focus first on *proximate causes*, making drive-by shootings harder to carry out, for example, by decreasing offenders' mobility and/or the availability of weapons. In addition, Dedel (2007, 16–23) suggests some combination of responses:

» *Targeting the activity, not the individual*—eliminating the perception that police are unfairly focusing on minorities and reinforcing their fair, unbiased approach to crime

» *Reducing weapon availability or prevalence* by conducting crackdowns, including saturating an area with patrols, using directed patrols, or setting up road blocks or checkpoints

» *Initiating "sweeps" targeting known offenders* in cooperation with parole and probation agencies; police can search offenders' residences, vehicles, and persons and confiscate any illegal weapons found

» *Obtaining consent to search for and seize weapons* from parents of at-risk youth who may be willing to consent, in exchange for a promise from police that neither the parents nor the youth will be charged or prosecuted if any weapons are found

» *Identifying situations with the potential for violence* by tracking current tensions and past altercations (many drive-by shootings are catalyzed by past altercations and ongoing tensions between individuals or among rival gang members); coordinating with hospitals

» *Prohibiting high-risk people from riding in cars with each other*, either as part of probation or parole conditions or as specified in a civil gang injunction

» *Making environmental changes* such as closing streets where drive-by shootings are concentrated, blocking entrances and exits, but coordinating these changes with first responders (e.g., firefighters, EMTs, ambulance drivers) to ensure their safe and efficient passage

» *Responding to incidents and increasing sanctions* by deploying response teams rapidly before physical evidence is destroyed or witnesses leave the scene or are influenced by discussions among witnesses and neighbors

» *Creating witness incentives* by minimizing the risks that witnesses who want to cooperate face, strengthening ties with the community, and offering support in the form of financial assistance and temporary relocation [to] encourage those with information to come forward

» *Implementing a "pulling levers" strategy* by targeting gang members with chronic involvement in serious crime, outlining the consequences for continued involvement in gun violence while offering prosocial alternatives (e.g., education and employment opportunities, drug treatment); in addition, if one member of the target group is involved in gun violence, all members of the group are subjected to intensified supervision and other forms of enhanced enforcement

Ideas in Practice

CEASE-FIRE TO PREVENT GANG VIOLENCE

In 1998 Rochester, New York, Mayor Johnson instituted a policing initiative called Cease-Fire to prevent gang activity and reduce youth violence. Cease-Fire is an interagency and community effort that focuses on homicides committed by gang members and operates under this basic strategy: When a gang member commits a homicide, the entire gang receives intense, special attention from law enforcement.

Cease-Fire partners include the mayor's office, Pathways to Peace, Rochester Police Department, Monroe County District Attorney's Office, Monroe County Probation, New York State Parole, U.S. Attorney's office, community leaders, defense attorneys, and professors from the Rochester Institute of Technology and Harvard University.

Cease-Fire operates by gathering intelligence on gangs and their alliances, enemies, activities, location, membership, and criminal records or police contacts. If a homicide is committed by anyone associated with any gang, law enforcement focuses suppression efforts on the people involved in the homicide as well as on all members of the gang. The Cease-Fire team meets biweekly to discuss law enforcement efforts, homicides, and gang activity.

A "Call-In," which occurs in response to a gang-related homicide, is convened for all gang members on probation, parole, and federal probation. The Call-In is held in a Monroe County Court Room and overseen by the Supervising Monroe County Supreme Court Judge. The judge takes attendance, and any gang member not present is issued an arrest warrant on the spot.

A Rochester police lieutenant informs the attendees as to why they are at the Call-In. The attendees then listen to speakers representing the community and law enforcement. The focus gang is highlighted for their crime and the consequences that followed. The message is simple: If you kill someone, you and your friends will realize a similar fate as the highlighted gang. "This is not business as usual. There is zero tolerance for homicides in this community." The attendees are instructed to go back to their neighborhoods and share this information with their friends and associates.

The Call-In ends with the dismissal of all speakers. Then members of the mayor's Pathways to Peace Initiative (Rochester's youth violence and gang outreach and intervention team) establish rapport with the attendees, validate the message they heard, and offer their services, to assist them with exploring and realizing alternatives to violence and crime.

The message of Cease-Fire is targeted for gang members who want to avoid enforcement by leading a law-abiding life, and in doing so they will be supported. Pathways to Peace has assisted participants who have requested help with education, employment, and other issues. Furthermore, many former gang members have been hired in private sector jobs and are currently working.

An extension of Cease-Fire entitled Juvenile Cease-Fire focuses on probationers under the age of 16. Because the enforcement actions for these youth are limited, those involved in violent acts will receive intensive probation supervision.

The Cease-Fire program's effectiveness is measured by the decrease in gang-related homicides, especially those among African American males between the ages of 16 and 30.

One of the major lessons learned is that it is important to make the initiative part of a long-term strategy and not merely use it as a short-term tactic that will fade away because of initial success or the emergence of other problems. Maintaining efforts even when it seems the objectives have been met is important because scaling back operations may result in re-emergence of the problems.

It is imperative to have a good working relationship between agencies. Alternative agendas, egos, and territory have no place in Cease-Fire. It must be understood by all partnering agencies that their role is permanent and their commitment must stand despite budget reductions, administrative changes, and other emerging issues. It is also important to maintain focus and not try to address too many issues under the initiative.

Source: Adapted from *Best Practices of Community Policing in Gang Intervention and Gang Violence Prevention*. Washington, DC: The United States Conference of Mayors, Best Practices Center, 2006, pp. 116–117. http://www.usmayors.org/bestpractices/community_policing_2006/gangbp_2006.pdf

Limited Effectiveness Responses Responses that appear to have limited effectiveness include targeting gun traffickers, teaching conflict resolution skills, implementing gun buyback programs, restricting entry to high-risk neighborhoods (which may anger residents and business owners and raise Fourth Amendment issues), and impounding cars that are not properly registered. The low yield of weapons and the inconvenience to residents suggest that impounding does not substantially decrease the number of drive-by shootings (Dedel, 2007, 23–25).

STRATEGIES TO RESPOND TO ILLEGAL GUN USE

Strategies to respond to illegal gun use include identification, prosecution, and aggressive punishment of those who commit multiple violent crimes, are armed drug traffickers, or have used a firearm in a crime; intensive education; and strict monitoring of offenders. Local gun courts may also prove an effective strategy.

Local gun courts deal exclusively with gun law violations; they reinforce community standards against violence and ensure swift punishment of violators. The country's first adult gun court was established in the Providence (Rhode Island) Superior Court in 1994 by a statute creating a separate gun court calendar with concurrent jurisdiction with all other superior court calendars. Within 4 months of its implementation, the backlog of gun-related cases was reduced by two-thirds.

All cases are tried within 60 days, and most carry mandatory prison terms, including 10 years to life for a third offense. The mayor obtained support from the National Rifle Association (NRA) and from local advocates of gun control—a tricky combination.

COMPREHENSIVE GUN VIOLENCE REDUCTION STRATEGIES

Comprehensive gun reduction involves partnerships through which the community, law enforcement, prosecutors, courts, and social services agencies undertake three objectives:

» Identify where gun violence occurs and who perpetrates it
» Develop a comprehensive plan
» Create strategies to carry out the plan

Partners in gun violence reduction identified by the Office of Juvenile Justice and Delinquency Prevention (OJJDP) include the U.S. attorney, chief of police, sheriff, federal law enforcement agencies (FBI, ATF, DEA), district attorney, state attorney general, mayor/city manager, probation and parole officers, juvenile corrections officials, judges, public defenders, school superintendents, social services officials, leaders in the faith community, and business leaders.

Reducing Access to Firearms

Child Access Prevention (CAP) laws, or "safe storage" laws, require adults to either store loaded guns in a place reasonably inaccessible to children or use a safety device to lock the gun if they choose to leave the weapon accessible. If a child obtains an improperly stored, loaded gun, the adult owner is criminally liable.

CAP laws also help reduce juvenile suicide by keeping guns out of the reach of children. For youths, particularly adolescents, rapid and intense fluctuations in mood are fairly common. A child going through a particularly difficult time emotionally may, with easy access to a firearm, turn a temporary situation into a permanent mistake.

Approximately one-third of U.S. households with children also have guns, and more than 40 percent of these residences do not keep their guns locked. Many children are unable to distinguish a real gun from a toy, and many toddlers are strong enough to pull the trigger on a real gun. Not surprisingly, children and teens commit more than half of all unintentional shootings in the United States ("Gun Safety," 2012).

Teaching Gun-Safe Behavior

When adults fail to keep firearms securely locked away or to teach others in the house, especially children, proper gun safety techniques, they place their entire family and anyone who may be in or near their house at tremendous risk. One police officer, despite educating her two young sons about gun safety and how to handle firearms, lost her older boy to an accidental shooting. He had gone next door to play with a neighbor, who had found a gun in one of the bedrooms and, while playing with it, accidentally shot his friend in the face. His mother, like many parents, had never considered asking the parents of her children's playmates if they kept guns in their house.

Although the ultimate responsibility for teaching kids gun-safe behavior lies with parents, many adults themselves need coaching in this area. *Project ChildSafe*, the nation's largest firearm safety education program, aims to ensure safe and responsible firearm ownership. Since 2003 it has distributed more than 35 million safety kits that include a cable-style gun-locking device and safety education materials. It has partnered with governors, lieutenant governors, U.S. attorneys, mayors, and local law enforcement to promote Project ChildSafe's safety education measures. It also helps local law enforcement agencies to schedule firearm safety events in their communities. Project Child Safe was funded by the U.S. Department of Justice with a $50 million grant (*Project ChildSafe*, 2004).

Right-to-Carry Laws

Right-to-carry (RTC) concealed handgun laws are a controversial issue. One fact is clear: Such laws do increase the number of concealed weapons on the streets. The argument in favor of such laws is that they will reduce crime and simultaneously give citizens a feeling of security.

Preventing gun violence may greatly affect the other types of violence discussed next: domestic violence and workplace violence.

SEXUAL VIOLENCE

Rape is one of the four violent crimes tracked by the FBI in its Uniform Crime Reports; however, the FBI documents only forcible rape of female victims, excluding all other illegal sex crimes. Rape or sexual assault is one of the most underreported crimes and, depending on the official source cited, the extent of the problem can be vastly underestimated. For example, in 2006 the FBI reported 90,427 forcible rapes. In contrast, that same year the NCVS reported 272,350 rapes/sexual assaults. The NCVS counts all types of rape, regardless of gender or of whether the force was physical or psychological.

Like other violent crimes, the vast majority of sexual assaults are committed by someone the victim knows. Although women fear random attacks by strangers, the reality is that most victims are attacked by an acquaintance. Few sexual assaults (only about 10–20%) are ever reported to authorities. For the most part, the ones that are reported are those committed by strangers. Several factors account for the reluctance of victims of nonstranger rape to report assaults, including a fear that they will not be believed or that they will be blamed for their own victimization. Some victims are afraid to report because of threats by the assailant. Furthermore, many victims of sexual assault feel shame, blame themselves, and dread revealing what is normally very private information to police, courts, and possibly the public. They may be reluctant to report the rape if they had been drinking alcohol in excess or illegally or if they had used illegal substances at the time of the assault.

The most effective response to sexual assaults employs a collaborative team approach, which includes a police officer, victim advocate, and the physician or nurse who conducts the sexual assault examination and collects evidence from the victim's body. Ideally, each of these professionals should have specific training in sexual assault and each should understand the roles of the others. Advocates can make all the difference in these cases because their role is to support the victim throughout the process, helping her understand her choices at each stage and making her comfortable enough to be able to provide the necessary information for an investigation to go forward.

A little-understood phenomenon that affects people who have been in a recent traumatic situation is a type of amnesia that causes the victim to temporarily forget facts so important that it would seem, to others, that they would be impossible to forget. It is only after a night's sleep, or even a couple of nights' sleep, that the victim is able to remember these facts. Police officers often have difficulty believing people who "suddenly" remember an important fact, but officers suffer the very same phenomenon after a major incident involving gunfire or other violent action. For that reason, departments are often advised to let officers involved in a shooting incident "sleep on it" before being questioned in detail about the event. Rape victims commonly experience the same temporary memory loss.

Although there are some exemplary examples of departments that conduct professional, unbiased investigations, it is probably fair to say the majority of sexual assault victims are poorly served by the criminal justice system.

Problem-Solving Approach to Acquaintance Rape of College Students

Rape is the most common violent crime on college campuses today (Sampson, 2011). Women between the ages of 16 and 24 are four times more likely to become rape victims than all other women, and college women are at more risk for rape and other sexual assaults than noncollege women of the same age, yet fewer than 5 percent of women who are victims or rape or attempted rape report the assault to the police (Sampson, 2011).

Some police officers believe the number of false rape reports is unusually high. This may result from the fact that the sexual assault training most police officers receive is focused on stranger rape, giving officers the idea that only stranger rapes are valid cases. Another reason officers are skeptical of rape reports is that police are subjected to the same social stereotyping about rape and victims as the rest of society. Yet another reason is that the FBI does not separately track false rape reports; it tracks the total number of *unfounded* reports, which consist of both baseless cases in which the elements of the crime were never met and false reports. Officers need to know that unfounded reports are *not* the same as false reports.

Some officers believe incorrectly that a rape report is unfounded or false if any or all of the following conditions apply (Sampson, 2011, 10):

» The victim had a prior relationship with the offender, including being intimate

» The victim used alcohol or drugs at the time of the assault

» There is no visible evidence of injury

» The victim delays reporting and/or does not have a rape medical examination

» The victim fails to immediately label her assault as a rape and/or blames herself

Most college rape prevention activities consist of the campus police providing self-defense training, doing environmental assessments of outdoor areas where rapes could occur, providing safe escort for women on campus, and recommending the installation of cameras, lights, locks, and so on. These approaches do not focus on preventing acquaintance rape. Such approaches are actually a disservice because they send a message that "real rape" is stranger rape and that stranger rape is what police are concerned with, whereas non-stranger rape can be dealt with by other campus departments or student organizations (Sampson, 2011).

Sampson (2011, 15) stresses: "Colleges have a legal duty to warn students of known risks and to provide reasonable protection. If a crime is foreseeable, then a college can be held liable for not sufficiently protecting against it. As noted, acquaintance rape is the most common violent crime on college campuses. If acquaintance rape(s) occur at predictable times and places, the school must make reasonable efforts to prevent a recurrence; the school may be liable if it fails to deal effectively with repeat student offenders, including rapists, whose conduct eventually results in more damage."

Responses to Sexual Assault on Campuses Appropriate responses to sexual assault on campuses might include conducting acquaintance rape prevention programs for college men in general; conducting acquaintance rape risk-reduction programs for college women; developing risk-reduction plans to prevent repeat victimization; educating police about acquaintance rape of college students; conducting acquaintance rape prevention programs for college administrators, campus judicial officers, and other key campus personnel; and conducting acquaintance rape prevention programs geared toward campus athletes and fraternities (Sampson, 2011, 27–30). Providing student escort and/or shuttle services and providing rape aggression defense training have limited effectiveness in preventing acquaintance rape on college campuses (Sampson, 2011, 31).

DOMESTIC VIOLENCE

Domestic violence is an area where the system response has a real potential to save lives. In the words of the late Robert Trojanowicz, a community policing pioneer: "We must remember that until we are all safe, no one is truly safe." Building trust with the victims of domestic violence is crucial. Those who have been victimized by spousal abuse, stalking, child abuse, or elder abuse can be of great assistance in community efforts to prevent such victimization. This part of the chapter focuses on strategies to reduce or prevent domestic violence. In addition to collaboration among criminal justice agencies, all other stakeholders in the community need to be involved in identifying problems and working toward solutions.

Intimate Partner Violence

intimate partner violence (IPV)

Violence that occurs between two people in a close (intimate) relationship, whether the partners are of the same or opposite gender; can involve physical violence, sexual violence, threats, emotional abuse, and stalking.

Intimate partner violence (IPV) is defined by the Centers for Disease Control and Prevention (CDC) as that which occurs between two people in a close relationship ("Understanding Intimate Partner Violence," 2012). It can involve physical violence, sexual violence, threats, emotional abuse, and stalking. It can involve partners of the same or opposite gender. IPV is a serious problem in the United States, with an estimated 30 percent of women and 10 percent of men in this country having experienced rape, physical violence, and/or stalking by an intimate partner. In 2007, 2,340 deaths were attributed to IPV, and the majority (70%) of victims were females ("Understanding Intimate Partner Violence," 2012). Trend data indicate that, between 1980 and 2008, female homicide victims were more likely than male victims—in every age group—to have been killed by an intimate. And while the proportion of intimate homicides by a spouse has decreased since 1980, the proportion committed by a boyfriend or girlfriend has increased (Cooper and Smith, 2011).

Important Research Findings—Who Is at Risk?

Information on risk factors is helpful in developing prevention strategies and interventions. It is important to recognize that risk factors associated with a greater likelihood of IPV victimization or perpetration are merely contributing

ON THE BEAT

Many violent acts occur in today's world, including domestic violence—a serious problem in our society. Our agency's policy is to protect victims of domestic abuse by making an arrest whenever it is authorized under the law. It is a crime that can potentially have severe, deadly consequences.

I recall a domestic situation where the violence escalated very rapidly. A woman in her fifties (I will refer to her as Gail) and the man she had been with for over 20 years (who was also in his fifties and will be referred to as Anthony) had a domestic dispute at an apartment complex. The first time I was called to Gail's apartment I was to serve a search warrant. I found a bloody trail leading to the unit from the street. Several hours earlier, Anthony had been found at an intersection bleeding profusely from multiple stab wounds. He refused to give officers any information. Officers went into the apartment and found several people inside, including Gail. I recovered the 10-inch butcher knife she had used against Anthony just hours earlier. This was only the first of more incidents to come.

The violence became more frequent and the relationship more toxic. I responded to the location enough times that Gail got to know my face and would give me the straight scoop when I interacted with her. I built up a certain level of trust with her, and I recall asking her why she stayed with Anthony despite all the abuse. She replied that he was all she knew and that despite everything, she loved him.

The domestic violence got to a point where Anthony literally set Gail on fire one night. It cannot get much more horrific than that. She survived that incident, but I think one of them would have ended up killing the other had Gail not died from her drug use. Maybe the drug use was due to the abusive situation; it's hard to say. The point is this is only one story of many, many terrible stories out there. Domestic violence is a serious problem in today's society, and more efforts need to be made to systematically curtail, prevent and hopefully stop this terrible crime.

—*Kim Czapar*

factors, not direct causes per se. Not everyone who is identified as "at risk" becomes involved in violence:

> Some risk factors for IPV victimization and perpetration are the same. In addition, some risk factors for victimization and perpetration are associated with one another; for example, childhood physical or sexual victimization is a risk factor for future IPV perpetration and victimization.

> A combination of individual, relational, community, and societal factors contribute to the risk of becoming a victim or perpetrator of IPV. Understanding these multilevel factors can help identify various opportunities for prevention.

Individual Risk Factors

» Low self-esteem

» Low income

» Low academic achievement

» Young age

» Aggressive or delinquent behavior as a youth

» Heavy alcohol and drug use

» Depression

» Anger and hostility

» Antisocial personality traits

» Borderline personality traits

» Prior history of being physically abusive

» Having few friends and being isolated from other people

» Unemployment

» Emotional dependence and insecurity

» Belief in strict gender roles (e.g., male dominance and aggression in relationships)

» Desire for power and control in relationships

» Perpetrating psychological aggression

» Being a victim of physical or psychological abuse (consistently one of the strongest predictors of perpetration)

» History of experiencing poor parenting as a child

» History of experiencing physical discipline as a child

Relationship Factors

» Marital conflict—fights, tension, and other struggles

» Marital instability—divorces or separations

» Dominance and control of the relationship by one partner over the other

» Economic stress

» Unhealthy family relationships and interactions

Community Factors

» Poverty and associated factors (e.g., overcrowding)

» Low social capital—lack of institutions, relationships, and norms that shape a community's social interactions

» Weak community sanctions against IPV (e.g., unwillingness of neighbors to intervene in situations where they witness violence)

Societal Factors

» Traditional gender norms (e.g., women should stay at home, not enter workforce, and be submissive; men support the family and make the decisions) ("Intimate Partner Violence: Risk and Protective Factors," 2010)

Women are more vulnerable to being assaulted or killed during separation and are particularly vulnerable when they are pregnant. A survey in Canada found that 21 percent of abused women were assaulted during pregnancy, and in 40 percent of these cases, this episode was the beginning of the abuse. The extreme vulnerability to violence by women in the sex trade often goes unnoticed. According to police reports submitted to Statistics Canada, between 1991 and 2004, 171 female prostitutes were killed. These cases are often never solved (Johnson, 2006).

Legislation to Prevent Stalking and Domestic Violence

Although several laws have been passed to prevent stalking and domestic violence, one law, the Violence against Women Act (VAWA), merits emphasis because it makes this serious problem a system-wide institutional priority. Passed in 1994 and re-authorized by the U.S. Congress in 2000, the Act was renewed in 2005 and extended for another 5 years. However, reauthorization of VAWA, due to occur in 2012, has stalled in Congress as this text goes to print.

Animal Abuse and Domestic Violence

When looking at domestic violence cases, animal abuse serves as a predictor of other violent and abusive behavior. Animal abuse is often found in the background of homicide, vandalism, and arson perpetrators. In addition, many serial killers and even students involved in recent school shootings have histories of abusing animals first before moving on to human targets. Animal abuse has been identified as one component of the "MacDonald Triad," a conceptual model of violence risk that has been linked to multiple homicide, homicide, and sexual offending, the other two components being enuresis (bed wetting) and fire setting (Vaughn et al., 2010).

The American Humane Association, in collaboration with the National Coalition against Domestic Violence, has presented the following data ("Facts about Animal Abuse and Domestic Violence," 2011):

» More than 7 out of 10 (71%) pet-owning women who enter shelters report that their batterer has either injured, maimed, killed, or threatened family pets for revenge or to psychologically control victims, and more than 3 out of 10 (32%) report that their children had hurt or killed animals.

» More than two-thirds (68%) of battered women say their pets had been treated with violence by someone else in the household. Three-fourths (75%) of these incidents occurred in the presence of the children, to psychologically control and coerce them.

» Between 25 percent and 40 percent of battered women chose to stay in an abusive situation because they worry about what will happen to their pets if they leave.

» One study found that 70 percent of animal abusers also had criminal records.[1]

---

[1] **Reprinted by permission of the American Humane Association.**

Also, a child who abuses an animal may be imitating parents who have abused them or other family members. The child may feel helpless and consequently hurt the only member of the family who is more vulnerable than he or she is—the family pet. Jeffrey Dahmer and Ted Bundy are "infamous examples" of this disturbing correlation.

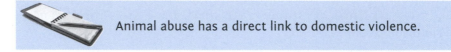

Animal abuse has a direct link to domestic violence.

First Strike: The Violence Connection campaign was created in 1997 to raise public and professional awareness about the connection between animal cruelty and human violence and to help communities identify some of the origins of violence, predict its patterns, and prevent its escalation. The campaign worked with local animal protection agencies around the United States to bring together animal shelter workers, animal control officers, social service workers, law enforcement officials, veterinarians, educators, and others to learn about the violence connection and to promote interagency collaborations to reduce animal cruelty, family violence, and community violence. *First Strike* (2008) provides investigative support, rewards, expert testimony, and information on the animal–human cruelty connection to law enforcement and prosecutors in high-profile animal cruelty cases. *First Strike* also works jointly with legislators and activists throughout the United States to press for the passage of well-enforced, felony-level anticruelty laws.

The Law Enforcement Response to Domestic Violence

Domestic violence victims are less likely than other victims to call police because of privacy concerns, a fear of reprisal by their abuser, and their desire to protect offenders. This adds to the challenge of an effective police response to domestic violence.

One controversial law enforcement response is a mandatory arrest policy, and research results on the effectiveness of arresting domestic violence offenders are mixed. The *Spouse Assault Replication Program*, a field study cosponsored by the NIJ and the CDC and carried out between 1981 and 1991, analyzed more than 4,000 domestic violence incidents, from six jurisdictions, in which males had assaulted their female intimate partners. The first of the six studies within the SARP was the Minneapolis Domestic Violence Experiment (MDVE), conducted by Lawrence Sherman and Richard Berk, which found that arresting batterers reduced the rate of subsequent abuse involving the same victim by 50 percent within a 6-month follow-up period. The five replication studies added support to the MDVE results by finding that arresting batterers was consistently associated with less repeat offending. However, subsequent criticism of the studies' methodology led to the results being questioned and follow-up studies being conducted. Later research by Maxwell, Garner, and Fagan (2001, 2) led to several key findings:

» Arresting batterers was consistently related to reduced subsequent aggression against female intimate partners, although not all comparisons met the standard level of statistical significance.

» Regardless of the type of intervention [arrest vs. no arrest], most suspects had no subsequent criminal offense against their original victim within the follow-up period.

» The research found no association between arresting the offender and an increased risk of subsequent aggression against women.

The finding that most battering suspects discontinued their aggressive behaviors even without being arrested suggests that mandatory arrest policies for all batterers may unnecessarily misdirect a community's limited resources away from identifying and responding to the worst offenders and the victims at greatest risk (Maxwell, Garner, and Fagan, 2001).

A national survey found that approximately 11 percent of police departments in the United States have a specialized domestic violence unit, most of which work within investigative units. The majority of departments (56%) with 100 or more sworn officers have specialized domestic violence units (Klein, 2009). Studies have found that specialized domestic violence units, which put emphasis on repeat victim contact and evidence collection, significantly increase the likelihood of prosecution, conviction, and sentencing of abusers; are more likely to result in the victim leaving their abuser sooner (within 4 months, as opposed to the average 14 months for victims who do not receive a specialized police response); lead to higher victim reporting of reabuse; and increase the likelihood that victims will seek and secure a protective order against their abusers (Klein, 2009).

Other Efforts to Prevent Domestic Violence

As in other problems related to violence, several approaches have been used.

Corporate Partnership to Combat Domestic Violence

Most executives and managers in the corporate sector have given little or no thought to the impact of partner abuse on the health and safety of their employees. Potential barriers to understanding and helping employees who are victims of partner abuse include lack of awareness; denial; embarrassment; privacy and confidentiality concerns; victim blaming; expectations of self-identification by abused women; fear of advocating for change; and concern that outreach to abused women may alienate male employees, damage the company image, or be too expensive.

A survey of employee assistance professionals (EAPs) found that a large majority of EAP providers had been faced with cases of partner abuse, including restraining order violations and stalking in the workplace. General policies on workplace violence exist, but few specifically address domestic violence. Among larger corporations, EAP staff use a range of practices to assist employees affected by abuse, including use of leaves of absence, medical leaves, and short-term disability. The affect of domestic violence on the workplace is discussed shortly.

The Lakewood (Colorado) Police Department and Motorola joined forces to apply sophisticated law enforcement and business principles to develop new strategies for managing domestic violence cases. The partnership uses **process mapping**, a program Motorola developed as part of its quality management process. An alternative to traditional top-down methods of internal

process mapping
A method of internal analysis that takes a horizontal view of a system, in contrast to the traditional vertical view. It involves personnel at all levels and uses flowcharts to visually depict how information, materials, and activities flow in an organization; how work is handed off from one unit or department to another; and how processes work currently and what changes should be made to attain a more ideal process flow.

analysis, process mapping takes a horizontal view of a system and involves personnel at all levels. It uses a series of flowcharts or maps to visually depict how information, materials, and activities flow in an organization and how work is handed off from one unit or department to another. It also identifies how processes work currently and what changes should be made to attain a more ideal process flow. The Lakewood Police Department chose to apply process mapping to domestic violence because of the complexity of such cases and how the crime affects not only the victim but also branches out to affect the victim's children, other family members, neighbors, colleagues, and others. With process mapping, police can more effectively monitor the activities of various agencies involved in the response. Thus the process mapping program not only identifies areas for improvement but also facilitates communication between the city, police department, and community.

A Domestic Violence Reduction Unit

In 1992 the Portland (Oregon) Police Bureau identified a need to provide additional services to families. In keeping with the community policing philosophy, the agency turned to the community to help define the new programs. They consulted more than 100 community leaders and groups. To design the administrative framework for their Domestic Violence Reduction Unit, the bureau looked for models other agencies had designed. It also held discussions with the district attorney and judges as well as leaders in the battered women's movement. The participants agreed that officers would not only vigorously enforce the laws but that they would become advocates for victims, and that increased cooperation would be needed between the police and other public safety agencies to enhance reporting and enforcement.

The unit's activities are not confined to working with individual cases. Their work is also a source of training for other officers and for community education outside the Portland Police Bureau. In addition, the officers have provided training to more than 20 other police agencies in the country.

When forming partnerships to prevent domestic violence, the issue of cultural diversity between male-dominated police organizations and female-dominated grassroots advocate groups must be addressed.

S*T*O*P Violence against Women

The Department of Justice's S*T*O*P Violence against Women grant program provides money directly to states and Native American tribes as a step in helping to restructure the criminal justice system's response to crimes of violence against women. The acronym stands for *services, training, officers,* and *prosecution,* the vital components in a comprehensive program for victims of domestic violence and its perpetrators. This program requires collaboration between victim advocates, prosecutors, and police. Funding from these grants can help build and maintain crisis centers and shelters for battered women, train and finance hundreds of new prosecutors for specialized domestic violence or sexual assault units, and help hundreds of volunteer coordinators run domestic violence hotlines.

Police–Community Partnership

A number of jurisdictions have attempted to bring together a wide range of criminal justice and social service agencies to provide a coordinated community response to domestic violence, an approach with the potential to positively impact both case processing and re-abuse (Klein, 2009). An estimated 65 percent of police departments have established partnerships with community-based victim advocacy groups, according to a national survey of 14,000 police departments (Klein, 2009).

The Police Executive Research Forum (PERF), with funding from the Community Oriented Policing Services (COPS) Office, explored the nature, function, and impact of police–community partnerships to address domestic violence. *Police–Community Partnerships to Address Domestic Violence* (Reuland et al., 2006) reports that about 62 percent of task force partnerships mentioned participation in coalitions or teams, and almost 60 percent of the partnerships listed victim services as an important component. On-scene responses were mentioned as an activity by only 42 percent. The majority of police respondents noted that the most important aspect of the partnership was how well the various parties communicate and work together to agree on the appropriate course of action and that they do it "almost automatically" despite their differences (Reuland et al., 2006, 29).

These partnerships are most successful in achieving those goals related to improving victim services and safety. Less success is noted for the goals of reducing the number of domestic violence incidents or repeated incidents. The predominant finding of this project is that partnerships between the police and a community-based organization have made tremendous improvements in the way agencies communicate and channel their energies toward a shared goal of improving safety for the victims of domestic violence (Reuland et al., 2006, 44).

Worst Mistakes The most frequently noted mistake a police department can make is not partnering with the community to address domestic violence (Reuland et al., 2006). Almost all community partner sources said their worst mistake would be to overstep the bounds of the advocate's role by telling officers what to do, interfering in the criminal aspects of the situations, or confusing their role with that of the officers.

Recommendations Based on research, communities that develop such partnerships with the police should:

» Involve as many stakeholders as possible when developing the partnership arrangements, including a wide range of community members (such as schools and animal shelters) and criminal justice agencies (such as prosecutors and judges).

» Develop strong personal relationships with partners, usually characterized by trust and shared goals; develop common ground by sharing frustration over the intractability of domestic violence and uncooperative victims.

» Demonstrate police leadership and commitment to addressing domestic violence by setting appropriate staff levels and developing mechanisms to enforce policy.

» Emphasize goals related to victim safety and services. Very few respondents focused on increased arrests *per se*. Instead, they hoped to increase victim safety, provide on-scene crisis intervention counseling, and ensure victim awareness of community resources to break the **cycle of violence** and get abuse victims out of their situation.

» Involve line-level staff (officers and counselors) in the process of developing and implementing partnership policies and procedures (Reuland et al., 2006, 44–45).

cycle of violence

Violent or sexual victimization of children can often lead to these victims becoming perpetrators of domestic violence as adults.

When the Batterer Is a Police Officer

"Domestic violence in police families has always been one of the original 'don't ask, don't tell' issues—alternately ignored, hidden, or denied, firmly protected by the blue wall of silence" (Gallo, 2004, 60). Several studies have shown that at least 40 percent of police families experience officer-involved domestic violence (OIDV) each year, compared with about 10 percent of families in the general U.S. population ("Police Family Violence Fact Sheet," 2005). Because of their training in using force, police officers can be the most dangerous of domestic abusers, but specialized training is only one factor that makes OIDV particularly perilous. The danger to victims of abuse by police officers is further heightened by the fact that the abuser has a gun; the weight of a close-knit, male-oriented police culture behind them; knowledge of the location of crisis centers and women's shelters; the ability and resources to track people down; and the know-how to manipulate the system to avoid penalty (Ammons, 2005).

Graves (2004) recommends a zero-tolerance posture against officer-involved domestic abuse, emphasizing the agency's commitment to maintaining community trust, discipline, and the like. He suggests that community members hold law enforcement officers to a higher standard of conduct both on and off duty: "No agency can afford the negative ramifications that come with a domestic abuse incident by one of their own" (Graves, 2004, 108).

Federal law prohibits anyone convicted of qualifying misdemeanor domestic violence crimes from possessing firearms. A qualifying misdemeanor domestic violence crime means that the crime has, as an element, the use or attempted use of physical force, or the threatened use of a deadly weapon, committed by a current or former spouse, parent, or guardian of the victim, by a person with whom the victim shares a child in common, by a person who is cohabiting with or has cohabited with the victim as a spouse, parent, or guardian, or by a person similarly situated to a spouse, parent, or guardian of the victim. The law does not exempt law enforcement officers and governmental employees (such as security guards or military personnel) ("Federal Law: Firearms and Ammunition Prohibitions," 2009).

The problem of partner abuse often also involves child abuse, whether it involves the trauma a child experiences witnessing such abuse or actually being physically abused as well.

CHILD ABUSE

The link between child abuse and spousal abuse and the risk factors involved in being abused as a child have been discussed. Figure 14.3 illustrates the overlap of child abuse and domestic violence, with data suggesting a 30-percent to 60-percent overlap between violence against children and violence against women in the same family.

 Children in violent homes face three risks: (1) the risk of observing traumatic events, (2) the risk of being abused themselves, and (3) the risk of being neglected.

Children Exposed to Violence

Johnson (2000) states: "[Children who witness violence] are the 'bystanders' to violence, the indirect victims. ... Children who witness violence in their homes and neighborhoods, recent studies suggest, may not be as resilient as medical and mental health specialists once believed. It turns out that kids exposed to violence—especially the estimated 3.3 million to 10 million kids a year who've seen brutality between people they love and trust—are often as traumatized as those who are directly victimized." One meta-analysis revealed strong evidence that children who witness interparental violence are at risk for a wide range of psychological, social, emotional, behavioral, and academic problems and that exposure to this type of violence may affect children more negatively than witnessing other forms of destructive conflict (Kitzmann et al., 2003).

Training Professionals to Recognize Child Victims

Hospital personnel, lawyers, justice system officials, and psychiatrists need training to enable them to recognize child victims of violence and abuse, understand their special needs, and act as their advocates.

A potential obstacle is that professionals such as lawyers and physicians may be reluctant to admit their inability to recognize and assist child victims. The American Academy of Pediatrics and the Center to Prevent Handgun Violence sponsor educational and training materials for pediatric health care professionals through the Stop Firearm Injury program. The program provides doctors and others with brochures, posters, reading lists, and other information to help them recognize child victims of gun violence and refer them and their families to other service providers as needed. Thousands of physicians have received and used the materials.

Figure 14.3   Overlap of Child Maltreatment and Domestic Violence

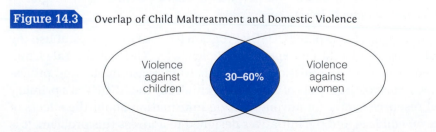

Source: Data from http://library.adoption.com/articles/in-harms-way-domestic-violence-and-child-maltreatment .html

The Child Development–Community Policing Model

The child development–community policing (CD–CP) model is a pilot initiative that emphasizes the importance of developing collaborative relationships between law enforcement and mental health communities to ensure that youths exposed to violence have access to a wide array of services offered in their communities.

 The CD–CP model emphasizes cross-training of criminal justice and mental health professionals to develop collaborative problem-solving techniques that go beyond the reach of either "system" acting alone.

The distinction between law enforcement and child protection agencies is beginning to blur, with police spending more time in noninvestigative activities and child protection workers spending more time as investigators. Their spheres of influence have come to overlap in many areas, and both have shifted emphasis from reactive to proactive responses when possible.

The CD–CP program began in New Haven, Connecticut, in 1991 and has been facilitated by resources of and researchers at the Yale University Child Study Center. Specifically, the CD–CP model's training and collaboration principles include:

» Child development fellowships for police supervisors, which provide supervisory officers with the necessary expertise to lead a team of community-based officers in activities and services related to children and families and create opportunities to interact with the child mental health professionals with whom they will collaborate in the future.

» Police fellowships for clinicians, which provide clinicians the opportunity to observe and learn directly from law enforcement officers about the responsibilities of community-based policing, while also building collaborative relationships with law enforcement officials.

» Seminars on child development, human functioning, and policing strategies for clinicians, community police officers, and related justice practitioners that incorporate case scenarios to apply principles of child development to the daily work of policing.

» Consultation services that give law enforcement the ability to make referrals and obtain immediate clinical guidance if necessary.

» Program conferencing, where CD–CP police officers and clinicians meet weekly to discuss difficult and perplexing cases (*Promising Strategies to Reduce Gun Violence*, 1999).

The pioneering efforts of the CD–CP Program led the OJJDP to establish the National Center for Children Exposed to Violence (NCCEV) at the Yale Child Study Center in 1999, the mission of which is to increase public and professional awareness of the effects of violence on children. The NCCEV is a primary national resource center for anyone seeking information about the effects of violence on children and the initiatives designed to address this problem. It is also a provider of training, technical assistance, and consultation to a variety of collaborative community programs across the country.

Forming a Multidisciplinary Team to Investigate Child Abuse

Unfortunately, failure to respond to reports of child abuse in a timely and appropriate manner has happened many times—and is continuing to happen—in probably every state in the country and almost always for the same reason—a lack of and coordination among the agencies investigating reports of possible abuse. A key to avoiding tragedies is the formation of a multidisciplinary team representing the government agencies and private practitioners responsible for investigating crimes against children and protecting and treating children in the community.

Legislation to Increase Child Protections

The Adam Walsh Child Protection and Safety Act was passed in 2006. Among the numerous provisions of the Act are four that are especially significant:

1. The Act integrates the information in state sex offender registries and ensures that law enforcement agencies will have access to the same information nationwide, "helping prevent sex offenders from evading detection by moving from state to state."

2. The Act imposes mandatory minimum prison terms for the most serious crimes against children and authorizes federal grants to the states to help

Second-grade students in Austin, Texas, look at a children's Internet safety program on library computers during a kickoff event for the "Cyber-Guardian for the Internet Age—Faux Paw the Techno Cat."

© Bob Daemmrich/The Image Works

them institutionalize, through civil commitment procedures, sex offenders found to be dangerous and about to be released from prison.

3. The Act aims to increase prosecutions of sexual predators who use the Internet to make contact with children, by authorizing funding for new regional Internet Crimes against Children Task Forces.

4. The Act establishes a new national child abuse registry and requires investigators to conduct background checks of prospective adoptive and foster parents before they are approved to take custody of a child. "By giving child protective service professionals in all 50 states access to this critical information, we will improve their ability to investigate child abuse cases and help ensure that vulnerable children are not put into situations of abuse or neglect."

WORKPLACE VIOLENCE

Yet another type of violence that community policing efforts, partnerships, and problem solving can help address is workplace violence. The Occupational Safety and Health Administration (OSHA) defines workplace violence as "any act or threat of physical violence, harassment, intimidation, or other threatening disruptive behavior that occurs at the work site. It ranges from threats and verbal abuse to physical assaults and even homicide. It can affect and involve employees, clients, customers, and visitors" ("Workplace Violence," 2012). The Bureau of Labor Statistics (BLS) Census of Fatal Occupational Injuries (CFOI) reports that 4,690 fatal injuries occurred in U.S. workplaces in 2010, 518 of which were workplace homicides. Homicide currently ranks fourth among causes of fatal occupational injuries in the country and is the leading cause of death for women in the workplace ("Workplace Violence," 2012).

The overall number of workplace homicides in 2010 represented a decline of 52 percent since 1994, the lowest total ever recorded by the fatality census. And although workplace homicides of men were down 8 percent in 2010 from the previous year's numbers, workplace homicides involving women increased by 14 percent in 2010 (*2010 Census of Fatal Occupational Injuries*, 2012).

Most study results and experts identify the driving forces behind workplace violence as being (1) an economic system that fails to support full employment (downsizing), (2) a legal system that fails to protect citizens and releases criminals from prison early because of overcrowding, (3) a cultural system that glamorizes violence in the media, and (4) the universal availability of weapons.

Common motivations behind violent behavior in the workplace include robbery, loss of a job, anger from feelings of mistreatment, substance abuse, and mental problems.

As with school shooters, many employees provide clues that they may become violent. Warning signs include unusual fascination with weapons, a display of unwarranted anger, irrational beliefs and ideas, feelings of victimization, talk of hurting self and others, substance abuse, inability to take criticism, constant complaining, attendance and productivity problems, and past threats or acts of intimidation.

Workplace violence shares many characteristics with school violence. School violence is, in fact, a form of workplace violence for school staff.

 Characteristics common to workplace violence and school violence include the profiles of the perpetrators, the targets, the warnings, the means, and the pathways to violence.

Who Is Vulnerable?

Workplace violence can strike anywhere; no one is immune. However, some workers are at increased risk, including workers who exchange money with the public; deliver passengers, goods, or services; or work alone or in small groups, during late night or early morning hours, in high-crime areas, or in community settings and homes where they have extensive contact with the public. This group includes health care and social service workers such as visiting nurses, psychiatric evaluators, and probation officers; community workers such as gas and water utility employees, phone and cable TV installers, and letter carriers; retail workers; and taxi drivers (*OSHA Fact Sheet*, 2002).

Protecting Employees

The best protection is a zero-tolerance policy toward workplace violence against or by employees. Employers should establish a workplace violence prevention program or incorporate the information into an existing accident prevention program, employee handbook, or procedure manual. The FBI's National Center for the Analysis of Violent Crime (NCAVC) publication, *Workplace Violence: Issues in Response* (2003, 19), suggests:

> As with most other risks, prevention of workplace violence begins with planning. Also, as with other risks, it is easier to persuade managers to focus on the problem after a violent act has taken place than it is to get them to act before anything has happened. If the decision to plan in advance is more difficult to make, however, it is also more logical. Any organization, large or small, will be far better able to spot potential dangers and defuse them before violence develops and will be able to manage a crisis better if one does occur, if its executives have considered the issue beforehand and have prepared policies, practices, and structures to deal with it.

Workplace Violence and Domestic Violence

Sometimes it is harassing phone calls to an employee or an angry spouse bursting into the workplace threatening violence or actually assaulting the partner. It may include homicide. Corporations are increasingly raising the profile of battered women and encouraging individuals, businesses, and communities to take action to prevent domestic violence.

Workplace Violence and Hospital Emergency Rooms

A strategy some communities are using to reduce the violence often experienced in hospital emergency rooms by violent patients and visitors is to train the staff in violence prevention. A survey of 103 hospitals in Los Angeles and other urban areas of California found that nearly 60 percent of hospital staff had been injured by visitors or patients. Hospital administrators, with the assistance of law enforcement, can develop partnerships with physicians, nurses, and staff to understand past events and devise training strategies and security policies to prevent further incidents.

The Changing Role of Law Enforcement

"In violence-prevention planning, threat assessment, and other preventive efforts, collaboration among law enforcement officers, employers' representatives, and other resources such as mental health workers will yield the best results in almost all situations" (*Workplace Violence: Issues in Response,* 2003, 38).

Ideas in Practice

WORKPLACE VIOLENCE INITIATIVE, BALTIMORE COUNTY, MARYLAND

After the Baltimore County Police Department responded to several workplace violence/stalking incidents in the suburban Cockeysville, Maryland, Precinct Seven area of the county, they realized they would be more effective if they could be proactive about these kinds of situations. The precinct had already handled two domestic workplace violence homicides in a 3-year period.

The officers did research on the issue of workplace violence, talking with leaders in the more than 750 businesses in the community. The information they gained, in combination with research results from the department's analysis unit, raised enough concern to lead to formation of a workplace violence prevention program.

With a focus on the *workplace avenger* and on domestic violence, which often spills over into the workplace, the department set up a workplace violence team as part of the behavioral assessment unit. The team set up a Web page with links and e-mail so that both police and businesses would have a confidential location to make requests and have their needs addressed. There is also an e-mail address for reporting potential problems anonymously to the police department.

The team also developed an internal tracking system for workplace violence cases. Previously, cases or calls were coded by offense because a workplace violence category did not exist; this system made it difficult to get a good idea of the scope of the problem. The new workplace violence tracking system has subcategories of assault, domestic violence, harassment, and stalking.

The team developed training seminars for managers, EAPs, and human resource professionals to address personnel problems and interventions. They offer help in case investigation, intervention, assessment, and management strategies for threats of violence and assistance with the prosecution of cases.

In the first 2 years, the team assessed 67 serious cases throughout Baltimore County. They have presented the training in workshops and at professional conferences throughout the country and appeared on television and radio to talk about workplace violence.

A workplace violence case protocol was created, and the team created a countywide workplace violence prevention committee. When they surveyed over 500 businesses in the targeted pilot area, 60 percent of them requested their assistance. The team assisted the Mid-Atlantic Region Community Policing Institute in designing manuals and handouts and worked with the Baltimore County state attorneys' office to have an assistant state attorney assigned to review and prosecute workplace violence cases.

The program expanded rapidly and was soon implemented throughout the county. It has received positive comments from other jurisdictions in the state of Maryland and across the country.

The new program was in step with the county's desire to attract and retain small and large businesses and with the police department's desire to assist the business community while improving the quality of life and safety for those who worked in the county.

Source: *Workplace Violence Initiative: Baltimore County.* POPS Office (2004).

A PROBLEM-SOLVING PARTNERSHIP IN ACTION

The 2002 Herman Goldstein Award was presented to the project entitled "Domestic Violence Intervention Project: Charlotte–Mecklenburg (North Carolina) Police Department" ("Domestic Violence Intervention Project," 2002).

Scanning

The problem was an apparent increase in domestic assaults in the Charlotte–Mecklenburg Police Department's Baker One District.

Analysis

Analysis of domestic assault reports showed that the average victim had filed nine previous police reports, most involving the same suspect but sometimes filing reports in more than one police district. Many of the prior reports were for indicator crimes—offenses such as trespassing, threatening, and stalking. Within the Baker One District, most repeat call locations were domestic situations. Further analysis suggested the desirability of regarding the victim and suspect as "hot spots" instead of the traditional fixed geographic location.

Response

Baker One officers developed a tailored response plan for each repeat offense case, including zero tolerance of criminal behavior by the suspect and the use of other criminal justice and social service agencies. A Police Watch Program and a Domestic Violence Hotline voicemail system for victims were implemented. Officers developed detailed case files and created a database with victim/offender background data. The database tracks victims and offenders as moving "hot spots" from one address to another and across district boundaries.

The officers felt that building on existing partnerships with other components of the criminal justice system was critical to intervene effectively in these cases. They established a stronger partnership with the district attorney's office to achieve increased evidence-based prosecution. The department's research showed many of the offenders had prior criminal records and were frequently still on probation. The Baker One officers reached out to community corrections and probation and parole officers for Mecklenburg County to garner their support and understanding of the concept and to help them focus on the behavior of domestic violence suspects who were in violation of the terms of their probation and/or parole.

A variety of stakeholders developed these intervention tactics, including domestic violence investigators and counselors, prosecutors, probation officers, and practitioners in social programs that offer services to domestic violence victims and offenders. The social services agencies participating included New Options for Violent Actions (NOVA), Victim Assistance, Legal Services of the Southern Piedmont, and the Battered Women's Shelter. All agreed to work with Baker One officers in dealing with these complex cases. Guidelines were established to provide as uniform a response as possible to each case.

Assessment

Repeat calls for service were reduced by 98.9 percent at seven target locations. Domestic assaults decreased by 7 percent in the Baker One District but increased by 29 percent in other areas of the city. In 105 cases with indicator crimes, only three victims later reported a domestic assault. Only 14.8 percent of domestic violence victims in the project reported repeat victimization, as opposed to a benchmark figure of 35 percent. No internal affairs complaints were generated by officer contacts with suspects.[2]

SUMMARY

Causes of violence may include ready availability of guns, drugs, and alcohol; a desensitization to violence; disintegration of the family and community; social and economic deprivation; and increased numbers of children growing up in violent families. A problem-solving approach to preventing violence must attempt to identify the underlying causes of specific violent situations that threaten a community before solutions can be devised.

Developing effective prevention tactics will require long-term collaborations between criminal justice and juvenile justice practitioners and other social service agencies. It also requires involvement of the entire community of which these agencies are a part. Strategies for general violence prevention include public dialogue and community mediation, and addressing violence as a public health problem.

Hate can be classified into two categories: rational and irrational. The majority of hate crimes are motivated by racial bias and involve violence.

Gun violence may be considered as a three-phase continuum: (1) the illegal acquisition of firearms; (2) the illegal possession and carrying of firearms; and (3) the illegal, improper, or careless use of firearms. The National Crime Prevention Council suggests that regulations and ordinances on gun licensing may interrupt sources of illegal guns. Gun interdictions may be an effective deterrent to illegal gun possessing and carrying.

Partners in gun violence reduction identified by the Office of Juvenile Justice and Delinquency Prevention (OJJDP) include the U.S. attorney, chief of police, sheriff, federal law enforcement agencies (FBI, ATF, DEA), district attorney, state attorney general, mayor/city manager, probation and parole officers, juvenile corrections officials, judges, public defenders, school superintendents, social services officials, leaders in the faith community, and business leaders.

Domestic violence is another type of problem in most communities. Animal abuse has a direct link to domestic violence. When forming partnerships to prevent domestic violence, the issue of cultural diversity between male-dominated police organizations and female-dominated grassroots advocate groups must be addressed.

Children in violent homes face three risks: (1) the risk of observing traumatic events, (2) the risk of being abused themselves, and (3) the risk of being neglected. The CD–CP model emphasizes cross-training of criminal justice and mental health professionals to develop collaborative problem-solving techniques that go beyond the reach of either "system" acting alone.

Yet another type of violence challenging communities is workplace violence. Common

---

[2] **Source: From "Domestic Violence Intervention in Charlotte–Mecklenburg,** *Problem Solving Quarterly,* **Vol. 16, No. 1, Spring 2003. Reprinted by permission of the Police Executive Research Forum.**

motivations behind violent behavior in the workplace include robbery, loss of a job, anger from feelings of mistreatment, substance abuse, and mental problems. Characteristics common to workplace violence and school violence include the profiles of the perpetrators, the targets, the warnings, the means, and the pathways to violence.

DISCUSSION QUESTIONS

1. Explain why some experts recommend a problem-solving approach to violence prevention.

2. What is the public health model of violence prevention?

3. Why do gun interdiction strategies frequently lead to charges that the police have targeted the minority community, and what can be done to allay such concerns?

4. Explain the difference researchers found between those who are violent to their partners and those who commit violent crimes against others.

5. What risks exist for children who live in homes where domestic violence occurs?

6. Corporations are suggested in this chapter as partners in violence prevention. Why would corporations have any interest in prevention or their ability to affect it?

7. Name some likely types of people who might pose a risk of violence in a workplace.

8. Discuss any instances of hate crimes in your community or your state. Does your state have mandatory reporting laws for hate crimes?

9. What type of person is the most likely victim of domestic violence?

10. What childhood experience increases the likelihood of being arrested later in life?

GALE EMERGENCY SERVICES DATABASE ASSIGNMENTS

ONLINE Database

- Use the Gale Emergency Services Database to help answer the Discussion Questions as appropriate.

- Research gun violence statistics in the United States, and compare what you find with statistics from other industrialized nations. How can the differences be explained? Be prepared to discuss your work with the class.

- Research either family violence or workplace violence. Write a brief (3- or 4-page) report on the topic of your choice. Be prepared to discuss your work with the class.

REFERENCES

Ammons, Jennifer. 2005. *Batterers with Badges: Officer-Involved Domestic Violence.* San Diego, CA: California Western School of Law. http://www.americanbar.org/content/dam/aba/migrated/domviol/priorwinners/Ammons1.authcheckdam.pdf

Best Practices of Community Policing in Gang Intervention and Gang Violence Prevention. (2006). Washington, DC: The United States Conference of Mayors, Best Practices Center. http://www.usmayors.org/bestpractices/community_policing_2006/gangbp_2006.pdf

Brennan, Shannon and Mia Dauvergne. 2011 (July). *Police-Reported Crime Statistics in Canada, 2010.* Ottawa, Ontario: Minister of Industry, Statistics Canada. http://www.statcan.gc.ca/pub/85-002-x/2011001/article/11523-eng.pdf

Bune, Karen L. 2004. "Law Enforcement Must Take Lead on Hate Crimes." *The Police Chief* 71 (4): 41–55.

Cooper, Alexia and Erica L. Smith. 2011 (November). *Homicide Trends in the United States, 1980–2008 (Annual Rates for 2009 and 2010).* Washington, DC: Bureau of Justice Statistics. (NCJ 236018)

Crime in the United States 2010. 2010. Washington, DC: Federal Bureau of Investigation, Uniform Crime Reports.

Dedel, Kelly. 2007 (March). *Drive-by Shootings.* Washington, DC: Office of Community Oriented Policing Services, Problem Specific Guides Series, Guide No. 47.

"Domestic Violence Intervention Project: Charlotte–Mecklenburg (North Carolina) Police Department." 2002. In *Excellence in Problem-Oriented Policing: The 2002 Herman Goldstein Award Winners*, 19–25. Washington, DC: Police Executive Research Forum.

Doyle, Michael. 2007. "Licensed Gun Dealers Down 79%." *The Seattle Times*, August 16. http://seattletimes.com/html/nationworld/2003838480_gundealers16.html

"Facts about Animal Abuse and Domestic Violence." 2011. Fact sheet. Washington, DC: American Humane Association. http://www.americanhumane.org/interaction/support-the-bond/fact-sheets/animal-abuse-domestic-violence.html

"Federal Law: Firearms and Ammunition Prohibitions." 2009 (February). Minneapolis, MN: Battered Women's Legal Advocacy Project, Inc. http://www.bwlap.org/publication/stream?fileName=Firearms__Federal__2.pdf

First Strike: The Violence Connection. 2008. Washington, DC: The Humane Society of the United States. http://www.humanesociety.org/assets/pdfs/abuse/first_strike.pdf

Gallo, Gina. 2004. "The National Police Family Violence Prevention Project Helps Departments Address Domestic Abuse in Police Families." *Law Enforcement Technology* (July): 60–64.

Graves, Alex. 2004. "Law Enforcement Involved Domestic Abuse." *Law and Order* 52 (11): 108–111.

"Gun Safety." 2012 (October 10). Bethesda, MD: U.S. National Library of Medicine, National Institutes of Health. http://www.nlm.nih.gov/medlineplus/gunsafety.html

"Hate and Extremism." 2012. Montgomery, AL: Southern Poverty Law Center. http://www.splcenter.org/what-we-do/hate-and-extremism

"Hate Crime—Overview." n.d. Washington, DC: Federal Bureau of Investigation. http://www.fbi.gov/about-us/investigate/civilrights/hate_crimes/overview

Hess, Kären M. and Henry M. Wrobleski. 2006. *Police Operations: Theory and Practice.* 4th edition. Clifton Park, NY: Cengage Learning.

"Intimate Partner Violence: Risk and Protective Factors." 2010 (September 20). Atlanta, GA: Centers for Disease Control and Prevention. http://www.cdc.gov/violenceprevention/intimatepartnerviolence/riskprotectivefactors.html

Johnson, Caitlin. 2000 (March 20). *Hidden Victims: Caring for Children Who Witness Violence.* SparkAction. http://sparkaction.org/node/180

Johnson, Holly. 2006. *Measuring Violence against Women: Statistical Trends 2006*, Ottawa, Ontario: Minister of Industry, Statistics Canada. http://ywcacanada.ca/data/research_docs/00000043.pdf

Kennedy, David M., Anthony A. Braga, and Anne M. Piehl. 2001 (September). "Developing and Implementing Operation Ceasefire." In *Reducing Gun Violence: The Boston Gun Project's Operation Ceasefire*, 5–54. Research report. Washington, DC: National Institute of Justice. (NCJ 188741)

Kitzmann, Katherine M., Noni K. Gaylord, Aimee R. Holt, and Erin D. Kenny. 2003. "Child Witnesses to Domestic Violence: A Meta-Analytic Review." *Journal of Consulting and Clinical Psychology* 71 (2): 339–352.

Klein, Andrew R. 2009 (June 5). *Practical Implications of Current Domestic Violence Research: For Law Enforcement, Prosecutors, and Judges.* Washington, DC: National Institute of Justice. (NCJ 225722)

Langton, Lynn and Michael Planty. 2011 (June). *Hate Crime, 2003–2009.* Special report. Washington, DC: Bureau of Justice Statistics. (NCJ 234058)

Maxwell, Christopher D., Joel H. Garner, and Jeffrey A. Fagan. 2001 (July). "The Effects of Arrest on Intimate Partner Violence: New Evidence from the Spouse Assault Replication Program." *Research in Brief.* Washington, DC: National Institute of Justice. (NCJ 188199)

OSHA Fact Sheet: Workplace Violence. 2002. Fact sheet. Washington, DC: Occupational Safety and Health Administration. http://www.osha.gov/OshDoc/data_General_Facts/factsheet-workplace-violence.pdf

"Police Family Violence Fact Sheet." 2005. Fact sheet. Beverly Hills, CA: National Center for Women and Policing. http://www.womenandpolicing.org/violenceFS.asp

Project ChildSafe. 2004. Washington, DC: Bureau of Justice Assistance. (NCJ 204959)

Promising Strategies to Reduce Gun Violence. 1999 (February). Report. Washington, DC: Office of Juvenile Justice and Delinquency Prevention. http://www.ojjdp.gov/pubs/gun_violence/173950.pdf

Reuland, Melissa, Melissa Schaefer Morabito, Camille Preston, and Jason Cheney. 2006 (March 20). *Police–Community Partnerships to Address Domestic Violence.* Washington, DC: Police Executive Research Forum and the Office of Community Oriented Policing Services.

Rosen, Marie Simonetti. 2006. *Chief Concerns: A Gathering Storm—Violent Crime in America.* Washington, DC: Police Executive Research Forum.

Sampson, Rana. 2011 (August). *Acquaintance Rape of College Students.* Washington, DC: Office of Community Oriented Policing Services, Problem-Specific Guide Series, Guide No. 17.

Stretesky, Paul R., Amie M. Schuck, and Michael J. Hogan. 2004. "Space Matters: An Analysis of Poverty, Poverty Clustering, and Violent Crime." *Justice Quarterly* 21 (4): 817–841.

2010 Census of Fatal Occupational Injuries. 2012. Washington, DC: U.S. Department of Labor, Bureau of Labor Statistics. http://www.bls.gov/iif/oshwc/cfoi/cfch0009.pdf

"Understanding Intimate Partner Violence." 2012. Fact sheet. Atlanta, GA: Centers for Disease Control and Prevention. http://www.cdc.gov/violenceprevention/pdf/ipv_factsheet-a.pdf

Vaughn, Michael G., Qiang Fu, Matt DeLisi, John Paul Wright, Kevin M. Beaver, Brian E. Perron, and Matthew O. Howard. 2010. "Prevalence and Correlates of Fire-Setting in the United States: Results from the National Epidemiologic Survey on Alcohol and Related Conditions." *Comprehensive Psychiatry* 51 (3): 217–223.

"Workplace Violence." 2012. Washington, DC: U.S. Department of Labor, Occupational Safety and Health Administration. http://www.osha.gov/SLTC/workplaceviolence/index.html

Workplace Violence: Issues in Response. 2003. Eugene A. Rugala and Arnold R. Isaacs, editors. Washington, DC: FBI Critical Incident Response Group. (NCJ 204462)

Workplace Violence Initiative. 2004 (January). Washington, DC: Center for Problem-Oriented Policing Web site. http://www.popcenter.org/library/awards/goldstein/2001/01-04.pdf

Understanding and Preventing Terrorism

> The terrorist attacks of September 11, 2001, sounded a clarion call to Americans: Our nation must prepare more vigorously to prevent and, if necessary, to manage the consequences of man-made disasters.
>
> —McDonald and McLaughlin

DO YOU KNOW ...

» What common elements in definitions of terrorism are?

» What motivates most terrorist attacks?

» How the FBI classifies terrorism?

» What methods terrorists may use?

» What federal office was established as a result of 9/11?

» What the two lead agencies in combating terrorism are?

» What the first line of defense against terrorism in the United States is?

» What keys to combating terrorism are?

» What two concerns related to the war on terrorism are?

» What dual challenges in combating violence community policing is facing?

CAN YOU DEFINE ...

asymmetric warfare
contagion effect
deconfliction
interoperability
jihad
terrorism

INTRODUCTION

The September 11, 2001, attack on America galvanized the United States into action: "Tonight we are a country awakened to danger and called to defend freedom. Our grief has turned to anger, and anger to resolution," announced then-President George W. Bush. The horrific events of September 11 pulled together and unified the American people. Patriotism was immediately in vogue. Thousands of volunteers helped search for victims and donated blood and money. The American flag flew everywhere.

451

The events of that tragic day also added a new dimension to American policing. Experience now tells us that the first responders to any future terrorist incidents will most assuredly be local police, fire, and rescue personnel. As a result, law enforcement officials must now strategically rethink public security procedures and practices to maximize the full potential of their resources. This chapter begins with an overview of terrorism, including definitions of and motivations for terrorism. Next is a discussion of the classification of terrorist acts as either domestic or international, followed by a look at terrorists as criminals; the methods used by such criminals to cause fear; and the ways terrorists generate funds for their activities. The federal response to terrorism is next examined, followed by a discussion of the local police response to terrorism. Next is a look at information gathering and intelligence sharing as applied to the war on terrorism, how community policing is addressing the challenge of terrorism, and the crucial role of partnerships in achieving homeland security. The chapter concludes with a discussion of concerns related to the war on terrorism, including civil rights issues and retaliation concerns against Arab Americans or Muslims.

A shell of what was once one of the twin towers of New York's World Trade Center rises above the rubble that remains after both towers were destroyed in a terrorist attack on September 11, 2001. The 110-story towers collapsed after two hijacked airliners carrying scores of passengers slammed into the twin symbols of American capitalism.

©AP Images/Shawn Baldwin

TERRORISM: AN OVERVIEW

Terrorism has occurred throughout history for a variety of reasons: historical, cultural, political, social, psychological, economic, religious, or any combination of these. White (2012, 31) notes: "Terrorism is a method of fighting. It allows a very weak force to attack a stronger power, disrupting the social organization of established authority. Terrorism fluctuates over time, and it transforms with multiple political, social, and psychological circumstances. This means that terrorism is dynamic and ever changing." Terrorism can be perpetrated by an individual, a small group, or a large organization. National governments have at times aided terrorists to further their own foreign policy goals. State-sponsored terrorism is a form of covert warfare, a means to wage war secretly through the use of terrorist surrogates (stand-ins) as hired guns. The U.S. Department of State designates countries as state sponsors of terrorism if they actively assist or aid terrorists, if they harbor past terrorists, or if they refuse to renounce terrorism. Four countries are currently designed as state sponsors of terrorism: Cuba, Iran, Sudan, and Syria (*Country Reports on Terrorism 2011*, 2012).

Definitions of Terrorism

There is no single, universally accepted definition of terrorism. The Federal Bureau of Investigation (FBI) uses the guidelines set forth in the United States Code of Federal Regulations, which defines **terrorism** as "the unlawful use of force and violence against persons or property to intimidate or coerce a government, the civilian population, or any segment thereof, in furtherance of political or social objectives" (28 C.F.R. Section 0.85). Terrorists aim to create fear as a way to bring about political change. All terrorist acts involve violence or the threat of violence committed by nongovernmental groups or individuals.

Terrorism is by nature political because it involves acquiring and using power to force others to submit to terrorist demands. Terrorist attacks generate publicity and focus attention on the organization behind the attack, creating their power. Terrorists usually attempt to justify their violence by arguing that they have been excluded from the accepted process to bring about political or social change. They claim terrorism is their only option. Whether one agrees with this argument often depends on whether one sympathizes with the terrorists' cause or with the victims of the terrorist attack. The label *terrorism* can be highly subjective depending on one's sympathies. However, terrorist acts—including murder, kidnapping, bombing, and arson—have long been defined in both national and international law as crimes. Even in time of war, violence deliberately directed against innocent civilians is considered a crime.

Despite the lack of a single, universally accepted definition of terrorism, most definitions do have common elements.

terrorism
The unlawful use of force or violence against persons or property to intimidate or coerce a government, the civilian population, or any segment thereof, in furtherance of political or social objectives.

Common elements in definitions of terrorism include (1) systematic use of physical violence—actual or threatened, (2) against noncombatants, (3) but with an audience broader than the immediate victims in mind, (4) to create a general climate of fear in a target population, (5) to cause political and/or social change.

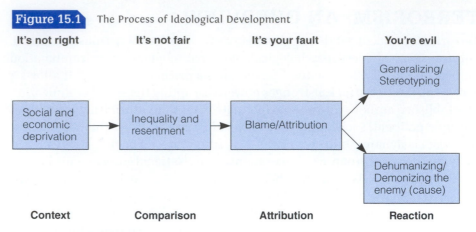

Figure 15.1   The Process of Ideological Development

Source: Randy Borum. "Understanding the Terrorist Mind-Set." *FBI Law Enforcement Bulletin*, July 2003, p. 9. Reprinted by permission.

Motivations for Terrorism

Terrorists act based on varying motivations.

 Most terrorist acts result from dissatisfaction with a religious, political, or social system or policy and frustration resulting from an inability to change it through acceptable, nonviolent means.

Religious motives are seen in Islamic extremism. Political motives include such elements as the Red Army Faction. Social motives are seen in single-issue groups such as antiabortion groups, animal rights groups, and environmentalists.

Extremists begin believing that a specific situation is not right and that it is not fair. They focus blame on another group and then determine that group is evil. This process of ideological development is illustrated in Figure 15.1.

Before looking at specific terrorist groups, consider how their actions might be classified.

CLASSIFICATION OF TERRORIST ACTS

Although there are several ways to classify terrorist acts, the FBI generally distinguishes between two categories of terrorism.

 The FBI categorizes terrorism in the United States as either domestic or international terrorism.

Domestic Terrorism

The FBI has defined domestic terrorism as "the unlawful use, or threatened use, of force or violence by a group or individual based and operating entirely within the United States or its territories without foreign direction committed against persons or property to intimidate or coerce a government, the civilian population, or any segment thereof, in furtherance of political or social objectives" (*Terrorism 2002–2005*, 2005, v).

The bombing of the Alfred P. Murrah Federal Building in Oklahoma City; the pipe bomb explosions in Centennial Olympic Park in Atlanta, Georgia, during the 1996 Summer Olympic Games; the 2009 shooting of a guard at the Holocaust Museum in Washington, DC; the 2009 shooting at Fort Hood in Texas; and the 2010 flight of a small airplane into the IRS building in Austin, Texas—these incidents highlight the threat of domestic terrorists. These terrorists represent extreme right- or left-wing and special-interest beliefs. Many are antigovernment, antitaxation, and antiabortion; and some engage in survivalist training to perpetuate a White, Christian nation.

The number of domestic terrorist attacks is almost double the number of international acts of terrorism.

International Terrorism

International terrorism is foreign based or directed by countries or groups outside the United States against the United States. International terrorism involves violent acts or acts dangerous to human life that violate the criminal laws of the United States or any state, or that would be a criminal violation if committed within the jurisdiction of the United States or any state (*Terrorism 2002–2005*, 2005). These acts are intended to intimidate or coerce a civilian population, influence the policy of a government by intimidation or coercion, or affect the conduct of a government by assassination or kidnapping. International terrorist acts occur outside the United States or transcend national boundaries in terms of the means by which they are accomplished, the persons they appear intended to coerce or intimidate, or the locale in which the perpetrators operate or seek asylum.

The 1990s saw multiple terrorist attacks against U.S. military installations in Saudi Arabia and embassies in East Africa. On February 23, 1998, Osama bin Laden declared **jihad**, a holy war, on the United States, calling on "every Muslim who believes in God and wishes to be rewarded to comply with God's order to kill Americans and plunder their money wherever and whenever they find it" (Savelli, 2004, 3). Bin Laden was placed on the FBI's 10 Most Wanted List in connection with the August 7, 1998, bombings of U.S. embassies in dar Es Salaam, Tanzania and Nairobi, Kenya. Unfortunately, he was not apprehended and grew capable of even more horrific attacks, as Americans learned on that fateful September day in 2001. Since then the U.S. government has been extremely aware of the threat of international terrorism and has shifted its focus from a war on drugs to a war on terrorism. Following a relentless 10-year search for this terrorist leader, U.S. special forces located and killed bin Laden on May 2, 2011, at his million-dollar compound in Abbottabad, Pakistan.

International terrorist groups are likely to engage in what is often referred to as asymmetric warfare. **Asymmetric warfare** refers to combat in which a weaker group attacks a superior group by not attacking the stronger adversary head on but rather attacking areas where the adversary least expects to be hit, causing great psychological shock. Asymmetric warfare gives power to the powerless and destroys the stronger adversary's ability to use its conventional

jihad
Holy war.

asymmetric warfare
Combat in which a weaker group attacks a superior group by not attacking the stronger adversary head on but rather attacking areas where the adversary least expects to be hit, causing great psychological shock and giving power to the powerless by destroying the stronger adversary's ability to use its conventional weapons.

weapons. A prime example is al Qaeda terrorists using box cutters to convert airplanes into weapons of mass destruction, costing billions of dollars of losses to the U.S. economy and tremendous loss of life—all at an estimated cost to the terrorists of $500,000.

According to the FBI's National Counter Terrorism Center (NCTC), more than 10,000 terrorist attacks occurred in 2011, affecting nearly 45,000 victims in 70 countries and causing over 12,500 deaths (*2011 Report on Terrorism*, 2012, 9): "The total number of worldwide attacks in 2011, however, dropped by almost 12 percent from 2010 and nearly 29 percent from 2007. Although the 2011 numbers represent 5-year lows, they also underscore the human toll and geographic reach of terrorism. The Near East and South Asia continued to experience the most attacks, incurring just over 75 percent of the 2011 total. In addition, Africa and the Western Hemisphere experienced 5-year highs in the number of attacks, exhibiting the constant evolution of the terrorist threat." More than half of those killed in 2011 were civilians, and 755 were children.

TERRORISTS AS CRIMINALS

A documented nexus exists between traditional crime and terrorism, involving fraudulent identification, trafficking in illegal merchandise, and drug sales as means to terrorists' ends (Loyka, Faggiani, and Karchmer, 2005). Polisar (2004, 8) observes: "Suddenly agencies and officers who have been trained and equipped to deal with more traditional crimes are now focused on apprehending individuals operating with different motivations, who have different objectives, and who use much deadlier weapons than traditional criminals."

Linett (2005, 59) notes another striking difference between dealing with a terrorist and a street criminal: "The difference is not just one of semantics; it is a matter of life and death. When fighting terrorists, it's kill or be killed, not capture and convict." This blurring of the line between crime and war has drawn law enforcement directly into a new type of battle: "Local law enforcement will be expected to handle complex tactical situations such as chemical, biological, and nuclear events" (Page, 2004, 87).

The Rand Corporation studied how terrorist groups end and found, among other things, that police and intelligence efforts are more effective at eliminating terrorist groups than is the military: "The United States cannot conduct an effective long-term counterterrorism campaign against al Qaida or other terrorist groups without understanding how terrorist groups end," said the study's lead author and a political scientist at the Rand Corporation, a nonprofit research organization. "In most cases, military force isn't the best instrument" ("U.S. Should Rethink 'War on Terrorism,'" 2008). The most common way terrorist groups end (43%) is by a transition in the political process. The second most common way they end (40%) is through police and intelligence services: "Policing is especially effective in dealing with terrorists because police have a permanent presence in cities that enables them to efficiently gather information" ("U.S. Should Rethink," 2008). That is one of the same reasons community policing is so successful. Police must also be familiar with the arsenal of methods terrorists use.

METHODS USED BY TERRORISTS

Terrorists have used a variety of techniques in furtherance of their cause. Figure 15.2 illustrates the methods used in international terrorist attacks during 2011. Note that armed attacks and bombings accounted for the vast majority (nearly 80 percent) of all terrorist attacks in 2011.

Figure 15.3 shows the number of attacks and deaths in 2011 by various weapon types. From these two figures it is seen that suicide attacks comprised only 2.7 percent of terrorist attacks in 2011 but were responsible for 21 percent of all terrorism-related fatalities, a fact that underscores their lethality (*2011 Report on Terrorism*, 2012).

Terrorists may use arson; explosives and bombs; weapons of mass destruction (biological, chemical, or nuclear agents); and technology.

Some terrorism experts suggest that incendiary devices and explosives are most likely to be used because they are easy to make.

Explosives and Bombs

From 1978 to 1996, Theodore Kaczynski, the notorious Unabomber, terrorized the country, apparently in a protest against technology, with a string of 16 mail bombings that killed three people. Ramzi Ahmed Yousef, found guilty of masterminding the first World Trade Center bombing in 1993, declared that he was proud to be a terrorist and that terrorism was the only viable response to what he saw as a Jewish lobby in Washington. The car bomb used to shatter the Murrah Federal Building in 1995 was Timothy McVeigh's way of protesting

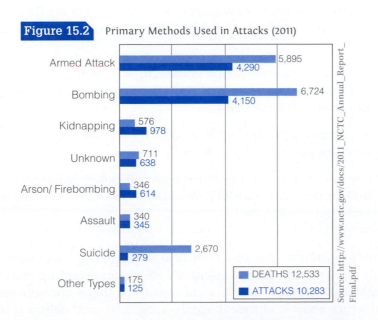

Figure 15.2 Primary Methods Used in Attacks (2011)

Method	Deaths	Attacks
Armed Attack	5,895	4,290
Bombing	6,724	4,150
Kidnapping	576	978
Unknown	711	638
Arson/ Firebombing	346	614
Assault	340	345
Suicide	2,670	279
Other Types	175	125

DEATHS 12,533
ATTACKS 10,283

Source: http://www.nctc.gov/docs/2011_NCTC_Annual_Report_Final.pdf

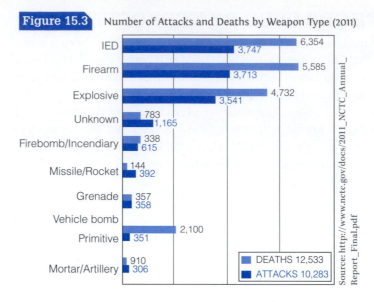

Figure 15.3 Number of Attacks and Deaths by Weapon Type (2011)

Source: http://www.nctc.gov/docs/2011_NCTC_Annual_Report_Final.pdf

- IED: 6,354 / 3,747
- Firearm: 5,585 / 3,713
- Explosive: 4,732 / 3,541
- Unknown: 783 / 1,165
- Firebomb/Incendiary: 338 / 615
- Missile/Rocket: 144 / 392
- Grenade: 357 / 358
- Vehicle bomb / Primitive: 2,100 / 351
- Mortar/Artillery: 910 / 306

DEATHS 12,533
ATTACKS 10,283

the government and their raid on the Branch Davidians at Waco, Texas. In 2002 Lucas Helder terrorized the Midwest by placing 18 pipe bombs accompanied by antigovernment letters in mailboxes throughout five states. Six exploded, injuring four letter carriers and two residents. The most horrific act of terrorism against the United States occurred on September 11, 2001, when two airplanes were used as missiles to explode the World Trade Center and another plane was used to attack the Pentagon. A fourth plane crashed in a Pennsylvania field before it could reach its destination.

Weapons of Mass Destruction

Weapons of mass destruction (WMD) are defined under U.S. law (18 USC §2332) as:

» Any destructive device as defined in section 921 of this title (i.e., explosive device)

» Any weapon that is designed or intended to cause death or serious bodily injury through the release, dissemination, or impact of toxic or poisonous chemicals, or their precursors

» Any weapon involving a biological agent, toxin, or vector (as those terms are defined in section 178 of this title)

» Any weapon that is designed to release radiation or radioactivity at a level dangerous to human life ("Weapons of Mass Destruction: Frequently Asked Questions," n.d.)

Chemical Agents The Aum Shinrikyo attack in the Tokyo subway in 1995 initially focused the security industry's efforts on detecting and mitigating chemical agent threats. That incident confirmed that a nonstate entity could manufacture a viable chemical agent—sarin gas—and deliver it in a public location. Unfortunately, anyone with Internet access and a Web browser can obtain the chemical formula for sarin in less than 40 minutes and can produce it inexpensively. The four common types of chemical weapons are nerve agents, blood/choking agents, blistering agents, and radiological agents (White, 2012). One agent, ricin toxin, is both a biological and a chemical weapon.

Biological Agents Bioterrorism involves such biological weapons of mass destruction (WMD) as anthrax, botulism, and smallpox, and the potential for bioterrorism in the United States has been identified as an increasingly unfortunate threat in the aftermath of the September 11 attacks and the anthrax scares (Hanson, 2005). Especially susceptible to bioterrorism are the nation's food and water supplies.

Nuclear Terrorism Although many people consider a nuclear weapon in the hands of a terrorist to be the most frightening scenario possible, it is a very difficult feat to accomplish: "It is much easier for terrorists to use conventional weapons than it is to build a nuclear weapon. Nuclear weapons are also difficult to obtain and detonate" (White, 2012, 143). Many scholars consider the probability of nuclear terrorism to be low based on the crime causation model where the victim, motivated offender, and opportunity to commit a crime intersect: "Al Qaeda—the only group that has made an effort to obtain a nuclear device—has the desire to make any one of their enemies victims, but it has consistently lacked the opportunity to strike. Further, there is no evidence to suggest that al Qaeda has the ability to obtain a nuclear weapon or to construct one" (White, 2012, 144).

WMD Team Local law enforcement agencies select and train officers to form a WMD team. The officers' time is not devoted solely to the unit, but they are ready if a need for their skills arises.

Technological Terrorism

Technological terrorism includes attacks *on* technology as well as *by* technology. The United States relies on energy to drive the nation's technology. An attack on the U.S. energy supply could be devastating. Likewise, an attack on the computer systems and networks critical to the functioning of businesses, health care facilities, educational institutions, the military, and all governmental agencies would be catastrophic. Cyberterrorism, a type of technological terrorism, has been defined as "the intimidation of civilian enterprise through the use of high technology to bring about political, religious, or ideological aims, actions that result in disabling or deleting critical infrastructure data or information" (Tafoya, 2011, 2).

Damage to critical computer systems could put the nation's safety and security in jeopardy. Each of the preceding types of terrorism poses a threat to national security.

FUNDING TERRORISM

Money is needed to carry out terrorism, not only for weapons but for general operating expenses. Many terrorist operations are financed by charitable groups and wealthy people sympathetic to the group's cause. Terrorist groups commonly collaborate with organized criminal groups to deal drugs, arms, and, in some instances, humans.

Fraud has become increasingly common among terrorists, not only as a way to generate revenue but also as a way to gain access to their targets. Fraudulently obtained drivers' licenses, passports, and other identification documents are often found among terrorists' belongings (Savelli, 2004). Common criminal methods of funding terrorist operations include kidnapping, extortion, robbery, fraud, larceny, smuggling, forgery, and counterfeiting: "Interpol estimates that counterfeiting and intellectual property theft is responsible for $200 billion in illegal profits in the United States alone" (White, 2012, 86).

THE FEDERAL RESPONSE TO TERRORISM: HOMELAND SECURITY

In 1996 the FBI established a Counterterrorism Center to combat terrorism. That same year, the Antiterrorism and Effective Death Penalty Act was passed, including several specific measures aimed at terrorism. This Act enhanced the federal government's power to deny visas to individuals belonging to terrorist groups and simplified the process for deporting aliens convicted of crimes.

In 1999 FBI Director Louis Freeh announced, "Our Number-One priority is the prevention of terrorism." To that end, the FBI added a new Counterterrorism Division with four subunits: the International Terrorism Section, the Domestic Terrorism Section, the National Infrastructure Protection Center, and the National Domestic Preparedness Office. These efforts, unfortunately, were not enough to avert the tragic events of September 11. It took a disaster of that magnitude to make the war on terrorism truly the first priority of the United States.

The National Counterterrorism Center (NCTC), created by Presidential Executive Order in 2004, is part of the Office of the Director of National Intelligence. NCTC serves as the primary organization in the U.S. government for integrating and analyzing all intelligence pertaining to terrorism possessed or acquired by the government (except purely domestic terrorism); serves as the central and shared knowledge bank on terrorism information; provides all-source intelligence support to government-wide counterterrorism activities; and establishes the information technology (IT) systems and architectures within the NCTC and between the NCTC and other agencies that enable access to, as well as integration, dissemination, and use of, terrorism information. NCTC's mission statement succinctly summarizes its key responsibilities and value-added contributions: *Lead our nation's effort to combat terrorism at home and abroad by analyzing the threat, sharing that information with our partners, and integrating all instruments of national power to ensure unity of effort* ("About Us," n.d.).

NCTC issues an annual *Report on Terrorism* to fulfill its mandate to collect statistics on the annual number of incidents of "terrorism," although its ability to track the specific groups responsible for each incident involving killings, kidnappings, and injuries is significantly limited by the availability of reliable open-source information, particularly for events involving small numbers of casualties or occurring in remote regions of the world. Moreover, specific details about victims, damage, perpetrators, and other incident elements are frequently not fully reported in open-source information. In deriving its figures for incidents of terrorism, the NCTC in 2005 adopted the definition of *terrorism* that appears in 22 USC §2656f(d)(2): "premeditated, politically motivated violence perpetrated against noncombatant targets by subnational groups or clandestine agents."

According to Gary LaFree (2009), Director of the National Consortium for the Study of Terrorism and Responses to Terrorism (START), University of Maryland:

> Compared to most types of criminal violence, terrorism poses special conceptual and methodological challenges. To begin with, the term "terrorism" yields varying definitions, often loaded with political and emotional implications. As PLO Chairman Arafat famously noted in a 1974 speech before the United Nations, "One man's terrorist is another man's freedom fighter." Defining terrorism is no less complex for researchers. Researchers have identified dozens of different definitions of terrorism, and it is not unusual for academic conferences to dedicate hours of discussion to exploring and defending competing definitions.

The FBI's *Strategic Plan 2004–2009* declares: "The events of September 11th have forever changed our nation and the FBI. Since that terrible day, the FBI's overriding priority has been protecting America by preventing further attacks." In their list of priorities, that is number one. Priority nine is to support federal, state, local, and international partners: "To achieve its mission, the FBI must strengthen three inextricably linked core functions: intelligence, investigations, and partnerships. … Partnerships are essential if the FBI is to effectively address evolving threats that are too complex or multijurisdictional for one agency to handle alone. To achieve its vital mission, the FBI is dependent upon the good-will, cooperation, and expertise of our local, state, federal and international partners" (*Federal Bureau of Investigation Strategic Plan 2004–2009*, 2004, 19). No new strategic plan has been made available.

One of the first federal initiatives after September 11 was the establishment of the Department of Homeland Security.

The Department of Homeland Security

The Department of Homeland Security (DHS) was established by Executive Order on October 8, 2001, in direct response to the September 11 attacks on the United States. Created through the integration of 22 different federal departments and agencies, either in whole or in part, the DHS is primarily responsible for protecting the country from terrorist attacks and responding to natural disasters. Agencies included under the umbrella of DHS include the U.S. Customs and Border Protection (CBP), U.S. Citizenship and Immigration Services (CIS), U.S. Immigration and Customs Enforcement (ICE), Domestic Nuclear Detection Office, Transportation Security Administration (TSA), Federal Law Enforcement Training Center (FLETC), Federal Emergency Management Agency (FEMA), U.S. Coast Guard (USCG), and U.S. Secret Service ("Department Subcomponents and Agencies," 2009). With 240,000 employees, DHS is the third largest U.S. federal government department.

 As a result of September 11, 2001, the Department of Homeland Security was established, reorganizing the departments of the federal government.

The mission of the DHS is stated in the department's Strategic Plan for 2008–2013 (*One Team, One Mission, Securing Our Homeland*, 2008, 3): "We will lead the unified national effort to secure America. We will prevent and deter terrorist attacks and protect against and respond to threats and hazards to the nation. We will secure our national borders while welcoming lawful immigrants, visitors, and trade." All U.S. attorneys have been directed to establish antiterrorism task forces to serve as conduits for information about suspected terrorists between federal and local agencies.

 At the federal level, the FBI is the lead agency for responding to acts of domestic terrorism. The Federal Emergency Management Agency (FEMA) is the lead agency for consequence management (after an attack).

The DHS serves in a broad capacity, facilitating collaboration between local and federal law enforcement to develop a national strategy to detect, prepare for, prevent, protect against, respond to, and recover from terrorist attacks within the United States. The DHS had previously established a five-level color-coded threat system which it used to communicate with public safety officials and the public at large. However, in April 2011, DHS Secretary Janet Napolitano announced that the five-tiered color-coded security advisory system would be replaced by a two-level National Terrorism Advisory System:

» Elevated Threat—warns of a credible terrorist threat against the United States

» Imminent Threat—warns of a credible, specific, and impending terrorist threat against the United States

Another effort to enhance national security was passage of the USA PATRIOT Act.

The USA PATRIOT Act

On October 26, 2001, President George W. Bush signed into law the Uniting and Strengthening America by Providing Appropriate Tools Required to Intercept and Obstruct Terrorism (USA PATRIOT) Act, giving police unprecedented ability to search, seize, detain, or eavesdrop in their pursuit of possible terrorists. The law expands the FBI's wiretapping and electronic surveillance authority and allows nationwide jurisdiction for search warrants and electronic surveillance devices, including legal expansion of those devices to email and the Internet. The USA PATRIOT Act significantly improves the nation's counterterrorism efforts by:

» Allowing investigators to use the tools already available to investigate organized crime and drug trafficking.

» Facilitating information sharing and cooperation among government agencies so they can better "connect the dots."

» Updating the law to reflect new technologies and new threats.

» Increasing the penalties for those who commit or support terrorist crimes.

Further, the USA PATRIOT Act makes it a federal crime to commit an act of terrorism against a mass transit system.

Increased Border Security

Enhancing security at our nation's borders is a fundamental step in keeping our citizenry safe. The DHS's United States Visitor and Immigrant Status Indicator Technology Program (US-VISIT) is an integrated, automated, biometric entry–exit system that records the arrival and departure of certain aliens (an *alien* is defined as any person not a citizen or national of the United States); conducts certain immigrations violation, criminal, and terrorist checks on aliens; and compares biometric identifiers (digital fingerprints and a photograph) to those collected on previous encounters to verify identity. The procedure applies to all non–U.S. citizens except Canadians applying for admission to the United States for business or pleasure ("Fact Sheet: Expansion of US-VISIT Procedures," 2009). The program was implemented in January 2004 at 115 airports and 14 seaports and has been expanded to all land points of entry as well.

The National Incident Management System

The National Incident Management System (NIMS) was implemented in 2004 and revised in 2008. It provides a systematic, proactive approach to guide departments and agencies at all levels of government, nongovernmental organizations, and the private sector to work seamlessly to prevent, protect against, respond to, recover from, and mitigate the effects of incidents, regardless of cause, size, location, or complexity, in order to reduce the loss of life and property and harm to the environment (*National Incident Management System*, 2008).

Although the federal government has increased its efforts in the area of terrorism prevention and response, a large degree of responsibility for responding to threats of terrorism rests at the local level.

THE LOCAL POLICE RESPONSE TO TERRORISM: HOMETOWN SECURITY

On October 16, 2001, a little more than a month after the devastating attacks on America, Bruce Glasscock (2001), then president of the International Association of Chiefs of Police (IACP), sent a letter to police departments throughout the country, in which he wrote: "The war against terrorism isn't limited to actions overseas, or even restricted to military actions. The fight against terrorism begins in our own backyards—our own communities, our own neighborhoods—and police chiefs need to prepare themselves, their officers, and their communities—the people they've sworn to protect—against terrorism."

State and local law enforcement agencies can and must play a vital role in the investigation and prevention of future terrorist attacks. Across the United States, there are nearly 17,985 state and local law enforcement agencies (U.S. Census Bureau, 2012). These agencies, and the 765,237 officers they employ, daily patrol our state highways and the streets of our cities and towns and, as a result, have an intimate knowledge of the communities they serve and have developed close relationships with the citizens they protect.

The IACP project *Taking Command* report, *From Hometown Security to Homeland Security* (2005, 2), suggests that our nation's current homeland security strategy "is handicapped by a fundamental flaw. It does not sufficiently incorporate the advice, expertise, or consent of public safety organizations at state, tribal, or local levels." The IACP has identified five key principles that should form the basis for a national homeland security strategy (*From Hometown Security to Homeland Security*, 2005, 3–7):

1. All terrorism is local.

2. Prevention is paramount.

3. Hometown security is homeland security.

4. Homeland security strategies must be coordinated nationally, not federally.

5. Bottom-up engineering; the diversity of the state, tribal, and local public safety community; and noncompetitive collaboration are vital.

A study conducted by Rowan University found that one of the most significant changes in policing since September 11 may be how the nation's lowest-ranking officers approach their daily patrols. The study found that street officers, who see themselves as first responders, also recognize that they would be the ones most likely to be on the front lines of a terrorist attack. Therefore, they pay attention to things they did not used to pay attention to ("9/11 Changed Culture, Attitude of Street Cops," 2006).

The first line of defense against terrorism is the patrol officer in the field.

Law enforcement officers must be aware of the possibility for contact with terrorists at any time during their normal course of duty: "Keep in mind how many of the 9-11-01 hijackers had contact with law enforcement officers in various parts of the country and how many unsuspecting law enforcement officers, in any capacity, may have such contact with terrorists today or in the future" (Savelli, 2004, 65–66). Consider these examples:

» September 9, 2001—Ziad Jarrah, hijacker of the plane that crashed in Shanksville, Pennsylvania, was stopped by police in Maryland for speeding. He was driving 90 mph in a 65-mph zone. He was issued a ticket and released.

» August 2001—Hani Hanjour, who hijacked and piloted the plane that crashed into the Pentagon, killing 289 persons, was stopped by police in Arlington, Virginia. He was issued a ticket for speeding and released. He paid the ticket so he would not have to show up in court.

» April 2001—Mohammed Atta, who hijacked and piloted the plane that crashed into the north tower of the World Trade Center, was stopped in Tamarac, Florida, for driving without a valid license and issued a ticket. He did not pay the ticket, so an arrest warrant was issued. A few weeks later he was stopped for speeding but let go because police did not know about the warrant.

This final incident underscores the critical importance not only of gathering information but also of sharing intelligence and data with the larger law enforcement community.

INFORMATION GATHERING AND INTELLIGENCE SHARING

According to Berkow (2004, 25):

> American policing is well into the post–September 11 era of new duties. Before the attacks, the world of counterterrorism, site security, and intelligence gathering were generally restricted to either the largest of police agencies or those departments that were responsible for specific identified threats. Most police agencies in the United States were neither trained to carry out these tasks nor focused on them. Since the attacks, every agency in the United States regardless of size or location has accepted these new homeland security missions to some degree. Every agency has now added a counterterrorism mindset to their regular mission and is focused on building and enhancing that capability.

It is not sufficient to simply gather data. Data must be analyzed and shared systematically with neighboring law enforcement agencies and also different levels of law enforcement (i.e., local, state, and federal) and other institutions, such as schools, hospitals, city departments, and motor vehicle divisions.

A distinction is made between *information* and *intelligence,* with intelligence broadening to become organized information: "Intelligence has come to mean information that has not only been selected and collected, but also analyzed, evaluated, and distributed to meet the unique policymaking needs of one particular enterprise" (Loyka, Faggiani, and Karchmer, 2005, 7).

The application of such information in efforts to combat terrorism can be visualized as an intelligence cycle (Figure 15.4). In a threat-driven environment,

Figure 15.4 The Intelligence Cycle

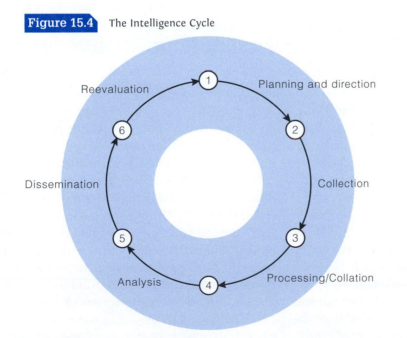

Source: Stephan A. Loyka, Donald A. Faggiani, and Clifford Karchmer. *Protecting Your Community from Terrorism: Strategies for Local Law Enforcement. Volume 4: The Production and Sharing of Intelligence.* Washington, DC: Community Oriented Policing Services and the Police Executive Research Forum, February 2005. Reprinted by permission of the Police Executive Research Forum.

intelligence requirements—identified information needs, or what must be known to safeguard the nation—are what drive investigations (Loyka, Faggiani, and Karchmer, 2005, 35). Intelligence requirements are established by the Director of Central Intelligence under the guidance of the president and the National and Homeland Security Advisors. The attorney general and the director of the FBI also participate in the formulation of national intelligence requirements.

The second step in the intelligence cycle is *planning and direction,* a function of the FBI. Third is the *collection of raw information* from local, state, and federal investigations. Fourth is *processing and exploitation* of the raw information—that is, converting the collected information to a form usable for analysis. Fifth is *analysis and production,* converting the raw information into intelligence. The final step is *dissemination,* which leads back to refinement of intelligence requirements.

Loyka, Faggiani, and Karchmer (2005, 36) explain: "The Intelligence Cycle is just that, a continuing cycle, which overlaps and drives each of its functions and in turn, drives the investigative mission. This cycle or process is used across all programs—Counterterrorism, Counterintelligence, Cyber, and Criminal—to counter all threats."

Local and state law enforcement agencies are critical to the third step in the intelligence cycle and benefit from the sixth step as well. Many of the day-to-day duties of local law enforcement officers bring them into proximity with sources of information about terrorism. Patrol operations, especially traffic officers, properly trained in what to look for and what questions to ask when

TECHNOLOGY IN COMMUNITY POLICING: THE DOMAIN AWARENESS SYSTEM

The New York City Police Department (NYPD) has partnered with Microsoft Corporation to develop the Domain Awareness System (DAS), a sophisticated crime-prevention and counterterrorism tool that aggregates and analyzes, in real time, information collected from the city's more than 3,000 closed-circuit surveillance cameras, license-plate readers, 911 calls, sensors, and other law enforcement databases. The system also archives information, allowing investigators and analysts to go back in time and track the movement of a suspect or vehicle before a particular event occurred. This technology provides law enforcement officers and investigators, public safety administrators, and intelligence analysts with a comprehensive view of criminal activity and potential threats. For example, DAS can notify analysts of suspicious packages

or vehicles, and data collected can allow NYPD investigators to actively search for suspects by mapping their criminal history geospacially and chronologically, thus revealing patterns to their behavior. Police Commissioner Raymond Kelly notes: "The system is a transformative tool because it was created by police officers for police officers." And although the system is expected to cost the city $30–40 million, it also has the potential to generate revenue—because DAS was built by NYPD in partnership with Microsoft, sale of the technology to other jurisdictions will bring in revenue to help New York fund more crime prevention and counterterrorism efforts.

Source: "New York City Police Department and Microsoft Partner to Bring Real-Time Crime Prevention and Counterterrorism Technology Solution to Global Law Enforcement Agencies." Microsoft News Center, August 8, 2012. http://www.microsoft.com/en-us/news/Press/2012/Aug12/08-08NYPDPR.aspx

interacting with citizens, can be a tremendous source of intelligence, not only for local investigators but also for their state and federal homeland security counterparts.

The Regional Information Sharing Systems (RISS)

The Regional Information Sharing Systems (RISS) program supports federal, state, and local law enforcement efforts to combat criminal activity, including terrorism. Six regional RISS intelligence centers provide investigative support services to law enforcement agencies across the nation. The RISS Program is the only multijurisdictional criminal intelligence system operated by and for state and local law enforcement agencies. The overall goal of the RISS Program is to enhance the ability of state and local criminal justice agencies to identify, target, and remove criminal conspiracies and activities spanning jurisdictional boundaries ("Regional Information Sharing Systems Program Fact Sheet," n.d.).

The National Criminal Intelligence Sharing Plan (NCISP)

Limitations on information sharing have caused tensions in the past because often information received by the FBI is classified. Rules of federal procedure and constraints associated with grand jury classified material also limit how much information can be shared.

A subtitle of the Homeland Security Act of 2002, called the Homeland Security Information Sharing Act, required the president to develop new procedures for sharing classified information, as well as unclassified but otherwise sensitive information, with state and local police. This charge was fulfilled in May 2002 when the IACP, the Department of Justice, the FBI, the DHS, and other representatives of the federal, state, tribal, and local law enforcement communities endorsed *The National Criminal Intelligence Sharing Plan* (NCISP). Originally published in 2003, this report was the first version of a plan intended to be a "living document" and periodically updated. The most recent update available was in 2005. Those charged with developing and implementing the plan will continue to solicit the involvement of the law enforcement and intelligence communities, national organizations and other government and public safety entities, in order to ensure that the plan is responsive to their needs for information and intelligence development and sharing.

Although progress has been made, obstacles persist to hamper the fluid exchange of intelligence.

Addressing Obstacles to Intelligence Sharing

Two barriers to effective exchange of intelligence are lack of deconfliction protocols and interoperability issues. Polisar (2004, 8) asserts: "For far too long efforts to combat crime and terrorism have been handicapped by jurisdictional squabbles and archaic rules that prevented us from forging cooperative work-ing relationships with our counterparts in local, regional, tribal, and federal law enforcement. This must end." The mass shooting at Fort Hood provided a more recent example of what can occur when information sharing is insufficient. On March 10, 2011, Senator Joseph Lieberman, who was chairing a Congressional Hearing of the Senate Homeland Security and Governmental Affairs Committee, stated: "This Committee's recent report on the Fort Hood attack shows that information sharing within and across agencies is nonetheless still not all it should be. And that allowed in that a case a ticking time bomb, namely Major Nidal Hasan, now accused of killing 13 and wounding 32 others at Fort Hood, to radicalize right under the noses of the Department of Defense and the FBI. So we need to continue improving our information sharing strategies" ("Senate Homeland Security and Governmental Affairs Committee," 2011).

A local networking module developed between local, state, and federal law enforcement agencies is the most effective way to discuss and share investigative and enforcement endeavors to combat terrorism. This networking module approach avoids compromising existing investigations or conducting conflicting cases and should have a built-in **deconfliction** protocol, which essentially means guidelines to avoid conflict. Deconfliction can be applied to declassified and confidential investigations (Savelli, 2004, 43).

The 9/11 attacks, besides bringing attention to defective or ineffective routes of interagency communication, highlighted the importance of communications. **Interoperability** is the compatibility of communication systems such as emergency medical services (EMS), fire and rescue, and police, and across levels of government. The 9/11 Commission cited the inability to communicate as a critical failure on September 11 and stated that compatible and adequate communications among public safety organizations at the local, state, and federal levels remains a problem. The commission's recommendations were finally adopted in August 2007, almost 6 years after the attacks of September 11 ("The 9-11 Commission Bill and 9-11 Commission Recommendations," n.d.).

deconfliction
Protocol or guidelines to avoid conflict.

interoperability
The compatibility of communication systems such as EMS, fire and rescue, and police, and across levels of government.

The keys to combating terrorism lie with the local police and the intelligence they can provide to federal authorities; how readily information is shared between agencies at different levels; and the interoperability of communications systems should an attack occur.

Hindsight reveals that many clues existed prior to the attack on September 11, but they were fragmented and never put together; thus, like a jigsaw puzzle with pieces scattered, the true scope of the picture went unrealized until it was too late. Seemingly insignificant information may be the one missing piece to put together an impending terrorist attack. Federal efforts rely on information from state and local officers. Local officers, in turn, will rely on citizen information and the networks formed through community policing.

LAPD MODEL FOR CRIME REDUCTION AND COUNTERTERRORISM

CompStat, Operation Archangel, and the Critical Incident Management Bureau (CIMB)

In Los Angeles, Police Chief William Bratton, former New York City police commissioner and one of the driving forces behind the implementation of CompStat at the New York Police Department (NYPD), is in the process of installing CompStat at the Los Angeles Police Department (LAPD) to fully integrate criminal and terrorism-related intelligence collection and sharing. According to the LAPD Plan of Action released in October 2004: "Improved crime-fighting and counterterrorism tools are the LAPD's top priority for technology, along with data integration, and CompStat software is the vehicle to deliver such tools. For the first time in the nation, new CompStat technology will allow a multijurisdictional CompStat approach to integrate crime information and counterterrorism-related information collected, analyzed, and used by the LAPD to reduce crime in the region and to prevent terrorism incidents" (Bratton, 2006, 2).

The LAPD is not only using CompStat to accomplish its crime-reduction and counterterrorism mission—an all-hazards approach that maximizes the effectiveness of scarce resources—but will also include a "new automated community policing problem-solving component as a strategic crime management tool." This will give officers in the field timely access to crime data and automate the inputting of crime locations, helping beat officers develop their own successful crime-reduction strategies.

To improve its ability to identify and protect critical infrastructure, the LAPD has also launched Operation Archangel, a partnership between the City and County of Los Angeles, the California Department of Homeland Security, and the U.S. Department of Homeland Security. Archangel is a proactive program used by the police to identify critical infrastructure locations in Los Angeles and develop a multiagency response. Archangel is geared toward facilitating the management of information and resources for the prevention, deterrence, response, and mitigation of major critical incidents. Again, at the heart of Archangel is a database-management tool that will "provide an automated system to assess threats and vulnerabilities to infrastructure, as well as the defenses available. The system will point out everything a responder would need to know before approaching a building, utility, or reservoir in an emergency."

The LAPD works closely in consultation with the owners and operators of critical infrastructure sites, who are asked to contribute detailed and up-to-date infrastructure information to Archangel, including floor plans, HVAC systems, entrances and exits, security centers, and fire-control stations. Archangel has been held up as a "proving ground for best practices as developed by the LAPD in conjunction with the Department of Homeland Security."

The LAPD has also taken the important step of institutionalizing its counterterrorism efforts through the creation of the Critical Incident Management Bureau (CIMB), which identifies critical infrastructure, coordinates security with private-sector partners, and coordinates applications for homeland security grants to fund training, technology, and intelligence-gathering programs at the LAPD. The CIMB has established a forward, proactive counterterrorism posture for the LAPD and uses its officers to network throughout the public and private sectors in Los Angeles to collect intelligence and preemptively disrupt potential terrorist attacks.

Finally, the CIMB has not been hesitant to share its knowledge and expertise with private-sector partners. The CIMB has developed and disseminated al Qaeda countersurveillance training not only for selected LAPD personnel but private security officers at critical infrastructure sites. This training allows police and private security officers to identify terrorists as they conduct surveillance under the Safe Cities Project on prospective targets. This training has been carefully based on actual training that al Qaeda target teams received in the training camps in Afghanistan. This not only improves the effectiveness of private security officers but also improves their ability to pass credible intelligence to LAPD officers.

The LAPD, under the leadership of Chief Bratton, is dedicated to building a world-class counterterrorism capability by building on the proven crime-fighting success of problem-solving policing, CompStat information technology, and the relentless focus of the department on updating its knowledge of terrorist methods and planning. Problem-solving policing is the backbone that allows the LAPD and the CIMB to aggressively identify and prosecute potential terrorism precursor crimes and maximize the department's ability to disrupt and interdict terrorists without compromising its traditional crime-fighting mission.

Source: Reprinted by permission of the Manhattan Institute.

COMMUNITY POLICING AND THE WAR ON TERRORISM

The September 11 attacks undoubtedly shifted the priorities of policing. Law enforcement agencies must not, however, let the "war on terrorism" tempt them into abandoning or diminishing community policing efforts in favor of a return to the traditional model of policing with its paramilitary emphasis: "To do so would not only be counterproductive but would also arrest the progress policing has made over recent decades which has taken it to the high level of societal acceptance it now enjoys" (Murray, 2005, 347). In noting how the community policing philosophy can dovetail with homeland security efforts, Docobo (2005) asserts:

> Both neighborhood crime and terrorism threaten the quality of life in a community and exploit the fear they create. Despite creative ways to stretch public safety budgets, local law enforcement cannot sustain two separate missions of traditional policing and terrorism prevention. Community policing and homeland security can share the same goals and strategies. Creating external partnerships, citizen involvement, problem solving, and transforming the organization to take on a new mission are all key elements of community policing and should be part of a comprehensive homeland security strategy. The lesson learned from fighting traditional crime is that prevention is the most effective approach in dealing with crime, fear, and social disorder. Fighting terrorism is no different.

A quote from former CIA director James Woolsey during his testimony before Congress in 2004 provides but one example of the invaluable role local police play in counterterrorism efforts: "Only an effective local police establishment that has the confidence of citizens is going to be likely to hear from, say, a local merchant in a part of town containing a number of new immigrants that a group of young men from abroad have recently moved into a nearby apartment and are acting suspiciously. Local police are best equipped to understand how to protect citizens' liberties and obtain such leads legally" (Newman and Clarke, 2008, 80).

The successful detection and prevention of terrorism depends on information, and a community–police relationship based on mutual trust is most likely to uncover matters helpful in identifying prospective terrorists. Chapman (2008) describes the importance of community partnerships:

> Partnerships with the community are integral to any crime-prevention effort and, in many respects, terrorism can be understood and addressed in terms of other crime threats. Just as state and local law enforcement entities serve as partners with their federal counterparts and are now a critical component of our nation's security capability as both "first preventers" and "first responders," so, too, do law enforcement partnerships with the community hold tremendous potential for thwarting acts of terrorism. Partnerships help to create trust and improve lines of communication between the police and the community....

> Just as street-level knowledge is important to breaking up narcotics activities in a neighborhood, community partnerships and trusting relationships will inspire the confidence of citizens to pass along information that can help to uncover terrorist individuals or cells. Both here and abroad, those who have

firsthand experience preventing terrorism incidents enthusiastically promote the importance of community partnerships to defeat terrorism. "It is not the police and the intelligence services who will defeat terrorism," according to Sir Ian Blair, the commissioner of the London Metropolitan Police Service. "It is communities who defeat terrorism" (Blair, 2006, 1). . . .

Examples of the value of strong community partnerships have been widely reported. In London, England, a strong, strange odor drifting from a flat and the strange group of visitors to the premises caused a London grandmother to report this activity to authorities, which helped to unravel a terror cell planning a poison gas attack. And in New York City, a resident who worked at an Islamic bookstore located next to one of the city's largest mosques so concerned local residents with his inflammatory anti-American rhetoric that the New York City Police Department tip line received a number of calls about his behavior. A subsequent investigation revealed plans to attack the Herald Square subway station around the time of the 2004 Republican National Convention.

Risk Assessment and Identifying Potential Terrorist Targets

Potential terrorist targets might be a transit system hub, a chemical storage warehouse, or high-level government officials' residences. Although jurisdictions necessarily focus efforts on protecting logical, high-profile targets for terrorist attacks, soft targets should not be overlooked. Soft targets, those that are relatively unguarded or difficult to guard, include shopping malls, subways, trains, sporting stadiums, theaters, schools, hospitals, restaurants, entertainment parks, compressed gas and oil storage areas, chemical plants, pharmaceutical companies, and many others (Hanson, 2005).

ON THE BEAT

I recall where I was on September 11, 2001: at college in an auditorium for a criminal justice course. The news came, and the auditorium fell silent as everyone watched the news on the large white screen. I remember the bewildered and frightened looks on people's faces. I don't think anyone who was alive on that date will ever forget it. I recall feeling like I needed to serve my country more than ever and felt even more convinced about my decision to become a police officer.

Terrorism can happen anywhere, and as a patrol officer I have to be ready. Being on the "front lines," so to speak, I can see things in the community that federal authorities may not be able to see. Gathering information in the field is crucial to the effort of protecting our homeland. Sharing this information is equally important, if not more so.

In this day and age, when terrorist attacks are happening around the world, it is more crucial than ever that agencies share information and communicate with one another.

—*Kim Czapar*

Being Proactive

As with gangs, domestic violence, and other areas of concern to community policing, a proactive approach to terrorism is advocated: "Securing the homeland begins at the local level and 'first responders' must see themselves in a more proactive role as 'first preventers'" (Doherty and Hibbard, 2006, 78). However, a poll conducted by the IACP revealed that 71 percent of the 4,500 agencies that responded to the survey reported being "not at all prepared" or "somewhat unprepared" to prevent terrorism. A mere 1 percent claimed that they were "adequately prepared" (Garrett, 2004, 6).

This lack of preparedness apparently extends to citizens in communities across the country. A *New York Times* poll shows that, whereas Americans are closely divided on their views of how prepared the United States is for another terrorist attack, the overwhelming majority of citizens have done nothing personally to prepare for such an attack (Sims, 2004). In addition, many Americans say they would probably ignore official instructions for how to respond to a terrorist attack. Clearly, community policing officers can do much to educate citizens in their jurisdiction on preparedness plans, including a meeting place in case of a terrorist attack.

Success in terrorism prevention might be enhanced by cultivating numerous community information sources such as these (Doherty and Hibbard, 2006, 79–80):

» Neighborhood Watch—supported by local law enforcement, easily contacted, and provides advisories of crime trends; source of information about suspicious activities

» Hotels (clerks, security officers, housekeepers, food service workers, and entertainment staff members)—source of information about suspicious guests

» Real estate agents—source of information about suspicious activities at properties and about location of wanted persons and undocumented residents

» Storage facilities—source of information about explosive or hazardous materials or other items in storage that could be connected to terrorist or criminal activity

» Religious groups—source of information about controversial religious speakers or visitors

» Fraternal, social, and civic clubs—source of information about upcoming events

» Colleges and universities (police officers, administrators, faculty clubs, student groups, and alumni association groups)—source of information about possession of hazardous materials, foreign exchange students, and controversial research, speakers, activities, and events

» Printing shops—source of information about threatening or illegal photos and about requests for development of multiple photographs for false IDs

» Business managers—source of information about purchasers of dangerous materials such as torches, propane, and blasting supplies

» Transportation centers and tourist attractions—target-rich environments for terrorism and source of information about suspicious persons and activities

» Major industrial enterprises (owners, security officers, and nearby neighbors)—source of information about potential threats and suspicious activities

» Schools (teachers and administrators)—source of information about suspicious activities

» School and office building custodians—source of information about students, employees, visitors, and after-hours activities

» Health care providers (EMS drivers, doctors, and hospital employees)—source of information about unusual injuries, such as radiation and chemical burns, as well as mandatory reports of firearms and cutting injuries

» Bar and liquor stores—source of information about suspicious conversations, observations, and activities

» Inspectors and code enforcers—source of information about suspicious activities and materials, such as a large amount of fertilizer where there is no agricultural activity

» Facility licenses—source of information about type of building, building plans, premise protection, fire suppression, and storage of hazardous materials

» Licenses and permits (handgun, firearm, liquor, hackney, parade and event, blasting, business occupancy, and other types)—source of information about the background of licensees and permit holders

» Delivery services (letter carriers, couriers, delivery drivers)—source of information about suspicious activities and packages

» Department of public works employees and refuse haulers—source of information about strangers in the neighborhood, foreign substances in trash, inactivity or increased activity at a residence, and other suspicious persons and things

» Housing managers (public housing, apartment complexes, and property management associations)—source of information about unusual rentals and other suspicious activities in the properties

» Meter readers—source of information about unusual observations

» Automobile and truck drivers—source of information about items left behind in rented vehicles, method of payment, and departure and return details that arouse suspicion

» Taxi and delivery drivers, many from countries of interest—source of information concerning activities and threats[1]

The extent of the preceding list illustrates how broad in scope a community's information network can be for law enforcement officers faced with tackling terrorism, and it makes clear that the police are most certainly not "in this alone." Partnerships are also critical in community policing efforts to fight terrorism.

---

[1] Reprinted from Stephen Doherty and Bradley G. Hibbard, "Special Focus: Community Policing and Homeland Security," *The Police Chief*, Vol. 73, No. 2, pages 78–86, February 2006. Copyright held by the International Association of Chiefs of Police, 515 North Washington Street, Alexandria, VA 22314 USA. Further reproduction without express written permission from IACP is strictly prohibited.

CRUCIAL COLLABORATIONS AND PARTNERSHIPS TO PREVENT TERRORISM

The importance of partnerships between law enforcement agencies at all levels cannot be overstated as it applies to the war on terrorism. However, although these partnerships are obviously critical, broader partnerships are needed.

Private security, a traditionally underutilized resource by law enforcement, can be an important partner in the war against terrorism. The 9/11 Commission confirmed just how dependent the nation is on private security, noting that the private sector owns and protects about 85 percent of the nation's infrastructure—buildings, power plants, utilities, transportation systems, and communications networks. The number of people employed in private security in the United States is estimated to be at least 2 million people—more than three times the number employed by public law enforcement (Morabito and Greenberg, 2005). The Law Enforcement–Private Security Consortium (2009, 10) notes:

> Viewing private security as a force multiplier does not mean ignoring the differences between police and private security in legal authority, training, or accountability. Rather, it acknowledges the following:
>
> > Private security works in certain critical areas that law enforcement simply cannot cover because it lacks the human resources, mandate, or technology. Private security is a growth industry, whereas the number of sworn local and state law enforcement officers is not projected to grow significantly in the future.
>
> The most recent U.S. data on employment in local and state law enforcement show that 2000 through 2004 was a period of slow growth overall. The number of sworn officers decreased in 20 of the nation's 50 largest police departments, including 6 of the 7 largest. The New York City Police Department saw a 10.7-percent decrease in sworn officers, with even greater declines in Newark, New Jersey (down 11.4%); Cleveland, Ohio (down 14.4%); Nassau County, New York (down 15.3%); and Detroit, Michigan (down 15.5%).
>
> The combination of increased demands and stagnant or declining local law enforcement resources makes it clear that, now more than ever, law enforcement agencies must pursue all reasonable avenues for collaboration with private security, as well as with each other.

A national summit held in January 2004 by the IACP was specifically designed to bring law enforcement and private security professionals together to build partnerships in a unified response to terrorism. The resulting 38-page report, *Building Private Security/Public Policing Partnerships to Prevent and Respond to Terrorism and Public Disorder* (2004), outlines five action items crucial to successful partnerships between the private sector and public policing:

1. Leaders of major police organizations and private security organizations should make a formal commitment to cooperation.

2. Fund research and training on relevant legislation, private security, and law enforcement–private security cooperation.

3. Create an advisory council to oversee the day-to-day implementation issues of law enforcement–private security partnerships.

4. Convene key practitioners to move this agenda forward in the future.

5. Local partnerships should set priorities and address key problems.

Community policing efforts should develop innovative approaches to community mobilization, including strategies such as community mediation to help engage the community in a positive manner and channel citizens' desire to get involved.

Tapping citizens' patriotism and inclination to voluntarily serve their community has, however, become more challenging as time has passed. In this regard, the very success of law enforcement in preventing further terrorist incidents on U.S. soil has, to some degree, worked against it. Many Americans have forgotten the shock, anger, and raw fear they felt on those days, weeks, and even months following September 11. Complacency has returned. In addition, some citizens have grown critical of a government they contend is too willing to infringe on individuals' civil rights in its overzealous attempt to keep Americans safe from terrorists. This is one of the basic concerns surrounding the war on terrorism.

CONCERNS RELATED TO THE WAR ON TERRORISM

After the bombings on the London transit system in 2005, the NYPD took the unprecedented step of making random checks of bags and backpacks at subway stations, buses, and commuter rail lines. The police department announced their intentions to the public a day in advance.

Two concerns related to the "war on terrorism" are that civil liberties may be jeopardized and that people of Middle Eastern descent may be discriminated against or become victims of hate crimes.

Concern for Civil Rights

The first guiding principle of the DHS is to protect civil rights and civil liberties:

> We will defend America while protecting the freedoms that define America. Our strategies and actions will be consistent with the individual rights and liberties enshrined by our Constitution and the Rule of Law. While we seek to improve the way we collect and share information about terrorists, we will nevertheless be vigilant in respecting the confidentiality and protecting the privacy of our citizens. We are committed to securing our nation while protecting civil rights and civil liberties. (*Securing Our Homeland*, 2004, 6)

Civil libertarians are concerned, however, that valued American freedoms are being sacrificed in the interest of national safety. For example, the Justice Department has issued a new regulation giving itself the authority to monitor inmate–attorney communications if "reasonable suspicion" exists that inmates are using such communications to further or facilitate acts of terrorism. However, criminal defense lawyers and members of the

American Civil Liberties Union (ACLU) have protested the regulation, saying it effectively eliminates the Sixth Amendment right to counsel because, under codes of professional responsibility, attorneys cannot communicate with clients if confidentiality is not assured. The ACLU has vowed to monitor police actions closely to see that freedoms protected under the Constitution are not jeopardized.

Retaliation or Discrimination against People of Middle Eastern Descent

Another concern is that some Americans may retaliate against innocent people of Middle Eastern descent, many of whom were either born in the United States or are naturalized citizens. In fact, such injustices have already occurred. Davies and Murphy (2004, 1), note: "Within hours of the Twin Towers' collapse and the attack on the Pentagon, U.S. residents and visitors, particularly Arabs, Muslims, and Sikhs, were harassed or attacked because they shared—or were perceived to share—the terrorists' national background or religion. . . . Law enforcement's challenge since then has been to maintain an appropriate balance between the security interests of our country and the constitutional rights of every American." We must remember the Japanese internment camps during World War II and make sure we do not repeat that mistake.

A comprehensive public opinion poll conducted by the Pew Research Center in the summer of 2011, nearly 10 years after the 9/11 attacks, found no indication of an increased sense of alienation among Muslim Americans but did find that the vast majority of Muslim Americans are concerned about Islamic extremism, both within the United States and abroad; Muslims in the United States reject extremism by much larger margins than most other Muslim populations around the world; and an increasing number of Muslim Americans view U.S. efforts to combat efforts as sincere ("Muslim Americans: No Signs of Growth in Alienation or Support for Extremism," 2011).

A survey of policing in Arab American communities after September 11 found the following (Henderson et al., 2008, 1–2):

> Surveys in 16 sites across the country where Arab Americans were geographically concentrated found that many Arab American respondents were troubled by increased government scrutiny of their communities following 9/11. Some reported they were more afraid of law enforcement agencies, particularly Federal agencies, than they were of being victims of hate crimes. They specifically mentioned fears about immigration enforcement, surveillance of their activities, and racial profiling.

> After September 11, law enforcement agencies on both the local and federal levels experienced great pressure to prevent further attacks. Some researchers and law enforcement officials suggested that local law enforcement agencies should play a greater role in intelligence-gathering and immigration enforcement. In addition, the FBI began to stress counterterrorism efforts, with Joint Terrorism Task Forces working in concert with local law enforcement agencies. Often, these efforts focused on Arab American communities.

> At the same time, local law enforcement agencies were called on to protect the Arab American community. After the attacks, some people of Arab descent

said they experienced increased levels of harassment, ranging from workplace discrimination to verbal abuse and vandalism to severe hate crimes such as assault and homicide. To ensure the safety of Arab Americans, some local law enforcement agencies felt it necessary to step up their outreach efforts.

Finally, some Arab Americans and law enforcement officers said that public suspicion of Arab Americans had led to an increase in false reporting. As one FBI special agent said, "The general public calls in some ridiculous stuff—it's really guilt by being Muslim." Because officers have to look into all reports, false reporting can be a significant strain on law enforcement agencies.

Arab American communities have been deeply affected by the events of September 11 in other ways. Before the attacks, many Arab Americans were well assimilated into the American mainstream. But after September 11, some members of Arab American communities came to believe that many of their fellow citizens—not to mention some in the media and government—regarded them with suspicion. Although Arab Americans report a fair amount of goodwill towards local law enforcement agencies, some Arab Americans said these developments have strained relations between their communities and those agencies.

The study (2008, 2) identified four obstacles to improved relations between police and Arab American communities. One barrier is a persistent mutual mistrust; a second is police agencies' lack of knowledge about and sensitivity to the culture and religion of Arab Americans. The two other barriers are language differences and Arab American concerns about immigration status and deportation.

The study—which included surveys of local law enforcement officers and FBI agents in local field offices at each site—also produced some recommendations for ways to improve relations between Arab American communities and local law enforcement agencies and officers. Many of the recommendations reflect the priorities and practices of community policing. Recommendations include the creation of a police–community liaison position within local police departments, the recruitment of police officers from Arab American communities, and the training of officers in the cultural and religious values of Arab American communities. Such training should include guidance on how to deal with Arab Americans' mistrust of law enforcement officers (Henderson et al., 2008, 3–9).

Local law enforcement can take these steps to prevent racial profiling and/or discrimination against Arab Americans (Henderson et al., 2006, 25):

» Increase communication and dialogue
» Develop person-to-person contact
» Provide cultural awareness training
» Identify community needs
» Create a community liaison position to work with the Arab American community
» Recruit more Arab Americans into law enforcement

Strategies for recruiting more Arab Americans into law enforcement include focusing on young people, translating recruitment materials into Arabic, providing incentives for Arabic-speaking officers, and expediting citizenship for recruits of Arab descent (Henderson et al., 2006, 26).

Another concern involves the media and possible exploitation of this forum by terrorists looking to "get the word out."

THE ROLE OF THE MEDIA IN THE WAR ON TERRORISM

The media can be a positive or negative influence on efforts to combat terrorism. Indeed, as the late Richard Clutterbuck, economics professor and expert on political violence, once observed, the media is like a loaded gun lying on the street—the first person to pick it up gets to decide how to use it. Governments try to use the media as their loaded gun by embedding reporters in active war zones, and terrorists use the media to justify their violent acts and spread their message: "One Algerian terrorist once said he would rather kill one victim in front of a news camera than one hundred in the desert where the world would not see them. His point should be noted: Modern terrorism is a media phenomenon" (White, 2012, 104). Certainly, without the 24-hour media coverage of the events of September 11 and the continuous stream of graphic visuals that poured into U.S. homes, the impact of that horrific attack would not have been so profound.

One report on how terrorists seek to influence media channels states: "Indeed there is recent evidence that contemporary jihadis show unabated zeal for media operations" (Corman and Schiefelbein, 2006, 4). In fact, the al Qaeda leader in Iraq, Abu Musab al-Zarqawi, has been quoted as saying: "More than half of this battle is taking place in the battlefield of the media. We are in a media battle in a race for the hearts and minds of Muslims" (Rumsfeld, 2006). Al-Zarqawi, the mastermind behind hundreds of bombings, kidnappings, and beheadings in Iraq, was killed in June 2006 by an air strike north of Baghdad.

contagion effect
The media coverage of terrorism inspires more terrorism.

White (2012, 120) raises the question of the **contagion effect**—that is, the coverage of terrorism inspires more terrorism. It is, in effect, contagious. This controversial issue leads to discussions about censorship in the war on terrorism, an idea to which the media is, not surprisingly, fundamentally opposed.

Law enforcement agencies attempting to engage the community in a collective effort to fight terrorism must, at some level, be aware of the negative undercurrent that exists among segments of society regarding the actions of the government, perpetuated in large part by the media.

A FINAL CONSIDERATION

Bucqueroux and Diamond (2002, 6) note: "Few people outside the field know about the pitched battle for the heart and soul of policing that has raged over the past decade. It is said that people get the police they deserve. If we are to maintain recent reductions in violent crime and uncover the terrorists living among us, while preserving the civil rights that make our society special, we must insist on community policing now more than ever before."

The dual challenges in combating violence facing community policing are countering terrorism while continuing to address crime and disorder.

Research suggests, however, that balancing traditional crime fighting and the new challenge of counterterrorism should not be a tremendous either/or proposition, as the philosophical principles governing each task complement each other and offer considerable overlap in policing's public safety mandate:

> As homeland security has gained contemporary recognition in an atmosphere of terrorism and fear, community policing has increasingly been relegated to far lesser importance by local, state, and federal organizations. However, through examining these two strategies, evidence suggests that they share a number of overlapping principles. Furthermore, community policing has been shown to satisfy the central concepts found within homeland security; namely, a) extensive information gathering, b) collaboration with local, federal, and state agencies, c) community involvement, and d) the formation of inter-agency cooperation. The value of community policing is revealed in the ability of law enforcement agencies, of varying styles and sizes, to adapt to community realities. Policy makers at each level of government will achieve better terrorism prevention and response when they wholly adhere to integrating the community policing philosophy into the homeland security strategy. (Friedmann and Cannon, 2007, 18)

 SUMMARY

The threat of terrorism has become a reality in America. Common elements in definitions of terrorism include (1) systematic use of physical violence—actual or threatened, (2) against non-combatants, (3) but with an audience broader than the immediate victims in mind, (4) to create a general climate of fear in a target population, (5) to cause political and/or social change. Most terrorist acts result from dissatisfaction with a religious, political, or social system or policy and frustration resulting from an inability to change it through acceptable, nonviolent means.

The FBI categorizes terrorism in the United States as either domestic or international. Terrorists may use arson; explosives and bombs; weapons of mass destruction (biological, chemical, or nuclear agents); and technology.

As a result of September 11, the Department of Homeland Security was established, reorganizing the departments of the federal government.

At the federal level, the FBI is the lead agency for responding to acts of domestic terrorism. The Federal Emergency Management Agency (FEMA) is the lead agency for consequence management (after an attack).

The first line of defense against terrorism is the patrol officer in the field. The keys to combating terrorism lie with the local police and the intelligence they can provide to federal authorities; how readily information is shared between agencies at different levels; and the interoperability of communications systems should an attack occur.

Two concerns related to the "war on terrorism" are that civil liberties may be jeopardized and that people of Middle Eastern descent may be discriminated against or become victims of hate crimes. The dual challenges in combating violence facing community policing are countering terrorism while continuing to address crime and disorder.

DISCUSSION QUESTIONS

1. Discuss the aphorism: "One man's terrorist is another man's freedom fighter." What kinds of examples can you think of that confirm this statement?

2. What can local law enforcement agencies do to prevent terrorism? What about communities? Will community partnerships have any effect on terrorism? How realistic do you think it is that any of these will affect terrorism?

3. Why does information sharing between government agencies seem like something they cannot or will not do, in spite of what's at stake?

4. Why was the Department of Homeland Security created? What is its purpose?

5. Police and private security rarely, if ever, collaborate. Why do you think this is so?

6. Discuss what is controversial about the USA PATRIOT Act. How did it change the government's ability to conduct investigations?

7. Is it *profiling* to focus security efforts on those who appear to be Middle Eastern or Arab?

8. Should the media report on terrorism events? How does media coverage affect terrorists?

9. The 9/11 Commission made recommendations to the government that would enhance safety for Americans. Why do you think that few of their recommendations have been adopted?

10. Do you think America's focus on fighting terrorism jeopardizes the progress of the community policing philosophy?

GALE EMERGENCY SERVICES DATABASE ASSIGNMENTS

ONLINE Database

- Use the Gale Emergency Services Database to help answer the Discussion Questions as appropriate.

- Read and outline the article "Understanding the Terrorist Mind-Set" by Randy Borum. Be prepared to share and discuss your outline with the class.

REFERENCES

"About Us." n.d. Washington, DC: National Counterterrorism Center. http://www.nctc.gov/about_us/about_nctc.html

Berkow, Michael. 2004. "Homeland Security: The Internal Terrorists." *The Police Chief* 71 (6): 25–30.

Blair, Ian. 2006. "Policing in the New Normality: The Connection between Community Policing and Combating Terrorism." *Subject to Debate* 20 (5) 2006: 1.

Borum, Randy. 2003. "Understanding the Terrorist Mind-Set." *FBI Law Enforcement Bulletin* 72 (7): 7–10.

Bratton, William J. 2006. "The Need for Balance." *Subject to Debate* 20 (4): 2–3.

Bucqueroux, Bonnie and Drew Diamond. 2002. "Community Policing Is Our Best Bet against Terror." *Subject to Debate* 16 (1): 1, 6.

Building Private Security/Public Partnerships Policing Partnerships. 2004 (October 7). Arlington, VA: International Association of Chiefs of Police.

Chapman, Robert. 2008. "Community Partnerships: A Key Ingredient in an Effective Homeland Security Approach." *Community Policing Dispatch* 1 (2).

Corman, Steven R. and Jill S. Schiefelbein. 2006. *Communication and Media Strategy in the Jihadi War of Ideas.* Phoenix, AZ: Arizona State University, Hugh Downs School of Human Communication.

Country Reports on Terrorism 2011. 2012 (July 31). Report. Washington, DC: U.S. Department of State, Office of the Coordinator for Counterterrorism. http://www.state.gov/j/ct/rls/crt/2011/195547.htm

Davies, Heather J. and Gerard R. Murphy. 2004. *Protecting Your Community from Terrorism: Strategies for Local Law Enforcement Series: Volume 2: Working with Diverse Communities.* Washington, DC: The Office of Community Oriented Policing Services and the Police Executive Research Forum.

"Department Subcomponents and Agencies." 2009 (June 15). Washington, DC: Department of Homeland Security.

Docobo, Jose. 2005. "Community Policing as the Primary Prevention Strategy for Homeland Security at the Local Law Enforcement Level." *Homeland Security Affairs* 1 (1). http://www.hsaj.org/?fullarticle=1.1.4

Doherty, Stephen and Bradley G. Hibbard. 2006. "Special Focus: Community Policing and Homeland Security." *The Police Chief* 73 (2): 78–86.

"Fact Sheet: Expansion of US-VISIT Procedures to Additional Travelers." 2009 (January 14). Fact sheet. Washington, DC: Department of Homeland Security. http://www.dhs.gov/us-visit-expansion-fact-sheet

Federal Bureau of Investigation Strategic Plan 2004–2009. 2004. Washington, DC: Federal Bureau of Investigation.

Friedmann, Robert R. and William J. Cannon. 2007. "Homeland Security and Community Policing: Competing or Complementing Public Safety Policies." *Journal of Homeland Security and Emergency Management* 4 (4): Article 2.

From Hometown Security to Homeland Security: IACP's Principles for a Locally Designed and Nationally Coordinated Homeland Security Strategy. 2005 (May 17). Alexandria, VA: International Association of Chiefs of Police. http://www.theiacp.org/LinkClick.aspx?fileticket=78X8uKjLa0U%3D&tabid=392

Garrett, Ronnie. 2004. "The Wolf Is at the Door: What Are We Waiting For?" *Law Enforcement Technology* (March): 6.

Glasscock, Bruce D. 2011 (October 16). "Letter to IACP Colleagues."

Hanson, Doug. 2005. "What's Next—Soft Target Attacks." *Law Enforcement Technology* (August): 18–27.

Henderson, Nicole J., Christopher W. Ortiz, Naomi F. Sugie, and Joel Miller. 2006 (June). *Law Enforcement and Arab American Community Relations after September 11, 2001: Engagement in a Time of Uncertainty.* New York: Vera Institute of Justice.

Henderson, Nicole J., Christopher W. Ortiz, Naomi F. Sugie, and Joel Miller. 2008 (July). *Policing in Arab American Communities after September 11.* Washington, DC: National Institute of Justice. (NCJ 221706)

Howard, Paul and Mark Riebling. 2005 (May). *Hard Won Lessons: Problem-Solving Principles for Local Police.* New York: Manhattan Institute for Policy Research, Safe Cities Project.

LaFree, Gary. 2009 (March 28). "Challenges and Recommendations for Measuring Terrorism." College Park, MD: University of Maryland, National Consortium for the Study of Terrorism (START).

Law Enforcement–Private Security Consortium. 2009 (July). *Operation Partnership: Trends and Practices in Law Enforcement and Private Security Collaborations.* Washington, DC: Office of Community Oriented Policing Services. (e08094224)

Linett, Howard. 2005. "Counter-Terrorism 101." *Police* (August): 58–64.

Loyka, Stephan A., Donald A. Faggiani, and Clifford Karchmer. 2005 (February). *Protecting Your Community from Terrorism: Strategies for Local Law Enforcement. Volume 4: The Production and Sharing of Intelligence.* Washington, DC: Community Oriented Policing Services and the Police Executive Research Forum.

McDonald, Kathleen and W. Sean McLaughlin. 2003. "First Responders: Ready or Not?" *Law Enforcement Trainer* 18 (3): 14–19.

Morabito, Andrew and Sheldon Greenberg. 2005 (September). *Engaging the Private Sector to Promote Homeland Security: Law Enforcement–Private Security Partnerships.* Washington, DC: U.S. Department of Justice, Bureau of Justice Assistance. (NCJ 210678)

Murray, John. 2005. "Policing Terrorism: A Threat to Community Policing or Just a Shift in Priorities?" *Police Practice and Research* 6 (4): 347–361.

"Muslim Americans: No Signs of Growth in Alienation or Support for Extremism." 2011 (August 30). Poll. Washington, DC: Pew Research Center, The Pew Forum on Religion and Public Life. http://www.pewforum.org/Muslim/Muslim-Americans--No-Signs-of-Growth-in-Alienation-or-Support-for-Extremism.aspx

National Incident Management System (NIMS): What's New. 2008 (December). Washington, DC: Federal Emergency Management Agency (FEMA). http://www.fema.gov/pdf/emergency/nims/NIMSWhatsNew.pdf

Newman, Graeme R. and Ronald V. Clarke. 2008 (July). *Policing Terrorism: An Executive's Guide.* Washington, DC: Office of Community Oriented Policing Services.

"New York City Police Department and Microsoft Partner to Bring Real-Time Crime Prevention and Counterterrorism Technology Solution to Global Law Enforcement Agencies." Microsoft News Center, August 8, 2012. http://www.microsoft.com/en-us/news/Press/2012/Aug12/08-08NYPDPR.aspx

"9/11 Changed Culture, Attitude of Street Cops." 2006. *Newswise,* August 2. http://www.newswise.com/articles/911-changed-culture-attitude-of-street-cops

"The 9-11 Commission Bill and 9-11 Commission Recommendations At-A-Glance." n.d. Prepared by the Democratic Staff of the Committee on Homeland Security. http://www.asisonline.org/toolkit/911bill.pdf

One Team, One Mission, Securing Our Homeland: U.S. Department of Homeland Security Strategic Plan Fiscal Years 2008–2013. 2008 (May 20). Washington, DC: U.S. Department of Homeland Security. http://www.hsdl.org/?view&did=235371

Page, Douglas. 2004. "Law Enforcement Renaissance: The Sequel." *Law Enforcement Technology* (March): 86–90.

Polisar, Joseph M. 2004. "The National Criminal Intelligence Sharing Plan." President's message. *The Police Chief* 71 (6): 8.

"Regional Information Sharing Systems Program Fact Sheet." n.d. Fact sheet. Washington, DC: Bureau of Justice Assistance.

Rumsfeld, Donald. 2006 (February 17). *New Realities in the Media Age: A Conversation with Donald Rumsfeld.* Transcript of an interview. Council on Foreign Relations. www.cfr.org/publication/9900

Savelli, Lou. 2004. *A Proactive Law Enforcement Guide for the War on Terrorism.* Flushing, NY: LooseLeaf Law Publications, Inc.

Securing Our Homeland: U.S. Department of Homeland Security Strategic Plan. 2004. Washington, DC: U.S. Department of Homeland Security.

"Senate Homeland Security and Governmental Affairs Committee Holds Hearing on Information Sharing in the Era of WikiLeaks." 2011 (March 10). *CQ Transcriptions, Congressional Hearings.* http://ise.gov/sites/default/files/Senate_HSGAC_Hearing_InfoSharing_Mar2011.pdf

Sims, Calvin. 2004. "Poll Finds Most Americans Have Not Prepared for a Terror Attack." *The New York Times,* October 28.

Tafoya, William L. 2011. "Cyber Terror." *FBI Law Enforcement Bulletin* (November): 1–7.

Terrorism 2002–2005. 2005. Washington, DC: Federal Bureau of Investigation. http://www.fbi.gov/stats-services/publications/terrorism-2002-2005/terror02_05.pdf

2011 Report on Terrorism. 2012 (March 12). Washington, DC: National Counterterrorism Center.

U.S. Census Bureau. 2012. *Statistical Abstract of the United States: 2012.* http://www.census.gov/compendia/statab/2012/tables/12s0344.pdf

"U.S. Should Rethink 'War on Terrorism' Strategy to Deal with Resurgent Al Qaida." 2008 (August 6). Santa Monica, CA: The Rand Corporation.

"Weapons of Mass Destruction: Frequently Asked Questions." n.d. Washington, DC: Federal Bureau of Investigation Web site. http://www.fbi.gov/about-us/investigate/terrorism/wmd/wmd_faqs

White, Jonathan R. 2012. *Terrorism and Homeland Security.* 7th edition. Belmont, CA: Wadsworth.

This available CourseMate has an interactive eBook and interactive learning tools, including flash cards, quizzes, and more. To learn more about this resource and access free demo CourseMate resources, go to **www.cengagebrain.com**, and search for this book. To access CourseMate materials that you have purchased, go to **login.cengagebrain.com**.

CHAPTER 16

What Research Tells Us and a Look to the Future

> The best way to predict the future is to create it.

> —Peter Drucker

DO YOU KNOW ...

» What is at the heart of experimental design?

» What issues are raised by experiments in criminal justice?

» Whether the American Society of Criminology supports experiments in criminal justice?

» What assistance is available to departments wishing to conduct experiments?

» What percentage of distributed surveys is required to validate an evaluation?

» What effect community policing is having on crime statistics?

» What other types of statistics might be more helpful?

» What the goals of futuristics are?

CAN YOU DEFINE ...

action research
coercive isomorphism
experimental design
isomorphism
mimetic isomorphism
normative isomorphism
random assignment
two-wave survey

INTRODUCTION

With the wealth of information related to community policing and strategies available in print and online, how can departments determine which ideas and programs are effective? Why is research important and what pitfalls might be encountered? What has been learned that will affect community policing efforts in the future?

Bratton (2006, 2) examines the relationship between practitioners and researchers and what can be done to improve and build on this critical—but often strained—relationship. In the evolving crime paradigm of the 21st century, intelligence-led policing will create new demands and challenges for law enforcement while simultaneously requiring law enforcement to combat the many facets of terrorism and cybercrime. Bratton calls for research partnerships focused on addressing these demands, maximizing the effectiveness and usefulness of the research conducted: "A great deal of the research in the last half of the 20th century was of little practical value to practitioners." He advocates working more closely with researchers to help focus their efforts.

This chapter begins with a discussion of reliable sources of law enforcement research and the importance of practical, relevant research. This is followed by an explanation of the kinds of research that can be conducted. Next research findings on community policing departments and community policing evaluation and crime statistics are discussed. This is followed by an evaluation of the Community Oriented Policing Services (COPS) Office and of community-based crime prevention programs. The chapter concludes with a look at the current status of law enforcement and community policing, the technology that is changing policing, how the economic downturn has affected law enforcement, and a look to the future, including the role of futurists.

RELIABLE SOURCES OF LAW ENFORCEMENT RESEARCH

Several reliable sources of information are provided by criminal justice research organizations in the United States. Following are profiles of eight of the most prominent sources.

The *National Institute of Justice (NIJ)* is the research, development, and evaluation agency of the U.S. Department of Justice and is dedicated to researching crime control and justice issues. The NIJ provides objective, independent, evidence-based knowledge and tools to meet the challenges of crime and justice, especially at the state and local levels. Among its high-priority goals are to: (1) identify ways police and law enforcement agencies can improve their effectiveness, efficiency, and productivity; (2) enhance officer safety while minimizing unnecessary risks to suspects and others; (3) improve the police organizations' ability to collect, analyze, disseminate, and use information effectively and to communicate reliably and securely; (4) identify procedures, policies, technologies, and basic knowledge that will maximize appropriate and lawful police actions; and (5) enhance local investigative resources by identifying and disseminating investigative best practices and by developing technologies and techniques that help locate suspects and establish guilt.

The *Justice Research and Statistics Association (JRSA)* is a national nonprofit association of state Statistical Analysis Center (SAC) directors, researchers, and practitioners throughout government, academia, and criminal justice organizations. The JRSA is dedicated to the use of applied research and data analysis for sound development of criminal justice policy. The JRSA Web site is a gateway to online justice resources, providing links to statistical analysis centers and access to publications on key justice issues. It also provides access to the InfoBase of State Activities and Research (ISAR), a clearinghouse of current information on state criminal justice research, programs, and publications as well as reports on the latest research being conducted by federal and state agencies, including the annual *Directory of Justice Issues in the States* and *The JRSA Forum* newsletter.

The *Police Executive Research Forum (PERF)* is a national membership organization of police executives from city, county, and state law enforcement agencies dedicated to improving policing and advancing professionalism through research and involvement in public policy debate.

SEARCH, the *National Consortium for Justice Information and Statistics*, is a national membership organization created by and for the states, dedicated to improving the criminal justice system through effective application of information and identification technology. Since 1960, SEARCH's primary objective has been to identify and help solve the information management problems of state and local criminal justice agencies confronted with the need to exchange information with other local agencies, state agencies, agencies in other states, or the federal government.

The *Justice Research Association* is a private consulting firm and "think tank" focusing on issues of crime and justice. The Justice Research Association links agencies and practitioners in the justice field with specialized professional service providers. The service is free to those seeking professional services, with fees provided by the providers recommended.

The *Police Foundation* conducts national research on law enforcement and policing. Their first foundation study was the classic "Kansas City Preventive Patrol Experiment," which showed that increasing or decreasing the level of routine preventive patrol—the backbone of police work—had no appreciable effect on crime, fear of crime, or citizen satisfaction with police services. Many attribute the beginning of community policing with this study. Another study, "Policewomen on Patrol," conducted in cooperation with the Washington (DC) Police Department, concluded that women perform patrol work as well as men and that gender is not a valid reason to bar women from such work. Their follow-on study, "On the Move: The Status of Women in Policing," revealed that women have made major inroads into policing, but it also suggests that much more progress needs to be made in recruiting, promoting, and retaining women in policing.

Other classic research findings by the Police Foundation include the "Newark Foot Patrol Experiment," which found that foot patrol reduces citizen fear of crime and increases overall satisfaction with police services, a finding seminal to the evolution of community policing. An evaluation conducted with the San Diego (California) Police Department concluded that one officer is as effective and safe as two officers in a patrol car and markedly less expensive. As a partner in the Community Policing Consortium, the foundation plays a principal role in developing community policing research and technical assistance.

The *Vera Institute of Justice* is a private nonprofit organization that conducts research and offers consulting services in the area of criminal justice. The institute works closely with leaders in government and civil society to improve the services people rely on for safety and justice. The Vera Institute develops innovative, affordable programs that often grow into self-sustaining organizations, studies social problems and current responses, and provides practical advice and assistance to government officials in New York and internationally.

Each Vera Institute project begins with an empirical investigation of how some part of the justice system really works. That exploration may lead to designing a practical experiment. In other cases, officials are brought together with their peers and constituents to plot a rational course for reform. The aim is to help government partners achieve measurable improvements in the quality of justice they deliver and share what they have learned with others around the globe. For more than 40 years the institute has been a pioneer in developing practical, affordable solutions to some of the toughest problems in the administration of justice.

The *International Association of Chiefs of Police (IACP) Research Center's* mission is to identify issues in law enforcement and conduct timely policy research, evaluation, follow-up training, and technical assistance and direction to law enforcement leaders, the justice system, and the community. The IACP calls for practical, relevant research in policing. The IACP's Research Advisory Committee (RAC) has published a nationwide, survey-based, focused research agenda to guide both police leaders and researchers as they undertake research initiatives. This *National Law Enforcement Research Agenda (NLERA)* is a list of priority research topics for law enforcement aimed at (1) promoting research on these topics, (2) encouraging police/researcher partnerships to conduct that research, and (3) ensuring that research topic selection results in relevant policy to assist the law enforcement community (*Improving 21st-Century Policing*, 2008). Using the information gained from all prior work, particularly the survey of IACP members, RAC members agreed on a final set of eight research areas that function as the core elements of the NLERA (*Improving 21st-Century Policing*, 2008, 4):

» Leadership
» Management and administration
» Training and education
» Systems approaches
» Technology
» Response to crime and victimization
» Emergency preparedness
» Emerging issues

The *NLERA* includes examples of specific research questions for each of the eight areas. For example, a few of the research questions included in the management and administration category are (*Improving 21st-Century Policing*, 2008, 11):

» What are the best practices in communicating policies and procedures to employees?
» What are the best practices in developing and implementing goals and objectives?
» How do agencies define community policing and measure its implementation and effectiveness?
» What is the impact of accreditation on an agency? How can the accreditation process be more effective?
» Is CompStat effective? What variations of the concept are most effective and for which types of agencies? Can CompStat accommodate community policing?
» What recruitment issues are agencies facing, and what strategies have agencies successfully employed to overcome them?

THE COMMISSION ON ACCREDITATION FOR LAW ENFORCEMENT AGENCIES

The Commission on Accreditation for Law Enforcement Agencies, Inc. (CALEA) was created in 1979 through the joint efforts of the International Association of Chiefs of Police (IACP), the National Organization of Black Law Enforcement Executives (NOBLE), the National Sheriff's Association (NSA), and the Police Executive Research Forum (PERF). The purpose in forming CALEA was to enhance law enforcement as a profession and to improve law enforcement by providing credentialing for law enforcement agencies that meet certain standards of professionalism ("The Commission," 2010).

The benefits for agencies that become accredited are many. Once accredited, they will have greater accountability within the agency; they will experience a reduced risk and liability exposure often reflected in reduced insurance costs; and they will have a stronger defense against civil lawsuits, staunch support from government officials, and increased community support.

The accreditation process is lengthy and requires agencies to examine their management practices and, in most cases, adjust those practices. Accreditation is also not free. CALEA charges agencies based on their size for the guidance, assessment, and other services they provide during the process. Once accredited, agencies must pay an annual fee to CALEA.

Hundreds of agencies across the United States and Canada have become accredited, and more are going through the process every year.

Source: "The Commission." Fairfax, VA: The Commission on Accreditation for Law Enforcement, 2010. Retrieved September 23, 2012 from http://www.calea.org/content/commission

» What programs and selection procedures are effective to recruit officers in agencies with various missions?

» What issues arise with combat veterans returning from active duty to policing? What methods are effective in facilitating that transition?

THE IMPORTANCE OF PRACTICAL, RELEVANT RESEARCH

"Contrary to conventional wisdom, law enforcement agencies are actually quite open to the research process. The problems that have been associated with police research have been related to the current exclusionary style of conducting research by academics who are more interested in publications than in providing useful information for departments. The emphasis on publications in the absence of practical accountability has led to police distrust for research" (Cosner and Loftus, 2005, 64–65). What is needed is a research model that includes those affected by the results and that is practical and relevant.

Research as a Partnership

Many partnerships between law enforcement leaders and academic researchers have been successful over the last 30 years (Sanders and Fields, 2009). Policing has been influenced by research projects leading to substantive, sound policy recommendations. Despite these successes, however, much remains to be done. Existing research partnerships often suffer from many unresolved problems.

Police agencies and researchers need to identify and locate each other, determine mutually interesting projects, and set ground rules for how the project will proceed. Partnerships between police agencies and academic researchers can benefit both groups.

Undoubtedly, for most researchers, the main benefit is access to data. Sanders and Fields (2009) suggest these benefits for police agencies:

» Employing data to make hiring decisions
» Applying job analysis data to make promotions more objective
» Collecting data for writing grant applications
» Surveying citizens about crime priorities or quality of life
» Gathering data to justify requests for money or equipment
» Using data to improve services in general (identifying priorities, understanding citizen fears)

In addition, through partnerships, agencies can provide internship opportunities for professors' students as well as potential future job opportunities for graduates. Police officers can also provide professors with such teaching aids as case studies and guest speakers, providing access to real-life examples of motivation, leadership, organizational structure, personnel issues, and organizational communication. A further mutual benefit is that networks at local colleges might provide future opportunities for adjunct teaching for police administrators with advanced degrees.

"Research is a partnership, and its best application and realization of meaningful results begins when the user is directly involved in the process" (Cosner and Loftus, 2005, 65). Experts in police research recommend that to improve police–researcher coordination, law enforcement agencies should:

» Partner with skilled researchers to carefully design research.
» Train their leaders in evaluating potential research to ensure their ability to identify suitable research partners and to recognize relevant research topics.
» Establish regular forums through which their own research interests and priorities are communicated.
» Be willing to initiate research partnerships on regional, national, and local levels.
» Use the action research model for conducting research in law enforcement.

Action Research

action research
Emphasizes full participation in the research by everyone directly affected by the process and results.

One of the best models for police–researcher alliance is an action research approach, first used by Lewin in the 1940s. **Action research** emphasizes full participation in the research by everyone directly affected by the process and results. When police officers participate in designing and conducting the research, they are more likely to use the results.

Kinds of Research

Research can be very formal and rigorous or more informal and less rigorous. It is important to recognize what type of research is being reported.

Experimental Design Among the most formal research is that based on an experimental design.

experimental design
Research method involving the random assignment of individuals to experimental (treatment) and control (no treatment) conditions.

At the heart of **experimental design** is the random assignment of individuals to experimental and control conditions.

In **random assignment**, the individuals participating in the study are selected with no definite design (randomly) and placed into an experimental (treatment) or control (no treatment) group purely by chance.

Although support for experiments is strong, experiments in criminal justice are not without critics.

Experiments in criminal justice raise ethical issues as well as privacy issues.

The ethical issue centers around denying those in the control group "treatment." However, the American Society of Criminology (ASC) conducted an email poll, which resulted in "virtually unanimous" support for random assignment.

Support for experimental research is also attested to by the formation of the Academy of Experimental Criminology in 2000, with Lawrence Sherman as its first president.

Assistance in experiments in criminal justice is available through the NIJ's Locally Initiated Research Partnerships in Policing.

In this NIJ initiative, partners share responsibility throughout the entire project, jointly selecting an area of interest to the department (locally initiated) and collaborating on the research design, implementation, and interpretation of findings. Started in 1995, the NIJ partnership program currently has 41 projects. Usually the partnerships involve a local police department or other law enforcement agency and a local university. Often graduate students are used and can receive credit for research projects.

At the heart of the partnerships is the Action Research Model, illustrated in Figure 16.1. The cyclical, multistep process starts with nomination of a research topic, continues with development and implementation of the research design, and ends with communicating and applying the findings.

random assignment
Dependence on a random number table or machine-generated random number that indicates the particular group to which an individual or entity will be assigned. Whether a person is a member of the treatment group or the control (no treatment) group is determined purely by chance.

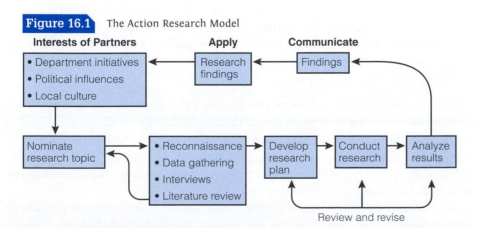

Figure 16.1 The Action Research Model

Source: Tom McEwen. "NIJ's Locally Initiated Research Partnerships in Policing Factors that Add Up to Success." *National Institute of Justice Journal*, Issue 238, January 1999, p. 7.

RESEARCH ON EYEWITNESS TESTIMONY

Eyewitnesses play a vital role in the administration of justice (Schuster, 2007). Their testimony can lead to identifying, charging, and convicting a suspect of a crime. In some cases it may be the only evidence available. Even the most well-intentioned witnesses can identify the wrong person or fail to identify the perpetrator of a crime, however. According to the American Judicature Society, misidentification by eyewitnesses was the leading cause of wrongful conviction in more than 75 percent of the first 183 DNA exonerations in the United States (Schuster, 2007). These exonerations have led to debate over the best way to obtain reliable eyewitness identification through lineups (Schuster, 2007, 4, 6):

> The most common lineup procedure in use by law enforcement is the simultaneous lineup. Researchers like Gary Wells, Ph.D., from Iowa State University, claim, however, that during simultaneous lineups, witnesses use "relative judgment," meaning that they compare lineup photographs or members to each other, rather than to their memory of the offender. This is a problem when the perpetrator is not present in the lineup because often the witness will choose the lineup member who most closely resembles the perpetrator.

> During sequential lineups, on the other hand, witnesses must make a decision about each photograph or member before moving on to the next, prompting them to use "absolute judgment." In other words, witnesses compare each photograph or person only to their memory of what the offender looked like.

> As the body of research into simultaneous versus sequential methods continued to grow, some researchers working in the lab discovered that the double-blind sequential method—in which the administrator does not know the identity of the suspect—produced fewer false identifications than the traditional simultaneous method. In 2003, the Illinois legislature put this research to the test. Lawmakers charged the Illinois State Police with conducting a yearlong examination of the double-blind sequential versus the simultaneous (commonly used) eyewitness identification procedure to determine which produced fewer false identifications.

> The results, published in March 2006, surprised many. Although the double-blind sequential lineup had produced more reliable outcomes in the laboratory, this was not the case in the field. Data collected from approximately 700 photo arrays and live lineups from urban, suburban, and semirural Illinois police departments revealed that the double-blind sequential procedure resulted in an overall higher rate of false identifications and a lower rate of "suspect picks" than the simultaneous lineup.

The stunning implications of the Illinois Pilot Program have since been marred, however, by questions about the methodology used, with a panel of social scientists criticizing the design of the Illinois Pilot Program, which compared double-blind sequential lineup procedures to traditional nonblind simultaneous procedures, as having "devastating consequences for assessing the real-world implications" (Schuster, 2007, 6).

Gaertner and Harrington (2009, 130) contend that two essentials in lineup reform are that lineups be sequential and that they be "blind" (conducted by someone who does not know who the suspect is); this finding is supported by more than a quarter century of scientific study. These two essentials were pilot tested in Ramsey County, Minnesota. After the yearlong pilot study proved successful, a new lineup protocol was adopted countywide. Gaertner and Harrington (2009, 130) conclude: "After almost 4 years of experience with this protocol, the county has concluded that it is feasible, practical, and superior to past eyewitness identification procedures."

A much more informal approach to research is through a survey.

Surveys

One commonly used method to evaluate the effectiveness of a strategy is the survey—either in person, mailed, or phoned. Sometimes a **two-wave survey** is used, the first wave consisting of a pretest before a strategy is implemented and the second wave a posttest after the strategy has been implemented for a given amount of time.

Other times surveys are used to determine what citizens feel a neighborhood's main problems are or how effective residents feel the police in their neighborhood are.

two-wave survey

Study method where the first wave consists of a pretest before a strategy is implemented, and the second wave consists of a posttest after the strategy has been implemented for a given amount of time.

To validate an evaluation conducted by survey, 60 percent of distributed surveys must be returned.

PERF has established a center for survey research to help agencies design, conduct, and analyze surveys. Surveys also play an important part in the *agency-level* Performance Measurement System that PERF developed for the law enforcement community: "The PERF measurement system is unique because it focuses law enforcement agencies' attention on a broader spectrum of activities—ones that have not been measured consistently, but are imperative to understanding what law enforcement agencies produce for their communities" (Milligan and Fridell, 2006, 5). Figure 16.2 illustrates how law enforcement outcomes contribute to overall community health.

Several surveys included in the Performance Measurement System will help agencies measure their performance and provide the accountability the public rightfully expects. Community surveys available in the Performance Measurement System include surveys that measure victimization of community members and businesses and self-reported delinquency surveys for juveniles. Self-reporting is an important way to measure crime in a community, as not all victims report crimes to the police. Also included in this list are measures that relate to perceptions of safety and security, confidence, trust, and satisfaction and traffic safety, since they clearly affect community safety. Departments wishing to use surveys might benefit from the Bureau of Justice Assistance's free report "A Police Guide to Surveying Citizens and Their Environment." Agencies might also consider using case studies to support reports on how a program is working when they are describing it to the public or applying for funding.

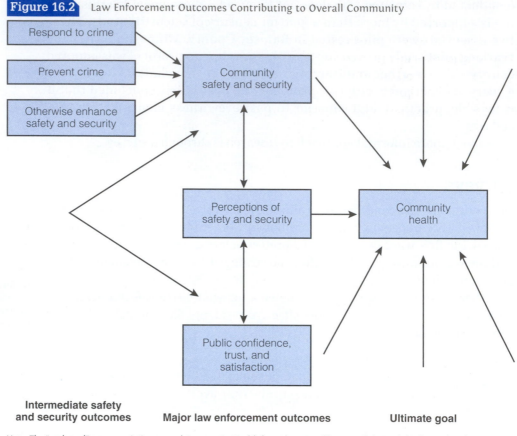

| **Figure 16.2** | Law Enforcement Outcomes Contributing to Overall Community |

**Intermediate safety
and security outcomes**   **Major law enforcement outcomes**   **Ultimate goal**

Note: The "orphaned" arrows pointing toward Community Health from the top and bottom of the model indicate that there are many other contributors to a community's health besides law enforcement. Certainly, a healthy community is partially defined by a low crime rate, residents' feelings of security, and residents' trust and confidence in local law enforcement agency, but it is also dependent on the actions of many other agencies, organizations and individuals.

Source: Milligan, Stacy Osnick and Fridell, Lorie. *Implementing an Agency-Level Performance Measurement System: A Guide for Law Enforcement Executives.* Washington, DC: Police Executive Research Forum, April 2006.

Case Studies

Much of what is known about community policing derives from case studies of community policing practices in cities throughout the country: "These case studies are diverse in their goals, design, length, and richness of detail. Collectively, they provide much-needed information about the stated purposes of community policing, in particular, places, strategic and structural components of community policing, implementation process and obstacles, and, occasionally, results. ... Case studies frequently provide readers with a strong sense of knowing what community policing is like" (Scott, Duffee, and Renauer, 2003, 411). Results of prior case studies often provide useful databases for measuring new concepts and examining relationships among variables: "When reading case studies ... one could have reasonable confidence in the following kinds of statements about police–community interaction:

» The kinds of steps taken by the police in a neighborhood to provide accessibility, improve responsiveness, and increase communication with residents (identification).

» The nature of issues or problems that residents and the police were addressing in a neighborhood and [the] extent to which those improvement steps included problem-solving characteristics (improvements).

» The kind of steps that the police took to encourage civic engagement by residents (encouragement).

» The kinds of decisions about the neighborhood that residents contributed to and the balance of decision making by police and the residents (participation).

» The kinds of organizations that the police interacted with in the course of identification, improvement, and encouragement activities and the contributions made by these other organizations (coordination)." (Scott, Duffee, and Renauer, 2003, 433)

A high degree of confidence may also be considered with the following statements (Scott, Duffee, and Renauer, 2003, 433–434):

» Whether or not identification efforts extended over the entire neighborhood and included most of the residents (the dispersion of identification)

» Whether or not improvement steps were concentrated (such as around business property) or widespread in a neighborhood (the dispersion of improvements)

» Whether the improvement steps were narrowly focused on crime and public safety or were more broadly gauged (the scope of improvements)

» Whether coordination occurred with a wide variety or a narrow segment of organizations important to the neighborhood (the scope of coordination)

Evidence-Based Policing

In 1998 criminologist Larry Sherman proposed a new model of law enforcement he called evidence-based policing (EBP): "Of all the ideas in policing, one stands out as the most powerful force for change: police practices should be based on scientific evidence about what works best." He notes that often, even after research has shown that something does not work, law enforcement continues to do it as a result of political pressure, inertia, or ignorance (Jensen, 2006, 98).

In reality, EBP is more a philosophy than a model to use when confronted with an issue or problem. As a starter, specific outcomes or goals should be established and used to drive every other aspect of a project. The next step is to determine best practices as identified in recent, relevant literature. A wealth of cutting-edge research is already available through most major city police departments and state police organizations and on the Internet. Sherman stresses that all research is not created equal. Some studies involve an adequate number of subjects and use random assignment and control groups; others do not. It is critical to understand how well a study was conducted.

After best practices are determined, the agency must adapt them to their local laws, agency policies, and community realities to formulate guidelines. What works in one jurisdiction may not work, or be acceptable, in another jurisdiction. Once guidelines are in place, they can be used to develop outputs or means to accomplish a task. Finally, and perhaps most important, is a means of measuring whether the plan actually works—that is, if it accomplishes what it was designed to do.

RESEARCH FINDINGS ON COMMUNITY POLICING DEPARTMENTS

The Chicago Internet Project conducted online surveys of target communities and provided feedback to those communities. The project was based on the premise that, while much has been done under the community policing and problem-oriented policing models, progress in reforming police organizations and communities has been restricted by failure to explore new measures of success and new methods of accountability that are grounded in the community (Rosenbaum et al., 2007, iii).

If police–community relations are a priority, accountability systems should examine the day-to-day interactions between police and citizens. The project sought to learn the police response to residents as victims, witnesses, suspects, complainants, callers, and concerned citizens, as well as to gain insight about how residents respond to the police.

The project developed, field-tested, and validated three primary types of community assessment: general assessments of police officers, experience-based assessments of police officers, and assessments of the police organization as a whole.

Rosenbaum and colleagues (2007, ix) suggest: "From management and research perspectives, the Internet allows for hundreds of performance comparisons within and across jurisdictions. This tool can be used, for example, to assess the impact of localized interventions (e.g., the impact of installing cameras in crime hot spots on residents' awareness, fear, and risk of detection compared to control locations), to compare performance across beats or districts (e.g., police visibility and response times across different Latino beats), or to compare performance across jurisdictions (e.g., perceived police demeanor during traffic stops in African American neighborhoods in Chicago, London, and Los Angeles)."

Institutionalized organizations may experience **isomorphism** or structural conformity becoming more like each other through three mechanism: mimetic, coercive, and normative (Willis, Mastrofski, and Weisburd, 2007). **Mimetic isomorphism** occurs when an organization copies or imitates another organization. **Coercive isomorphism** occurs when organizations adopt something as a result of pressure either from the state or other organizations, with perhaps the greatest source of coercive isomorphism being the U.S. Justice Department, which controls billions of dollars in funding. **Normative isomorphism** results from professionalism, with influences coming from such organizations as PERF and IACP.

COMMUNITY POLICING, EVALUATION, AND CRIME STATISTICS

The effectiveness of community policing is often measured using crime rates for a given jurisdiction. Decreasing crime rates would indicate success. As discussed in Chapter 10, the national decline in violent crime rates from the

isomorphism
Similar in structural characteristics. Isomorphism results in a one-size-fits-all approach to community policing; in contrast to refraction.

mimetic isomorphism
Occurs when an organization copies or imitates another.

coercive isomorphism
Occurs when organizations adopt something due to pressure either from the state or other organizations.

normative isomorphism
Results from professionalism, with influences coming from other organizations involved in the same profession.

late 1990s through 2004 was attributed by many to the implementation of community policing throughout the country. Some, however, suggest that community policing is just one factor, others being a robust economy, a graying population, and fewer teenagers. The COPS Office has added thousands of officers, but whether these officers are implementing community policing strategies is not as clear.

When using crime reduction as a measure of community policing's effectiveness, the question often arises as to whether crime is, instead, simply displaced—moved to another community. Another question, in the case of crime actually being prevented, concerns how to measure incidents or events that do not happen.

 Crime statistics are seldom sufficient to understand the extent and character of a particular strategy's impact. Most research on community policing strategies shows only modest and statistically insignificant effects on crime rates, drug abuse and trafficking, and fear of crime.

If departments want more effective approaches to evaluating community policing efforts, they must incorporate communitywide information in the process. It is especially important to use data collected and maintained by public and private agencies other than law enforcement agencies.

To evaluate the effectiveness of specific community policing strategies, police departments should consider data from the health care system (especially emergency rooms), schools, housing and licensing departments, and community surveys.

When evaluating the effectiveness of family violence prevention programs, the number of abused women referred by medical personnel to shelters may be a more reliable indicator of program success or lack thereof than the number of domestic violence arrests. Similarly, strategies aimed at youths might use data on truancy, suspensions, and expulsions as one means of measuring effectiveness.

Several researchers have suggested that law enforcement not concentrate on crime statistics but rather focus on whether community policing efforts are able to build stronger communities—a major goal of the philosophy. One such measure might be the number and nature of citizen complaints. However, in some studies community policing and traditional policing officers generated a similar proportion of complaints, similar types of complaints, and a similar number of complaints.

EVALUATION OF THE COPS OFFICE

The Government Accountability Office's (GAO) *Interim Report on the Effects of COPS Funds on the Decline in Crime during the 1990s* (2005) reported various successes resulting from the COPS Office grants in the 1990s. The report is based on a broad, exhaustive survey of 13,144 local law enforcement agencies, extensively reviewed and investigated by groups of criminologists, economists, statisticians, and the National Research Council of the National Academy of Sciences. This independent study found that COPS grants have consistently contributed between 10 percent and 13 percent to the yearly reductions in violent crime at the height of their funding.

In addition, the COPS Office has increased the number of sworn officers per capita by 3 percent nationwide and has also had a significant effect on the adoption of new and effective police practices. The report concludes: COPS grants work. In its strongest years (from 1994 to 2001), the COPS Office and its grants have been effective in combating crime, adding officers to the street, and improving practices known to help fight crime and strengthen relations with the community.

THE THREAT OF TERRORISM

Local police play a crucial role in homeland safety and security. Although some agencies may fall back on more traditional methods of policing because of immediate policing concerns, they should not abandon community policing. Chapman and Scheider (2002) set forth the following reasons in support of community policing:

» The community policing philosophy emphasizes organizational changes such as delegating decision-making power to line-level officers and assigning them to fixed geographic areas This can be valuable in a crisis.

ON THE BEAT

Quantifying different approaches in community policing can be a daunting task. Take the SARA model, for instance (scanning, analyzing, responding, assessment). Police officers are often great at scanning, analyzing, and responding but not so great at the assessment piece. This is where researchers could really fit into the equation. Without assessment to see if the efforts you are putting forth are working, you might be spinning your wheels and not getting very far. You need to understand how effective your efforts were and ultimately understand whether the problem was actually solved. Assessment becomes crucial for formulating strategies and making changes to them. These changes can lead to better results.

Community policing efforts are often hard to quantify. For instance, you can count the number of burglaries reported in a year but it is extremely difficult to count the number you prevented by using different community policing initiatives. Although it may be impossible to have firm statistics on issues such as these, community policing strategies, I feel, may be the direct cause of community building. Community building is invaluable any way you look at it. Connecting with the community, empowering residents to improve home security, and educating them on different ways to keep themselves safe—these things work. We just need to figure out a way to quantify the results. The future may hold more answers!

—*Kim Czapar*

» Community policing also helps to build trust between the community and law enforcement, which in a crisis can help law enforcement deal more effectively with community concerns.

» The problem-solving model is also well suited to the prevention of terrorism.

» As law enforcement is only one of many entities that respond to community problems, partnering with other agencies and community groups is central to community policing.

» The threat of terrorism provides a unique opportunity to create these partnerships.

THE IMPACT OF THE ECONOMIC DOWNTURN ON POLICING IN THE UNITED STATES

According to the COPS Office: "Police agencies are some of the hardest hit by the current economic climate. Curtailing revenues nationwide have forced local governments to make cuts in spending across the board, which includes public safety operating budgets. While budget cuts threaten the jobs of law enforcement officers, the duties and responsibilities to ensure public safety remain" (*The Impact of the Economic Downturn*, 2011, 3). The most recent economic downturn, which began in 2008 and marked the tenth such decline since World War II, is projected to negatively impact law enforcement agencies for at least the next 5 to 10 years (until about 2021). It may have longer lasting effects, the permanence of which will be driven not by the economy alone but also by local government officials who may determine that allocating 30–50 percent of their general fund budgets for public safety costs is no longer fiscally possible (Melekian, 2011).

Faced with the need to cut budgets and continue to "do more with less," law enforcement administrators must not only identify different ways to deliver police services more cost effectively but also articulate what the revised public safety models will look like to their communities (*The Impact of the Economic Downturn*, 2011). Highlighting the importance of community policing during tough financial times, the COPS Office notes that many of the cost-saving techniques being implemented by agencies throughout the country are directly related to community policing efforts (*The Impact of the Economic Downturn*, 2011, 33–34):

> The three tenets of community policing—community partnerships, organizational transformation, and problem solving—are of increased importance when facing budget cuts that reduce the number of officers on the streets.

> Collaborative partnerships to develop solutions to problems and increase trust in police can be seen in many of the solutions police agencies are using in light of the economic downturn. Specifically, the use of volunteers, partnerships between the police and private agencies, and the use of social media as a means to communicate effectively with the community in order to meet their needs, are all examples of how collaborative partnerships act as a cost-saving tool.

Organizational transformation exists through the alignment of organizational management, structure, personnel, and information systems to support community partnerships and proactive problem solving. From its inception, community policing's goal is one of forging strong relationships between law enforcement and the communities they serve. It aims to redesign the practice of public safety into a collective, collaborative effort....

The current economic crisis, which has thwarted many police activities, requires police agencies to place a greater emphasis on problem-solving techniques. By engaging in the proactive and systematic examination of identified problems and developing and rigorously evaluating effective responses, they will be able to best use the limited resources that are available to them.

Unfortunately, when agencies are forced to make widespread budget cuts, some have done so by reducing or eliminating some of their community policing programs. In fact, according to the [Major Cities Chiefs Association] MCCA survey, 39 percent of respondents who have reduced budgets stated that those budgets cuts were made to their community policing efforts.

Herein lies one of the major fallacies as it relates to community policing. Community policing should not be viewed as a particular program within a department, but rather as a department-wide philosophy. Programs are typically initiated as a response to a specific problem, in which only a small portion of the organization is involved and once the problem has been addressed the program is dissolved. Instead, community policing must be understood as a philosophy that promotes the systematic use of partnerships and problem-solving techniques to proactively address the conditions within a community that are cause for public concerns over crime and social disorder issues....

Some have made the argument that these economic challenges may compel us to abandon community policing because we simply cannot afford it. However, experience has shown that community policing is a more cost-effective way of utilizing available resources than simple traditional policing practices, for a number of reasons. Primarily, community participation in crime-prevention amplifies the amount of available resources, while community partnerships used to address problem solving provides a more efficient distribution of combined police and community resources than simply reactive policing program models.

RETHINKING THE "GET TOUGH" ON CRIME APPROACH

Armed with an increasing body of empirical data regarding "get tough" measures and criminal recidivism, many jurisdictions are now revisiting their mandatory minimum laws, three-strikes laws, and other nondiscretionary sentencing schemes, particularly for low-level drug offenders. Many of our nation's correctional institutions have become severely overcrowded by the long-term warehousing of these repeat, albeit generally nonviolent, offenders. As the economic recession has worsened, many policy makers have been forced to examine whether we can afford to continue the "get tough" approach of incarcerating the mass number of offenders who "strike out." Data provided by the National Conference of State Legislatures (NCSL) indicates that, of the 24 states that passed three-strikes laws during the 1990s, at least 16 have since modified their legislation to allow judges more discretion in sentencing or to narrow the types of crimes that count as a "strike" (Michels, 2012). In addition, at least 14 states have either eliminated mandatory minimum sentencing for low-level drug offenders or have granted greater judicial discretion concerning correctional alternatives to incarceration (Michels, 2012).

HOW INNOVATIONS IN TECHNOLOGY ARE TRANSFORMING POLICING

Technology was the topic of a recent Police Executive Research Forum (PERF) Executive Session as part of their Critical Issues in Policing Series. At this conference, police chiefs unanimously expressed how impactful technology has been in helping bring crime rates down and helping their officers be more efficient and effective (*How Are Innovations in Technology Transforming Policing?*, 2012). They also all agreed that a new Age of Technology will sweep through American policing in the next two decades, as the technologies that have recently emerged begin to take hold and technologies no one is yet aware of are developed and become available:

> Policing today bears very little resemblance to the policing of the 1970s. For those of us who have been watching this happen day by day, the differences are simply stunning. Back then, police officers thought they were doing a fine job if they responded quickly to calls for service and investigated crimes thoroughly. Today's police departments have given themselves a much larger and more important mission: working with their communities to solve crime problems, and in so doing, [using technology to] actually [prevent] crimes from being committed and [reduce] crime rates. (Wexler, 2012, iii)

Technologies discussed at the session included gunshot detection systems, license plate readers, use of communication technology/social media, cameras in squads, body cameras, cameras in hot spots, wireless video streaming, online crime reporting and case tracking for crime victims, and the use of GPS (global positioning systems) to track criminals and officer locations, Readers are encouraged to give a closer look to the PERF report generated from that Executive Session: *How Are Innovations in Technology Transforming Policing?* (also available online at policeforum.org).

Other technologies not mentioned at the PERF Executive Session that have been implemented by various law enforcement agencies throughout the country include:

» Camera-equipped aerial drones—These can be controversial in that while such technology enables officers to obtain a bird's-eye view of a crime scene in an emergency, such surveillance capabilities also raise privacy concerns.

» Tablet computers—Portable, lightweight devices, such as the Apple iPad, can be used to take notes and record victim and witness statements in the

Technology is making policing safer and more efficient.
Here an officer is shown
wearing a portable camera
that travels along with him
on patrol.

© AP Images/Kitsap Sun, Josh Farley

field. Various police-specific applications are available, such as crime scene
diagramming tools.

» GPS vehicle pursuit darts—Squads involved in potentially dangerous high-
speed pursuits can fire an adhesive GPS-equipped "dart" at a fleeing vehicle
and then track the vehicle's movements from a safe distance.

» Throwable robotic cameras—A robotic camera is a small remote-controlled
device that can withstand being thrown over a wall and then right itself,
climb stairs, and maneuver into small, poorly lit spaces to allow officers to
view potential threats from a safe distance.

A LOOK TOWARD THE FUTURE

The FBI forecasts that subnational and nongovernmental entities will play an
increasing role in world affairs for years to come, presenting new "asymmetric" threats to the United States. Although the United States will continue to
occupy a position of economic and political leadership, and although other
governments will also continue to be important actors on the world stage, terrorist groups, criminal enterprises, and other nonstate actors will assume an
increasing role in international affairs. Nation-states and their governments will
exercise decreasing control over the flow of information, resources, technology,
services, and people.

Globalization and the trend of an increasingly networked world economy will become more pronounced within the coming years. The global economy will stabilize some regions, but widening economic divides are likely to make areas, groups, and nations that are left behind breeding grounds for unrest, violence, and terrorism. As corporate, financial, and nationality definitions and structures become more complex and global, the distinction between foreign and domestic entities will increasingly blur. This will lead to further globalization and networking of criminal elements, directly threatening the security of the United States.

Most experts believe that technological innovation will have the most profound impact on the collective ability of the federal, state, and local governments to protect the United States. Advances in information technology, as well as other scientific and technical areas, have created the most significant global transformation since the Industrial Revolution. These advances allow terrorists, disaffected states, weapons proliferators, criminal enterprises, drug traffickers, and other threat enterprises easier and cheaper access to weapons technology. Technological advances will also provide terrorists and others with the potential to stay ahead of law enforcement countermeasures. For example, it will be easier and cheaper for small groups or individuals to acquire designer chemical or biological warfare agents and correspondingly more difficult for forensic experts to trace an agent to a specific country, company, or group (*Federal Bureau of Investigation Strategic Plan 2004–2009*, 2004, Section I).

How Futurists Work

Law enforcement tends to focus on the immediate future, dealing with problems that need resolution, trying to stay "on top of things," and "putting out fires." It is not surprising that a mere 2- to 4-percent increase in the crime rate may go unnoticed. The crisis faced today is probably a minor one that was ignored yesterday. The terrorist attacks on September 11, 2001, should not have been the surprise they were had law enforcement paid more attention to what was happening in the present and how it could affect the future.

Futurists operate under three fundamental premises (Tafoya, 1983, 15):

» The future is not predictable.

» The future is not predetermined.

» Future outcomes can be influenced by individual choice.

The third premise is critical to law enforcement because the choices made today will affect law enforcement in the future. As has been said, "The future is coming. Only you can decide where it's going."

How can futuristics be used in law enforcement? Tafoya suggests three primary priorities or goals (1983, 17):

Goals of futuristics:
- Form perceptions of the future (the possible).
- Study likely alternatives (the probable).
- Make choices to bring about particular events (the preferable).

Futurists' Look at the Role Police Will Play in the Years Ahead

Proteus USA is "an international consortium and 'think tank' that promotes further discourse, study, and research focused on examining uncertainty, enhancing creativity, gaining foresight, and developing critical analytical and decision-making processes to effectively provide insight and knowledge to future complex national security, military, and intelligence challenges" (Cetron and Davies, 2008). This group released a research report, *55 Trends Now Shaping the Future of Policing*, as part of their 55 Global Trends Series.

According to the report, more than 1 in every 100 adults in the United States were in prison at the end of 2007, the highest rate of imprisonment in American history. Nationwide, the prison population has tripled in three decades, to 1.6 million. Some 723,000 more are being held in local jails.

At the same time, the number of police officers is stable or declining. In Boston, there were 1,800 officers a decade ago. Now there are fewer than 1,400. In Ohio, there are 1,500 state troopers, just as there were in the mid-1970s.

In Western societies, populations are living longer due to improved health care and are growing more diverse due to continued immigration. As societies age, they are likely to see fewer violent crimes, because violence is generally associated with young people, but financial crimes will increase because in the modern world the elderly tend to be relatively well-off. A shift in policing will be required to meet the needs of older citizens, and more officers will need training in handling financial crimes. Territorial conflicts may increase between police agencies and private security firms that look after the day-to-day needs of corporations and wealthy communities. Security will be one of the great growth industries of the next 20 years.

The panel of law enforcement experts who contributed to this report of the future of policing listed the top 10 most important trends for policing (from Cetron and Davies, 2008):

1. Technology will increasingly dominate both the economy and society (9). A vast array of technological advances will alter police operations, from surveillance, to detection of weapons of mass destruction (WMDs), to enhancements in databases and the way information is gathered and intelligence is developed.

2. Societal values will continue to change, possibly rapidly (12), which may lead to increasing tension among cultures and a rise in the number of hate crimes aimed at the foreign-born population.

3. The global economy will become more integrated (14), facilitated by the Internet. This will, in turn, lead to a spread in economic crimes that cross national boundaries, making investigation of such crimes considerably more complex and costly.

4. Militant Islam will continue to spread and gain power (15), requiring Western nations, and the United States in particular, to become more vigilant in protecting against violent attacks.

5. Mass migration will redistribute the world's population (17), creating new challenges for law enforcement in Western developed countries in terms of

citizen diversity and increasing the need for police officers who can speak and understand many languages and different cultures.

6. Privacy rights, once a defining right for Americans, will continue to erode (19) as society's security concerns clash with individual privacy protections.

7. The population of the developed world will live longer (20), including police officers, who will have longer retirements and whose pension costs will rise across the industrialized world. The growing elderly population will also require both increased private security and increased police services.

8. Continuing urbanization will aggravate most environmental and social problems (22), including an increased concentration of citizens living in urban poverty under conditions that foster crime and violence.

9. Specialization will continue to spread throughout the law enforcement profession (23), with more sharing of resources and outsourcing to consultants. Educational and training requirements will increase for officers, and accreditation will gain prominence. Civilianization of positions not requiring the use of sworn, armed law enforcement will expand, including dispatch, crime scene investigation, general investigations, crime and intelligence analysis, and information technology.

10. The work ethic will continue to fade away (25), creating new challenges for police managers and administrators: "The new generation of workers cannot simply be hired and ignored. They must be nurtured, paid well, and made to feel appreciated, or they will quickly look for a friendlier, more rewarding workplace. ... Without the opportunity to learn new skills, young people will quickly find a job that can help them prepare for the rest of their professional life. This may make it difficult for law enforcement to recruit and retain personnel willing to accept the rigors of a police career" (Cetron and Davies, 2008).

Future Trends in Law Enforcement Recruiting and Training

Church (2007) points out that recruiting is at a crossroads, lacking enough "qualified bodies" to fill existing openings. He predicts a growing involvement of state training and certification agencies, commonly called Peace Officers Standards and Training, or POST, in assisting local agencies. He also foresees more nonprofit organizations getting involved in mentoring candidates and even funding them through the academy.

Where does community policing fit into the context of basic police academy training? Shults (2007) examined this question and found clear support from police training experts for community policing training to become an integral part of basic police training academies. In both 2002 and 2006, more than 90 percent of academies provided basic training on community policing topics. Additionally, 90 percent of academies provided basic training on terrorism-related topics in 2006, up from 80 percent in 2002 (Reaves, 2009).

As this chapter has discussed, and as is aptly stated by John Schaar, American writer and scholar: *"The future is not some place we are going to, but one we are creating. The paths are not to be found, but made, and the activity of making them changes both the maker and the destination."*

SUMMARY

At the heart of experimental design is the random assignment of individuals to experimental and control conditions. Experiments in criminal justice raise ethical issues as well as privacy issues. Assistance in experiments in criminal justice is available through the NIJ's Locally Initiated Research Partnerships in Policing.

Surveys are commonly used by police departments. To validate an evaluation conducted by survey, 60 percent of distributed surveys must be returned.

Crime statistics are seldom sufficient to understand the extent and character of a particular strategy's impact. Most research on community policing strategies shows only modest and statistically insignificant effects on crime rates, drug abuse and trafficking, and fear of crime. To evaluate the effectiveness of specific community policing strategies, police departments should consider data from the health care system (especially emergency rooms), schools, housing and licensing departments, and community surveys.

The goals of futuristics are (1) to form perceptions of the future (the possible), (2) to study likely alternatives (the probable), and (3) to make choices to bring about particular events (the preferable).

DISCUSSION QUESTIONS

1. Why has the relationship between law enforcement practitioners and researchers often been difficult?

2. How can partnerships make research more effective?

3. What percentage of returned surveys is required for validation, and why?

4. Why do crime and arrest statistics fall short of explaining the success or failure of a particular strategy? What other kinds of data should also be looked at?

5. Discuss the importance of research in criminal justice.

6. Some police agencies conduct citizen surveys to gauge public attitudes toward the police. Discuss the impact different methods of conducting surveys can have on the results.

7. Do the 10 trends affecting policing listed by Proteus USA appear valid in your community?

8. How does the availability of funding affect patterns of community policing within police departments?

9. What is a two-wave survey, and when might it be appropriate to use?

10. What do you think will be law enforcement's biggest future challenge and why?

GALE EMERGENCY SERVICES DATABASE ASSIGNMENTS

ONLINE Database

- Use the Gale Emergency Services Database to help answer the Discussion Questions as appropriate.

- Crime researchers in Canada have formed the Network for Research on Crime and Justice, which allows researchers to network and share knowledge, avoid duplication of effort, and build on existing findings. The network's Research in Brief page on its Web site includes results from U.S. Department of Justice research on the continued decline of serious crime levels in 1999. Discuss the measures used in this research and the sources of the data. Also explain what NCVS and UCR mean.

REFERENCES

Bratton, William J. 2006. "Working Together to Meet the Challenges of 21st-Century Policing." *Subject to Debate* 20 (9): 2.

Cetron, Marvin J. and Owen Davies. 2008. *55 Trends Now Shaping the Future of Policing.* Carlisle Barracks, PA: Proteus USA.

Chapman, Rob and Matthew C. Scheider. 2002 (Fall). "Community Policing: Now More Than Ever." Washington, DC: Community Oriented Policing Services Office.

Church, Jeffrey. 2007. "Future Trends in Law Enforcement Recruiting." *Officer.com*, February 15. http://www.officer.com/article/10250151/future-trends-in-law-enforcement-recruiting

"The Commission." 2010, Fairfax, VA: The Commission on Accreditation for Law Enforcement. http://www.calea.org/content/commission

Cosner, Thurston L. and Greg M. Loftus. 2005. "Law Enforcement-Driven Action Research." *The Police Chief* 72 (10): 62–68.

Federal Bureau of Investigation Strategic Plan 2004–2009. 2004. Washington, DC: Federal Bureau of Investigation.

Gaertner, Susan and John Harrington. 2009. "Successful Eyewitness Identification Reform: Ramsey County's Blind Sequential Lineup Protocol." *The Police Chief* 76 (4): 130–141.

How Are Innovations in Technology Transforming Policing? 2012 (January). Washington, DC: Police Executive Research Forum, Critical Issues in Policing Series.

The Impact of the Economic Downturn on American Police Agencies. 2011 (October). Washington, DC: U.S. Department of Justice, Office of Community Oriented Policing Services. http://www.cops.usdoj.gov/files/ric/publications/e101113406_economic%20impact.pdf

Improving 21st-Century Policing through Priority Research: The IACP's National Law Enforcement Research Agenda. 2008 (September). Arlington, VA: IACP Research Advisory Committee.

Interim Report on the Effects of COPS Funds in the Decline in Crime during the 1990s. 2005 (June 3). Washington, DC: Government Accountability Office.

Jensen, Carl J. 2006. "Consuming and Applying Research: Evidence-Based Policing." *The Police Chief* 73 (2): 98–101.

McEwen, Tom. 1999. "NIJ's Locally Initiated Research Partnerships in Policing Factors that Add Up to Success." *NIJ Journal* 238 (January): 2–10.

Melekian, Bernard. 2011. "Director's Column: July 2011." *Community Policing Dispatch* 4 (7). http://cops.usdoj.gov/html/dispatch/07-2011/DirectorMessage.asp

Michels, Scott. 2012. "Rethinking 'Tough on Crime.'" *The Crime Report*, June 28. http://www.thecrimereport.org/news/inside-criminal-justice/2012-06-rethinking-tough-on-crime#

Milligan, Stacy Osnick and Lorie Fridell. 2006 (April). *Implementing an Agency-Level Performance Measurement System: A Guide for Law Enforcement Executives.* Washington, DC: Police Executive Research Forum.

"A Police Guide to Surveying Citizens and Their Environment." 1993 (October). Monograph. Washington, DC: Bureau of Justice Assistance. (NCJ 143711) https://www.ncjrs.gov/pdffiles/polc.pdf

Reaves, Brian A. 2009 (February 26). *State and Local Law Enforcement Training Academies, 2006.* Special report. Washington, DC: Bureau of Justice Statistics. (NCJ 222987)

Rosenbaum, Dennis P., Amie M. Schuck, Lisa M. Graziano, and Cody D. Stephens. 2007 (November 25). *Measuring Police and Community Performance Using Web-Based Surveys: Findings from the Chicago Internet Project Final Report.* Chicago, IL: Center for Research in Law and Justice, Department of Criminal Justice, University of Illinois at Chicago.

Sanders, Beth A. and Marc L. Fields. 2009. "Partnerships with University-Based Researchers." *The Police Chief* 76 (6): 58–61.

Schuster, Beth. 2007. "Police Lineups: Making Eyewitness Identification More Reliable." *NIJ Journal* 258 (October): 2–9.

Scott, Jason D., David E. Duffee, and Brian C. Renauer. 2003. "Measuring Police–Community Coproduction: The Utility of Community Policing Case Studies." *Police Quarterly* 6 (4): 410–439.

Shults, Joel F. 2007 (August). *The Future of Community Policing in the Context of Basic Police Academy Training.* D.Ed. dissertation. Columbia, MO: Graduate School of the University of Missouri–Columbia.

Tafoya, William L. 1983 (March). "Futuristics: New Tools for Criminal Justice Executives: Part I." Presentation. San Antonio, TX: Academy of Criminal Justice Sciences, Annual Meeting.

Wexler, Chuck. 2012 (January). "Introduction." In *How Are Innovations in Technology Transforming Policing?*, iii–iv. Washington, DC: Police Executive Research Forum, Critical Issues in Policing Series.

Willis, James J., Stephen D. Mastrofski, and David Weisburd. 2007. "Making Sense of COMPSTAT: A Theory-Based Analysis of Organizational Change in Three Police Departments." *Law and Society Review* 41 (1): 147–188.

A HELPFUL RESOURCE

The Criminal Justice Distance Learning Consortium. 1999. *The Definitive Guide to Criminal Justice and Criminology on the World Wide Web.* Upper Saddle River, NJ: Prentice Hall.

GLOSSARY

Number in parentheses indicates the chapter in which the term is introduced.

A

acculturation—Occurs when a society takes in or assimilates other cultures. Also called *assimilation*. (6)

action research—Emphasizes full participation in the research by everyone directly affected by the process and results. (16)

Alzheimer's disease (AD)—A progressive, irreversible, and incurable brain disease with no known cause that affects four million elderly Americans; the classic symptom is memory loss. (6)

Americans with Disabilities Act (ADA)—Legislation signed in 1990 that guarantees that persons with disabilities will have equal access to any public facilities available to persons without disabilities. (6)

analysis (in SARA)—Refers to evaluating how effective the intervention was; was the problem solved? (4)

assessment (in SARA)—Examines the identified problem's causes, scope, and effects; includes determining how often the problem occurs and how long it has been occurring, as well as conditions that appear to create the problem. (4)

assimilation—Occurs when a society takes in or assimilates various other cultures to become a "melting pot." Also called *acculturation*. (6)

asymmetric warfare—Combat in which a weaker group attacks a superior group by not attacking the stronger adversary head on but rather attacking areas where the adversary least expects to be hit, causing great psychological shock and giving power to the powerless by destroying the stronger adversary's ability to use its conventional weapons. (15)

attention deficit hyperactivity disorder (ADHD)—A common disruptive behavior disorder characterized by heightened motor activity (fidgeting and squirming), short attention span, distractibility, impulsiveness, and lack of self-control. (6)

B

bias—A prejudice that inhibits objectivity; can evolve into hate. (6)

bias crime—A criminal offense committed against a person, property, or society that is motivated, in whole or in part, by an offender's bias against an individual's or group's race, religion, ethnic/national origin, gender, age, disability, or sexual orientation. *Hate crime* and *bias crime* are considered synonymous. (14)

bias incident—Use of bigoted and prejudiced language; does not in itself violate hate crime laws. (14)

bifurcated society—The widening of the gap between those with wealth (the "haves") and those living in poverty (the "have-nots"), with a shrinking middle class. (3)

binge drinking—Five or more drinks in a row during the previous 2 weeks. (11)

bowling alone—A metaphor referring to a striking decline in social, capital, and civic engagement in the United States. (3)

broken windows phenomenon—Suggests that if it appears no one cares about the community, as indicated by broken windows not being repaired, then disorder and crime will thrive. (3)

bullying—Name calling, fistfights, purposeful ostracism, extortion, character assassination, repeated physical attacks, and sexual harassment; also called *peer child abuse*. (12)

C

call management—Calls are prioritized based on the department's judgment about the emergency nature of the call (e.g., imminent harm to a person or a crime in progress), response time, need for backup, and other local factors. (7)

call stacking—A process performed by a computer-aided dispatch system in which nonemergency, lower-priority calls are ranked and held or "stacked" so the higher priorities are continually dispatched first. (7)

change management—The development of an overall strategy to examine the present state of an organization, envision the future state of the organization, and devise a means of moving from one to the other. (5)

closed drug market—Dealers sell only to people they know or who are vouched for by other buyers. (11)

cocoon neighborhood watch—Focusing on only those living around at-risk places rather than an entire neighborhood. (10)

coercive isomorphism—Occurs when organizations adopt something due to pressure either from the state or other organizations. (16)

collaboration—Occurs when a number of agencies and individuals make a commitment to work together and contribute resources to obtain a common, long-term goal. (7)

communication process—Involves a sender, a message, a channel, a receiver, and, sometimes, feedback. (6)

community—The specific geographic area served by a police department or law enforcement agency and the individuals, organizations, and agencies within that area. (3)

community justice—An ethic that transforms the aim of the justice system into enhancing community life or sustaining communities. (3)

community mobilization—Strategy to address the gang problem that includes improved communication and joint policy and program development among justice, community-based, and grassroots organizations. (13)

community policing—A philosophy or orientation that emphasizes working proactively with citizens to reduce fear, solve crime-related problems, and prevent crime. (1)

community relations—Efforts to interact and communicate with the community—team policing, community resource officers, and school liaison officers. See also *public relations.* (1)

conditional threat—The type of threat often seen in extortion cases; warns that a violent act will happen unless certain demands or terms are met. (12)

conservative crime control—Comes down hard on crime; wages "war" on crime and drugs. (11)

contagion—Suggests that when offenders notice one criminal opportunity they often detect similar opportunities they have previously overlooked; crime then spreads; the broken windows theory is an example. (10)

contagion effect—The media coverage of terrorism inspires more terrorism. (15)

CPTED—Crime Prevention through Environmental Design—altering the physical environment to enhance safety, reduce the incidence and fear of crime, and improve the quality of life. (9)

crack children—Children who were exposed to cocaine while in the womb. (6)

crime-specific planning—Uses the principles of problem solving to focus on identified crime problems. (4)

crisis behavior—Results when a person has a temporary breakdown in coping skills; not the same as mental illness. (6)

critical mass—The smallest number of citizens and organizations needed to support

and sustain the community policing initiative. (5)

cycle of violence—Violent or sexual victimization of children can often lead to these victims becoming perpetrators of domestic violence as adults. (14)

D

DARE—Drug Abuse Resistance Education—a program aimed at elementary-age school children, seeking to teach them to "say no to drugs." (9)

decentralization—An operating principle that encourages flattening of the organization and places decision-making authority and autonomy at the level where information is plentiful, usually at the level of the patrol officer. (5)

deconfliction—Protocol or guidelines to avoid conflict. (15)

demographics—The characteristics of a human population or community. (3)

developmental assets—Forty ideals, experiences, and qualities established by the Search Institute to "help young people make wise decisions, choose positive paths, and grow up competent, caring, and responsible." (12)

diffusion—Occurs when criminals believe that the opportunity blocking of one type of criminal activity is also aimed at other types of criminal activity. (10)

direct threat—Identifies a specific act against a specific target and is delivered in a straightforward, clear, and explicit manner. (12)

discretion—Freedom to make choices among possible courses of action or inaction, for example, to arrest or not arrest. (2)

displacement—The theory that successful implementation of a crime-reduction initiative does not really prevent crime; instead it just moves the crime to another area. (3)

diversion—Turning youths away from the criminal justice system, rerouting them to another agency or program. (3)

DOC model—Dilemmas–Options– Consequences challenges officers to carefully consider their decisions and the short- and long-term consequences of those decisions, with the goal of fusing problem solving and morality. (4)

E

EBD—Emotionally/behaviorally disturbed. (6)

effectiveness—Producing the desired result or goal; doing the right things. (4)

efficiency—Minimizing waste, expense, or unnecessary effort; results in a high ratio of output to input; doing things right. (4)

empirical study—Research based on observation or practical experience. (9)

empowered—Granting authority and decision making to lower-level officers. (5)

ethnocentrism—The preference for one's own way of life over all others. (6)

experimental design—Research method involving the random assignment of individuals to experimental (treatment) and control (no treatment) conditions. (16)

F

fetal alcohol syndrome (FAS)— The leading known cause of mental retardation in the Western world; effects include impulsivity, inability to predict consequences or to use appropriate judgment in daily life, poor communication skills, high levels of activity, distractibility in small children, and frustration and depression in adolescents. (6)

flat organization—Unlike a typical pyramid organization chart, the top is pushed down and the sides are expanded at the base. In a police department, this means fewer lieutenants and captains, fewer staff departments, and fewer staff assistants but more sergeants and more patrol officers. (5)

formal power structure— Includes divisions of society with wealth and political influence such as federal, state, and local agencies and governments, commissions, and regulatory agencies. (3)

frankpledge system—The Norman system requiring all freemen to swear loyalty to the king's law and to take responsibility for maintaining the local peace. (1)

G

gang—An ongoing group of people that form an allegiance for a common purpose and engage in unlawful or criminal activity. See also *street gang* and *youth gang*. (13)

gateway theory—Teaches that milder illicit drugs—such as marijuana—lead directly to experimentation with and an addiction to hard drugs such as crack cocaine and heroin. (11)

geographic information system (GIS)—Creating, updating, and analyzing computerized maps. (4)

geographic profiling—A crime-mapping technique that takes the locations of past crimes and, using a complex mathematical algorithm, calculates probabilities of a suspect's residence. (4)

ghetto—An area of a city usually inhabited by individuals of the same race or ethnic background who live in poverty and apparent social disorganization. (3)

graffiti—Painting or writing on buildings, walls, bridges, bus stops, and other available public surfaces; used by gangs to mark their turf. (13)

Guardian Angels—Private citizen patrols who seek to deter crime and to provide a positive role model for young children. (9)

gun interdiction—Local police direct intensive patrols to specific geographic areas with high rates of gun-related incidents of violence. (14)

H

hate crime—A criminal offense committed against a person, property, or society that is motivated, in whole or in part, by an offender's bias against an individual's or group's race, religion, ethnic/national origin, gender, age, disability, or sexual orientation. *Hate crime* and *bias crime* are considered synonymous. (14)

heterogeneous—Involving things (including people) that are unlike, dissimilar, different; the opposite of *homogeneous*. (3)

homogeneous—Involving things (including people) that are basically similar, alike; the opposite of *heterogeneous*. (3)

hot spots—Areas where incidents of crime and disorder tend to cluster in close proximity to one another. (4)

hue and cry—The summoning of all citizens within earshot to join in pursuing and capturing a wrongdoer. (1)

human relations—Efforts to relate to and understand other individuals or groups. (1)

I

impact evaluation—Determines if the problem declined. (4)

incident—An isolated event that requires a police response; the primary work unit in the professional model. (4)

incivilities—Occur when social control mechanisms have eroded and include unmowed lawns, piles of accumulated trash, graffiti, public drunkenness, fighting, prostitution, abandoned buildings, and broken windows. (3)

indirect threat—Tends to be vague, unclear, and ambiguous; the plan, the intended victim, the motivation, and other aspects of the threat are masked or equivocal. (12)

informal power structure—Includes religious groups, wealthy subgroups, ethnic groups, political groups, and public interest groups. (3)

interoperability—The compatibility of communication systems such as EMS, fire and rescue, and police, and across levels of government. (15)

intimate partner violence (IPV)—Violence that occurs between two people in a close (intimate) relationship, whether the partners are of the same or opposite gender; can involve physical violence, sexual violence, threats, emotional abuse, and stalking. (14)

isomorphism—Similar in structural characteristics. Isomorphism results in a one-size-fits-all approach to community policing; in contrast to refraction. (16)

J

jargon—The technical language of a profession. (6)

jihad—Holy war. (15)

K

kinesics—The study of body movement or body language. (6)

L

leakage—Occurs when a student intentionally or unintentionally reveals clues to feelings, thoughts, fantasies, attitudes, or intentions that may signal an impending violent act. (12)

least-effort principle—Concept proposing that criminals tend to commit acts of crimes within a comfort zone located near but not too close to their residence. (4)

liberal crime control—Emphasizes correctional policies and broader social reforms intended to expand opportunities for those "locked out" of the American Dream; wages "war" on poverty and inequality of opportunity. (11)

Lucifer effect—The transformation of good people into evil. (2)

M

magnet phenomenon—Occurs when a phone number or address is associated with a crime simply because it was a convenient number or address to use. (4)

mediation—The intervention of a third party into an interpersonal dispute, where the third party helps disputants reach a resolution; often termed alternative dispute resolution (ADR). (4)

mimetic isomorphism—Occurs when an organization copies or imitates another. (16)

mission statement—A written declaration of purpose. (2)

moniker—A nickname, often of a gang member. (13)

N

negative contacts—Unpleasant interactions between the police and the public; may or may not relate to criminal activity. (2)

news media echo effect—The theory that the media have the power, through their coverage of isolated, high-profile cases, to influence the operations of the criminal justice system and even the disposition of individual cases. (8)

NIMBY syndrome—"Not in my backyard"; the idea that it is fine to have a halfway house—across town, not in my backyard. (3)

911 policing—Incident-driven, reactive policing. (2)

nonverbal communication—Includes everything other than the actual words spoken in a message, such as tone, pitch, and pacing. (6)

normative isomorphism—Results from professionalism, with influences coming from other organizations involved in the same profession. (16)

O

open drug market—Dealers sell to all potential customers, eliminating only those suspected of being police or some other threat. (11)

opportunity blocking—Changes to make crime more difficult, risky, less rewarding, or less excusable; one of the oldest forms of crime prevention. (10)

organizational development—A law enforcement strategy to address the gang problem that includes special police units and special youth agency crisis programs. (13)

P

PAL—Police Athletic League—developed to provide opportunities for youths to interact with police officers in gyms or ballparks instead of in a juvenile detention hall. (9)

paradigm—A model or a way of viewing a specific aspect of life such as politics, medicine, education, and the criminal justice system. (1)

paradigm shift—A new way of thinking about a specific subject. (1)

participatory leadership—A management style in which each individual has a voice in decisions, but top management still has the ultimate decision-making authority. (5)

patronage system—Politicians rewarded those who voted for them with jobs or special privileges; prevalent during the political era. Also called the *spoils system*. (1)

peer child abuse—Another term for *bullying*—name calling, fistfights, purposeful ostracism, extortion, character assassination, repeated physical attacks, and sexual harassment. (12)

perp walks—The police practice of parading suspects before the media, often simply for the publicity provided by news media coverage. (8)

place—A very small area reserved for a narrow range of functions, often controlled by a single owner and separated from the surrounding area. (10)

plea bargaining—A practice in which prosecutors charge a defendant with a less serious crime in exchange for a guilty plea, thus eliminating the time and expense of a trial. (3)

police culture—Incident-driven, reactive policing. (2)

police–school liaison program—Places an officer in a school to work with school authorities, parents, and students to prevent crime and antisocial behavior and to improve police–youth relationships. (9)

political era—Extended into the first quarter of the 20th century and witnessed the formation of police departments. (1)

posttraumatic stress disorder (PTSD)—A persistent reexperiencing of a traumatic event through intrusive memories, dreams, and a variety of anxiety-related symptoms. (6)

poverty syndrome—Includes inadequate housing, education, and jobs and a resentment of those who control the social system. (6)

privatization—Using private security officers or agencies to provide services typically considered to be law enforcement functions. (3)

proactive—Anticipating problems and seeking solutions to those problems, as in community policing. The opposite of *reactive*. (1)

problem-oriented policing (POP)—A department-wide strategy aimed at solving persistent community problems by grouping incidents to identify problems and to determine possible underlying causes. (4)

problem-solving approach—Involves proactively identifying problems and making decisions about how best to deal with them. (4)

process evaluation—Determines if the response was implemented as planned. (4)

process mapping—A method of internal analysis that takes a horizontal view of a system, in contrast to the traditional vertical view. It involves personnel at all levels and uses flowcharts to visually depict how information, materials, and activities flow in an organization; how work is handed off from one unit or department to another; and how processes work currently and what changes should be made to attain a more ideal process flow. (14)

professional model—Emphasized crime control by preventive automobile patrol coupled with rapid response to calls. The predominant policing model used during the reform era (1970s and 1980s). (1)

progressive era—Emphasized preventive automobile patrol and rapid response to calls for service. Also called the *reform era*. (1)

protective factor—A condition, characteristic, or variable that increases the likelihood that a child will avoid delinquency; often the opposite of a *risk factor*. (12)

PSAs—Public service announcements. (9)

public information officer (PIO)—An officer trained in public relations and assigned to disseminate information to the media, thereby providing accurate, consistent information while controlling leaks of confidential or inaccurate information and managing controversial or negative situations to the department's benefit. (8)

public relations—Efforts to enhance the police image. See also *community relations*. (1)

pulling levers—Refers to a multiagency law enforcement team imposing all available sanctions on gang members who violate established standards for behavior. (13)

Q

qualitative data—Examines the excellence (quality) of the response, that is, how satisfied were the officers and the citizens; most frequently determined by surveys, focus groups, or tracking complaints and compliments. (4)

qualitative evaluations—Assessments that are more descriptive and less statistical than empirical studies; the opposite of quantitative evaluation. (9)

quantitative data—Examine the amount of change (quantity) as a result of the response; most frequently measured by before-and-after data. (4)

R

racial profiling—A form of discrimination that singles out people of racial or ethnic groups because of a belief that these groups are more likely than others to commit certain types of crimes. Race-based enforcement is illegal. (6)

random assignment—Dependence on a random number table or machine-generated random number that indicates the particular group to which an individual or entity will be assigned. Whether a person is a member of the treatment group or the control (no treatment) group is determined purely by chance. (16)

rave—A dance party with fast-paced electronic music, light shows, and use of a wide variety of drugs and alcohol. (11)

reactive—Responding after the fact; responding to calls for service. The opposite of *proactive*. (1)

reform era—Emphasized preventive automobile patrol and rapid response to calls for service. Also called the *progressive era*. (1)

representing—A manner of dress to show allegiance or opposition to a gang; uses an imaginary line drawn vertically through the body. (13)

response (in SARA)—Acting to alleviate the problem, that is, selecting the alternative solution or solutions. (4)

restorative justice—Advocates a balanced approach to sentencing that involves offenders, victims, local communities, and government to alleviate crime and violence and obtain peaceful communities. (3)

risk factor—A condition, characteristic, or variable that increases the likelihood that a child will become delinquent; often the opposite of a *protective factor*. (12)

risk factor prevention paradigm—Seeks to identify key risk factors for offending and then implement prevention methods designed to counteract them. (10)

routine activity theory—Principle of environmental criminology that states crime occurs at the intersection of a motivated offender, a suitable target, and an absent or ineffective guardian. (4)

S

scanning (in SARA)—Refers to identifying recurring problems and prioritizing them to select one problem to address. (4)

selective enforcement—The use of police discretion, deciding to concentrate on specific crimes such as drug dealing and to downplay other crimes such as white-collar crime. (2)

social capital—Refers to the strength of a community's social fabric and includes the elements of trustworthiness and obligations. Two levels of social capital are local and public. (3)

social contract—A legal theory that suggests that for everyone to receive justice, each person must relinquish some individual freedom. (3)

social intervention—Strategy to address the gang problem that includes crisis intervention, treatment for youths and their families, outreach, and referral to social services. (13)

social opportunities—Strategy to address the gang problem that includes providing basic or remedial education, training, work incentives, and jobs for gang members. (13)

soundbites—Good, solid information stated briefly, that is, within 7 to 12 seconds. (8)

spoils system—Politicians rewarded those who voted for them with jobs or special privileges; prevalent during the political era. Also called the *patronage system*. (1)

stakeholders—Those people who have an interest in what happens in a particular situation. (7)

stereotyping—Assuming all people within a specific group are the same, lacking individuality. (6)

strategic planning—Long-term, large-scale, futuristic planning. (5)

straw purchasers—Weapons buyers fronting for people linked to illegal gun trafficking. (14)

street gang—A group of people whose allegiance is based on social needs, who have an identifiable leadership, who claim control over a specific territory in the community, and who engage in acts injurious to the public; the preferred term of most local law enforcement agencies. (13)

suppression—Strategy to address the gang problem that includes tactics such as prevention, arrest, imprisonment, supervision, and surveillance. (13)

symbiotic—Describes a relationship of mutual dependence upon each other. (8)

syndrome of crime—A group of signs, causes, and symptoms that occur together to foster specific crimes. (3)

synergism—Occurs when individuals channel their energies toward a common purpose and accomplish what they could not accomplish alone. (10)

T

target hardening—Refers to making potential objectives of criminals more difficult to obtain through the use of improved locks, alarm systems, and security cameras. (10)

tattling—Something done to get someone in trouble, in contrast to telling or reporting to keep someone safe. (12)

terrorism—The unlawful use of force or violence against persons or property to intimidate or coerce a government, the civilian population, or any segment thereof, in furtherance of political or social objectives. (15)

thin blue line—The distancing of the police from the public they serve. (1)

tipping point—That point at which an ordinary, stable phenomenon can turn into a crisis. (3)

tithing—A group of 10 families. (1)

tithing system—The Anglo-Saxon principle establishing the principle of collective responsibility for maintaining local law and order. (1)

traffic calming—Describes a wide range of road and environmental design changes that either make it more difficult for a vehicle to speed or make drivers believe they should slow down for safety. (10)

TRIAD—A three-way partnership among the American Association of Retired Persons (AARP), the International Association of Chiefs of Police (IACP), and the National Sheriffs' Association (NSA) to address criminal victimization of older people. (7)

turf—Territory occupied by a gang, often marked by graffiti. (13)

two-wave survey—Study method where the first wave consists of a pretest before a strategy is implemented, and the second wave consists of a posttest after the strategy has been implemented for a given amount of time. (16)

V

veiled threat—One that strongly implies but does not explicitly threaten violence. (12)

vision—Intelligent foresight; starts with a mental image that gradually evolves from abstract musings to a concrete series of mission statements, goals, and objectives. (5)

W

White flight—The departure of White families from neighborhoods experiencing racial integration or from cities experiencing school desegregation. (3)

working in "silos"—Occurs when agencies with common interests work independently with no collaboration. (7)

Y

youth gang—A subgroup of a street gang; may refer to a juvenile clique within a gang. (13)

Z

zero tolerance—A policy of punishing all offenses severely, no matter how minor an offense may be. (12)

AUTHOR INDEX

SUBJECT INDEX

Key: figure (*f*), table (*t*)

H

I

Neighborhood Activity Log, 331*f*
Neighborhood Anti-Crime Center of the Citizens
  Committee
  for New York City, 334–336
Neighborhood Environmental Assistance Teams
  (NEAT), 302
Neighborhood Foot Patrol Program of Flint, Michigan,
  250–251
neighborhood gangs, 389
Neighborhood-Oriented Policing (NOP), 32
neighborhood policing, 17
neighborhoods, building partnerships in, 209
neighborhood theories, crime mapping and, 107
Neighborhood Watch, 32
neighborhood watch program, 140–141, 242
Nevada, Reno PD, police training, 133
Newark Foot Patrol Experiments, 251–252
New Hampshire, Durham PD, strategic planning, 129
New Jersey
  Camden, gunshot detection technology, 285
  consolidated services in, 204
  Newark Foot Patrol Experiments, 251–252
  schools, T-PASS, safe schools, 374
  Trenton, Safe Haven program, 302
New Options for Violent Actions (NOVA), 447
newsletters, police community anticrime, 263–264
news media echo effect, 224
news release ideas, 229*f*
New York
  Albany, community dispute resolution centers, 260
  Brooklyn, Citywide Vandals Task Force, 211–212
  community courts in, 199, 200*f*
  Long Island, DNA tracking, 327
  Manhattan, Blockos in, 80
  Manhattan, 210 Stanton, 80
  New York City, combat auto theft (CAT) program, 293
  New York City, Domain Awareness System (DAS), 466
  New York City, drug abuse in, 334–336
  New York City, order maintenance and, 65
  New York City, police magnet schools, 347
  New York City, V-Cops, 167
  NYPD, CompStat and, 105–106
  police department, immigrant communities
    and, 159
  Rochester, Cease-Fire violence prevention
    program, 427
New York Times, 80
night watchmen, 6, 7
NIJ. *See* National Institute of Justice
NIMBY syndrome, 75
9/11 Commission, 474
Nixle, 227, 285
No Child Left Behind law, 361
no comment, in media interviews, 224–225
nonreporting victimization, 178
nonverbal communication, 152–153
normative isomorphism, 494

North Carolina
  Charlotte, neighborhood violence reduction program, 322
  Charlotte-Mecklenburg, domestic violence intervention
    program, 447–448
  Wilson, Operation Broken Window, 332
nuclear terrorism, 459
nuisance break-ins (schools), 362

O

oath of office, 29–30
obsessive-compulsive disorder, 171
Occupational Safety and Health Administration (OSHA), 444
Occupy Wall Street, 19
Office for Victims of Crime (OVC), 178
Office of Community Oriented Policing Services (COPS), 7,
  25, 110, 128, 133, 184
  impediments to implementation, 139
  Portland, Oregon PD strategic plan, 133–135
Office of Juvenile Justice and Delinquency Prevention
  (OJJDP), 355–356, 400, 403–405
Office of Management and Budget (OMB), 352
Office of National Drug Control Policy (ONDCP), 313, 314
Office of the Director of National Intelligence, 460
Officer Friendly, crime prevention program, 248
"off the record" comments, 220–221
Ohio
  Canton, prostitution, 297
  Cleveland, gun exchange program, 231
  Columbus, Community Crime Patrol, 302
  Dayton, Urban High School Disorder Reduction
    Project, 378
OJJDP, Office of Juvenile Justice and Delinquency Prevention,
  403–405
Oklahoma
  Norman, citizen police academies, 195–196
  Oklahoma City, Alfred P. Murrah Federal Building,
    455, 457
  Tulsa, low income housing drug reduction, 330
Olweus Bullying Prevention Program, 366
omission, acts of, 54*f*
One Percenter (OMGs), 388
online reporting, call management, 194–195
On the Beat
  building trust, 188
  community policing model, 137
  crime prevention programs, 247
  disabilities encountered by police, 169
  domestic violence, 433
  gang activity, 407
  geographic information systems (GIS), 286
  media police relationship, 230
  mission statements, 32
  peace officer, 22
  Police Reserve program, 82
  problem solving, 109
  research, 496

W